Start With A Story

The Case Study Method of Teaching College Science

Start WITH A Story

The Case Study Method of Teaching College Science

Edited by Clyde Freeman Herreid

NSTApress
NATIONAL SCIENCE TEACHERS ASSOCIATION
Arlington, Virginia

NATIONAL SCIENCE TEACHERS ASSOCIATION

Claire Reinburg, Director
Judy Cusick, Senior Editor
J. Andrew Cocke, Associate Editor
Betty Smith, Associate Editor
Robin Allan, Book Acquisitions Coordinator

ART AND DESIGN, Will Thomas, Jr., Director

PRINTING AND PRODUCTION, Catherine Lorrain, Director
Nguyet Tran, Assistant Production Manager
Jack Parker, Electronic Prepress Technician

NATIONAL SCIENCE TEACHERS ASSOCIATION
Gerald F. Wheeler, Executive Director
David Beacom, Publisher

Library of Congress Cataloging-in-Publication Data
Herreid, Clyde Freeman.
 Start with a story: the case study method of teaching college science / by Clyde Freeman Herreid.
   p. cm.
 ISBN-13: 978-1-933531-06-9
1. Science--Study and teaching (Higher)--United States. 2. Science--Study and teaching--Case studies.
3. Teachers--Training of--Case studies. I. Title.
Q183.3.A1H44 2006
507.1'173--dc22
                    2006027392

NSTA is committed to publishing quality materials that promote the best in inquiry-based science education. However, conditions of actual use may vary and the safety procedures and practices described in this book are intended to serve only as a guide. Additional precautionary measures may be required. NSTA and the author(s) do not warrant or represent that the procedure and practices in this book meet any safety code or standard or federal, state, or local regulations. NSTA and the author(s) disclaim any liability for personal injury or damage to property arising out of or relating to the use of this book, including any recommendations, instructions, or materials contained therein.

Permission is granted in advance for photocopying brief excerpts for one-time use in a classroom or workshop. Permissions requests for coursepacks, textbooks, electronic reproduction, and other commercial uses should be directed to Copyright Clearance Center, 222 Rosewood Dr., Danvers, MA 01923; fax 978-646-8600; *www. copyright.com.*

This material is based upon work supported by NSF under Grants #0341279, #0618570, and #9752799 and a Higher Education Reform Grant from The Pew Charitable Trusts. Any opinions, findings, conclusions, or recommendations expressed in this material are those of the authors and editor and do not necessarily reflect the views of NSF or The Pew Charitable Trusts.

Contents

SECTION XI: LARGE CLASS METHODS 219

SECTION XII: INDIVIDUAL CASE STUDY METHODS 237

SECTION XIII: HYBRID CASE METHODS 251

SECTION XIV: THE DIRECTED CASE METHOD 299

SECTION XV: HOW NOT TO TEACH WITH CASE STUDIES 331

SECTION XVI: HOW TO WRITE CASE STUDIES.................349

Dedication

For Jan

Kimberly, John, Ky, Jennifer

Sierra, Roxanna, Miranda, Phoebe, and Ayden

Teachers and Students All.

Foreword

Clyde (Kipp) Herreid's work in creating and compiling case studies for undergraduate science instruction and developing case methods previously reserved mainly for law and medical students stands as a major contribution to undergraduate science instruction, fulfilling the vision we had when we invited him to write a regular column on case instruction for the Journal of College Science Teaching more than a decade ago. The quality of those columns was so high and their content often so innovative that we soon invited him to prepare an extra annual issue devoted exclusively to case instruction.

For many of us who had experienced much of our science preparation through lectures, the cases presented in Kipp's columns were often exciting to read because they gave us a new methodology that clearly had the potential to enrich our own teaching. Instead of only helping students master material in a text, we had to think about the case problem and ways to approach it. In addition, these cases were interesting enough that we would read cases in disciplines other than our own, often finding issues and connections requiring cross-disciplinary approaches. Cases provide ample opportunity for students to think creatively. They can be used as stand-alone activities or in combination with texts and journal articles. Used thoughtfully, they can help instructors convey a sense of scientific inquiry that more traditional approaches might find difficult to match.

Watching Kipp leading NSF Chautauqua short courses on the case method for college faculty was always illuminating because of the way he involved participants, It is not easy to sustain any group's interest during three solid days of instruction, to say nothing of the challenge of motivating experienced instructors, but by using cases, Kipp was able to do so with aplomb. He made it look easy, but he is a master teacher with many years of experience. Now, this special volume will enable us to have at our fingertips Kipp's thoughtful analyses of ways to use cases in many classroom settings. This fine collection deserves a place on the book shelf of all those who want to enrich their own teaching and should surely be standard issue for new faculty and graduate teaching assistants. Our community of teaching scientists has a rare resource here and we have Kipp Herreid, his colleagues at the National Center for Case Study Teaching in Science and the other contributors to this volume to thank for it.

Les Paldy, Editor Emeritus, Journal of College Science Teaching , Distinguished Service Professor, Stony Brook Univesity, State University of New York

INTRODUCTION

I first heard about case study teaching from a neighbor—a lawyer who had taught at Cornell University and had been trained at Harvard. He and I were standing in the middle of our country road talking about teaching and education, as it was in the first few hours of our acquaintance. I asked him how he taught law. He paused and then said the magic words, "I use case studies."

He explained that lawyers used real cases in their classrooms to teach the principles of law and precedence. They discussed this with their students, teaching law as they used case after case. They had been doing this for a hundred years.

I had been searching for new ways of teaching for a long time. The lecture method had paled for me over time. I didn't know it then, but well over a thousand studies had demonstrated the inferiority of the lecture method compared to active learning strategies. I had started out my teaching career like so many young PhDs without a shred of training and was thrown into the classroom and told to "teach." So, I taught like my mentors—I lectured. As I suffered through my first year's teaching, racing through my lectures, pouring out all of the information that I had gleaned the night before, scrambling to keep ahead of the students, never once did it occur to me that there were other ways to teach. True, I had heard strange rumblings that other methods were being used on the other side of campus. There were rumors that people in "the humanities" actually used something called DISCUSSION. Now here was my neighbor talking about it again.

To be truthful, I had tried holding a discussion with students in my class from time to time with notable failure. Without warning, in the middle of my physiology lectures, I tried asking a few questions in moments of heroic chutzpa, but to no avail. I would ask questions like "What is the simple abbreviation for sodium?" Not a single eye met my inquiring gaze. None of the students dared look at me for fear that their gaze might be misinterpreted as being willing to speak. Pleading for an answer was beneath me, so like so many teachers before me, I started lecturing again. Only later, did I realize that even if someone had answered my sodium question, this would hardly lead to a discussion. But, my quest for different teaching methods was not to be stopped. I could not get over the fact that I, like so many of my colleagues, was giving a large percentage of F, D, and Withdrawal grades in my introductory science classes, 40% to be exact. This hardly seemed like success.

Years later, I ran into a paper discussing an experiment at Arizona State University. The chemistry department was teaching large numbers of introductory students. They had several sections of the course taught by faculty of different abilities. All of the sections had a common exam. When they compared the grades of the students in the different sections, they found to their surprise that there were no differences among the different sections regardless of the teaching reputation of the instructors! Physics teacher Richard Hake reported similar findings in his survey of 6,000 students taking introductory physics: The skill of the lecturer did not appear to make much difference in the student performance on tests. With these results, you can see why I might look for an alternate approach to teaching.

In my quest for the perfect method, I ran into work by Professor James Conant, a chemist at Harvard, who was President Franklin Delano Roosevelt's science adviser during World War II. He returned from his experience convinced that the public did not understand the way science worked and vowed to change his teaching at Harvard as a result. He created a science course using case studies. This was a lecture course where Conant explored the discovery of great principles, such as the second law of thermodynamics. Over a series of lectures he traced the development of the idea as it came to fruition through fits and spurts, good and bad science. The course apparently did not survive him, although his lectures did make it into print.

Then I heard about McMaster University's medical school, in Ontario, Canada. They, too, were using a case study approach to teaching. But no lectures at all! They based their entire curriculum around cases using a method called Problem-Based Learning. They put all of their students in small groups of, say, a dozen students with a faculty facilitator. Students were given a patient's history and asked to diagnose the problem. When this was complete they received another case. And so it went—case after case, small groups learning the subject on a need-to-know basis, receiving the problem in sections.

So, here was my dilemma: In three different situations I had found people using the term *case study teaching*. All were enthusiastic. Yet, plainly they were doing very different things in the classroom: law professors were leading discussions; Conant was lecturing; and the medical professors were using small groups. The conclusion was obvious: The definition of case studies could not depend upon the method of instruction.

So what was the essence of case studies? I decided to make it simple. "Case studies are stories with an educational message." That's it. The moment that I realized this, I was suddenly free to create stories with different formats for different purposes. Moreover, when I started running workshops, many faculty who only knew of the Harvard discussion model and were dreadfully afraid of it suddenly saw that there were other excellent methods that they could capitalize on the use of stories.

What's the magic of stories? People love stories. Stories put learning into context. Lectures often don't do this. They are abstract with mountains of facts. Sheila Tobias, in her book *They're Not Dumb, They're Different*, described the disagreeable nature of the lecture method. She pointed out that science majors are much more tolerant of the dull recitation of facts than non-majors. Even the redoubtable Richard Feynman spoke of his frustration with science education in the preface to his *Lectures in Physics* saying, "I think the system is a failure." He summarized, "The best teaching can be done only when there is a direct individual relationship between a student and a good teacher—a situation in which the student discusses the ideas, thinks about the things, and talks about the things. It is impossible to learn very much simply by sitting in lecture."

Clearly, I agree. And several granting agencies have been willing to give me a chance to find out if the method(s) can be used to teach basic science. For this I thank them most gratefully: The U.S. Department of Education Fund for the Improvement of Postsecondary Education; The Pew Charitable Trusts; and the National Science Foundation. In addition, I thank my colleagues who have helped develop many of the ideas that form many of the essays in this collection, especially my Co-PI on several of these grants: Nancy Schiller.

Together, we have been able to establish the National Center for Case Study Teaching in Science *(http://ublib.buffalo.edu/libraries/projects/cases/case.html)*. This center puts on workshops and conferences where we extol the virtues of case study teaching to thousands of faculty over the years. Its website has hundreds of cases and teaching notes written by faculty across the world and has thousands of visitors each day. This is truly amazing to me and is a remarkable testimony to the fact that faculty are finally trying out different teaching methods. The case study method has come of age.

In this book I have gathered together many of the columns that I have written for the *Journal of College Science Teaching* over the years. Les Paldy, longtime editor of the journal, was kind enough to ask me to start publishing these essays a dozen years ago and indeed it was he who suggested that I put this collection together so that readers could more readily access the articles. This book is the result. I have not attempted to modify the essays themselves. They stand as they were written. As a consequence, there is some redundancy and perhaps some gaps. I have attempted to smooth over the bumps by writing commentary along the way. Also, I have asked several of my colleagues to contribute to this book by including their essays that deal with important aspects of the case study approach. Hopefully, readers will find the essays useful.

It seems fitting to put case study teaching into a larger context. There is no one better able to do this than the late Carl Sagan, whose work in astronomy and relentless search for ways to engage the public resulted in outstanding books and a television special, *Cosmos*. In his last public appearance reported in the *Skepical Inquirer* (29: 29–37, 2005), knowing he was dying of cancer, he was asked a question: "Do you have any thought on what path might be taken to remedy [the bad name of science]?"

Sagan replied,
"I think one, perhaps, is to present science as it is, as something dazzling, as something tremendously exciting, as something eliciting feelings of reverence and awe, as something that our lives depend upon. If it isn't presented that way, if it's presented in very dull textbook fashion, then of course people will be turned off. If the chemistry teacher is the basketball coach, if the school boards are unable to get support for the new bond issue, if teachers' salaries, especially in the sciences, are very low, if very little is demanded of our students in terms of homework and original class time, if virtually every newspaper in the country has a daily astrology column and hardly any of them has a weekly science column, if the Sunday morning pundit shows never discuss science, if every one of the commercial television networks has somebody designated as science reporter but he (it's always a he) never presents any science (it's all technology and medicine), if an intelligent remark on science never has been uttered in living memory by a president of the United States, if in all of television there are no action-adventure series in which the hero or heroine is someone devoted to finding out how the universe works, if spiffy jackets attractive to the opposite sex are given to students who do well in football, basketball, and baseball but none are given in chemistry, physics, and mathematics, if we do all of that, then it is not surprising that a lot of people come out of the American educational system turned off, or having never experienced science."

Sagan has set us a lofty goal. Case study teaching is a step in the right direction.

▶   ▶   ▶

Section I

The Case for Cases:
We Need a New Approach

This section presents the essence of the book: Our educational system fails large numbers of students. There must be a better way. The first two chapters describe the inadequacy of science education in the United States and then propose some solutions, including the use of storytelling, i.e., case studies. The first article was written a dozen years ago for the journal of the Association for General and Liberal Studies, *Perspectives*.

In rereading it, I am stuck with the fact that not much has changed:

1. Student scores in standardized science tests indicates that the United States still lags far behind other developed nations;
2. The United States's status in the world economy has slipped even more as many nations are speedily catching up, as Thomas Friedman argues in his book *The World Is Flat* (2005). But things have changed in the dozen years that have passed since I wrote that article. It is no longer Germany and Japan that worry American leaders but the emerging economic juggernauts of China and India;
3. The student dropout rate in science still is severe, although we can applaud that women are much more in evidence in most of the sciences;
4. Pseudoscience still attracts large numbers of Americans; and
5. Science literacy among adults seems as questionable as ever. The search for solutions goes on.

Storytelling as a method of education has much to recommend it, as I contend in the last chapters in this section. It is teaching in context. Aesop knew it. Homer knew it. We are storytelling animals. The Bible is the most widely published book in history: It is filled with one story after another. Arguably, one can make the case that its great appeal to the public is not because it is a deep philosophical treatise but because it is a profound storybook.

Chicken Little, Paul Revere, and Winston Churchill Look at Science Literacy

By Clyde Freeman Herreid

One day Chicken Little was picking up corn in the corn yard when, whack!—something hit her upon the head. "Goodness gracious me!" said Chicken Little, "the sky's a-going to fall; I must go and tell the king."

—*English Fairy Tales*, Joseph Jacobs (ed.)

We have heard tell of the reporter who visited a recent Harvard graduation and found practically no one who knew why we have seasonal changes on Earth. The graduating seniors almost unanimously declared that it was because the Earth was further from the Sun in winter than summer. They were surprised to hear that the reverse is true, and that the seasons occur because of the Earth's tilt and the angle of the Sun's rays as they hit the planet. If Harvard students are so scientifically illiterate, what can we expect from the average citizen? Jon Miller (1988), director of the Public Opinion Lab at Northern Illinois University, can tell us. He has tracked American scientific literacy for years with National Science Foundation support. Miller reports that only 5% of American adults can be considered scientifically literate. Other authors say this sets the stage for not only national embarrassment, but a national catastrophe as well. It looks like Chicken Little might be on to something: Perhaps, indeed, the sky is falling.

Concern for the status of science education seems to come from five areas, says D. W. Mullins (1993) of the University of Alabama: (1) The results of standardized tests of students; (2) "the declining of fortunes and international competitiveness of American business and industry;" (3) the dropout of students from science and engineering programs (the pipeline problem); (4) a prevalence of nonsense in American society; and (5) surveys showing the degree of science literacy in American adults. Let us review these points of alarm.

THE RESULTS OF STANDARDIZED TESTS

It has been well reported that the International Assessment of Educational Progress compared American elementary, middle, and high school students with the achievement of students in other countries (IAEEA 1988; Garfield 1988; Beardsley 1992). In 1990–1991 tests, the United States placed 13th among 15 countries for the knowledge of science among 13-year-olds. Similar results were noted for our graduating high school students. When these scores were announced, many educators argued that the results could be readily explained because only the elite students of other countries took their exams while most Americans were involved in ours. Not so.

A study by the American Federation of Teachers and the National Center for Improving Science Teaching, reported in the *American Educator* (1994), puts the results in perspective. They decided to analyze American success in high school biology. They chose this field because 95% of U.S. students take this subject in contrast to only 45% taking chemistry and 20% taking physics. In England, Wales, France, Germany, and Japan, 30% to 50% of all 18-year-olds take the national exams, which are roughly comparable to our Advanced Placement Exams. One-fourth to one-third of these 18-year-olds pass these rigorous tests. In contrast, only 7% of Americans take the AP exams and only 4% pass! Hans Andersen, when president of the National Science Teachers Association, was quoted as saying

only 7% of American high school graduates are ready to pursue science programs in college while 85% of the students in the Soviet Union were ready.

Why are these countries so successful? Two reasons stand out. First, they have a rigorous and mandated national curriculum. Second, they have national or standardized exams that students must pass in order to graduate from high school (rather than simply passing a series of courses). Further, they must pass exams in order to gain entrance into college or the university. Consequently, everyone has an unequivocal understanding of what constitutes success within the school system.

AMERICA'S ROLE IN THE WORLD'S ECONOMY

Business and political leaders have bemoaned the rise of the economic might of many countries, which has apparently occurred at the expense of the U.S. leadership. Particularly galling has been the rise of German and Japanese economies, our old enemies in World War II. With our increasing reliance on high tech workers and the need for a sophisticated workforce, many pundits proclaim that the U.S. educational system must be blamed for the decline of our competitiveness internationally (*Business Week* 1988; U.S. Congress, Office of Technology Assessment 1988). They worry when they see row upon row of white clad Asian workers assembling computer chips to run our cameras, autos, and factory robotics, not to mention our VCRs.

THE PIPELINE PROBLEM

Throughout our school system there is a dramatic decline in the number of students who say they are interested in science and engineering careers. For example, Sheila Tobias in her book, *They're Not Dumb, They're Different,* cites these statistics: 18% of high school sophomores claim interest but by the time they're sophomores in college, 9% have this desire and as graduating seniors the figure is 5%. Only 1.5% become graduate students and 0.24% become PhDs. The decline is even worse for women who make up over 50% of the population and 45% of the American workforce but are only 13% of the scientists and engineers. The picture for some ethnic minorities is even more dismal; African Americans and Hispanic Americans are practically nonexistent in the pipeline. African Americans in 1993 received only 2% of the doctorates in the life sciences and 1% in the physical sciences (MacIlwain 1995). Naturally, there are complex reasons for this state of affairs.

Why do students drop out of the pipeline? An NSF study of college freshmen who switched out of science and engineering reported that 31% said it was too hard, 43% found other fields were more interesting, and 26% said that there were better job prospects elsewhere. *Science* magazine in 1991 reported that poor teaching and unapproachable faculty were cited as major factors why college students switched fields. Even non-switchers complained of these conditions. The science dropout problem has been extensively analyzed by Seymour (1992), who interviewed 350 students at seven colleges and universities. Her study debunks the common myth that students who switch out of science, math, or engineering are incapable of such rigorous work. Switchers' grade point averages were 2.9 at the time they left their majors. Tobias (1990) nailed the problem neatly when she hired non-scientists to take science courses and to keep detailed journals of their experiences. She cataloged the transgressions of the unfriendly science and technology field where the lecture style, multiple-choice tests, megaclasses, and a hostile competitive cutthroat environment reigned. Students who survive this initiation into the field and remain science majors appear to love the subject in spite of the agony or they develop a support network of friends and mentors. It is interesting to note that mathematician Uri Treisman gained notoriety at Berkeley and celebrity nationally for his extraordinary success with African Americans in calculus classes when he convinced them to work together developing a support network, which is so frequently found among successful Asian students.

THE PREVALENCE OF NON-SENSE IN AMERICAN SOCIETY

The public is infatuated with pseudoscience. Our tabloid newspapers and television produce a steady stream of alien abductions, ESP, UFOs, and facilitated communication—all of them treated seriously. This is a recent phenomena; things were not always so. Although a shift in reading matter seems obvious to those of us viewing the tabloids in line at the supermarket, few studies are available to document the impact of these stories. But the report by Stewart (1992) on animistic beliefs serves us well. In 1954, college students finishing a college biology class were asked if they thought an automobile tire felt anything when it blew out, or if the Sun was in any way living, or if the sea knew where lost ships were. Practically no one said yes in 1954. But when college students at Michigan State University were asked this in 1989, upwards of 25% said yes to those questions.

Not all paranormal beliefs have changed to the same extent. Belief in ESP by Americans has stayed roughly constant at 50% from 1978 to 1990, whereas belief in devils increased from 39% to 55%, and belief in ghosts more than doubled from 11% to 25% (Gallup and Newport 1991). Perhaps the latter is not so surprising in view of the fact that almost half of the paranormal newspaper stories at that time were on the subject of poltergeists and ghosts (Klare 1990).

There are many reasons for the shift in American culture. It is not simply a lack of scientific literacy by the public. Surely they are more sophisticated and knowledgeable as a whole than they were fifty years ago. But their skepticism and suspicions are gone. Heinz Pagels, late director of the New York Academy of Science, wrote in his book *The Dreams of Reason*, "According to some pollsters, about 70% of all U.S. college undergraduates believe in some kind of psychic or supernatural focus lying outside of natural science." He argues it is because students have been brought up on TV fare and scientifically irresponsible books and magazines. It is hard not to blame the media and its quest for money and sensationalism. Yet the reporters and producers of nonsense are not ignorant or uneducated. They simply have been seduced or corrupted by their greed as they look for any edge over their competitors.

My daughter provides a case in point. She is an investigative reporter at one of the leading television stations in Colorado. Daily she must go on the air and report drive-by shootings, rape, mayhem, fires, and plane crashes. The station lives by its ratings, especially during the ratings period when everyone gears up to find stories that will stretch over several days. Reporters are forever pressured by station managers to look for new angles, new stories, anything that will catch the interest of the viewer. Cattle mutilations have been big news in Colorado over the years. The carcasses of dead cattle on the range appear in various stages of decomposition and every once in a while a rancher will claim that these must be the work of aliens or a satanic cult. These stories reach the press and are just as rapidly debunked and the stories fade away. For several years they have been old hat and not seen to be newsworthy and they get no airtime.

However, a couple of weeks ago as the ratings period approached, my daughter and the station manager conferred together. There was a new angle on the story. Black helicopters had been reported recently around Colorado and some folks thought maybe they were

dropping mutilated cattle over the range. Now that's a story! In spite of my daughter's protests, she was forced to do the story, collecting the usual weird quotes and counterquotes by the "worthies" and "unworthies." This is about the best one can hope for from a reporter who wants to keep her job: balanced reporting. One may view this as a simple anecdote, out of place in a serious analysis of scientific literacy. However, three weeks after I wrote these words, an article appeared in the *Buffalo Press*: "Black copters are the fad in latest paranoia" (Margolis 1995). In the old days—during the slow days of the summer silly season—such stories would be seen as jokes, fluff, or trash. Today, they appear on primetime, are treated seriously, are seldom balanced, and are everywhere in the media. *New York Times* critic John O'Connor (1994) recently wrote, "Take the supernatural and paranormal, sprinkle liberally with paranoia, and you have a substantial chunk of what increasingly seems to be television's entertainment agenda for the 1990s." He continued, "In the past, the line between fantasy and reality was usually clearly delineated. Today that line gets fuzzier and fuzzier as television, expanding on the success of 'Unsolved Mysteries,' does its peculiar based-on-fact and news magazine dances." There is every reason to believe that such programs will significantly increase the gullibility of Americans (see Sparks, Hansen, and Shah 1994).

SURVEYS OF ADULT LITERACY IN THE UNITED STATES

When Jon Miller reported that only 5% of adult Americans were scientifically literate, i.e., they could identify a number of well-established facts, he went on to say that the results varied with the amount of education. The literacy trend is not surprising: A dismal 0% of those without high school diplomas are scientifically literate; 3% with high school diplomas; 12% of college graduates; and only

18% with post-graduate degrees, excluding scientists. Even the highest rates are not impressive. If you don't get your science in school, you probably won't get it at all.

To put such figures in perspective, here is a series of recently collected statistics, again focusing upon the factual content of scientific literacy. A poll in 1994 by the American Museum of Natural History found that 46% of Americans don't believe that humans evolved from other species, and 65% don't know how many planets there are in our solar system. A 1993 Science and Engineering Indicators survey out of Washington, D.C., found that 41% of adults don't know that DNA regulates inherited characteristics of all plants and animals and that 92% can't correctly identify the cause of acid rain.

Not all of the survey news is bad. Many people have a positive attitude toward science: The American Museum of Natural History poll found that 67% are interested in subjects such as plants and trees, peoples of the world, and the history of life; 76% said they enjoyed learning about science for its own sake; and 68% said science will solve many of the world's problems. Yet, a 1993 North Carolina survey found that 58% of the population said that science and technology made the world a riskier place.

There is clearly a love-hate relationship with science and technology. Hollywood's Frankenstein's monster was weird and wonderful, yet caused death and mayhem. Nuclear energy is seen in a similar light as miraculous and powerful, yet dangerous and potentially out of control. Michael Crichton's book and the movie *Jurassic Park* had a similar theme. The application of DNA technology led to a world of dinosaurs on the loose and cinematic chaos.

Scientific illiteracy seems to pervade our society from the youngest to the oldest citizens. Chicken Little seems to be on target. Yet we can't let her go without raising this issue: If our nation is in such bad shape, how can we illiterate boobs produce so many Nobel laureates in science? Part of the answer lies in the fact that many of these Nobel winners were educated in other countries. Part of the answer lies in the fact that the United States spends enormous amounts of money on research and development, and provides an excellent training environment for numerous postdoctoral fellows and graduate students. We have an academic environment that promotes young scientists. And part of the answer lies in the fact that our system of education doesn't stifle a few of the brilliant students. But since this is an article about the average citizen and not the elite, let us send Chicken Little on her way.

WHAT ARE THE SOLUTIONS, PAUL REVERE?

Paul Revere, an American patriot and silversmith from Boston, rode "through every Middlesex village and farm, for the country folk to be up and arm." He was reputed to call, "The British are coming! The British are coming!" The citizenry awoke and beat back the invaders. Can America now do likewise? Can we solve the problems of scientific illiteracy? Indeed, what are the solutions? The simple answer is to teach more science; to teach better science. Let's take these answers in turn.

Teach More Science

John Moore of the University of California at Riverside doesn't beat around the bush. He says 20% of the time in the elementary, middle, and high schools should be devoted to science. Today, we devote probably less than 10% to this enterprise. For illustration, in a national study prepared for the National Science Foundation, Weiss (1987) found teachers spent only an average of 20 minutes per day on science in the K–3 classroom and 35 minutes in the grade 4–6 classroom. These numbers have not changed much over a decade and there is little reason to believe they are different today.

The situation in college and university education is even worse. Most schools require only two semesters of science/mathematics. This works out to be about 6% of the liberal arts curriculum for math and science combined. The American Association for the Advancement of Science has argued 15–16 semester credit hours should be devoted to science. This is about 12.5% of the course load. Practically no school has such requirements. My own institution, The State University of New York at Buffalo, is an exception. After years of debate within departments and committees, the Faculty Senate passed a liberal arts curriculum requiring 13 credits in the sciences and 8 credits of math for about 15% of the general curriculum. Our program was so novel that we received a major U.S. Department of Education (FIPSE) grant to assist in the implementa-

tion of our program and to train our faculty. Regrettably, five years later, because of budgetary problems and university politics, the program is in jeopardy.

The solution to teach more science obviously can significantly improve literacy rates. Recall that Miller (1988) found more schooling (and more science) leads to higher literacy, and Astin (1993), surveying hundreds of thousands of students at dozens of institutions, reported that the greatest knowledge comes when more course work is required. Yet simply more science in the curriculum will clearly not solve all our problems.

Teach Better Science

In his quest to become the "Education President," George Bush met with the nation's governors at a summit conference in 1989. He said our goal should be to make the U.S. students first in science and math by the year 2000. I say—Not a chance! This is not to say that there are not a lot of folks out there trying. There are major organized efforts to improve science education. The National Research Council (NRC), the National Science Teachers Association (NSTA), and the American Association for the Advancement of Science (AAAS) are all striving to set reasonable national standards for science education.

The AAAS (1993) has a major effort in the works with its 2061 project. (This is the date for Halley's comet to return.) The project is to develop guidelines for student learning by the second, fifth, eighth, and twelfth grades. The National Academy of Sciences has likewise developed a draft of science education standards for three grade levels: K to fourth grade, fifth to eighth grade, and ninth to twelfth grades. All of these efforts are to be commended for the substance of these contributions as well as for the publicity they engender. Someday, someone might treat the problem seriously. The citizenry must heed Paul Revere's call to arms.

WHAT KIND OF SCIENCE SHOULD WE TEACH?

The national organizations' efforts to set standards of science literacy are to be commended for they treat scientific literacy as more than a collection of facts. Scientific literacy has three major dimensions: (1) the substantive concepts in science (facts, phenomena, content), (2) the nature of scientific activity, and (3) the role of science in society (Bauer 1992). Unfortunately, many faculty, parents, and textbook publishers are fixated on only the teaching of facts, principles, and terms as are the pollsters and researchers who follow trends of scientific literacy! Let us address the other two dimensions.

Teaching the Nature of the Scientific Process

This cannot be accomplished by simply memorizing the steps of the scientific method. Students must experience the process. They must make observations, ask questions, make and test hypotheses and predictions, collect data and evaluate their results. Most people don't have a clue about most of this process. Part of the problem comes from the nature of our school laboratories. Most of the lab exercises are not discovery-based but simply demonstrations or skill-developing exercises. Hence, many students think that is what goes on in research labs. They conclude that research labs are performing confirmatory exercises rather than generating new knowledge. These students function at the lowest stages of the Perry Model of Cognitive Development (Perry 1970): *That truth is known and the student's job is to learn it or ferret it out from books or lab assistants.* When confronted with a lab exercise, students know there is a correct answer and the best of them try to find it. When their results do not jibe with their expectation, they assume their answer is wrong. Many instructors do not take this golden opportunity to explore the reasons for the mismatch in the data and predictions.

They simply say, "You're wrong," or mark the paper wrong. It is no wonder that students don't know how the scientific process functions. To their credit, the national organizations are making serious efforts to correct this deficiency.

The Role of Science in Society

This topic receives little treatment in traditional science teaching. One aspect of its importance can be highlighted if we pay more attention to the history of science. Most science texts and instructors give this topic short shrift, perhaps condescending to dropping a famous scientist's name every once in a while. Seldom is there an effort to put previous scientific beliefs in context. Scientists themselves pay little homage to history, especially of failed ideas. They tend to function in the present and they teach this way. Perhaps this isn't such a great tragedy, but the lack of history in our teaching tends to reinforce the notion that scientific ideas just drop from the sky or are known all along, just waiting confirmation. Consequently, students miss hearing about the revolutions which periodically occur in science and the gestalt shifts involved. Whether you agree with Thomas Kuhn (1970) that these events are revolutionary or with other authors that these events are evolutionary matters little. What is important is to emphasize periodically that people of the past did not hold the same view of the world as we do today, and it is unlikely that later generations will see the world as we do.

Another aspect of the problem is this: Through our science teaching, students must gain some sense of how technology and the values of our society affect the kinds of problems we tackle, the hypotheses we advance, the data we collect, and our evaluation of ideas. To take a simple technical example, without the development of microscopes, it is unlikely that we would have much of a concept about the cell theory. Or consider how government funded basic research has changed the American scientific enterprise and drawn the world's greatest scientists to our shores. Or consider how our need for an atomic bomb led to the nuclear energy industry, the use of radiation to the treatment of cancer, the development of radioactive isotopes to the study of metabolism, and so on.

Our values and perspectives may also be determined by our cultural biases. Some people argue that science, being largely a white western male enterprise, has been contaminated by this unique viewpoint. Steven Jay Gould's book, *The Mismeasure of Man,* traces the history of a group of scientists who measured the brain volume of skulls and concluded that blacks are an inferior race. Would such a question even arise in a colorblind society? Would we be raising similar issues about I.Q. and race in the recent book, *The Bell Curve,* if it were not for the fact that the social scene sets the stage for certain questions that might not be asked otherwise? The recent search for a "gay gene" would probably not be high on our list of concerns if it were not for the vigorous debate about the rights of the homosexual community.

In a similar vein, a group of feminists has charged that the way biologists have interpreted primate behavior reflects the bias of our male-dominated science. They argue that primatologists have long interpreted monkey and ape behavior as a male dominated society because white western males first studied the animals. Enlightened scientists today realize that many primate societies are in fact based more on female/offspring relationships. Feminists are convinced that the old view could only have occurred because of our male-based science. I beg to differ. There are simple methodological reasons for the bias of the early primatologists. Early studies of primates were done rapidly and on different species than those today. Males do, in fact, set much of the obvious social structure in many primates. Further-more, it requires years of study to tease out family relationships and discover the social impact. Society may affect our interpretations to some extent, but not every error of science can be so naively assigned to politically incorrect viewpoints.

The conclusion from the above is evident: The scientific enterprise is affected by society and vice versa. This reciprocal relationship should be made explicit in any teaching. The obvious examples include the impact of science upon warfare (dynamite, radar, the atomic bomb), medicine and public health (water purification, vaccines, drugs), and chemistry (nylon, plastics). But science brings with it ethical dilemmas as well: Should we use the atomic bomb, or even threaten to use it? Who should have birth control pills? Should amniocentesis be used to tell a parent the sex of a child if the parent is likely to abort female children (as is reputed to occur in China)? Should we tell a patient that she is a carrier of the fatal Huntington's chorea and will die of this genetic disorder? Do we inform her insurance agent? Once genetic manipulation of our children becomes possible, is it ethical to use genetic engineering to produce the specimen of choice? Where in our educational system are such issues discussed?

So if facts, the process of science, and society's interactions with science are the three legs of scientific literacy, what do we do with our knowledge? Paul Revere is calling "The British are coming!" and so are the Germans, the Chinese, the Japanese, the Koreans ... and we're not ready.

THE "I LOVE LUCY" SYNDROME

We cannot continue to do what we have been doing: There are too many facts and too little time. I call this the *I Love Lucy* Syndrome. You will remember the episode in the TV series: Lucy and her friend Ethel are on the assembly line in the candy factory, wrapping each candy as it passes. They can't keep up. The candy comes faster and faster. They stuff them in their pockets, aprons, mouths and all available nooks and crannies. Still the assembly line races on. So it is with science information. There is no way to keep up nor is there any way to stop the machine.

Those of us in our 60s were born into a world of crystal sets and radios and now we have TV, computers, virtual reality, and the internet; we were born into a world with Model Ts and Piper Cubs and now we have Concorde jets and Stealth bombers; we were born into a world with 48 chromosomes and genes and now we have 46 chromosomes, DNA, RNA, and genetic engineering that can put human genes into bacteria. If the doubling time for information in the field of genetics is seven years and that of biochemistry five years as some scientists claim, how can we cope? We cannot, and nothing can prepare our students for these changes if we insist on teaching only facts. The facts will not stay facts for long. Textbook publishers haven't figured out how to deal with this information overload. They publish introductory college texts that bulge over 1,300 pages—adding, always adding.

To tell us to teach more science, set national standards, and give graduation exams and entrance exams is useful but distant from the average teacher's classroom. What can we as individual instructors do? I look first to Winston Churchill for inspiration.

THREE THINGS WE CAN DO

Ultimately the battle of scientific literacy is fought in the classroom. Great teachers can overcome a poor curriculum. Poor teachers cannot be saved by a great curriculum. What can the average science teacher do to fight the good fight, without surrendering to the advancing armies of scientific illiteracy?

Focus on a Few Select Topics

If we cannot keep up with the deluge of facts, at least we must decide what is most important and what has good longevity. These are "keepers." So what are the most vital topics?

I argue that the major paradigms of science are the topics to be taught. The word *paradigm* is used in the sense of Thomas Kuhn (1970). Paradigms are the most major, encompassing ideas that bind an entire scientific discipline together. In geology it might be the concept of plate tectonics. This single idea explains much of what is known about continental drift, mountain building, volcanoes, earthquakes, and the distribution of many fossil and living organisms. Other major paradigms of science are not hard to identify: The cell theory, molecular biology's central dogma, the big bang theory of the origin of the universe, evolution theory, atomic theory, and quantum theory, to name several. I have two additional points to stress. First, the paradigms taught should be few in number. No discipline should claim more than two or three, otherwise we risk diffusing the focus. Second, the topics should be taught in sufficient depth so that students really understand where each paradigm comes from, why we believe it to be true, what weaknesses exist in the model, and what solutions the paradigm provides.

By choosing to teach paradigms rather than a plethora of unconnected factoids and principles, we gain real power and real access to scientific literacy. First, paradigms are obviously important and central to understanding an entire discipline; there is no chance for trivia here. If we understand the central paradigms of the discipline, we should understand many of the new discoveries in the future. Second, because these are the central ideas, there is little chance that the paradigm will be overturned in a person's lifetime. Or if it is, the person will readily understand the revolutionary implication of the paradigm shift. Finally, facts and principles that are part of a paradigm are easier to recall by a student because they are taught in context, not as isolated bits of information; historical figures become major players on the stage of discovery and are more readily remembered for their contributions.

Teach in Context

Case study teaching in science has had few advocates. In the 1940s, the president of Harvard University, James B. Conant, advocated its use, but few if any teachers took him up on his suggestion. His view of case study was limited to the use of the lecture method for the explication of a historical case such as the overthrow of the phlogiston theory of heat. More recently, I have tried to entice instructors to see the enchantment of the method by exploring some of the various ways cases can be used: in discussion, debates, trials, public hearings, and with small groups (Herreid 1994).

Cases engage students like few other devices in the classroom. Why? Because people like stories. Learning in the context of a story is easier, is more likely to be retained, and is more fun. For over 70 years the method has been used successfully in Harvard business and law schools and other institutions. It has been virtually untried in the teaching of science.

I think the best cases to use are those that are based on real events, especially those that involve unresolved questions, are current and contentious, and involve public policy issues. If you want to teach the structure of DNA, use the example of the O. J. Simpson trial and DNA fingerprinting. If you want to teach people about radiation, use a case study on sunburn lotion, or the recent revelations about radioactive experiments in the 1940s, or cellular phones generating electromagnetic radiation that might induce cancer, or the bombing of Hiroshima. If you want to teach about immunology, teach a case about AIDS, using the basketball player Magic Johnson or Olympian diver Greg Louganis for a storyline. If you want to teach about extinction use the case of the Northern spotted owl.

If we use such cases we solve several major problems that seem inherent in the teaching of science. Cases show the process of science in action better than almost any other teaching experience—short of doing original work oneself. Since the issues of contemporary cases are unresolved, there can be no smug pontificating on how stupid scientists were in the past not to see the solution to a particular problem. Moreover, in contentious issues, the humanity of the scientific enterprise is exposed. On many occasions after I have used case studies, students have pointedly commented on how surprised they were to find that scientists acted "just like people." Scientists argue, they make both bright and stupid remarks, they make mistakes, they persevere, sometimes they succeed in solving a problem, and sometimes they fail. It is the humanness of the enterprise that is missing from most science teaching. When we exclusively teach from textbooks that have been stripped of drama and excitement, we reinforce one of the myths of the scientific method, that scientists are cold, calculating individuals devoid of passion and error.

By using cases involving public policy issues, such as those involving the government regulations for the clearance of drugs, or regulations for nuclear waste disposal, students readily see the societal interaction of science and the ethical implications of many decisions. These issues may not be emphasized in a class discussion but they are part of the background nevertheless. With case studies, students can often see the need for basic science as well as applied science; unresolved problems remain unresolved because the basic science hasn't been done. Finally, the use of cases provides many opportunities to explore the differences between tabloid science and original science reporting. It gives chances to explore the difference between science and pseudoscience.

Use Cooperative/ Collaborative Learning

For generations, elementary school teachers have had small groups of students working together on projects. The use of small learning groups in college and universities has gained attention more recently. Over 600 studies comparing this style of learning with the more traditional methods of individual work have been published (Johnson and Johnson 1989). The data are overwhelmingly in favor of the cooperative mode over the lecture method. Students in such cooperative classrooms retain more information, are more enthusiastic for their subject, have more social skills and tolerance for different opinions, and they have a greater sense of personal worth. In addition, this form of teaching is more appealing to women and ethnic minorities than traditional classrooms. Sheila Tobias (1990), writing in her

book, *They're Not Dumb, They're Different,* tells how alienating the science classroom can be with its lectures, memorization, authoritarian tone, and multiple-choice tests. It is no wonder we turn off students. Our science-teaching methods are medieval. In the colleges of the Middle Ages, before books were widespread, the professor professed—passing his knowledge on to the notes of his students. Surely, we should have progressed. Scientists are among the worst offenders, especially in universities with their monstrous classrooms and impersonal approach. If we wanted to design the worst environment for learning, we could hardly do better. Yet even in these megaclasses it is possible to use interactive techniques such as "think-pair-share," or Mazur's interrupted lecture, feedback lecture, or guided lecture (see Bonwell and Eison 1991; Tobias 1992). But since we have so few serious teacher training programs in universities, such methods are not generally known.

It is not enough to change national curricula, set standards, and make up screening examinations; we must change our teaching as well. We can and must do it. Winston Churchill said it well: "We must never surrender."

So what is the final message here—the bottom line? It is this: We must prepare students for the science that has yet to be discovered, for the books that are yet to be written, for the ethical problems that are yet to be posed. This must be done at every level of the educational system. All of us must be engaged: the national organizations, the state and local committees, and especially the classroom teachers who are ultimately responsible for the good and the bad.

If we can pull this off, we will leave Chicken Little in the farmyard and ride with Paul Revere through the countryside, ultimately to celebrate victory with Winston Churchill. And our problems of scientific literacy should disappear.

REFERENCES

American Association for the Advancement of Science (AAAS). 1994. *Benchmarks for science literacy.* New York: Oxford University Press.

American Federation of Teachers. 1994. Excerpts from what college-bound students abroad are expected to know about biology. Exams from England and Wales, France, Germany and Japan. *American Educator* (Spring): 7–30.

Astin, A. A. 1993. *What matters in college? Four critical years revisited.* San Francisco: Jossey-Bass.

Bauer, H. H. 1992. *Scientific literacy and the myth of the scientific method.* Chicago: University of Illinois Press.

Beardsley, T. 1992. Teaching real science. *Scientific American* 267(4): 98–102.

Bonwell, C. C., and J. A. Eison, 1991. Active learning: Creating excitement in the classroom. *ASHE-ERIC Higher Education Report No 1.* Washington, DC: George Washington University.

Business Week. 1988. Human capital: The decline of America's workforce (September 19): 100–141.

Gallup, G., Jr., and E. Newport. 1991. Belief in paranormal phenomena among adult Americans. *Skeptical Inquirer* 15: 137–146.

Garfield, E. 1988. Science literacy. Part 1. What is science literacy and why is it important? *Current Contents* 31: 3–9.

Herreid, C. E. 1994. Case studies in science: A novel method of science education. *Journal of College Science Teaching* (Feb): 221–229.

International Association for the Evaluation of Educational Achievement. 1988. *Science achievement in seventeen countries.* New York: Pergamon Press.

Johnson, D. W., and R. T. Johnson. 1989. *Cooperation and competition: Theory and research.* Edina, MN: Interaction Book Company.

Klare, R. 1990. Ghosts make news. *Skeptical Inquirer* 14: 363–371.

Kuhn, T. S. 1970. *The structure of scientific revolutions.* Chicago: University of Chicago Press.

MacIlwain, C. 1995. After 20 years, prospects remain bleak for minorities in U.S. science. *Nature* 373: 645–646.

Margolis, J. 1995. Black copters are the fad in latest paranoia. *Buffalo News* (March 26): 7–11.

Miller, J. D. 1988. The five percent problem. *American Scientist* 72(2): iv.

Montague, A., and E. Darling. 1967. *The prevalence of nonsense.* New York: Dell.

Mullins, D. W., Jr. 1993. The science education crisis and existential appreciation. *Forum for Honors* (Spring/Summer): 18–31.

O'Connor, J. J. 1994. TV's infatuation with the mystical. *New York Times* (June 30).

Perry, W. G. 1970. *Forms of intellectual and ethical development in the college years: A scheme.* Troy, MO: Holt, Rinehart, and Winston.

Seymour, E. 1992. The "problem iceberg" in science, mathematics, and engineering education: Student explanations for high attrition rates. *Journal of College Science Teaching* 21(4): 230.

Sparks, G. G., T. Hansen, and R. Shah. 1994. Do televised depictions of paranormal events influence viewer's beliefs? *Skeptical Inquirer* 18: 386–395.

Stewart, B. 1992. Science or animism? *Creation/Evolution* 12: 18–19.

Tobias, S. 1990. *They're not dumb, they're different: Stalking the second tier.* Tucson, AZ: Research Corporation.

Tobias, S. 1992. *Revitalizing undergraduate science: Why some things work and most don't.* Tucson, AZ: Research Corporation.

U.S. Congress, Office of Technology Assessment. 1988. *Elementary and secondary education for science and engineering: A technical memorandum.* U.S. Government Printing Office (TA-TM-SET-41), December.

Weiss, I. R. 1987. Report of the 1985–86 national survey of science and mathematics education. *Research Triangle Institute Report*, North Carolina 27709-2194.

The Maiden and the Witch

The Crippling Undergraduate Experience

By Clyde Freeman Herreid

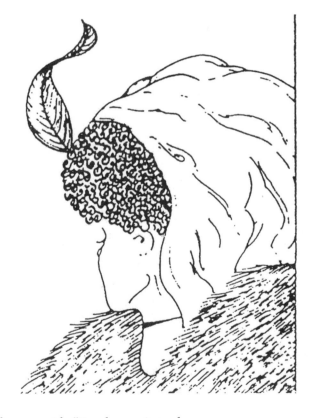

A colleague came up to me a couple of days ago and said something that startled me. It shouldn't have because deep down I knew it. In fact, I had been saying something like it for years. And yet, I had never put the idea into quite the right words where the force of the statement was so dramatic. You know the feeling when you look at something familiar in a new light, like the childhood optical illusion of the beautiful maiden that suddenly looks like an old witch!

We were chatting together before a case study workshop that we run in Buffalo each summer. These workshops draw people from many disciplines and many places around the world. Understandably, I am shamelessly partisan about these affairs. At a moment's notice I will wax enthusiastic about how case teaching connects students to the real world, how cases put learning into context, and although they may not be a panacea for all educational problems, their use in the science classroom will bring joy to students' hearts. I think you get the picture.

But after a few moment's agreement, my colleague said, "You know, it took me about four years to get over my undergraduate education."

I stopped cold. I asked her to repeat what she had said. She did and went on. "All those lectures. All of that memorization. We never really used any of it except to answer test questions. We learned the same thing over and over each semester and never remembered much between one semester and the next, because we never used it."

"Are you saying that the undergraduate experience was disabling—debilitating?"

"Yes, undergraduate teaching isn't just neutral—it's hurtful."

Of course, she was right. I had had the same experience, but not her insight. It wasn't until graduate school that I really began to think my way through problems that weren't strictly academic paper-and-pencil exercises. I had to do this in order to design experiments and write a dissertation, of course. This ability was a long time coming. And as it began to happen, I assumed that this was just a normal stage of development in my maturity; it would take a long time to be able to think on my own. My colleague seemed to be suggesting that this wasn't the case—that the college process was defective and perhaps even responsible for my ineptness.

What if she was right?

The first year I started teaching I was particularly struck by my inadequacies in taking textbook knowledge and putting it to work in real-life situations. I had finished my PhD, done postdoc research, published a bevy of papers (for that is the way to academic nirvana if not world enlightenment), then found myself in my first teaching position. I was lecturing away in a class on animal physiology. I think I was talking about temperature regulation (how appropriate, for my first teaching job was at the University of Alaska). I was ticking off the adaptations for low temperature survival when suddenly an older student, crew cut, tall, and in a flannel shirt interrupted.

"I wonder if that is how the rock rabbits survive the Alaskan winters?"

I asked him what he meant. He proceeded to take all of the esoteric abstract points that I had just enumerated and relate them to his observations in the wild. I was floored. This student had just done something that I had never done—leave the world of the classroom and academic tomes and connect the concepts to his own firsthand experiences. In a flash. This was truly a humbling experience for me.

As the years rolled by, I got better. I also began to wonder how I could encourage students to make these connections sooner than I had. I started sprinkling my lectures with more and more examples and stories. It wasn't enough. They still thought of the material in the class in an isolated way: stuff to be memorized for the teacher, for the exams and nothing more. Years passed and I pushed these bits of anxiety into the background as I received high teaching evaluations, awards, and kudos. That was nice. I appreciated it. But as is probably true for most teachers, I felt not really successful. There were simply too many Ds and Fs in my classes for me to feel complacent. Surely, these students couldn't bear all of the blame. In fact, the Swiss developmental psychologist, Piaget, put his finger on the point when he said something like this: "Every teacher should have been an animal trainer sometime in his career, because when the animal doesn't do the trick, you don't blame the animal!"

Surely, we teachers bear some of the fault.

It was when I came upon case study teaching that the connections between textbook and the real world really dropped into place. Here it was obvious that you have to put your learning to use in order to analyze the situation, decide what the problem is, figure out what you need to know to solve it, and if it is a dilemma case, decide what the hero should do.

So, even though I had been using case studies for years and extolling their virtues, it had never struck me until this conversation that the undergraduate experience with its lectures and labs where you are told what to do and what to learn was—there is no other way to say it—crippling.

Good Lord, what an awful thought.

Let's look at it this way. Question: What does our current teaching method produce? Answer: A cadre of students who if they remember anything about science, it is facts, facts, and more facts that can be used to answer questions on *Jeopardy, Wheel of Fortune,* and *Who Wants to be a Millionaire?* We produce people who can't see the reason why they need to understand mitosis or the second law of thermodynamics because they know deep in their hearts they will never need to know this. What good is this information? We clearly fail to convince them. It's not that they try to forget this information, it just never gets into their long-term memory banks. The lecture method just isn't up to the job.

We never seem to teach students how to solve real-world problems, or analyze data, or read a newspaper critically, or be a skeptic when they hear people claim to have paranormal powers, or demand sensible answers of politicians. We have to teach topics like pH and mitosis over and over again because the students just don't get it. It isn't connected to anything.

We faculty just don't get it. Even though we passed through the same mind-numbing process ourselves and have "learned" the same things and forgotten them just as fast, we seem to think that everyone has to pass through the same hazing process we did. After all, we survived. Someday in graduate school or beyond we might finally figure out how to use the "book learning." But perhaps not. It will never dawn on most of us that there must be a better way.

What a pity.

Saint Anthony and the Chicken Poop

An Essay on the Power of Storytelling in the Teaching of Science

By Clyde Freeman Herreid

T he Garden of Eden must have been in northern New Mexico. In early Christian iconography Adam and Eve were always depicted buck-naked: no fig leaves. As anyone knows, there are no fig leaves in New Mexico—and in fact, covering one's private parts with pine needles is painful to even contemplate—hence, the nudity of the first couple is easy to explain.

They lived in northern New Mexico, and Bethlehem is a little south of Albuquerque. With that insight, tongue in cheek, anthropologist Charles Carrillo began his New Year's lecture in Santa Fe.

On two occasions in my life I have heard lectures that were completely structured around a series of stories. Only two! That's quite remarkable when you consider I have lived long enough to hear literally thousands of lectures.

The first occasion was shortly after the collapse of the Soviet Union, and the country had opened its doors to tourists. There, on a ship floating down the Volga River, I heard a lecture from a Russian government

A 16th-century painting of the Virgin Mary with St. Anthony of Padua (left) and St. Roch. St. Anthony, the subject of this chapter's "Case Study," is known in the Catholic Church as the "finder of lost objects."

tour guide who told us about her country through a series of stories. She believed she could best capture the spirit and essence of her homeland with tales from the past. I was not only captivated by her stories, but also intrigued by the method of conveying information. I have often reflected upon this approach to teaching.

The second occasion was right after New Year's. I happened to be in Santa Fe, New Mexico, at a luncheon meeting. The speaker for the day was an anthropologist, Charles Carrillo. Although he had earned his PhD at the University of New Mexico, he was making his living as a santero, carving and painting icons of Christian saints.

As a Hispanic who could trace his ancestry back to the arrival of the Spanish conquistadors, he had long been impressed with the fact that anthropologists had oft analyzed Indian pottery, but the Hispanic ceramic tradition had been virtually neglected. This was a source of distress to him and ultimately led to his dissertation and the inspiration for his life as a santero. His lecture was about three unassuming pots—a bean pot, a coffee mug, and a tiny cosmetic pot. But before that he had to tell us about St. Anthony and the chicken poop.

Holding a small statuette of St. Anthony of Padua, Carrillo told us that he had discovered it was made by a santero in the early 1800s. Although apparently carved of wood, he had discovered using x-rays that only the core of the statue was made of wood and that layers of gypsum had been applied on top of the wood to build up the features of the saint. This discovery was to serve as part of his PhD thesis.

To his sorrow, the statue was missing a tiny figurine of the baby Jesus, who traditionally was held in the arms of the saint. Carrillo related how he had discovered a solitary Christ child figurine in an antique shop in California. There, lying in a forgotten corner of a doll collection, was the baby Jesus. Careful exami-

nation revealed it had come from the same santero's workshop where his St. Anthony had been crafted. It looked like a perfect fit. Perhaps it was not the missing Jesus, but it made a nice story and became another part of his thesis.

I doubt that the chicken poop story got into his thesis. Carrillo told us that Hispanic homes invariably had saint statuettes. St. Anthony was clearly his favorite for familial reasons, if no other. His grandmother revered St. Anthony because he had figured significantly in her life.

Chili peppers are a staple of every meal in Hispanic households. Even during the Thanksgiving dinner, turkey, cranberries and pumpkin pie are garnished with green and red chilies. Many Hispanic families of New Mexico raise their own crop of garden chilies. The best are raised with a rich mixture of manure.

The recipe in Grandmother Carrillo's time consisted of mixing a pail of chicken poop with an equal amount of cow dung and adding to that a bit of water to make a slurry. Then dried seeds of chili peppers were added. The housewife would take the concoction and, stepping through the garden, poke a hole in the ground. With three fingers she would reach into the mixture to obtain a pinch of seeds and manure.

One year as Grandma was following the ancient tradition, stooping to the earth and depositing the seed and manure mixture one step at a time, she discovered that a terrible thing had happened. She had lost her wedding ring! Somewhere in the garden the ring had slipped from her finger.

What to do? Like any God-fearing woman of the 1930s, Grandma went back to the house for her St. Anthony. Returning to the garden with the statuette in hand she implored St. Anthony to find the ring. This petition was totally appropriate, for the Roman Catholic Church depicts St. Anthony as "a finder of lost objects" and reveres him as a patron saint of miracles. Grandma Carrillo needed a miracle for sure. She placed St. Anthony in a hole in a nearby tree overlooking the garden, admonishing him that he would not gain reentrance to the house until the ring was recovered.

There St. Anthony stayed day after day. But this year the usual dry conditions familiar to residents of the Southwest didn't come to pass. No, this was the best growing season in memory. The rains came frequently. The chilies grew profusely. With each rain not only was the soil moistened but also water dripped steadily on St. Anthony's head, wearing away his plaster countenance.

One day, as Grandma was tending the garden, she looked in on St. Anthony. She discovered to her dismay that the water had worn away his head. Realizing the futility of leaving St. Anthony to suffer further climatic indignities, she retrieved the statuette from the tree. After all, St. Anthony no longer had eyes to search for the ring, and "What good is a man without a brain, anyway?" she reasoned.

As she lifted St. Anthony from the tree she got the surprise of her life: There, sticking to the bottom of the statuette's feet, was her ring. St. Anthony had indeed produced the demanded miracle! Thanks be to God. A family legend was born, one that would be told for generations of Carrillos.

What good are such stories of pots and saints?

Carrillo answered it this way: Stories are a way to connect to the past—to hold on to the memories of who we were and are. He encouraged his audience to "Go home and write about yourselves, not just your genealogy, but your personal history and where you come from."

I have often been struck with how little scientists care about history. It is today that matters. Indeed, researchers' publications seldom note a reference more than 10 years old. This same temporal provincialism exists in Americans collectively, for we seldom know or care much about our ancestors prior to Grandpa or Grandma. Surely, there is more to know. After all, our lineage stretches back over 3.5 billion years.

Scientists are as fond of stories as the next person. Experimentalists tell them all the time, though their stories are stilted tales of lab and field studies in journal articles of research. Those are still stories. Astronomers, paleontologists, and evolutionary biologists spin grand Homeric tales of the universe and Earth. Yet, in spite of our obvious concern that "history matters," we seldom convey this connection to our students. Where are the stargazers, the lab workers, the diggers of fossils in our classroom lectures? A Charles Darwin or Richard Feynman gets a pat on the head, but the rest of our "artwork" is unsigned.

It is often said that the field of science is impersonal and objective. That is its strength, we are told. We scientists are out to seek and reveal "truth," which is independent of the observers. This has led to the god-awful writing style that has permeated our journals for decades where the use of the personal pronoun "I" is shunned and the use of the passive voice praised. We scientists are to remain in the background, above the fray—as mere observers and recorders, scientific voyeurs; peeping toms, prying out nature's secrets.

As teachers, we scientists are supposed to just deliver "the facts, ma'am, just the facts" (as Joe Friday in TV's *Dragnet* was fond of saying). As a result, we have sucked the life out of science, as a student of mine recently said to me about a professor who was teaching ecology. I wouldn't have believed it possible to do that to ecology—a field filled with wonderful tales of adventurous discoveries. But it happened because the teacher filled each lecture with nonstop equations, modeling this and that. What a shame. Now this may appeal to some types of learners, but certainly not to most. I have nothing against equations and models.

I can appreciate the argument that it is a sign of maturity when a field of science can express its principles mathematically (even though, as is in the case of ecology, most of these heuristic models have little empirical basis). But to have reduced the personas of the lynx and the snowshoe hare to nothing more than squiggles on graph paper or symbols in a Lotka-Volterra equation is indeed sucking the life out of the field.

Storytelling even in the field of science is not entirely dead. Jane Goodall and other notable field biologists (many of whom are women) studying animal behavior have chosen to present many of their findings in narrative form. The life in their science is still there—vibrant and alive. We do still see the scientist as a human being even as we can see the abstract architecture of their science. Compelling stories do that for us.

Donald McCloskey, professor of economics and history at the University of Iowa, made some interesting comments in an essay in the February 1995 issue of *Scientific American*. Economics has trod its own path away from the narrative style of Adam Smith to become extraordinarily mathematical and abstract. He pointed out that "the notion of 'science' as divorced from storytelling arose largely during the last century. Before then the word—like its French, Tamil, Turkish, and Japanese counterparts—meant 'systematic inquiry.' The German word for the humanities is *Geistewissenschaft,* or 'inquiry into the human spirit,' as opposed to *Naturwissenschaft,"* which is our inquiry into nature.

McCloskey goes on:

Most sciences do storytelling and model building. At one end of the gamut sits Newtonian physics—the *Principia* (1687) is essentially geometric rather than narrative. Charles Darwin's biology in the *Origin of Species* (1859), in contrast, is almost entirely historical and devoid of mathematical models. Nevertheless, most scientists and economists among

them hate to admit to something so childish-sounding as telling stories. They want to emulate Newton's elegance rather than Darwin's complexity. One suspects that the relative prestige of the two methods has more to do with age than anything else. If a proto-Darwin had published in 1687, and a neo-Newton in 1859, you can bet the prestige of storytelling versus timeless modeling would be reversed.

Storytelling in science is largely verboten. We seldom hear of the passion, emotion, or personal matters of a Newton, Einstein, Lavoisier, Lyell, or Pasteur—such things are regarded as asides or diversions from truth, the grand structure of the universe that exists separate from the observer. So, many students sit in class waiting for the suffering to be over, or they change majors to other more human-centered fields where the subjective, the individual, matters.

Some years ago, I read about someone who was asked what one thing he would most like to keep in his possession if he had to fly off to another planet to start another civilization—a copy of Newton's *Principia*, Darwin's *Origin of Species*, Einstein's papers on relativity, or Shakespeare's plays. He answered, Shakespeare's plays. All of the other works could be regenerated. They were objective. Other scientists would duplicate them. Only Shakespeare's plays were unique and personal.

Even if we accept that science is objective, must we suck the life out of our teaching by neglecting our roots? James Conant, chemist, science adviser to President Franklin Roosevelt, and eventually president of Harvard University, thought we must not. He responded by pioneering the use of storytelling case studies within the lecture method framework. He built an entire course around this approach that he described in his book, *The Growth of the Experimental Sciences* (1949).

Case study teaching, whether it is done via the lecture method, the discussion method, or small group Problem-Based Learning method, puts a human face on science. It is not that case teachers deny the ultimate reality of the universe or refuse to accept that the universe will some day be described by a set of mathematical models. But the case study approach using stories gives us a context within which to learn.

Not only are stories captivating, they make it easier to learn and recall facts, figures, and yes, equations. Moreover, stories tell us who we are as a people—the problems we face, the values we cherish, the barriers we must surmount, whether personal or societal. They help tie us with an umbilical cord of DNA to our heritage—to those who have gone before us and to those who struggle in today's world in ways we would not otherwise know.

So what value are pots and saints? They represent the mundane and spiritual. They can put the life back into teaching, where it was sucked dry before.

Storyteller's Box

Opening the Doors to Science Case Studies

By Clyde Freeman Herreid

I went to the Denver Art Museum just before Christmas 2000. After wandering through the splendid Southwestern art exhibit and the incredible display of Native American artifacts, I was drawn to the Asian section to reminisce over the Buddhist and Hindu sculptures that have been my favorites ever since I had a sabbatical in India many years ago.

Looking at Indian art I have found new deities, cultural remarkables, and surprising polychrome color combinations undreamed of in our Western traditions. In Denver I wasn't disappointed. Tucked in a far away corner, I discovered a storyteller's box.

Here was a blood red, rectangular wooden box, perhaps two feet tall. The front had two doors hinged on each side so that when they were closed they met in the middle. But the doors didn't merely open and close. Their ornamentation promised splendors within!

When swung open, each door was really a series of panels hinged together that could be opened in sequence, each one as it was uncovered revealing another. When fully opened, the box would look like it had hinged wings. On each panel were a series of small paintings much like the layout of a comic book. These paintings revealed the classical tales of India. They told of Krishna and his boyhood pranks, of the comings and goings of the monkey god Hunuman and his various buddies and foes, along with the tribulations and triumphs of the sundry deities that populate the Indian pantheon.

This enchanted box would be carried from town to town by the storyteller and his family. The travelers would settle in a corner of the local market or under a banyan tree and attract a crowd. They might have to compete with a fakir who could pierce his flesh with needles, a snake charmer and his basket of cobras, or a magician and his cups and balls, but eventually they would be surrounded by a small gathering of adults and children.

Before the story began the box was closed. What mysteries lay within? The spectators could only wonder about the fantasy about to unfold. Then, with suitable solemnity, the storyteller would weave his verbal tapestry as the innards of the box were slowly revealed, one panel after the other opening like the pages of a pleated book. The wings of the storyteller's box would transport the listeners into their cultural chronicles. These mythical epics were Homerian in scope and symbolism. At the climax of the story the deepest recesses of the box would be unveiled, and two inner doors would be seen. Behind them, were two small statuettes depicting the deities that were the *deus ex machina* of the story.

A story well told should be rewarded, of course. A few rupees were welcome not as a *baksheesh* or charity but as a contribution to the spiritualism and meaning the story brought to the listeners.

I never tire of learning about stories and storytellers. Surely, stories are part of what makes us human. Because I am so captivated with stories at a visceral level, I am convinced that they are important avenues to learning. Stories are seldom used by us as educators in colleges and universities. Why don't we have storyteller boxes that we carry from gathering to gathering or class to class to tell of science and scientists and *their* trials and *their* tribulations?

Well, in a way we do. Our stories are called case studies. Our storyteller's box is this book, devoted entirely to yarns, narratives, and parables that can be used in the classroom. As you open the panels of the box you will find dilemmas, heroes, and heroines ready to fly. Enjoy the feast, and don't forget a small *baksheesh* for the storytellers.

Section II

What Are Case Studies?

The definition of a case study varies enormously, as I have found when I ask folks at workshops for their definition. Having struggled with that very topic for many years early in the game, I believe it important to get to the heart of the matter right from the start. It took me some time to reach my present broad definition, which is: "A case study is a story with an educational message."

The first chapter in this section, "Case Studies in Science: A Novel Method of Science Education," gives an overall approach to the topic as seen from my vantage point in 1994 and covers many of the different types of cases, how to write them, and how to teach them. This article was my first overarching stab at these problems. The themes are revisited throughout the book in different essays. The three chapters that follow in this section delve into the history a bit more in "What Is a Case?" and pick up some basic rules that the teachers in business schools espouse in "What Makes a Good Case?" and "The Business End of Cases." These serve as worthy models, although they are focused solely upon the discussion method of teaching. Truth to tell, I am far more eclectic.

Case Studies in Science

A Novel Method of Science Education

By Clyde Freeman Herreid

Science education in the United States has been faulted by politicians, laymen, and scientists. Comparisons among countries using standardized mathematics and science tests repeatedly show the United States trailing many European and Asian nations. J. Miller's National Surveys of American Scientific Literacy (1983) reveals large percentages of people who believe in astrology, occult experiences, extraterrestrial landings on Earth, and creationism, along with a woeful misunderstanding of basic science concepts.

Our deficiencies in science have been cited as a harbinger of the demise of America's preeminence in technology. Its long-term economic leadership has been questioned. Educators have been quick to point out that science education is not user-friendly, disproportionately turning off large numbers of women and minorities.

How to correct the many perceived ills of our science education has occupied the attention of many scientific societies, including the National Academy of Sciences and the American Association for the Advancement of Science (*Project 2061: Science for All Americans*). Sheila Tobias says in her book, *Revitalizing Undergraduate Science* (1992), that some 300 reports on the problems of American science and mathematics have appeared since 1983, yet with notable exceptions, "it is difficult to show that these reports have had much impact." Schools around the nation are seeking curriculum reform and classroom innovations to aid in rectifying the deficiency in scientific literacy.

One innovation that holds exceptional promise—yet has had little trial among science teachers—is the case study method.

CASE STUDIES AS A TEACHING TECHNIQUE

Case studies have rarely been used in undergraduate science teaching except as occasional stories told by an instructor, perhaps as historical footnotes to general lectures. James B. Conant of Harvard was apparently the first science educator to try and organize an entire course around this mode of teaching (Conant 1949). However, unlike the current practice in business and most other fields that present cases within a framework of discussion or Socratic dialogue, Conant presented cases entirely in a lecture format. Conant's model did not survive him and other attempts to use the method are not widely known.

In contrast, business and law schools have had a long tradition of using real or simulated stories known as cases to teach students about their field. Harvard University has been the leader in developing cases in these subjects (Christensen 1986) and has produced faculty who have carried their enthusiasm for the method to other institutions. Valuable case books in the field have been written about the pedagogy (Erskine, Leenders, and Mauffette-Leenders 1981). Other disciplines such as medicine, psychology, and teacher training have used the method to capture the imagination of students. The monograph *Using Cases to Improve College Teaching* (Hutchings 1993) is the newest effort in the field of teaching.

In these disciplines, cases are typically written as dilemmas, which give a personal history of an individual, institution, or business faced with a problem that must be solved. Background information, charts, graphs, and tables may be integrated into the tale or appended. The teacher's goal is to help the students work through the facts and analysis of the problem and then consider possible solutions and consequences of their actions.

For the past four years, we at the State University of New York at Buffalo have used case studies in three types of situations:

- As the core material of a general education course, Scientific Inquiry;
- as part of two general education "Great Discoveries" courses where three paradigms are discussed in the form of cases in the classical sense of a historical story as envisioned by Conant; and
- as an occasional case used in the laboratories and lecture of a large biology course.

We draw several conclusions from these experiences.

(1) Like case teachers in business, medicine, and law before us, we note that the case method involves learning by doing, the development of analytical and decision-making skills, the internalization of learning, learning how to grapple with messy real-life problems, the development of skills in oral communications, and often teamwork. It's a "rehearsal for life."

(2) Cases have strong appeal for many students who are turned off by traditional science courses oriented around a lecture format with a concentration on facts and content rather than the development of higher-order thinking skills. In a current course of nonscience majors using cases, we have 95% attendance while normal lecture courses have 50–65% attendance.

(3) Faculty must be shown how to write and to teach from cases, especially if discussion methods are used. These are techniques not common in the science classroom.

(4) A method of dissemination must be established so that teachers across the country can have access to the new material.

(5) The case method of presentation is extraordinarily flexible as a teaching tool, as I hope to illustrate with a few examples.

Robert Merry (1954) wrote that the case process is inductive rather than deductive. He adds, "The focus is on students learning through their joint, cooperative effort, rather than on the teacher conveying his/her views to students." Charles Gragg (1953) wrote a captivating article entitled "Because Wisdom Can't Be Told," in which he stressed that the purpose of case teaching is to develop analytical and decision-making skills. Erskine, Leenders, and Mauffette-Leenders (1981) noted that students "are developing in the classroom, a whole set of skills of speaking, debating and resolving issues. They are also gaining a sense of confidence in themselves and relating to their peers." I would add that the use of case studies in science should encourage students to critically appraise stories about science they hear through the media, to have a more positive attitude about science, to understand the process of science and its limitations, and to be able to ask more critical questions during public policy debates.

In short, the goal in most of our case method teaching is not so much to teach the content of science (although that does clearly happen) but to teach how the process of science works and to develop higher-order skills of learning. Looking at Bloom's (1956) taxonomy of cognitive learning, we focus less on "knowledge" than on comprehension, application, analysis, synthesis, and evaluation. Cases seem ideally suited to illustrate the relevance of science in society. Cases are equally suited to the collaborative / cooperative learning format in small groups but can easily be used in large discussion classes, as exemplified in law and business schools. They can even be adapted for megaclasses of students.

How to Write a Case

There are two basic questions that face anyone interested in using the case method. The first is, how am I going to write the case? The second is, how am I going to teach the case? The two questions are clearly related, for the case often will be written differently for different teaching formats.

How much work is required in writing the case varies enormously depending upon the materials you decide to provide the students. One of my colleagues, Michael Hudecki, uses a single 100-word paragraph from the *New York Times* as the basis for an entire class period. As class begins, he gives the students this brief announcement of an experiment in memory loss in mice. He asks them to write concise responses to the following questions: What is the problem being investigated? What are the details of the experimental method apparently used? What are the pertinent results? What specific conclusion can you draw from the study? Then, with gentle and probing questioning, he is able to draw out a miraculous number of vital points about the scientific process. Before the students realize it, they are creating control groups, hiring research personnel, spending taxpayers' money, and curing Alzheimer's disease. At the end of the class period, the blackboard is a blizzard of speculations, experiments, and conclusions, and virtually all of the students are eager to read the original research article published in the *Proceedings of the National Academy of Science* to see if their suppositions are correct.

At the other extreme, cases may take elaborate preparation requiring dozens of pages of text and extensive research. Business cases may require over a year of information gathering and interviews along with thousands of dollars of investment to develop a case that may extend over several class sessions.

Mount Holyoke College has put such an investment into an interdisciplinary course called Case Studies in Quantitative Reasoning (Pollatsek and Schwartz 1990). Designed and taught by members of at least eight departments, it uses only three cases in a semester to develop reasoning and evaluation skills. The first case is on Salem Village witchcraft and involves writing a paper "formulating and discussing a hypothesis about the relationship between wealth and power as reflected in the historical records for Salem Village during the 17th century." The second case deals with measurement and prediction: SAT scores and GPA. The final case deals with rates of change: modeling population and resources. Obviously these cases have required major investments of preparation time, finances, and class time. As with any case study approach, Mount Holyoke faculty have carefully laid out a series of detailed objectives that each of these cases illustrates. These objectives are attained through one lecture, two discussions, and a computer lab each week.

Preexisting Materials

Case materials can be found prepackaged almost anywhere: in newspapers, magazines, novels, cartoons, videos, and television dramas. The motion picture *Jurassic Park*, based on Michael Crichton's novel, is an ideal story to consider questions about scientific responsibility as well as DNA technology. Criminal trials reported on in the press may be used to highlight the recent use of DNA fingerprinting to identify suspects. The play *Inherit the Wind* is an excellent vehicle to discuss evolution and its place in the public school system. Advertisements for health food, vitamins, and pharmaceutical agents are prime materials for cases. Gary Larson's cartoons from the *Far Side* are a rich source of biological case material, as are tabloid papers with their outrageous stories. These need not be dressed up with extensive writing to work as case material.

For the very adventuresome, there are detailed medical cases published each week in the *New England Journal of Medicine*. Many teachers may find these intimidating but the cases need not be used intact. They can be edited to suit the occasion. In fact, some of the most interesting cases can be developed by taking one or two graphs and tables from any scientific article and asking the students to interpret the graphs or plot the data, postulate the methods, and speculate on the conclusions of the author.

Another technique is to simply collect a series of articles focused around a single topic. These articles are put on library reserve, or copied with permission from the journal involved and then given to the students. If accompanied by a short series of questions to guide their reading, an outstanding case can be developed. For example, in 1988 there were several articles and letters to the editor published in the journal *Nature* about the spectacular claims from the laboratory of the French immunologist Jacques Benveniste (Devenas et al. 1988). The paper theorized that water may hold the "memory" of a substance that it once contained. This caused an uproar in the scientific community. Claims and counterclaims were flung across the Atlantic with a magician being part of a "fraud squad" brought in to help settle the dispute. While this is hardly a flattering moment for science, the letters and articles are especially enlightening to focus upon questions of data interpretation, suitable experimental design, double blinds, and the role of editors in the publication process.

In summary, preexisting materials are cheap and easy to find. They come from familiar sources and are recognizable as authentic parts of the student's world. There is an immediacy in their use; one can see an article in the press in the evening and be using it in the classroom the next day.

Writing Cases

Many cases are best developed from scratch. This is the process used for most business cases and although it requires considerable time, it has the advantage that only essential material is included in the writing. The case may be customized exactly to meet the teacher's goals. Reynolds (1980) has classified cases into three basic types:

(1) Decision or Dilemma Cases present problems or decisions that need to be made by a central character in the drama. The case usually consists of a short introductory paragraph setting up the problem to be considered and may introduce the decision maker at the moment of crisis. A background section fills in the historical information necessary to understand the situation. A narrative section then presents the recent developments leading up to the crisis that our protagonist faces. Exhibits (appendices) follow, including tables, graphs, letters, or documents that help lay the foundation for a possible solution to the

problem. Examples might include a woman who has been disfigured in an auto accident trying to decide about having a breast implant, or an FDA official faced with a decision of releasing a controversial AIDS remedy with serious possible side effects, or President Clinton trying to decide what to do about the logging industry and spotted owl controversy.

The University of Minnesota has published a book entitled *Decision Cases for Agriculture* (Stanford el al. 1992) that has examples of how the method might be applied in that field. These cases follow the business school format; they are multipage documents based on real cases and with extensive data. Another approach is used by David Newton (1992) in *Science and Social Issues*, which consists of brief dilemma cases obviously contrived for students yet based on important realistic problems.

(2) Appraisal Cases ("Issue" Cases) are used to teach students the skills of analysis. The material is focused around answering questions like "What is going on here?" It frequently lacks a central character in the drama and generally stops short of demanding that the students make a decision. Examples would be a description of the Valdez oil spill, or a collection of papers and data showing the possible effects of vitamin C on the common cold, or a selection of articles arguing whether HIV virus is the causative agent of AIDS. Ricki Lewis (1994) has put together the *Case Workbook in Human Genetics*, which deals with issue cases. While obviously a student exercise book, it gains in credibility because it deals with real people.

(3) Case Histories are largely finished stories and are generally less exciting than decision or appraisal cases. They can serve as illustrative models of science in action and they provide plenty of opportunities for Monday morning quarterbacking. Science is replete with cases of this type: for example the Copernican revolution, cold fusion, or the Tuskegee syphilis study where several hundred black syphilis patients were studied for decades without modern medical treatment being provided.

HOW TO TEACH A CASE

Eighty years of using the case method of teaching at Harvard and other institutions has led to dozens of articles and books on the topic. Virtually all of these publications center their attention on the discussion mode of teaching cases. This is too limited a view of the method and I offer a few alternatives that are suitable to many scientific cases. However, in almost all methods there is a common approach. The instructor must have his or her objectives clearly in mind, must structure the presentation to develop the analytical skills of the students, and must be sure that student participation is maximized.

Discussion Format

The discussion technique is the one classically used by business and law schools to deal with cases. Students are usually presented with decision or appraisal cases. The instructor's job is to identify, with the student's help, the various issues and problems, possible solutions, and consequences of action. On the surface, the method is simple: The instructor asks probing questions and the students analyze the problem depicted in the story with clarity and brilliance.

Case discussion instructors vary enormously in their classroom manner. On the one hand, you have the strong intimidating approach used by Professor Kingsley in the movie and television series *The Paper Chase*. This strong directive questioning approach is often called the Socratic Method. The "all-knowing" instructor (acting as inquisitor, judge, and jury) tries to extract wisdom from his or her student victim. In its worst form, the questioning can be a version of "I've got a secret, and you have to guess it." In its best form, it can bring about an intellectual awakening as insights emerge from a complex case.

On the other hand, you can have almost nondirective class discussion. The instructor can practically stay on the sidelines while the students take over the analysis. The instructor may start the discussion with a minimum of fuss saying, "Well, what do you think about the case?" From that moment on, the instructor may merely act as a facilitator or "traffic cop," being sure that some semblance of order is kept and students get to voice their views. Finally, the class may end without any resolution of the issue or summation. The virtues of this nondirective approach versus the directive Socratic approach may be debated, but most practitioners of the discussion method prefer a middle ground. William Welty (1989), writing on the "Discussion" method in *Change* magazine, argues for such an approach with proper introduction, directive but not dominating questioning, good blackboard work to highlight the essential issues, and an appropriate summary.

Many experts argue that the best class size for discussion is perhaps 20 to 60 students. When class size is too small there is not enough diversity of opinion. When it is too large the chances that a given student can participate even once a semester becomes small. There is little incentive to prepare adequately.

Debate Format

Debates used to be common in the American educational system, and many aspiring politicians and lawyers got their start in debating clubs and societies. Few people have seen formal debates and have the presidential debates as their only frame of reference.

Debates are well suited for many types of cases where two diametrically opposed views are evident. Propositions such as the following are ideal for the debate format: "HIV virus is the causative agent of AIDS"; "Nuclear energy must be an essential part of our energy production system over the next 100 years"; "Abortion must be available for women."

A good format for the debate is to follow the procedure of moot court competition. Two teams of students each prepare written briefs on both sides of the issue and are prepared to argue either side. Just before the actual debate, they draw lots or flip a coin to see which side they must argue. The debate itself starts with the pro side presenting for five minutes. Then a member of the con side speaks for five minutes. There is a five-minute rebuttal by a second speaker on the pro side, followed by five-minute rebuttal on the con side. This is then followed by three-minute summaries by each side. In a classroom setting where some members of the class are not participating in this particular debate, it is valuable to permit questions from the audience and to ask them to evaluate the content and presentation of the debate.

The team sizes can vary, with three individuals per side being logical. However, there can easily be larger numbers: These "extras" can be used in several ways. One possibility is to use the two or three extras to help prepare the teams for the debate, help write the briefs and be on hand to answer questions, or to give rapid advice during the debate itself.

Public Hearing Format

Public hearings are part of many procedures in the United States. They are used by Congress and by public agencies and regulatory bodies. They are an ideal format to allow a variety of people to speak and different views to be expressed. Their use in case studies has similar strengths and has the added virtue of mimicking real-world events.

Public hearings are structured so that a student panel, role-playing as a hearing board, listens to presentations by different student groups. Typically, the hearing board (e.g., Environmental Protection Agency, Food and Drug Administration) establishes the rules of the hearing at the outset (e.g., time to speak, order of presenters, rules of conduct, regulations and criteria governing their decision making). This is followed by individuals or groups role-playing particular positions. Members of the panel often ask follow-up questions of the presenters. After all of the presentations are completed, the panel makes its decision or recommendation.

Teachers using this method may find that the public hearing approach works most effectively over more than one class period. This permits students the maximum chance to see the entire procedure play out and the preparations to be extensive.

Trial Format

Trials have inherent fascination because of their tension and drama. In the trial format, there are two opposing sides, each represented by an attorney, with witnesses and cross-examination. The case I will use to illustrate the method (The Case of the Northern Spotted Owl) could effectively be presented by any of the methods we have already mentioned but for pure drama, the trial method is hard to beat. Here is the way I ran this for an evolutionary biology class of 370 students. It serves as a reminder that not all case studies must be done in small classes and that a single case in an otherwise lecture course can serve as a wonderful stimulus for class interest.

The case is the conflict between environmentalists wishing to preserve the spotted owl and the lumber industry of the Pacific Northwest. Although these two sides of the issue can be framed in extreme terms, I believe it is best and more realistic to frame the argument with more subtlety. There are not just two positions in the debate nor are there just two solutions. Environmentalists cannot simply be dismissed as long-haired, dirty-fingernailed, bootwearing, tree-worshipping nuts. Nor can the logging industry be characterized as slobbering capitalist pigs with no concerns except the almighty dollar. There are bright, concerned people on both sides of the question and there are more solutions than either clear-cutting the forest or destroying the logging industry. It is important that students understand this. As a consequence, in the trial we have tried to use "witnesses" with different views. The 20-page case, which we handed out to all students before the trial, was written to represent different perspectives, as well. The case finishes with four different plans to deal with the problem.

In presenting this trial before a student audience, I used undergraduate teaching assistants who help in the laboratories of the course. I used two assertive, confident individuals as attorneys and team leaders. Together they and the other teaching assistants worked out the roles, the basic script, and format of the presentation. We decided not to treat this in a spontaneous, unrehearsed fashion, because too many important points might not get developed. Instead, we developed a script where each "witness" knew the essential points they must develop in their presentation and the points to mention during cross examination.

The format of the trial was as follows: After a brief introduction by myself, the attorneys for the two sides took over. First the logging interests were presented by an attorney and three witnesses. Each witness was allowed three minutes followed by two-minute responses during cross examination by the opposing attorney. The first witness for the logging industry was a "scientist" who described the owl and the basic problem. He presented the possibility that the owl might become extinct regardless of the cessation of logging. The second witness was a "member of the U.S. Forest Service," who supported multiple uses of government land. The last witness was a "logger," who not only presented his personal plight, but the economic problems that would occur if logging ceased.

The opposing view for the owl and environmental concerns were first represented by a "member of the Fish and Wildlife Service" who was seeking some sort of compromise, but was most assuredly against clear-cutting. The second witness was a "representative of the local Audubon Club," who was concerned about the cultural and aesthetic issues in the case—the preservation of our basic heritage. The final witness was a "representative of the Sierra Club," who strongly advocated a no-touch policy, arguing with facts and figures that the logging industry will soon be out of business in the Pacific Northwest regardless of whether it cuts the forest or not.

The trial proceeded with each side alternating its witnesses and cross examination. Following the last witness, the attorneys for each side summed up their positions in three minutes, finishing with the logger's position.

It was essential that the student audience not see this case as merely entertainment. There were two methods to get student involvement. First, prior to the trial, we asked that students work in teams to develop two position papers, one favoring the extreme environmental stand and the other the extreme logging interest stand. These were to be short (two-page) outlines listing the key arguments on each side. These papers were turned in at the time of the trial. Second, at the end of the trial, all students were asked to write two-minute reaction papers. They were to respond to two questions: Which plan did they prefer to resolve the issue and why. These papers were then collected as the students left class.

Problem-Based Learning Format

Medical schools have used the case method of instruction for years. Seasoned physicians have always posed problems to interns, residents, and students as they made their rounds. Not until McMaster University of Canada developed the method for its entire curriculum was the full potential of the approach realized. Since then, the method has spread to other medical schools that have been frustrated with the fact-crammed lectures in traditional curricula. A review of the method is provided by Barrows (1986) and an unpublished review by Koschmann, Myers, Feltovich, and Barrows (1994).

Problem-Based Learning is faculty-intensive, for it uses one tutor for every four or five students. They stay together for the entire term, working through a series of cases. The cases are typically linked by some common area of study or progressive shift in complexity.

A typical case passes through several stages. In their first meeting, the instructor presents a short written account of the patient, with some symptoms and background. The faculty and students together try to identify the points they think they understand and determine those terms, tests, procedures, and symptoms for which they need more information. At the end of this meeting, students agree on how each will divide up the responsibilities to search for the needed information in the libraries.

In the second meeting, students discuss their findings and share opinions. Their search for the correct diagnosis narrows down. By the end of the class meeting, the students have determined what new information they need to uncover and go their separate ways to find it.

At the third meeting, students share their thoughts, data, and understanding. They try to reach closure on the diagnosis and treatment. This is the last step in the process and generally students will not find out the "real" answer to the problem. The knowledge and understanding of the case comes from the search for answers, not from "the answer" to a particular case. The power of this method is its interactive approach between thinking, discussion, and searching for more information. Consequently, it mimics the approach we usually use in real life.

Scientific Research Team Format

The essence of most scientific research is the case method. As scientists, we are constantly confronted by problems, questions, or dilemmas. We usually have a large background of information that we can use to "solve the problem." We are likely to use some version of the hypothetico-deductive method where we ask questions, make hypotheses, make predictions, test our predictions by observation and experiment as we collect data, compare the results with our predictions, and make evaluations arid draw conclusions. Students usually have dim and faulty understanding of these steps, although they can usually recite some version of "The Scientific Method." Cases involving the above steps of science are particularly valuable for students. The more students take charge of the process, the more they are likely to appreciate what scientists actually do.

Depending upon the sophistication of the students and the facilities available, there are large numbers of real experiments that students may try. Typical lab experiments are poor substitutes for real science. So any attempt on the part of a teacher to have students question and gather data that are novel is to be commended.

Here are two examples of student research projects that generate interest and simulate certain types of science. The first involves the simple collecting of rain samples in different regions of the campus or city and measuring pH. The data collected over a semester will yield lots of tables and graphs for comparison with other regions of the country and lead to discussions of acid rain and its effect upon the ecosystem. Mundane though this project seems, it instills in students a great sense of many steps in the collection and analysis of data.

The second example involves the testing of astrological claims. It is easy to have students devise tests of the likely validity of forecasts made by astrologers that I provide. Over several class periods, I ask them to work in small groups to come up with experimental protocols. They compare and criticize the protocols, collect preliminary data, then revise their experimental designs. Often at this stage they recognize the problem they will have in analyzing the data, and consequently simplify

their approach. Again, they go out and collect more data, analyze it, and write a full-blown research paper using the standard format of Introduction, Methods, Results, Discussion, and References. The papers are group efforts and may differ significantly because the experimental designs may differ.

The papers are exchanged between groups, and the students evaluate each other's efforts, using the normal peer-review process familiar to journal publication. They will criticize all sections, evaluating the design, adequacy of methods, presentation of results, and validity of the interpretation. Finally, they will accept, reject, or accept the paper with revision. Whatever the commentary, all groups will revise their papers and submit them to the instructor for grading. At the end of this process, students feel they have an understanding of the process of science and the publication of papers.

Team-Learning Format

Michaelsen (1992) of the University of Oklahoma and his colleagues have devised a novel use of the case method that they call "Team Learning." It uses cooperative/collaborative learning strategies with small groups involved in a large classroom setting. The technique requires a radical overhaul of the typical classroom syllabus. It is not for the faint-of-heart, but it solves many problems that plague faculty trying to get students to prepare for and attend classes, and it largely overcomes one of the major complaints against the use of the case method: that it doesn't cover enough facts and fundamental principles.

In brief, Team Learning involves setting up the class in permanent heterogeneous small groups of students (four to seven students per group). The syllabus of the course is typically subdivided into learning units, perhaps 5 to 10 in number. Each learning unit is approached the same way: (1) Individual reading assignments are given and read. These assignments cover the essential facts and principles of the unit. (2) A short (15-minute) multiple choice and true/false test covering the central points of the reading is given to individual students. (3) Then small groups of students immediately take the same test together. (4) Both individual and group tests are scored in the classroom (preferably using a portable testing scoring machine, for example Scantron). (5) The groups of students discuss their answers using textbooks and may make written appeals to the instructor. (6) The instructor clarifies points about the test and reading. Steps 2–6 generally occur in one class period. (7) Students now apply the facts and principles they have learned from the reading to a problem or case. This application phase occupies perhaps 80% of the course.

Here is an example drawn from my Scientific Inquiry course for nonscientists. The purpose of the course is to acquaint students with how scientists actually go about their work and how they interact with other scientists and society. Their first assignment is to read the National Academy of Sciences publication *On Being a Scientist* (1989), which covers the major principles of scientific conduct. The students are then tested on the material as individuals and as groups. Written appeals are received and discussed briefly. As part of the application process the groups are asked to generate a list of scientific commandments that apply to scientists and their code of behavior. They are asked to put their commandments in the form of "Thou shalt not..." or "Thou shalt...."

The groups are then asked to read a review of Pons and Fleishman's reported "discovery" of cold fusion, and are asked to compare and score the behavior of Pons and Fleishman with their group's list of commandments.

It is easy to see how the Team Learning approach can be used with most of the case study methods mentioned above. However, its particular strength is that it captures the power of small groups even in large classes of over 200 students.

PLUSES AND MINUSES OF THE CASE METHOD

The case method cannot solve all of the ills in the teaching of science. Even devotees admit that it is not the best method to deliver a plethora of facts, figures, and principles. However, the case method is ideal to develop higher-order reasoning skills, which every science teacher claims they strive for. When cases are used occasionally within a course, they spice up the semester and show students how their esoteric learning impacts on the world and is dependent on political and social currents. However when used only occasionally, neither teachers nor students become comfortable with the method.

When cases become the predominant method of instruction this problem is avoided, but the question of information coverage becomes an issue. Traditionalists argue they can't cover the same amount of information using cases. This is true. Also, they warn that when social issues are involved in a science debate, it is always tempting for ill-prepared students to concentrate on the opinion issues. Naturally, teachers must be alert to keep the discussion on the science, evidence, and analysis side. Faculty must develop teaching skills many do not now possess.

Cases are most easily used in general education courses dealing with science and society. There is little tradition to worry about or proprietary interest involved. However, the use of cases in science courses will probably be viewed with suspicion and skepticism. Faculty who have themselves survived and succeeded in traditional lecture courses, and have years of yellowed lecture notes, will be loathe to give way to what may seem an educational novelty. Yet this "novelty" has had a long history in the education of some of our finest lawyers, physicians, and business leaders. Cases can do equally well for scientists, especially if we wish them to care about how their work affects society.

REFERENCES

American Association for the Advancement of Science (AAAS). 1989. *Project 2061: Science for all Americans*. Washington, DC: American Association for the Advancement of Science.

Barrows, H. S. 1986. A taxonomy of problem-based learning methods. *Medical Education* 20: 481–486.

Bloom, B. S., ed. 1956. *Taxonomy of educational objectives: Handbook I: Cognitive domain*. New York: David McKay Company, Inc.

Christensen, C. R., and A. J. Hansen. 1986. *Teaching and the case method*. Boston: Harvard Business School.

Conant, J. B. 1949. *The growth of the experimental sciences: An experiment in general education*. New Haven, CT: Yale University Press.

Davenas, E. et al. 1988. Human basophil degranulation triggered by very dilute antiserum against IgE. *Nature* 333: 816–818.

Erskine, J. A., M. R. Leenders, and L. A. Mauffette-Leenders. 1981. *Teaching with cases*. Waterloo, Canada: Davis and Henderson.

Gragg, C. I. 1953. Because wisdom can't be told. In *The case method of teaching human relations and administration*, ed. K. R. Andrews, 3–12. Cambridge: Harvard University Press.

Hutchings, P. 1993. *Using cases to improve college teaching: A guide to a more reflective practice*. Washington, DC: American Association for Higher Education.

Koschmann, T. D., A. C. Myers, P. J. Feltovich, and H. S. Barrows. 1993. Using technology to assist in realizing effective learning and instruction. *Journal of the Learning Sciences* (3).

Lewis, R. 1994. *Case workbook in human genetics*. Dubuque, IA: W. C. Brown Communications.

Merry, R. W. 1954. Preparation to teach a case. In *The case method at the Harvard Business School*, eds. M. P. McNair, and A. C. Hersum. New York: McGraw-Hill.

Michaelson, L. K. 1992. Team learning: A comprehensive approach for harnessing the power of small groups in higher education. *To Improve the Academy* 11: 107–122.

Miller, J. D. 1983. Scientific literacy: A conceptual and empirical review. *Daedalus* 112 (2): 29–48.

National Academy of Sciences. 1989. *On being a scientist*. Washington, DC: National Academy Press.

Newton, D. E. 1992. *Science and social issues*. Portland, ME: J. Wesson Watch.

Pollatsek, H., and R. Schwartz. 1990. *Case studies in quantitative reasoning. An interdisciplinary course*. Extended syllabi of the New Liberal Arts Program. Stony Brook, NY: Dept. Technology and Society, SUNY/Stony Brook.

Reynolds, J. I. 1980. Case types and purposes. In *Case method in management development: Guide for effective use*, ed. R. I. Reynolds. Geneva, Switzerland: Management Development Series No. 17, International Labour Office.

Stanford, M. J., R. K. Crookston, D. W. Davis, and S. R. Simmons. *Decision cases for agriculture*. Minneapolis, MN: Program for Decision Cases, University of Minnesota.

Tobias, S. 1992. *Revitalizing undergraduate science*. Tucson, AZ: Research Corporation.

Welty, W. M. 1989. Discussion method teaching. *Change* (July/Aug): 41–49.

What Is a Case?

Bringing to Science Education the Established Teaching Tool of Law and Medicine

By Clyde Freeman Herreid

The first sign that a baby is going to be a human being and not a noisy pet comes when he begins naming the world and demanding the stories that connect its parts. Once he knows the first of these he will instruct his teddy bear, enforce his world view on victims in the sandlot, tell himself stories of what he is doing as he plays, and forecast stories of what he will do when he grows up. He will keep track of the actions of others and relate deviations to the person in charge. He will want a story at bedtime.

—Kathryn Morton

Cases are stories with a message. They are not simply narratives for entertainment. They are stories to educate. Humans are storytelling animals. Consequently, the use of cases gives a teacher an immediate advantage; she has the attention of the audience.

The best way to start this column is with a glance at the history of case study teaching in academia. I do not propose to start with *Homo erectus* in my search for the origin of cases, but you can be sure that those of us interested in historical antecedents and animal behavior might pick up the elements of storytelling even in beehives, where workers return from their flower hunts and dance out messages to their apian colleagues. Avoiding such temptations, I leap ahead to Harvard Law School at the turn of the 20th century, where the formal use of cases entered the academic scene. I am helped in my historical musings by a 1991 article by Katherine Merseth, "The Case for Cases in Teacher Education," a publication of the American Association for Higher Education (AAHE).

Law as a discipline is essentially composed of criminal and civil cases. New decisions, new cases, and new laws are built upon old decisions. Students learning the profession must study the cases of the past and use them as examples of judicial reasoning.

Students come to appreciate that there is a correct answer to many of the cases they see in the classroom. Socratic interrogation, as seen in the popular movie and television series *The Paper Chase*, is a common method of instruction. We witness Professor Kingsfield leading, nay browbeating, his law students through cases leading to predetermined correct answers. The cases are closed ended.

The use of the case method in medicine is not much different. The life of a physician is nothing if not a succession of cases—particular examples of general physiological systems gone awry. The physician's job is to reason deductively from general principles to reach the solution of a particular problem. Correct diagnoses exist and "woe be unto you" (and lawsuits) if you make mistakes.

Modern medical education in the United States prepares students for their awesome responsibilities by having them spend two years taking basic courses in anatomy, physiology, embryology, and biochemistry before unleashing them into the clinical setting where they are allowed contact with patients. Recently, a couple dozen medical schools have revolutionized their curricula and set up physician education completely around the study of cases. Small groups of students and faculty tutors work through one case after another as they learn about medicine. This is the Problem-Based Learning Curriculum pioneered by McMaster University in Canada.

Thus, in both medicine and law, cases are real stories dealing with people in trouble. Students attempt to figure out what went wrong and how to fix it. The cases are chosen because they serve to illustrate general principles and good practices; correct answers and facts have a high priority.

In the 1940s, after the ravages of World War II, chemist James Conant returned from the Manhattan Project to life as a professor at Harvard convinced that our educational system in the sciences was flawed. He realized that laymen and politicians did not understand how scientific discoveries were made. Determined to correct this academic oversight, Conant began what he called "case study teaching" using the lecture method.

Conant would take an important historical event such as the discovery of oxygen and the overthrow of the phlogiston theory and painstakingly describe the steps and misadventures of the protagonists in the setting of the time. His book, *On Understanding Science,* describes his case method as he reveals scientists in action, following false leads, stumbling upon correct ideas, having brilliant insights one minute and making stupid errors the next, and serendipity always popping up unexpectedly.

Once again, cases are real stories—examples for us to study and appreciate, if not emulate. Facts and principles have importance but the value of the case is to show great scientists in action. Since these are historical lessons, the student is not an active puzzle solver but an observer of human nature. The instructor is a storyteller. The student is the audience.

At the other end of the spectrum, we have the cases used in business schools. Harvard professors introduced cases for the first time to give students practical experience for use in the real world. For instance, businessmen were invited into the classroom to tell students about actual problems. The students held discussions and offered solutions, thus the start of "The Case Method." It has become a model that is emulated across the world with thousands of cases now offered for sale. A typical business case may devote 15 pages plus appendices to documenting a business dilemma (e.g., a marketing decision by Coca-Cola to change its classic formula). The student would be expected to prepare for the class discussion by closely analyzing the background data leading to the decision. The class would then discuss the case in an organized way with the instructor moving through various critical topics as he or she outlined the problem on the board with help from the students.

Business cases employed in today's classrooms are real and told in narrative form. Instructors give the cases to the students in an incomplete state, and have the class analyze and discuss them to determine what action should be taken. Like cases in medicine, they are puzzles to be solved, but unlike the latter there is no predetermined correct answer. The purpose of the method is to produce managers who both know and act. Harvard business school professor C. Roland Christensen states: "When successful, the case method of instruction produces a manager grounded in theory and abstract knowledge, and more important, able to apply those elements." Cases allow the student to deal with situation-specific dilemmas. Consequently, a business school instructor never expects a discussion to go the same way twice; there are always novelties and unexpected turns in the conversation.

Two characteristics distinguish the use of cases in law (and medicine) from business, according to Merseth. The first is that law and medical practice depend upon a well-defined knowledge base as a starting point, whereas in business much of the knowledge is in flux. Conditions are always changing in the business environment. Second, business education stresses the human condition and the subjective view.

According to Christensen, "Any problem may well be understood differently by individuals and groups and that perception changes." In law and medicine, deductive logic and lines of precedent make the individual or specific context of a case less compelling. Merseth concludes, "To a remarkable extent, the purposes and uses of the case method turn on the nature of the body of knowledge that exists in the professional field."

Given this historical preamble, what can we say in summary? First, it is evident that in all instances cases are stories, usually real stories. Second, it is evident that teachers using cases are not all delivering these stories the same way. There is no "case method" (except perhaps in business). Conant used cases with the lecture method. Law school professors use Socratic questioning. Business school instructors use discussion leading. Medical school tutors use small group cooperative learning called problem-based learning. Third, the subject matter definitely determines the nature of the cases and their expected conclu-

sions. Some cases (and perhaps the method of teaching) are fact driven and deductive, i.e., there is a correct answer. Other cases are context driven, i.e., multiple solutions are reasonable. The best answer depends upon the situation at the moment.

Depending upon the case, instructors might employ different types of teaching methods. So where does this leave us on the matter of using cases in science? My answer is that we are in the catbird seat.

Science is a body of facts, concepts, principles, and paradigms that forms the core of scientific knowledge. This is textbook science. We want our students to know a substantial amount of information, such as how the heart works, the definition of the second law of thermodynamics, what pH is, the concept of plate tectonics, and so on. Instructors traditionally teach these subjects through lecture and need substantial work and creativity to come up with cases dealing with these scientific topics.

On the surface, the situation appears to demand closed-ended cases with correct answers. This is not necessarily the case. Instead, many fact-driven cases are open-ended and have multiple solutions because the data are inadequate or emotions are involved, and ethical or political decisions are at stake. Consider, for example, a case involving a mother trying to decide whether to enroll her child in an experimental program to cure a genetic disorder such as muscular dystrophy. Or think about cases involving government decisions on global warming, pollution control, human cloning, or NASA space probe funding to find life on Mars. All such cases can be loaded with facts but many of the decisions to be made are necessarily open ended. Moreover, all cutting-edge science, "frontier science," is necessarily contentious. Science philosopher Stephen Cole put it this way: "In frontier knowledge different scientists looking at the same empirical evidence can reach different conclusions. Frontier knowledge is accepted by scientists not as true but as claims to truth of particular scientists." So all kinds of case structures should be available to us depending upon the goals at the moment.

Personally, I feel liberated knowing that I do not have to conform to a particular method or someone else's vision about what a case is. Nor do I feel obligated in any way to always use cases in my teaching. There are moments when the standard lecture approach is appropriate, inspirational, and superior to other methods. Surely it makes sense to mix and match our teaching techniques to reach the best arrangement possible. Using cases is simply another arrow in our pedagogical quiver. But when we do choose to use cases, we are responding to the child in all of us, who once demanded there be heroes and heroines and mysteries galore in our stories at bedtime.

What Makes a Good Case?

Some Basic Rules of Good Storytelling Help Teachers Generate Excitement in the Classroom

By Clyde Freeman Herreid

Modern storytellers are the descendants of an immense and ancient community of holy people, troubadours, bards, griots, cantadoras, cantors, traveling poets, bums, hags, and crazy people.

—Clarissa Pinkola Estes

I wish Estes had mentioned teachers. Teachers should be in that lineup. Stories are their natural allies in the transmittal of the wisdom of the tribe from one generation to the next. Although I am not taken by Dr. Estes's notion of the Jungian archetype she so eloquently argues for in her book, *Women Who Run With Wolves,* I do agree there is something in stories that touches our fundamental nature. Estes again:

> Stories are medicine. I have been taken with stories since I heard my first. They have such power; they do not require that we do, be, act anything—we only need listen. The remedies for repair or reclamation of any lost psychic drive are contained in stories. Stories engender the excitement, sadness, questions, longings, and understandings that spontaneously bring the archetype...to the surface.

> Stories are embedded with instructions, which guide us about the complexities of life.

But not all stories are created equal. Some are better than others. And that brings us to the issue of this chapter: What makes a good case? Rather than begging the question or ignoring it altogether, I propose that we look at research that has been done in one of the citadels of case study instruction, Harvard University. John Bennett and Balaji Chakravarthy wrote an article for the 1978 *Harvard Business School Bulletin* presenting the results of detailed interviews and questionnaires of faculty and students. Later, Dorothy Robyn of the Kennedy School of Government wrote a note on "What makes a good case" (N15-86-673). I mixed and matched their conclusions that I amended for our purposes:

A good case tells a story. It must have an interesting plot that relates to the experiences of the audience. It must have a beginning, a middle, and an end. The end may not exist yet; it will be what the students need to supply once the case is discussed.

A good case focuses on an interest-arousing issue. Malcolm McNair has written, "For the case to be a real living thing and for the student to forget that it's artificial, there must be drama, there must be suspense.... A case must have an issue."

A good case is set in the past five years. To appear real the story must have the trappings of a current problem. This is not to denigrate classical or historical cases, but unless a case deals with current issues and the student feels the problem is important, some of its power is lost. If a student has just seen the problem mentioned in the media so much the better. Thus, a case on human cloning will awaken the students' interest before one on the Copernican revolution. Even a case on cold fusion is old news today and lacks the luster it did in the chaotic days of the original report.

A good case creates empathy with the central characters. We should create empathy not only to make the story line more engaging but because the personal attributes of the characters will influence the way a decision might be made. Certain decisions are beyond the scope of the characters' personalities and powers. It may be unrealistic for us to expect President Clinton to declare human cloning illegal all over the world by fiat, or for him not to comment about the NASA "Life on Mars" episode.

A good case includes quotations. There is no better way to understand a situation and to gain empathy for the characters than to hear them speak in their own voices. Quotations add life and drama to any case. Quotations from documents and letters should be used as well. Quotations give realism.

A good case is relevant to the reader. Cases should be chosen that involve situations the students know or are likely to face. This improves the empathy factor and makes the case clearly something worth studying. Thus, for a graduate student in science, a case involving people arguing about authorship of a paper is of greater interest than a discussion about sand flies in Uganda.

A good case must have pedagogic utility. Only an educator would use such jargon, but the point is valid. What function will the case serve? What does it do for the course and the student? What is the point of the story in the education of the student and is there a better way to do it?

A good case is conflict provoking. Robyn argues, "Most cases are fundamentally about something controversial"; if not, what is there to talk about? She goes on, "Is this an issue about which reasonable people could disagree?" If so, you have the beginning of a good case.

A good case is decision forcing. Not all cases have to be dilemmas that need to be solved, but there is an urgency and a seriousness that is involved with such cases. We can easily second-guess the owners of the shipping lines about the *Valdez* oil spill in retrospect, but at the time many of their decisions may have seemed quite reasonable. In dilemma or decision cases, students cannot duck the issue but must face problems head on. Without a dilemma in the case, a student can sit back and *tsk-tsk* the way that a case unfolded. When they are forced to take a position, they are thrust into the action of the case.

A good case has generality. What good is a case that is so specific that one can use it only for a curiosity? Cases must be of more use than a minor or local problem; they must have general applicability. If one writes a case about the cold fusion affair, there must be more to it than to state that Pons and Fleishman made a mistake or that particular chemical reactions are not going to solve the world's energy problems.

A good case is short. It is simply a matter of attention. It is easier to hold someone's attention for brief moments than long ones. Cases must be long enough to introduce the facts of the case but not so long as to bore the reader or to make the analysis tedious. If one must introduce complexity, let it be done in stages. First, give some data and then a series of questions and perhaps a decision point before more information is introduced. After all, that is the way life plays out...little bits at a time.

So now that we have the recipe, can we bake the cake? Can we take a subject that tickles our fancy and write a case that will work? Let us try an exercise to see how some of these ideas work out in practice. I have written two versions of an incident to emphasize the key points. Since readers of this chapter come from different disciplines, we will take a problem familiar to all teachers: cheating.

A CASE OF CHEATING?
Version I

A teacher was instructing 24 students in an introductory physics course during the summer. She was using a version of cooperative learning where students worked in small groups throughout the term. She gave daily quizzes, first individually and then in groups. The professor had a habit of leaving the classroom during the quizzes. All went well until the last day of class when she heard from one of her best students that cheating had occurred during the taking of quizzes. When she gave out peer evaluation forms for the students to rank their teammates, she gained additional information. Two Asian students in adjoining

groups had been cheating. Six separate students wrote about how the two friends had cheated and that they had been told to stop by their teammates but to no avail. There were no more class periods left, only the final exam. What should the teacher do?

Version II

"I couldn't stand it! I had to move. They were cheating. I study hard to get my 'A' and they were cheating."

Physics professor Margaret Blake looked hard at the young woman in front of her quietly telling her story. Paula was one of Margaret's best students. Margaret asked her why she had suddenly moved during the daily quiz.

"Lang, the guy in the group next to us, writes his multiple-choice answers in large letters on his quiz paper. He holds it up for Mengfei who is in our group to see while you are out of the room. We all told them to stop, but they keep doing it."

Margaret replied, "I wish you had told me sooner, we could have done something. Today is the last regular day of class. Friday we have the final exam. There isn't much we can do now. Well, at least today we are having the peer evaluation where students rank the contributions of the rest of their group members. Be sure you write down your complaint."

"I guarantee that lots of us will complain."

Not long after the class was over, Paula's words came true. Six students had pointedly written about the cheating between the two Asian students. One student in Mengfei's group was especially angry: "Meng gets such a low mark because he is never prepared. He comes to lab whenever he feels like it, and he and his buddy cheat every single day. Did you see how badly Meng did on the quiz when you stood behind him? And he always changes his answers on his bubble sheet and pretends they were scored wrong. I HATE CHEATERS! AARRRGH!"

Margaret sat there in her office stunned. She always thought that group learning prevented this sort of thing, otherwise she never would have left the room during the quizzes. Now what? Paula's last words rang in her ears, "They were cheating. What are you going to do about it?"

QUESTION AND EVALUATION

Most people, I believe, would find the second case more compelling than the first. Why? Both versions tell essentially the same story. Both deal with an interesting issue and are recent, relevant, pedagogically useful, conflict provoking, decision forcing, have generality, and are brief. But while the first version is a rather cold rendition of the facts, the second gives us a feel for the characters through their speech and thoughts. We can identify and empathize we them. They seem real, and because of this we care about the decision. If we had spent a little more time we could have even shared Margaret's anguish as she wondered about her own culpability in the situation. Had she expected too much from the students? Was this a cultural problem? Were these Asian students really aware of the rules in her classroom? What were her responsibilities to the rest of the students?

So what is the essence of a good case? It is this: A good case has ambiguities and it requires space to give a richness of texture to a story. The audience never knows how it will all come out, and that is at least half of the magic. And this half of the magic matters greatly in the classroom where the case will be "solved." No two discussions will ever be the same in a great case. There should be new flecks of gold to be panned each time the stream is visited.

If uncertainty, richness, and options are one half of the magic of a good case, what is the other half? I would argue it is the realism that is captured in the story line. The best cases conjure up the sounds, smells, and sights besetting the protagonists. It is not essential that the story line be so compelling that the reader can literally feel the deck of the Titanic as it slips beneath the waves or hear the cries of the winged monkeys as they carry Dorothy off to the castle of the Wicked Witch. But it must be real enough to make the reader believe the problem is worth solving and care what the solution should be. Given that, the battle is won. And if the storyteller is good enough that the readers can indeed close their eyes and believe the knight is there on a white charger, lance in hand, and feel the hot breath of the dragon, so much the better. It is something to strive for in case writing. Such magic is hard to find.

See chapter 55 for further discussion of this case study.

The Business End of Cases

By Clyde Freeman Herreid

N o, this isn't an article on how to make a fortune writing case studies. And it isn't a financial analysis of what would happen if you suddenly gave up lecturing in favor of the case study approach or wanted to be a poster child for active learning.

Nope. This is a retrospective look at how the folks in business schools look at the case method. After all, they have been at this business a long time and have produced *beaucoup* cases. We in the sciences are mere babes in the woods compared to the long-beards on the other side of campus.

I have just finished reading a trio of books on case study teaching in business by the writing team of James Erskine, Michiel Leenders, and Louise Mauffette-Leenders. The authors—who have over 30 years of case study experience combined—hail from the University of Western Ontario, the home of over 2,000 case studies in business. In the books *Teaching with Cases, Writing Cases,* and *Learning with Cases,* the reader learns lessons about case studies that the authors have shared with over 15,000 workshop participants worldwide. They and the European Case Clearing House, the Harvard Business School, and the Darden Graduate School of Business Administration are the major distribution centers of the world in their field.

According to the authors, the use of case studies in management is relatively new, being predated by the fields of law and medicine. The case study approach in business started at the Harvard Business School in 1910, when Dr. Copeland was advised by Dean Gray to add student discussion to his classes. During the next decade, business executives visited Copeland's classes to present their problems and listen to student analyses and recommendations. Copeland wrote the first textbook of cases in 1921.

The legacy of cases in business may seem short in the eyes of our Canadian authors but it is positively ancient when compared to the use of cases in the basic sciences, which began to take hold in the 1990s. But surprisingly, in spite of its impeccable academic pedigree (or perhaps because of it) and its hoary longevity, there seems to be little literature on the success of the method; virtually no assessment data in business, law, or public policy teaching seems to exist. Amazing! Years ago when I was first getting interested in cases, I asked one case study wag about the evidence and he simply shrugged with a twinkle in his eye saying, "Well, Harvard uses it."

This lighthearted response would not suffice today for any granting agency that is being asked to pony up a couple of million dollars to introduce case studies into the science curriculum. Nor should it. In contrast, people using Problem-Based Learning cases have been much more serious about assessment and now it is one of the best-studied teaching methods we have.

Returning to the business school approach, I would like to summarize the case method described by the Canadian authors because their books are the clearest and most unequivocal stand on case teaching and writing that I have seen. For starters, here is the way they define the case method:

The case method is a discussion-based learning methodology that enables participants, through the use of cases, to learn by doing and by teaching others.

Here is their definition of a case:

A case is a description of an actual situation, commonly involving a decision, a challenge, an opportunity, a problem or an issue faced by a person or persons in an organization. The case requires the reader to step figuratively into the position of a particular decision maker.....The repetitive opportunity to identify, analyze, and solve a number of cases in a variety of settings prepares learners to become truly professional in their field of work.

There are a number of points to highlight from the above definitions and other readings from the books:

1. A case study must be real. No lies. No fabrications. No fantasy. It must involve real events, real problems, and real people. Nothing is made up. The case is developed in collaboration with company officials with interviews and real data. The companys and individuals' names may be disguised if necessary. A release must be signed by a company official. If the information isn't real it doesn't deserve to be called a case—an exercise, a problem, an article, a simulation, perhaps, but a case, never.

2. Once the case has been accepted, it cannot be changed by anyone except the original case authors; otherwise it is a copyright infringement. Indeed, if the case author makes substantial changes, then another release may be required.

3. Business schools sell their cases. The more copies they sell to students the more money the schools make. There is no surprise here; after all, they are called business schools for a reason. They use this money to pay for the writing of new cases; there is a finite longevity for many cases because the situation changes over time, and both students and teachers prize cases that are up-to-date.

4. Business cases are usually dilemma cases. The students are asked to place themselves in the shoes of the decision maker. This is where the distinction between armchair cases and real cases is relevant: *The student takes the cases writer's word for it that a "Mr. Park" or "Ms. Lee" really existed, and the case material was based on a real situation. The moment the student starts doubting the reality of the situation described, his or her ability to give the case full attention and to take the task seriously diminishes. Academic honesty requires disclosure of the source of the data and the research methodology used.*

5. The method of teaching business cases is via whole class discussion; the instructor is in charge like a conductor leading his or her orchestra. The extent that he or she commands attention can vary. Some teachers see their roles as coaches or facilitators, while at the other extreme, some instructors are more dictatorial. In the middle of this spectrum both students and teacher achieve a true partnership. The authors look at case

teaching as a three-step process. First, there is individual study and analysis of the material. Second, there is an optional small group work by the students outside of class as they get together to briefly talk through the case. Finally, there is the whole class discussion.

6. The cases themselves have a clear and formulaic structure. A single paragraph makes up the introductory section. The decision maker is introduced, named, and his or her role in a specific company established at a specific point in time and space. In the final sentence we learn the question that the person is grappling with. The second section presents the company's background, and the third section gives more specific details about the part of the company where the decision maker works. The fourth section focuses on the details of the specific problem. The fifth section gives the alternatives and a final section gives a conclusion with a deadline as to when the decision has to be made (Figure 1).

I don't know the extent that this approach is used in other business schools, but I do think that the very predictability of the case structure should provide a student with a confidence that the answer is to be found within the document, perhaps in specific sections. This allows the case student to rapidly peruse the case and have a reasonably good chance of getting the essence of the material in about 15 minutes (the Short Cycle Process). But even using the Long Cycle Process, the case preparation should take only one to two hours.

Some years ago, I came to the conclusion that this highly structured approach was not for me. Reading the case study literature, it seemed evident that the term *case study* historically had been used to cover a variety of teaching methods rather than just whole class

FIGURE 1.

Normal case outline.

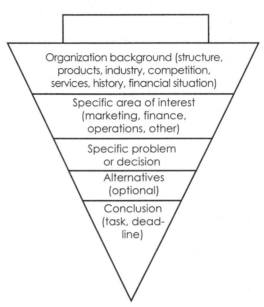

Organization background (structure, products, industry, competition, services, history, financial situation)

Specific area of interest (marketing, finance, operations, other)

Specific problem or decision

Alternatives (optional)

Conclusion (task, deadline)

Reprinted with permission from L. Mauffette-Leenders, J. Erskine, M. Leenders 3rd ed. Ivey Pub. University of Western Ontario, Canada.

discussion. For example, Harvard's James Conant taught cases using the lecture format. And McMaster University's medical school used cases with small groups and the progressive disclosure of information. I concluded that the essence of a case study approach was not in the style of teaching, not in the use of real cases per se, and not in the use of dilemmas where a character necessarily has to solve a problem. And I certainly felt that selling cases was not in the best interest of science education where few teachers had heard of the method (where was the market?). Instead, I have vigorously argued in this very journal that the essence of the case study approach is that it uses a story line to engage the student. And the story can be told in many ways.

Now, I have no quarrel with the University of Western Ontario authors' approach for their clients. Indeed, their slant seems eminently reasonable. But if we were to limit ourselves to their approach, large numbers of exercises, which have been used for a hundred years in business and law schools, would no longer qualify as cases. Nor would Problem-Based Learning cases or most of the science cases that we have published in *JCST* over the years. So, let us continue to explore the use of stories in their various forms in the classroom and celebrate them as cases even though we may from time to time get a disapproving tsk-tsk from north of the border.

Section III

Types of Case Studies

Four years after I wrote my first article devoted to case study teaching I had the itch to reorganize the classification of cases. Taxonomists are forever fussing with their genera and species, so why couldn't I? Indeed, a look at the newest classification schemes for all organisms reveals that even the higher taxa are not immune from the fussbudgets of biology. We even have a new major category that supersedes Kingdoms: We are told that there are three Domains in biology into which all organisms fall. So, I cannot be blamed for my transgressions here in "Sorting Potatoes for Miss Bonner." In this chapter I categorize cases around the teaching methods applied, and indeed I have organized this book around this approach. Yet, as you will see later on, Miss Bonner hardly has the last word on this, for new species of cases are being discovered even as we speak.

Sorting Potatoes for Miss Bonner

Bringing Order to Case Study Methodology Through a Classification Scheme

By Clyde Freeman Herreid

And out of the ground the Lord God formed every beast of the field and every fowl of the air; and brought them unto Adam to see what he would call them: and whatsoever Adam called every living creature, that was the name thereof.

—Genesis 2:19

To classify, order, name, and organize is a very human endeavor. In Genesis, God has Adam doing it right off the bat. The first man gets to name all the cattle, the fowl, and every beast of the field even before he is put into a deep sleep, deribbed, and meets up with Eve. Although I am not attempting so august an enterprise, I would like to take up the challenge to catalog some of the types of case study approaches that have captured my attention.

In high school, I had an old Latin teacher who was as fond of a story as she was of Virgil and the *Aeneid*. She was the quintessential Latin teacher, short, white haired, and with sparkling blue eyes set in a round face. I can see her smiling in a spring-flowered print dress. She was unfailingly kind and liberally dispensed A grades to lure callow youths into her under-enrolled classes. I think I was one of her favorites as I progressed from *amo, amas, amat* to become the Latin Club president, whose only known function was to preside over the annual Roman festival of milling students clad in sandals and bed sheets.

Miss Bernice Bonner told a favorite story to successive years of students extending back perhaps to Romulus and Remus themselves. She invariably told it when faced by a hesitant freshman who was conjugating verbs and groping for the proper ending.

Once there was a man who was hired to sort potatoes into two piles—big potatoes placed in one corner and small potatoes into the other. That was all he had to do. It was a simple task, requiring a couple of hours. His employer left him there in the morning and returned in the afternoon. He was stunned. The pile was untouched. Not a single potato had been sorted. What was wrong? The man was still sitting in front of the pile with a potato in each hand, looking worriedly back and forth, shaking his head muttering to himself, "Decisions, decisions, decisions."

Forty-five years have not made the story any funnier, but it was memorable, for I recall it now as I approach the problem of categorizing types of case studies. Much like sorting potatoes, decisions must be made, otherwise we will be left with a heap of indiscriminate spuds.

In 1994, I took a crack at cataloging the types of case study methods in an article published in the *Journal of College Science Teaching* (February 1994, pp. 221–229). I mentioned eight techniques where cases could be employed: lectures, discussions, debates, public hearings, trials, problem-based learning, scientific research teams, and team learning. Several years later, I, like a taxonomist exploring the kinds of ants in the jungle, found that I had seriously underestimated the number of extant species and had to revise my scheme. Now I am prepared to throw the following methods into the hopper: dialogues, structured controversy, role-playing, poster sessions, symposia, and a cluster of other formats. I will explore many of these approaches in the columns to come, but at the moment, I wish to discuss the basis for my classification scheme.

I have four major classification headings: individual assignment, lecture, discussion, and small group activities. These are based upon who will do the case analysis. In all instances, we deal with stories with a message (my definition of a case), but the role of the students and instructor will vary as will the case material itself. In one format (individual assignment) the student largely works alone. In another format (lecture) the faculty instructor works alone. In the other two formats there

is collaboration in analyzing the case. In discussion the instructor (especially in Socratic questioning) is still the controlling force in the analysis. In small group activities the tables are reversed with the students largely controlling the flow of analysis.

Individual Assignment Format. There is no need to dwell on this format for we all have experienced it, though we probably have not thought of calling it a case study approach. I argue for its inclusion as many assignments involve students building a story line—anytime a student is asked to write a historical account of events seems to fit. Many term papers, dissertations, theses, book reviews, plays, and written dialogues qualify, even though you may believe I am pushing the envelope too much. If it is a story with a message it counts.

Lecture Format. James Conant, chemist and past president of Harvard University, introduced his lecture version of the case method in the 1940s. His freshman-sophomore course for nonscientists was constructed around long elaborate case histories that illustrated how great discoveries were made. Described in his book, *The Growth of the Experimental Sciences,* he wished students to see science in the historical and human setting of the time. Few faculty have followed Conant's lead.

Yet all teachers tell stories. It is hard to call these off-the-cuff vignettes case studies. Many are brief anecdotes to whet the interest of the audience, but some stories are more elaborate and memorable. My first-year biology instructor at Colorado College, Robert Stabler, a parasitologist, used an entire class period to tell his puzzled students about the life of Moses and the perils of his people: starvation, plagues, and spiritual deprivation. Wondering what this long preamble had to do with biology, we were at last rewarded in the final minutes of class. Stabler spoke of diseases afflicting people of the Middle East, especially the guinea worm, *Dracunculus medinensis.* The female worms, which could reach a meter in length, lived just under the skin releasing eggs out of a small wound when an infected person waded into water. The people still removed these "fiery serpents" from their legs with the same folk remedy used by Moses. They used a forked stick to nip the end of the worm protruding from the skin and slowly rolled the parasite out over several days. Modern medical techniques are not as colorful. More to the point: I never forgot the story of the "fiery serpents."

Zoology professor Richard Eakin of Berkeley went even further. He became known for his dramatic presentations dressed as famous scientists. He lectured as Pasteur, Mendel, and Darwin complete with accent and costume, enchanting students with a glimpse of these scientific giants and their time.

Also fitting into this case lecture category are dialogues and debates. Occasionally, two instructors may work together in front of a class covering a story line with different perspectives and arguments. A single instructor may even do this using an intriguing method called a "Two Hat Debate." Here a teacher will "debate" himself, first giving an argument on one side of a contentious problem, then arguing the other side. In its most theatrical form, the teacher will literally change hats as he changes perspectives. He might don a beret as he argues the French viewpoint that Dr. Luc Montagnier discovered the HIV virus first. Then he could wear a baseball cap to represent the American viewpoint that Dr. Robert Gallo of the United States was first.

Discussion Format. The best-known method for conducting a case study is by discussion. This is the case method used in both business and law schools. The instructor to varying degrees questions the students about their perspectives on a case. The technique requires great skill to ensure that the students do not simply have a "bull session" and do have a sense of completion once the case is over.

Most business cases are dilemmas where a decision must be made. These cases require significant time and money to prepare. Harvard University, the University of Virginia, and the University of Western Ontario each have a major collection of business cases that can be purchased by instructors from other universities. The University of Minnesota has a similar arrangement for cases written on the topics of agriculture, food, natural resources, and environmental problems (*www.decision.edu*). The State University of New York at Buffalo has a number of science cases and teaching problems that are free to the public on its case study website *(http://ublib.buffalo.edu/libraries/projects/cases/case.html)*. If case study teaching is to become common in science, it seems clear that we must have a national repository so we each do not have to write all of our own cases.

One of the greatest problems in the use of dilemma cases is that most teachers do not know how to use them. Raised and nurtured via the lecture method in our youth, we are not usually skilled discussion leaders. In writing science cases we should follow the lead of business cases and provide extensive teaching notes. For an illustration, see chapter 16 on the Tuskegee syphilis experiments. This style should become standard practice.

Small Group Format. If we are to believe the extensive meta-analysis of over 1,200 studies by the Johnson brothers at the University of Minnesota, the use of cooperative learning strategies in small groups is the best method for learning. This may prove to be true for case study teaching as well. Let us take a look at some of the interesting strategies that have evolved.

In the November 1997 issue of the *JCST*, instructors at The College of St. Catherine in St. Paul, Minnesota, wrote about how they set up research teams of students to carry out long-term projects and had them set up poster sessions to summarize their work. Frank Dinan of Canisius College has used Michaelson's team learning strategies to teach

TABLE 1. Case study teaching.				
Teaching Method	**Individual Assignment**	**Lecture**	**Discussion**	**Small Group**
Thesis	X			
Term Paper	X			
Directed Case Study	X			
Storytelling		X		
Theoreticals		X		
Socratic Method			X	
Symposium			X	
Trial			X	
Hypotheticals			X	
Public Hearing			X	
Structured Controversy			X	
Debate Role Playing				X
Interrupted Case				X
Journal Article Cases				X
Promo Presentation				X
				X
Poster Presentation				X
Team Learning				X
Problem-Based Learning				X
Research Team				X
Book/Paper Review	X	X	X	X
Dialogue	X	X	X	X

organic chemistry with great success. Permanent groups of students took individual and group tests, solved problems, and analyzed case studies without formal lectures.

Problem-based learning, pioneered by McMaster University Medical School in Hamilton, Ontario, is a spectacular success story in the use of cases. This medical school, and a couple of dozen others, completely revamped their curricula around patient cases. Students working in small groups with a faculty tutor deal with a new case every three class periods. On the first day, they receive a new case, a patient with a set of symptoms, and some clinical test results. (They may actually see the patient in the flesh or on video.) The students with reference books in hand analyze the case. With the help of the tutor, they decide what the issues are and what they need to find out to deal with the patient. They subdivide the workload among themselves then leave class for the libraries and the internet. When the students return to the next class they share the fruits of their labors. Again, they ponder the problem and perhaps receive more clinical information before adjourning for another search through the literature. The following class brings the case to closure as the group pools its knowledge, finishes its diagnoses,

and plans its final report. As this class period ends, they are given their next case to begin anew. The University of Delaware *(www.udel. edu/pbl)* has taken this model and applied it to undergraduate courses in physics, chemistry, and biology with great success.

So much for the taxonomy. It is evident that many of the stories (cases) that we might cover in a class may be put into any format—individual assignment, lecture, discussion, or small group. Take the problems of global warming, toxic waste disposal, or species extinction. All would work in any format.

Many of the specific teaching methods can be used in more than one format. For instance, a dialogue might be a written assignment, used as a lecture, discussion, or small group. In contrast, a public hearing or symposium is restricted to the discussion format. The accompanying chart (see Table 1) gives an overview of the case study landscape. The Xs show where the method is most likely to be used. Perhaps you will view the chart as too inclusive. Perhaps you feel that I would classify everything as a case study approach if I could. Perhaps you are right. But at least give me this: I think that Miss Bernice Bonner would approve. There are no more potatoes on the floor. Decisions have been made.

Section IV

How to Teach With Case Studies: An Overview

There are many ways to teach with cases, each with their strengths and weaknesses. In this section I will consider the major approaches a teacher can take. But no matter what method is chosen, there are some generalizations to be made. The chapters in this section make several key points:

1. Although case studies can be used to present facts, their greatest strength is that they integrate material across many fields and demand critical thinking in assessing information;
2. The first few days of class are critical, especially if you are doing something totally new;
3. A teacher must get to know the students by name and they must get to know one another. Fruitful discussions are impossible between strangers; and
4. If you really want to know what the students are thinking about a case, course, or a teaching approach, ask them to help. In fact, I am so taken with using students as critics that I use the strategy that I describe here in all of our five-day summer workshops. Undeniably, faculty participants consider such student input the highlight of the workshops.

Can Case Studies Be Used to Teach Critical Thinking?

By Clyde Freeman Herreid

Everyone says they want to teach critical thinking. I have seen these words used as talismans on untold numbers of grant proposals. It falls from the lips of curriculum reformers of every stripe. It has to be the number one phrase David Letterman would put at his top 10 list of clichés of grant entrepreneurs. It is the equivalent of the Holy Grail for educators—not necessarily teachers, but "educators."

Yet average professors don't appear to give a hoot about the term. They are content to go into the classroom and get on with the job of ripping through their lectures so they can get back to their labs and do the university's real work—research—which ideally will bring fame and fortune to themselves and their universities.

Like many of us, I have given a lot of thought to the use of the term *critical thinking*. Just what does it mean? There are whole books written on the subject, and they haven't helped me one bit. Except to make me feel guilty that I may not be putting enough emphasis on critical thinking in my classroom—even if I don't know what it is.

Let me think out loud here for a minute. Critical thinking can't be just the content of a discipline, can it? It sounds more important than that. Yet, certainly, content must be involved; otherwise, one can't really think about a subject about which he or she knows nothing. But then, how would that explain my daughter, who was a television reporter and often knew little about the subject she was covering? She had an uncanny ability to ask great questions and to pull information out of even the most irascible academician. But still, content knowledge must be in there somewhere. If this is true then, every teacher in some way must automatically be teaching critical thinking.

Surely, we must mean more than "pedagogical content knowledge" (a favorite phrase of educator Lee Schulman); otherwise critical thinking would be a trivial phrase. And our colleagues cannot be accused of pursuing trivial chimeras, can they? So, this leads me to think about process. Critical thinking must have something to do with the way we think—the way we go about problem solving and asking questions. But I struggle with this, too.

More Than a Mind-Set

I am currently a consultant to a drug company, even though I know little about the pharmaceutical business, except what I read in *Reader's Digest* and on the back of pill bottles. The company has asked me to develop case studies to help their employees acquire a "drug hunter mind-set." After long discussions, the only thing I can get out of this phrase is the obvious point—they want a streamlined way to avoid all of the pitfalls and cost of going off in the wrong direction as they search the pharmacopoeia for miracle cures for aging, baldness, cancer, impotence, sleepwalking, and mean-spiritedness.

I have not found any magic wand to do this; if it existed, others would have been there long ago. But I do believe there are better ways to solve problems—by developing habits of mind that speed things along. They include problem solving, skepticism, flexibility, and seeing alternative strategies when others see only one way.

Let's take problem solving. Once again, this seems tied to specific content. I know that there are problem-solving exercises some authorities recommend—the "thinking out of the box" thing—but I don't know of any evidence to support that they improve one's approach to problems. Maybe the data exist, but I don't know of any. It is hard to imagine that working crossword puzzles, reading Ann Landers's opinions about personal crises, or letting your inner child out to play with finger paints helps you achieve the drug hunter mind-set. But maybe it does. Frankly, I think if you want to improve people's ability in chemistry, you ought to have them do chemistry and grapple with chemical problems.

Pardon me, but I am back to the idea that critical thinking is discipline-specific. What you really want in someone is creativity, curiosity, and skepticism in problem solving—someone who really wants to know the answers. I don't know, really, how you achieve this. We all know some people who really want to know answers, and we know hundreds who don't. Perhaps it is a genetic or a learned trait that is bestowed upon us early. But even if it is, I think we can train people to be more inquisitive.

If I had to choose one general characteristic that cuts across smart people it would be skepticism—the ability to ask oneself and others if the conclusions and data are correct. Smart people silently or openly say, "What is the evidence for this or that idea? Why should I believe this? Are there other explanations for the data? Is there another way to explain the data? What do you mean when you say this?" If you routinely ask such questions, even when dealing with subjects out of your own area of expertise, you will be well off. Certainly, this is true in the political arena. We have just had a terrible brouhaha—fiasco, is more like it—over the war in Iraq. Assumptions and hearsay, rather than evidence, dominated the debate.

Would that we could imbue skepticism into the American public about UFOs, psychic healing, astrology, creation "science," and a host of other paranormal claims. This goes for TV infomercials touting hair replacements, exercise equipment, vitamin therapy, and so forth. And it goes for supposed experts in our own disciplines as well. Asking to see the evidence is a good thing. It helps if you have a little background in statistics too!

Now, how can we develop this habit of mind in our students? The best way is to model it ourselves. Constantly, in lectures and discussions, we should openly ask: "Why should we believe this?" But this isn't enough. Most of us only got good at this in our careers as graduate students. It happened as we gained experience, read original literature, and attended journal clubs where articles were repeatedly attacked. Then we rose eagerly to the challenge. Soon we were emulating our mentors and sneering at claims of authors and doubting everything. There was probably even a stage where we were apt to be hypercritical and see nothing of worth in even excellent papers because of some trivial transgression in procedure. If this scenario is correct, then skepticism can be taught!

This brings me to case studies. If reading, arguing, and challenging are hallmarks of critical thinking, then case studies are the poster children for the process. Most of them are discipline specific, certainly. But they all grapple with the essence of critical thinking—asking for evidence—developing a habit of mind that should permeate everyday life. Many case studies deal with real social problems such as global warming, pollution, environmental degradation, and medical problems. I like the ones that deal with general problems: How to develop a dossier when seeking a job. Does prayer help heal the sick? Does acupuncture work? Such cases can be used in many different disciplines because of their general nature.

Best-Case Scenario

The best-case technique that I know is one called the "Interrupted Case Method." Readers can see a version of it titled "Mom Always Liked You Best" in chapter 27 of this book. The method begins when the teacher gives students (ideally working in groups) a problem faced by real researchers. He or she asks the students to come up with a tentative approach to solving the problem. After students work for about 15 minutes, the professor asks them to report their thoughts. Then the teacher provides some additional information about the problem, saying that the real scientists who struggled with the problem decided to do it in a certain way.

The professor tells of additional difficulties and asks students to brainstorm solutions. Again, they report after discussions. Then, perhaps the teacher provides additional data for their interpretation. Students consult with their teammates and report out. Again, the instructor gives them the interpretation offered by the original authors. And so on.

The interrupted case has enormous virtues. Students struggle with a real research problem and challenge each other and the data. Most importantly, they see different groups offering alternative approaches to the problem, and they see model behavior from the experts. I love this method because it is the way real science works—we have to work with incomplete data, make tentative hypotheses, collect more information, refine our hypotheses, make more predictions, get more data, and so on. In fact, this interrupted method is the very one that I use in workshops with the pharmaceutical industry, training folks there to attack problems. They like it, too.

So, I would argue that the case method has the real potential to develop the same skepticism that we all developed in graduate school when we analyzed research papers and saw what went on in the collection of data. The trouble with the lecture method is that it seldom exposes students to what really happens in the process of collecting data. Once students see this, they are forever changed. They rapidly recognize that there are alternative ways of attacking a problem and alternative interpretations of the data. They begin to doubt.

Most textbooks and lectures give purported facts as if they were received wisdom—wisdom that is certain and irrefutable. This is a great disservice. Students are not likely to question how we know a particular fact if we speak *ex cathedra*. We cannot develop a drug hunter mind-set this way, or any other type of inquiring mind.

William Perry, the Harvard psychologist famous for outlining the Perry model of student development, pointed out that the earliest stage in the maturity of students is the "dualist." The dualist student sees the teacher and parents as absolute authority figures and everything in the textbook as correct. There are always right and wrong answers to questions. The job for these students is to learn that what teachers say is truth and regurgitate it back on the tests. The trouble with the lecture method is that it perpetuates this stage in students. Further, it distorts the actual way that science is accomplished. Students are left with the idea that Newton, sitting under an apple tree, was bonked on the head and gravity was born—it was all "Eureka!"

Case studies don't do this. They show the messy, get-the-hands-dirty approach that is the real science. Cases demand skepticism, flexibility, and the ability to see alternative approaches. Problem solving is its *sine qua non*. In short, cases demand critical thinking.

REFERENCE

Herreid, C. F. 2001. Mom always liked you best: Examining the hypothesis of parental favoritism. Available online from the National Center for Case Study Teaching in Science at *http://ublib.buffalo. edu/libraries/projects/cases/case.html*.

Naming Names

The Greatest Secret in Leading a Discussion Is Using Students' Names

By Clyde Freeman Herreid

I attended our honors graduation ceremony in early May. Then, as each year before, I was struck by the tour-de-force performance of my colleague, Josephine Capuana, administrative director of the Honors Program. She read the names of 350 honors students—flawlessly. That may not seem too impressive, but impressive it is.

Our university, like so many public institutions of higher learning, has a spectacularly diverse student body. Dozens of different countries and cultures are represented in each graduating class. To read the names of students from Thailand, India, Poland, Greece, China, Korea, Chile, and a host of other nations flawlessly is no mean feat.

But I know how she does it. First, she calls all of the students whose names are unfamiliar to her and asks them for the correct pronunciation. She writes their names phonetically on cue cards. *Her first secret, then, is to care enough to get the names right.*

Her second secret is confidence. She says the students' names with such verve and *joie de vie* that even if she gets it wrong, the parents are convinced that they are hearing their children's names pronounced correctly—if only for the first time!

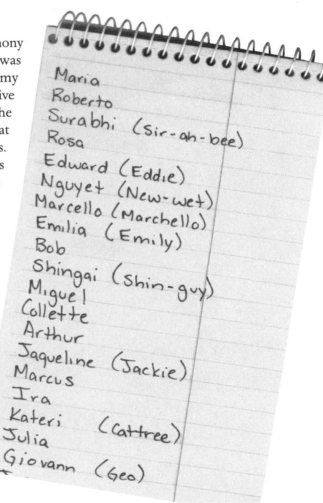

Maria
Roberto
Surabhi (sir-ah-bee)
Rosa
Edward (Eddie)
Nguyet (New-wet)
Marcello (Marchello)
Emilia (Emily)
Bob
Shingai (shin-guy)
Miguel
Collette
Arthur
Jaqueline (Jackie)
Marcus
Ira
Kateri (Cattree)
Julia
Giovann (Geo)

Names are vital. Adam's first task after his naked appearance in the Garden of Eden was to get to work naming the beasts around him. Naming things needs to be done if we are to put our world in order. Names allow us to communicate with other folks. Taxonomists know this. They are the CPAs of the scientific world. They keep our world organized, tidy, categorized—and familiar.

Carolus Linneaus, a peripatetic Swede from Uppsala University, made the world of plants and animals a safe place to visit when he came up with the Binomial System of Nomenclature to which all students thereafter had to pay homage if they were to pass General Biology. Before his enlightening work, the terminology of Adam's world was a bewildering array of names for God's biological handiwork. Scientists had a devil of a time figuring out whether a potato should be called a "papa" or a "pomme de terre" or a "dirt tuber." Our Swede solved it and said it is *Solanum tuberosum* no matter where you are.

Latin is the thing—no one uses it anymore; it is a stable language; it's not going to change. So use Latin to name the organisms of the planet. And while you are at it, give your tuber two names so that it shows its ancestral connections. Like the names for human beings. Most of us have at least two names (except for personages of the likes of Cher and Madonna). Names reveal to us family connections. Some of us even have three or more names, like I do. My first name is a given name; my middle name comes from my grandmother's maiden name, and my last name is from my father's side of the family, coming through untold generations of Norwegian farmers. We all can tell similar tales. It isn't surprising that Linneaus felt that the scientific name must do the same thing, and so it is that our potato's species name (*tuberosum*) is equivalent to our given name and the genus name (*Solanum*) is equivalent to our family name.

Names do more than allow us to pigeonhole things and give us relationships. They give us a sense of ownership. Once we put a name to things we get a sense that we understand something about the essence of the thing itself. This may be entirely wrong, but nonetheless we feel secure that our world is more orderly. And we can go on.

There is more to it, argue some philosophers and psychologists. They say that it is difficult to think about things if they do not have names. Indeed, language and nouns set the framework for our analytical processes. Hobbes put it, "We cannot think about things but only about the names of things."

The naming of a child is no trivial matter. We name our kids after saints, heroes, and ancestors in hopes that they will receive some of the virtues or wealth of the individual whose name is used. And using the name can lead to magical and dangerous results. Consider the plight of Rumplestiltskin, who was doing just fine in the German folklore tale until his captive maiden discovered his name and gained her release.

Name taboos exist in many cultures. The Kiowa Indians say you cannot utter the word "bear" unless you are named for the bear. Otherwise you will be driven mad. One must be especially careful dealing with the names of gods and demons—or before you know it, they may be at your doorstep demanding your soul or more mundane things, like your life. Indeed, using names is no trivial matter.

Dale Carnegie was passionate about names. His famous book, *How to Win Friends and Influence People*, and his training seminars emphasize the importance of learning and using names to become a paragon of success. Perhaps the greatest key to fame and fortune is to remember a person's name. Who doesn't feel flattered when someone recalls their name? This is especially true if the person who remembers us is someone in authority. "He recognizes me. I must be important," runs our inner dialogue. This recognition reaffirms our existence, our value. Nothing is more personal than our names.

So perhaps we can understand the personal hurt and insult that can occur when someone mispronounces, or worse, misprints our name—there is hardly a greater sin. Harry Houdini, the renowned escape artist of the early 20th century, said he didn't care what the newspapers printed about him—be it good or ill—as long as they spelled his name correctly. That's what mattered.

The point of this essay is simple. *Learn your students' names.* Use them constantly. This will repay you a thousandfold in relationships with students. No longer can students hide in the anonymity of the classroom. They will start to behave more like responsible citizens than the children we are so used to seeing, being irresponsible and whining and behaving—well—like students! A Swedish colleague of mine, Arne Tarnvik, professor at Umea University, has put it well. He said that using students' names is the most cost-effective way of getting a good discussion started and to keep it going. Call on students by name. Use those names whenever possible. No longer will the group be composed of strangers; if not friends, they will become at least colleagues together on a quest.

How many of us have suffered this ignoble fate in our classrooms? We ask a question and get no response. Students avert their eyes and start writing furiously on their papers. We wait in vain for someone to say something intelligent. If not intelligent, at least something. Anything. We give up. And start lecturing again. Surely, not many among us have not sweated through this scenario. There are several ways to survive this embarrassment, but undoubtedly, the simplest is to use students' names. They can hardly not respond if you call on them by name.

There are many ways to do this. But first you must find out their names. You know the ways. Use assigned seating and seating charts. Use nametags stuck to their bodies or on their desks. Take snapshots in one of the first class periods and learn who's who. Whatever you do, devise some system to get the job done.

This is the way I handle it. If I am in a class or workshop with say 40 people, I have them each write their name down on an index card in bold letters using a felt tip marker. This card is folded lengthwise and placed on their desk with their name facing me. It is useful to have them write their name on the other side as well if there are people seated to their side or behind them. The next step is to use their names constantly. Whenever I ask a question, I direct that question to a person and use their name. "Anna, what do you think about the suggestion that Bill just made?" "Does anyone have a different viewpoint than Jessica's?" "Frank, will you expand on that idea." And so on.

Use names repeatedly, and in the course of a 50-minute class, you can learn 20 to 40 names. Just as importantly, students will begin to use each other's names as well. This sets the stage for a good class discussion.

It won't solve all of your problems in getting students engaged in an intelligent case discussion. But it will go a long way. You will still have to be brilliant yourself. You will still have to give engaging assignments. You will still have students that will not prepare. But there will be fewer of them—they can no longer hide. Because you know their names!

Opening Day

Getting Started in a Cooperative Classroom

By Frank J. Dinan

Star for star, the players from places like Lithuania or Puerto Rico don't rank well versus Americans, but when they play as a team, when they collaborate better than we do, they are extremely competitive.

—Comments on why the USA is no longer dominant in Olympic basketball, from Thomas L. Friedman's *The World Is Flat*.

Since 1993, I have been teaching organic chemistry in a team-oriented, cooperative learning manner (Dinan and Frydrychowski 1995; Dinan 2002). Over the years I have come to realize that the time and effort spent during the first days of a new semester are key to the success of the class that lies ahead. What happens during these first days can set a tone that inspires students to work actively and cooperatively to achieve success in the new semester, or to sit back and assume a "here we go again" attitude. With this in mind, I begin each new year with activities designed to convince my students that they are valued as individuals, activities that will help them to get to know each other and to begin to appreciate the diversity, character, and knowledge of their fellow students. Most importantly though, I set out to demonstrate the great power that working together in cooperative teams has to enhance their learning.

I begin the first class by introducing myself. In this introduction, in addition to a brief review of my academic background, I tell students about some of my interests (baseball, films, and cycling), explain how I came to fall in love with organic chemistry, and share how I came to the conclusion that organic chemistry could be taught effectively using the cooperative learning techniques. All of this is intended to help students to think of me more as someone who wants to help them learn, and less as an obstacle to be overcome to complete the course.

We then move on to an interactive review of the course syllabus. I begin by distributing a copy of the syllabus to each student. The syllabus is more complex than most because, in addition to the usual administrative content, it describes how the essential elements of the cooperative learning technique that we will be using—problem-based team learning (PBTL)—will interact to form the backbone of the course that lies ahead. Additionally, the syllabus describes how case studies, peer evaluations, and individual and team grading will be used in the determination of their final grades.

After allowing students adequate time to complete their individual readings of the syllabus, I pointedly *do not* ask if there any questions. Instead, I ask each student to pair with a neighbor, exchange names, and discuss the questions and ambiguities that arose for each of them during their individual readings of the syllabus. After allowing some time for this discussion, I ask each of the student pairs to get together with another pair of students, exchange introductions, and discuss their observations and questions. I then ask each group of four to decide on a spokesperson who will present any points the groups may wish to have clarified, or any observations they may wish to make about the syllabus.

After responding to the group's questions and comments, I tell students that we are about to start learning each other's names. We do this by forming 8–10-person circles. A student begins by giving his or her first name, and the student next to that student repeats the first student's name and gives his or her own first name. The third student repeats the previous two names and gives his or her own name. This pattern continues until everyone has been involved. I actively participate in this process. After we have gone around the circle, I give a tennis ball to one student in each circle, and tell that student to throw the ball to anyone else in the circle. The person to whom the ball is thrown must give the name of the thrower and may then throw the ball to another person. If the receiver can't identify the thrower, then the thrower repeats his or her name and play resumes. Again, the pattern continues until everyone in the circle has been named.

By now, most of the allotted time for the first class has passed. I inform students that at the next class I will announce the composition of the cooperative learning teams that will be together for the remainder of the semester. Before our next class meeting, I obtain the grades each of the students in my class achieved in related classes taken in the past.

Using this information, as well as my personal observations from the first class, I determine the composition of the four-person learning teams. I put these teams together to maximize their diversity in terms of academic ability, gender, race, personality, and so on.

At the beginning of the second class, I announce the composition of the learning teams and ask the team members to gather, place their chairs in a tight circle, and exchange the information they will need to stay in touch with each other during the semester ahead. While this is underway, I take a digital photograph of each learning team. A student assistant prints these photos within minutes. I then give each team its photo and ask students to write their full name under the picture and write the name they wish to be called in class in parentheses under their full name. Studying these photos allows me to know each student's name by the time the third class begins. This, I find, is a big help in establishing the informal classroom atmosphere that I prefer and that most students seem to value. I post the learning team photos and names on the webpage for each class so they are available to all of the students.

With students still gathered together in their teams, I continue to help them to get to know each other by asking them to each share the funniest experience that they can recall involving food. This exercise is designed to get students talking and sharing light, personal information. I ask each team to select one of their stories and share it with the whole class. This exercise is not only a great icebreaker, it also leads to the telling of some very funny tales that help to bring the class closer together.

The remainder of the second class is taken up playing the NASA game. This is an exercise designed by NASA in the 1960s to convince the early astronauts of the power of cooperative decision-making. These astronauts were all test pilots, accustomed to making critical life-or-death decisions on their own in the cockpits of the planes they were testing. The power of cooperative decision-making had to be convincingly demonstrated to them because they would now be acting as members of cooperative teams in the spacecraft they would jointly occupy. The game was designed to demonstrate to the early astronauts that they had greater problem-solving power when they acted cooperatively than when they tried to solve complex problems as individuals. In the classroom, the NASA game vividly demonstrates to students how much the members of their learning teams can help each other by sharing their knowledge cooperatively.

To start the game, each student is given a description of a situation in which a space crew finds itself: Their ship has crash-landed on the dark side of the Moon, about 320 meters from the mother ship that they must reach. Students are each given a list of the items that were left undamaged in the crash, and, working individually, they must rank the items in terms of their importance and ability to help in making the journey to the mother ship. After this task is complete, each student team is then given one new copy of the same list of items and told to work cooperatively to reach a consensus decision on the ranking of the same items. When the teams have arrived at their new consensus ranking, they are given the ranking of the items that was determined by NASA experts. They then calculate the difference between their individual scores and the experts' ranking, and their team's score and the NASA rankings. Almost always, the team rankings are much closer to the NASA rankings than are those made by any of the individual students that comprise the teams. I record all of this information on the board so that everyone can see how well the teams have done relative to their individual members. Students are impressed by how well the teams do working cooperatively relative to any individual team member working alone. This exercise provides students with a clear demonstration of the power their teams have to solve complex problems when they work cooperatively.

Occasionally, one student's individual ranking of the items is closer to the NASA rankings than the team's consensus score. This situation offers an excellent opportunity to ask the teams to analyze how this could happen in a cooperative decision-making setting. The answer, of course, lies in a failure to communicate effectively. Either the knowledgeable student did not communicate his or her knowledge well, or the members of that team did not pay attention to his or her contribution. Either way, the team is made aware of a problem that it has and can begin to deal with it. The other teams, too, benefit from listening to and observing this discussion. Students find the outcome of this exercise very impressive and refer to it often during the months ahead. (For further details about this game, visit *http://corrections.com/nic/pdf_mirror/05112005_SpaceSurvivalExercise.pdf*.)

The NASA game ends the second day of the new semester. We are now ready to settle down to our task for the semester ahead: learning organic chemistry. The question is, have these two days helped to prepare the nascent class to do this? Would the two class days be better spent immediately delving into the meat of the course? Obviously, I don't think so.

Success in a cooperative learning approach depends on—even demands—good communication skills, trust, and a feeling that we are all in this together, that we can help each other to learn and to become better learners. The exercises described above are designed to begin to develop these attitudes. My experience indicates that they pay off richly by starting students moving along the path to good interpersonal relationships, making them feel comfortable in their new learning environment, and convincingly illustrating the power of cooperative decision-making. The cost that is paid for these desirable, highly valuable outcomes is a small one: two class periods. The outcome, as the credit card commercial says, and as many new semesters have demonstrated, is "priceless."

REFERENCES

Dinan, F. J., 2002. An alternative to lecturing in the sciences. In *Team-based learning: A transformative use of small groups,* eds. L. K. Michaelsen, A. B. Knight, and L. Dee Fink, 101–108. Westport, CT: Prager Publishers.

Dinan, F. J., and V. J. Frydrychowski. 1995. A team learning method for organic chemistry. *Journal of Chemical Education* 72 (5): 429–31.

Using Students as Critics in Faculty Development

By Clyde Freeman Herreid and Arnold I. Kozak

As part of a reinvented undergraduate curriculum, several new science courses were developed at the State University of New York at Buffalo (SUNY Buffalo). To help faculty prepare to teach the new courses, summer workshops were held to allow faculty to try out new material and different methods of presentation for an audience of 16 students who had been hired as professional critics. Both faculty and students praised the experience highly. On the basis of the success of these workshops, the authors believe that students should be included in faculty development workshops as critics and consultants whenever possible to provide "reality checks."

Most faculty dislike teaching new courses, especially those outside their research specialty. Professors come to know their subject and to revel in their expertise. They feel secure knowing they have nothing more to do for tomorrow's lecture than to dust off old notes just before walking into the classroom. The more adventuresome faculty members read a few new articles or revise a small section of their course each semester. But most faculty seldom contemplate, much less accomplish, a major revision of their syllabus. A change in teaching style by a seasoned veteran is rare indeed, because professors become comfortable.

This equilibrium is upset, and dramatically, if faculty are confronted with teaching a radically new course to different kinds of students. The trauma increases exponentially if several new courses and dozens of faculty in multiple disciplines are involved. Those struggling with curriculum reform are trying to avoid this recipe for disaster, especially because thousands of students may be put at risk in the upheaval. Such a scenario occurred at the State University of New York at Buffalo (SUNY Buffalo) when faculty faced the reality that they were about to implement a curriculum no one knew how to teach. The following is an account of how students helped show the way out of this predicament.

CURRICULUM REFORM AT SUNY BUFFALO

For six years, faculty at SUNY Buffalo labored over the redesign of the entire undergraduate program. Their vision was to reinvent the modern liberal arts curriculum. By the spring of 1991, members of the Faculty Senate decided that this goal had been reached and approved the program. The new curriculum would be implemented for the entering class of 1992. With new courses such as World Civilization, American Pluralism, and Scientific Inquiry coming on board, the practical realities of teaching the revamped curriculum began to loom larger. Put bluntly, the faculty asked, "How are we going to teach these courses?"

The problem was particularly acute for science and math courses, because a major increase in requirements had been adopted: a beginning year of mathematics, statistics, or computer science and a sophomore year of basic laboratory science (biology, chemistry, astronomy, physics, or geology), followed by two new, upper-division, one-semester courses, Great Discoveries in Science and Scientific Inquiry. Great Discoveries would focus on the historical development of three paradigms: how great ideas originate, how they are challenged, and how they change. One version of Great Discoveries—Macroworld—would examine the big bang model of the origin of the universe, plate tectonics, and evolution. The other version—Microworld—would examine quantum physics, atomic theory, and the central dogma of molecular genetics. Each of the Great Discoveries courses would illustrate different kinds of science in action: Microworld would deal with experimental sciences and small events in time and space, whereas Macroworld would focus on historical sciences and large-scale events.

Scientific Inquiry was designed to show how scientists perform their jobs in real life and to develop students' critical thinking skills in science. Unlike most science courses, whose primary emphasis is content, Scientific Inquiry would concentrate on process. Its purpose would be to show scientists in action within their own field and within society at large—designing experiments, collecting and analyzing data, and succeeding or failing and trying again. The case study method would be used, and the cases selected would be current, contentious, and relevant to public policy. AIDS, anabolic steroids, DNA testing, cold fusion, the use of animals in research, silicone breast implants, carcinogenic agents in the environment, the ozone layer, and global warming all would be appropriate topics.

It is evident that courses such as Microworld, Macroworld, and Scientific Inquiry were sufficiently novel that few faculty felt ready to teach them. To help faculty "retool" for the new curriculum, outside funding for faculty development was sought. The U.S. Department of Education's Fund for the Improvement of Postsecondary Education (FIPSE) came to the rescue. A FIPSE grant was awarded to support the development of a cadre of faculty who would be willing and able to work through the problems of the new curriculum.

SUMMER WORKSHOP FOR FACULTY

To accomplish the faculty development goals, a four-week science workshop with an unusual approach was held immediately after spring commencement. Each faculty member who agreed to participate received a summer stipend and in return was required to teach one of the pilot courses during the next academic year.

The purpose of the workshop was to give faculty an opportunity to try out new methods of teaching and to develop creative projects for the science courses. It was believed that this aim could be realized only by introducing faculty to new methods of instruction and by encouraging them to reflect on their teaching. Consequently, during the first week of the workshop, intense seminars were held daily on topics such as scientific literacy, how students learn, and differences in learning styles (including evaluation methods such as the Myers-Briggs scheme, the Perry model, and the Kolb learning styles inventory). Gender issues and ethnic differences in learning were also discussed. Because case studies would be a crucial element of the new courses, especially Scientific Inquiry, a couple of days were devoted to guidance on how to write and teach cases. Finally, outside consultants were brought in to lead workshops on cooperative learning and classroom assessment.

The first-week program greatly increased the faculty's knowledge of and receptiveness to new approaches. During the next two weeks, faculty met in subgroups to discuss their specific course assignments (Microworld, Macroworld, or Scientific Inquiry) for the next year. They worked on syllabi, sample lectures, demonstrations, cases, and lab experiments to prepare for a full-scale dress rehearsal.

HIRING STUDENTS AS CRITICS

For the last week of the workshop, 16 undergraduates were hired to critique faculty performance in delivering the new course material. The students were junior and senior nonscience majors chosen from a pool of respondents to an ad in the student newspaper. The group was representative of the normal student population, with an even mixture of males and females, juniors and seniors, a 37% ethnic presence, grade point averages ranging from 1.7 to 4.0, and 12 major fields of study in the social sciences and the humanities.

Employing students as critics has clear precedents. Redmond and Clark (1982) reported bringing consultants into the classroom to conduct assessment sessions with students whose remarks were then passed on to the instructor. This technique is used at many universities today. In another instance, Tobias (1990) described how she hired nonscience stu-

dents to keep journals about their experiences in science classes. The students' entries gave Tobias insight into some of the factors that discourage students from pursuing science. Using students as a sounding board for the teaching methods of the new science courses was intended to prevent such an outcome. The assessment efforts at SUNY Buffalo were unique in that students were involved *before* the faculty actually taught the courses.

During the last week of the program, each faculty participant delivered at least one planned class presentation to the audience of hired students and other faculty participants. The presenters were encouraged to try novel approaches to teaching, based on the earlier discussions about cooperative learning, different learning styles, and case studies. To their credit, the faculty responded courageously and became pedagogically adventuresome.

Each morning or afternoon session followed the same protocol. First, the faculty member explained which course was involved and where the presentation would fall in the semester's work. Then the faculty member either delivered a lecture, led a discussion or a case (based on a reading assignment given the students), performed a demonstration, or conducted a lab exercise. During the presentation, the students and other faculty listened, took notes, and participated. Meanwhile, the presentation was videotaped.

After the presentation, the faculty and student audience was asked to answer a detailed checklist of questions and to write a short paragraph each about the most interesting and the most difficult parts of the presentation. These brief essays were modeled on the one-minute assessment method set forth by Angelo and Cross in *Classroom Assessment Techniques* (1988). The entire assessment process took perhaps 15 minutes.

At the end of the assessment, the evaluations and the videotape were given to the faculty presenter, who was then asked to leave the room. Over the next half hour, the students and other faculty held a forum on the presentation just witnessed. If it was a lecture, the audience talked about substance and style, including delivery, pacing, speech patterns, and body language. For faculty who had led a discussion, the audience evaluated the questioning pattern, use of the Socratic method, chalkboard work, importance of the first question, whether or not a summary was required, and so on. For faculty who had tried collaborative techniques, the audience probed the effectiveness of small group work, the importance of heterogeneous versus homogeneous groups, the value of permanent versus temporary groups, and the nature of group assignments. For faculty who had presented laboratory or demonstration projects, the audience discussed the worth of such experiences in comparison to the standard lecture, exploring whether the time and effort involved were well spent.

These evaluation sessions were extraordinarily fruitful. First, the sessions made it possible to clarify and understand the students' views so that their remarks could be passed on to the presenter in a nonthreatening manner. More important, however, the faculty in the audience had an opportunity to hear students talk about which instructor behaviors they value and which they disparage. The faculty audience also had a chance to pursue certain arguments with students. Because the students had been told to be candid yet civilized, and because they were not dependent on these faculty for grades, forthright discussions of teaching occurred. Another benefit was that the students became immersed in their own educational process. They asked questions of themselves that few students do, such as, How do I learn best? Perhaps for the first time, the students had the opportunity to deliberate this question as a legitimate issue.

The facilitators of the evaluative discussion often asked students to diagram an interest curve for the presentation. First, the students were instructed to outline the major events or topics of the presentation as a time line on a chalkboard. Then, small groups of students working together were asked to graph their interest level in the presentation at each point. Finally, group representatives were invited to draw their graph on the board and to give a brief explanation of their rationale. Follow-up questions inevitably focused on what made a particular topic boring or exciting and what the instructor could do to make the material come alive.

In many ways, these evaluations were the most important part of the final week, because they directly exposed faculty to student thinking about teaching. Sometimes the point was lost. A faculty member chastised a facilitator after one session for not defending the presenter vigorously enough against the student comments. This faculty member had momentarily adopted a typical defensive posture—the students were at fault—rather than seeking ways to circumvent the situation. Fortunately, such lapses were rare.

EVALUATION OF THE WORKSHOP

To assess the impact of the four-week workshop, several questionnaires were developed for both faculty and students. In addition, a final roundtable discussion was held to determine "lessons learned" from the experience. The comments from this discussion, which are summarized below, revealed that the workshop produced both predicted and unanticipated benefits. The students' views were perhaps most interesting, especially because there had been no expectation that the students would be affected by the experience. The only intention had been to receive their assistance, but as frequently happens in dialogues, both parties were changed.

STUDENT FEEDBACK

The students were unfailingly gentle in their remarks and often more perceptive than faculty about how to improve a presentation.

They approached the task with an enthusiasm and a maturity that they generally did not display during a normal semester. Surprised by the apparent incongruity in their behavior, the facilitators once asked the students why they were so responsible and perceptive in the workshop setting when this did not seem the case during the academic year. "You're paying us" was only part of the answer. The hired critics said that they felt an obligation to improve the learning experience for the students who would follow them. A sampling of their views is instructive.

Overall impression. The students were impressed by the faculty's desire to improve and to present science in a new way. They empathized as instructors struggled through new techniques and methods, and their respect for faculty increased as a result. The students also appreciated the nonauthoritarian approach that most faculty adopted. Nearly all the students found it rewarding to be involved in the process, not only because they learned something new, but also because they had a sense of making a difference. One student commented,

> I thought the workshop was an excellent idea. It was an opportunity to deal one on one with other students as well as faculty. I feel that much was accomplished, not only for the new curriculum, but possibly for the professor's regard for student input and vice-versa. More workshops like this should be done in the future.

Changes in perception of science. Students who were already interested in science reported little change in their perception of this subject area. Other students, however, indicated that their perception of science did change: They discovered that science is important and can be interesting. Some felt less intimidated and more open to learning. One student wrote,

> I learned that I am not as bad a science student as I thought I was. I used to have the impression that I was unable to grasp any kind of science, but I'm happy to say that I was presented with some difficult scientific ideas and I think I understood them quite well. I am not as down on science as I used to be because it was made to be fun and interesting.

Changes in perception of science education. The students endorsed the importance of science education and were concerned that the teaching of science not be superficial. Some realized that there is more to science than memorizing formulas. They also recognized the connection between science education and critical thinking skills. Nontraditional teaching techniques helped change perceptions by making science more accessible. One student, however, believed that science should not be forced upon students. A representative comment was,

> I suppose the fact that the professors are here proves that they care about undergrad education. I've always felt that professors view undergrads as necessary evils they *have* to deal with in order to conduct their research and work with grad students. Maybe science is different.

Benefits of participation. The students were exposed to new teaching techniques and areas of science they found interesting. Many started to think about issues they had not considered before. The students also reported that the workshop increased their respect for faculty, improved their critical thinking and learning skills, and gave them an opportunity to meet people and make friends. A typical comment was,

> I got a chance to see that some faculty members genuinely are concerned about the way they teach their students. I also got

to see the views of my peers on the same issues and while not always agreeing with them, I learned that it is important to take everybody's views into account.

The students listed the following as the most valuable aspects of the workshop:
- New teaching techniques;
- Learning about oneself through working in groups;
- Personal contact with faculty; and
- Group discussion.

One representative comment was,

The evaluations following the week were valuable in that I was able to learn more about how I can take in information in class. I was also able to learn how to function in a group, which will be a helpful skill outside of school.

Another student wrote that "group exercises, group and interpersonal discussions were highly rewarding, both personally and intellectually."

The least valuable aspects of the workshop, according to the students, were the following:
- Over-the-head lectures;
- Interference from faculty during small group discussions; and
- The faculty's desire to impress students.

Faculty Feedback

Overall impression. The faculty were equally enthusiastic. They expressed genuine appreciation for the entire workshop and the way it gave them new perspectives on teaching and learning. The discussion of the Perry model especially interested many of the science faculty, because it enabled them to better understand differences in students' approaches to material and responses on examinations. The workshop's value was summed up by one faculty member:

If nothing else, the workshop was a wonderful occasion to look at myself—my role as an educator—what I teach, how I teach, and whom I teach. Some items in my role were confirmed, i.e., I do belong to a faculty, who like myself, care about teaching, care about students, and want to be effective. Some items in my role were laid bare for all to see, i.e., a forum was created that allowed for introspection and self criticism without penalty. I felt free to expose my weaknesses as well as my strengths. By this process I was the benefactor.

Value of the presentations before students. Two themes emerged on this subject during the debriefing of faculty. First, many commented that they now had a better sense of how to teach technical material to nonscientists without losing student interest or diluting the material. The faculty developed a much clearer picture of their audience in terms of background, interests, and intelligence. They were surprised that the nonscientists grasped concepts so well and asked bright questions, but the faculty also felt frustrated over their personal difficulties in explaining concepts adequately to students. Such inadequacies are seldom exposed by the traditional lecture format, because faculty who use this format may tend to blame students exclusively for poor performance in a course. In the workshop setting, however, immediate assessment and feedback from both student and faculty participants quickly dispelled this presumption of faculty innocence.

Second, the workshop provided abundant opportunity to hear about and try different methods of teaching. Only a couple of faculty used lectures, and even these individuals included brief demonstrations or small group activities. Most faculty were more adventuresome and spent the entire presentation period on cooperative or collaborative learning, case studies, or team learning (Goodsell, Maher, Tinto, Smith, and MacGregor 1992; Herreid 1994; Johnson, Johnson, and Smith 1991; Kadel and Keehner 1994; Michaelsen 1992). One typical comment was, "I learned several new approaches to classroom instruction, some of which are suitable for incorporation into my classes (group work, especially, I intend to try)." Enthusiasm for group learning was high, after initial skepticism. The evaluations revealed that the faculty appreciated witnessing group activities. One faculty member remarked, "The groups did better than my expectations in the session I conducted." Another saw the workshop "as a safe place for me to actually try out a case. I can immediately see how it will work and how to fix problems." This thought was echoed in many variations as faculty expressed a "willingness to try alternative methods of teaching." Others reported that their views about all teaching, even in science courses, would change. One professor wrote, "I will be more innovative as a result. I am even more impressed by the limitations of a poor lecture."

AFTERTHOUGHTS ON THE WORKSHOP

Twenty-five faculty members from eight different science departments were trained in two separate summer workshops. The faculty and student participants gave both workshops near unanimous acclaim. Following that summer, 16 pilot science courses, each involving 10 to 60 students, were taught with varying degrees of success. All the faculty said that the workshop prepared them to adjust to nonscience students and gave them a good start in organizing a syllabus. However, the workshop experience definitely did not prevent all of the problems of adapting to a new curriculum and new kinds of students. Faculty who were committed to lecturing, unless they were superb practitioners of the art, experienced the most difficulties with students and the highest absenteeism. Faculty who were bold enough to switch to cooperative and collaborative techniques had extraordinary success and negligible absenteeism.

At this point, it is reasonable to ask whether the benefits of the workshop could have been realized at a lower cost and in other ways. The answer is probably *yes,* but two other approaches tried since were not as successful. These "experiments" are noteworthy. The first effort was aimed at increasing the pool of trained, committed faculty by conducting a series of two-hour, afternoon seminars every two weeks for medical school faculty who "were volunteered" for participation in the new curriculum. The seminars were sponsored by the Vice-Provost for Undergraduate Education and nominally approved by the Dean of the Medical School, with a hesitant imprimatur from the respective chairs of the medical school departments. The seminars dealt with many of the same subjects that had been discussed in the summer workshops: scientific literacy, the new curriculum, assessment, collaborative and cooperative learning, and so on. However, there were no practice sessions before student critics. The seminars failed, as interest waned and the number of attending faculty dwindled. Only one person who attended the seminars joined the curriculum converts, and he is steadfastly devoted to the lecture method.

The second attempt to engage faculty in the curriculum and to alter their teaching methods involved using students as critics once again. The Vice-Provost asked that a one-week summer workshop be offered to assist faculty who were teaching math and the first-year science laboratory courses that were part of the new curriculum. Participating in this workshop were engineers and scientists, who were compensated with stipends. Because the math and the science lab courses were directed toward younger nonscience students, 16 sophomores with diverse backgrounds were hired to act as critics. The faculty in this one-week workshop never met as a group and had only a general idea of the new university curriculum overall. During the week, students watched faculty presentations, many of which were laboratory exercises. After each presentation, the students wrote a critique and participated in an oral evaluation session, but without the involvement of other faculty.

The results were perhaps predictable. The faculty did receive valuable feedback on the teaching methods they tried and did develop a much better sense of the students they would be instructing. The students described the experience as positive. However, the lack of faculty interchange, the lack of serious discussion about pedagogical alternatives to standard lectures and labs, and the lack of early conversations on learning theory and assessment methods, which would have sensitized faculty to student needs, kept the workshop from being a transforming experience. Unlike the results of the previous workshops, "the scales did not fall off faculty eyes," and attitudes did not change.

Conclusion

Students can be extremely informative about the educational experience if they are asked pointed questions about particular class presentations. They also can be led to discuss serious pedagogical issues if they are made to feel like partners, rather than mere receptacles, in the educational process. One faculty member observed, "My experience has taught me that students care about their learning if their opinion is taken *seriously*, and their right to opinion is *respected*."

Faculty gain insight into the educational process when their own presentations are dissected in detail by students. But they gain even more when they see other faculty making mistakes and having successes and then discuss the pedagogical process with students and other faculty. Student criticism without faculty dialogue is apt to be too vague to be useful. Faculty learn little from a student's comment that "The presentation was boring," or "I don't understand." Students need to be asked specific questions to glean information that will help in correcting problems.

Teaching workshops devoid of student input are likely to be too theoretical and to lack a "reality check." Faculty need to face the fact that their expectations of what should happen in the classroom are frequently wrong. The experiences at SUNY Buffalo suggest that all teaching workshops should include student representatives. In the workshop setting, faculty and students form a true partnership from which learning results. One faculty member summed up this symbiotic interaction as follows:

What I guess needs to be said is that my *attitude* has changed. I can approach a subject in different ways now. In the past I might have looked upon a subject being taught in really only one way (my way, my perception). Now I can fully look upon a subject in a variety of ways—and importantly, many of these ways will come from *the students themselves.*

References

Angelo, T. A., and K. P. Cross. 1988. *Classroom assessment techniques: A handbook for faculty.* San Francisco: Jossey-Bass.

Goodsell, A., M. Maher, V. Tinto, B. L. Smith, and J. MacGregor. 1992. *Collaborative learning: A sourcebook for higher education.* University Park, PA: Pennsylvania State University, National Center for Postsecondary Teaching, Learning, and Assessment.

Herreid, C. F. 1994. Case studies in science: A novel method of science education. *Journal of College Science Teaching* 23: 221–229.

Johnson, D. W., R. T. Johnson, and K. A. Smith. 1991. *Cooperative learning: Increasing college faculty instructional productivity* (ASHE-ERIC Higher Education Rep. No.4). Washington, DC: George Washington University.

Kadel, S., and J. A. Keehner. 1994. *Collaborative learning: A sourcebook for higher education* (Vol. 2). University Park, PA: Pennsylvania State University, National Center for Postsecondary Teaching, Learning, and Assessment.

Michaelsen, L. 1992. Team learning: A comprehensive approach for harnessing the power of small groups in higher education. *To Improve the Academy* 11: 107–122.

Redmond, M. V., and D. J. Clark. 1982. Student group instructional diagnosis: A practical approach to improving teaching. *AAHE Bulletin* 34(6): 8–10.

Tobias, S. 1990. *They're not dumb, they're different: Stalking the second tier.* Tucson, AZ: Research Corporation.

Reprinted with permission from *Journal on Excellence in College Teaching:* 17–29 (1995). *http://ject.lib.muohio.edu*

Section V

Whole Class Discussion: The Classical Method

Originally, case studies were scenarios from the world of law or business. Teachers or guest lecturers presented real stories to a class of students and then ran discussions about these cases. Teaching this way, with whole class discussions, has the virtue that everyone hears essentially the same information and deliberations. It works best in small classes where everyone can chime in and have their say. Law and business schools today still use the method even in classes that reach 70–90 students. Moreover, participation in class discussions may be required, but plainly not everyone can contribute at each class session.

Such discussion cases can be classified either as Analysis (Issues) Cases or Dilemma Cases. In the former, the students' job is to simply analyze what happened in the case. In the latter, the students have to both analyze the situation and then suggest what might be done. Analysis Cases (sometimes also called Appraisal Cases) can be further categorized as contemporary (any recent event in the news such as the Enron scandal) or historical (something so far back in time where conditions were quite different politically, socially, or scientifically, such as the Stock Market crash of 1929.) This categorization is useful for science cases as well.

Analysis (Issues) Cases ask, "What happened?" or "What is happening?" These cases may be categorized as Contemporary Cases (for example, the Challenger shuttle disaster, ozone depletion in the atmosphere, or Hurricane Katrina's effect on New Orleans) or as Historical Cases (Galileo at the Inquisition, the influenza epidemic of 1918, or the Tuskegee Syphilis Project, for example).

Dilemma (Decision) Cases ask, "What happened and what do we—or the protagonist in the story—do about it?" Examples include the physician's diagnosis and treatment of a patient, global warming, and an FDA official deciding whether to release a new drug for the treatment of AIDS.

How do we teach discussion cases? Here is my approach: If it is an Analysis Case, I want to establish the essential facts of the case by asking probing questions of the students that address the who, what, why, where, when, and how of the story. When I have achieved that, the case is finished.

For a Dilemma Case, I still want to analyze the case first to get the essential facts out in the open to be sure that everyone has a general understanding of what happened. Then I turn to the problem of what decision(s) the protagonists should make. I want to explore the short-term (immediate) decisions that might be made and their risks and benefits. Afterward I explore the possible long-range solutions to the dilemma.

One of the critical problems facing any teacher of cases is to be sure that s/he has a clear idea of the goals of the case. Once that is in hand, it is important to decide what the opening question should be to get to these goals. This is vital. If the instructor chooses the wrong question s/he might immediately be diverted into uncharted and unproductive waters. For example, if a teacher starts off by asking what the hero of the story should do, without establishing the facts, this may lead to unnecessary disagreements because no one is certain of the data. That is why I choose to work through the analysis portion of a case first; I want to get to the science right away. If, instead, I prematurely get drawn into a conversation on decision making, there are invariably political, social, and ethical problems involved, and these tend to overpower the science. And students are all too willing to talk about these topics even if they haven't a clue about the science. Be wary of that first question.

A final point on closure: How an instructor finishes a case discussion is important. At the end of the case some faculty briefly summarize what the class has accomplished that day. This gives the instructor a chance to clarify key points and to add structure to sometimes an otherwise formless discussion. Other teachers ask a student to do the honors, although that has some risks. Finally, some instructors prefer to just stop when they run out of time, leaving a case unresolved. They do this knowing that life doesn't just stop at the end of a set period; also, they know that an unresolved case is likely to plague students enough that they may continue to puzzle over it—perhaps indefinitely.

The chapter list below categorizes the different styles of discussion cases explored in this section.

- Chapter 14: Using Novels as Bases for Case Studies: Michael Chrichton's *State of Fear* and Global Warming [Analysis Case—contemporary]
- Chapter 15: Journal Articles as Case Studies: *The New England Journal of Medicine* on Breast Cancer [Dilemma Case]
- Chapter 16: Bad Blood: A Case Study of the Tuskegee Syphilis Project [Analysis Case—historical]
- Chapter 17: Case Study Teaching in Science: A Dilemma Case on "Animal Rights" [Dilemma Case]
- Chapter 18: Is There Life on Mars? [Dilemma Case]

Using Novels as Bases for Case Studies

Michael Crichton's State of Fear and Global Warming

By Clyde Freeman Herreid

Some books are to be tasted, others to be swallowed, and some few to be chewed and digested.

—Francis Bacon

Every time an English professor assigns a novel, poem, or play for a class to analyze, he or she is using the case study method. Why shouldn't we scientists do the same? We don't always have to write our own material. After all, there are some pretty good writers out there, and some of them actually slip a lot of science into the nooks and crannies of their plots. Indeed, in the case of Michael Crichton, author of *Jurassic Park, The Andromeda Strain,* and more recently *State of Fear,* science is front and center—with graphs and footnotes to actual scientific papers no less. So let's consider the novel as a basis for a case study.

NOVEL TEACHING

Each spring I teach an honors seminar called Scientific Inquiry: Case Studies in Science. Enrolling a couple of dozen students, my main objective is to give them a better idea of how science is really accomplished. That's easier said than done. (Most students—and indeed, most folks—don't have a clue as to the really messy nature of science and the reasons that we can't always give simple answers to questions. Lawyers take full advantage of this when they put scientists on the stand as expert witnesses.) Case studies can show how scientists act on a day-to-day basis. That's what I am after in this course.

To accomplish this, over the years I have developed and used a covey of case studies. More imaginatively, I have had students create cases themselves and then go into the community to teach their cases to high school classes. This year, I tried a slightly different approach. I still had students develop cases and go into the community, but I started the course off using a novel as the basis of a case.

On the first day of class, I had each student list the top 10 problems in the world—similar to a David Letterman survey. Not surprisingly, they named subjects like overpopulation, pollution, the ozone hole, deforestation, loss of exotic species, and extinction. What surprised me momentarily was that many of them also included natural disasters. But this was explicable, because we had just passed through the rough hurricane season and a horrendous tsunami had swept away hundreds of thousands of people in Indonesia and India. But, predictably, the single topic that was on almost everyone's list was global warming. That's where Crichton's new book, *State of Fear*, comes in. Global warming is the theme that drives the book, so I thought why not use it?

Before students read the book, they needed in-depth background in the subject. There is no question that the subject of global warming is important. A week rarely passes without a media story flickering across our television screens; anything out of the ordinary in weather merits a comment from some pundit about how the anomaly is connected to global warming. But the primary literature is humongous, complex, and overwhelming. *Science* and *Nature* publish an article on the subject in almost every issue. If we were going to use the global warming theme, we really had to do our homework.

During the second class, I reported that, on the basis of students' lists, we were going to concentrate on global warming and were going to read Crichton's novel. But we had to prepare for it. To start, I asked them to list all the lines of evidence they could think of that might indicate that global warming was indeed occurring. Once the list was made and placed on the blackboard, I assigned small groups of students different aspects of the problem—temperature, ice caps, sea level, gases in the atmosphere and the greenhouse effect, and ozone. Although ozone is not actually indicative of global warming, I let this topic stand because laypeople and the media often bring up the ozone hole when talking about global warming.

The groups had two weeks to research the topic and write a 20-page paper. I asked for one volunteer in each group to write the paper (this person would have reduced duties in the collection of data); this is a common strategy in teams of engineering professionals. This approach ensured that there would be coherence in the writing style and an integrated approach to the report. Groups who write separate sections and then splice them together invariably have messy papers.

After the reports were turned in, graded, and returned, I asked each student to write two different types of case studies on their portion of the case. They prepared for this by presenting a couple of case studies on other topics in class so they learned what I was after. I also suggested that they look at the cases on the website of the National Center for Case Study Teaching in Science for further examples. Plus, I asked them to write teaching notes for their cases.

When the papers were handed in, the case study portions turned out pretty well, but most of the lesson plans for teachers were woefully inadequate. Not surprisingly, students do not have much insight into how something should be taught. I must hurriedly add that many faculty who do know how to teach also have difficulty writing good teaching notes.

But now I come to Crichton. There we were, a third of the way through the semester, and spring break was coming. A student pleaded with me, "Please, no more global warming!"

But I was relentless and said, "Over the next couple of weeks I want you to read Crichton's *State of Fear* and write a critique of the book. When next we meet, we will discuss the book. And, oh, by the way, write another case study on any other topic that was on your original list of the top 10 important issues. Have a nice spring vacation."

There were no revolts. No crying or whining. Well, not much. Almost all of the assignments were done by the time we got together again, although there were a couple of "My grandmother died" and "I had a personal crisis" pleas. All was well after spring break. The students looked rested and ready to go.

GETTING TO THE SCIENCE

On the day of the discussion, I primed students to talk about Crichton by first having them look at critiques written by other members in their group. Then I said, "Let's talk about *State of Fear*."

Just like in any other case discussion, it was necessary to have a distinct plan of attack for this one. My strategy was to first have students discuss what they thought of the basic plot. This was an easy question to field, which was good because an opening question in a case should be nonthreatening—something easily handled by anyone. And it was; everyone got into the act. There were lots of comments about the ease of the read ("a page turner"), the improbability of the events ("Come on, how reasonable is it to haul around a tiny octopus just to kill someone?"), the character of Dr. Kenner ("Know-it-all Rambo"), the role of the women ("As a feminist, I don't think the character Jennifer is a good role model"), the main character Evans ("Why is this guy going along to the Antarctic, Greenland, New Guinea, and Arizona? What good is he?"), and the gruesomeness of the cannibal scene ("Geesh"). It was clear they had read the book!

The second stage of my plan was to get to the science. The way I approached it was to turn to each group that specialized in a topic and ask them to comment on the accuracy of the data presented in the novel itself and in the author's personal remarks at the end. Interestingly, the students largely supported Crichton's assessment of the global warming argument (that there is considerable hype but little concern for the immediate future).

As they worked their way through the graphs, students noted that the evidence supported the view that small changes in the gas composition of the atmosphere were occurring and that global temperature was rising slightly. Yet there was really no way to assess whether or not this is due to human activities or normal climate variations. Moreover, the groups looking at the sea level and ice cap data, in which there are extreme difficulties in measurement, simply threw their hands up and said the data were inconclusive. And most of them sided with critics of modeling because of the questionable accuracy of forecasting years into the future.

Crichton would be pleased, especially as sundry internet critics have bashed him for his contrarian views about global warming. He definitely had friends in this class.

Leaving the discussion, I assured the young lady who earlier wished that we could abandon the global warming topic that we could now get on with solving other problems in the world, like cancer. She seemed satisfied. (And … there is Lance Armstrong's book about testicular cancer, *It's Not About the Bike*.)

Journal Articles as Case Studies

The New England Journal of Medicine on Breast Cancer: Promoting Critical Thinking in Science

By Clyde Freeman Herreid

A common argument against the use of case studies in science springs from the issue of "coverage." Skeptics argue that they do not have time for case discussion in their lecture-dominated syllabus.

Thus ecologists cannot linger over the serious arguments on both sides of the spotted owl vs. logging controversy. Molecular biologists cannot squeeze in a case dealing with DNA fingerprinting. Chemists cannot dally over a debate about cold fusion, although it may be permissible to throw in a deriding remark in passing. They must get on with their lecturing. Any topic that smacks of a social issue tends to get little "airtime" in the normal science course. The argument against inclusion of such topics is typically, "I can't spare the time." But it is equally likely that the teacher is just plain uncomfortable dealing with social issues.

In the last several years, I have been experimenting with the case method in the teaching of science and have discovered a method that is highly appealing to many previous skeptics of the case study approach. It is the use of a journal article and its analysis. This type of case method has the advantage of being rich with information and full of opportunities to teach critical thinking in science.

The use of journal articles clearly fits the broad definition of a case—a story, which is used as a moral or object lesson to instruct or inform the audience. Journal articles, of course, do have a storyline laid out in bold relief. In the article's introduction, the authors lay out a basic problem and reason for their search for its solution. Their Methods and Materials section tell of their approach. The Results and Discussion sections speak of the outcome of their quest for answers and what they may mean.

This is a storytelling format fundamental to all of us in the scientific guild, yet students seldom hear of these tales until they have been stripped down and reworked into a few sentences in textbooks where they appear as revealed truths to the naive reader. It is no wonder that students seldom understand the human side of science.

I would argue that it is in telling of these original tales found in the primary literature where the student has the most to learn about how science goes about its real business. Since we educators often claim that is one of our goals, by using journal articles as sources for our case materials we have an unusual opportunity to help students understand both the content and the process of science.

How to Use Journal Articles

Almost any journal article can serve as the basis of a case. My approach is to cut the article up into pieces and give the students only some of these fragments, asking them to reconstruct the missing parts. Depending upon which article the teacher uses, the fragments revealed, and the sophistication of the students, this exercise can teach content, process, and critical-thinking skills.

The best way to understand how to use the method is to see an example, and I have included such an article published in the *New England Journal of Medicine* (July 29, 1993: 329 (5): 326–331), which has kindly given me permission to edit it for teaching purposes. The article deals with the possible linkage between breast cancer and insurance coverage; it is especially timely in view of the media coverage about health reform and the serious concern about breast cancer.

This type of a case is called an "issue" or "analysis" case, where the focus of attention is on developing skills of analysis and an understanding of a particular problem. The approach is to give students only the introduction section of the article along with the tables and figures and then guide them through a series of questions that help them think through many of the important details within the paper. This format is especially good for students who are just beginning case study work and need some guidance. It is also a secure type of case for a beginning case teacher because the questions lend structure to the analysis. After significant experience, the guiding questions could be left out and the teacher might simply open the discussion with open-ended questions such as "What's happening here? Let's see if we can make sense out of the data. Who has some ideas?"

This case was designed for a junior/senior general education course called Scientific Inquiry, at the State University of New York at Buffalo. The purpose of the course is to help students understand how scientists go about their work, and to develop critical-thinking skills. The course is based upon the case study method. The cases selected are those that are controversial, unresolved, have a solid core of science, and involve important social issues and public policy. The breast cancer case is one of the first cases examined in the semester. However, before turning to the actual journal article, let me summarize the reasons why this type of case is so powerful.

Ten Reasons to Use the Method

The use of an edited journal article has many strengths:

- First, the approach works in any field of science that publishes a journal.
- Second, it uses preexisting material. There are no long writing preparations to be done.
- Third, consequently, it can be used either on classical or contemporary publications arriving on your desk as recently as today.
- Fourth, it deals with the stuff of real science—real methods, real results, and real problems.
- Fifth, it illustrates how there are alternative ways to perform experiments and interpret data. For aficionados of

the Perry model of development, it moves students along the scale from dualism to multiplicity, relativism, and commitment stages of development. For followers of Bloom's Taxonomy it promotes higher-order thinking.

- Sixth, it works with practically any level of high school, college, or graduate students, provided you choose the articles appropriately.

- Seventh, it is ideal to show weaknesses in the journal article's experimental design and faulty logic. It is especially useful to examine claims of the paranormal and pseudoscience where experimental flaws commonly exist.

- Eighth, because it can deal with facts, figures, data, jargon, and the lexicon of true science, an edited journal case cannot be faulted for its lack of content. If you want "rigor," edited journals are ideal.

- Ninth, it is perfect for those people who wish to experiment with the case method, for an instructor can easily insert a single case in the middle of a normal lecture course. It fits perfectly wherever you might want it in your course outline using as much or as little time as you might wish.

- Tenth, it is practically risk-free. Many science teachers do not have the skills or training to run effective classroom discussions. They feel ill equipped to know how to ask open-ended, thought-provoking questions. Their only experience in the discussion format might have been disastrous, a nightmare of blank stares, averted eyes, and deadly silence. Using journal articles, a set of working questions, plus having students work in small groups prior to a general discussion is almost a guarantee of an exciting, productive class period.

THE CASE STUDY
Breast Cancer and Insurance Coverage: Is There a Link?

To the Student:

The following case focuses upon one of our most pressing medical problems, breast cancer. It does so in the context of one of our most urgent social and political problems, the access to adequate medical care. There are several reasons for studying this case, aside from gaining a better understanding of the disease and the societal issues. Remember we wish to have you become familiar with how scientists attack problems in general. So examining the material from this medical paper should give you a better idea of

1. How medical "experiments" are designed to extract information from existing data;

2. How to interpret data presented in tables and graphs;

3. How statistical terms and concepts enter into the interpretation of data;

4. How caution must be exerted in drawing conclusions and how your social agenda can influence the "meaning" of data; and

5. How original science articles are structured (Abstract, Introduction, Methods, Results, and Discussion).

In the following case, we have given you the introduction and tables and figures from the results section of a recent paper. This material will permit you to see clearly what the authors were after and the results they obtained. We expect you to approach the data in the same way that scientists do, with some preconceived ideas about what to expect and with a curiosity as to what really happened.

First, read the introduction. Second, answer the set of questions about each table and figure. These questions are exactly the types of questions scientists would ask themselves and the answers would be part of the results section. Finally, consider the general questions. Many of these points would be addressed in the discussion part of the paper.

To the Teacher:

This case illustrates many points about one type of case study:

1. It is an "issue" or "analysis" case in contrast to a "dilemma" case. The latter usually has a central character who has to grapple with a problem. The reader's job is not only to analyze the problem, but to come up with one or more solutions and consider their consequences. Issue cases are used to teach students the skills of analysis, and they typically stop short of asking students to make a decision. Although we do ask students to make policy recommendations, this decision is not central to the case.

2. This case makes use of "prepackaged" materials. That is, we use parts of an article from the *New England Journal of Medicine* as the case rather than composing and writing a case from scratch. The use of existing materials, such as motion pictures like *Jurassic Park*, TV documentaries, plays, newspaper articles, and so on, is fast, timely, engaging, and relatively easy compared to writing a case *de novo*. This particular approach, where a scientific article is dissected, is especially familiar to scientists, who have spent much of their graduate and professional careers doing just that. Scientists are secure discussing methods, tables, graphs, and experimental design. Working through part of an article or several articles joined together is a comfortable start for casework.

3. The case involves serious real issues that are of vital concern to many people. The content is likely to be inherently interesting especially as it is apt to be discussed in the media. However, using highly charged, controversial topics can easily divert a discussion into social speculation rather than rigorous appraisal of the evidence. A teacher must walk a delicate balance to capitalize on the excitement of the issue without being drawn into an emotional "black hole."

4. The analytical skills and processes being developed within this case—graph and table interpretation, experimental design, and so on—are generalizable to other problems. They are often the most important aspects of any case. Science problems come and go over time, whereas the methodological approaches are apt to be more universal.

5. This case structure is easily adapted to classes where an instructor is not totally comfortable with an open, free discussion. Students are asked to work through a sequence of exercises. How much discussion occurs is up to the instructor. There are several obvious options. The case could be given as a homework exercise and never discussed at all. In this case, the instructor should take care to remove the author's name and alter the article's title to prevent students from taking the easy way out by simply looking up the paper. At the other extreme, the case could be handled entirely in small groups in class with group reports being handed in. Or as a compromise, the reading (with authors expunged and title altered) and questions could be given out before class. During class, the questions might first be discussed in small groups and finally summarized by the entire class. The staging of the questions gives a safe, controlled approach to the case.

6. This case is especially valuable for students to improve their understanding of retrospective study design, because it is so common in medicine today. Many reports seen on TV and in newspapers are based upon retrospective analysis

of hospital data rather than prospective data gathering. In retrospective studies scientists are concerned with analysis of events already past and data already gathered for other purposes, whereas normal experimental (prospective or predictive) studies are those set up to examine a specific hypothesis or problem. The breast cancer data being retrospective provides a prime opportunity for the class to discuss the difficulty in collecting information from hospital records where proper controls may not be in effect, unanticipated errors may crop up, and incomplete data are the norm. Clearly, correlation between two variables in retrospective studies are much less likely to be directly a result of cause and effect than in experimental studies with tight controls in place with good experimental design.

7. An effective conclusion to this case is to hand out copies of the complete journal article on breast cancer. This permits students to see how close their analysis and speculations came to those of the authors.

ANALYSIS OF CASE

Introduction

Depending upon your class, your purpose, and your teaching plan, the article's introduction might serve as an important launching pad for a serious preliminary discussion of breast cancer and the health-care system. If so, prior readings on the etiology, pathology, and epidemiology of breast cancer along with the psychology of patients might be in order along with information on the insurance system, Medicaid, and so on. If on the other hand you are primarily focused on the study's design, then these topics can be largely bypassed by turning to the essential questions of the paper:

1. "Do uninsured patients and those covered by Medicaid have more advanced breast cancer than privately insured patients when the disease is first diagnosed?"

2. "And do these patients die sooner, on average, than privately insured patients during the 7.5 years after breast cancer is diagnosed?"

Since these questions are so clearly identified in the introduction, an instructor might simply restate the questions as a prelude to the table and graph analyses. Or the instructor might ask students to consider how they might collect information to answer such questions. This could lead into a discussion of the differences between a retrospective study, which is being presented here, and an experimental study, which has tightly matched controls. These topics can be easily deferred until later in the analysis.

Another possible introductory concern might involve a discussion about why so few previous studies have looked at possible links between insurance coverage and health outcomes, a point raised by the authors. However, if an instructor is primarily interested in data analysis and study design, they should be wary of these socially bewitching questions.

Table 1

1. The general purpose of the table (p. 95) is to establish the demographic background of the patients and to establish differences that exist in the insurance categories. Students should identify that the largest number of women analyzed in this study were privately insured patients and be curious as to why this was so and if this affects the conclusions. They should readily see that the women that were uninsured and covered by Medicaid were younger, less likely to be white or married, and came from households with a lower income than privately insured patients.

2. Students may have difficulty with the category "Number of coexisting diag-

noses," which means that diseases other than breast cancer have been identified. Could the lower percentage of coexisting diagnoses in privately insured patients be due to better medical care? Students may have difficulty in the statistical statements and understanding t-tests and chi-squared tests. This is probably not the time to open up such questions for serious study. If students have not had statistics, it is probably sufficient to explain that P values are estimates of error. For example, it looks like uninsured women are younger (on average) than privately insured women. So a P = 0.03 estimates that in only 3 chances out of 100 will a person be wrong making such a conclusion based on these data. There is even less chance of being wrong by saying Medicaid patients are likely to be younger than those privately insured because P<0.001. (The chances of error are less than 1 in a 1,000.)

3. This is a direct question leading to a discussion of the methods the investigators had to use in collecting data. The instructor has an excellent chance to explore here the potential problems involved in gathering such information. Refer to the original paper.

4. Privately insured patients are more likely to be white, older, married, economically more advantaged and have fewer coexisting diagnoses than patients who were uninsured or covered by Medicaid. The typical privately insured patient is white, 52.7 years old, married, with a high median household income, with breast cancer but no other diagnosed illnesses. The typical patient covered by Medicaid would be white, 49.8 years old, unmarried, have a low median household income, with breast cancer and one or more additional diagnosed ailments.

5. Much of the data can be displayed in either a bar graph or pie chart. An instructor could ask for an example of this method of presentation. It helps some students get a clearer grasp of data presentation.

Table 2

This table (p. 96) compares how the stages of breast cancer differ among women with various levels of insurance coverage. Both uninsured and Medicaid patients had a higher percentage of individuals with cancer at regional and distant stages. Students should have little difficulty speculating what this terminology implies about the spread of the disease. The methods section, of course, clarifies the terms *local*, *regional*, and *distant*. Students might further infer that private coverage leads to earlier diagnosis before the cancer has spread. Again, the statistical Wilcoxon rank-sum test does not have to be explained in order to understand what the P values mean.

Table 3

This table (p. 96) shows how the severity of stages of cancer differs among women with various levels of insurance coverage. Students generally have little difficulty guessing that the stages represent a scale of severity; however, some instructors may wish to use the opportunity to discuss the definitions and diagnostic features of each stage, which are described in the article's methods section.

The table clearly shows how privately insured women with breast cancer tended to be in the earlier stages of the disease at the time of diagnosis, whereas those uninsured and on Medicaid were in the more advanced stages. Students might infer that private coverage leads to earlier diagnosis.

A question should be raised as to why the sample sizes are drastically smaller in this table than in the previous table.

Figure 1

This figure (p. 97) focuses on the estimated survival rates of patients with local-stage breast cancer. A discussion of the Kaplan-Meier methodology is not necessary in order to see that the poorest survival rate is in the Medicaid patients while the best is found in the privately insured women. Students should speculate why this might be so, even though at the time of diagnosis the women in the graph had only a local expression of the cancer. Yet by 24 months their curves (survival rate) began to differ.

Figure 2

This figure (p. 97) shows the survival rates for women after they have been diagnosed with regional-stage breast cancer. Students should readily note that both Medicaid and uninsured patients show a similar and lower survival rate than those privately insured. All survival rates are poorer than those shown in Figure 1.

Figure 3

This figure (p. 97) shows the survival rates for women after they have been diagnosed with distant-stage breast cancer. The survival curves for all patient groups do not differ much from one another and they are sharply lower than the rates shown in Figures 1 and 2.

Comparing the three figures, students should recognize the progressive drop in survival rates of all insurance groups if the cancer has been diagnosed at later time periods. To illustrate the point, the instructor can ask how many Medicaid patients out of 100 would be living after six years (72 months) if they had been diagnosed with local-stage

TABLE 1.

Characteristics of women in New Jersey, 35–64 years of age, in whom invasive breast cancer was diagnosed in 1985–1987, according to insurance coverage.

Characteristic	Privately insured	Uninsured	Covered by Medicaid
No. of women	4,283	277	115
Mean age (yr)	52.7	51.6*	49.8†
White race (%)	88.3	70.8‡	64.4
Median household income (%)			
Low	30.9	53.8‡	72.6‡
Intermediate	34.1	28.5	17.7
High	35.0	17.7	9.7
No. of coexisting diagnoses (% of women)			
0	58.9	48.8‡	38.3‡
1	20.6	18.8	12.2
2	10.0	16.2	19.1
>3	10.5	16.2	30.4

*p = 0.03 by the t-test for the comparison with the privately insured women.
†p<0.001 by the t-test for the comparison with the privately insured women.
†p<0.001 by the chi-square test for the comparison with the privately insured women.

breast cancer? This value should be compared with regional- stage and distant-stage breast cancer.

GENERAL QUESTIONS

1. If methodology has not been discussed previously, this is the place where the various possible study designs should be clarified. The instructor should be sure that students get a clear sense of how the results might be biased unless care is used to collect the data. For example, how should the patients be chosen? How will the patients' data be obtained? Will we collect data primarily from the large cities? How many samples are reasonable? Also, this is an opportunity to touch upon an ethical issue: Do patients need to be informed

TABLE 2.

Summary stage of breast cancer at diagnosis, according to insurance coverage, in women 35–64 years of age, in all New Jersey counties, 1985–1987.

Insurance Coverage	No. of Women	Local	Stage Regional %	Distant	P Value*
Privately insured	4,283	53.9	38.8	7.3	—
Uninsured	277	44.4	43.3	12.3	<0.001
Covered by Medicaid	115	46.1	36.5	17.4	0.01

*For the comparison with the privately uninsured women, according to the Wilcoxon rank-sum test.

TABLE 3.

Stage of breast cancer at diagnosis, according to insurance coverage, in women 35–64 years of age, in Essex, Hudson, Passaic, and Union Counties, 1985–1987.

Insurance Coverage	No. of Women	Stage Percentages					P value*
		I	IIA	IIB	III	IV	
Privately insured	969	29.7	34.9	23.3	4.2	7.9	—
Uninsured	82	15.9	21.9	41.5	7.3	13.4	<0.001
Covered by Medicaid	35	17.1	31.5	28.6	5.7	17.1	0.02

*For the comparison with the privately insured women, according to the Wilcoxon rank-sum test.

Tables 1, 2, 3

1. What is the purpose of each table?

2. Are there any unclear terms or confusing aspects of the table?

3. How do you think the data were obtained?

4. What points may be inferred from each table?

5. Could you graph any of these data using a bar graph or pie chart?

6. Describe the "typical" person in each insurance category in Table 1.

Figures 1, 2, 3

1. What is the purpose of each figure?

2. Are there unclear terms or confusing aspects of the figures?

3. What points may be inferred from the figures?

4. How do you think the data were obtained?

5. Why are the figures different from one another?

General Questions

1. Write a summary of the methods that you believe the scientists used to collect and analyze the data.
2. How would you answer the two questions that the authors posed in the beginning of their article? Indicate which tables or figures support your claim.
3. What are the results that might account for the main results?
4. What are some risky conclusions or misinterpretations that might be drawn from the data?
5. What questions arise from this study that warrant further analysis? Design another study that could answer one of your questions.
6. What policy recommendations might you make on the basis of this study?
7. Write an abstract for this paper.

FIGURE 1.

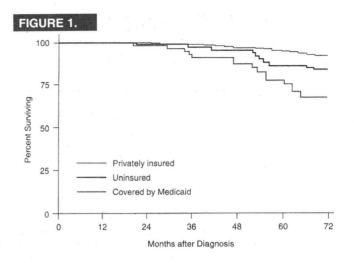

FIGURE 2.

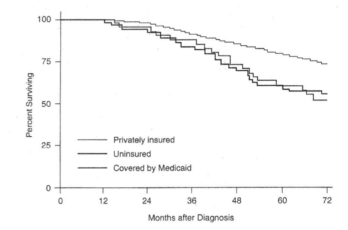

FIGURE 3.

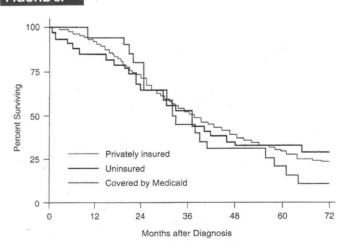

that they are part of the survey? Or do they have no control over their hospital or physician's records? Is this an infringement of privacy?

2. The first question: Do uninsured and Medicaid patients have more advanced cancer at the time of diagnosis than privately insured patients?

   Answer: Yes, and this is clearly shown by the data in Tables 1 and 2. The cancer has spread to more distant sites and is in a more advance stage in uninsured and Medicaid patients.

   The second question: Do uninsured and Medicaid patients die sooner, on average, than privately insured patients during the 7.5 years after breast cancer is diagnosed?

   Answer: Yes, Figures 1, 2, and 3 illustrate to varying degrees the differences in survivorship. In cases where the cancer is either local or regional, privately insured patients clearly fare better, whereas in distant-stage breast cancer survival is poor in all women, suggesting that differences among patient care may make little difference in this condition.

3. It appears likely that women with private insurance are diagnosed earlier and have better subsequent treatment than other patients. Thus they have relatively higher survival rate.

4. This may not be a simple cause-effect relationship. Women with private insurance also are better off financially and have better health and have very different lifestyles (for example, note marriage data). This may affect the progress of the disease, so even if uninsured and Medicaid patients had private insurance it may be that their survival rates would be unaltered. If this is true, a massive overhaul of the health insurance system may not have the desired effects.

5. One experiment that might be done to clarify the relationship is to provide a group of uninsured patients with coverage that is comparable to that of privately insured patients. Ideally, not only would their subsequent disease conditions and survival be tracked, but their actual use of health-care facilities could be followed. It would not surprise most experts to find that even with equal coverage these women coming from different socioeconomic groups might still differ in breast cancer epidemiology.

6. The questions set the stage for a major social policy discussion. Unless you wish to develop this aspect of the study, it will be sufficient to point out that your policy recommendations might be very different depending upon what the result of the experiment in answer five will be. Moreover, even if the authors are correct that women without private health insurance "would benefit from improved access to screening and optimal therapy," what is an acceptable cost to improve survival rates? Such questions are contentious to say the least and they lie at the heart of all health-care reform.

ACKNOWLEDGMENT

This work was supported by a grant from the Fund for the Improvement of Postsecondary Education, U.S. Department of Education.

REFERENCE

Ayanian, J. Z., B. A. Kohler, T. Abe, and A. M. Epstein. 1993. The relation between health insurance coverage and clinical outcomes among women with breast cancer. *New England Journal of Medicine* 329 (5): 326–331.

Bad Blood

A Case Study of the Tuskegee Syphilis Project

By Ann W. Fourtner, Charles R. Fourtner, and Clyde Freeman Herreid

Syphilis is a venereal disease spread during sexual intercourse. It can also be passed from mother to child during pregnancy. It is caused by a corkscrew-shaped bacterium called a spirochete, *Treponema pallidum*. This microscopic organism resides in many organs of the body but causes sores or ulcers (called chancres) to appear on the skin of the penis, vagina, mouth, and occasionally in the rectum, or on the tongue, lips, or breast. During sex the bacteria leave the sores of one person and enter the moist membranes of their partner's penis, vagina, mouth, or rectum.

Once the spirochetes wiggle inside a victim, they begin to multiply at an amazing rate. (Some bacteria have a doubling rate of 30 minutes. You may want to consider how many bacteria you might have in 12 hours if one bacterium entered your body, doubling at that rate.) The spirochetes then enter the lymph circulation that carries them to nearby lymph glands, which may swell in response to the infection.

This first stage of the disease (called primary syphilis) lasts only a few weeks and usually causes hard red sores or ulcers to develop on the genitals of the victim who can then pass the disease on to the someone else. During this primary stage, a blood test will not reveal the presence of the disease, but the bacteria can be scraped from the sores. The sores soon heal and some people may recover entirely without treatment.

Secondary syphilis develops two-to-six weeks after the sores heal. Then flulike symptoms appear with fever, headache, eye inflammation, malaise, joint pain, a skin rash, and mouth and genital sores. These symptoms are a clear sign that the spirochetes have travelled throughout the body by way of the lymph and blood systems where they now can be readily detected by a blood test (for example, the Wassermann test). Scalp hair may drop out to give a "moth-eaten" type of look to the head. This secondary stage ends in a few weeks as the sores heal.

Signs of the disease may never reappear even though the bacteria continue to live in the person. But in about 25% of those originally infected, symptoms will flare up again in late or tertiary stage syphilis.

Almost any organ can be attacked, such as the cardiovascular system, producing leaking heart valves and aneurysms, balloon-like bulges in the aorta which may burst leading to instant death. Gummy or rubbery tumors filled with spirochetes may develop on the skin covered by a dried crust of pus. The bones may deteriorate, as in osteomyelitis or tuberculosis, and may produce disfiguring facial mutilations as nasal and palate bones are eaten away. If the nervous system is infected, a stumbling, foot-slapping gait may occur or, more severely, paralysis, senility, blindness, and insanity.

THE HEALTH PROGRAM

The cause of syphilis, the stages of the disease's development, and the complications that can result from untreated syphilis were all known to medical science in the early 1900s. In 1905, German scientists Hoffman and Schaudinn isolated the bacterium that causes syphilis. In 1907, the Wassermann blood test was developed, enabling physicians to diagnose the disease. Three years later, German scientist Paul Ehrlich created an arsenic compound called salvarsan to treat syphilis. Together with mercury, it was either injected or rubbed onto the skin and often produced serious and occasionally fatal reactions in patients. Treatment was painful and usually required more than a year to complete.

In 1908, Congress established the Division of Venereal Diseases in the U.S. Public Health Service. Within a year, 44 states had organized separate bureaus for venereal disease control. Unfortunately, free treatment clinics operated only in urban areas for many years. Data, collected in a survey begun in 1926 of 25 communities across the United States, indicated that the incidence of syphilis among patients under observation was "4.05 cases per 1,000 population, the rate for whites being 4 per 1,000, and that for Negroes 7.2 per 1,000."

In 1929, Dr. Hugh S. Cumming, the Surgeon General of the U.S. Public Health Service (PHS), asked the Julius Rosenwald Fund for financial support to study the control of venereal disease in the rural South. The Rosenwald Fund was a philanthropic organization that played a key role in promoting the welfare of African Americans. The fund agreed to help the U.S. PHS in developing health programs for southern African Americans.

One of the fund's major goals was to encourage their grantees to use black personnel whenever possible as a means to promote professional integration. Thus, the mission of the fund seemed to fit well with the plans of the PHS. Macon County, Alabama, was selected as one of five syphilis-control demonstration programs in February 1930. The local Tuskegee Institute endorsed the program. The institute and its John A. Andrew Memorial Hospital were staffed and administered entirely by African American physicians and nurses. "The demonstrations would provide training for private physicians, white and colored, in the elements of venereal disease treatments and the more extensive distribution of antisyphilitic drugs and the promotion of wider use of state diagnostic laboratory facilities."

In 1930, Macon County had 27,000 residents, 82% African American, most living in rural poverty in a shack with a dirt floor, with no plumbing and poor sanitation. This was the target population, people who "had never in their lives been treated by a doctor." Public health officials arriving on the scene announced they had come to test people for "bad blood." The term included a host of maladies and later surveys suggest that few people connected that term with syphilis.

The syphilis control study in Macon County turned up the alarming news that 36% of the African American population had syphilis. The medical director of the Rosenwald Fund was concerned about the racial implications of the findings, saying, "There is bound to be danger that the impression will be given that syphilis in the South is a Negro problem rather than one of both races." The PHS officer assured the fund and the Tuskegee Institute that demonstrations would not be used to attack the images of black Americans. He argued that the high syphilis rates were not due to "inherent racial susceptibility" but could be explained by "differences in their respective social and economic status." However, the PHS failed to persuade the fund that more work could break the cycle of poverty and disease in Macon County. So when the PHS officers suggested a larger scale extension of the work, the Rosenwald Fund trustees voted against the new project.

Building on what had been learned during the Rosenwald Fund demonstrations and the four other sites, the PHS covered the nation with the Wassermann tests. Both blacks and whites were reached with extensive testing, and in some areas mobile treatment clinics were available.

THE EXPERIMENT

As the PHS officers analyzed the data for the final Rosenwald Fund report in September of 1932, and realizing that funding for the project would be discontinued, the idea for a new study evolved into the Tuskegee Study of Untreated Syphilis in the Negro Male. They would convert the original treatment program into a nontherapeutic human experiment aimed at compiling data on the progression of the disease on untreated African American males.

The precedent existed for such a study. One had been conducted in Oslo, Norway, at the turn of the century on a population of white males and females. An impressive amount of information had been gathered from these patients concerning the progression of the disease. However, questions of manifestation and progression of syphilis in individuals of African descent had not been studied. In light of the discovery that African natives had some rather unique diseases (for example, sickle cell anemia—a disease of red blood cells), a study of African males could reveal biological differences during the course of syphilis. (Later, the argument that supported continuation of the study may even have been reinforced in the early 1950s when it was suggested that native Africans with the sickle cell trait were less susceptible to the ravages of malaria.)

In fact, Dr. Joseph Earle Moore of the Venereal Disease Clinic of the Johns Hopkins University School of Medicine stated when consulted, "Syphilis in the negro is in many respects almost a different disease from syphilis in the white." The PHS doctors felt that this study would emphasize and delineate these differences. Moreover, whereas the Oslo study was retrospective (looking back at old cases), the Macon Study would be a better prospective study, following the progress of the disease through time.

It was estimated that of the 1,400 patients in Macon County admitted to treatment under the Rosenwald Fund, not one had received the full course of medication prescribed as standard therapy for syphilis. The PHS officials decided that these men could be considered untreated because they had not received enough treatment to cure them. In the county, there was a well-equipped teaching hospital (John A. Andrew Memorial Hospital at the Tuskegee Institute) that could be used for scientific purposes.

Over the next months in 1932, cooperation was ensured from the Alabama State Board of Health, the Macon County Health Department, and the Tuskegee Institute. However, Dr. J. N. Baker, the state health officer, received one important concession in exchange for his approval. Everyone found to have syphilis would have to be treated. Although this would not cure them—the nine-month study was too short—it would keep them noninfectious. Dr. Baker also argued for the involvement of local physicians.

Dr. Raymond Vonderlehr was chosen for the fieldwork that began in October 1932. Dr. Vonderlehr began his work in Alabama by spreading the word that a new syphilis control demonstration was beginning and that government doctors were giving free blood tests. Black people came to schoolhouses and churches for examination—most had never before seen a doctor. Several hundred men over 25 years old were identified as Wassermann-positive who had not been treated for "bad blood" and had been infected for over five years. Cardiovascular problems seemed particularly evident in this population in the early days, reaffirming that blacks might be different in their response. But nervous system involvement was not evident.

As Dr. Vonderlehr approached the end of his few months of study, he suggested to his superior, Dr. Clark, that the work continue for 5–10 years because "many interesting facts could be learned regarding the course and complications of untreated syphilis." Dr. Clark retired a few months later and in June 1933 Dr. Vonderlehr was promoted to director of the Division of Venereal Diseases of the PHS.

This promotion began a bureaucratic pattern over the next four decades that saw the position of director go to a physician who had worked on the Tuskegee Study. Dr. Vonderlehr spent much of the summer of 1933 working out the study's logistics that would enable the PHS to follow the men's health through their lifetime. This included gaining permission from the men and their families to perform an autopsy at the time of their death that would give the scientific community a detailed microscopic description of the diseased organs.

Neither the syphilitics nor the controls (those men free of syphilis, who were added to the project) were informed as to the study's true objective. These men knew only that they were receiving treatment for "bad blood" and money for burial. Burial stipends began in 1935, funded by the Milbank Memorial Fund.

The skill of the African American nurse, Eunice Rivers, and the cooperation of the local health providers (most of them white males), were essential in this project. They understood the project details and the fact that the patients' available medical care (other than valid treatment for syphilis) was far better than that for most African Americans in Macon County. The local draft board agreed to exclude the men in the study from medical treatment when that became an issue during the early 1940s. State health officials also cooperated.

The study was not kept secret from the national medical community. Dr. Vonderlehr in 1933 contacted a large number of experts in the field of venereal disease and related medical complications. Most responded with support for the study. The American Heart Association asked for clarification of the scientific validity, then subsequently expressed great doubt and criticism concerning the tests and procedures. Dr. Vonderlehr remained convinced that the study was valid and would prove that syphilis affected African Americans differently than those of European descent. As director of the PHS Venereal Disease Division, he controlled the funds necessary to conduct the study, as did his successors.

Key to the cooperation of the men in the Tuskegee study was the African American PHS nurse assigned to monitor them. She quickly gained their trust. She dealt with their problems. The physicians came to respect her ability to deal with the men. She not only attempted to keep the men in the study, she many times prevented them from receiving medical care from the PHS treatment clinics offering neoarsphenamine and bismuth (the treatment for syphilis) during the late 1930s and early 1940s. She never advocated treating the men. She knew these treatment drugs had side effects. As a nurse, she had been trained to follow doctor's orders. By the time penicillin became available for the treatment of syphilis, not treating these men had become a routine that she did not question. She truly felt that these men were better off because of the routine medical examinations, distribution of aspirin pink pills that relieved aches and pains, and personal nursing care. She never thought of the men as victims. She was aware of the Oslo study. "This is the way I saw it: that they were studying the Negro just like they were studying the white man, see, making a comparison." She retired from active nursing in 1965, but assisted during the annual checkups until the experiment ended.

By 1943, when the Division of Venereal Diseases began treating syphilitic patients nationwide with penicillin, the Tuskegee study men were not considered patients. They were viewed as experimental subjects and were denied antibiotic treatment. The PHS officials insisted that the study offered even more of an opportunity to study these men as a "control against which to project not only the results obtained with the rapid schedules of therapy for syphilis but also the costs involved in finding and placing under treatment the infected individuals." There is no evidence that the study had ever been discussed in the light of the Nuremberg Code, a set of 10 ethical principles for human experimentation developed during the trials of Nazi physicians in the aftermath of World War II. Again the study had become routine.

In 1951, Dr. Trygve Gjustland, then the current director of the Oslo study, joined the Tuskegee group to review the experiment. He offered suggestions on updating records and reviewing criteria. No one questioned the issue of contamination (men with partial treatment) or ethics. In 1952, the study began to focus on the study of aging, as well as heart disease, because of the long-term data that had been accumulated on the men. It became clear that syphilis generally shortened the lifespan of its victims and that the tissue damage began while the young men were in the second stage of the disease (see Tables 1–3).

In June 1965, Dr. Irwin J. Schatz became the first medical professional to object to the study. He suggested a need for PHS to reevaluate its moral judgments. The PHS did not respond to his letter. In November 1966 Peter Buxtin, a PHS venereal disease interviewer and investigator, expressed his moral concerns about the study. He continued to question the study within the PHS network.

In February 1969, the PHS called together a blue ribbon panel to discuss the Tuskegee study. The participants were all physicians. Not one had training in medical ethics. None was of African descent. At no point during the discussions did anyone remind the panel of PHS's own guidelines on human experimentation (established in February 1966).

According to records, the original study had been composed of 412 men with syphilis and 204 controls. In 1969, 56 syphilitic subjects and 36 controls were known to be living. A total of 373 men in both groups were known to be dead. The rest were unaccounted for. The age of the survivors ranged from 59 to 85, one claiming to be 102.

The outcome of this meeting was that the study would continue. The doctors convinced themselves that the syphilis in the Tuskegee men was too far along to be effectively treated by penicillin and that the men might actually suffer severe complications from such therapy. Even the Macon County Medical Society, now made up of mostly African American physicians, agreed to assist the PHS. Each was given a list of subjects.

In the late 1960s, PHS physician Dr. James Lucas stated in a memorandum that the Tuskegee study was "bad science" because it had been contaminated by treatment. PHS continued to put a positive spin on the experiment by noting that the study had been keeping laboratories supplied with blood samples for evaluating new blood tests for syphilis.

Peter Buxtin, who had left the PHS for law school and was bothered by the study and the no-change attitude of the PHS, contacted the Associated Press. Jean Heller, the reporter assigned to the story, did extensive research into the Tuskegee experiment. When interviewed by her, the PHS officials provided her with much of her information. They were men who had nothing to hide. The story broke on July 25, 1972. The study immediately stopped.

STUDY QUESTIONS

1. Carefully analyze this case. When you

examine the paper and the appendices, what information appears to have been gained from this study? That is, what kind of argument can be made for the benefits of the study?

2. What do you believe were the motives for the people to become involved in the study, specifically: The subjects? The PHS personnel? The Tuskegee staff? The Macon County physicians? Nurse Rivers?

3. What kind of criticisms can you offer of this study?

4. What were the factors underlying the cessation of the project?

5. Could this project (or one similar to it involving AIDS or radiation effects) be conducted today?

INTRODUCTION

This case is a synopsis of events described by James H. Jones in his book *Bad Blood: The Tuskegee Syphilis Experiment*. (All direct quotes in the case study are from this book.) It was first published in 1981 and later updated in 1993 with the addition of a chapter called "AIDS: Is it genocide?" The book has led to a play, a motion picture, and a PBS Nova special. The Tuskegee study became an instant classic on the ethics of human experimentation once the Kennedy congressional hearings in 1973 occurred.

This case is an example of a "historical" case in the sense that it happened sufficiently long ago that there are few of the major participants alive and there are no more major decisions or actions to be made. The story is largely finished. Further, the social and ethical climate is significantly different today than when the events in the case transpired. Many of the key decisions could not be made today in light of present legal and moral guidelines.

Why do we study such a case? The answer in simple: to understand the evolution in our thinking on issues of science, human experimentation, and race and to see how they are colored by our culture. In addition, we can emphasize certain long-standing principles of science that have not changed over the century; for example, proper controls are still seen as essential. Also, there are clear parallels in dealing with disease conditions within special segments of the population today (for example, breast cancer, AIDS) that lead to special research projects, with political and legal overtones.

TEACHING THE CASE

This case seems ideally suited for the classical case discussion format used for decades in business schools, although it can easily be adapted for small group cooperative learning teams.

It is divided into three parts: *the disease, the public health program,* and *the experiment.*

- The section on the disease is a straightforward account of the symptoms of syphilis, and it normally figures only in a modest way in the discussion except as a backdrop to the case. The instructor can highlight the disease by an early focus on the disease symptoms, perhaps with graphic photos and review of included data and readings from original papers.

- The section on the public health program should be viewed from the perspective of concern regarding the extent of disease in rural southern America, the need to establish a health vehicle to address the problems of disease, and the concern of an expanding civil rights movement regarding health care and health care professionals.

- The section on the experiment itself leads to several lines of inquiry that should be pursued in discussion.
  1. Rationale for loss of funds.
  2. Rationale for study on untreated African American males and societal acceptance of such experimentations.

3. The medical importance of longitudinal studies.
4. Rationale for continuing study after penicillin was discovered.
5. The use or inappropriate use of "control" groups.
6. The meaning of "informed consent." That is, can you ever be fully informed?
7. What is the Nuremberg Code and does it really pertain to this study?
8. Of what use are the data collected from this study? Do there appear to be any significant conclusions? Review the contamination aspect of various degrees of treatment.
9. Can scientists become so intimately associated with their projects that they lose objectivity?
10. Why was the consistent care provided by one person throughout the study so necessary?

There are a myriad of other questions that the discussion could develop by reading the case study. If small groups are used, these questions and others can be divided among them to provide different perspectives on the case. These views would be shared in a general group discussion. However, our remaining comments about teaching will emphasize the group discussion technique.

In writing this case we have kept the account relatively straightforward, eschewing emotion-laden phrases, keeping in mind the science and ethics earlier in the century. It has a documentary feel to it; that is intentional. As a result, we hope to accomplish two things: (1) To keep the reader focussed on the science first; and (2) To avoid the easy criticism that comes from second guessing events that took place over 50 years ago. It helps to dampen the tendency of some individuals to use this case as a platform to deride racism without serious analysis. There is always a risk of polemics when we deal with scientific cases that im-

TABLE 1.

1963 Viability data of Tuskegee group.

	Dead		Alive		Unknown	
	number	%	number	%	number	%
Syphilitics	242	59	85	21	85	21
Controls	78	45	66	34	39	20

From Rockwell, Yobs, and Moore (1964)

TABLE 2.

Abnormal findings in 90 syphilitics and 65 controls.

	Syphilitics		Controls	
Abnormality	number	%	number	%
Electrocardiographic	41	46	21	32
Cardiomegaly via x-ray	37	42	22	34
Peripheral neuropathy	12	13	5	8
Hypertension d.b.p.>90	38	43	29	45
Cardiac murmurs	24	27	20	31
Urine	28	36	21	33

From Rockwell, Yobs, and Moore (1964)

TABLE 3.

Aortic arch and myocardial abnormalities at autopsy.

	Aortic arch		Myocardial	
	number	%	number	%
Syphilitics (140)	62	44	48	34
Controls (54)	8	15	20	37
	X2P<0.005		X2P>0.25 not different	

From Caldwell et al. (1973)

pinge on the public welfare. These moments are seldom enlightening. Careful preparation on the part of the instructor can help head off such events.

BLOCKS OF ANALYSIS

Every case has its major points for discussion; these vary with the teacher and audience. In this instance, we have identified three major issues for analysis: the science; the ethics of human experimentation; and the racial issue. We choose to start with the least volatile of the issues just as we would in the classroom.

The Science

Basically, was this good science? Questions that illuminate this issue include: What was the purpose of the project? How did the purpose shift through time? Was the experimental design adequate? What were the contributions of the study? On one side of the argument we have the view that many of the so-called untreated men were in fact treated and this invalidated all conclusions that might be drawn. Furthermore, one might argue that there was no need to repeat a study on untreated people since the Oslo data were adequate.

Clearly, physicians involved with the project did not agree, for they thought it likely the black population might differ, especially in their cardiovascular and neurological response to syphilis. Also, we have statements that the blood from these men was used to develop standardized blood tests, that the project served as a training ground for many PHS and other medical staff, and that the project led to several scientific publications. The Tuskegee data still serve as the reference for understanding syphilis.

Ethics of Human Experimentation

Our view of human experimentation has changed markedly over the past century. There are numerous examples of soldiers, prisoners, and citizens who have unwillingly or unknowingly participated in life-threatening "experi-

ments" (Barber 1976). The 1993 revelation that Americans were unwillingly exposed to potentially harmful doses of nuclear radiation during tests of the 1940s and 1950s is only the most recent example.

Historically, one might think that development of the Nuremberg Code would have prevented such work. This does not seem to be the case. The notorious Nazi medical experiments, which were brought to light after World War II during the war crimes trials, led to the development of a code of ethics called the Nuremberg Code. This set of 10 principles asserts "the subjects' right to decide whether or not to become research subjects." It defines what physicians may or may not do even with the permission of the subject. An investigator must take all precautions to avoid the remote possibility of injury, and the degree of risk involved to the subject must be commensurate with the "humanitarian importance of the problem." In spite of the widespread publicity of the Nuremberg trials there appears to be no suggestion that any of the physicians in the Tuskegee syphilis experiment thought the Nuremberg Code applied to them. Nor for that matter has it appeared to have had any impact on the development of our own ethical framework in the United States (Annas and Grodin 1992).

Not until the thalidomide scandal of the 1960s did the U.S. scientific community seriously engage on the question of human experimentation. Only in the past few years have we seen universities and the National Institutes of Health establish guides for human experimentation.

How much of this checkered past needs to be part of the discussion is up to the instructor, but it might be useful to give students your school's or a local drug company's guidelines on human experimentation or ask them to develop their own principles. Certainly, any discussion on these issues will include the "right" of people to choose whether they will be part of an experiment. Also, there will be questions of whether it is possible to truly inform a person about the consequences of an experiment and whether this knowledge will influence the results of the work itself. Lawsuits have been won on the basis that even if a person signs a release, he or she cannot be held accountable; he or she may be acting under coercion or stress and without proper understanding of the work. For example, how much would you accept as adequate compensation in such an experiment: $5, $50, $500, $5,000?

The Racial Issue

This is potentially the most volatile issue in the case. If terms such as *genocide* can be applied to the AIDS crisis, so might they be applied to the syphilis epidemic and the Tuskegee study. Here is a documented case of a government agency withholding medical treatment from an ethnic minority.

If an instructor wishes to explore this issue, he or she would presumably focus on how it is possible to view the same event from different perspectives. There is evidence that the Rosenwald Fund had a long history of helping black Americans and one of its concerns about funding the second phase of the Tuskegee project was that its motives could be misconstrued. Furthermore, there is documented evidence that the prime motive for early work was to see if the progress of syphilis in the black male was similar to that first studied in the European male in Oslo. Also, we have clear cooperation of black physicians, nurses, and administrators of Macon County and the Tuskegee Institute. Yet evidence of this type can be viewed through another lens. The perspective of a person arguing the genocide scenario is captured simply with this question: Would this study have occurred (especially once penicillin was discovered) if it involved white middle-class Americans as subjects? Speculation will not provide sure answers, yet the recent revelation that such citizens have been exposed to life-threatening radiation by our government is worth considering as a model.

For instructors using the small group approach to teaching, these issues can be assigned to separate groups to discuss. Also, it is helpful to assign one group to take the affirmative side of the issue and another group to take the negative side.

The First Question

The opening question to the class is one of the most critical features of case teaching. It determines the entry point into the case, and if one chooses the wrong question or wrong person to respond, the instructor may have difficulty getting back on track. Your question will depend upon your goals in teaching the particular case. Nonetheless, good opening questions share several characteristics in that they:

(1) Encourage participation.
(2) Move toward a specific goal.
(3) Set up a discussion of the facts.
(4) Elicit different perceptions of the case.
(5) Help formulate (define) a problem.
(6) Get personal involvement.

Consider three examples of questions for the Tuskegee case:

(1) *Some people have argued that there are racial overtones in this project, yet Eunice Rivers, a black nurse, was an important participant in the experiment. Are these two points of view compatible?* This question will likely catapult the class squarely into the racial issue. It meets many of the goals of a good opening question, but it will probably not suit the tastes of most scientists as the best entry point into the discussion.

(2) *As we look at this study, one cannot help but wonder if it was ethical, given that the men were simply informed that the doctors were studying "bad blood." How important is it to have informed consent?* This question launches the class into the ethics of human experimentation and once again meets many of the qualifications of a good opening question, but if the scien-

tific data are of prime concern, the next question may be better.

(3) *The Tuskegee experiment has been criticized because its experimental design was inherently flawed. Is that really so? And even if it is true that the study was not ideal, were there valuable results to emerge from this 40-year study?* This question, although less exciting than the previous two, starts the class on an exploration of the scientific issues and facts of the case. Below we have identified some of the questions that might be addressed under each issue.

BLACKBOARD WORK

Practitioners of the Case Study Discussion almost invariably make extensive use of the blackboard or flip charts. This provides a tangible structure to the discussion. If instructors do not use the board, they are throwing away one of their most important tools in teaching. Discussion has the inherent problem that it often seems aimless. Good board work provides students with a sense that something valuable is being accomplished. When the instructor writes a brief phrase on the board summarizing a student's thoughts, he or she shows that he or she values this contribution to the discussion. This encourages other students to participate, especially if the instructor is able to use the student's name. For instance, the teacher might comment: "If I understand Kimberly's point correctly, she is arguing that we do not have an adequate control population to make the claim that the men actually suffered in this study. She's arguing that men not in the study in any way probably had much poorer health than either the experimental subjects or the official controls." As this point is summarized, the instructor might note on the board "Inadequate control for claim that men suffered in study," perhaps even jotting Kimberly's name or initials next to the writing.

The final board outline is seldom neat and tidy; rather it has phrases, arrows, circles,

and lines connecting ideas from different parts in the discussion. Yet a clear pattern should emerge leaving students with a sense of "Look what we have accomplished!" To bring about order out of the emerging discussion is part of the art of case study. It not only requires practice but it requires preparation. In the current case it is logical to arrange the board around the major issues. For example if the instructor were to begin the discussion with the science issue, he or she might label it as such on the left side of the board, jotting down notes and phrases as they are developed. When other ideas pop up, the instructor might momentarily move over to other places on the board to write down these ideas, only to return to the science issue later. The teacher might set up the center of the board to develop the human experimentation theme, adding notes to other places on the board as they appear appropriate. The instructor might then shift to the right hand side of the board to develop the racial issue, making connections with previous points by moving back and forth among the issues as neglected points emerge. Thus the board has given structure to the discussion regardless of how freewheeling it might have been.

CLOSURE

How to finish a class discussion has different answers. Some case teachers simply stop when class time runs out. They feel no obligation to give their perspective on the discussion. "Life is messy," they argue. "There are no simple solutions. It is counterproductive to the development of higher-level critical thinking to give an instructor-biased viewpoint."

Other case teachers seriously disagree. Instead, they recognize the value of a good two- or three-minute summary of the class's discussion, and some instructors turn to the students themselves for assistance, asking one or two bold souls to wrap it up. A summary,

Suggested Question Outline

A. THE SCIENCE

1. What kind of disease is syphilis?

2. What did we know about the disease in 1930?

3. What was the original purpose of the study? Was the goal accomplished?

4. How did the goals of the project change over time?

5. What was the logic behind the choice of subjects?

6. What kinds of data were collected in the project and what conclusions resulted from the work?

7. What kind of scientific criticisms of the research can we offer?

B. HUMAN EXPERIMENTATION

1. What benefits did the men gain from the experiment?

2. What evidence do we have that the men were harmed by their participation in the project?

3. Was it possible to inform the men about the true goals of the experiment, given their educational status?

4. Given that men who participated in this study received health benefits, status, attention, and money, could they reasonably be expected to exercise good judgment about their participation in this project?

5. Are there circumstances that you could imagine where informed consent would interfere with an experiment?

6. Are there any circumstances where the overall good of an experiment to society overrides the harm done to a small group?

C. THE RACIAL ISSUE

1. What evidence do we have that race might have been a factor in the experiment?

2. What motivated the PHS investigators to choose Macon County as one of its study sites?

3. What differences were present in the experimental designs of the Tuskegee and Oslo studies?

4. If the Tuskegee and Oslo studies had shown racial differences, how would that information have been used?

5. Is it reasonable to conclude that the administrators of the Rosenwald Fund failed to fund the second PHS project because they identified racial bias in the work?

6. Is there any way to fund research on special groups in the U.S. population without running the risk of being accused of bias?

7. Given that certain segments of the population have special health problems, is there any way not to fund research on these groups without running the risk of being accused of bias?

of course, does not imply that you have solved the problems, it merely identifies some of the signposts along the way.

REFERENCES

Annas, G., and M. Grodin, eds. 1992. *The Nazi doctors and the Nuremberg Code.* Oxford University Press.

Barber, B. 1976. The ethics of experimentation with human subjects. *Scientific American* 234 (2):25–31.

Caldwell, J. G. et al. 1973. Aortic regurgitation in the Tuskegee study of untreated syphilis. *J. Chronic Dis.* 26: 187–199.

Jones, J. H. 1993. *Bad blood: The Tuskegee experiment.* Free Press.

Rockwell, D. H., A. R. Yobs, and M. B. Moore. 1964. The Tuskegee study of untreated syphilis: The 30th year of observation. Arch. Inter. Med. 144: 792–798.

Case Study Teaching in Science:

A Dilemma Case on "Animal Rights"

By Clyde Freeman Herreid

ontinuing our series on case study teaching, we turn to the most well-known method of case instruction, the "dilemma case." Here a protagonist is thrust into the middle of a crisis and must make a decision. Students studying the case gain an understanding of the issues and then suggest possible solutions to the dilemma. In the process they develop their critical-thinking skills and speaking abilities.

THE CASE: SAM BALLARD REQUESTS...

"And so if there are problems with registration, please see Ms. Lampier up here now. She'll be over in that corner." Professor Bill Torkey waved his hand to the right. "I'll be over here to handle all other questions that I may not have answered in my general discussion of the course. Remember, labs don't start until next week. See you next Wednesday."

Torkey quickly straightened his notes and slipped them into the brown file folder and watched the chaos develop at the front of the large lecture hall. The first day of general biology at the university was always the same—300 young, strained faces peering from dozens of rows into the lecture pit wondering what was going to happen here. Torkey knew they had heard the usual stories about the course—"It's incredibly tough, but rewarding if you work your tail off." The lectures were "exciting," but the exams "impossible." The labs were a mixed bag—some "too simple," others "ridiculous" in what they demanded in the way of memorization, but there was one compensation—the teaching assistants were heralded as "superb."

This was due in large part to the demands of their professor. Torkey had a reputation among the graduate students for insisting on excellence in their preparation for each lab session, and he held long training sessions each Friday to work out problems that might develop during their teaching. He had even gotten university honors students to volunteer to help the graduate students, so that each of the 14 lab sections had two teaching assistants.

The first class of the year began heading for the exits. Students with problems—there were always a lot the first day—headed for the front. The anxious types who were afraid of getting closed out of the class made a hurried scramble for Ms. Lampier who, implacably as ever, began the process of sorting problems and handing out sign-up sheets. Torkey looked at the swirling sea of faces about him clamoring for his attention and had one last thought before he turned to the individuals awaiting his attention: what an array of diversity he saw now in this public university in New York. The university's population had changed dramatically in his 25 years of teaching. Students from every conceivable culture were there sitting in his classroom: Chinese, Vietnamese, Japanese, Colombian, Russian, Iranian, African, and Indian, along with second- and third-generation Europeans. There were even a few Native Americans in his class this year. The classroom was an incredible display of the American "melting pot."

Then the questions came. "I have a conflict with the first exam. Can I arrange an alternate time?" "Can I change my lab from Mondays to Tuesdays?" "Do you have any more handouts?" "I haven't been able to buy the book—will this one do just as well?" "Should I...?" "Will you...?" "Can we...?" Torkey rapidly answered or delayed most of the questions that bubbled up from the 40 students clustered about the lectern. He had timed the process well. Charles Sargent from the philosophy department had the classroom next and his students were coming in. Sargent's day was just beginning.

One last student remained for Torkey—Sam Ballard, a serious-faced young man he had seen before in one of his freshman honors seminars last semester. "Well, Mr. Ballard,

what's on your mind?" Torkey asked him.

"I would like to speak to you about a serious conflict that I may have with some of the laboratories. I didn't want to cause any difficulties so I waited until the other people were gone. It's about the dissecting labs, I am philosophically opposed to them."

Torkey sighed, realizing that this question would take more than just a moment to resolve. "Come on over to my office so we can talk about this. Do you have a minute?"

After a brief stroll across campus, while they talked amiably about other matters, Ballard sat in Torkey's office.

"Let me see if I understand this, Sam. You don't want to dissect any animals because you're philosophically opposed to it?"

"Yes. I don't believe that I should be a party in the death of any animal."

"Why is that?"

"All animals have the right to be free of pain. And I don't think any one has the right to subjugate and exploit animals simply for their own end."

"Sam, this is a biology course. You knew when you signed up that there was dissection involved. Why did you take this class? You could have taken physics, chemistry, or geology to complete your science requirements."

"Well, I considered that. But I like biology. In fact, I am majoring in environmental studies, and that department requires that I take this course in order to graduate. I don't have any choice."

"Sam, I agree with them. It's logical that you know something about animal anatomy and physiology if you are going to study environmental studies. In fact, I think every student should know the fundamentals of anatomy regardless of their major. It's part of becoming an educated person. And it sure doesn't make any more sense for a major in environmental studies to be allowed to bypass dissection than it does for someone who is a pre-vet or pre-med student. It's part of understanding the animal."

"But I plan to be a lawyer and specialize in environmental law. I don't see why I need to have the experience of working on a pickled dead animal which doesn't look anything like the real thing in order to pass this course or to graduate."

"Obviously, I don't agree with you. Nor, for that matter, does the Department of Environmental Studies. It is their requirement, not mine, that you take this course. So what do you suggest is the solution to this problem?"

"I'm not asking that you drop all of the dissection labs, although I think that is the correct thing to do. What I am asking is that I not be forced to dissect an animal. I would be happy to work on models, or look at videos or look at diagrams in textbooks to learn the material. I'll take the same tests as everyone else. I will be happy to do any extra work, a paper or project or anything. I just don't want to kill or cut up anything."

Torkey leaned back in his chair, listening. This wasn't his first student to challenge the time-honored dissection approach to biology labs, but Sam Ballard was certainly the most serious. Torkey was willing to acknowledge that biology wasn't the same as it used to be. It was mostly cellular and molecular stuff today. Did students really have to dissect a frog, fetal pig, starfish, or earthworm to get a good education?

And what in the world was a lab about, anyway? Torkey knew that most students hated the dissection labs. There was nothing new to be discovered by poking around in a poorly preserved frog dripping with preservative. It had been done hundreds of thousands of time before. For what? Should he reevaluate his approach? What effect would his waiving this requirement for Sam have on the other students? What if some of them wanted other alternatives as well? What the devil should he do? He had skirted this problem long enough.

TEACHING NOTE

This is an excellent example of a dilemma case in which the character must make an important decision. The problem posed is a serious one in today's American classroom. The "animal rights" movement has emerged as a political force in the United States in the last few years. With varying degrees of success, students have challenged the traditional use of animals in the classroom.

The issues surrounding "animal rights" have grown more complex with the development of cell and molecular biology, both fields in which whole organisms are seldom seen or used. Methods of tissue culture and computer simulation hold out the promise that animals may not have to be used for certain types of drug testing. Videos, computer simulation, CD-ROMs, and interactive software programs, along with traditional models and multicolored textbooks, suggest that we may have reached the stage where animals do not have to be used in the classroom. This argument has become more pointed as many species have become threatened with extinction, and even sources for laboratory frogs have become scarce.

On the other hand, there is perhaps even more need today for the use of organisms in the classroom. The urbanization of the nation has removed most people from direct contact with plants and animals. City dwellers may see a pigeon, dog, cat, or rat, but little else. Their notions of how animals behave are colored less by the occasional documentary film than by Bambi and thousands of cartoon figures dancing across their Saturday morning television. With the devastation of the world's native habitats, there is a renewed urgency for educated people to understand the earth's flora and fauna. This cannot be done by simple behavioral observations or superficial understanding of anatomy and physiology. One must see, touch, smell, and hear the organisms with their own senses. Learning is not an abstract process that arrives simply from reading books. Learning is *doing*. That's what student laboratories are all about. The answer is not to do away with them, but to make them more meaningful.

Around these two polarized positions swirl issues of animal pain, medical experimentation, animal rights (if they exist), learning strategies, academic freedom, and a student's right in the classroom. Discussion of the case can easily involve topics such as rodeos, vegetarianism, circuses, bullfights, the use of leather and fur, ecoterrorism, zoos and their role, and national park philosophy. Instructors using the case should have a firm grasp of their aims, for the potential for emotionalism runs high.

BLOCKS OF ANALYSIS

Educational value of the dissection issue. The pros and cons of this central question must be discussed. What evidence can we bring to bear that actually cutting open and examining an organism changes a student's understanding of a subject? Perhaps it is useful to look for parallels in other fields where actually *doing* something is compared to reading about or seeing the activity. Is it apt to make the analogy that one doesn't learn to play basketball by simply watching Michael Jordan, or learn to play the piano just by listening to Van Cliburn?

Could a person who has only seen a video really "know" what a heart looks like? Watching the movie *Out of Africa* is hardly the same as standing on the Serengeti plain. But are the differences fundamental to the appreciation of biology? Anyone who has ever tried to perform a dissection or interpret the anatomy of an actual organism using a textbook, model, or video realizes how frustrating the experience can be. Things just don't look the same in real life. In fact, biologist Libbie Hyman, who wrote the best vertebrate anatomy textbook 40 years ago, virtually shunned all photos and figures because she argued they were actually deceptive in their simplicity. Living things don't look like that.

The issue of whether it is essential for a nonscience major to dissect organisms should be raised. Does the answer differ for students with different majors and career expectations? Or should all educated people be knowledgeable at this rudimentary level, especially in view of the many career changes students are apt to make over the courses of their lives? In what way is it essential that an environmental studies student who has done dissection differ from one who has not? Will their decisions in life differ? What about Sam Ballard's point that he is going to be a lawyer and argue environmental cases? Would his behavior as a lawyer be different *with* the dissection experience, as opposed to without it? Is it realistic to expect to find adequate video, model, or computer simulation material for Sam? Does it even exist in today's marketplace or is the argument strictly theoretical?

The animal rights issue. Sam Ballard makes the point in the case that "all animals have the right to be free of pain." He goes on to state that no one "has the right to subjugate and exploit another animal simply for his own end." These arguments need to be carefully explored, for they lie at the heart of most animal rights discussions.

One must ask what animal rights *are* and where they come from. Comparisons will be immediately made with human rights issues. Arguments for animal rights almost invariably are made by appeals to fairness, and arguments by analogy will be made to slavery, civil rights, and women's rights. All of these are strong, emotionally charged subjects. One will hear how animal use (abuse) is analogous to Nazi torture, human slavery, and the subjugation of women. In reply, there will be those who say these analogies are not apt; humans are unique, having reasoning ability, and are smarter than other organisms, therefore giving us the right to exploit other species. An animal rightist would respond that if we use this logic, then we should be able to use mentally handicapped people or infants for our experiments, as they are less intelligent than many animals, such as apes, dogs, or dolphins. Surely, we cannot use intelligence as the deciding factor. The important criteria should be the presence of a nervous system and the capacity for suffering. All animals with these attributes should be spared, unless there is some reason that is *so* compelling that we would actually be willing to use people. Only under those circumstances is the use of animals justified.

A major counterargument is that the "specialness" of humans does not lie merely in their nervous system or intelligence, but in the fact that we are a unique species, period. The argument may be of several types:

Power: "Might" gives humans the right to do as they wish.

Religious: Judeo-Christian tradition teaches that God gave "man" dominion over the animals. Orthodox Jewish tradition, in fact, demands that ritualized kosher slaughter be used on animals, a more brutal form of slaughter than many non-kosher methods.

Evolutionary: All species are distinct, and DNA analysis allows us to easily identify humans. Humans are members of a gregarious species, who, to varying degrees depending upon cultural differences and circumstances, cooperate with one another for mutual benefit and exploit other species for their own ends. Our altruistic behavior leads us to take care of our aged, infirm, impaired, and young because historically it has been selectively advantageous to behave this way. We see our obligations in terms of genetic similarities to us: families come first; other humans come second.

Animals that are similar to ourselves receive our concern because they evoke our sympathies when they give distress signals similar to our own, triggering our emotions. The less similar an animal is to humans, evolutionarily, the more unlikely it will have similar anatomy or physiology or suffer pain in any similar way. But, more importantly, an injured starfish (for example) does not send off recognizable distress signals that we respond to.

The issue of student rights and responsibilities. What are Sam's rights in this case? Can, or should, he be forced to do something that is against his conscience? How do we distinguish between a justifiable argument and one that is frivolous? In Sam's case, it does not appear that the argument is based on religious grounds, but it might be for another student. Although no major religious group objects to dissection, some sects do direct their followers to abstain from the practice. Is that a situation that should be handled differently than this one?

If Torkey granted Ballard's request, what would be a suitable alternative assignment? Torkey could quite reasonably request that Ballard sit next to students performing a dissection in the lab and watch their procedures. This would assure Torkey that Ballard had at least seen the actual specimens, and would be capable of taking any practical exam in the course. In this compromise, Ballard would not be responsible for the demise of any organism, but simply would be taking double advantage of the material. How might Ballard respond to this suggestion? What would be the effect of such an arrangement on the other students, especially Sam's neighbors who might be asked to share their frog or fetal pig? And what about the real possibility that Sam, vocal and articulate as he is, might actually begin to proselytize the other students in the class, urging them to likewise boycott the labs? How much leeway should Torkey allow the teaching assistant to have in dealing with this issue?

Faculty rights and responsibilities. At the outset, this case appears to be solidly in the hands of Torkey as the instructor. However, it could quickly involve other individuals if Torkey does not handle the situation so that Ballard is satisfied. Ballard could carry the problem to the department chairman, the dean of the college, president of the university, and the school newspaper, and he could bring in outside legal assistance. Questions of academic freedom, promotion and tenure, school politics, and publicity could more easily arise in some institutions than others. Since Torkey is a veteran professor at a public university, we might expect him to have less difficulty maintaining his position than, say, a young professor at a small private institution.

Whom Is the Case For?

This case has been used in student classes and in faculty workshops. However, the emphasis given by the participants and the ensuing discussion differs remarkably. Used in a faculty workshop, the educational value of labs and the issues of classroom control and faculty versus student rights become the central issues. Faculty—especially science faculty—are not especially intrigued with the animal rights issue. It's often a nonissue.

In contrast, students can be enthralled with the problem, and they look for ways to accommodate Sam's wishes. For students, the issue "Do animals have rights?" is particularly important since this lies at the heart of all animal liberation debates. It is the most challenging topic; it sets the parameters for the debate. If a class decides that animals have rights, they must decide the limits of those rights and what the consequences of their actions will have for education, medicine, food, and product processing. If a class decides that animals do not have rights and that we may therefore exploit them mercilessly, the consequences of their actions must be followed through. But, ultimately, the discussion must come to grips with what Torkey should do with Ballard.

The First Question

The first question asked in a discussion always sets the tone of the debate. It can be general or specific, emotionally charged or pedantic. It can come without warning to a student—a "cold call"—or come to a student who has been warned ahead of time—a "warm call." Consider how different the dis-

cussion might be if the following questions were used to start the discussion:

- What should Professor Torkey do?
- What, essentially, is the problem that Sam Ballard—or Professor Torkey—faces?
- Do you think that students should be forced to dissect animals if they don't want to?
- In what way can the dissection and use of animals be compared to the Nazi torture?
- Where do you think that Sam Ballard developed his animal rights concerns?
- Suppose you were the chair of the environmental studies department and heard about the controversy. How might you look at the problem?

The first question immediately jumps to the solution of the case. Discussion leaders starting here will have to rapidly branch out the discussion to consider the reasons behind the decision—the pros and cons of the argument, along with the consequences of any decision. It is a good, sensible starting point, as long as the leader circles back to pick up the main arguments.

The second question pitches the discussion at a personal level. It humanizes the problem in terms of the main characters. However, the discussion will be quite different depending upon whether it is Ballard's concerns or Torkey's concerns that are first examined. For Ballard, the issues are animal rights and his right as a student to control his education. For Torkey, the issues are the integrity of the educational system and his rights and responsibilities as a faculty member.

The third question is emotionally charged and will certainly get the discussion rolling. Opinions are apt to fly fast and furiously, without much analysis, unless the leader takes strong control and redirects the discussion. The fourth question is even more volatile, and there is a decided risk that the discussion never will deal with some of the critical issues.

The fifth question again personalizes the issue from Sam's point of view and will open up the historical and cultural basis for the animal rights issue first. Finally, the last question puts the discussion into an outsider's perspective. Faculty discussing this point will likely focus on faculty rights, academic freedom and politics, not a particularly auspicious beginning for an animal rights discussion. Students given this opening question will likely have little to say, except they may see the administration as a lever for Ballard to pull to force Torkey to agree to his request.

Consequently, the entry point for the topics is quite different depending upon the first question. Once started, the discussion can flow readily from one issue to the other, almost without warning. However, certain patterns are more likely than others. For example, if one talks about student rights, the issue of faculty rights is sure to follow, along with talk of who is in control in the classroom and who is in control of the educational process. The question of animal rights can easily be lost unless the instructor brings it back into focus. But if one starts with the educational issue, discussion can equally easily move to animal rights, student rights, or faculty rights.

Boardwork and Discussion Flow

Most successful case discussion leaders use the chalkboard extensively. They chart the progress of the discussion. Without visible evidence of the day's discussion points, many people are helplessly confused about the group's accomplishments. In fact, its absence leads students to undervalue the discussion method of teaching with the glib phrase, "It was all hot air."

Although there are many ways to handle a board, a reasonable approach might be the one

FIGURE 1.

A suggested chalkboard diagram for the discussion of this case.

Analysis of the Problem				Actions to be Taken	
Educational Issue	Animal Rights Issue	Students Rights Issue	Faculty Rights Issue	Short-Term Action	Long-Term Action

shown in Figure 1. Major issues in the case are laid out from left to right, with the appropriate ideas developed below. To the far right of the board, one might write the short-term and long-term actions that Torkey might take.

The issue headings can be placed on the board immediately to structure the discussion, but most experienced case discussion leaders would prefer to have the issues emerge from the audience and then be written in their appropriate spot. How much control the instructor wishes to exert is a matter of experience and taste. However, most practitioners usually will try first to explore the issues and be sure everyone has a good understanding of "what's happened" before they move to the question of what are the possible short-term and long-term solutions to the problem and their "consequences."

Closure on the case can either be avoided, as is the practice with some case leaders, or the instructor can wind up the discussion with a summary of the case or ask a student to do the honors. Finally, since this is a real case, the instructor can tell the audience what really happened. Many instructors will eschew this step... but in case you have a curious bent, "Bill Torkey" and "Sam Ballard" did indeed reach a compromise, and Ballard was willing to sit next to other students and assist them without using extra animals. Torkey continued to use this "solution" for the occasional student who requested the option. However, Torkey eventually was to face a more belligerent student. And that, of course, is another case altogether.

Is There Life on Mars?

Debating the Existence of Extraterrestrial Life in a Classroom Dilemma Case

By Bruce C. Allen and Clyde Freeman Herreid

Michael King let his mind wander as he waited for the meeting to begin. Although still young, he had earned a reputation as a competent planetary geologist through years of hard work at the University of Arizona. He attributed his success in part to an excellent education that stressed the validity of the scientific method.

Michael fully understood the need to proceed cautiously whenever scientists contemplated the announcement of a new discovery. Such a situation developed from the discovery in Antarctica in 1984 of a meteorite from Mars known as ALH84001. That was why he was both astonished and dismayed when then-NASA Administrator David Collins called with the news that the "Life on Mars" investigation would be shared with the public at an upcoming press conference.

As part of the investigative team, Michael felt that such an announcement was premature. He did not want to risk his reputation and career by rushing to make a public disclosure before the work was validated. He tried to imagine the public and professional reactions if the first report of life on another planet was ultimately proven false. The repercussions would be far worse than the simple disappointment many felt when the *Viking Lander* soil experiments produced negative indications of life on Mars 20 years earlier.

Michael stopped musing and turned his attention to the meeting. Dr. Collins was trying to explain the situation. "We are here because word has leaked that we have discovered evidence of life on Mars. If we let this get out of control, we could have a public relations nightmare. A news blackout will do more harm than good. So, we are going public tomorrow at 1:00 p.m. with a televised press conference." Michael wished he could find an argument against a well-orchestrated press release as the best method of rumor control. He could not, so he kept quiet.

Peter Kraft, a geochemist with the Johnson Space Center (JSC) and the lead author, spoke next. "Let's review the project. We received a sample of an SNC (shergottite, nakhlite, chassignite) class meteorite, ALH84001, for analysis two years ago from LPI (Lunar and Planetary Institute). Microscopic and chemical analysis of the sample led us to conclude that there was biologic activity on early Mars. Four lines of evidence were developed in support of our hypothesis: 1) the meteorite and the calcium carbonate it contains came from Mars, 2) the mineralogy and chemistry of the carbonate globules are compatible with biologic origin, 3) the meteorite contains organic material from Mars, and 4) there are microfossils within the globules. Any of these data have alternate interpretations, but, taken collectively, they are indicative of ancient Martian life."

Kenneth Holland, also a geochemist with JSC, picked up where Peter left off. "I've prepared a brief history of the meteorite. Mars began solidifying 4.5 billion years ago. The meteorite's parent rock formed at that time according to Rubidium-Strontium radiometric dating. Early in Martian history, the surface was considerably warmer and wetter than it is now. Approximately 3.6 billion years ago, calcium carbonate globules precipitated from chemical solutions flowing through fractures within the parent rock. At the same time microorganisms were present and became trapped in the carbonate. Moving ahead to about 16 million years ago, an asteroid-sized object impacted Mars and ejected ALH84001 from the surface. It traveled through space exposed to cosmic rays until it landed in Antarctica 13,000 years ago. In 1984 it was recovered by a joint NASA/NSF (National Science Foundation)/Smithsonian team and classified as a diogenite. Nine years later it was recognized as a Martian meteorite. Then, as Peter said, we received a sample in 1994."

Michael interjected. "Remember that ALH84001 is three times older than any other SNC. That makes it very unusual and casts some doubt on its origin."

"Look Mike," Kenneth responded. "We've been over this before. Most meteoriticists agree that it's from Mars and so do most members of this team. So, put it to rest." Kenneth did not like to be challenged.

Claudia Morgan from Lockheed-Martin took this opportunity to speak. "ALH84001 is an igneous rock. Its most interesting features are those carbonate globules that Ken mentioned. Transmission electron microscopy (TEM) reveals the black color around the rims is due to a high concentration of magnetite crystals. We consider the magnetite to have been formed by organisms based on three criteria: distinctive shapes, chemical composition, and environment of deposition. The cuboid and teardrop shapes of the magnetite crystals are consistent with magnetofossils produced by terrestrial bacteria. The same is true of the chemical composition, which is very pure. Furthermore, the isotopic compositions of the globules suggest they were formed in a low temperature, aqueous environment. The simplest explanation for these features is that they are by-products of Martian life."

Claudia's presentation was cogent and concise, but Michael still had doubts. "Claudia, you know the minerals are anhydrous and often found in environments hot enough to fry any bacteria. And what about the magnetite? Terrestrial bacteria are thought to navigate with it in Earth's magnetic field, but Mars has no magnetic field! So, why is it there?"

Peter interrupted before Claudia could answer. "Mike, this meeting is not a debate. It is simply a review in preparation for tomorrow. So, let's move on. All right?"

Peter signaled that Brian Murphy from UCLA was next. "I found PAHs (polycyclic aromatic hydrocarbons) that correlate with the position of the globules, but I admit they can be found in organic combustion products ranging from soot to burned steak. However, the observed mass spectrum is much simpler than typical for a meteorite. That suggests simple organic decay instead of combustion. Moreover, the concentration of PAHs in the meteorite increases with depth from the surface. If the PAHs were Earth contaminants we would find most at the surface."

Michael knew that was true. Frictional heating from high-speed entry into the Earth's atmosphere would burn off the PAHs in the outer layers of the rock. On the other hand, he knew that nonliving processes could form PAHs. They are found virtually everywhere.

Then Kenneth reviewed the scanning electron microscope (SEM) photos for the group. "The cylindrical forms in the globules could be dried clay, but they strongly resemble in both size and shape the microphotos of terrestrial nanobacteria. Segmentation present in some examples suggests cellular structures."

Michael could not let those last remarks pass without comment. "But Ken, how are you going to handle questions about the lack of cellular walls? There are no confirming biochemical signatures of life: no DNA, no protein, not even a trace of an amino acid! You know that bacteriologists will realize these things are 10 times smaller than anything previously recognized as life. To conclude these structures are microfossils is unjustified and to refer to them as similar to 'terrestrial nanobacteria' is misleading at best. There simply are no confirmed reports of nanometer-sized bacteria, anywhere!"

"I don't agree, Michael," retorted Ken. "I've been in touch with an excellent mineralogist that says he has found fossil bacteria of the same scale as ours in copper deposits in Chile. So, let's leave that issue for the biologists to sort out."

The discussions continued for some time. When they were finally over, Michael was still left with a feeling that the issues were unresolved and would be until further evidence was gathered. He was not sure what he should do personally. Should he risk his career by backing the project publicly, or should he play the role of the skeptic, or even resign from the team? For the right decision, the rewards could be enormous. For the wrong decision, the penalties to his career could be devastating. Suddenly, it all became clear to him. There was only one way to preserve his personal and professional integrity, but it meant he would not get much sleep that night.

STUDY QUESTIONS

- *Why do we think that ALH84001 is a meteorite from Mars?*
- *What are the arguments for believing that the rock harbors microfossils?*
- *What are the reasons for being skeptical of the microfossils?*

NOTE

A web page devoted to this case can be found at: *http://ublib.buffalo.edu/libraries/projects/cases/case.html*

REFERENCES

Kerr, R. 1997. Martian 'microbes' cover their tracks. *Science* 276: 30–31.

Letter to Editor. 1997. Nanobacteria: Size limits and evidence. *Science* 276: 1773–1774.

McKay, D. S., E. K. Gibson Jr., K. L. Thomas-Keprta, H. Vali, C. S. Romanek, S. J. Clemett, X. D. F. Chillier, C. R. Meechling, and R. N. Zare. 1996. Search for past life on Mars: Possible relic biogenic activity in Martian Meteorite ALH84001. *Science* 271: 924–930.

TEACHING NOTES

This is a case that deals with the question "Was there past life on Mars?" The matter received sensational attention when a group of scientists associated with the National Aeronautics and Space Administration decided to hold a press conference on August 7, 1996. At the press conference, they revealed evidence favoring the presence of life on Mars 3.6 billion years ago.

These findings were publicized days in advance of *Science* magazine's report published on August 16. NASA's approach was largely unprecedented and generally condemned by the scientific community.

This conflict sets the stage for the case. It has several elements: scientific, ethical, and personal. First, it deals with the basic science of the "discovery," how we know or say we know something. Second, the case touches on ethical questions and problems created by going public prematurely. Third, it encompasses a personal story (fictional) of a young scientist who is skeptical about the evidence and must mull over his personal involvement in a press conference that he feels is premature. The events of the case are real but the conversation is fictional.

BLOCKS OF ANALYSIS

The Science

Many scientific issues cutting across several disciplines are embedded in the case. These will be emphasized differently by different instructors. Nevertheless, the case allows extensive opportunities to address these questions.

- *What is the evidence ALH84001 is a meteorite from Mars?* The evidence includes (1) a fusion crust (burnt exterior) on the outside of the rock, (2) discovery on top of an Antarctic glacier, (3) evidence of alteration due to impact shock, and (4) composition similar to SNC meteorites from Mars identified by comparisons with data from the Mars *Viking Lander* Project.

- *What evidence exists about the age of ALH84001?* Four ages are offered in the case: The date the rock was formed (4.5 B.Y.B.P.), the date the carbonate globules were deposited (3.6 B.Y.B.P.), the date the rock was blasted off Mars (16 M.Y.B.P.), and the date the rock landed on Earth (13,000 Y.B.P.). These questions naturally require a discussion and understanding of radiometric and cosmogenic isotope dating techniques.

- *What is the evidence that ALH84001 harbors fossils (i.e., past life)?* This is the most contentious part of the scientific story. Three lines of evidence are used to support the life on Mars argument: (1) scanning electron micrographs show rod-like shapes in the rock that resemble bacteria, (2) magnetic mineral (magnetite Fe_3O_4) crystals are found in the rock similar to those discovered in some terrestrial bacteria, and (3) organic molecules, polycyclic aromatic hydrocarbons (PAHs), are found in the rock. As the case points out (and the students should verify themselves when they consult the literature), there are problems with all three lines of evidence.

The Ethics

It is highly unusual to hold a press conference before data are published. Such an event is typically condemned. Students can get a better appreciation for the arguments involved in releasing data in a public forum by discussing the case with practicing scientists.

Arguments in favor of a press conference before publication:

- To establish priority for a discovery before a competitor publishes the same findings. This seems to have been a factor in the Cold Fusion fiasco but does not appear to be important in the Mars case.

- To be sure the correct story is presented without distortions. A leak did occur before the Mars paper was published.

- To be sure that NASA funding was maintained. Cynics argue that NASA was in serious financial trouble prior to the press conference and might have orchestrated the leak itself. The sensationalism that followed the actual media event did appear to offset any thoughts about curtailing NASA programs.

Arguments against a press conference before publication:

- To prevent error. When a variety of scientists and journal editors examine the data and conclusions they are likely to catch errors of method and logic.
- To prevent the appearance of self-aggrandizement, self-promotion, and hucksterism that pervades much of life.
- To maintain the role of scientists as impartial seekers of truth.
- To protect reputations against mistakes and to preserve the credibility of science so that people may depend upon the untainted word of scientists.

Career Issues

The dilemma feature of the Mars case involves Michael King and his role in the press conference. Scientists reading this case have various opinions as to what Michael should do and this ambiguity is ideal for a case.

Michael's concerns fall into two categories: (1) Scientific concerns. This would include Michael's obligation to "seek truth," that is, to be sure that things are scientifically accurate and credible. His own reputation is tied into that responsibility. (2) Career concerns. Michael could be worried that he will miss out on a great discovery if he does not join in the press conference or that he will look like a fool if they are wrong. He runs the risk of alienating colleagues within the NASA team and beyond and jeopardizing future jobs, grants, and promotions.

TEACHING THE CASE
Discussion Method
To teach this case in 90 minutes requires that students come prepared. They must read the background literature in the references or on the internet to be able to discuss the science involved. It is reasonable to begin the class discussion by asking students to write down a single sentence that encapsulates the major scientific claims made. By asking a few students to read their sentences, the instructor can write on the blackboard the list of claims and have the class discuss the evidence enumerated. Closure to this section can be reached by asking the class to rank the level of certainty for each claim on a scale of 1 to 10.

The issue of the prepublication press conference can be considered next, followed by Michael's personal dilemma. The latter may be approached by first listing his concerns, then his options, and finally discussing the possible consequences of his choices. As class ends, ask the students to choose the best option and vote by a show of hands. It might be useful to point out that in the real press conference a skeptic who was a member of the NASA team did participate by pointing out problems with the interpretations.

Small Group Method
If the case is taught using small teams of students, as in Problem-Based Learning, the case might be covered in parts of three classes. In the first session, teams would read the case and identify the scientific issues. Students would then divide the work and seek information for the next session. In the second session, teammates would share information. They would clarify the science and summarize the evidence in a report. For example, teams could write the key assertions and give the evidence why the NASA scientists believe what they do. Next, a general discussion with the entire class summarizing the points might be appropriate. Before leaving the second class, the students might then spend a brief time identifying the ethical and personal issues at stake for Michael. To research this they might each leave with the goal of interviewing scientists about the case. The third session would focus on the sharing of their views in the small groups with a final general discussion and/or paper.

Section VI

Small Group Methods: An Overview

I have a bias: I believe small group methods are best for case study teaching. Lectures are still lectures even if cases are used. Discussions run by faculty still limit the opportunity for student participation. The data seem clear. Small groups are best. Cooperative learning strategies have been evaluated hundreds of times. When students get together to argue, discuss, and persuade with other students, the information becomes their own. They quickly find out if they understand the material when they try to explain it to other students.

My arguments for small groups are laid out in the first three chapters in this section. But a point that does not appear strongly enough in these writings is that "The positive effects of small-group learning [are] significantly greater for members of underrepresented groups (African Americans and Latinas/os)" according to a meta-analysis of studies in science, math, engineering, and technology (SMET) courses by Springer, Stanne, and Donovan (*Review of Educational Research* 1999. 69: 21–51). In the last chapter I describe a workshop at Pima Community College that has a large contingent of minority students, where three interesting approaches were taken in presenting cases.

Why Isn't Cooperative Learning Used To Teach Science?

By Clyde Freeman Herreid

I t is a shame that more scientists don't read the education literature, for they would be aware of the quiet revolution taking place in teaching. In the past 30 years, cognitive psychologists have made significant headway in understanding how people learn. Many of these principles have found their way into the hands of educators, and from there into some of the nation's K–12 classrooms. As usual, educators in institutions of higher learning lag behind.

The revolution that I speak of is called cooperative learning. Its message is simple: Put students into small interactive groups of four or five, give them projects, problems, tests, or case studies to analyze and they will learn more effectively. Unlike many fads in education, which are enthusiastically touted but poorly investigated, cooperative learning may be the most thoroughly studied educational technique ever utilized. Johnson and Johnson (1989, 1993) of the University of Minnesota have performed a meta-analysis of over 1,200 studies in which researchers have compared the performance of students educated using cooperative learning strategies with that of students taught by traditional methods, such as the lecture method.

The results of this meta-analysis are unequivocal and overwhelming: Cooperative learning promoted higher individual knowledge than did competitive and individualistic learning, whether the task required verbal, mathematical, or physical skills. Most important, the retention of knowledge was greater. Cooperative learning has striking additional benefits. Students enjoy the experience more, have a better attitude toward the subject, develop better social skills, become more articulate, and end-up respecting differing viewpoints more than when they are taught in the traditional teaching modes. Clearly, these are outstanding plusses, especially for the field of science, in which educators are concerned about our failure to engage the majority of students.

Cooperative learning holds out the possibility of offsetting the scientific illiteracy that plagues Americans. Evidence of this illiteracy is in the following signs (Mullins 1993; Herreid 1995): The results of standardized tests, in which American students perform poorly compared to those of other nations; the declining fortunes and international competitiveness of American industry and business; the increasing prevalence of the occult, pseudoscience and paranormal non-sense in the media; the high dropout rate of students from science and engineering programs (the "pipeline problem"); and the finding that adult scientific literacy in the United States is as low as 5% (e.g., Miller 1988). In addition, science as a field is not attractive for many women or members of ethnic minority groups. For example, African-Americans in 1993 received only 2% of the doctorates in the life sciences and 1% in the physical sciences (MacIlwain 1995). In the United States, women make up 50% of the population and 45% of the American workforce but only 13% of the engineers and scientists.

Small group learning is well suited for many individuals and is especially effective for the very groups not currently enchanted by our current pedagogy. Uri Treisman (1985) of the University of California-Berkeley pioneered the teaching of college calculus in groups. He noticed that African American students failed freshman calculus at a higher rate than other minorities, whereas Asian American students outperformed all others. He found that the African-American students tended to work alone, whereas the Asian American students tended to study in groups. When Theisman set up study groups for the African Americans, their performance improved spectacularly.

Similarly, Frederick Mostellar teaching statistics at Harvard found distinct improvement in students who were placed into learning groups, and improvement was especially significant for women (Light 1990).

The findings of Light's (1990, 1992) Harvard Assessment Seminar Reports, which involved 100 faculty members from 24 colleges and universities, are especially noteworthy. When students were asked why they do not take science courses, they pointed to the fact that science courses have more grade competition among students than classes in other areas, a view reinforced by Sheila Tobias (1990). Light (1992) emphasized the importance of small study groups. "For some students, whether or not they work in a study group outside of class is the single best prediction of how many classes in science they take. Those who work in small groups take more" (p. 66).

WHAT IS COOPERATIVE LEARNING?

"Cooperative learning is the instructional use of small groups so that students work together to maximize their own and each others learning" (Johnson, Johnson, and Holubec 1993, p. 6). But beware: Cooperative learning is more than throwing students together and expecting learning to occur. This casual approach is a recipe for failure (see Feichtner and Davis 1985.) Five elements are essential to successfully implement cooperative learning (Johnson and Johnson 1989).

Positive interdependence. The groups must be given a clear task and group goal, the success of which demands that several individuals work together to complete the job. Students understand that they will either sink or swim together. In other words, they must cooperate or fail, because the task is too complex or time-consuming to do alone.

Individual and group accountability. Not only must the group be held accountable for achieving its goals, but each person must be held accountable for his or her own contributions. There must be no "hitchhikers" on the work of others.

Face-to-face (promotive) interaction. Students need to encourage and help one another by exchanging resources, providing feedback, challenging conclusions, and acting in trusting and trustworthy ways; in short, they need to care about one another's success. Thus, most advocates of cooperative learning strongly recommend using class time for group work.

Interpersonal skills. As Johnson, Johnson, and Holubec (1993) point out, "People must be taught how to work in groups. Leadership, decision-making, trust-building, communication and conflict-management skills have to be taught just as purposefully and precisely as academic skills" (p.10)

Group processing. Students must constantly assess how well their group is functioning and if things aren't going well, fix them. Fortunately, groups that work well together over long periods tend to resolve many initial problems on their own.

STRATEGIES FOR COOPERATIVE LEARNING

Cooperative learning is quite variable in form (Johnson, Johnson, and Holubec 1993). However, all of the strategies are based on the knowledge that learning is enhanced when people explain their ideas to one another.

Informal cooperative learning groups are brief groupings of students for only a few minutes or perhaps one class period. For example, a lecturer may pause and ask the students to work a genetics problem and then, moments later, ask them to turn to their neighbor and compare answers while explaining their reasoning.

Formal cooperative learning groups are larger groupings of students, lasting from one class period to several weeks. For instance, students in a general biology class may be formed into temporary debate teams to collect information about human cloning and then argue its merits. In a physiology class, groups might design an experiment or present a poster on recent advances in the field.

Cooperative base groups are groupings of students that last for months or years. For example, an ecology class might have a semester-long project to study a river, in which permanent teams of students gather data on hydrology, water chemistry, plants, and invertebrates. For years, I have taught a course titled "Science, Technology, and Society" using Michealsen's (1992) team-learning approach, which places students into permanent teams in which they take group tests and work on case projects together.

Teamwork is not an alien concept to scientists. After all, scientists function within research teams and departments. They know that groups often produce better results than individuals. Indeed, many science projects could never be duplicated by a single individual. However, scientists rarely consider the impact that group interactions can have on education or their obligations to provide students with opportunities (such as cooperative learning) to enhance their social skills. The need for such training is emphasized by the data of Pettit (quoted in Light 1990) who reported that 80% of the alumni from 35 liberal arts colleges said that the prime ingredient for success in their chosen field was the ability to work in groups and with people. Most alumni reported that virtually no time had been spent developing that skill in the normal classroom. Hildebrandt and Murphy (1984) make the point another way: They note the number one reason that people lose their jobs is interpersonal conflict!

Cooperative learning works extraordinarily well in science, math, and engineering courses. One of its noted practitioners, Karl Smith, of the Engineering School of the University of Minnesota, summarizes some of the reasons why cooperative learning works effectively (1993, p. 11):

"Whoever organizes, summarizes, provides elaboration, justification, explanation, etc. learns. The person who does the intellectual work, especially the conceptual work, learns the most.

More learning occurs in an environment of peer support and encouragement because students work harder and longer.

Students learn more when they're doing things they enjoy.

Learning that is informal, social, and focused on meaningful problems helps create 'insider knowledge.' Gaining insider knowledge is a major part of becoming a member of a community of practice."

OBSTACLES TO CHANGE

Although cooperative learning can be very successful, there are several potential problems. Johnson and Johnson (1993) point out there is always the danger that many faculty will implement cooperative learning poorly on the basis of inadequate training and become disillusioned. Fortunately, there are numerous workshops around the country and a national journal that will help alleviate the problem; nonetheless, gaining skill in cooperative learning is not simple. Also, there are increasing numbers of centers for teaching excellence on university campuses where cooperative learning strategies may be acquired

Nevertheless, three groups of individuals will provide resistance to implementing any change in science teaching: the faculty, the students, and the administration. Each group has its own doubts, and its concerns must be addressed.

BARRIERS FOR FACULTY

Few scientists have implemented cooperative learning and its cousin, collaborative learning, in their classes in spite of their demonstrated superiority over traditional teaching (Bruffee 1995; Matthews, Cooper, Davidson, and Hawkes 1995). There are several possible explanations for this situation.

Science faculty rebel at the thought of things "educational." Many university science teachers have not heard of group learning techniques. In addition, they are apt to dislike what they often perceive as jargon, "mushy methods," and "touchy-feely" approach of "education." They believe the field of education is for K–12 teachers and has little to say to the college instructor. Consequently, even if they have heard of the cooperative learning process, they find it easy to dismiss. Professors of education and professors of science tend to remain in their private worlds. The two groups are in different places physically, pedagogically, and philosophically; they attend different meetings; they read different journals; they do not speak the same language; and they cooperate on little or nothing. In fact, only a few scientific societies have teaching sections in their journals and many authors seem unaware that a rich literature exists for higher education.

Science faculty know only how to lecture. Scientists have been trained by the lecture method. They have grown up with it. Even if they haven't been trained how to teach (and few have), they knew what was expected of them when they stepped into their first classroom: lecture. If they were lucky, they got better. If they tried to lead discussion in class it was probably a failure. They asked a question and were greeted by averted eyes and silence, or a brief response from one of their braver students. Getting even brief responses was like pulling teeth—painful. Soon they were lecturing again. They simply do not know any other way to teach. Discussion leading is a skill which most scientists do not have, and cooperative learning is something altogether foreign, even to those who might want to try it.

Science faculty do not want to spend the time retooling their teaching methods and revising their teaching materials. Cooperative learning takes time, and lots of it, because a teacher cannot rely on the old lecture notes. New exercises for groups must be carefully crafted and projects graded. Standardized tests and well-known textbooks can be used, but most are clearly out of step with the higher-level thinking that cooperative learning demands of students. Hence, the instructor is soon forced into writing new materials. The result is more work.

Some faculty are convinced they are such good lecturers that they do not need other teaching methods. Some stellar lecturers are loathe to relinquish center stage. The ego satisfaction can be enormous. Why give up something you are good at, especially when your teaching evaluations say you are the best?

Faculty don't know how to handle group grades. Cooperative learning strategy demands that groups produce some evidence of their progress. Most of the time they must turn in a tangible product (a paper, proposal, model, report). How should this be evaluated? Some experts argue that no group grade be given, that rewards only be given to the individual through normal testing and grading policy. They argue that students will work on the group project because it promotes their individual understanding of the material. Moreover, since the instructor uses numerous opportunities (at least one per class) to have the groups analyze their social dynamics, looking for ways to improve the group's effectiveness, the group will stay motivated (Johnson, Johnson, and Smith 1991).

There is another school of thought: That group work needs to be a part of the grade to ensure that students will be sufficiently motivated to work together. Such assignments prepare students for the real world, which works this way. That is, many projects cannot be done by a single individual and must be worked on and evaluated collectively. Also, from the instructor's viewpoint, grading group work cuts down the workload; there are fewer papers to correct. But even if instructors buy into group grading, how can they determine if all students have contributed equally to the project? How can they ensure that the grading is fair? This can be solved simply by the use of peer evaluation. But peer evaluation methods raise the hackles of some teachers while others use the method with aplomb.

Faculty using cooperative learning may be seen by colleagues and administrators as flakes, kooks, or worse (in some large universities) as someone too interested in teaching. Instructors, especially young nontenured individuals, run a serious risk teaching in an unorthodox way. It might lower their teaching ratings. (A young assistant professor recently told me that I should try telling the dean that her dip in student ratings was only temporary!) Obviously, any innovation needs to be explained adequately to colleagues and superiors. Ideally, several in-

dividuals in a department should be committed to trying the new methods, after suitable training. A local support group can help one another through the rough spots.

Faculty don't have lessons, exercises or cases to use in cooperative learning strategies. These can take many days or weeks to prepare. On the other hand, a few people have been working to develop this material in the last few years and case files are beginning to develop and to appear in publications such as the *Journal of College Science Teaching,* and on websites devoted to case-based teaching: University of Minnesota's cases on agriculture, food, natural resources, and environmental problems (*www.decisioncase.edu*); and the University of New York at Buffalo's National Center for Case Study Teaching in Science (*http://ulib.buffalo.edu/libraries/projects/cases/case.html*). However, many exercises can be easily drawn from news articles or journal articles and others can be written in one or two paragraphs (Herreid 1994a; 1994b). Case studies for teaching need not be 15 pages with 5 appendices requiring months to put together such as we see in business school.

Faculty claim that they can't cover as much material if they don't lecture. There may be some truth to this claim, depending upon the cooperative learning method chosen. Nevertheless, Dinan and Frydrychowski (1995) teaching organic chemistry using Team Learning (Michaelsen 1992) actually covered more material than with the previous lecture method, so the generalization isn't universally true.

Most cooperative learning techniques generally do not put a premium on coverage. Rather, they emphasize higher-order learning skills—that is, analysis, synthesis, evaluation, and critical-thinking skills. Facts as such have a lower priority. The use of case studies are an illustration (Herreid, 1994a). Teaching by case studies puts the learning into context, and it is difficult sometimes to put together a sequence of cases that will get in all of the facts an instructor wishes to cover. Indeed, medical students at McMaster University in Hamilton, Ontario, trained by the problem-based learning method, were found to have some gaps in their background (Albanese and Mitchell 1993). These gaps were readily filled in during residency because these students had learned how to learn and find information. Their great strength—problem solving—was far more important to their careers as physicians than the accumulation of a few facts whose absence was easily remedied.

Finally, as all teachers recognize, just because an instructor covers the material, does not mean the students learn it. Cooperative learning stresses learning rather than coverage, which explains why it produces better retention than traditional methods even if fewer facts are taught.

Faculty argue they can't use cooperative learning in large classes. Cooperative learning has traditionally been used for small classes, perhaps 30 students or less. But much larger classes have tried cooperative learning successfully. Dental school classes of 70 students have proved workable (Scannapeico and Herreid 1994). Michaelsen (1992) writes that Team Learning has been effective with student numbers in the hundreds. A major limitation in using cooperative learning in large lecture halls is that the seats are all fixed to the floor. However, students can work with their neighbors, and with the people in front of and behind them, if they are encouraged to do so. Also large science classes frequently have laboratory sections or recitation sections in which students meet in small groups, providing excellent opportunities for cooperative learning.

BARRIERS FOR STUDENTS

By the time most students reach college, they have adjusted to the lecture method used by so many of their K–12 instructors. They have become passive listeners. Anything out of the ordinary in the classroom is greeted with suspicion, especially by students who have done well in the previous mode. They have a right to question any changes.

Students can be threatened by the new approach to learning. When cooperative learning is the dominant method of teaching, students may perceive that they are doing everything whereas the teacher does nothing. Students may complain that they have to teach themselves! They don't recognize that is one of the goals of education.

Student evaluations may slump during the first couple of years that cooperative techniques are set in place. Then after the instructor has become more skilled, evaluations soar. I have even had a student refuse to fill out a teaching evaluation form because he said it wasn't applicable to me because I didn't teach. Yet, when students are asked to evaluate cooperative learning courses they almost universally have positive remarks to make about working in groups.

Students can be hostile to cooperative learning modes. Science majors, especially ones who get good grades, are survivors of the current system. The lecture method suits them just fine. If it is not ideal for their learning style at least it is familiar, and they have mastered it. Even if the lectures are disorganized and boring, science majors are attracted by the subject matter and have a long-term faith that things will get better. It should not surprise instructors that such students, when first confronted with a new technique, have a healthy skepticism about it. Such skepticism seems especially likely in professional schools, such as schools of dentistry (Scanneipco and Herreid 1994) and medicine (Albanese and Mitchell 1993), all of whose students are there by virtue of their excellence in receiving grades by the traditional route. Cooperative learning strategies, especially if only a single course is involved, are a hard sell indeed for science majors who have done well in the traditional lecture system. By contrast, as Tobias (1990) reported, nonscientists are different; they do not have an inherent love for the sciences.

When the teaching is uninspired, they often give up on the sciences, even though they may be good students. Such individuals often welcome cooperative learning with open arms.

There is another danger: Students become discontented if they believe they are part of an experiment; they sense the instructor's insecurity and blame any setbacks on the teacher and the method. Moreover, discontent with their teammates, sometimes for very good reasons, is likely to lead to problems unless the faculty member is a seasoned problem solver. Beginning instructors are particularly vulnerable in trying cooperative learning. They must grapple with both the novelty of the method and the normal problems of any classroom.

Students do not have the social skills to survive the stress in small group learning. The competitive nature of our society is mirrored in the classroom, and much of a college student's early life is locked in a struggle with rigid grading schemes in which there are few As. Small group work can be a terrible experience (Feichtner and Davis 1985), especially for good students who feel they have been taken advantage of by their classmates. To be successful, cooperative learning techniques must solve the social problems that threaten all groups: the dominant person, the shy nonparticipant, the personal conflicts over control, and so on.

Barriers for Administrators

Administrators must deal with the spillover of problems faced by the students and faculty. If their problems are not dealt with adequately, the trouble lands resoundingly on the chairman's, dean's, or even president's desk.

Administrators question the use of novelty if it generates problems for students. Department chairs are usually the first administrators to hear of difficulty in the classroom. But sometimes, unhappy students go straight to administrators at higher levels: My first experience using small group work was so clumsy that a student delegation went to the dean to appeal for relief.

Administrators in large schools may rebel if class sizes drop. Cooperative learning classes are frequently small. So, if an instructor wants to switch from the lecture method to cooperative learning, reducing class size may be necessary. This may be unacceptable to an administrator, especially if budgetary concerns are involved. The problem may be insoluble unless the instructor manages to incorporate cooperative learning into recitation sections or labs or can figure out how to implement cooperative exercises into the large lecture hall.

Administrators often view teaching as interfering with research. This phenomenon is common in "publish or perish" institutions. Faculty promotions and tenure decisions hinge on the publication list and grant success of the candidates. Despite lip service to the contrary, teaching in large public universities is often seen as getting in the way of research. Time used in creating new exercises, correcting papers, and meeting with student groups—all standard demands of cooperative learning—is time taken away from the lab bench, field station, and grant writing.

Overcoming the Barriers

With all of the negatives, why would anyone change his or her teaching to cooperative learning? For four reasons: First, over 1,200 studies testify that the traditional mode of teaching is less effective than cooperative learning. Second, instructors have demonstrable evidence in their own classrooms that with the traditional methods, large numbers of students fail or barely pass. It is too easy to blame the students for all of the failure. The comment of cognitive psychologist Jean Piaget is telling: He says that teachers should do some animal training, "since when that training fails, the trainer is bound to accept that it is his own fault, whereas in education failures are always attributed to the pupil" (Kraft 1990, p. 69).

Third, it may be that even a "good" lecturer is no better a teacher than a "poor" lecturer.

In science courses in which multiple sections were taught by different people of widely differing lecture skills and teaching evaluations, student grades on standardized tests were identical (Birk and Foster 1993). When good lecturers hear these data, they are at first disbelieving. They then immediately challenge the standardized test as an accurate method of measuring the impact of their teaching. Of course, if the standardized test is not an accurate measure, why is it so widely used in lecture courses? Something is wrong here.

Fourth, attendance is dramatically improved with cooperative learning. In my institution and many others, even fine lecturers may have 30–50% absenteeism in their classes after the first few weeks of the semester. In cooperative learning classes, attendance is 95–100% because students do not wish to let their teammates down. Given that there is a persuasive case for small group learning, how can the barriers outlined above be overcome? Here are several suggestions.

Recognize that all things "educational" are not just fluff, but are based on decades of rigorous testing by thousands of researchers. Some studies are good, some are poor, but virtually all say cooperative learning is superior to the lecture method. Communication between scientists and educators must be improved.

Read the education sections of scientific discipline journals. In addition, subscribe to the *Journal of College Science Teaching*, which has articles from teachers in all types of universities and colleges. There are frequent articles on the use of exercises for small group learning.

Learn how to use small group teaching methods and active learning strategies. Read key works and attend workshops and seminars on the topic. For example, subscribe to the cooperative learning newsletter, and attend conferences (such as Lily Conferences) devoted to the art of teaching.

Start small. Add a cooperative learning exercise now and again until you gain profi-

ciency and are secure with the method. Few instructors have the nerve to suddenly convert a class to small group learning overnight. A slow beginning also means that it will not be necessary to devote massive amounts of time to designing new exercises. But there is a catch: Group work takes practice for students, so if cooperative learning is only an occasional activity, the payoff is likely to be low. Also, I have found that it takes no more time to design a cooperative learning class than to design a new lecture. Both require thought and creativity.

Use peer evaluation if you use group grades. Kegan (1995) makes strong arguments against group grading, noting that this grading method is blatantly unfair, debases report cards, undermines motivation of high achievers, and violates individual accountability. The disadvantages Kegan mentions disappear if it is possible to determine who is doing the work. Thus, the group grades can be apportioned accordingly. For instance, in problem-based learning, tutors who sit in on groups can easily assess who does the work. When tutors are not used, peer evaluation techniques will work. For example, students in a five-person group can each be given 40 points to distribute among the four other group members. People averaging 10 points receive 100% of the group grade; those with an average of 9 receive 90% of the group grade, and so on. The instructor can reserve the right to overrule the peer evaluation if he or she believes that there is an injustice in the result.

Encourage your colleagues to use cooperative learning. The best solution is for several faculty at an institution to try out the method in different classes. Then, by meeting periodically, perhaps over a brown-bag lunch, they can talk over their experiences. The members of such a local support group can do wonders to help each other over the rough spots.

Beg, borrow, or steal group exercises from one another to use in the classroom. It takes significant time to build up a supply of excrcises. Why reinvent the wheel? Fortunately, in the last few years exercises and case studies are beginning to develop and to appear in publications such as the *Journal of College Science Teaching* and on websites such as the University of Minnesota's cases on agriculture, food, natural resources, and environmental problems (*www.decisioncase.edu*); the State University of New York at Buffalo's Case Studies in Science (*http://ulib.buffalo.edu/libraries/projects/cases/case.html*); and the University of Delaware Problem-Based Learning cases (*www.udel.edu/ppl*).

Give up the idea that coverage of the material is the same as learning. Students forget most of the lecture material as soon as the course is over. Cooperative learning and other small group methods deliver far better retention. What good is it to cover the book when few remember it?

Refuse to accept the fact that cooperative learning cannot be used in large classes. Eric Mazur's "concept test" is a case in point. This Harvard physics instructor delivers 15-minute lectures, then stops the class and asks students to privately write down the answer to a multiple-choice question. He then asks the students to turn to their neighbor, compare notes, and justify their answers. Following this two-minute pause, he asks for a show of hands on each of the multiple-choice answers. If a high percentage of students has answered wrong, he lectures further to clarify the concept. The interruption of the class period by these concept tests generates feedback and excitement.

Constantly give and receive feedback from the students. Explain why you are using small group methods, soothe their concerns about grades, and talk to them about their responsibilities to their group. Have them write and talk together in their groups about how they can improve their own effectiveness. If you are using peer evaluations, run practice sessions so that individuals will have opportunities to correct their behavior before disaster strikes. Warn them that absenteeism and tardiness

are the two worst offenses in a cooperative learning setting.

Tell the department chair about the benefits of cooperative learning. Jim Cooper, editor of the *Cooperative Learning and College Teaching Newsletter*, has recently written the article "Ten Reasons College Administrators Should Support Cooperative Learning" (Cooper 1995). He notes that cooperative learning increases student retention, values diversity, enhances the success of technology in the classroom, develops critical thinking, fosters the goals of liberal education, prepares students for the world of work, builds a sense of community, revitalizes faculty, responds to learning styles, and promotes cooperation in university governance.

Following these suggestions will overcome most of the barriers to implementing cooperative learning. In addition, it is important to remember that students do figure out how to handle many of the difficulties themselves, especially if student groups are kept constant. It takes time to learn to work as a team; at least one-third to one-half of a semester is generally needed. Even then, it takes a certain maturity before students recognize that they do not have to like their teammates to work with them. Under the best of circumstances, perhaps 10–20% of groups have significant difficulty working together. Thankfully, most of these problems are fixable if the instructor intervenes by meeting with the troubled group members individually and collectively. Finally, I should note that in my experience, as many as 15% of students will still prefer the familiar lecture method even if they have had a good experience with cooperative learning.

Conclusion

Practitioners of cooperative learning must have not only skill but patience for they are flying in the face of student expectations and tradition. They must expect challenges from students who for the first time have been empowered by the group process to openly voice their concerns about the educational process. They must be prepared to experience greater highs and lows than they will probably have experienced before in teaching. The lecture method allows the instructor to operate at a distance, to treat students as a mass audience, while he or she is the authority figure at center stage. By contrast, cooperative learning strategies force the teacher to see students as individuals. For the first time, the instructor has ample opportunity to watch student interactions often leading to profound insights about the learning process. When one gives up being "the sage on the stage" to being a "guide on the side," teaching will never again be the same.

REFERENCES

Albanese, M. A., and S. Mitchell. 1993. Problem-based learning: A review of the literature on its outcomes and implementation issues. *Academic Medicine* 68: 52–81.

Birk, J. P., and J. Foster. 1993. The importance of lecture in general chemistry course performance. *Journal of Chemical Education* 70: 180–182.

Bruffee, K. A. 1995. Sharing our toys. *Change* (Jan/Feb): 12–18.

Dinan, F. J., and V. A. Frydrychowski. 1995. A team learning method for organic chemistry. *Journal of Chemical Education* 72: 429–431.

Feichtner, S. B., and E. A. Davis. 1985. Why some groups fail: A survey of students' experience with learning groups. *Organizational Behavior Teaching Reviews* 9(4): 58–73.

Herreid, C. F. 1994a. Case studies in science: A novel method of science education. *Journal of College Science Teaching* 23: 227–229.

Herreid, C. F. 1994b. Journal articles as case studies: The *New England Journal of Medicine* on Breast Cancer. *Journal of College Science Teaching* 23: 227–229.

Herreid, C. F. 1995. Chicken Little, Paul Revere, and Winston Churchill look at science literacy. *Perspectives* 25: 17–32.

Hildebrandt, H. A., and H. W. Murphy. 1984. *Effective business communications*, 4th ed. New York: McGraw Hill.

Johnson, D. W., R. T. Johnson, and K. A. Smith. 1991. *Active learning: Cooperation in the classroom*. Edina, MN: Interaction Book.

Johnson, D. W., R. T. Johnson, and E. J. Holubec. 1993. *Circles of learning: Cooperation in the classroom*, 4th ed. Edina, MN: Interaction Book.

Johnson, D. W., and R. T. Johnson. 1993. Cooperative learning: Where we have been, where we are going. *Cooperative Learning and College Teaching* 3(2): 6–9.

Light, R. J. 1990. *The Harvard assessment seminars: First report*. Cambridge, MA: Harvard Graduate School of Education.

Light, R. J. 1992. *The Harvard assessment seminars: Second report*. Cambridge, MA: Harvard Graduate School of Education.

MacIlwain, C. 1995. After 20 years, prospects remain bleak for minorities in U.S. science. *Nature* 373: 645–646.

Matthews, R. S., J. L. Cooper, N. Davidson, and P. Hawkes. 1995. Building bridges between cooperative and collaborative learning. *Change* (July/Aug.).

Michaelsen, L. K. 1992. Team learning: A comprehensive approach for harnessing the power of small groups in higher education. *To Improve the Academy* 11: 107–122.

Penick, J. E. 1995. New goals for biology education. *Bioscience Supplement* S-52-S63.

Smith, K. A. 1993. Cooperative learning and problem solving. *Cooperative Learning and College Science Teaching* 3(2): 10–12.

Tobias, S. 1990. *They're not dumb, they're different*. Tucson, AZ: Research Corp.

The Bee and the Groundhog

Lessons in Cooperative Learning—Troubles With Groups

By Clyde Freeman Herreid

You've got trouble. Right here in River City.
Trouble with a capital T and it rhymes with G
And that stands for groups!

—With apologies to Meredith Wilson

I'm thinking of two animals, the bee and the hedgehog. The bee is the essence of cooperation in song and fable; the groundhog has had little press except when February 2 rolls around and an ersatz groundhog is rolled out into view in Punxsutawney, Pennsylvania, as a rodent soothsayer to ponder the coming of spring.

The lack of media coverage for groundhogs is understandable for they are solitary beasts, not just during the winter somnolence, but during most of the rest of their lives as well. They are loners.

Here are two extremes of interactions: On the one hand, there is the bee whose entire life is involved with communal feeding, nest tending, and communication among her sisters who have completely given up their privilege to mate so their mother can reproduce. (Is this altruism or what?) On the other hand, there is the groundhog, a veritable recluse, who stakes out his territory and will not stand for interlopers in his world.

Between the two extremes of cooperation and competition, humans fit in somewhere. Homo sapiens live, work, and thrive together as gregarious beings, but they fight, fuss, and maim one another at the drop of a hat. The tension is legendary. Humans build together what they could never build alone, yet their individualism threatens to destroy any cooperative enterprise. So it is no surprise that when groups of humans get together, this polarization is often evident.

In the microcosm of the classroom the tensions are hardly a titanic struggle of nations for the control of continents, nor battles to sway the hearts and souls of millions, but they are no less real to the combatants. Let us look in at a typical group of students struggling to survive a general biology course taught with case studies using cooperative learning.

Here is Anju, an average student whose heart is in the right place, who wants to cooperate and get a good grade, but is struggling with the material. She would probably get a D or an F in a normal lecture course. She is usually on time and tries to do her share but her work is invariably average or worse.

Then there is Heidi, a pretty good student who has a strong Puritan strain running through her veins. She is friendly and tries mightily. Essay questions demanding that she use her knowledge give her difficulty. She is always on time. She is probably a B student in a lecture course. In her group she is totally dependable; she has hopes for medical school.

And there is William. He is a theater major taking this course for general education credit. He is laid back, pleasant, and bored to tears with the course material. He falls asleep whenever there is a lull and almost certainly would fail or slip by with a D in a normal semester.

Margaret is an older student in the group. She is working a full-time job as an accountant. By her own admission, she is a loner, an independent learner who likes to be given a job and left alone. She is bright, articulate, and "no nonsense." She is an A student and cannot abide laziness. She is taking this course because she has decided to go to medical school. She is highly skeptical of group projects because she has been burned in the past.

Finally, there is Raoul, a Puerto Rican, good looking, and bright. He is working two jobs. He is brash, verbal, and he too wants to go to medical school. He cuts corners whenever possible, faking and bluffing his way through discussions. Within two classes his group has caught on to the fact that they cannot depend upon him. He could get an A in the class, but chances are he would end up with a D if it were not for his teammates.

There you have them: Anju, Heidi, William, Margaret, and Raoul, locked into a relationship not of their own choosing because the instructor has followed the time-honored protocol of cooperative learning to form diverse groups.

This is one of many groups that I have faced in the last several years: a problem group—one that struggled throughout the school term with Margaret gritting her teeth and doing the brunt of the work; Raoul thinking he was getting away with his meager performance; William not caring much because he only needed to pass the course but giving a much needed spark of levity to the group meetings when tensions ran high; Anju, clinging to Heidi for support as she slipped further behind in course load while Heidi struggled valiantly with high anxiety to get her A.

Case study teaching in many of its incarnations relies on groups. Indeed, the best-known case study strategy, Problem-Based Learning, is totally dependent on group success. In its classical form in medical school, tutors are used in every group to help solve interpersonal problems as they arise. But the normal cooperative classroom that relies on groups has no such luxury. The professor is alone, faced with the dilemma of controlling, cajoling, and corralling the efforts of many groups and personalities, the equivalent of herding butterflies.

What are the problems that groups face as they go through their evolution from "forming, storming, norming, and performing." Thinking about the problems of groups, I am reminded of the opening words of Tolstoy's *Anna Karenina*, "Happy families are all alike, every unhappy family is unhappy in its own way." So too with groups; the problems are particular, unique, and sometimes painful.

Let's take a closer look at Raoul's group. What was the problem here? It was not a gender issue, nor a racial one, nor a struggle for group dominance. It was the unevenness or inequity in the individuals' contributions to the group enterprise. It was Anju who tried and wasn't always up to the task intellectually. It was William who did not try or care for he only needed a D to pass. It was Raoul who always just slid by, sure he was fooling everyone, doing reasonably well in his individual work but failing miserably in group projects. Heidi and Margaret were left picking up the pieces.

Some practitioners of cooperative learning argue that group work should not be graded. There are strong reasons to accept their wisdom. But others, myself included, believe that group projects if they are constructed correctly have great value. The instructor must have a method for ensuring that "hitchhikers" in the group get their just desserts if they do not deliver and see to it that the "workhorses" are rewarded. There must be justice.

I think I bypassed many of the problems that arise in group work. I did not make assignments that required the groups to meet outside of class. This is almost impossible in today's classrooms where commuters are common and work schedules and family commitments intervene. Group activities should be exclusively in the classroom.

The Problem-Based Learning model is ideal. Students working in permanent groups are given a case or a problem to solve. They analyze the problem, discover what they do and do not know. They divide up the workload and go off to the library or the internet to seek out the necessary information that will be shared the next class period. This is where Raoul's group ran into trouble.

At this point you may ask, what would possess any instructor to follow the cooperative learning mode? I leave that question for another column, but here I address the problem by asking, how often do we see problem groups? Is this a rarity—the social equivalent of an asteroid crashing through our atmosphere causing the dinosaur's extinction—or is it more like the number of beetle species in the world, pervasive, ubiquitous, and over-

whelming? (J. B. S. Haldane, a prominent British scientist, when asked what, if anything, he had learned in his long and distinguished career answered, "God has an inordinate fondness for beetles." I do not believe God would say the same about problem groups.)

My curiosity piqued, I asked several hundred faculty who are experienced in cooperative learning to estimate the percentage of groups that develop problems. Their answers ranged from 5% to 50%. But, the average seems to be around 20%. That seems about right to me: one in five. When I have asked the follow-up question, "What percentage of that number are fixable?", the answer seems to be about 95%. That's good news. Most problems can be patched up if not solved all together.

How to deal with problem groups depends, doesn't it? The drastic solution of permitting a group to "fire" a nonparticipant has few supporters. What would the outcast do in a cooperative classroom? A "divorce and remarriage," where a person leaves one group and goes to another is equally unattractive. No, the problem must be dealt with.

Here are two generic solutions:

- Be sure and have many classroom moments when groups must analyze their process of working together. This can be accomplished many ways. Classroom assessment forms can be used to ask the students to rank how well their groups are doing and explain how things can be improved. Summary discussions can be held within groups as a follow-up. Johnson and Johnson, gurus of cooperative learning, argue that frequent discussions are essential to group cohesiveness. They document that academic achievement rises with group feedback (*Cooperation and Competition*. 1989, Edina, MN: Interaction Book Company).

- Use peer evaluations. These ask each group member to assign a given number of points to teammates based upon their relative contribution to the group. Say, in a group of five people, each person would have 40 points to distribute among their teammates. If all team members are contributing equally, each would end up with an average of 10 points. If a student ends up with an average of eight points, he/she is clearly doing too little according to the teammates. If he/she receives an average of 12, that person is doing too much. I go so far as to tell the students that if they receive a score of seven or below, they will fail.

I used both of the above approaches in dealing with Raoul's group, but it was peer evaluation that had the greatest impact. After about a third of the school term was over and the groups had established certain patterns of interactions, I handed out peer evaluation forms telling students that this was a practice for the kind of evaluation they would have to complete for their teammates at the end of the semester. Their evaluations would be kept confidential and they were encouraged to be honest in their appraisal so that if any problems existed, everyone would be warned in time to correct their errant ways.

I then collected their evaluations and calculated the averages. In Raoul's group the consensus was clear: Anju, Heidi, and even William ended up with about a 10 average. (Students are amazingly forgiving if they sense a positive attitude and a willingness to try.) Margaret received over a 12 and Raoul near seven. There was indeed trouble in River City.

I gave out cards to the students with their personal averages written down and delivered a speech reminding them of what the numbers meant. After class I pulled Raoul aside for a heart-to-heart talk. Now I had his attention. After the usual remonstrations, Raoul agreed that he had better mend his ways. So with gnashing of teeth, he was off.

Now I'm not going to tell you that all was suddenly right in River City or that Margaret, Heidi, and Raoul are running an HMO together. But I am going to tell you that things got better and livable for the rest of the semester. Margaret and Heidi got their As; Anju her C+; William his C; and Raoul squeaked out a C–. Along the way, they learned some biology and something about teamwork.

Humans are not bees laced with altruistic DNA, nor are we groundhogs, solitary and reclusive. We are something in between. It isn't always easy but there are times we need one another. Jane Howard said it clearly, "Call it a clan, call it a network, call it a tribe, call it a family. Whatever you call it, whoever you are, you need one."

I Never Knew Joe Paterno

An Essay on Teamwork and Love

By Clyde Freeman Herreid

The reason we were so good, and continued to be so good, was because he [Joe Paterno] forces you to develop an inner love among the players. It is much harder to give up on your buddy than it is to give up on your coach. I really believe that over the years the teams I played on were almost unbeatable in tight situations. When we needed to get that six inches we got it because of our love for each other. Our camaraderie existed because of the kind of person Joe was.

—Dr. David Joyner

I was a Nittany Lion for a couple of years when I was in my last stages of graduate school. I transferred to Penn State when my thesis adviser decided to pack up and leave Johns Hopkins University and head to real football country. Not that he was interested in football, but the Penn State prowess with the pigskin was a bonus. Joe Paterno, Penn State's all-time great coach, was still in the future, so I didn't get to have even a glimpse of this gray eminence on campus.

I regret this chronological faux pas, for Joe Paterno is clearly one of the great teachers of teamwork in the world of sports. He has been voted coach of the year for an unprecedented four times and has won more gridiron victories than any other major active collegiate coach. He does it not by browbeating, but by

developing love between his players. This is the kind of teacher that many of us aspire to be.

People love sports almost as much as they love stories. And the most popular sports are team events: football, basketball, baseball, and, of course, the world's leading sport, soccer. This is notwithstanding the current craze for wrestling, which hardly qualifies for a sport but ranks right up there with the best of soap operas as an emotional bouillabaisse.

What is it about team events that seem to transcend individual events such as track, swimming, tennis, or ice skating as spectator sports? If you will let me get away with a little pop psychology here, I believe it is a reflection

of both the competitive and cooperative sides of our human nature. To see the basic human nature exposed for what it is, we only have to turn to that sensational TV show *Survivor,* where 16 strangers were placed on an island for a few weeks. There they acted as perfect primates, working together by forming alliances yet at the same time acting as conniving selfish individuals to the bitter end. The show quickly captured the fancy of the public and catapulted the last survivors into media darlings. Yup, that's us—in the raw.

Not much in our world can get done without teams. We don't have to turn to examples of building the pyramids or space rockets to see this. Teams are everywhere from the operating room to the boardroom. Cooperation is a valued trait even if it is tainted with a bit of self-interest. "I will pay more for the ability to deal with people than any other ability under the sun." This, ironically, was said by oil executive John D. Rockefeller, whose maverick ways won him a fortune.

It's not surprising that teams might be useful in the teaching business, too. Indeed, teams are the modus operandi for two prime methods of using case studies in the classroom: problem-based learning and team learning. Both strategies depend upon the instructor setting up permanent teams of students in a class where no formal lectures are given. And both, from my perspective, are the best ways to teach cases.

Let me pause for a moment to make the argument that groups work best for learning. The brothers Johnson (David and Roger), along with Karl Smith from the University of Minnesota, have produced a string of books on the power of cooperative learning. They have performed a meta-analysis of over a thousand studies comparing the effectiveness of cooperative-learning strategies with the traditional lecture-based classroom. Guess what? The data are unambiguous: Groups are the best way to go. Students working in groups retain information better, like the subjects better, develop a better appreciation for a diversity of opinions, and develop better skills in self-expression. Better. Better. Better. Lectures don't come close to delivering the goods.

I don't know about you, but that impresses me. I like data. So, right away, with my bias toward stories, I am going to be looking for a way to combine cases with small group teaching. Stories delivered via lecture are nice but it is still a lecture. (And I can't help remembering the Arizona study where several professors with a wide range of skills as lecturers taught different sections of general chemistry. Yet, their students all performed at about the same level on the tests, regardless of who their instructor was. Those of us who pride ourselves on our lecture style need to pause and reflect a moment on this one.)

Stories (cases) delivered by the discussion method (as in the business school model) are nice, too, but they are still orchestrated by a professor standing in front of the room hand waving. No matter how good the sage is, he is still the head honcho, center stage, and has most of the "air time." There are limited opportunities for students to explore their own ideas.

That brings us to groups. For the moment, don't ask me for tips on how to make groups work; we'll save that for another day. Let's start with the powerful point that groups get the job done better than lectures. But success is not attained when groups are merely thrown together and told to discuss things. Careful planning is required so that the basics of cooperative learning are accomplished. That is, one must choose group tasks that can't be successfully accomplished alone.

Let's take a look at the five basic tenets of cooperation. These are the things that we must accomplish or the whole enterprise falls apart.

(1) *Positive interdependence.* Students must understand that they sink or swim together. The tasks we set as instructors must really be group activities that require many hands and minds to get the job done. Either the task must be too complex to do it alone or it must be too large to get it done in the time available. If the students know that they can do it better alone, they won't buy into the notion of a group activity.

(2) *Face-to-face interaction.* The instructor must promote situations where the students are physically together helping, encouraging, and explaining things to one another.

(3) *Individual accountability.* The teacher must set up a system where the efforts of the individual are identifiable so that students can't hitchhike on the work of others.

(4) *Social skills.* Students must be taught social skills that allow them to be effective in groups. They must learn leadership, decision making, trust building, communication, and conflict management skills. Group roles such as leader,

recorder, and reporter need to be rotated regularly so everyone has a crack at these tasks.

(5) *Group processing.* Groups must analyze how they are doing. They need to discuss what they can personally do to make the group perform better. They should periodically turn in a written analysis that is signed by everyone. This debriefing process is essential because it forces students to come to terms with their own role in the success of the group.

It isn't easy to accomplish all of these things; but neither is it easy to deliver a great lecture.

So, that brings me to case study teaching and groups. Obviously, it is possible in any classroom, even where lectures are normally given, to suddenly put students into small groups and hand them a case. Although this will surely spice up your day, it is not the most ideal arrangement. Students are like the rest of us, they need practice to get good at anything. There is an apocryphal tale about the eminent violinist Jascha Heifetz that makes the point. Heifetz, who was known to wander the streets of New York as an old man, was stopped one day by a bewildered tourist and asked, "How do you get to Carnegie Hall?" Heifetz pondered this a moment and responded, "Practice. Practice. Practice." So it is with us; we must practice if we wish to get to Carnegie Hall.

Problem-Based Learning (PBL) is one of the most successful methods of integrating cases into the classroom on a regular basis. For the past 25 years or so it has been used to teach medical students at McMaster University in Canada. Cases are a natural way to teach in medical school for each patient is a case study. At McMaster, virtually the entire curriculum is a collection of cases, and a couple dozen other medical schools in the United States and in other countries have followed suit because of its success.

On the undergraduate level, there are two major efforts to use PBL. The first is at the University of Delaware, where they began to use the method in science courses in the early 1990s. This initiative soon broadened to other disciplines. Take a look at their website at *www.udel.edu/pbl.*

More recently, Samford University in Alabama has taken the plunge into PBL wholeheartedly with a large curriculum effort across the disciplines. They just held a conference on the method and their website is at *www.samford.edu/pbl/pbl_main.html.*

PBL develops independent critical thinkers better than any method I know. Students are placed into small groups with a facilitator who is generally a faculty member or an experienced student. They stay together for the semester since it takes time to develop the bonds that are necessary for success in group work. Every two or three class periods, the groups are given a new case to analyze.

You can see examples of such cases laid out in the textbook written by Deborah Allen and Barbara Duch, *Thinking Toward Solutions: Problem-Based Learning Activities for General Biology* (1998, Saunders College Publishing).

PBL cases come in parts, with the students receiving them piecemeal over several class periods. This has become known as "progressive disclosure." When they receive the first part of the case, the groups read it over and decide what they know about the unfolding problem and what they need to research. They divide up the jobs among the group members and everyone heads off to the library, the lab, or the internet to search out the answers. The next time the class gets together, the students in their groups share their findings with their teammates. The process is repeated as the case unfolds and the denouement is reached.

One of the big knocks against the use of PBL is the question of coverage. Critics lament that using cooperative methods limits the amount of material that can be covered by an instructor. True enough. But let us recall that "covering the material is not the same thing as learning." Surely we have enough Fs and Ds in our classrooms to remind us of this fact! Also, it is well to remind ourselves that we faculty are survivors of the lecture system. No wonder we love it. Do students with different learning styles always have to head off to the social sciences and humanities to find a home?

You say you're not satisfied? You say that you must cover 14 chapters of your 1,000-page organic chemistry text otherwise your students will never be able to compete? Stay in your seats, for help is on the way. Here is team learning coming to your rescue. This innovative technique was developed by Larry Michaelsen at the University of Oklahoma (see *The Organizational Behavior Teaching Review* 1984–1985).

Team learning involves several steps:

(1) *Individual study.* Students are given reading assignments, which they must read or they fall into a flaming abyss, as you will see in a moment.

(2) *Individual quizzes.* Students are given 15 to 20 multiple-choice questions over the readings almost the moment they walk into the classroom each day.

(3) *Group quizzes.* Students working in their permanent groups take the same multiple-choice quiz that they did moments before, but this time they talk over the questions together to reach a consensus on the answers. Both individual and group quizzes are immediately graded by the students using a portable Scantron scoring machine in the classroom so they get *immediate* feedback.

(4) *Preparation of written appeals.* The students are given a brief time to consult their textbooks and write appeals if they think that the questions are unfair or ambiguous. These must be signed by all group members and are best read by the instructor after class to avoid incessant bickering.

(5) *Instructor input.* The teacher gives a short mini-lecture to clarify any issues that may crop up during the test. And that's it. The 50-minute class is over.

Now this sequence of activities can be repeated day after day as you march through the textbook. Frank Dinan of Canisius College in Buffalo, New York, has taught his organic chemistry course just this way and was able to cover more chapters than ever before and the students got higher grades than when he used the traditional lecture approach!

But a full appreciation of the method occurs when cases are used with the mini-quizzes. Michaelsen says that step six, *application-oriented activities,* should occupy a major part of team learning. This is when some classes are turned over to group projects such as case studies. For example, when I am teaching evolutionary biology and the students have covered a topic like species formation, I give them a case study on the Galapagos Islands to work on in their groups. Case studies drive the central points of the readings home.

Team learning gives teachers the luxury of depending on the students to cover the major points of a topic without lecturing so that class time can be devoted to understanding of real problems. In my experience using the method for nearly 10 years, there are other bonuses.

The students get higher grades. I get to know the students much better than when I lecture. The students almost universally prefer the method, although some grumble about the hard work when they realize there is no hiding from their responsibilities. Plus, there is the striking fact that there are practically no absences! And why is that? Because the students invariably say they simply can't let their classmates down. Compare that to the traditional classroom.

So the bottom line here is love, although I doubt that a student would go so far as to use the word. But another hard-nosed football coach, Vince Lombardi of the world champion Green Bay Packers, had no trouble with the "L" word, saying, "Love is loyalty. Love is teamwork. Love respects the dignity of the individual."

I never knew Vince Lombardi either, but he and Joe Paterno got it right.

The Pima Experience

Three Easy Pieces

By Clyde Freeman Herreid

I just returned from a delightful five-day stay in Tucson, Arizona. As the guest of the Desert Vista Campus of the Pima Community College System, I was plied with margaritas and tamales—the essence of the good Southwestern lifestyle. I was giving a workshop on the use of case studies in science during my semester break and, incidentally, taking in the Desert Museum perched high above the city where it sits next to Old Tucson, the site of dozens of old Western movies. Coyotes and cacti and mountain lions—oh my! This was John Wayne territory.

What brought me here in the dead of winter? Skeptics will doubt me, knowing that I hail from Buffalo, but it was not the sunny weather. Nor was it the wining and dining pleasure. Nor even the prospect of meeting old friends. No, it was because a couple of years ago, when we were writing an NSF grant proposing to disseminate the case study method throughout the land, we had proposed traveling thither and yon to spread the "good word." This included going to both large and small schools, public and private institutions, research universities and community colleges.

So there I was at Pima, one of the nation's premier minority/majority systems where there is a significant Hispanic, Native American, and African American population. I was hoping to inspire some of the faculty to forsake their holiday vacation to learn about the joys of case study teaching.

The workshop unfolded as usual, with me pontificating about the pleasures and problems, and the whys and wherefores of changing our method of teaching in the classroom. This included a quick historical account of Harvard's innovations with the case study method 100 years ago and McMaster Medical School's problem-based learning foray into cooperative learning more than 30 years ago. Over the next couple of days I demonstrated the classical discussion method and several variations of the case study approach.

All the while, the participants developed their own cases, in preparation for their performances on Thursday and Friday. On those days, the faculty presented their cases to a group of students that we hired to act as expert critics. The faculty, usually in pairs, presented their cases to the students as if it were their own class. When each case was over, the students wrote comments about the efficacy of the case and offered suggestions.

Following this written evaluation, I conducted a discussion with the students about the case, asking them pointed questions about the various strategies that the instructor used. The faculty that ran the case remained silent, unless called upon. Other faculty listened at the back of the room to these critical comments—and hopefully gained some insight into the minds of the students—something that we as faculty seldom get to hear, unless they are complaints about grades.

So that was the structure of the workshop. But that is not the reason I bring this to your attention. It is rather that whenever I do these functions, I am always impressed at how creative the faculty can be. They take a basic concept such as case teaching in science, and once they are freed from the fact that classes do not have to be lecture, lecture, lecture, they develop all sorts of innovative ways of teaching. Often the most creative teachers are those from teaching and community colleges. In fact, three of the cleverest approaches to case study teaching that I've ever seen emerged during my desert days at Pima.

FIRST-PERSON ORAL NARRATIVES

Let me tell you about Cindy Rankin and Lillie Hansen who nipped over from the University of Arizona, also in Tucson, to put together a case on homeostasis—a topic that is often mentioned in physiology courses but seldom emphasized. This is unfortunate because the regulatory systems of the body are key to our survival.

Cindy opened the case by telling a 10-minute true story about something that happened to her just a couple of weeks earlier. She narrated a harrowing adventure that occurred when she and her husband were scuba diving off the coast of Mexico. While underwater admiring the wonders of the deep, a violent storm swept their boat away, leaving them stranded

two miles from shore. Swimming below the surface waves, they struggled to the beach and then hiked overland only to be confronted with another inlet of water that separated them from the marina. There was nothing to do except to get back in the water and swim the distance. The students and listening faculty were enthralled—who doesn't love a good story?

When the tale ended, Cindy asked the students to make a list of the different environments to which she and her husband had been exposed. They were to write in an adjoining column the physiological reactions that she experienced in her struggle to survive. Lillie summarized this information on the blackboard. Cindy then focused on one of the physiological responses—body temperature variation—and asked the student groups to predict what happened to her body temperature as she experienced her adventure.

After due consideration, student representatives from the groups drew their predictions on the board. Cindy followed this by drawing her real core body temperature through the ordeal, which revealed only minor variations in contrast to the students' predictions. Finally, Cindy asked what compensatory devices the body used to achieve this constancy. This led to the final summary comments about how this was an excellent example of homeostasis in action.

Despite my brief synopsis of an exciting case, it should come as no surprise that during the debriefing exercise, students enthusiastically praised the oral presentation of the case. They had received a written copy of it after the narration was completed, but most of them did not use it. They completed the case without needing written material. It is well to keep the power of the spoken word in mind when designing cases—it is just possible that this is the best method for capturing interest and holding attention.

EXPERT WITNESSES

During the workshops, faculty are faced with

a difficult mission. They have to design a case to present to a group of students they have never seen. This situation is artificial to say the least. If they were to use cases in their normal classes, they would know the students and would have given them background information in preparation for the case. In the workshop environment, the instructors are not only dealing with strangers, but their cases must be self-contained. There is no opportunity to give homework or follow-up assignments. It is a wonder that the faculty can pull this off so successfully! But they do, and usually the cases are outstanding. The reasons for this include the fact that any faculty member who is apt to attend the workshop is highly motivated and ready to try something new, plus they are usually veterans of the classroom.

They solve the background problem in various ways. Some give an introductory mini-lecture telling their audience that they would know the following things… (*a*, *b*, and *c*). Others give students a handout with necessary facts to which they can refer throughout the case presentation. A third approach is to use an expert witness. Part of the way through the case, when certain information is needed, the instructor can literally or figuratively put on a white lab coat and rattle off some important information. This does not have to be didactic; in fact it is much better to ask the students what information they would like to know to help them solve the case. The instructor can then respond to their questions with appropriate information.

In the workshop situation, faculty often work in pairs, and it is simple for one of them to assume the role of an expert witness. In their own course at home, they could accomplish the same thing by inviting a real expert on the topic to field questions. This is a common case approach. Indeed, the expert can introduce the case itself to the class. This gives a further advantage—an outside person lends variety to the classroom.

INTIMATE DEBATE

The debate format is a common technique for cases. There are several versions of this method. In the first, two teams research a controversial topic such as the proposition, "The United States should sign the Kyoto Treaty on global warming." They should be prepared to argue both sides of the question. Then on the day of the debate, a flip of a coin determines which team will represent the pro side and which will handle the con side of the argument. The teams alternate presentations as follows:

- pro (5 minutes) then con (5 minutes) offer their opening remarks;
- pro (5 minutes) and con (5 minutes) give their rebuttals; and
- con (3 minutes) and pro (3 minutes) finish with summary statements.

The student audience can have a question period introduced after the rebuttal and before the summary as a way to keep their interest piqued. And, of course, they can vote on who won the debate and write a follow-up paper justifying their position. As an added fillip to the method, I have on some occasions had the same teams reverse their positions in the following class period and argue from the opposite side.

While at Pima I saw a clever variation on the debate strategy. Becky Richardson from Cochise College, receiving advice from facilitator Mary Lundeberg from Michigan State University, designed a dilemma case on the subject, "Should college students be required to have the meningococcal vaccine?" To start, Becky placed her students into groups of four, two individuals sitting across the table opposite the other two. Then they read a story about a young man who had not been vaccinated, contracted the bacterium, and died 24 hours after reporting symptoms.

Students on one side of the table represented the parents of college students who were strongly advising the state legislature of Arizona to pass a law requiring the vaccination procedure; they received a handout with details supporting their views. The two students sitting opposite represented state legislators concerned with costs and the politics of the problem; they received a somewhat different set of data.

After the teams had a few minutes to digest the material and to chat among themselves, the parent team had four minutes to present their side of the argument. The legislators could only listen and ask questions for clarification. Then it was the legislators' turn to present their side while the parents listened. Then there was a chance for the two teams to argue back and forth briefly.

Moments later, Becky told the two teams to literally get up and switch places at the table. They had to take their notes with them, including their original fact sheet. The two teams then had to argue on the opposite side of the question—four minutes for the new team representing parents and four for the new legislators. If they did not take good notes, they would be at a disadvantage be-

cause they did not have access to the facts describing their opponent's position.

Finally, Becky asked students at the different tables in the class to make a personal decision about the question; they had debated both sides of the issue and should have been able to come to an informed decision for themselves. After a few minutes, Becky polled the class and found, not surprisingly, that the tables had come to different conclusions. She finished her case with a short summary discussion on the current legislative positions on this issue in the country.

This case method was particularly effective at getting students to examine an issue from both sides and is a method often termed "constructive controversy." I call it an "Intimate Debate."

There you have it—three neat, simple methods to inspire your next casework. You can thank the folks at Pima for their creativity, even though you didn't get the benefit of their tamales and margaritas. Hasta la vista y buena suerte con sus casos estudios!

Section VII

Problem-Based Learning

Problem-Based Learning (PBL) got its formal start in the late 1960s in Canada at the McMaster University Faculty of Health Sciences when it established a new medical school. Disappointed with the traditional lecture method of educating physicians, they wished to produce graduates who worked well in teams, were lifelong learners, and excellent problem solvers. They graduated their first class in 1972. About the same time, the College of Human Medicine at Michigan State developed a PBL track and other newly established medical schools in the Netherlands (Maastricht) and Australia (Newcastle) soon followed suit. Today, there are dozens of medical schools using some variation of PBL. Other health-related professions such as dentistry, nursing, physical therapy, and occupational therapy are also trying out their versions of the method.

Problem-Based Learning moved into undergraduate programs beginning in the early 1990s when science faculty at the University of Delaware became aware of the medical school model and contracted with the medical school at the University of New Mexico to assist them in setting up PBL courses across the curriculum. Delaware has given numerous workshops and has established a web-based clearinghouse for PBL cases. Several books have been published on the use of PBL in the undergraduate classroom (*Bringing Problem-Based Learning to Higher Education: Theory and Practice*; *The Power of Problem-Based Learning*). Nonetheless, it seems to me that the term "PBL" has become so elastic that it means any case that starts off with a problem to be solved. As you can tell from the first chapter of this section, I prefer its original connotation.

In chapter 24, I present a case using the PBL model, which focuses upon the question, what is the causative agent of AIDS? Although this issue is largely resolved in the scientific literature, it still has echoes today in politics, especially in South Africa.

In the final chapter in this section I present a classical discussion-based case, but in the teaching notes I refer to an approach where the case can be readily converted to a three-step PBL case. The existence of global warming, the subject of the case, was still being seriously debated in 1998 when the case was written. Today, according to almost weekly articles in the journals *Science* and *Nature,* most experts report they are convinced that we are experiencing global warming that is due, at least in part, to human activities. The media have picked up on this as well as the potential consequences (e.g., unusual weather patterns, severe hurricanes, flooding, droughts) of the phenomenon become evident. Today, the issue is not whether global warming is occurring, but how fast is it happening, what will be its impact, and can we stop it? The case is still relevant because it asks students to explore the evidence for our convictions.

REFERENCES

Duch, B., S. Groh, and D. Allen, eds. 2001. *The power of problem-based learning.* Sterling, VA: Stylus Publishing.

Wilkerson, L., and W. H. Gijselaers. 1996. *Bringing problem-based learning to higher education: Theory and practice.* San Francisco, CA: Jossey-Bass.

The Death of Problem-Based Learning?

By Clyde Freeman Herreid

T his past summer I went to a conference on Problem-Based Learning (PBL) hosted by the University of Delaware. This conference was attended by several hundred faculty members from around the world—all interested in PBL. I was asked to present the plenary talk at the conference on the future of PBL. What I didn't know then, because I was the kick-off speaker, was the extent to which PBL isn't PBL anymore. In session after session, people were not talking about the classic method of PBL at all, yet they persisted in using the term without apology or explanation. In fact, I speculate that no one is using the pure version anymore. Let me explain.

Problem-based learning was pioneered by McMaster University Medical School in Hamilton, Ontario, about 30 years ago. From the beginning it seemed a spectacular success story in the use of case study teaching. Real patient problems became the entire basis for their curriculum. Inspired by this success, a couple dozen other medical schools in the United States and abroad also revamped their curricula around patient cases. Albanese and Mitchell (1993) have written an extensive review of its strengths and weaknesses.

Early on, PBL began to be defined and re-defined in various ways (e.g., Barrows 1986), but let's stick with the classical method: Students work in small permanent groups with a faculty tutor and deal with a new case every three class periods. On the first day, they receive a new case: a story about a patient with a set of symptoms and some clinical test results. Sometimes they actually see the patient in the flesh or on video. The students, with reference books in hand, analyze the case to determine as best they can what the trouble with the patient might be. With the help of the tutor, they decide what the issues are and what they need to find out to deal with the patient. They subdivide the workload among themselves, then leave class to search for information in the library or on the internet.

When students return to the next class, they share the fruits of their labors. Again, they ponder the problem and perhaps receive more clinical information before adjourning to continue their search of the literature. The following class brings the case to closure as the group pools its knowledge, finishes its diagnoses, and plans its final report. As this class period ends, they are given their next case to begin anew. Often in this session, the group becomes introspective about their various problem-solving strategies with the hope that they will improve with later cases.

About 10 years ago, the University of Delaware took this model and applied it to undergraduate courses in physics, chemistry, and biology (online at *www.udel.edu/pbl*). I consulted on some of their early experiments. Not surprisingly, as with any educational innovation, the folks who used it in the classroom modified it. Some faculty, still wanting to lecture, sprinkled in heavy doses of didactic wisdom; some didn't want to use permanent groups

all of the time; some had classes too large to use groups, yet they wished to use problems for discussion; some didn't want the cases to drag on over three class periods; some wanted to do simple classroom exercises (more like back-of-the-chapter problems) rather than the full-blown story lines that are typical of medical cases; and on and on, the variations went. Some of these innovations were highly successful, as we find in Harold White's biochemistry course where the entire semester is devoted to the historical analysis of our understanding of hemoglobin using journal articles as the basis for analysis (1992).

Perhaps most importantly, the University of Delaware discovered that the notion of having a faculty tutor for every student group was prohibitively expensive. Almost immediately some faculty members tried running classes without tutors; they had just one instructor in the room with several groups. They had clearly shifted toward a model of cooperative/collaborative learning.

Deborah Allen and Harold White attempted to solve the tutor problem by using peer instructors. They trained undergraduate students who had been through the course in a previous semester to be facilitators. These tutors-to-be had to attend a course where they read PBL literature, created cases themselves, discussed classroom strategies, and were shown videotapes demonstrating problem situations they were likely to face. Under the guidance of a faculty expert, they discussed the possible ways the problem might be resolved. By all accounts, the peer tutor approach was highly successful and Allen and White continue to use the approach today.

It was interesting to me to see many of these variations played out again when I was a consultant at Stamford University in Alabama when they embarked on a massive PBL program several years ago. Few of the attempts at the method bore much resemblance to the original model, yet everyone insisted on calling what they were doing PBL. Perhaps it didn't matter, because lots of interesting teaching was going on.

Now let me tell you of another chapter in this saga. Recently I visited two medical schools, Ohio State University and Umea University in Sweden. They had the same request. They wanted me to show them how to use different methods of case study teaching in their medical programs. These schools had been using PBL for some of their students and thought that it wasn't working. That wasn't true. It was working just fine but they simply couldn't sustain the program.

I had heard rumblings like this for years from medical school people (including at my own university's medical school) that jumped on the PBL bandwagon. And now I had a chance to see the situation firsthand.

The story they all told me was: "The ideals of PBL are fine. The basic idea sounds great. The lecture method is too passive and lacks the hands-on experience students need to deal with real-world problems. We want to turn out physicians who are in tune with patients' problems. We want them to be problem solvers, to be independent learners, to work well together in groups, for this is the wave of medicine in the future—group practice."

But reality set in. When many medical schools tried to implement this program, they first had to get a commitment from their faculty to serve as tutors. They needed lots of them—one for every 6 to 12 students. This wasn't always easy because the reward structure, like that of most universities, is heavily weighted toward those who publish like mad and receive massive amounts of money through grants. (You know the system well.) So, it was not always easy to find volunteers for tutoring. Making the problem worse was the fact there were the usual skeptics certain that this was one more innovation that was bound to fail.

Despite the skeptics, the program got off the ground in some schools. But within three or so years, the programs began to falter. The initial group of tutors began to tire of the extra burden that PBL placed on them. Remember, in most medical schools the faculty have extraordinarily light teaching loads, often a handful of lectures for the year. The rest of the time they are supposed to do research—present papers, write articles, and generate grant funds. Some have clinical duties as well.

Because the PBL experiences were normally add-ons to their lives, the PBL enthusiasts soon began to chafe under the pressure. Even though they often felt that PBL was the best way to teach (and most students tended to agree), they received no reward for their contributions. In fact, they clearly suffered because they weren't holding up the research end of the deal.

The upshot of this was that the tutors began to demand replacements. They were seldom forthcoming. Not enough replacements were standing in the wings. The system just couldn't be sustained—too many tutors were required. Naturally, some schools tried using a combination of graduate students and faculty in this role, which worked for a while. But it became plain to most folks that major modifications needed be made to the original PBL model.

Now let me stop for a moment and tell you my bias: PBL is simply one method of case study learning. The case study method started around the turn of the century in Harvard's law and business schools—perhaps 60 years before PBL was born. Harvard defined the method as students solving real cases with real dilemmas. The instruction method was for an instructor to give students a written case, allow them time to analyze it, and then discuss the case in the classroom, examining the background for the problem and searching for alternative ways to solve it.

Classrooms had several dozen students involved with a single instructor. The problems were generally open-ended; no single solution existed. Not infrequently, problems had several parts to them and extended over several days. Students frequently set up study groups to work on the problems, and faculty members sometimes had short warm-up sessions with small groups of students before the general discussion got started. There was great variation among instructors using cases right from the beginning.

In the 1940s, James Conant, a well-known chemist from Harvard, was invited to be President Franklin Roosevelt's science adviser during the war years. Conant returned to teaching a chastened man from his dealings with laymen and the Washington bureaucracy. He believed that science education must be improved. (Does this sound familiar?) He decided to follow the case study model he had seen used so effectively in law and business, but like many science educators today he simply couldn't give up lecturing. I suspect for the usual reasons—so much material, so little time. He felt he needed to get across the facts so he designed a course using case histories in science. The entire course dealt with great discoveries in science, such as the discovery of oxygen. He regaled his Harvard students with stories of how science discoveries were made. He recounted experiments, both good and bad, and politics, both good and bad.

I heard about this approach when educator Lee Schulman gave a talk about innovations in teaching and he called it a case study method. He also referred to McMaster's PBL approach as a case study method. How could such apparently different pedagogies all be case study teaching? The answer seemed evident: They all were using stories with an educational message. The definition obviously could not depend on the method of delivering the story—discussions were used sometimes, lectures on other occasions, and small groups and tutors in still other classes. I have written about the many variations in case study teaching over some years starting in the *Journal of College Science Teaching* in 1994.

This leads me to argue that PBL has always been simply one way to deliver the case (story). It rightly deserved special terminology when it started; there were open-ended dilemma cases to be solved over several classes with time for research and reflection by a tutor and a few students working in small permanent groups. Almost all of that is gone now. The methods of teaching are eclectic. I cannot identify any one factor that makes PBL unique. This is exactly what happened to the original case study approach—decades earlier. Everything has blurred together. I would go further: Because PBL's unique methodology has been eroded away, there is no longer any reason to mislabel what we are doing as PBL. It is case study teaching all the way.

Do I believe that people will stop using the term Problem-Based Learning? Of course not. The cachet and publicity of PBL is such that people will continue to use the words in any way they want. Remember how Lewis Carroll, writing in *Alice Through the Looking Glass,* put it when he had Humpty Dumpty say, "When I use a word, it means just what I choose it to mean—neither more nor less."

But Alice replied: "The question is whether you *can* make words mean so many different things."

"The question is," Humpty Dumpty shot back, having the final word, "which is to be the master—that's all."

REFERENCES

Albanese, M., and S. Mitchell. 1993. Problem-based learning: A review of literature on its outcomes and implementation issues. *Academic Medicine* 68: 52–81.

Barrows, H. 1986. A taxonomy of problem-based learning methods. *Medical Education* 20: 481–486.

White, H. 1992. Introduction to biochemistry: A different approach. *Biochemical Education* 20(1): 22–23.

AIDS and the Duesberg Phenomenon

By Clyde Freeman Herreid

T he topic of acquired immunodeficiency syndrome, AIDS, is ideal for case study teaching. The topic is complex, important, and controversial and has public policy implications. It is of vital interest, and in every course where I have used case studies, those cases involved with AIDS always receive the highest marks from students.

In the 1990s, the scientific community was alternately challenged, irritated, frustrated, and bemused by Dr. Peter Duesberg of the University of California at Berkeley, and his position on AIDS. Duesberg, a renowned virologist and a member of the prestigious National Academy of Science, did not believe that HIV causes AIDS. Rather, he claimed that AIDS was the result of recreational and anti-HIV drugs. Virtually all scientists who studied the issue believed Duesberg's opinions to be extreme, although some maintained that HIV was not the sole cause of AIDS. A December 9, 1995 issue of *Science* devoted an eight-page special report on "The Duesberg Phenomenon." Nevertheless, Duesberg believed his views had not received the attention they deserved and his research program was seriously affected because of his unpopular position. He did not receive any grant support since becoming embroiled in the controversy according to reports in *The Scientist* (March 20, 1995). In that publication, he is quoted explaining why the AIDS community has rejected his views and why he can't get funded for research:

> "A whole generation of AIDS scientists, retrovirologists—in the last 10 years their names, their papers, not to mention their fortunes, solely and exclusively rest on one thing, on HIV. If HIV is not what it is said to be... all these people... would be nobody.... In fact, worse than that: Many would be rightfully blamed for having intoxicated 200,000 Americans with AZT every six hours and panicked millions of people with a positive AIDS test.... They would have done unbelievable harm in the name of this hypothesis, if this hypothesis were proven wrong. So these people cannot afford in the least bit to consider an alternative that might end their careers."

STUDENT ASSIGNMENT

The following assignment is basically that used by practitioners of Problem-Based Learning. The case requires part of three class periods. It involves the use of papers from the literature rather than a written scenario. I have used it for groups of 3–6 students working in permanent groups without tutors with reasonable success. Basically, I give the groups sets of papers and ask them to identify the learning issues and to educate themselves about AIDS.

I give out two 1988 *Science* magazine articles: A short critique by Duesberg entitled "HIV Is Not the Cause of AIDS," and an opposing article: "HIV Causes AIDS," by noted experts Drs. Blattner, Gallo, and Temin. I also include copies of their rebuttals to one another.

On Day One, the students' basic task is to identify the issues that are important in the papers, as well as to identify the terms, concepts, and information they need in order to resolve the problem as they see it. Then the students subdivide the workload, and after class go to the library, the internet, and their texts to try and resolve their questions.

On Day Two of this case, the students pool their information and summarize their knowledge. To aid the process, I give them a couple of additional papers to be sure that certain points are addressed. For example, Duesberg's (1991) article highlights his views especially well. Also, Moore's (1996) review of Duesberg's book *Inventing the AIDS Virus* is useful, as is the *Scientific American* (1995) article, "How HIV Defeats the Immune System" by Nowak and McMichael.

With these papers in hand, the students are asked to again identify any new issues, terms, and information they need. Once again they set out and collect the information for the next class.

On Day Three of the case, the students pool their information for the last time and prepare to deal with the final assignment. In their groups I ask them to evaluate the nine points that Duesberg made in his original *Science* article, where he claimed "HIV is not the cause of AIDS because it fails to meet the postulates of Koch and Henle, as well as six cardinal rules of

virology." In class, the groups write brief summaries about each of the nine points in light of our most recent information.

On pages 159–160, I show one student group's paper, written in 1996. The paper is not ideal, but it gives an idea of what can be accomplished in an introductory biology course. Today, its criticisms would be much more pointed, given our extended knowledge of AIDS. When I checked a few minutes ago, the listing of AIDS on Google yielded 469 million articles! A search for "AIDS + Duesberg" produced 286,000 references! Today, the politics of the disease in Africa would come much more into play, as Duesberg maintains the majority of African AIDS cases may be explained away as malnutrition, parasitic infection, and poor sanitation. Unfortunately, some African leaders have followed his lead and delayed the introduction of antiviral drug therapy.

REFERENCES

Blattner, W., R. C. Gallo, and H. M. Temin. 1988. HIV causes AIDS. *Science* 241: 515.

Blattner, W., R. C. Gallo, and H. M. Temin. 1988. Blattner and colleagues respond to Duesberg. *Science* 241: 514, 517.

Duesberg, P. 1988. HIV is not the cause of AIDS. *Science* 241: 514.

Duesberg, P. 1988. Duesberg's response to Blattner and colleagues. *Science* 241: 515–516.

Duesberg, P. 1991. AIDS epidemiology: Inconsistencies with human immunodeficiency virus and with infectious disease. *Proceedings of the National Academy of Science* 88: 1575–1579.

Goodman, B. 1995. A controversy that will not die: The role of HIV in causing AIDS. *The Scientist* 9(6): 1, 6–7.

Moore, J. 1996. À Duesberg, Adieu! *Nature* 380: 293–294.

Nowak, M. A., and A. J. McMichael. 1995. How HIV defeats the immune system. *Scientific American* (August): 58–65.

STUDENT RESPONSE TO DUESBERG

Duesberg's theory contains nine parts, saying: HIV is a harmless retrovirus that may serve as a marker for people in AIDS high-risk groups; AIDS is not a contagious syndrome caused by one conventional virus or microbe; AIDS is probably caused by conventional pathogenic factors: administration of blood transfusions of drugs, promiscuous male homosexual activity associated with drugs, acute parasitic infections, and malnutrition; and drugs such as AZT promote AIDS, rather than fight it. In our opinion Duesberg is a biological flake.

Duesberg's first three parts to his theory rely on Koch's 1st, 2nd, 3rd postulates: (1) Free virus is not detectable in most cases of AIDS; (2) Virus can only be isolated by reactivating virus in vitro from a few latently infected lymphocytes among millions of uninfected ones; and (3) Pure HIV does not cause AIDS upon experimental infection of chimpanzees or accidental infection of healthy humans (Duesberg 1989). First, we know Koch's postulates are more of historical interest than practical use. We know for a fact that people who receive HIV tainted blood become HIV+ and come down with AIDS. People who receive HIV-free blood don't get AIDS (unless they get HIV somewhere else). Thus, it is the HIV, not the transfusion, which causes AIDS. As far as HIV not being able to be isolated in 20–50% AIDS cases as Duesberg points out, we know that with a few recent exceptions, everyone with an AIDS-like immune deficiency tests positive for HIV. Everyone with HIV apparently gets AIDS eventually, after an average of 8 years. (There may be some exceptions for people having natural immunity.) In summary with his first three parts to his theory, Duesberg is trying to fit a new virus into old postulates.

In his fourth part, Duesberg is claiming HIV doesn't kill enough T-cells to cause AIDS. This can be proven wrong with the definition of apoptosis, which is a natural suicide mechanism by which the body takes care of exten-sively damaged cells, especially when their chromosomal DNA is damaged or cleaved. Apoptosis in mature T-cells has been proposed to be induced in at least two prominent ways by HIV. The first involves signals generated upon binding of HIV surface proteins to CD4 of activated T-cells. This cannot only occur upon binding of HIV itself to the T-cells, but also upon binding of infected T-cells, having viral protein gp120 on their surface, to uninfected cells. The second mechanism involves modification of accessory-cell functions by HIV, changing the balance of activation signals required to prevent apoptosis in the mature T-cells. This can be accomplished either by enhancing the amount of apoptic signals or reducing the amount of balancing preventive signals (Blattner, Gallo, and Temin 1988).

In his fifth part to his theory, Duesberg says that HIV remains inactive during AIDS and therefore it can't be the cause. What Duesberg could not have known in the 1980s is that the common cause of AIDS is due to the fact that opportunistic infections generally happen because of a dysfunctional immune system, and the cause of this disjunction is HIV infection (Moore 1996). Of course, there can be other causes—genetic or environmental—but rarely is the dysfunction as devastating as that found in the later stages of HIV infection, and never is it as common.

In his sixth part to his theory, Duesberg is saying that the eight-year period between the onset of antiviral immunity and AIDS is unusual, and that AIDS should occur early when HIV is active. What Duesberg has to realize is that AIDS occurs after the immune system has been broken down. HIV causes this breakdown by depleting the T-cells of the immune system and this process takes a long time because as Duesberg points out in his fourth part of his theory—the body is very good at regenerating T-cells to compensate losses to HIV.

In his seventh part of his theory, Duesberg points out that retroviruses are not cytocidal and, on the contrary, they often promote cell growth. We now know that retroviruses are divided into 3 categories, two of which fit Duesberg's description (oncoviruses and spumaviruses), and the third of which are called lentiviruses and are noncogenic which fuse into and kill their host cells, and this is what HIV is.

These lentivirus particles are spherical having a conical nucleoprotein covered by a bilayered phospholipid envelope with surface glycoprotein embedded. They are exogenously acquired viruses and are associated with slow, persistent and debilitating life long infections, inducing pathological changes in the immune system of the animals which result in severe immunodeficiency syndromes (Moore 1996).

In the eighth part of his theory, Duesberg is saying that the contagious rate from HIV infection to AIDS depends greatly on the country and risk group membership, so HIV isn't sufficient to cause AIDS. What we know is that HIV is directly correlated to the lifestyle risk factors such as homosexuality, drug use, and continued nonprotective heterosexual activity. So in Africa, where condoms are not commonly used, there is an equal distribution of AIDS between the sexes. Whereas in the United States, AIDS began specifically among homosexuals because of the lack of condom use. Therefore, it is not country specific, but it is risk group specific. No matter what country you're in, if you engage in any one of the lifestyle risk group factors you have the chance of getting HIV. But it all comes down to HIV causing AIDS. For example, people who engage in homosexuality, drug use, etc., but aren't exposed to HIV don't get AIDS. On the other hand, people who aren't members of "risk groups" but are exposed to HIV get AIDS.

Duesberg's ninth part to his theory claims that viruses are products of gradual evolution, therefore proposing that viruses HIV-1 and HIV-2 evolving within a few years is highly improbable. What we know now is that HIV-1 is the more prevalent of the two kinds of viruses around the globe, but as Duesberg points out, there is another less virulent strain HIV-2, endemic to certain populations of West Africa. And this does represent a fascinating jigsaw puzzle that we don't know how to put together yet. So Duesberg's claim is the only one of the nine that could still be valid.

Now in 1996, since we know so much about HIV, Duesberg's theories no longer hold true with the exception of the ninth postulate. It is clear that the advent of HIV really puzzled Duesberg, and made him somewhat of an ancient retrovirologist. HIV does not fit Koch's postulates. It is a new type of virus for a new age in time, and it needs to be dealt with by virologists who have an open mind, and are ready for any surprises that they may run into, leaving Mr. Duesberg "in the dust."

REFERENCES

Blattner, W., R. C. Gallo, and H. M. Temin. 1988. HIV causes AIDS. *Science* 241: 514–516.

Duesberg, P. H. 1988. HIV is not the cause of AIDS. *Science* 241: 514–516.

Duesberg, P. H. 1989. Human immunodeficiency virus and acquired immunodeficiency syndrome: Correlation but not causation. *Proceedings of the National Academy of Sciences* 86 (Feb.): 755–764.

Duesberg, P. H. 1991. AIDS epidemiology: Inconsistencies with human immunodeficiency virus and infectious disease. *Proceedings of the National Academy of Sciences* 88: 1575–1579.

Moore J., 1996. À Duesberg, Adieu! *Nature* 380: 293–294.

The Petition: A Global Warming Case Study

By Bruce C. Allen and Clyde Freeman Herreid

"**S**ign it, Mike!" Professor Dan Carlson's suggestion was unequivocal. "So it's overstated, maybe a little extreme. So what? Sign the petition or crumple it up and throw it out. Either way, let's get back to work!" Dan had little time or patience for paperwork.

"It is not just an exaggerated statement. There are ethical concerns," geophysicist Michael King responded. The meeting was not going as he expected. He had hoped to rally the other faculty members of the geology department against an organization named the *Petition Project*. Yet, after only five minutes of this special staff meeting, his hopes were rapidly fading.

Dan spoke again. "You know that 11,000 years ago a glacier covered North America. That ice sheet is gone because Earth warmed up without any influence from humans or our industries. Cooling and warming cycles have occurred repeatedly over Earth's history. There is paleoclimatological evidence that suggests variations in Earth's spin axis and orbital shape drive climatic oscillations or it may be directly related to solar output. But now, because the environmentalists have cast Nature and Mother Earth as victims, the blame falls to the 'evil humans.' Well, that thinking is misguided at best. It is not science. It's political correctness."

"Nevertheless," Toni Daniels, not one to keep quiet when a good argument presented itself, added, "a global warming trend is emerging that can't be dismissed out of hand! Until recently, it was questionable that temperatures have risen significantly over the past century. It looked like clouds and aerosols were offsetting any atmospheric warming generated by greenhouse gases. But the evidence is mounting and is already quite convincing.

"An ongoing project in the Arctic, named Ice Station Sheba, has found the pack ice is thinning rapidly," Toni continued. "It is 100 miles further north than expected and is only seven feet thick. That is three feet less than expected. These findings are supported by measurements of reduced salinity in the upper strata of the Arctic Ocean. If that isn't enough, now the weather service says this is the warmest year on record. And a recent tree-ring study indicates this is the warmest decade in six hundred years. Also, there are indications that heat-driven weather phenomena, such as cyclonic

A pulp and paper mill at Luke, Maryland. Rising temperatures have been correlated to increasing carbon dioxide emissions by industries.

storms and El Niño episodes, are escalating in frequency and intensity. These signs of climatic change correlate well with the 25% rise in atmospheric CO_2 levels above the pre-Industrial Age value. So, regardless of the root cause, it is likely greenhouse gases play a role in global warming."

There was a momentary pause as Dan and those that sided with him tried to think of a strong counterargument. Michael took the opportunity to restate his problem.

"Look," he began, "there is more to this than who is right and who is wrong about global warming. In front of you are copies of the letter and petition I received yesterday morning. The project is an effort to convince Congress to reject the United Nations-backed Kyoto Treaty. If ratified, the treaty would limit the use of fossil fuels, such as coal and oil, by approximately one-third of the 1990 levels by 2012. The projected result is a drop of 10% or less in greenhouse gas emissions, particularly carbon dioxide (CO_2), by industrialized nations. Listen to this excerpt from the cover letter that was signed by a past president of the National Academy of Sciences:

'This treaty is, in our opinion, based upon flawed ideas. Research data on climate change do not show that human use of hydrocarbons is harmful.'

"Sounds reasonable, doesn't it? In fact, it echoes my thoughts on the matter. Now listen to the actual petition:

'The proposed limits on greenhouse gases would harm the environment, hinder the advance of science and technology, and damage the health and welfare of mankind.'

"There is the problem. It is not opposition to the Kyoto Treaty. It is the premise on which that opposition is based. I find it hard to believe this petition is being circulated by professional scientists. This kind of melodramatic absoluteness sounds like the language of a would-be religious prophet."

Michael continued, "If that were the end of it, maybe it would be better to ignore the petition rather than draw attention to it. However, it gets worse. Again, in the stacks in front of you, you'll find copies of an *unpublished* professional paper. The authors are from the Oregon Institute of Science and Medicine (OISM) and the George C. Marshall Institute. However, the format is an exact duplicate of that used by the National Academy of Sciences journal *Proceedings*. The apparent intent is to make the paper appear as though it has been through the peer-review process.

"In my mind the overstated case, coupled with the misrepresented paper, is outright fraud! What really disturbs me are the websites for the Marshall Institute and OISM. Both sites present a biased perspective on global warming, and the OISM page contains a list of several thousand supporters' names. Among them are some of the country's top scientists. I believe the scenario has been engineered to convince Congress and the public that the sponsor's position represents a consensus of the scientific community."

"Well, it seems perfectly reasonable to me," responded paleontologist Robert Peters. "I intend to support it." As the senior member of the department, Peters' opinion carried considerable weight. "In fact, I think the department should support it." Michael's arguments seemed to be falling on deaf ears, but by this time he was no longer surprised.

"Maybe there are ethical issues," Peters continued, "but maybe a little white lie or two is just what we need. The public has been brainwashed into believing anything on the evening news is truth. The media have been pushing global warming for its sensationalistic value. All the dire predictions are emphasized while the arguments against global warming are ignored. It is never mentioned that global temperatures were higher in medieval times when grapes were growing in Scotland and the Vikings were inhabiting Greenland. Civilization wasn't destroyed then and the coastlands were not inundated. I think we owe it to the public to set the record straight. If that means fighting fire with fire then, so be it."

"Isn't it our responsibility as scientists to present a balanced picture of the facts as we understand them?" Michael countered. "Grandstanding and extreme advocacy are hallmarks of politics, not science. I am not convinced that support is the appropriate response."

Dan Carlson was a friend of Michael's. He felt he may have been too harsh earlier, so he tried a more moderate tone. "Michael, you've been following my research. You know that I've been working with Global Circulation Models for years now. If I have learned one thing, it's that we can't yet model atmospheric physics well enough to predict next year's weather, let alone the climate of the next century. We simply don't know Earth's level of climatic sensitivity to the input parameters like solar output, volcanoes, clouds, aerosols, or the suspect gases. In fact, we don't even know that we have identified all the parameters. We have to 'tune' the models significantly just to get them to represent anything near reality. That doesn't leave me with much confidence in predictions based on their output. I say let's not do anything we might regret later like limit the use of fossil fuels."

Toni Daniels clearly sided with Michael. She had a strong background in physical geography. "We must be advocates for truth and nothing else. Promoting a cause through deception is exactly what the petition backers are doing by adopting that level of advocacy. Besides, they are simply wrong. As I already stated, there is ample evidence for global warming. More importantly, we are running out of time to avert disaster. It no longer matters whether or not anthropogenic greenhouses gases are the fundamental cause of global warming. We all know their effect so we all know that controlling their emission will at least help reduce the rate of warming. The Kyoto Treaty may not be perfect but it is better than nothing! We certainly cannot support any petition that opposes it or that takes an anti-global warming posture!" Toni was adamant. Michael was impressed by her, although he did not agree with everything she said.

Scientists in Antarctica prepare a balloon to take measurements in the ozone layer, where a plunge in ozone levels has created a "hole" over the South Pole. Models suggest greenhouse gases may trigger a new ozone hole over the North Pole.

Dan responded. "Claims of impending disaster are certainly unjustified! Even if it turns out that human-made carbon dioxide is the primary cause of global warming, the prospects for the future may not be all that bleak. My garden is full of plants bigger and healthier than I have ever seen before. Agronomists are claiming that plants everywhere are experiencing the same effect because of increased atmospheric carbon dioxide. This could mean restoration of our rain forests due to the increased growth rates of trees. Higher grain yields would mean more food for more people. Deserts could become greener. Areas under ice and snow in the high latitudes could open up. New lands would be available for human occupation. Remember, carbon dioxide levels have risen only 25% in over 200 years. An offsetting amount of new vegetation is entirely possible and could bring the system back under control, limiting the average global temperature to roughly its current level. So, Michael, why would we want to block an effort to stop the Kyoto Treaty?"

"Dan, I am concerned about scientific integrity."

STUDY QUESTIONS

1. *What is meant by the term "global warming" and why may it be a problem?*

2. *What is the most probable cause of "global warming"?*

3. *What lines of evidence support or refute "global warming"?*

4. *Can we do anything about "global warming"?*

REFERENCES

Jones, P. D., and T. M. L. Wigley. 1990. Global warming trends. *Scientific American* (August): 84–91.

Mahlman, J. D. 1997. Uncertainties in projections of human-caused climate warming. *Science* 278 (November 21): 1416–1417.

Schneider, S. H. 1989. The changing climate. *Scientific American* (September): 70–79.

Suplee, C. 1998. Unlocking the climate puzzle. *National Geographic* 193(5): 38–71.

WEBSITES

- National Oceanic and Atmospheric Administration: *www.noaa.gov*
- Environmental Protection Agency: *www.epa.gov/docs/globalwarming*
- American Geophysical Union: *www.agu.org/sci_soc/barron.html*
- USGS Global Change Research Program: *http://geochange.er.usgs.gov*
- Global Warming Home Page: *www.globalwarming.org*
- Oregon Institute of Science and Medicine: *www.oism.org/pproject/s33p37.htm*

TEACHING NOTES

Introduction/Background

This case is complex, important, and timely. It can be used in a variety of courses such as biology, geology, chemistry, physics, meteorology, economics, political science, and ethics.

The way the case plays out will depend upon which course is involved, the resources and reading provided, and the classroom time devoted to it. We have used it twice, once in a general biology class of 20 students working in cooperative learning teams of five members with one instructor. On a second occasion it was used in a faculty development workshop with 200 people. There, 16 faculty facilitators trained in problem-based learning ran 70-minute sessions with a dozen faculty in each team. This was preceded and followed by 30 minutes of introduction and closure.

The faculty ranged over the entire spectrum of academic disciplines. Below is a partial list of objectives they identified for the case.

Case Objectives

The goal of this case study is to learn about: the greenhouse effect, global warming and its possible causes, how temperature and CO_2 changes can be estimated, what controls weather patterns, geochemical cycles, how to read graphs and interpret data, how humans may impact the Earth's environment, the politics and economics of scientific issues, how and why experts may differ, and faculty responsibility in dealing with ethical and political issues.

Blocks Of Analysis

There are many issues embedded in the case. We can touch on a few by focusing on the big questions in the case.

What is global warming?

This question should be addressed early in the discussion. A general sense of what is meant by the phrase is essential.

What is the evidence that global warming is occurring?

Several lines of evidence are cited in the case: The ice pack in the Arctic is thinning and has retreated. Salinity in the Arctic Ocean is reduced because of melting ice. The weather service says 1998 is the warmest year on record. A tree-ring study indicates this is the warmest decade in 600 years. Unusual weather phenomena, storms, and El Niño episodes now occur regularly.

The counterargument is that temperature variations have existed over the Earth's history, and there is no clear trend that over the past century global warming has really existed, especially as related to human activities.

As this question is explored, instructors must either have the students seek information in the literature or provide them with graphs. Their answer to the question depends on the time scale considered: 10 years, 1,000 years, 1 million years, 200 million years, and so forth.

What is the evidence that humans are the cause of global warming?

The argument is three-pronged:

- Temperatures are clearly rising recently, and this phenomenon is correlated with an increase in CO_2 in the atmosphere.
- Rising CO_2 levels plus increases in greenhouse gases are due to human activity and cause a greenhouse effect that traps more heat.
- Mathematical models suggest that the increases in greenhouse gases can account for the temperature increases we see.

The counterargument runs:
Good temperature and CO_2 records are very recent and older records are less reliable.

Even if we accept the data, note that CO_2 levels varied historically before the industrial revolution and even before humans were around. As a dramatic example, in the Cretaceous period, 145–65 million years ago when dinosaurs roamed the Earth, CO_2 levels were eight times higher than today.

Earth's geochemical cycles, the Sun's activity, volcanoes, changes in the Earth's tilt, and so forth are clearly responsible for CO_2 and temperature shifts. (Again, these issues can only be appreciated by reference to the literature or handouts.)

What are the consequences of global warming?

The literature is replete with possible scenarios. It is useful to have students list both "good" and "bad" effects that might occur if temperature and CO_2 levels rise, coastal areas flood, and precipitation patterns alter.

The Environmental Protection Agency has outlined the potential impacts in the categories of health, agriculture, forest, water resources, coastal areas, and species and natural areas. The impact could be enormous. Students need to consider these but realize there are great uncertainties in these speculations.

Can we do anything about global warming?

People arguing "yes" are persuaded that the recent warming trend is at least partially driven by our burning of fossil fuels and other human activities. They argue that even with the uncertainties, we must try corrective measures because the consequences of global warming will be devastating.

People arguing that we cannot affect global warming are persuaded that CO_2 and temperature changes are geochemical in nature and out of our reach. They note that we are monstrously ignorant about such patterns, mentioning that even experts are befuddled because they cannot account for over 40% of the CO_2 that is released by people today. Where has it gone?

They also know that only trivial amounts of CO_2 are in the air as compared to the total amount of planetary carbon. Over 130,000 times more is locked up in the rocks and buried organic matter, another indication that the geochemical cycles are responsible for regulating atmospheric CO_2 within a time scale of millions of years.

Should the United States sign the Kyoto agreement?

People arguing "yes" agree with 174 countries that have ratified the United Nations Framework Convention on Climate Change, which aims at "the stabilization of greenhouse gases in the atmosphere at a level that will prevent dangerous anthropogenic interference with the climate system."

The Kyoto Protocol sets targets (based on 1990 standards) for developed countries to help achieve these goals by reducing their fossil fuel emissions and those from terrestrial ecosystems. Countries of the European Union will cut their emissions of greenhouse gases by 8% before 2012, with individual countries varying in their commitment: Germany will cut emissions by 22.5%, but Portugal can increase by 24%.

A recent report by the Union of Concerned Scientists and the Tellus Institute claims that the United States could easily achieve the United Nations target of 7% with a net savings to the economy.

People arguing that the United States should *not* sign the treaty are first convinced that the science behind the global warming argument is inadequate and flawed. To base major economic decisions that will greatly affect our economy on poor science is an error.

They concur with James Sensenbremmer, chair of the U.S. House of Representatives Science Committee, who said that compliance with the treaty would "wreak havoc on U.S. businesses and families." Obviously, the thousands of scientists who have signed the petition mentioned in the case agree that we should not sign the treaty.

RUNNING THE CASE

If this case is run as a general discussion, students should prepare by researching answers to the study questions. Alternately, graphs and tables can be given to the student as appendices to the case. Some of these are included in our website version of the case and others are in the references (*http://ublib.buffalo.edu/libraries/projects/cases/case.html*).

The case is best considered by teams of students working in the Problem-Based Learning tradition over several days. Although the case is not written in three parts students can consider the case in distinct steps. For instance: first, they might deal with the evidence and causes of global warming. Second, they might deal with its possible consequences. Third, they might consider whether we can do anything about it.

At each step they must decide what they need to find out in order to answer the questions, then do the research. A way of closing the topic is to have a wrap-up discussion where the students are asked, "Would you sign the petition to stop the United States from signing the treaty?"

Section VIII

Interrupted Case Method

The Interrupted Case Method is the technique most favored by faculty who attend my case study workshops. Information is provided piecemeal to the students as they work through a problem. It is one of the simplest methods for a teacher to try, especially one who is coming from the lecture mode. It allows the instructor a large amount of control over the pacing of the material without forcing her/him to lead long discussions—a talent that is seldom developed by scientists coming from the lecture tradition. As I indicate in the first chapter of this section, the Interrupted Case Method is a close relative of PBL, except that it is accomplished in a single class period.

Chapter 27—"Mom Always Liked You Best"—shows the method in action. I have used this case in dozens of classes and workshops with faculty and students from both high school and college. Even nonscientists have been participants and all seem to do enormously well with the case, which focuses on the scientific method. Special expertise is not needed—only the ability to think critically.

The Interrupted Case Method

By Clyde Freeman Herreid

There are many ways to tell a tale. This issue of the journal demonstrates that point as it devotes itself once again entirely to case studies.

The classical method of teaching cases is the discussion method used by Harvard law professors for over 100 years. We have come a long way since then. Far and away the most popular tactic for many faculty when teaching a case is the method of *progressive disclosure*, where the story is provided piecemeal to students, who must act as detectives to solve the mystery. This is the approach used in Problem-Based Learning (PBL) pioneered by the medical school at McMaster University. Students are given a "patient problem" and over several days are required to diagnose it as they seek information outside of class.

Here, I wish to describe a method related to PBL that I have been using for many years in classrooms and faculty development workshops. I call it the *Interrupted Case Method*. Like the classical method of PBL, information is fed piecemeal to students working in small groups, and the Interrupted Method shares with PBL the great virtue of engaging all students in problem solving. But unlike PBL, in the Interrupted Method the case is presented in one class period rather than over several days. And (here is the real beauty of the method) science faculty find they can easily write and teach cases of this type!

A little background: The *New England Journal of Medicine* used to publish a Clinical Problem column where data about a real patient were presented in stages to an expert clinician who responded to the information, sharing his or her reasoning with the reader. This exercise was done in a series of steps: first, the case writer provided a paragraph or two of information about the patient. The clinician then revealed his thinking about the case, speculating on possible diagnoses and perhaps suggesting a test that might be performed. Next, the case writer gave some more information about the patient. Again, the clinician responded. Several more rounds of case writer and clinician remarks followed, usually ending with the case author providing a summary analysis.

This method of case analysis, where a problem-poser's remarks alternate with a problem-solver's remarks, can be used in the classroom in several effective ways. The most obvious but least inspired method is to use the lecture method. The teacher must develop a problem and then write the appropriate script—a dialogue between the problem-poser and the problem-solver (expert or novice). In the classroom, the instructor might present the case using the "two hat" technique—first acting as the problem-poser, and then switching hats and acting as the problem-solver. Alternatively, students could take turns reading the parts in the dialogue. This method of case presentation is largely passive, yet it does illustrate how an expert (or novice) reasons his or her way through a problem. It has the same weaknesses of any passive form of presentation unless the instructor stops periodically and has a discussion with the students.

A more exciting way to use the idea is to actively involve all of the students in a problem-solving exercise using the Interrupted Case Method. Perhaps the easiest way to use the method is to select an article from a scientific journal. The instructor chooses a question drawn from the introduction section of the paper. Small groups of students are asked to design an experiment to solve the problem that the article raises. After a suitable time for discussion, groups are called upon to present their experimental design and explain the reasons for their approach. Commentary is then solicited from other class members on the appropriateness of the approach.

In the next stage the instructor briefly describes how the authors of the paper decided to attack the problem. Their actual methods are described. Then the groups are asked to predict what the results might look like. Perhaps a blank table or blank graph is given to the groups to fill in. Once again, groups are asked to report their solutions to the entire class with their reasoning made clear to all. Commentary from students and teacher follows.

At this point the instructor reveals the actual data published in the article. The groups are asked to interpret the results and draw conclusions in light of the original hypothesis. After a suitable discussion, the instructor reveals the author's actual interpretation of the results and their conclusions. Closure follows.

You will see the potential for the method by looking at the case in chapter 27, "Mom Always Liked You Best." In fact, you will see several versions of this method in the following pages. Indeed, this method of presentation is arguably the favorite case approach for most science teachers; it mimics how we all have to make decisions based upon incomplete data and must constantly revise our conclusions as more information becomes available. Read on and enjoy!

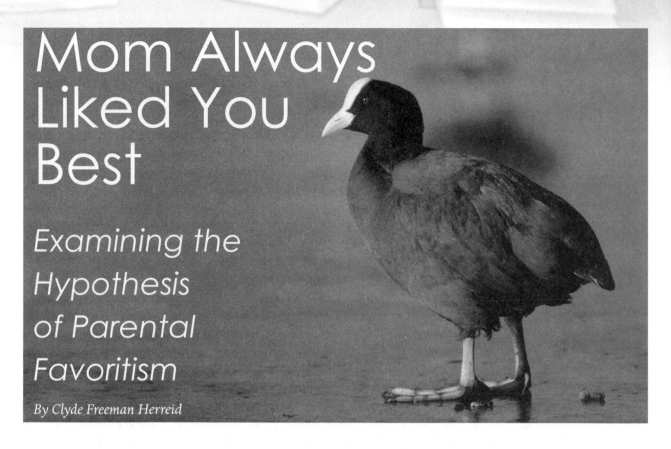

Mom Always Liked You Best

Examining the Hypothesis of Parental Favoritism

By Clyde Freeman Herreid

In this interrupted case study, based on a journal article on the parenting behavior of American coots, students are given information and data from which they must develop hypotheses and design experiments, mimicking the way that scientists conduct research. The case is appropriate for courses in biology, especially those focusing on evolution and ecology, but can also be used to great effect in nonscience majors' courses as an example of the scientific method.

THE CASE

Part I—What is the problem?

Many birds have bright, ornamental plumage. Most often it is displayed by the male of the species, who is believed to use the plumage to attract females. The female may select male breeding partners on the basis of this feather advertisement, perhaps assessing their health. According to evolutionary theory, it behooves the female to choose a strong, healthy male to be the father of her chicks, not only because the male helps to feed them, but also because the chicks will carry dad's healthy genes. Darwin labeled such mate choice as "sexual selection."

Another possible explanation of plumage selection has been studied by biologists in Canada. They think that the parents of certain bird species may select the "prettiest" chicks out of a nest as favorites and feed them better (why they might do this is an interesting question).

American coots are birds that live in the marshes of western North America. As adults they are grayish-black with white beaks. The chicks are unusual, for unlike most birds whose nestlings are usually drab, coot chicks are surprisingly conspicuous. They have long, orange-tipped, slender feathers, brilliant red papillae around their eyes, a bright red bill, and a bald red head (see Figure 1). The chicks lose this colorful appearance at three weeks. The Canadian biologists speculated that the plumage may make some chicks more attractive to their parents; possibly the most "attractive" chicks might be able to successfully beg for more food from their parents and have a better chance of survival. That seems possible because about one-half of all chicks die from starvation. But how could the authors test such an unusual notion?

Here is your challenge:

- First, identify the specific question(s) the researchers are asking.
- Second, what is the hypothesis that they suggest?
- Third, what predictions (deductions) can you make if the hypothesis is correct?
- Fourth, how can we test the predictions, such as: What exactly might we do if we were the researchers who had studied coots for several years?

Part II—The biologists find a method to attack the problem.

During the breeding season of 1992, Bruce Lyon, John Eadie, and Linda Hamilton studied 90 pairs of coots nesting in the marshes of British Columbia. They decided to try and alter the plumage of the chicks by dyeing them. Unfortunately, the dye made the chicks sick and it removed the oils from their feathers. They next tried to alter the appearance of the chicks by cutting the orange tips off their body feathers. This produced black chicks that seemed to act the same as the normal orange chicks. The scientists now began a test of their hypothesis using this technique. What do you expect they might do?

Part III—What should be measured?

The biologists decided to set up three types of nest conditions. In the first group of nests (let's call this the experimental group), they trimmed half of the chicks and made them black and left half of the brood with orange feathers. In a second group (call this a control group), all of the chicks were trimmed so they appeared black. In a third group of nests (call this another control group), all the chicks were left their natural color, orange. In all three groups, the chicks were captured within a day of hatching and were generally handled the same way even though some were trimmed. The chicks were kept in captivity for 30 minutes before being replaced in their nest. To control for hatching order in the experimental groups, the first chick hatched was randomly assigned to be trimmed or left orange. Thereafter, treatments were alternated with hatching order. The biologists worried about what kinds of data to collect, how to collect the data, and what kinds of results to expect. What would you suggest they do?

Part IV—At last, some data!

The biologists decided to compare the feeding, relative growth, and survival rates of the chicks in the different nests. Since the chicks had been individually color-marked, they could be easily observed and identified from floating blinds. To estimate growth rates, swimming chicks were photographed at known distances and their body length at waterline was estimated from projected slides. This measure of size is strongly correlated with body mass ($r = 0.97$, $n = 43$). Part of the data has been reproduced in Figure 2. Predict the results of the other values by plotting the values on the graph. Why have you made these predictions?

On the left side of the figure (panels a, c, and e) are the values for the two control groups (nests with either all orange chicks or nests with all black chicks). But the only data shown are for the nests composed entirely of orange chicks. Remember this is the normal situation that we find in the wild. The values shown are the medians, interquartile ranges, and 10–90 percentiles. With this knowledge, plot the values on the graph you would expect for the control black chicks raised with only black nest mates.

On the right side of the figure (panels b, d, and f) is a space for the expected values for the chicks in the experimental broods. Here, half of the chicks are black and half are kept orange. Now plot what you predict the values will be *if the researchers' hypothesis is correct.*

Part V—The rest of the story.
In Figure 3, you will see the real results that the researchers collected. How do the data compare with your predictions?

The values shown are the medians, interquartile ranges, and 10–90 percentiles.

Note: There are no statistical differences between orange and black chicks (controls) in separate nests. In the experimental nests, there were significant differences between the orange and black chicks in feeding, growth, and survival rates.

The biologists ran a series of statistical tests and noted that there were no significant differences between the two control groups in any of the measures—that is, when the orange and black chicks were in separate nests, they had similar feeding, growth, and survival rates.

But in the experimental group where both black and orange chicks occurred together and the parents had a true choice of which to feed, statistical analysis showed that the orange chicks fared better. Orange chicks were fed at a higher rate, had a higher growth rate, and enjoyed a higher survival rate than the black chicks in the same brood. What conclusions might the biologists make about their original hypothesis? For example:

FIGURE 1.

Photo of baby coots prior to color loss.
http://ublib.buffalo.edu/libraries/projects/cases/coots/coots.html

- Do black chicks survive more poorly simply because they are black or because they are "inferior" relative to the orange?
- Do the data support the hypothesis?
- Do the data prove the hypothesis?

TEACHING NOTES
This case is based on a fascinating article that appeared in 1994 in *Nature* entitled "Parental choice selects for ornamental plumage in American coot chicks" (Lyon, Eadie, and Hamilton 1994) and the commentary published in the same issue entitled "Parents prefer pretty plumage" (Pagel 1994).

As the case reveals, the authors of the original paper concluded that coot parents "feed ornamented chicks over non-ornamented chicks, resulting in higher growth rates and greater survival for ornamented chicks." They sum up "that parental preference is relative, rather than absolute, an important element in the evolution of exaggerated traits. These observations provide the first empirical evidence that parental choice can select for ornamental traits in offspring."

I use this case in courses whenever I wish to emphasize how scientists solve problems. Obviously, the subject matter of the case is appropriate for courses in biology, especially those focusing on evolution and ecology. Yet the case is accessible to students without any background in science at all, and I have also used it in a nonscience majors course called Scientific Inquiry. The way the case unfolds mimics the way that scientists go about their work: Scientists do not have all of the facts all at once; they get them piecemeal, as in this case.

OBJECTIVES

There are several objectives for this case beyond teaching coot biology:

- To give students practice in making predictions and interpreting data.
- To give students practice in designing experiments.
- To give students an explicit experience with the hypothetico-deductive method of reasoning (the "scientific method"), where a question is asked; a hypothesis suggested; predictions or deductions made in light of the hypothesis ("if the hypothesis is true, then such and such should occur"); tests accomplished; and the data evaluated supporting or rejecting the hypothesis. To reinforce this model, it is essential at every opportunity, as new information and questions are added, that the instructor always ask the students what they now expect if the hypothesis were true.

CLASSROOM MANAGEMENT

This case is an example of something I call the *Interrupted Case Method*, where information is fed piecemeal to students working in small groups. The basic technique is to give the students a problem to work on in small groups (in this case I give them a real research problem reported in *Nature*). Then, after the groups discuss the problem for a short time, I supply them with additional information and let them go back to work. This sequence is repeated several times as the problem gets closer to resolution. Just before I give them new information, I ask each group to briefly report their conclusions so that other groups can hear their progress. This has the effect of keeping the groups alert to other possible interpretations of the data and information.

It is important to note that the only parts of the case I hand out to the students are Part I and Figures 2 and 3. I do not hand out Parts II–V, but instead read this information out loud to the entire class.

This case takes about 75 minutes for analysis, but it can be easily shortened or lengthened. Here is how the timing of the case works along with my strategy for teaching it at each stage.

In Part I, students work in small groups and report before receiving new information. I use about 15 minutes for this. I first hand out Part I to each person in the class sitting in their groups. I instruct them to read the case and, as a group, answer the questions at the end of the page. (It is sometimes preferable to give each group only one copy of the case. This forces them to cooperate from the outset. If this is not done, individuals tend to read the case and then start making notes alone. It often takes them a long while to start talking together. To prevent this isolation, you must emphasize that the answers must be a group effort.)

After the small group discussion of Part I is in full swing, about five minutes along, I walk around the room with a color copy of the cover of *Nature* magazine (September 15, 1994), which has a photograph of the orange baby coots (see Figure 1). The students don't know it at the time (some hardly glance at it, others are simply enamored with how cute the babies are), but what the young coots look like is essential to what the authors did in the study. I then put a color overhead of the cover of the magazine on the projection screen for the rest of the class period so that the coots are omnipresent.

When the 15 minutes have passed, I interrupt the discussion, and ask for a representative from each group to *tell me what they*

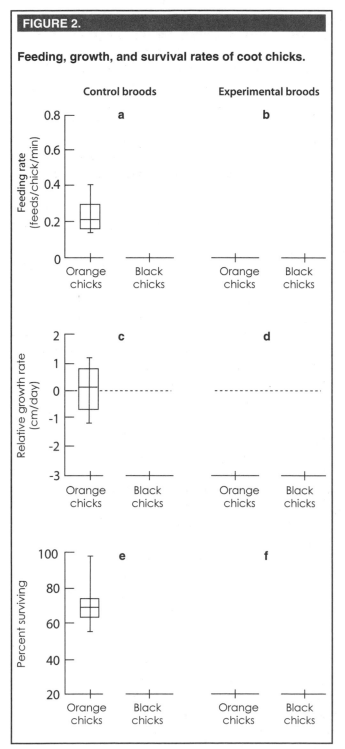

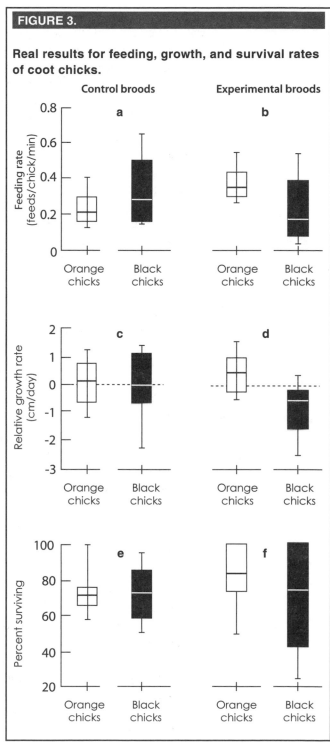

thought the question was that the researchers were addressing. I quickly have the groups report their conclusions. I do not comment at this point. There are always differences of opinion as to the question, usually because some groups have been specific, focusing on coots, while others have focused on the big evolutionary picture.

After this round-robin is over, I ask the groups to *quickly report on the hypothesis they think the researchers are pursuing.* Again, when the reporting is done, it will be apparent that there are differences among groups. I choose not to comment as this process is occurring except to say that clearly people differ even though they have the same information. At this point I say that I know that they have begun to consider the ways that the authors might test their hypothesis, but to help students on their way I thought that they might like to hear a little bit more from the biologists who conducted the actual study.

I now read Part II out loud. I finish by saying that now that they know what the researchers are up to, they are to use the method of clipping the feathers and design an experimental program that will test the hypothesis. It is essential at this point to emphasize that, yes, there are other ways to attack the problem, but use the researchers' approach. If you don't do this, some groups tend to go off on their own and produce radically different designs. Although this might be productive in some ways, it will surely be diversionary to the present case strategy.

I give the groups about 10–15 minutes to come up with an experimental design using the feather clipping method from the *Nature* article. As the discussion occurs, I move from group to group, checking on their progress and making sure they are using the authors' method. I try not to answer many coot questions. If they ask questions about the coots, I simply say that, yes, I know that they don't know much about coots but they should just make some reasonable assumptions as they

design their experiment. I do reassure them that they don't need to worry about budget at this point. Their goal is simple: Design an experiment to test the hypothesis.

When the time is up, I ask each group in turn to report its findings. (Incidentally, I always take the groups in a different order each time they report.) Most groups will have very similar experimental designs now. All will have decided to have a nest with orange chicks and to have another with all black chicks. Some will stop there, not realizing that they need to have a third group, a nest condition with 50% black and 50% orange. It is only in this situation that the parents will have a choice between the two conditions. Also, there will be variations in which data to collect and how to collect it. Once again, I don't comment except occasionally to ask questions for clarification.

I then read Part III out loud, telling the students what the researchers really did. This passage is instructive because it reveals details about how the authors of the study handled the coots that some of the student groups will have considered. At the end of the passage, I specifically ask them to decide which data the authors should collect and how they might do that. The groups now have a chance to revise their ideas in light of other groups' comments and the further information. Also, it is essential to emphasize that they should begin to seriously think about what the data might show.

After about five minutes, I have the groups briefly report their proposals. There will be a few surprises here, as some groups will have some novel and often very expensive ways to monitor the birds.

Next I read Part IV out loud and then hand out Figure 2 to everyone. Sometimes I only hand out a single copy of the data per group to save paper and to force each group to work together. After they have had a moment to look at the figure I go over it with them pointing out that the figure shows only the results for the nests where the birds are all the normal orange color. I ask them to plot what the missing data might look like *if the hypothesis were correct*. I suggest that they first plot the data for the experimental nests where half of the chicks are black and half are orange; that is, where the parents have a choice between black and orange chicks. When that is done they should turn their attention to what would happen in the nests where there are only black chicks. I emphasize that anything might really occur, but what would be the ideal data that one might like to have.

The plotting of the data will take about 10 minutes and, after some hemming and hawing, most groups end up with the appropriate predictions. I walk around the room as this is going on and when I find a group that thinks it is finished, I ask them to consider how they would interpret the data if the black control group were different. When most groups are finished, I hand them a completed version of what happened (Figure 3). After they have had a few moments to compare their predictions with the real data, I ask the entire class to respond to the questions listed at the end of the passage in Part V. By this point students will recognize the distinction between "support" and "prove." Also, at this point I ask students to consider how they might interpret the data if the chicks in the all-black control nest had survived more poorly than those in the all-orange nest. I challenge them to tell me why black chicks might not do well. It doesn't take long for them to suggest a myriad of possibilities, including temperature control, predation, parasitism, lack of parental recognition that they are chicks rather than adults, etc. I finish with the statement "Isn't it great that the authors used this control group, because without it they would never know if these factors were involved in the experimental nests. It appears clear now that they were not involved."

At this point I stop. The case is over but the work is not. The authors are still working on the problem. To intrigue students further I might mention what the authors say at the end of their abstract: They write, *"The survival benefits from increased parental care did not accrue to all orange chicks in experimental broods, but depended strongly on a chick's position in the hatching order. Late-hatched orange chicks had dramatically higher survival than late-hatched black chicks, but there was little difference in survival between early-hatched black and orange chicks."*

We could continue the case by giving the students the graph depicting hatching order and ask them what they make of it. As a last point, the authors of the *Nature* article suggest three possible answers to the question "Why do parents prefer orange-feathered chicks?"

- Ornamental plumage may be a signal of a chick's high genetic or phenotypic quality, leading the parents to invest more care-giving in them.
- Orange plumage may be a signal of age, allowing parents to selectively feed the chicks in an optimum way.
- The color preferences may not be directly related to feather color but simply due to a parent color preference for other reasons. Perhaps it is the chick's head color that signals the offspring's need.

What experiments might resolve the issue?

REFERENCES

Lyon, B. E., J. M. Eadie, and L. D. Hamilton. 1994. Parental choice selects for ornamental plumage in American coot chicks. *Nature* 371: 240–243.

Pagel, M. 1994. Parents prefer pretty plumage. *Nature* 371: 200.

Section IX

Intimate Debate Method

Formal debate is practiced among high school and college students and is often seen as a prelude to the training of a lawyer. Indeed, Moot Court debates are a normal exercise among aspiring law students. I consider debates a case study method because there is an inherent story involved as the two side's battle it out. And they are exciting. Debates do one thing exquisitely well: They reveal the positives and the negatives of each position in bold relief. Since debaters typically have to prepare for either side of the argument they become informed about the issues. The downside to debates is that they are all about winning and losing, not about reaching a sensible conclusion.

In this section I describe a debate method that has the strength of the debate strategy but ends with a meeting of the minds. It is a powerful method for dealing with case topics that involve controversy, such as whether to legalize marijuana, provide federal funding for cloning research, legalize euthanasia, abandon the Hubble space telescope, or permit Intelligent Design to be taught in the science classroom.

The Intimate Debate Method

Should Marijuana Be Legalized for Medicinal Purposes?

By Clyde Freeman Herreid and Kristie DuRei

No great advance has ever been made in science, politics, or religion without controversy.
—Lyman Beecher

Testimony is like an arrow shot from a long bow; its force depends upon the strength of the hand that draws it. But argument is like an arrow shot from a crossbow, which has equal force if drawn by a child or a man.
—Robert Boyle

The first duty of a wise advocate is to convince his opponents that he understands their arguments, and sympathizes with their feelings.
—Samuel Taylor Coleridge

Classroom debates used to be familiar exercises to students schooled in past generations. The Lincoln versus Douglas presidential disputations were often held as a model of formal debate style. These are seldom seen anymore except in speech classes or special clubs devoted to forensic competitive debate. Yet they can be powerful when used appropriately in a course, if the object is to understand the nuances of the different sides of the argument. Still, they are extremely artificial, although politicians would often like us to think otherwise. There are not just two sides to most questions. Typically there are multiple sides. And certainly winning is not the higher goal of most scientific discussions. We like to think that seeking "truth" is in there somewhere and that frequently "truth" lies somewhere in the middle of extremes.

Here I wish to describe the technique that I call Intimate Debate. It is known by cooperative learning specialists as "Structured Debate" and sometimes as "Constructive Debate." Basically, two pairs of students face off across a small table, arguing first one side and then switching to argue the other side. At the end of this exercise they must abandon their formal position and try to come to a consensus as to what is a reasonable solution to the problem being debated. I briefly described the method in chapter 22, "The Pima Experience: Three Easy Pieces."

Here is one simple way to configure the debate.

Step 1: Arrange groups and assign roles. Let's say that the debate is over the legalization of marijuana. Suppose there are 24 students in the class. Take two groups of 6 students (12 students altogether) and assign them the pro side of the argument. Assign the other 12 students (in two groups of 6 students) to the con side. Give each group information sheets that deal with the major arguments from their prospective; i.e., the pro groups only get pro arguments and the con groups only receive con arguments. (Note: I could have all of the pro students—12 in all—talking together and sharing information; but this group size is a bit clumsy and not everyone gets a chance to speak.)

Step 2: Tell the groups to discuss their information and organize it around the major talking points (arguments) that they can make from their respective side. Tell everyone they are individually responsible for keeping notes because their current teams are going to be split up. If you fail to inform them of this point, they will not be adequately prepared. This general discussion takes 10–15 minutes.

Step 3: Take two students from a pro group and seat them facing two students from a con group. This is repeated for all students. In my hypothetical example, I started with 24 students so I would have 6 debates about to start. The opponents should be either seated across small tables or seated in chairs facing one another.

Step 4: To start the debate, tell the students on the pro side of the argument to speak for 4 minutes to their con opponents. The students representing the con side may not interrupt. Tell all students that the cons must take good notes because they will soon be arguing the pro side and they will not have the pro information sheet to guide them; i.e., they must listen carefully to the other side's remarks. At the end of 4 minutes, the instructor calls a halt.

Step 5: Tell the students for the con side they may speak for 4 minutes to their pro opponents without interruption. The pros must listen carefully and take good notes. The instructor calls a halt when the time is up.

Step 6: Allow all teams 3 minutes for a caucus. The teacher explains to the class that now the roles will be reversed: Pro speakers must shift to con side and visa versa. But they only have their notes for assistance. Therefore, during the caucus time, the pairs should briefly consult about their best arguments and get ready for a new debate.

Step 7: To start the next round of the debate, the new pro teams will have only 2 minutes to make their best arguments while the new cons listen.

Step 8: Then the new con team has 2 minutes to make their arguments while the new pros listen.

Step 9: Inform all students to abandon their formal positions. In their groups of four, their job is now to come up with what they believe to be a reasonable solution to the controversy. If possible, they should try to reach a consensus. This usually takes the students about 5 minutes.

Step 10: As an instructor you now ask the groups to report the results of their deliberations. This can take as little as 5 minutes or considerably longer, depending upon how much discussion the instructor wishes to instigate. The entire intimate debate process lasts about 45 minutes.

Students usually enjoy this case approach. It is exciting and fun. But if the teacher provides all of the information to the students in the manner I just described, the conversation is severely limited. A much richer discussion is possible if the instructor tells the class several days prior to the debate what they have in store for them. S/he informs them of the topic of the debate and tells them that they will be debating both sides of the issue, first on one side then the other. Thus, they should look up all the information they can on a topic and organize their notes in the two categories, the pro arguments and the con. When the debate is to be held, the instructor still can hand out information sheets, but the students can now add their own information to the pool.

Below are information sheets developed for the marijuana debate. References can be provided to the students depending upon the teaching goals.

PRO: MARIJUANA SHOULD BE ALLOWED FOR MEDICAL PURPOSES

Foremost in our society, marijuana is known as a recreational drug. However, for the many people in the United States who suffer from a number of diseases, marijuana may appeal to them as a purposive medicinal drug. This has become a very controversial issue because the U.S. government has placed the "war on drugs" very high on its domestic priorities list and making marijuana legal to serve a medical function could send mixed signals to the public. However, many Americans believe that if this drug can relieve the pain and suffering of so many, then it needs to be considered for a medical purpose.

In 1972, after reviewing the scientific evidence, the National Commission on Marijuana and Drug Abuse concluded that while marijuana was not entirely safe, its dangers had been grossly inflated. Since then, researchers have conducted thousands of studies of humans, animals, and cell cultures, none of which expose any findings significantly different from those expressed by the National Commission in 1972. In 1995, based on 30 years of scientific research, editors of the British medical journal *Lancet* deduced that "the smoking of cannabis, even long term, is not harmful to health."

In a 2003 article, the American Civil Liberties Union explains that no one has ever died from an overdose from marijuana used as a recreational or medicinal drug.

According to the Drug Policy Alliance, marijuana has been shown to be effective in lessening the nausea induced by cancer chemotherapy, rousing appetite in AIDS patients, and reducing intraocular pressure in people with glaucoma. There is also substantial evidence that marijuana reduces muscle spasticity in patients with neurological disorders. A synthetic capsule is available by prescription only, but it is not as effective as smoked marijuana for many patients. Pure THC may also produce more unpleasant psychoactive side effects than smoked marijuana.

In regards to cancer, marijuana can stimulate the appetite and alleviate nausea and vomiting, which are common side effects of chemotherapy treatment.

In the book *The Emperor Wears No Clothes*, Jack Herer states that researchers at the Medical College of Virginia discovered that cannabis (marijuana) is an incredibly successful herb for reducing many types of tumors, both benign and malignant.

In the article "Hemp and Health," Nelson describes that THC and CBN (the primary chemicals in marijuana) have inhibited primary tumor growth from 25% to 82% and increased the life expectancy of cancerous mice to the same extent. The anti-tumor property of THC and CBN is very selective, as it reduces tumor cells without damaging normal cells.

Joycelyn Elders, M.D., wrote in a March 26, 2004 editorial published in the *Providence Rhode Island Journal*: "The evidence is overwhelming that marijuana can relieve certain types of pain, nausea, vomiting and other symptoms caused by such illnesses as multiple sclerosis, cancer and AIDS—or by the harsh drugs sometimes used to treat them. And it can do so with remarkable safety. Indeed, marijuana is less toxic than many of the drugs that physicians prescribe every day."

Britain's Medicinal Cannabis Research Foundation published on their website in November 2001 that medicinal use of marijuana could provide a dramatic improvement in quality of life for people with AIDS wasting syndrome, glaucoma, Alzheimer's disease, hypertension, arthritis, multiple sclerosis, asthma, nail patella syndrome, brain injury/stroke, nausea (which accompanies chemotherapy), Crohn's/colitis, chronic pain, depression/mental illness, phantom limb pain, eating disorders, migraine, epilepsy, spinal cord injury, fibromyalgia, and Tourette's syndrome. This improvement in quality of life results from marijuana's lessening effect of chronic pain, spasm, bladder dysfunction, and nausea.

Researchers from GW Pharmaceuticals wrote in an article published in the *Journal of Cannabis Therapeutics* that in practice it has been found that, compared to the equivalent amount of cannabinoid given as a single chemical entity such as Marinol, extracts of cannabis offer greater relief of pain (pharmaceutical-quality Marinol provides standardized THC concentrations).

Cannabinoids taken by mouth begin working more gradually and are absorbed more unpredictably than inhaled marijuana, so many patients prefer the latter, University of Montreal pharmacologist Mohamed Ben Amar wrote in a paper posted in March 2006 by the *Journal of Ethnopharmacology*.

Marijuana is the most popular illegal drug in the United States today, states the Drug Policy Alliance. Therefore, people who have used less popular drugs such as heroin, cocaine, and LSD are likely to have also used marijuana. Most marijuana users never use any other illegal drug. Indeed, for the large majority of people, marijuana is a finishing point rather than a gateway drug.

None of the medical tests, as per the Drug Policy Alliance, presently utilized to detect brain damage in humans have found harm from marijuana, even from long-term high-dose use. An early study detailed brain damage in rhesus monkeys after six months' exposure to high concentrations of marijuana smoke. In a recent, more carefully conducted study, researchers failed to find evidence of brain abnormality in monkeys that were forced to inhale the equivalent of four to five marijuana cigarettes every day for a year. The claim that marijuana kills brain cells originated in a provisional report dating back a quarter of a century that has not been sufficiently corroborated.

CON: MARIJUANA SHOULD NOT BE USED AS A MEDICINAL DRUG

Foremost in our society, marijuana is known as a recreational drug. However, for the many people in the United States who suffer from a number of diseases, marijuana may appeal to them as a purposive medicinal drug. This has become a very controversial issue because the U.S. government has placed the "war on drugs" very high on its domestic priorities list and making marijuana legal to serve a medical function could send mixed signals to the public. However, many Americans believe that if this drug can relieve the pain and suffering of so many, then it needs to be considered for a medical purpose.

According to the article "Signs of Marijuana Addiction and Abuse," short-term side-effects of marijuana include: sleepiness, difficulty keeping track of time, impaired or reduced short-term memory, reduced ability to perform tasks requiring concentration and coordination (such as driving a car), increased heart rate, potential cardiac dangers for those with preexisting heart disease, bloodshot eyes, dry mouth and throat, decreased social inhibitions, paranoia, hallucinations, impaired or reduced short-term memory, impaired or reduced comprehension, altered motivation and cognition (making the acquisition of new information difficult), psychological dependence, impairments in learning and memory, perception, and judgment, difficulty speaking, listening effectively, thinking, retaining knowledge, problem solving, and forming concepts, intense anxiety or panic attacks

Long-term effects of marijuana, as per "Signs of Marijuana Addiction and Abuse," are enhanced cancer risk, decrease in testosterone levels and lower sperm counts for males, increase in testosterone levels for women and increased risk of infertility, diminished or extinguished sexual pleasure, and psychological dependence requiring more of the drug to get the same effect

One study has indicated that a user's risk of heart attack more than quadruples in the first hour after smoking marijuana, states the National Institute on Drug Abuse. The researchers suggest that such an effect might occur from marijuana's effects on blood pressure and heart rate and reduced oxygen-carrying capacity of blood.

Reported on the National Institute of Drug Abuse website, researchers have found that THC changes the manner in which sensory information gets into and is acted upon by the hippocampus. This is a component of the brain's limbic system that is imperative for learning, memory, and the integration of sensory experiences with emotions and motivations. Investigations have shown that neurons in the information processing system of the hippocampus and the activity of the nerve fibers are suppressed by THC. In addition, researchers have determined that learned behaviors, which depend on the hippocampus, also deteriorate. Recent research findings also indicate that long-term use of marijuana produces changes in the brain similar to those seen after long-term abuse of other major drugs.

Someone who smokes marijuana regularly may have many of the same respiratory problems that tobacco smokers have, as ascertained by the National Institute on Drug Abuse. These individuals may have daily cough and phlegm, symptoms of chronic bronchitis, and more frequent chest colds. Continuing to smoke marijuana can lead to abnormal functioning of lung tissue injured or destroyed by marijuana smoke.

As maintained in *Marijuana Myths and Facts,* the amount of tar inhaled by marijuana smokers and the level of carbon monoxide absorbed are three to five times greater than among tobacco smokers. This may be due to the marijuana users inhaling more deeply and holding the smoke in the lungs.

Regular use of cannabis can lead to psychological habituation for some people making it difficult for them to quit. According to Erowid, studies have estimated that between 5% and 10% of those who try smoking marijuana once, will become daily users sometime during their life, but most of these smokers will have given up the habit by age 30 and few remain daily smokers after age 40. Most people do not experience signs of physical addiction, but with regular daily use, mild to medium withdrawal symptoms usually occur for less than a week, but can extend for as long as six weeks.

Several studies have indicated that cannabis use (like many other strong psychoactive drugs) can precipitate neuroses or psychoses in those who are already at risk.

Walters states in "Happy Trails Paraphernalia Pushers" that making medicinal marijuana legal would destroy the societal norm that drug use is dangerous. It would undercut the goals of stopping the initiation of drug use to thwart addiction.

The article "Are Legal Alternatives to MMJ Effective?" states that the alternative to medicinal marijuana is Marinol. It provides consistent THC content, while marijuana does not provide standardized THC content and often contains impurities (including leaves, mold spores, and bacteria).

Marinol has already been approved by the FDA in the treatment of nausea and vomiting associated with cancer chemotherapy in patients.

Marijuana is a gateway drug that can lead to the eventual use of "harder" drugs such as cocaine or heroine.

In the article "Marijuana Myths, Marijuana Facts," Zimmer and Morgan state that used over time, marijuana permanently alters brain structure and function, causing memory loss, cognitive impairment, personality deterioration, and reduced productivity.

REFERENCES

American Civil Liberties Union. 2003. Stop the assault on medical marijuana. Available online at *www.aclu.org/drugpolicy/medmarijuana/10769 res20030510.html*

Are Legal Alternatives to MMJ Effective? 2006. Available online at *http://cannabisnews.com/news/21/thread21652.html*

Clear Haven Center. 2006. Signs of marijuana addiction and abuse. Available online at *www.clearhavencenter.com/substance-abuse-treatment-resources/signs-of-marijuana-use.php.*

Elders, J. 2004. Editorial on marijuana use. *Providence Journal* (March 24).

Erowid (2006). Cannabis Basics. Available online at *www.erowid.org/plants/cannabis/cannabis_basics.shtml*

GW Pharmaceuticals. 2001. Peer-reviewed scientific studies involving cannabis and cannabis extracts 1990–2005. Available online at *www.medicalmarijuanaprocon.org/pop/studychart.htm*

Herer, J. 1998. *The emperor wears no clothes: The authoritative historical record of cannabis and the conspiracy against marijuana.* Phoenix, AZ: Paper Master Trade.

Mittleman M. A., R. A. Lewis, M. Maclure, J. B. Sherwood, and J. E. Muller. 2001. Triggering myocardial infarction by marijuana. *Circulation* 103(23): 2805–2809.

National Institute on Drug Abuse (NIDA). 2004. Drug facts: Marijuana. NIH Publication No. 04-4036. Available online at *www.nida.nih.gov.*

National Institute on Drug Abuse (NIDA). 2004. Marijuana: Facts parents need to know. Available online at *www.nida.nih.gov.*

Nelson, R. A. 1999. Hemp and health. Available online at *www.rexresearch.com/hhusb/hmphlth.htm#hhl2e.*

Office of National Drug Control Policy. 2002. Marijuana myths and facts: The truth behind 10 popular misconceptions. Available online at *www.whitehousedrugpolicy.gov/publications/marijuana_myths_facts/index.html.*

Rubin, R. 2006. Cesamet joins Marinol in June. *USA Today* (May 17).

ThinkQuest New York City. 2001. Marijuana: Medical uses. Available online at *www.tqnyc.org/NYC063394/marijuana/medical_uses.html.*

Walters, J. 2004. Happy trails paraphernalia pushers. *The Coalition* 8(1): 20.

Zimmer, L., and J. Morgan. 1997. Marijuana myths, marijuana facts. Available online at *www.drugpolicy.org/marijuana/factsmyths.*

Section X

Team-Based Learning

Team-Based Learning is the brainchild of Larry Michaelsen. It is a form of cooperative learning where permanent groups of students are used throughout the semester. There are no lectures, only teamwork. The students do individual study and come to class. They take an individual quiz to ensure they have done the reading. This is followed by a group quiz using the same questions. The quizzes are graded immediately and the students have a chance to appeal. This is followed by a group project, such as a case study, wherein the students apply the terms and principles that they have read.

In the first two chapters of the section, I review the details and history of the method. This is followed by an example of how we used the method in a dental school and some data showing its success. The last chapter is an example of a case on extinction where the team method is extensively employed. There is nothing special about a case that is used for Team-Based Learning. The reason that I bring the method to the readers' attention is that Team-Based Learning is a complete, self-contained system where cases can be used and still cover large amounts of content. Thus it circumvents one of the criticisms offered against case study teaching.

Larry Finally Wrote His Book

Team-Based Learning Has Its Bible

By Clyde Freeman Herreid

Larry Michaelsen has finally written his long-awaited treatise on Team-Based Learning—with a little help from his friends. The book, entitled *Team-Based Learning: A Transformative Use of Small Groups,* was written and edited by Larry K. Michaelsen, Arletta B. Knight, and L. Dee Fink (2002).

Larry and I met about a dozen years ago when we were both invited to a day of faculty development at Vanderbilt University. We were asked to give presentations on two different approaches to effective teaching. My presentation was a lecture on how to lecture, immodestly titled, "The Ten Commandments of Teaching." Larry's workshop was on something he called "Team Learning." He never came to my presentation; he had given up lecturing. I went to Larry's workshop, and it transformed my approach to teaching, just as his book's subtitle promises to do for readers.

Let me tell you about the book. The first several chapters, primarily written by Larry and his co-editors, give "The Key Ideas of Team-Based Learning." They give the rationale for the method and the nitty-gritty details of how to do it. The second part of the book, called "The Voices of Experience," is a series of chapters written by teachers who are smitten by the method. I am one of the converts, as are chemistry professor Frank Dinan of Canisius College (Buffalo, New York) and hydrobiology and ecology professor Jiri Popoveski of Charles University (Prague, Czech Republic). We are the pure scientists in the parade of authors.

The other science folks who contributed to this book include Patricia Goodsen, who writes of her success "Working with Non-traditional and Underprepared Students in Health Education," and Melanie Nakaji, who tells a remarkable success story about "A Dramatic Turnaround in a Classroom of Deaf Students." Finally, because Michaelsen is a distinguished professor of management at The University of Oklahoma, the book includes chapters written by business and legal studies colleagues.

The third section of the book, the appendix, should not be overlooked; it is loaded with good stuff. Here, Michaelsen answers "Frequently Asked Questions about Team-Based Learning," explains how to calculate peer evaluation scores, provides team building exercises, and gives a plethora of other interesting exhibits. Good value for your dollar.

So, what's all the applause about? *Team-Based Learning* is not a book about teaching tips—it is a complete strategy for teaching. It reveals the power of small groups to provide a compelling learning environment. Unlike most cooperative/collaborative learning approaches, team-based learning is not simply a collection of small group exercises but is an integrated strategy set up to optimize learning. And, after all, that is the bottom line, isn't it? Larry Spence, writing in *Change* magazine, said that's where our emphasis rightly belongs: "It's not the teaching, stupid, it's the learning!" (2001).

QUALITY VERSUS QUANTITY

Team-Based Learning had its start 25 years ago when Michaelsen was forced to increase his class size from 40 to 120 students. Despite this challenge, he was unwilling to give up his approach in smaller size classes where he used group activities. He rejected advice from colleagues who said he should start lecturing. Instead, he created Team-Based Learning. Having done so, he realized three unanticipated accomplishments. One, students did not see the large class as a negative; in fact, it was beneficial. Two, the method prompted students to take responsibility for their own learning. And, three, he was having fun.

What is the essence of Team-Based Learning? It is this: There are no lectures. Students work in small permanent groups and learn on their own with carefully crafted quizzes and exercises. There are six steps:

- *Assign readings.* The teacher gives students carefully chosen reading assignments to be completed before class. These constitute the basic concepts the instructors believe to be essential. Typical textbook chapters may not work; they are usually too detailed and filled with trivia unless the teacher provides

a study guide. If you think the students won't read these assignments, think again, and read on.

- *Give individual quizzes.* When students first walk into class, they take a mini-test on the assigned readings. These are multiple-choice and true/false quizzes consisting of about 20 questions. The questions deal with only the basic points in the reading; minutiae are avoided. Once completed, the quizzes are set aside without being graded.

- *Give group mini-tests.* When all group members are finished with their individual quizzes, they pull their chairs together and take the same quiz again. They discuss their answers as a group and fill out a single answer sheet representing the group's consensus. After they have finished, they grade both the group quiz and their individual quizzes. This is done either with an electronic scoring machine or an answer key provided by the instructor. All groups work at their own pace. The groups post their scores on a blackboard for all to see. This invokes an *esprit de corps* within teams as they look to see how their performance compares with that of other groups.

- *Allow appeals.* After the mini-tests are graded, student groups reevaluate their answers and compare them to the key. Then, if they wish to challenge an answer or a question, they may make a written appeal. During this process, students may use their textbooks to look up basic information. Only groups can write appeals; individuals cannot. A warning here: To avoid intense arguments with students, the instructor should not attempt to evaluate these in the classroom. Instead, in the cool of the evening, perhaps with a mint julep in hand, he or she should evaluate the appeals and write out a reasoned response. If the instructor grants the appeal, both the group and individual scores are changed. Groups that do not challenge a question do not benefit from another group's appeal.

- *Give instructor input.* After the appeal process is over, the instructor takes a few minutes to clarify problems that have emerged. It is not a time to discuss the quiz *per se*; that can lead to incessant argument. Instead, it is simply a time for clarification of major issues the instructor feels are important. The entire quiz/appeal process is called the Readiness Assurance Process (RAP). It occupies an entire 50-minute class. The RAP is usually not done every class period but at the beginning of classes when a new unit of material is covered.

- *Apply the knowledge.* Once students have studied the readings, taken individual and group quizzes, and received feedback on both group quizzes and the appeal process, they are ready to apply their knowledge. The instructor gives the class an exercise, problem, or case study that uses the material students have learned from the textbooks. These exercises must be carefully designed to be large enough or complex enough so students must work together to successfully complete the project.

That's it: Reading assignments, RAPs, and applications. The cycle is repeated for every unit. When class periods are long, such as in a 3-hour summer school class, the instructor can get through the entire process in one class period. Adjustments have to be made for shorter class times. For 50-minute classes (the least ideal arrangement) the instructor might give a reading assignment and a RAP for two or three classes in a row to get through essential material. Then, he or she could give a case application that integrates material from the previous classes and might last one or more classes. Then, it is time to move on to another unit with a reading assignment, RAP, and case. A sample sequence of events that I arranged for a general education course called "Scientific Inquiry" is shown in the sidebar on page 193.

A WORD ABOUT GRADING

Instructors handle this in different ways, but Michaelsen suggests three elements be involved—individual work, group work, and peer evaluation. *Individual work* includes individual quizzes, homework assignments, and midterm and final exams. *Group work* consists of group quizzes and group assignments that grow out of projects assigned during case study work.

Finally, Michaelsen and the chapter authors argue strongly that one must have *peer evaluation* to get students to contribute equally to the team. Once or twice during the semester students evaluate one another's contribution to the group projects by an anonymous scoring system.

As an example, each student in a five-person group gets 40 points to distribute to other group members based on the effort they have made for the project. I have published a form showing the approach (Herreid 2001). If a student receives an average score of 10 from his or her four teammates, it is equivalent to 100%, and that student will receive the entire grade that the group earned on the group work. If, on the other hand, a student receives only an average score of 8, then he or she will only receive 80% of the group grade, and so on.

So, a student's final course grade is a combination of individual and group grades (as modified by the peer evaluation). After trying different weighting schemes, I have found that a 75% individual to 25% group score ratio works well. Other schemes are outlined in Michaelsen's magnum opus.

WHAT'S THE PAYOFF?

Attendance is virtually 100%! Students in Team-Based Learning classes soon realize that they must not be absent or late, as their grades will instantly suffer. Not only will they miss the quizzes but also their teammates will not forgive them. Absenteeism and tardiness are the two factors that most influence peer evaluations negatively. More importantly, students realize they do not want to let their groups down by being absent, and they like attending class.

Students get higher grades. This happens for many reasons, but the bottom line is, groups do better than their best individual member. The result: Whereas in my large lecture classes I may have 30% Ds and Fs, in my Team-Based Learning classes, I have less than 5% Ds and Fs.

Students learn more and retain it better. Students must keep up with the material; they cannot wait to study and cram at the last minute. The pace is relentless; students cannot be passive in the classroom. They must constantly interact with the material during their reading, individual quizzes, group quizzes, appeals, and case studies that integrate the material and put the learning in context. Students cannot hide like they can in a lecture.

Coverage of subject matter is at least as great as in a lecture course. Sometimes it is even greater. Chemistry professor Frank Dinan reported that his organic chemistry class covered two more chapters than normal, and students attained higher grades on a national exam than did those who had been taught by the traditional lecture method. Insufficient coverage of the material is the big rap against using the case method to teach—as if coverage of material is equivalent to learning the material, an unholy falsehood if there ever was one.

Students like it better. They say so in their course evaluations, and I believe them. Not all of my students prefer it, of course. In my experience, about 15% of students like the lecture approach better even if they have had a good experience with Team-Based Learning. Some students enjoy being passive. Some are even good at learning by the lecture method. So were we when we were students, otherwise we would not have made it through the system.

We are the survivors of the lecture method, and this explains our strong bias for its use. Yet, there is another way—Team-Based Learning. You can see it in action in a video sold by the National Center for Case Study Teaching in Science at *http://ublib.buffalo. edu/libraries/projects/cases/case.html.* Once you try it, you'll be a convert too!

REFERENCES

Herreid, C.F. 2001. When justice peeks: Evaluating students in case study teaching. *Journal of College Science Teaching* 30(7): 430–433.

Michaelsen, L. K., A. B. Knight, and L. D. Fink, eds. 2002. *Team-based learning: A transformative use of small groups.* Westport, CT: Praeger.

Spence, L. 2001. The case against teaching. *Change* 33(6): 10–19.

SIDEBAR: SAMPLE TEACHING SEQUENCE

Date	Topic	Readings
Aug. 25	Course organization	
27	Establish groups and negotiate grade guidelines	
Sept. 1	Mini-test: "On being a scientist"	Handout
3	Case: Cold fusion	Handout
8	Mini-test: Chapter 1 (sampling)	Text
10	Mini-test: Chapter 2 (experimentation)	Text
15	Case: Vitamin C	Handout
17	Case: Aspirin and heart disease	Handout
22	Mini-test: Chapter 3 (measurement)	Text
24	Case: "Will women soon outrun men?"	Handout
29	Holiday	
Oct. 1	Case: "Can water remember?"	Handout
6	Mini-test: Chapter 4 (distributions)	Text
8	Mini-test: Chapter 4 (distributions)	Text
13	Case: Smoking and cancer	Handout
15	Case: Smoking and cancer	Handout
20	Mini-test: Chapter 5 (correlation/causation)	Text
22	Case: Is homosexuality genetic?	Handout
27	Case: Is homosexuality genetic?	Handout
29	Case: Astrology (design of experiment)	Handout
Nov. 3	Mini-test: Chapter 7 (probability)	Text
5	Case: Astrology preliminary data review	Handout
10	Mini-test: Chapter 8 (statistical reasoning)	Text
12	Case: Astrology review of papers	Handout
17	Case: DNA fingerprinting	Handout
19	Case: Carcinogenic agents	Handout
24	Case: Use of animals in experiments	Handout
26	Holiday	
Dec. 1	Mini-test: AIDS	Handout
3	Case: AIDS drug approval	Handout
8	Final Exam	

Source: Moore, D. 1991. *Statistics: Concepts & Controversies.* New York: W. H. Freeman and Co.

Using Case Studies in Science—And Still "Covering the Content"

By Clyde Freeman Herreid

Many professors worry about shifting to small groups and other forms of active learning because of a fear they will not be able to cover as much content. Herreid used case studies with team-based learning and found his students learned as much or more, and comments on why this was so.

In the summer of 1992, I was invited to come to Vanderbilt University and give a lecture on the art of teaching. They were having a faculty colloquium, an annual event hosted by their Office of Teaching Effectiveness. They had invited me to lecture on how to lecture. I entitled my talk "The Ten Commandments." I am sure they thought they were getting something divinely inspired. Not willing to dissuade them of their fantasy, I went calling.

I gave my presentation to a large and generous audience. Not long afterward, I found myself seated at lunch with another presenter who was scheduled to speak in the afternoon on something called "team-based learning." In our brief exchange I found out that Larry Michaelsen had given up lecturing and was enthralled with a new method of presenting material that was a cross between collaborative learning and mastery teaching. He did not attend my lecture; I suppose it would have been antithetical to his newfound wisdom.

For years I had been looking for alternative forms of teaching, reasoning that I had exhausted the nuances of the lecture method and was ready to move on. I was mid-career and still found many students failing my classes. They complimented me on my presentations, yet there was always an eternal stream of students coming to office hours complaining that they did not understand why they could not absorb the material and perform better on the tests. They looked like intelligent students; they sounded like intelligent students; they said everything was clear to them when they heard the lecture; and yet, they were failing. Indeed, what was the problem? Could it be the lecture method itself?

Team-based learning sounded as if it might be the antidote. I attended the afternoon session and I felt as though the scales had fallen from my eyes. I rushed home to Buffalo determined to try out the method immediately. I had a course called "Scientific Inquiry" that was scheduled to begin in a few weeks; its purpose was to show nonscientists how science really works. The course was a new addition to our State University of New York at Buffalo curriculum and was required for general education credit. The basis for the course was Case Method Teaching. I had never tried using case studies before but had become convinced by Bill Welty of Pace University that this style of instruction might be a solution to my dissatisfaction with lecturing. When I heard of team-based learning it seemed that I could combine the two methods into a perfect medley.

At this same time, my son was teaching a course in informal logic for the first time as a graduate student in the Department of Philosophy at Buffalo and he also became enthused about team-based learning when he heard of my trip to Vanderbilt. He decided to use the method in his course. Our experiences turned out to be radically different. Although my course went smoothly one week after the other, he had problem after problem using team-based learning. Students continually challenged him in the use of this novel method.

What was the difference between us? I will return to this topic at the end of the chapter, but for the moment let me turn to what I have learned over the past seven years about using the method in science courses, especially in my field of biology.

Let us begin by taking a look at one of my initial concerns: "Could I possibly cover all of the content?" Then we'll move on to examples in which I have successfully used team-based learning, how students responded to this method, and how I am now living happily ever after.

CONCERNS ABOUT COVERING THE CONTENT

A couple of years ago I wrote an article entitled "Why Isn't Cooperative Learning Used to Teach Science?" (Herreid 1998). I listed at least a dozen barriers that faculty, students, and administrators need to surmount if the method is to be successful. None are unique to the sciences, but the problem that most science faculty cite as their biggest stumbling block is the question of content. They argue that cooperative methods always slow down the process of learning. They say they cannot cover as much material: "It's all right for the people in the humanities or social sciences to do it, but we can't afford to cut back on the content. We have other courses that follow this one that depend upon this knowledge and we have national standards to meet."

There is some truth to this claim for some styles of cooperative learning, such as Problem-Based Learning (PBL). Not as much subject matter can be covered, but the learning is much deeper. What good is it if a faculty member covers the material and the students do not remember it?

More to the point, team-based learning is an exception because it does permit the coverage of the same amount of material as a normal lecture course. I have no difficulty covering exactly the same subjects to the same extent in my summer team-based learning class as during the fall lecture course. And I have the added luxury of teaching several wonderful evolution cases. It is significant to note that Frank Dinan reports that he has been able to cover even more material using team-based learning in his organic chemistry courses than when he used the traditional lecture method and students received higher grades (Dinan and Frydrychowski 1995). So team-based learning is ideal for the sciences in which content is the issue.

EXAMPLES OF WHERE I CURRENTLY USE TEAM-BASED LEARNING

I use team-based learning whenever I have a small class. This means that I use it to teach my evolutionary biology course in the summer when I have only two dozen students. This is a course designed for freshmen, although many upper-division students take it as well. There is no occasion for me to use this method during the normal fall semester, when I teach this course to 500 students in a fixed-seat amphitheater. The best I can do in that situation is to do some interactive lecturing. The other setting in which I use team-based learning regularly is in honors seminars, in which, again, I teach about two dozen students.

The largest courses in which I have used team-based learning were an honors colloquium with 100 students, and a scientific inquiry course for 70 students. I found the latter two experiences workable but frustrating because I could not deal well with the application part of the method, when I give out case studies or problems for the groups to solve. I simply cannot be everywhere to ask questions and probe for answers. Similarly, people using problem-based learning, in which permanent teams are established, also find they cannot keep track of the group work during their case teaching without the use of tutors as a central part of each of the teams. Yet, I hasten to add that I have heard of instructors who have successfully used team-based learning in classes with up to 280 students. However, it is essential in larger classes that the application phase of team-based learning be especially well designed so that students cannot simply divide up the workload. The assignment must require that students work cooperatively to complete the tasks.

WHAT KINDS OF PROJECTS DO I ASSIGN IN TEAM-BASED LEARNING?

Typically, the assignments I use in team-based learning are case studies. I have published many of these in the *Journal of College Science Teaching* as well as on the Web page for our National Center for Case Study Teaching in Science, supported by the National Science Foundation and the Pew Charitable Trusts: *http://ublib.buffalo.edu/ libraries/ projects/ cases/ case.html*.

Most of my cases extend for several class periods. Part of the case is presented on each day and the students are provided time between classes to look up material in the literature or on the internet. When they reconvene, they pool their resources, try to solve problems, and are given another piece of the case. This follows the classic PBL strategy. For example, in my evolutionary biology course, I have one case that deals with the discovery of the first fossil bird, *Archaeopteryx,* and the evolution of flight. Other cases deal with the importance of the Galapagos Islands in the process of speciation, the possibility of life on Mars, and human evolution. All of these cases are on our website, along with detailed teaching notes explaining exactly how I handle them in the classroom.

To give you a flavor of these cases and how they fit into a course structure, let me walk you through the Galapagos case. I teach this about halfway through the summer course in evolutionary biology, in which class periods are two-and-a-half hours long. There is a reading assignment in the textbook for each day. I start each class briefly answering any questions from the students about the reading material. This is followed by the usual team-based learning Readiness Assessment Test (RAT), grading with a Scantron, and written appeals to ensure that students are familiar with key concepts. Then we take a brief break (after all, the classes are long). When the students return, it is on to the case.

The Galapagos case takes up part of four class periods; that is a lot of time, but it is worth it because of its importance in covering many of the principles of evolution. On day one, I give out the first part of the case, which involves a graduate student named

"Kate," who is considering what her research topic should be and musing on the history of the islands. There are many questions embedded in the piece that must be answered by the groups. Following the typical problem-based learning model, the students identify the learning issues and then subdivide the work so that when they leave class they know what to search for.

On day two, after the RAT exercise, the students share information with their team members. As a group, they must turn in a written set of answers to key questions about the formation and colonization of the islands by the flora and fauna. They are then given the second part of the case, which involves Kate talking to the director of the Darwin Research Station as he tells her about speciation problems. Again, the students ferret out the learning issues, subdivide the workload, and leave class to search for the answers to their questions.

On day three, after they have shared their information and answered the key questions, they get part three of the case and read it. Here is a new wrinkle based on a real incident: Kate is caught in a crisis. Sea cucumber fishermen who have had a running argument with the government of Ecuador have taken over the Darwin Research Station and are holding scientists hostage along with a lab colony of endangered Galapagos tortoises. Now the students are told that each group must take on the role of one of the stakeholders in the controversy: fishermen, tourists, scientists, storeowners, conservationists, and Ecuadorian politicians. Each group must outline its demands and develop a negotiating position on how to deal with the question of accessibility to the unique islands.

On day four, I give the groups 30 minutes to clarify their positions. Then I form negotiating teams, splitting up the group members. Each negotiating team has a politician in charge and includes a fisherman, storeowner, scientist, and conservationist. The groups

are all charged to draft a compromise policy statement that would form the basis for a law governing the islands; each member must be faithful to his or her own constituency yet must be committed to devising an equitable settlement. The policy document must be outlined by the end of the period and the politician must write it out in detail for the next class. The other members of the group individually must write out an analysis of Kate's research options in light of the crisis, which jeopardizes her thesis work. (This teaching strategy is the well-known Jigsaw Method. First, expert groups are formed—fishermen, scientists, storeowners, conservationists— these groups establish their common goals. Then the groups are split up and rearranged so that new groups are formed where there will be a representative from each category to hammer out a compromise.)

Turning to another course, scientific inquiry, in which the purpose of the class is to have students understand how scientists really go about their work, human foibles and all, I follow the usual team-based learning approach with RATs, and so on. Again, I use cases involving contentious issues such as DNA fingerprinting, AIDS, and the Tuskegee syphilis project. But first, so that students understand the background of the scientific enterprise, I have them read an essay on the ethics and canons of science developed by the National Academy of Sciences entitled "On Being A Scientist." After a RAT on the reading, I give them their first application exercise. I ask the teams to develop a list of "commandments" describing what is appropriate and inappropriate behavior on the part of scientists. In 30 minutes they must develop at least 30 statements that begin with either "Thou shalt" or "Thou shalt not." For example, "Thou shalt repeat experiments," and "Thou shalt not plagiarize." The purpose of the list, which they hand in for my evaluation and criticism, is to solidify in their minds what ethical standards scientists must meet daily in their work. Then, to show how the scientific enterprise really functions, I have them read reports and articles about the cold fusion affair for the next class period. On the basis of the reading, in the ensuing class the groups must evaluate the problematic behavior of the scientists who claimed that they had discovered cold fusion. I have the teams rank on a scale of 1 to 10 how Professors Pons and Fleishman lived up to each of the standards of science the students had previously described in their commandments. Teams finish the evaluation with a brief written summary of their overall assessment of the scientists' behavior.

Another very effective application approach that I have used has been to have students develop lesson plans for K–12 students. This is the requirement that I made for students taking my Science and the Paranormal course. The purpose of this course is to develop critical-thinking skills in students by asking them to analyze extraordinary scientific and pseudoscientific claims. Student teams had to examine one paranormal phenomenon such as pyramid power, ghosts, hypnotism, and so forth. They had to research it and develop a lesson plan with activities for a K–12 classroom, with the purpose of sharpening these students' critical-thinking skills. Teams had to give an oral report to the class on their subject, turn in a written lesson plan, teach it to a K–12 class, prepare a poster for display in the library, and develop a website for a national skeptics' organization, the Committee for the Scientific Investigation of Claims of the Paranormal. By the time the teams had finished the project, they had an excellent grasp of the nature of "evidence" for various paranormal claims. They also had developed a healthy skepticism of the media and learned one of the fundamental tenets of science: "Extraordinary claims require extraordinary proof." Just as importantly, they produced work that could be used by instructors in classrooms across the country.

GRADES AND PEER EVALUATIONS

I think peer evaluations are essential if we expect students to take group work seriously. Many students have worked in groups somewhere along the line, and frequently have had an awful experience. This is especially true for good students. The use of peer evaluations not only serves as an encouragement for all students to contribute their fair share, but can serve as a remedy for any misbehaving team members. The good students will get their just reward for the extra work they put in and the laggards will get their just deserts.

In setting up my grading schemes, I have found that individual scores should be worth about 75% of the grade and group work 25%. I have experimented with other strategies, such as permitting the students to collectively decide at the beginning of the course to set the grade proportions for the semester, but I have found that grade inflation sets in because group grades are typically higher than individual scores. A way to compensate for this is to shift the grading curve upward because the conventional "90% equals an A" is no longer appropriate. However, I have found that such an upward curve shift causes more dissension than it is worth. I solve the problem by a 75%–25% split, which keeps the grades more in line with expectations.

I use peer evaluations as a modifier of the group work score. Each student must evaluate his or her teammates anonymously using a numerical scale at the end of the course. If there are, say, five individuals in a group, they each have 40 points to distribute to their teammates. In a group that is functioning perfectly, each person should receive an average score of 10 points. Any student receiving an average of 10 will receive all the points his team has earned for group work. On the other hand, if he receives an 8, he will receive only 80% of the group score. I have also set a lower limit on the peer evaluation score that a student can obtain. That is, if a student receives less than an average of 7 from his teammates, I will fail him regardless of his individual or group score. I give them fair warning of this rule in the syllabus. Originally, I devised this scheme because our school has a regulation that allows students to take some of their courses on a pass-or-fail basis. Students choosing this option invariably did not contribute to their groups, expecting to slide by with a pass and crippling their groups in the process. I created the rule to stop this behavior. I have continued using this grading rule even in courses in which the pass-or-fail option does not exist, because it prevents any student from coasting through the course satisfied with a C or D effort. This strategy has almost always stopped lazy behavior.

What Kinds of Responses Do Students Have to Team-Based Learning?

Whenever I have done evaluations of team-based learning and other cooperative strategies in which we set up permanent groups, invariably students say the thing they liked best about the class was working in groups. Most even enjoyed taking examinations with one another. Clearly, however, whenever people are thrown together, it takes time to adjust. Groups pass through a series of stages that have been described as "forming, storming, norming, and performing." I believe that it takes at least a third to a half of a semester before students are comfortable with the method.

The use of peer evaluations tends to make students work harder at getting along. I always have the groups do a practice peer evaluation about a third of the way into the semester. By this time the groups have been together long enough for any interpersonal problems that exist to be evident. I have them turn in their practice peer evaluations to me and I tally the individual scores. At the next class period I hand students their scores with the comment that anybody that does not like their score needs to correct the situation by

asking their group what they can do to improve the situation. In addition, I may have to take some people aside and have a conversation with them about their work. This usually sets matters right. Recalcitrant students getting low peer evaluation scores generally make amends rapidly.

I am often asked how frequently groups have problems in getting along (Herreid 1999). Over the years I have queried hundreds of faculty who have attended workshops I have given on collaborative learning. The average answer seems to be that around 15–20% have difficulties, and that is my experience as well. Nonetheless, I have been able to fix virtually all of these problems by using practice peer evaluations and by talking to the students involved. Additionally, I find it useful to have the groups evaluate their own progress in teamwork. This is especially valuable during the early days of the course. To do this, I might ask them to write a list of characteristics that identify good and poor team members; this starts a little introspection about their own behavior. Alternatively, I might hand out profiles of fictional students and ask the groups what kind of peer evaluation they would give to these individuals. Or I might ask them to use a numerical scale and to rank how well their group is performing and ask what they could do as individuals to improve the team's work. All of these techniques make the students aware of how individual performances can be improved to produce a better group project.

What Are the Outcomes of Team-Based Learning?

First, I notice a dramatic difference in student attendance in classes using team-based learning or any other type of collaborative learning in which permanent teams are used. At my institution, the average attendance when the lecture method is used may fall to 50%. In contrast, collaborative learning strategies produce an attendance of about 95%. The students tell me there are several reasons for this: (1) the in-class RATs determine a large part of their grade, so they can't afford to miss them; (2) group projects are done in class and figure significantly in their grade; and (3) most important, they feel that they cannot let their teammates down. This is not only because I use peer evaluation, but also because once groups have bonded, the students realize their absence hurts their new friends.

Second, the grades in the course are always higher than during the normal year when the lecture method is used. With team-based learning, most of the grades are As and Bs. Part of the reason is that a significant portion of the grade comes from group work and the groups usually produce higher scores on quizzes and projects than individuals. Additionally, students work much harder at grasping the material, and retain it better once they have to work on their own to digest the reading and have to apply the general principles they have learned to real-life problems. They cannot escape the workload. It is relentless. In normal lecture-based classes, students can remain passive, hidden throughout the semester. This is impossible to do in team-based learning. They must keep up with the work or everyone will know it. It is no wonder the grades are better.

HINTS FOR USING TEAM-BASED LEARNING

I have often been asked by faculty how much time it takes to prepare for a team-based learning class. My answer is that if you are devising a new course, then you will need to put in the same amount of effort to prepare either the lectures or team-based learning material. There is a huge investment of time required either way. On the other hand, if you have been teaching a lecture course for years and have the bulk of the work done, then there is a large extra investment of time needed to convert to team-based learning. You must create RATs and applica-

tions for every class. Lots of teachers understandably balk at this. Furthermore, you might even have to create original written material for the students to read. Textbook readings are not designed for teaching using this approach. When using the lecture method, we are apt to give assigned readings in almost a casual way, more as an enrichment than as a central part of the learning. The content or the quality of the chapters doesn't necessarily have to be right on target. In contrast, in team-based learning, in which the students must get everything from their reading materials, such an approach will not work. As a result, many of us find we must write our own text material to get the job done right or at least we must write study guides to aid the students as they wade through a morass of text material. This takes a lot of time.

Fortunately, there are some helpful ways to survive without the heroic effort of rewriting the text. In evolutionary biology, I use a commercial textbook. Consequently, I take special care to provide a detailed list of important key points that the students must know in the assigned reading. For each chapter I give them a printed list with three columns. Its headings read: "Must Know," "Good to Know," and "Nice to Know." Under each heading I list the appropriate key words and concepts, depending on their level of importance. Students pay close attention to these helpful signposts while doing their reading. I also place the lists on my course website, where students may take practice quizzes on the reading. In a similar fashion, I have heard of a physics instructor who produces an audiotape reading guide for his text that the students listen to at the start of their reading and study sessions, and a statistics professor who uses web-based problem walk-through examples in his course. These aids are always helpful in any course, but particularly valuable when there are no lectures. Naturally, these guides have the added advantage that the students see that you really are earning your salary (something they are not always sure about when they see you standing by as they work feverishly in their groups).

Finally, let us turn to the problem(s) that bedeviled my son in his one and only foray into team-based learning. First, let me say that my son seemed like a natural for team-based learning. His undergraduate schooling was at St. Johns College where all of the classes were seminars. He had the patience of Job in helping students. Furthermore, he did not covet the lecture platform, nor was he concerned about relinquishing power in the classroom. He had no apparent barriers to a successful team-based learning experience. What was it then?

I think it was his lack of experience in the classroom. Here he was, a new instructor trying out a new method never seen before by him or his students. Not only was he facing the task of dealing with a new teaching style in which he had to give up a lot of authority to the students, but he did not have the depth of experience in dealing with the normal classroom problems. As a graduate student, he did not have the stature of a professor, nor was he considered by them a seasoned veteran. He did not have ready responses to such age-old questions as "I wasn't able to finish my homework. May I have an extension?" Or, "I have a conflict with the test time. May I take the test on another day?" Or, "What can I do for extra credit?" and "Are you going to curve the grades?" His uncertainty in how to deal with these problems as well as team-based learning produced an anxiety in him as well as in his students. He was vulnerable to attack by the students, who were not accustomed to working in groups and didn't know what group grading, individual grading, or peer evaluation were all about. His was a disastrous experience, and he has never tried to teach with team-based learning again.

It is not always that way with beginning teachers. I know of several young assistant professors who were so captivated by team-based learning that they immediately started using the method—successfully. It clearly depends on the person and the circumstances. The key variable seems to be how comfortable the instructor is

in being challenged by his students. There are veteran teachers who cannot abide it and there are those who thrive. Still, the bottom line is that I do think inexperienced teachers have a more difficult task in instituting team-based learning. They should be especially cautious in adopting it if they are in a school that is not tolerant of novel teaching or if their tenure depends on a high productivity in research.

IS TEAM-BASED LEARNING WORTH THE EFFORT?

The answer to whether team-based learning is worth the effort is obviously "yes" in my case. One great benefit for me in using team-based learning, or any other collaborative learning strategy, is that I get to know my students extraordinarily well. In a lecture course, I see the students sitting there taking notes as I pontificate on weighty matters. I assume all is well. I am doing a good job. All is right with the world. Then comes the exam. There are all those Fs and Ds. Well, I think, it was their fault: They were lazy or stupid. And yet?

In lecture classes, I generally did not see students as individuals. They were simply there—as an audience. All of this changed the moment I started using team-based learning. While students are working on their projects, I have plenty of time to observe every nuance of their interactions with the material and with each other. The openness of the classroom is much like a second-grade class in which a certain amount of chaos reigns. Students have less hesitancy to ask me questions or to approach me as a human being rather than as an authority figure. Not surprisingly, I get to know them; most are neither stupid nor lazy.

I began to have real fun in the classroom again. And that was not all. There were the better grades.

The better retention.

And they liked it—

a whole lot.

So did I.

REFERENCES

Dinan, F., and V. A. Frydrychowski. 1995. A team-based learning method for organic chemistry. *Journal of Chemistry Education 72:* 429–431.

Herreid, C. F. 1998. Why isn't cooperative learning used to teach science? *Bioscience 48:* 553–559.

Herreid, C. F. 1999. The bee and the groundhog: Lessons in cooperative learning—troubles with groups. *Journal of College Science Teaching 28*(4): 226–228.

An Application of Team Learning in Dental Education

By Frank A. Scannapieco and Clyde F. Herreid

While the most used teaching method in both basic science and preclinical dental curricula is the lecture, there has been significant widespread dissatisfaction with this learning format in professional education. While much material can be covered by lecturing, the assumption that students learn most lecture content may not be valid (Penner 1984). Learning by lecture is often passive and nonparticipatory. In this teacher-centered environment, students frequently do not achieve their full learning potential, do not learn how to learn, and do not become accustomed to working with their peers.

Despite these concerns, there are several reasons why the lecture has come to dominate professional education. The lecture format is convenient, efficient, and inexpensive to implement. One instructor can easily lecture to a class of 100–200 students, a class size typical of many American medical and dental schools. Unfortunately, most students tend to be passive participants in a lecture quietly taking notes and asking only an occasional question. Evaluation methods used in large lecture courses are mostly objective tests using questions of low intellectual order (e.g., testing the recall of facts or the comprehension of simple relationships).

Recognizing the deficiencies of the lecture format, many medical and dental schools are now searching for alternative teaching methods that promote "active learning" (Meyers and Jones 1993). Active learning methods involve students in the learning process by promoting participatory activities such as writing, problem solving, and discussion. Such activities provide frequent opportunities for students to explore their attitudes, values, and the limits of their knowledge and thus, their understanding of a subject (Bonwell and Eison 1991). One approach that has recently evolved to promote active learning in higher education is Team Learning (Michaelsen 1992). This model of cooperative learning assumes that students enter the classroom with a diversity of experience and knowledge. Rather than having the instructor present the entire course knowledge base to students, Team Learning attempts to construct a framework for learning that exploits the knowledge students already possess. This framework thus allows new knowledge to more likely become the student's own. Team Learning encourages student collaboration and cooperation through sharing of respective experiences and knowledge background as they master the course material.

A course organized for Team Learning exhibits a number of interesting features. These include the assignment of students to permanent heterogeneous groups; grading based on a combination of individual performance, group performance, and peer evaluation; and the use of the majority of class time in small group activities where students apply concepts by solving problems and analyzing case studies (Michaelsen 1992). Importantly, implementation of Team Learning requires relatively few faculty and a minimum of resources. This chapter describes our experience in applying the Team Learning method to an introductory course in clinical dentistry.

COURSE DESCRIPTION

"Introduction to Clinical and Preventive Dentistry" was taught during the fall 1993 semester to 77 first-year dental students. This course, which is assigned 2.5 semester hours of credit, is the first in a series of didactic and clinical courses in clinical and preventive dentistry. The broad objectives of this course were to (1) actively engage students in the acquisition of basic knowledge of oral health and disease; (2) provide experience in the recognition of oral health and disease; and (3) introduce fundamental clinical procedures designed to prevent disease and preserve oral health.

The topics presented in this course are listed in Table 1. This multidisciplinary content was chosen to provide the basic knowledge necessary for a student to manage a patient in the Preventive Dentistry Clinic the following semester. Note that the topics and reading material were integrated with group work and clinic activities. The coordination of didactic instruction and application-oriented group work is essential to the success of Team Learning.

This course had been taught for many years by the presentation of lectures followed by clinical exercises. For the fall 1993 semester, the course was reorganized using the Team Learning method as described by Michaelsen (1992). The class convened each week for a single, four-hour session. Ten groups of seven to eight students were formed, with an effort to make the groups heterogeneous with respect to previous college grade point average and gender. These groups met during the first two hours of each session for classroom work that typically introduced a concept, a problem, or a task relevant to clinical preventive dentistry (Table 1).

Each week, students prepared for class by studying an assigned reading of 10 to 20 pages usually prepared by the course instructors. Every classroom session began with a 10 to 15 objective question minitest that was based on the assigned reading. Minitest questions were written not only to assess student progress and to encourage student preparation, but also to emphasize the important issues relevant to the topic and to provide a focus for student group discussions. Upon completion of the minitest, each student handed in a completed computer-scorable answer sheet. The students then proceeded to take the same minitest with their assigned group members. Discussion of each question was encouraged so that a group consensus on the correct answers was reached. Each group then handed in a completed answer sheet reflecting the consensus. Both the individual and group minitests were corrected in class using an electronic scoring machine, and the corrected answer sheets were returned to the students immediately upon completion of the group test. The students then had the opportunity to review those questions that they answered incorrectly and were encouraged to appeal any questions they found to be ambiguous or factually incorrect. Written appeals were accepted from groups only, not from individuals. These appeals were acted upon by the instructor following class (this diminished the potential for arguments between students and instructor). The minitest process usually required 40–50 minutes to complete.

Didactic (Reading) Component	Clinical Exercise	Group Activity
Table 1. Content of the Course		
1. Introduction	Operation of the Dental Unit, Patient Positioning	
2. Infection Control, Instrument Handling	Infection Control Procedures Instrument Handling	
3. History and Physical Evaluation	Extra- and Intra-Oral Soft Tissue Examination, the Dental and Medical History	
4. Dental Plaque Formation: Detection and Control Oral Hygiene Techniques	Plaque Score, Oral Hygiene Techniques	
5. Dental Caries: Etiology and Role of Sucrose	Sucrose Intake Analysis	Epidemiology of Caries
6. Dental Caries Detection	Tooth Examination, DMFS, Dental Charting	Problems of Caries Detection
7. Periodontal Disease: Etiology and Classification	Gingival Score I, Periodontal Screening and Recording	Classification of Periodontal Diseases
8. Supragingival Scaling	Supragingival Scaling, Instrument Sharpening, Grasps	Typodont Scaling
9. Prevention of Caries: Fluorides and Sealants	Supragingival Tooth Scaling	Toxicity of Fluorides
10. Assessment of Caries and Periodontal Risk	Risk Assessment (Saliva Collection, Microbial Testing Demonstrations)	
11. Medical Considerations, Oral Cancer	Blood Pressure Measurement	Oral Cancer Case Conference
12. Introduction to Tobacco Cessation	Supragingival Tooth Scaling	Counseling for Tobacco Cessation
13. Case Presentation	Gingival Score II	Rampant Caries: Report of a case
14. Final Examination		

The minitest was followed by the application phase of Team Learning, a group activity or activities that attempted to relate the information learned through the readings and minitest to problems or tasks having clinical significance. These applications took various forms, all of which were designed to stimulate discussion of relevant concepts within the groups. For example, in one session a clinical case conference was held concerning a young woman who presented with rampant caries. The complete medical and dental history, projected clinical slides, and radiographs were presented to the student groups, who were then asked to describe the clinical findings, construct a problem list and develop a treatment plan. Another type of group activity involved the presentation of data (e.g., graphs or tables) from a recently published research paper. Students were asked to interpret the data, list conclusions, and critique the research design. Groups were always asked to hand in a summary of the group work, which formed the basis for group grading and which were returned to the group to provide feedback.

Each classroom session usually concluded with a 10 to 15 minute minilecture that summarized and highlighted the important points addressed during the day's activities described above. This time was also used to answer questions and provide clarification of important concepts. Throughout the course students kept their own records, including the individual and group scores. These records were remarkably accurate, with weekly audits finding no instances of faulty record keeping.

The second two hours each week were devoted to another type of application, the clinical exercises. Students within each group worked in pairs to practice the clinical procedures learned in the groups during the previous two-hour classroom session. In most cases, student pairs were asked to join their learning group at the end of each clinical exercise to discuss a clinical problem, report on a clinical finding, or compile a list of data they collected during the clinical exercise. For example, following their learning about caries detection and dental charting, each student was asked to provide data of the DMFT (Decayed, Missing, and Filled Teeth) scores for all group members. These data were then compiled into a group and class summary and distributed by the instructor the following week to share with the class as a basis for discussion of the caries prevalence of their cohort.

The final grade for the course was based on cumulative performance scores obtained from the weekly activities (75%) and on a final examination (25%). Grading for both the weekly activities and the final examination was based on three performance areas: individual performance, group performance, and peer assessment. At the beginning of the course the students were allowed to choose the relative weight that each performance area would contribute to the final grade. The class described here decided that the final grade would be composed of 20% individual performance, 60% group performance, and 20% student peer review.

Course Evaluation

To help determine their entering knowledge, students were asked at the beginning of the course to respond to a 50-item survey of dental knowledge. The survey sampled concepts and terminology randomly selected from the course content. Students were asked to indicate their level of understanding of each item, from complete unfamiliarity to good understanding of the concept. The items included in the survey ranged from highly specific subject matter pre-

sented in this course (e.g., xerostomia) to more general terms (e.g., dental caries). For comparative purposes, several items were included that were never mentioned during the course. For the 46 items covered in some fashion during the course, a mean of 22% of students indicated that they had at least a "pretty good understanding of the idea" before the start of the course. Following the course, this percentage increased to 83%. For four items never mentioned during the course, a precourse mean of 6% indicated a good understanding of the term or concept, while the average postcourse mean for these items was 13%.

A 10-item questionnaire was administered that gave the students the opportunity to provide feedback of this course (Table 2). All 77 students registered for the course responded to the questionnaire. Students' attitudes toward the course changed between the midterm and its completion. While many students were critical of the course at the midterm, by its end a majority of students seemed generally satisfied with the course. At midterm, an average of 37% of the students agreed with the statements listed in Table 2, whereas, 58% of the students on average agreed with these statements at the final examination. This improvement reflects Michaelson's experience, that the powerful features of Team Learning require time to be appreciated. The gradual acceptance may be especially pronounced among professional students, whose prior experiences center around attainment of individual success.

Students were also asked at the conclusion of the course what aspect of the course they liked most. Forty-seven of 77 reported they enjoyed the clinical experience, 14 endorsed the group learning method, and 10 felt that the weekly minitest stimulated their learning throughout the semester. Students were also asked to list aspects of the course they felt needed improvement. Significant problems cited included too few instructors in the clinic (22 students made this comment, probably because only four instructors were available to supervise 77 students); the need for more clearly written course materials (noted by 21 students); the cramped and poorly ventilated classroom (eight students); ambiguity with written test questions (seven students); and improper sequencing of lectures and testing (five students). None of these complaints criticized the Team Learning method per se; rather, they centered on deficiencies in staffing and the physical infrastructure.

The same final 3Q-question, multiple-choice test given to students taught by the lecture method during the fall 1992 semester was given to the class taught during fall 1993 semester by Team Learning. The students in the 1992 class had a mean score of 79.18 (:t 9.42, S.D.), while the mean score for the 1993 class was 75.25 (:t 8.77). This 4% difference, while found to be statistically significant (p<0.0001) when analyzed by student's t-test, is consistent with Michaelson's previous experience that there is little difference in performance among students taught by Team Learning and lecture method. However, performance in standardized objective testing should not be the only criterion by which learning is measured. Retention of information long after the course has ended, commitment to the subject discipline, increased tolerance for diversity of opinion, development of critical-thinking skills, and improvements in interpersonal skills can and should also be benchmarks of successful learning (Johnson, Johnson, and Smith 1991). Although difficult to quantify, we did note improvements for all of these areas in our students during the course of the semester.

While attendance at lectures at the start of the 1992 course, as in previous years, was observed to be 100%, it gradually diminished so that by the last week of the course only about 50% of the students regularly attended class. In sharp contrast, student attendance under the Team Learning format was 100% throughout the semester. The weekly minitest no doubt

Table 2. Results of Midterm and Final Course Critique				
	Percent of Students who			
	agree or strongly agree with the statement		disagree or strongly disagree with the statement	
	Midterm	Final	Midterm	Final
1. This course seemed well planned and organized.	21	52	56	44
2. The course goals and objectives were clear to me.	29	64	33	39
3. The course policies, procedures, and requirements were clear to me.	52	59	38	39
4. The readings used in this course were helpful to my learning.	23	72	57	47
5. The clinic component of this course was helpful to my learning.	72	68	15	43
6. The workload required for this course was manageable.	80	79	12	6
7. The instructional format used in this course facilitated my learning.	12	41	59	8
8. The course promoted my critical thinking and problem-solving through active learning.	31	57	43	43
9. The student evaluations (test, quizzes, projects, etc.) were fair and reflected the course objectives.	7	51	81	16
10. Overall, I feel that I learned much in this course.	37	77	21	18

motivated students to attend class, as did peer pressure. It is also possible that students found the course to be more interesting, involving, and enjoyable when taught by Team Learning than did the students who took the lecture-based course. Our experience is consistent with other Team Learning courses in particular and cooperative learning in general (Michaelsen 1992; Johnson, Johnson, and Smith 1991).

As a result of the weekly minitest, most students appeared to come well prepared to each class. This preparation resulted in an observable increase in the number and quality of questions asked by the students in contrast to questions asked by students in the prior year's lecture course. In the lecture setting, students' questions were found to be considerably fewer in number and usually asked for repetition of a concept or fact. Again, the observed increase in the quantity and quality of student questioning is the norm for cooperative learning (Johnson, Johnson, and Smith 1991).

Much better student performance was observed during the clinical activities under Team Learning. In prior years, most students would attend clinic sessions, but would tend to rush through the exercises to complete them as quickly as possible. Students taught by Team Learning spent more time in clinic, seemed to be better prepared for each session, and were very enthusiastic and interested in the activities. This observation is consistent with that of Johnson, Johanson, and Smith (1991) who reported that over 600 studies collectively show that collaborative learning enhances long-term interest in course subject, in contrast to individual-centered classes.

DISCUSSION

Team Learning represents a promising approach to promote active learning for courses in clinical dentistry. The Team Learning method has many strengths when compared to alternative active learning methods of instruction. Laboratory exercises, which can promote active learning, require considerable faculty participation, costly supplies, and teaching space to implement. Case presentations, which can be very effective in challenging students to use their knowledge, are best implemented with a relatively small class size and require considerable instructor expertise in this teaching method. Problem-based learning, currently in vogue at several medical and dental schools, requires many instructors, extensive instructor training, and the availability of an appropriate number of classrooms and other resources. Many of the effective aspects of these methods can easily be incorporated into the Team Learning approach during the application phase of instruction.

There are several caveats inherent to the implementation of Team Learning that should be pointed out. It is of paramount importance to accurately define the learning objectives for each unit of instruction and to choose (or write) succinct readings that accurately fulfill these objectives. Construction of weekly minitests and group activities can be quite laborious and time consuming. Consideration of appeals can also take considerable time, especially if there are many student groups and if minitest questions are poorly written. The design of effective applications requires considerable creativity and a perception for real-world problems that students will

encounter. It is imperative that any course utilizing Team Learning be well structured, with minitest and group activities reasonably paced and all of the students' time accounted for. Given these caveats, Team Learning can provide an exciting approach to implement active learning strategies. This learning format seems well-suited to dental education, since the goal is often to apply principles toward the performance of specific tasks rather than to simply learn concepts in the abstract. Perhaps most importantly, Team Learning encourages cooperation and the development of interpersonal skills, traits important to the successful practice of dentistry.

ACKNOWLEDGMENTS

Dr. Ernest Hausmann originally developed the precursor of this course in preventive dentistry. His contributions and encouragement over the years are greatly appreciated. We also thank Dr. Jeffrey Hollway for his critical review of the manuscript.

REFERENCES

Bonwell, C. C., and J. A. Eison. 1991. *Active learning: Creating excitement in the classroom.* Washington, DC: George Washington University, School of Education and Human Development.

Johnson, D. W., R. T. Johnson, and K. A. Smith. 1991. *Cooperative learning.* Washington, DC: George Washington University, School of Education and Human Development.

Meyers, C., and T. Jones. 1993. The case for active learning. In *Promoting active learning: Strategies for the college classroom*, eds. C. Meyers, and T. Jones, 3–17. San Francisco: Jossey-Bass.

Michaelsen, L. K. 1992. Team learning: A comprehensive approach for harnessing the power of small groups in higher education. *To Improve the Academy* 11:107–122.

Penner J. 1984. *Why many college teachers cannot lecture.* Springfield, IL: Thomas.

Of Mammoths and Men

A Case Study in Extinction

By Nancy A. Schiller and Clyde Freeman Herreid

The recent discovery of a mammoth frozen in the Siberian tundra is the backdrop for this case study, which explores the various theories for the extinction of the great Ice Age mammals and Homo neanderthalensis. Students research evidence for and against the various hypotheses and then meet in class to discuss the merits of each.

RAISING THE DEAD

The 26-ton ice block containing the frozen carcass of the mammoth was safely set down on the airport tarmac. The helicopter, which had lifted the mammoth out of its snowy grave in the Taimyr peninsula of Siberia and flown it over 200 miles to Khatanga, landed a few minutes later. A small group of reporters stood nearby, huddled against the cold. They had been awaiting the arrival of the expedition's leader. Now they surged forward to question him.

"Are you claiming this as some sort of scientific first?" asked one of the reporters.

"Maybe not a scientific first," replied Derek, the leader of the recovery team. "But if this mammoth is intact and its internal organs have been preserved, it will be a significant find."

"Why is that? What do you hope to learn from a mammoth frozen in the ground for more than 20,000 years?" asked another reporter.

"We could learn a great deal—not only about its anatomy and physiology, but also about the time and place in which it lived and maybe how it died. The extinction of the woolly mammoth, in fact the mass extinction of all the large Ice Age mammals at the end of the Pleistocene, is the subject of intense controversy among scientists. Some believe they were hunted to extinction. Others think they were killed off by a rapid change in climate or a deadly virus. This mammoth may provide us with clues to that mystery. Of course, we're also interested in the mammoth because of the role it played in the evolution of modern man."

"You spoke of clues just now. What kind of clues?" asked a reporter from the Associated Press.

"Pollen in the mammoth's hair and the permafrost surrounding it could provide us with insights into the type of vegetation in Siberia 20,000 years ago, but also possibly verify the mammoth's cause of death. Right now we are speculating that this animal crashed through the ice and either drowned or starved to death, trapped in a crevasse.

"Its teeth and tusks can provide us with other clues. The teeth can help us estimate the age of the animal. And the rings on the tusks, although they may not strictly speaking reflect annual growth like tree rings, can tell us something about how healthy the animal was during its lifetime and the environmental conditions in which it lived. Faster growth would indicate times of plenty, and slower growth times of food scarcity.

"Then there are the internal organs. Its stomach is likely to contain what it ate just before it died. Sixty-five percent of the plants in the diet of Siberian mammoths match up to the fossilized pollen at mammoth sites in Utah, down to the family level. It looks like they were eating the same things and that mammoths ate fairly specific foods. This may have something to do with the extinction of mammoths in Siberia, where the grasslands turned to wetlands when the Ice Age ended."

"What are you going to do with the carcass?" interrupted the AP reporter.

"We're going to keep it frozen in an ice cave here in Khatanga, where we plan to study it as we slowly thaw it out. It's going to be a slow process, but we'll be sure to keep the press up-to-date on our progress," said Derek.

A DEADLY DUET OF EVOLUTION AND EXTINCTION

"So, you would like to know what the woolly mammoth has to do with the evolution of man." Derek was inside one of the airport hangars having a cup of coffee with a journalist who had stayed on after the press conference. "What paper are you with?"

"I don't work for a newspaper. My name is Michael Shreve. I'm a science writer. My publisher sent me. We think there might be a book in all of this."

Derek sipped his coffee and then said, "Well, humans and mammoths go back a long way—and they both have their beginnings in Africa. The ancestors of woolly mammoths probably split off from the ancestors of today's African and Asian elephants 5 million years ago, about the time of the rise of the first hominids. Then, around 3 to 2.5 million years ago, the first mammoths appeared in Europe. Eventually their range extended from the British Isles to eastern Siberia, and from there into North and South America."

"I understand they were specialized for the cold," interjected Michael.

"Yes, they were. They had a thick skin and a heavy, woolly coat. When we dug this one out of the permafrost we were able to see and touch its hair, which was golden brown in color. The woolly mammoth also had small ears and a small tail to conserve body heat. It was highly specialized for the Ice Age world, like the Neanderthals they shared that world with. But, by the end of the Pleistocene, both the Neanderthals and the mammoths had disappeared. I should add that other large animals of the period went extinct, too, including mastodons, woolly rhinos, and the giant ground sloth. So did their predators, like the saber-toothed tiger and the cave bear."

"Who, or should I say what, survived?" asked Michael.

"Middle-sized and smaller animals. And man, of course. Modern man, that is. Homo sapiens. But keep in mind that the disappearance of the Ice Age mega-fauna didn't just happen in Eurasia. It was repeated around the globe, in North and South America—and in Australia, too. Some of the large flightless birds, like the giant moa, also died out during this period."

"But what has all this got to do with humans?" Michael asked.

"For humanity, the Ice Age was the 'crucible of evolution,' as one paleontologist has rather poetically put it. It was the time of our origins. At the start we're Australopithecines—ape-like creatures living in Africa. At the end of the Ice Age, only 10,000 years ago, we're humans, Homo sapiens, living on every continent except Antarctica.

"According to that same paleontologist, the Pleistocene was the backdrop against which a 'deadly duet of evolution and extinction' first played itself out between humans and elephants. That humans were responsible, at least in part, for the demise of the large mammals of the Ice Age ought not to surprise us. There are several modern cases in which overhunting by man has nearly exterminated a species. You're an American. Think of the American bison. And the problem continues today for African rhinos and for the mammoth's closest living relatives, Asian and African elephants."

"So, what's the mystery then? It was us—we brought about the mammoth's demise, right?" said Michael.

"Not necessarily," replied Derek. "Mass extinctions are complex phenomena. As the ice retreated at the end of the Pleistocene, the plant communities upon which mammoths depended became increasingly fragmented, less diverse, and less able to support a variety of animals. Many scientists believe that mammoths may have been in decline during the last four millennia of the Pleistocene and that the change to a warmer climate, combined with the stress of predation by man, pushed them over the edge."

In the Crucible of Evolution

"You mentioned the Neanderthals earlier. What about them?" Michael inquired.

"Ah, for that I'll have to turn you over to our visiting physical anthropologist." Derek called toward the back of the hangar: "Hey, Susan, I have a journalist over here asking about Neanderthals, your great Ice Age hunter. Can you field some questions from him?"

"Sure," said Susan, as she joined the two men at the table. "What would you like to know?"

"To begin with, who were the Neanderthals? What were they like?" asked Michael.

"Maybe I should start by saying that we know what we know about them primarily from studying the fossil record, though techniques used in molecular biology have recently begun to provide us with some new information." With a wry look at Derek, Susan added, "We can't hope to find a Neanderthal preserved in the permafrost like Derek here with his frozen woolly mammoth, you know."

Susan continued. "I'll give you my minilecture, okay? The first Neanderthal specimen recovered was found in 1856 in a cave in the Neander Valley in Germany. The fossilized remains of several hundreds of individuals have been discovered since then. Based on the current evidence, they flourished in Europe and Western Asia from about 150,000 to 30,000 years ago. For a long time we thought that they lived until about 35,000 years ago, but recent discoveries have pushed that date back, suggesting they may have survived up until 28,000 years ago."

"Derek mentioned earlier that they were specialized for the cold," Michael said.

"Yes, they were the first humans to live in Ice Age conditions, surviving by hunting—some say by scavenging—the big Pleistocene mammals, including the woolly mammoth. Like the woolly mammoth, they were built for the cold—short and stocky with strong powerful limbs and jaws. We know they fashioned tools out of stone and clothing from animal skins, and that they used fire and lived in caves."

"I grew up in New York City," Michael interrupted, "and I remember that the natural history museum had an exhibit on the Neanderthals that made them look like the stereotypical caveman—stupid and savage."

"I know. They've since revamped that. You should see how different it is now."

"But I've read that the Neanderthals were incapable of symbolic thought and that they didn't have any culture to speak of—at least not compared with early moderns," countered Michael.

"Oh, I don't know about that," said Susan. "Their average brain size, you know, was slightly larger than ours. There is evidence that they buried their dead. And some of them lived to middle age and older, a few with crippling diseases or injuries, suggesting that the old and sick were not cast out but were cared for."

"Were Neanderthals some sort of intermediate form in the evolution of modern man then?" asked Michael.

"I'm sure you know there are different theories. Some scientists believe they're a closely related subspecies of modern human, which would make them *Homo sapiens neanderthalensis* to our *Homo sapiens sapiens*. Others think that they represent a side branch of *Homo erectus*, related but not ancestral to modern humans. We do know that Neanderthals and modern man lived at the same time for about 5,000 to 10,000 years in Europe. In the Middle East, the fossil record suggests they coexisted for much longer. So, some people argue that if they lived together, they must have exchanged culture, at least traded with one another, maybe even interbred."

"What happened to them?" asked Michael.

"We're not really sure. *Homo sapiens* migrated to Europe and then from there to Asia somewhere between 40,000 and 30,000 years ago. Five thousand to 10,000 years later, the Neanderthals disappeared. Their disappearance may have been due to the dramatic changes in climate at the end of the Pleistocene. Or maybe with our more sophisticated tools and culture we simply 'outhunted' them, outcompeted them. I think there's a good chance we killed them off—you know, genocide. Of course, there's a more benign view that they 'disappeared' because they became us, through interbreeding. What we do know is that the Neanderthals, like the woolly mammoth, pass into history—or rather prehistory—at the end of the Pleistocene, until their bones are discovered tens of thousands of years later and scientists begin to piece together for the first time ideas about the extinction—and evolution—of species."

Teaching Notes

This case was developed for use in a general biology course that includes a section on evolution. Instructors of courses in anthropology and paleontology might also find it appropriate. We have used it in a freshman evolutionary biology course as the last case in the term after studying the general principles of evolution, genetics, and biodiversity.

Objectives

To examine

- the general principles and causes of extinction;
- possible causes for the extinction of

mammoths, especially the "overkill" hypothesis and the climate change hypothesis;

- possible causes for the extinction of the Neanderthals, especially the replacement hypothesis and the interbreeding hypothesis;
- the recent phylogeny of humans;
- the differences between speculation and evidence;
- the ways of marshalling evidence in support of an argument; and
- the relative merit of fossil versus DNA evidence.

BLOCKS OF ANALYSIS

The theme of this case is extinction. Within that overall theme, the major thrusts of this case fall along two lines: What happened to the mammoths? What happened to the Neanderthals?

Mammoths. When we taught this case study in the summer of 2000, the focus was on the problem of what happened to the Neanderthals. Mammoths were a side issue, although in another setting they could be the dominant focus.

The woolly mammoth, like the Neanderthal, is one of the quintessential symbols of the Ice Age. Tall and shaggy with a hump back and tusks that twist in an upward spiral, it ranged over northern parts of Eurasia and North America. It was hunted for food and clothing by early humans, who also used its bones and tusks as building materials.

The case opens with the actual recent discovery of a woolly mammoth carcass frozen in the Siberian tundra. The dramatic recovery in the fall of 1999 of the Jarkov mammoth (named for the nomadic reindeer herder who originally found it) was the subject of numerous news stories and articles as well as a two-hour Discovery Channel television special. Although not the first discovery of its kind, the Jarkov mammoth was believed to be in-

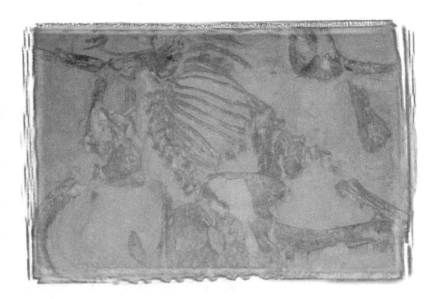

tact and its internal organs preserved.

Mammoths figure in this case in a number of ways. As a food source for early humans in Eurasia, scientists have speculated that their availability—and eventual disappearance—may have played a role in the extinction of the Neanderthal as well as the evolution and development of modern man. In addition, it has been hypothesized that mammoths along with other large Ice Age mammals became extinct because they were overhunted by humans (the "overkill" hypothesis), although other scientists argue that climate shifts that occurred during the Late Pleistocene as the Ice Age was coming to a close led to the mammoth's extinction.

Whatever the cause of their demise, mammoths and Neanderthals are linked in the minds of many experts, if for no other reason than that they lived at the same place and time and both became extinct. The dramatic discovery and recovery of the Jarkov mammoth, then, provides a hook into the case at the same time it helps to set the stage for exploring the causes, questions, and controversies concerning the extinction of species.

Neanderthals. The central focus when we taught the case was "What happened to the

Neanderthals?" Originally cast as a stooped, shuffling, ape-like brute, we now know that the large-brained Neanderthals successfully occupied Europe and western Asia for over 200,000 years, surviving the bitter cold of the Ice Age and the daily vicissitudes of prehistoric life. Once thought too stupid and too slow to do more than scavenge for food, recent evidence from Croatia indicates that they were skilled hunters able to kill large animals, including rhinos. Analysis of animal and human remains as well as stone and bone tools found in a cave in Croatia inhabited by Neanderthals suggests that they hunted medium to large mammals.

There are two general hypotheses put forward on the extinction of the Neanderthals:

1. They were eliminated by either indirect competition or "war" with the more advanced *Homo sapiens*. The argument runs this way: Back in Africa at the time of *Homo erectus*, some populations of early humans migrated into Europe and Asia. There they developed into specialized regional populations. One line of *Homo erectus*, primarily in Europe, became specialized for surviving the cold and this group became the Neanderthals. They survived for hundreds of thousands of years, developing stone tools and a culture we can only guess at based upon scanty evidence, such as the presence of fossilized pollen at sites where their remains have been found, suggesting to some that they buried their dead with flowers.

Meanwhile, back in Africa about 200,000 years ago, *Homo erectus* gave rise to *Homo sapiens*. One or more populations of *Homo sapiens* migrated from Africa into Europe and Asia (and eventually beyond). They reached the areas inhabited by the Neanderthals. In some regions it appears that they displaced Neanderthals; in others, such as in Spain, they apparently lived side by side for at least 10,000 years before the Neanderthals disappeared.

Several theories have been put forward (again with scanty evidence to support them) to explain how *Homo sapiens* may have caused the Neanderthals' demise: *Homo sapiens* may have outcompeted Neanderthals with their more sophisticated technology and advanced hunting skills or via faster breeding and greater longevity; diseases carried by *Homo sapiens* may have eliminated the Neanderthals; or *Homo sapiens* may have waged "war" against the Neanderthals, annihilating them.

2. The second major hypothesis is that Neanderthals and *Homo sapiens* interbred and became modern humans. (Before we had such clear evidence of the two groups living together, an earlier version of this hypothesis was that Neanderthals were a direct ancestor of *Homo sapiens*.) Two lines of evidence are used to bolster this "fusion" argument. First, that the two coexisted and thus may have traded with one another, perhaps even lived together, in which case why wouldn't they have interbred as well? Second, the recent discovery of the fossilized skeleton of a 24,500-year-old child in Portugal with apparently a mixture of Neanderthal and *Homo sapiens* traits suggests to some that they were interbreeding.

Strong counterevidence against this hypothesis has recently come to light. Mitochondrial DNA (mtDNA) isolated from the bones of the first Neanderthal fossil is sufficiently different from living moderns' mtDNA, convincing many scientists that modern humans are unlikely to be descendants of the Neanderthals. However, the researchers who conducted the mtDNA studies have themselves cautioned that the results come from a single individual and that the Neanderthals may have contributed other genes to modern man. Proponents of this hypothesis agree, maintaining that Neanderthal genes may not have persisted to the present time but were there in the beginnings of modern man's evolutionary history.

CLASSROOM MANAGEMENT

This case was handled in one 80-minute class period. The class was small, consisting of 20 students who were divided into four groups of five students each. The groups were permanent throughout the term and were well acquainted with group work.

This course is the first semester of a general biology sequence. In the summer it is taught using team learning, a technique devised by Larry Michaelsen of the University of Oklahoma (see Michaelson, L. K., 1992, Team learning: A comprehensive approach for harnessing the power of small groups in higher education. *To Improve the Academy* 11:107-122). No lectures are given. Instead, students have reading assignments and take both individual and group quizzes based on the reading. They then work on case studies that pertain to the reading.

This case was the culmination of a section on human evolution. In preparation for the case, the students had read a chapter detailing hominid and primate phylogeny, with the following question posed: "What happened to the Neanderthals?" In the laboratory preceding the case (see *http://ublib.buffalo.edu/libraries/projects/casesmissing_link_ intro.html*), students in their groups examined a large number of primate skulls and were asked to make up a phylogeny based upon their observations. At the end of this lab, the case was handed out to the students with instructions that they were to research individually the various hypotheses that had been suggested to account for the disappearance of the Neanderthals. They were told to list the hypotheses and give evidence for and against each one. Also, they were told to be ready to discuss these at the next class period.

During the next class, after the daily quizzes were given, we asked the students in their groups to compare notes and discuss the relative merits of the different hypotheses about the Neanderthals. After about 15 minutes, we then had student scribes from each team write

down all possible hypotheses on the board. They listed about eight. Among these were: "*Homo sapiens* exterminated the Neanderthals," "Neanderthals evolved into *Homo sapiens*," "Climate changes killed off the Neanderthals," "*Homo sapiens* outcompeted the Neanderthals," and "Neanderthals and *Homo sapiens* interbred," as well as a few "fringe" theories, such as "Neanderthals were still living." We then asked the groups to choose the hypothesis that most appealed to them (each group had to choose a different hypothesis) and gave them about five minutes to marshal evidence in support of their chosen hypothesis.

Next, we ran a discussion, listing on the board for each of the four hypotheses the groups' assertions and their evidence for these, allowing other groups to challenge the points made. This lasted about 30 minutes, although more time should have been allotted to develop these ideas more fully.

At this point we asked the students to imagine that an isolated group of Neanderthals had been found. We asked them: "What do you think we should do with them? Put them in zoos? Use them in experiments? Enroll them in our schools? (After all, they appear to be a different species.) Study them? (Suppose they didn't want to be studied?)."

After posing these questions, we gave the groups five minutes to think of a series of questions they would like to know the answers to before making a decision about the fate of the surviving Neanderthals. We then let each group ask us, the experts, their questions. The questions they asked had to do with culture, diet, cognitive abilities, language, and whether or not they could mate with us and produce viable offspring. After a couple of question-and-answer rounds, we asked the class to vote on the choices.

Students can earn up to 25 points of extra credit if they write a dialogue paper on the disappearance of the Neanderthals. Writing a good dialogue requires students to have a firm grasp of the facts and simultaneously understand several sides of a sensitive and controversial issue. We find that this kind of an assignment is a good way of stimulating critical thinking. The paper must follow a particular format: it must be at least five typewritten, double-spaced pages and in the form of a dialogue between two people arguing on opposite sides of the question. In addition, it must be written in the form of a script or play. For example,

Sam: Shirley, did you see that TV report about the recent discovery that Neanderthal DNA is quite different than that of modern humans? That just about cinches it; clearly they became extinct and didn't just interbreed with *Homo sapiens.*

Shirley: Look, a single sample of a tiny DNA fragment doesn't prove anything. The DNA has been around thousands of years and could have been contaminated, and we don't have a clue as to the variability of the DNA of Neanderthals. I still say that Neanderthals simply merged with *Homo sapiens.* There certainly isn't any reason to believe that modern humans killed them off.

Students are instructed that there should be at least 20 exchanges between the peo-

ple speaking, i.e., as shown in the example above, Sam should speak at least 20 times and Shirley should speak at least 20 times. The exchanges must be serious, substantive, and courteous comments made between two intelligent people grappling with an important issue. A short introductory paragraph is required indicating where the dialogue is occurring and what the circumstances surrounding the discussion are. In addition, the paper must end with a paragraph in which the student gives his or her personal opinion and the reasons behind it. The paper is graded primarily on the basis of the number of issues explored and the depth of the coverage.

NOTE

When we taught this case we didn't give the students references but told them to search the library and the internet for information. Citations to a number of articles you might want to give your students to get them started researching these topics can be found online at *http://ublib.buffalo.edu/libraries/projects/cases/mammothnotes.html*. References for instructors can also be found at that URL.

Section XI

Large Class Methods

It is tough to run discussions in large classes, i.e., classes with over a hundred students. Even though some teachers have heroically struggled to overcome the limitations of fixed-seat amphitheaters, for most of us a large class means that we have no choice but to lecture. Interactive classes and case studies seem to be impossible. Where can you even begin? Here we argue that all is not lost—clicker cases are the future.

"Clicker" Cases

Introducing Case Study
Teaching Into Large Classrooms

By Clyde Freeman Herreid

Case study teaching is difficult in large classes, especially in fixed-seat amphitheaters. The development of audience response systems, or "clickers," for use in classrooms has opened up exciting new possibilities for creating and implementing interactive case studies, particularly in large introductory science courses.

Large numbers of students do not like science (Seymour and Hewitt 1997; Kardash and Wallace 2001). Surely, this will come as no surprise. Most U.S. students receive their first college science training in large lecture classes in fixed-seat amphitheaters. A high proportion of these students withdraws or fails. Tobias (1990) found that science majors have a high tolerance for the cut-and-dried approach epitomized by most lecture styles—facts, facts, and more facts—whereas nonscience students are often bored to death, even though they may receive high grades. We know that the impersonal nature of the lecture, its lack of real-world application, and its prioritization of facts and memorization over critical analysis, synthesis, and discussion deter many bright students from a career in science.

Can we do anything to alter this state of affairs? Yes, if the following example is any indication. In his introductory astronomy class at the University of Colorado, Duncan (2005) reported that at the beginning of his course only 10–15% of students indicated that they liked science. He was able to modify the perceptions of most of them by strikingly reducing the traditional lecture component of the course and developing interactive exercises, demonstrations, and peer instruction. At the end of the course, Duncan again polled his students anonymously, and 80–90% had changed their views to a more positive opinion of science.

Reinforcing this observation that active learning strategies are important even in large classrooms, Hake (1998) reported the results of a study on 6,000 students in 62 introductory physics courses at different schools. Courses with active learning strategies were far superior in producing learning gains than traditional lectures. Indeed, the worst of the interactive courses did better than most of the lecture courses. Furthermore, there was little difference among lecturers, regardless of their perceived skill.

Clearly, case study teaching with its emphasis on active learning and problem solving within complex and real-world contexts has something to offer here. But we have to face facts. In spite of its demonstrated effectiveness in small classes and tutorials, the use of case studies in large classes is severely hampered. Discussion in such settings is often negligible. Typical question and answer interactions in large classrooms are often dominated by a small minority of students, and it is difficult and often impossible to hear a student speak in a large auditorium. Even discussions among student groups, one of the key techniques of many forms of case teaching including, for example, Problem-Based Learning, is restricted because of the fixed-seat amphitheaters that we use for large classes.

Large lecture classes are a fact of life in universities, especially in the introductory science courses. They are clearly cost effective. A single instructor can present material to hundreds of students at a time. Once lectures are prepared, only modest annual revisions are typically required. Multiple-choice exams (the normal testing procedure) are easy to concoct and readily available from textbook companies, and they are easy to grade via electronic scoring services available in universities.

But there are many well-documented disadvantages of large lecture classes including problems with attendance, discipline, learning, and the general alienation of students (Tobias 1990; Pinet 1995; DeCaprariis 1997; McConnell, Steer, and Owens 2003; Greer and Heaney 2004). Attendance in the normal lecture class frequently dips below 50%, and the percentage of students that drop introductory science courses or receive D or F grades is often 40% (Hatch, Jensen, and Moore 2005).

Attempts to offset the problems of lectures in large classes include using Think/Pair/Share, Just-In-Time Teaching, Peer Instruction, ConcepTests, computer-based instruction, recitation sections, case study teaching in lab sections, and more recently student response systems (Mazur 1997; Hatch, Jensen, and Moore 2005; Smith et al. 2005;

Twigg 1999). Some of these approaches show significant changes in student attitudes and learning gains. The critical feature in these positive experiences is that the instructors are using feedback systems that transform the classroom into an interactive experience. Mazur, teaching physics at Harvard, argues that his 10-year experience using Peer Instruction does not depend on a particular feedback method (Crouch and Mazur 2001). *Interactive feedback* is the key. It is the feedback pedagogy that is the driving force for success, not the particular technological method involved (Byrd, Coleman, and Werneth 2004; Draper, Cargill, and Cutts 2002; Judson and Sawada 2002). Nonetheless, today we have a new feedback system—"clickers." They are practical and economical. And their use allows us to effectively introduce case study teaching into large classrooms.

CLICKERS IN THE CLASSROOM

Student response systems, audience response keyboards, or "clickers," as they are often called, have been commercially available for the past 15 years, although they were preceded by fixed electronic response systems (Judson and Sawada 2002). Made famous by their use in the TV quiz show *Who Wants to Be a Millionaire?*, clickers are rapidly infiltrating higher education classrooms. They provide instant feedback to students and faculty regardless of the size of the class, and have a clear value in socialization, making impersonal classes more intimate. The technology also seems to resonate with students' fascination with interactive media.

For years, some instructors have attempted to garner responses to questions by asking students to hold up their hands, say in ConcepTests, as used in Peer Instruction (Mazur 1997). Unfortunately, students regularly alter their votes in front of their peers. This problem is avoided when clickers are used, as they are perceived to be anonymous, making it possible to collect more accurate data in the classroom. If truly anonymous results are desired, the instructor can ask students to switch devices with their neighbor.

Clickers are similar to a TV or stereo remote control with numbered buttons that students can push to register their votes. Typically students respond to questions framed in a multiple-choice format. Transmitted by either infrared or radio frequency signal, a receiver picks up the answers and then relays them to a classroom computer. The results can be immediately displayed as a chart on the computer screen and projected for the class. The data can be stored and retrieved later, either as an anonymous record or by identification with a personal ID (Greer and Heaney 2004).

The appropriate and successful use of clicker technology is associated with a variety of educational and psychological theories. Its use has been linked to increased attention (Jackson and Trees 2003; Horowitz 1988), which facilitates long-term memory storage. The recent success of clickers has been attributed to a shift from usage grounded in behavioral learning theories to that which encourages individual and social constructivist learning environments (Crouch and Mazur 2001; Draper, Cargill, and Cutts 2002; Dufresne et al. 1996; Judson and Sawada 2002; Roschelle, Penuel, and Abrahamson 2004). Research on various forms of instructional feedback, all of which can be provided by clicker systems, has indicated direct relationships between feedback and improved student learning (Guthrie and Carlin 2004). It has also been argued that clicker use improves motivation (Crouch and Mazur 2001), which may lead to cognitive persistence (Dufresne et al. 1996) and increased mastery goal setting (Roschelle, Penuel, and Abrahamson 2004).

In his book *Clickers in the Classroom: How to Enhance Science Teaching Using Classroom Response Systems*, Duncan (2005) lists 11 ways faculty use clickers: to measure what students know prior to instruction (i.e., preassessment); to measure student attitudes; to find out if students have done the reading; to get students to confront misconceptions; to transform the way they do demonstrations; to increase students' retention of the material they have been taught; to test students' understanding; to make some kinds of assessment easier; to facilitate testing of conceptual material; to facilitate discussion and peer instruction; and to increase class attendance.

Fundamentally, clickers are used in two different ways: either by individuals or by small groups of students. When individuals use them, either the school loans them out or instructors require that students purchase them from the bookstore. If being used by a group, they are handed out each class period and retrieved at the end of the session, as done at the University of Georgia (Brickman 2005).

There are few formal assessments on the use of student response systems because they are new on the educational scene. Nonetheless, some results are available (Judson and Sawada 2002; Greer and Heaney 2004; Hatch, Jensen, and Moore 2005; Duncan 2005), from which we have learned the following:

- Student enthusiasm for clickers is high. Whether it is their novelty or actual educational value is not clear. Nonetheless, students, particularly in large science classes, report they enjoy using them and believe they help them understand the material and prepare for exams.
- Student attendance is strikingly improved, changing from below 50% in the lecture method to over 80% when clickers are used. This observation is confounded because many instructors give points for attendance, which can now be closely monitored. Nonetheless, because grades are strongly correlated with attendance, this effect must be applauded.
- Student learning appears improved (although this may be because of their

novelty, as in the well-known Hawthorne Effect).

- Faculty enthusiasm is high, at least for those individuals willing to experiment.
- Student apathy is much less evident.

The disadvantages are several:

- There is a steep learning curve for faculty as they negotiate the "ins" and "outs" of the clicker software. Like any classroom technique, clickers can be used well or poorly. In a study at the University of Massachusetts, students' ratings of professors improved as professors became more experienced (Duncan 2005). So any project using clicker technology must have a training period associated with it.
- Clickers are particularly effective for eliciting responses to questions at the lower level of Bloom's (1956) taxonomy where questions involving facts are involved. With care, critical-thinking questions can be devised that focus on synthesis, evaluation, and analysis. However, designing effective clicker questions at the highest levels of Bloom's taxonomy requires significant creativity and time.
- The technology can be problematic, especially for large classes and when using infrared systems; these difficulties are largely eliminated with radio frequency.
- Cheating (one student bringing a friend's clicker to class) can occur and must be strongly discouraged and penalized.
- Rules and strategies must be established for lost, forgotten, or inoperable clickers; usually dropping the clicker scores for three to four classes out of the total will take care of the problem.
- The cost can be a deterrent as can be the storage of clickers. These potential difficulties can be minimized if students buy their clickers as part of the textbook package and are made responsible for them.
- Schools are scrambling to standardize their clicker systems so that students do not have to purchase multiple clickers for different classes. Five major clicker companies are competing for their share of the business: Turning Point, PRS (Personal Response System), CPS (Classroom Performance System), H-iTT (Hyper-interactive Teaching Technology), and Quizdom Student Response System.

The disadvantages of clickers are minor when compared to their advantages, hence their rapid assimilation into the nation's classrooms. In the near future, electronic response systems will rapidly improve to allow students to do more than answer multiple-choice questions; ideally, they will permit a student in the middle of an amphitheater to speak or transmit their version of a graph or diagram. There are already prototype systems that use cell phones and others that use laptop and tablet PCs and PDAs as student input devices. We can expect these to become integrated with learning management and course management software (such as Blackboard or ANGEL) as we push the boundaries of classroom communication systems (Beatty 2004). Thus, clickers are merely a first step to using interactive techniques with case study teaching in large classes.

CLICKER CASES

The ongoing evolution of personal response systems has made it feasible to marry interactive and case study teaching methods, producing what we call "clicker cases."

We have found one method of case teaching in particular to be ideally suited for use with clickers. Called the Interrupted Case Method (Herreid 2005), the case is delivered in parts, or stages. After each stage, students are asked to respond to questions posed by the professor. The method mimics what real scientists experience as they work their way through a problem—they identify key questions, develop hypotheses, design ways to test them, gather data, and draw conclusions, in an iterative process, refining their thinking about how to attack the problem as more information becomes available. Moreover, this method of teaching cases has been shown to be the most popular among science faculty (Yadav et al. 2006).

The Interrupted Case Method has proved successful in small classes, but is difficult to administer in large fixed-seat amphitheaters. However, Brickman (2005) has had significant success, even in classes of several hundred, using permanent small groups and Team Learning (Michaelsen, Knight, and Fink 2004) with clickers. At the University at Buffalo, we have used the method with clickers with great success in a general biology class of 450 students.

The way that we have used it is simple: An instructor selects a topic, such as the HIV virus replication cycle. In class, the instructor takes students through a series of carefully developed scenarios drawn from students' texts and recent literature. At each stage, students are given information and asked to predict what might happen if such and such were done. As a hook into the problem, for example, the tragic story of tennis great Arthur Ashe, who contracted AIDS from a contaminated blood transfusion, is introduced. Also, some of the history and spread of the disease is presented.

With this as background, students are asked at what point scientists might attempt to interrupt the viral reproduction cycle. Students are shown a series of options and asked to vote using their clickers, with their choices displayed as a histogram on a PowerPoint slide to the whole class. They are told of one early attempt to control the disease using the drug AZT. Students are asked to predict what would happen if AZT were administered to a patient if the treatment worked, and shown a series of graphs following the number of virus particles

in the blood over time. Before voting, they can consult with their neighbors. The instructor, using a microphone, asks a few students their thoughts. After students vote, the real results are shown. Then another experimental scenario is presented, which continues the story line in our understanding of HIV.

It is important to emphasize that this case method integrates lecture material, case scenario material, student discussion with their neighbors, clicker questions, clarification of the answers, more lecture, and data. And the cycle is repeated. The data we have collected indicate that attendance jumps dramatically (90%) and students write that they greatly value this approach over the traditional lecture. Performance on critical-thinking questions also improves and class grades rise. Using clicker cases promises to offset many of the criticisms that have been leveled at science teaching, especially in large enrollment science courses, as it engages students in real-world problems and challenges them to think every step of the way.

REFERENCES

Beatty, I. 2004. Transforming student learning with classroom communication systems. *Educause Center for Applied Research (ECAR) Research Bulletin* ERB0403 2004 (3): 1–13. *http ://www.utexas.edu/academic/ cit/services/cps/ECARCRS.pdf.*

Bloom, B. 1956. *Taxonomy of educational objectives: Book 1, cognitive domain.* New York: Longman.

Brickman, P. 2005. Case studies in large-enrollment courses. Presentation at the Annual Conference on Case Study in Science, University at Buffalo, State University of New York.

Byrd, G., S. Coleman, and C. Werneth. 2004. Exploring the universe together: Cooperative quizzes with and without a classroom performance system in Astronomy 101. *Astronomy Education Review* 3 (1): 26–30. *http://aer.noao.edu/AERArticle.php?issue=5 &section=2&article=3.*

Crouch, C. H., and E. Mazur. 2001. Peer instruction: Ten years experience and results. *American Journal of Physics* 69 (9): 970–77.

DeCaprariis, P.P. 1997. Impediments to providing scientific literacy to students in introductory survey courses. *Journal of Geoscience Education* 45: 207–10.

Draper, S., J. Cargill, and Q. Cutts. 2002. Electronically enhanced classroom interaction. *Australian Journal of Educational Technology* 18 (1): 13–23.

Dufresne, R. J., W. J. Gerace, W. J. Leonard, J.P . Mestre, and L. Wenk. 1996. A classroom communication system for active learning. *Journal of Computing in Higher Education* 7: 3–47.

Duncan, D. 2005. *Clickers in the classroom: How to enhance science teaching using classroom response systems.* San Francisco: Pearson Education Addison Wesley and Benjamin Cummings.

Greer, L., and P. J. Heaney. 2004. Real time analysis of student comprehension: An assessment of electronic student response technology in an introductory earth science course. *Journal of Geoscience Education* 52 (4): 345–51.

Guthrie, R. W., and A. Carlin. 2004. Waking the dead: Using interactive technology to engage passive listeners in the classroom. Proceedings of the Tenth Americas Conference on Information Systems. New York, NY. *http://www.mhhe.com/cps/docs/CPSWP_WakindDead082003.pdf*

Hake, R. 1998. Interactive engagement versus traditional methods: A six-thousand student survey of mechanics test data for introductory physics courses. *American Journal of Physics* 66 (1): 64–74.

Hatch, J., M. Jensen, and R. Moore. 2005. Manna from heaven or "clickers" from hell: Experiences with an electronic response system. *Journal of College Science Teaching* 34 (7) :36–42.

Herreid, C.F. 2005. Mother always liked you best: Examining the hypothesis of parental favoritism. *Journal of College Science Teaching* 35 (2): 10–14.

Horowitz, H.M. 1988. Student response systems: Interactivity in a classroom environment. *http://www.qwizdom.com/download/interactivity_in_classrooms.pdf*

Jackson, M., and A. Trees. 2003. *Clicker implementation and assessment.* Boulder, CO: Information and Technology Services and Faculty Teaching Excellence Program, University of Colorado. *www.colorado.edu/ftep/ technology/FTEPMichele%20jack.pdf*

Judson, E., and D. Sawada. 2002. Learning from past and present: Electronic response systems in college lecture halls. *Journal of Computers in Mathematics and Science Teaching* 21 (2): 167–81.

Kardash, C.M., and M.L. Wallace. 2001. The perceptions of science classes survey: What undergraduate science reform efforts really need to address. *Journal of Educational Psychology* 93 (1): 199–210.

McConnell, D., D. Steer, and K. Owens. 2003. Assessment and active learning strategies for introductory geology courses. *Journal of Geoscience Education* 51: 205–16.

Mazur, E. 1997. *Peer instruction: A user's manual.* Upper Saddle River, NJ: Prentice Hall.

Michaelsen, L., A. Knight, and L. Fink, eds. 2004. *A transformative use of small groups in college teaching.* Sterling, VA: Stylus Publishing.

Pinet, P. R. 1995. Rediscovering geological principles by collaborative learning. *Journal of Geoscience Education* 43: 371–376.

Roschelle, J., W. R. Penuel, and L. Abrahamson. 2004. Classroom response and communication systems: Research review and theory. Paper presented at the 2004 Meeting of the American Educational Research Association, San Diego, CA.

Seymour, E., and N. M. Hewitt. 1997. *Talking about leaving: Why undergraduates leave science.* Boulder, CO: Westview Press.

Smith, A., R. Stewart, P. Shields, J. Hayes-Klosteridis, P. Robinson, and R. Yuan. 2005. Introductory biology courses: A framework to support active learning in large enrollment introductory science courses. *Cell Biology Education* 4 (2): 143–56.

Tobias, S. 1990. *They're not dumb, they're different: Stalking the Second Tier.* Tucson, AZ: Research Corporation.

Twigg, C. 1999. *Improving learning and reducing costs: redesigning large-enrollment courses.* Troy, NY: The Pew Learning and Technology Program. *http://www.thencat.org/Monographs/ImpLearn.html*

Yadav, A., M. Lundeberg, K. Dirkin, M. DeSchryver, N. Schiller, C. F. Herreid, and K. Maier. 2006. Teaching science with case studies—a national survey of faculty perceptions. Paper presented at the Annual Meeting of the American Educational Research Association, San Francisco, CA.

ACKNOWLEDGMENTS

The author thanks M. Lundeberg, M. DeSchryver, and N. Schiller for their help in the preparation of the manuscript.

The Case of the Druid Dracula

A Directed "Clicker" Case Study on DNA Fingerprinting

By Peggy Brickman

This chapter describes how case studies have been successfully implemented in an introductory biology course of 300+ students using available technologies ranging from WebCT, used to assign students to permanent small groups (as well as assign groups to regions of a large lecture hall), to hand-held response systems (aka "clickers"), which students use to collaboratively solve cases during class.

I use case studies in my one-semester, three-credit-hour introductory biology course with typical class sizes of 300+ students. Taken primarily by freshmen and sophomores to fulfill a general education requirement, the course consists of three 50-minute weekly meetings in a lecture classroom with no recitation section, although 65% of students are enrolled in an optional one-credit-hour lab section.

Using case studies in large-enrollment courses can be challenging. I have found that it can be done successfully with a little creative technical support. Before describing the technology I use, I'd like to discuss the kind of case study that I have found works best in this setting.

I recommend that the case study be short and self-contained, controllable, and gradable. For my purposes, I use cases that focus on the acquisition by students of important course-related concepts and facts and provide an opportunity for them to practice interpreting data and drawing inferences from observations. As *directed* cases, the focus of the case studies I use is more on the dissemination of facts and principles and less on analyzing all of the possible options and solutions to a problem. I have found that the best format for achieving my goals is the Interrupted Case Format, where students receive the information in parts, or sections. Each section builds on the information and data presented in the previous section and are punctuated by questions that drive students' learning. I use multiple-choice questions that have specific, correct answers. Students answer the multiple-choice questions in class using hand-held response systems, or "clickers," as they are more commonly known (more on those in a moment).

Students work on the cases during the 50-minute lecture period in permanent small groups, which I institute the very first day of class. These groups, which consist of six students to a group, are randomly assigned using the Group Generation tool in WebCT, the online course management system adopted by the University of Georgia. Each group has an assigned seating location in the "stadium-style" lecture hall (see Figure 1), and each group keeps handouts, grades, exams, and an attendance sheet in folders that they pick up in class each day. In their groups, students work daily on in-class activities that account for 15% of class time. Individual test and quiz scores determine 80% of each student's grade. An additional 20% of their grade is determined by group tests as well as mid- and end-of-semester peer evaluations.

CLICKERS IN THE CLASSROOM

Clicker technology has allowed me to successfully manage and encourage the type of classroom discussion and feedback critical for case study success in my classroom of 300+ students. I have turned to clickers because quality instruction depends on regularly assessing student comprehension and generating student discussion. The re-description by the student during discussion or questioning is a powerful way to promote learning that is unfortunately inhibited in very large classes.

Clickers are wireless transmitters used by students to instantly, accurately, and anonymously answer questions posed by the instructor. In my classroom, students use them to collaboratively solve cases during class. Each group is assigned a clicker that a member of the group picks up at the beginning of class and turns back in when class is over. Using the device, student groups tackle the multiple-choice "clicker questions" associated with a case. I then call on groups to provide an explanation to the rest of the class of their problem-solving strategies rather than just giving them the correct answer. This allows me to encourage the re-description that promotes learning as well as uncover sources of confusion and misconception.

THE CASE OF THE DRUID DRACULA

"The Case of the Druid Dracula," reprinted in Figure 2, is based on a lurid crime featured on the BBC program *Crimewatch UK* in December 2001 (Forensic Science Services Case Files) that was solved thanks to forensic DNA analysis. Students learn how the structure of DNA and the mechanism used by cells to duplicate DNA were critical to the forensic analysis. They then determine the statistical validity of the forensic data in the same way a prosecutor would prepare the case for a courtroom.

The case consists of three parts with questions that can be completed within a single 50-minute lecture session. In terms of the timing, there is approximately 15 to 20 minutes of student discussion punctuated by three "mini-lectures," each lasting about 10 minutes.

The case requires some preexisting knowledge on the part of students. My students receive a brief introduction to the biochemistry of DNA in a previous lecture and in their pre-class textbook reading (Krogh 2005).

Students also need to understand the chromosomal differences between men and women in the total human karyotype.

LEARNING OBJECTIVES

Upon completion of the case, students will:

- Understand the similarities and differences in the DNA of humans and how those differences can be exploited for forensic identification.
- Understand the structure of DNA and how hydrogen bonds between the nucleotide bases dictate the complementary nature of the double helix. Students will be able to predict the nucleotide sequence of one strand of DNA in a double helix if given its complementary strand.
- Describe the technique of polymerase chain reaction (PCR) and relate it to the normal cellular process of DNA replication. Students will be able to predict the sequence of PCR primers that would amplify just one short stretch of DNA out of an entire genome.
- Understand how short tandem repeats (STRs) within human chromosomes can be used to generate fingerprints and how to interpret these fingerprints to match the DNA to a specific person.
- Use statistical prevalence of STRs to determine the probability that someone else at random in the population could have DNA that matched a sample found at a crime scene.

CASE MANAGEMENT

I hand out Parts I, II, and III of the case on opposite sides of a single sheet of paper at

FIGURE 1.

Seating chart showing organization and location of student groups.

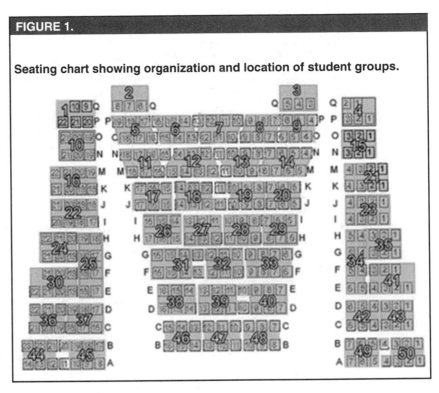

the beginning of class (with Part I on one side and Parts II and III on the other). I ask students to read the case, then describe to them the purpose of the case and ask them to answer two pre-assessments using their clickers on the structure of DNA from their pre-class reading, shown in Figure 3. If student responses to the pair of questions are below 90% correct, I will begin a quick review of the structure of DNA.

PART I—DNA STRUCTURE AND PCR

Part I of the case describes the murder of Mabel Leyshon and the evidence collected at the crime scene. I begin this part of the discussion and analysis with a short lecture describing the amelogenin gene. Found on the X chromosome, the amelogenin gene (AMELX) encodes a protein that is critical for the formation of the enamel on teeth. Individuals with deletions in this gene can have problems forming the normal thickness of enamel on their teeth, and problems in the mineralization of

"The Case of the Druid Dracula."

Part I: DNA structure and PCR

In the northernmost corner of the Isle of Anglesey in Wales, in a village called Llanfairpwll, the windswept beaches and ancient Druid ruins provided a surreal backdrop for the murder of 90-year-old Mabel Leyshon. Her murder was not only brutal—her heart had been hacked out—but also creepy. It appeared as if the killer had collected Mabel's blood in a small kitchen saucepan that had lip marks on the rim indicating the contents had been tasted. The murder showed other signs of the occult: a candlestick and a pair of crossed pokers had been arranged near the body. Further investigation indicated that this was no supernatural villain at work. The murderer had worn tennis shoes, which left distinctive footprints under the glass door that had been shattered with a piece of broken garden slate in order to gain entrance to the victim's home. Inside the house, a windowsill had bloodstains on it. With luck, the evidence recovery unit hoped to use it to find the killer.

Questions

DNA differences can be used to identify people. For example, there is a gene found on both the X and Y chromosomes called amelogenin, but the version of the gene found on the X and Y chromosomes differs in length, so it can be used to tell if a blood stain, such as the one found on the windowsill inside Mabel Leyshon's house, was left by a man or woman. This stretch of nucleotides shows one strand of the DNA double helix for the amelogenin gene. What is the sequence of the other, complementary strand?

5'CCCTGGGCTCTGTAAAGAATAGTGTGTTGATTCTTTATCCCAGATGTTTCTAAGTG3'

a. 3'ACTGTTAGATTTCCCTTTTTAGGTCTAGGTCCGTCGGCCTTATTTCCGAGGAATAA5'
b. 3'GGGACCCGAGACATTTCTTATCACACAACTAAGAAATAGGGTTTACAAAGATTCAC5'
c. 5'GGGACCCGAGACATTTCTTATCACACAACTAAGAAATAGGGTTTACAAAGATTCAC3'
d. 3'CCCTGGGCTCTGTAAAGAATAGTGTGTTGATTCTTTATCCCAGATGTTTCTAAGTG5'
e. 5'CCCTGGGCTCTGTAAAGAATAGTGTGTTGATTCTTTATCCCAGATGTTTCTAAGTG3'

To assist the investigators with the crime, you will need to perform polymerase chain reaction (PCR) to create copies of this gene so the sizes can be compared to determine if the blood was from a man or woman. During PCR it will be necessary to break the hydrogen bonds of the base pairs. Where are those hydrogen bonds normally found?

a. Between two nitrogen-containing bases in a single strand of DNA.
b. Between the phosphate and sugar of the same nucleotide.
c. Between the sugar of one nucleotide and the phosphate of a different nucleotide.
d. Between one nitrogen-containing base on a single strand of DNA and another nitrogen-containing base on the complementary strand of DNA.
e. Between one phosphate on a single strand of DNA and a sugar on the complementary strand of DNA.

PCR creates copies of DNA using the exact same mechanism used by your cells to copy their own DNA (replication). Place the steps listed below in the order in which they occur during replication:

A) Two strands, one new and one original template, wind together to form the double helix.
B) Short stretch of primer (~20 nucleotides exactly complementary to the gene that is going to be copied) is made.
C) Separation of the double helix from two parental DNA strands.
D) Use of parental DNA as a template so that nucleotides are covalently bonded together to form a new chain that is complementary to the bases on the original template.

   a. A, B, C, D
   b. B, C, A, D
   c. D, B, C, A
   d. C, B, D, A

PCR can be used to selectively duplicate one single gene out of thousands because the only primers available to start replication are the one unique pair that is complementary to the regions on both sides of the gene. Which of these primers (one for each strand) could you use to copy just the stretch (highlighted in gray) of the amelogenin gene that differs between the X and Y chromosomes?

3'GGGACCCGAGACATTTCTTATCACACAACTAAGAAATAGGGTCTACAAAGAGTTCACCAGGACTTTACAGTTCCTACCAC-CAGCTTCCCAGTTTAAGCTCTGAT5'
5'CCCTGGGCTCTGTAAAGAATAGTGTGTTGATTCTTTATCCCAGATGTTTCTCAAGTGGTCCTGAAATGTCAAGGATGGTGGTC-GAAGGGTCAAATTCGAGACTA3'

a. 3'GGGACCCGAGACATTTCTTATCAC5' and 5'CCCTGGGCTCTGTAAAGAATAGTG3'
b. 5'CCCTGGGCTCTGTAAAGAATAGTG3' and 5'GTCGAAGGGTCAAATTCGAGACTA3'
c. 5'CCCTGGGCTCTGTAAAGAATAGTG3' and 3'CAGCTTCCCAGTTTAAGCTCTGAT5'

Part II: The report

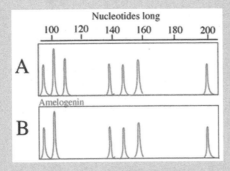

Question

Which of the above (A or B) represents the profile of a man?

Part III: More analysis

The crime was featured on BBC's *Crimewatch* program in December 2001 and North Wales Police received over 200 calls. Following up reports of a teenager who had attacked a German student, the police went to the home of Matthew Hardman (suspect 1), who gave police a cheek swab. During their visit, officers found a pair of Levi shoes. Forensic Science Service (FSS) scientists matched Hardman's shoes to the footwear marks found at the murder scene. Profiling, however, suggested a much older offender, so another suspect was also asked to give a cheek swab (suspect 2). Because both suspects were men, the officers needed to test for other genetic differences. They focused on STRs (short tandem repeats), stretches of DNA that exist in all people, but in different numbers of repeats. The allele ladder below shows all varieties in a population.

Questions

Did suspect 1 or 2 commit the crime?

a. suspect #1

b. suspect #2

There are only a few different numbers of repeats that are seen in our population—only five different TPOX STRs for example. By testing thousands of DNA samples, researchers know the distribution of these different STRs in the general population; those allele frequencies are shown in the table below. Using these frequencies, one can determine the probability that someone else at random would have the same matching pattern. For example, what is the likelihood that someone else at random would have the same pattern of Matthew Hardman (a 5- and 7-repeat for the THO1 STR)?

THO1	TPOX	CSF1PO
5: 1/200	8: 1/2	9: 1/40
6: 1/4	9: 1/8	10: 1/5
7: 1/6	10: 1/18	11: 1/3
8: 1/7	11: 1/5	12: 1/3
9: 1/6	12: 1/20	13: 1/10
9.3: 1/3		14: 1/50
10: 1/100		

a. 1/200

b. 1/206

c. 1/1,200

d. 1/2,600

e. 1/20,060

What is the probability that someone else at random would have that same pattern of THO1 5 & 7, TPOX 8 & 9, and CSF1PO 11 & 12?

a. 1/1,600

b. 1/7,200

c. 1/17,600

d. 1/172,800

e. 1/1,555,200

Pre-assessment "clicker" questions.

DNA is composed of nucleotides that are joined together by covalent bonds between which two portions of each nucleotide?
a. between deoxyribose and a phosphate group
b. between two deoxyribose groups
c. between the nitrogen-containing rings
d. between a phosphate group and the nitrogen-containing ring
e. between the phosphate groups of both nucleotides

In the hydrogen bonds between nitrogen-containing bases ____.
a. A always pairs with C
b. A always pairs with G
c. C always pairs with T
d. G always pairs with T
e. G always pairs with C

the AMELX and AMELY. PCR products generated from AMELX will be 106 base-pairs in length; PCR products from AMELY will be 112 base pairs in length.

After covering this material, I ask students to answer clicker questions 1 and 2 for Part I. I follow successful responses to these questions with a brief lecture on DNA replication and describe how the knowledge was exploited to create the technique of duplicating DNA in polymerase chain reaction (PCR). Before I go over the steps of PCR, I ask them to answer clicker question 3 to assess their understanding. After assessing their comprehension of normal replication, I lecture on the steps of PCR using animations on the internet (Dolan DNA Learning Center) or the PowerPoint presentations that can be downloaded from the National Institute for Science and Technology's website (Kline, Redman, and Butler 2001). To determine if they understand the idea of the primers, I ask them to answer clicker question 4. After five minutes of discussion, I call on groups at random to provide answers to the question. I ask them to explain why they chose the answer they did and try to probe for any confusion. If I discover major confusion, I will try to fill in any knowledge gaps. I then lecture on the

the enamel, so that their enamel may remain softer than normal (OMIM). A duplicate version of the amelogenin gene can be found on the Y chromosome in primates (AMELY), but there are significant differences between these two amelogenins. One of those differences is found in intron 1 of AMELX, which is missing 6 nucleotides found in AMELY. PCR can be performed using primers flanking this region to amplify DNA sequences from both

The sequence from the intron 1 of the AMELY gene.

The sequence reads:
3'G GGACCCGAGA CATTTCTTAT CACCCACCTA AGAAGTAGGG TTTATTTCAC CAAAGAGTTC ACCAGGGTTA
5'C CCTGGGCTCT GTAAAGAATA GTGGGTGGAT TCTTCATCCC AAATAAAGTG GTTTCTCAAG TGGTCCCAAT

3'TTTACAGTTC CTACCATCAG CTTCCCAGTT TAAGCTCTGA T-5'
5'AAATGTCAAG GATGGTAGTC GAAGGGTCAA ATTCGAGACT A-3'

The sequence from the intron 1 of the AMELX gene lacks 6 nucleotides compared to AMELY and reads:
3'G GGACCCGAGA CATTTCTTAT CACACAACTA AGAAATAGGG TCT-----AC -AAAGAGTTC ACCAGGACTA
5'C CCTGGGCTCT GTAAAGAATA GTGTGTTGAT TCTTTATCCC AGA-----TG -TTTCTCAAG TGGTCCTGAT

3'TTTACAGTTC CTACCACCAG CTTCCCAGTT TAAGCTCTGA T5'
5'AAATGTCAAG GATGGTGGTC GAAGGGTCAA ATTCGAGACT A3'

The actual primers used for both regions generate a 106 bp fragment from AMELX and 112 bp fragment from AMELY.
5'-CCCTGGGCTCTGTAAAGAATAGTG-3'
3'-CAGCTTCCCAGTTTAAGCTCTGAT-5' (backward 5'-TAGTCTCGAATTTGACCCTTCGAC-3')

way that the two different copies of the amelogenin gene (on the X versus the Y) would generate different sized PCR products (see Figure 4).

After explaining this to students, I describe how the technique of gel electrophoresis can be used to separate pieces of DNA like these two by size, again making use of the excellent animations available online (Dolan DNA Learning Center).

Obviously, this information only tells you the gender of the suspect who left the sample. It doesn't help with much else; that's where DNA fingerprinting comes in.

Background on DNA Fingerprinting Techniques Used in Parts II and III

DNA fingerprinting has been used since the 1980s when Alex Jeffreys took advantage of regions of the human genome that have repetitive sequences that vary in number. These short stretches of DNA can be found in all humans, and consist of the same sequence of nucleotides repeated a different number of times in tandem (hence one of the names, short tandem repeats, STRs). For example, a person could have five copies of one of these STRs, the THO1 sequence (TCAT), found on chromosome 11 on one homologue (a 5-repeat) and 6 repeats on the other homologue (6-repeat). Another person might have a 7-repeat and a 9-repeat, and therein lies the difference that can be used to match with a DNA evidence sample.

The procedure used to identify the number of repeats can vary. Most textbooks describe a technique called restriction fragment length polymorphism (RFLP) analysis. In this technique, researchers cleave chromosomal DNA with a restriction enzyme that recognizes restriction sites outside the repeat region so that the chromosome with the 6-repeat would yield a slightly longer fragment than the chromosome with the 5-repeat. Since smaller DNA fragments move farther into a gel during gel electrophoresis (toward the positive-charged electrode), a 5-repeat will appear as a band lower in the gel than a 6-repeat. In this way, you can create a lineup of fragments with these repeats, with the largest number of repeats at the top of the gel, the one with the smallest number of repeats at the bottom, and the rest lined up in between. In reality, it is difficult to view fragments of DNA in a gel if the DNA concentration is low. So researchers transfer the DNA fragments from the gel to a membrane (Southern blotting), probe the blot with a labeled piece of DNA complementary to the nucleotide sequence of the repeat, and expose the blot to x-ray film to detect hybridization.

The likelihood that anyone else at random has the same repeat pattern was determined by sampling DNA from thousands of individuals. For example, scientists have discovered that only about 1/200 of all chromosomes have the 5-repeat, but 1 out of 4 chromosomes has a 6-repeat (Brenner). So, the overall chance that someone else at random in the population has both of those repeats can be determined by multiplying the two probabilities together: $1/200 \times 1/4 = 1/800$. This is much better than the odds that someone at random would have the same blood type as that left at a crime scene, such as if 38% of the population has type O positive blood, but it is far from ideal. The beauty of using these STRs is that they occur in different regions of the human genome and the sequence of the repeats differs at these locations. So, researchers could subsequently probe this first blot for one of these different STRs (for example, TPOX found on chromosome 2) and determine that the DNA sample had an 8-repeat (1/2 probability) and a 9-repeat (1/8 probability). The probability that someone at random would have this pattern is $1/2 \times 1/8 = 1/16$. But the probability that someone at random would have a 5, 6-repeat at THO1 *and* an 8, 9-repeat at TPOX is the product of these two probabilities, or $1/16 \times$

1/800 = 1/12,800. Analysis with more STRs decreases the likelihood that someone else in the population could by random chance match the profile, thus increasing the validity of the data for use as evidence linking one suspect to the crime.

As the demand for analyzing DNA evidence grew in the last decade, it became imperative to use a cheaper and quicker way to generate these DNA fingerprints. The FBI began using specific PCR primers designed to amplify just those stretches of DNA with tandem repeats (Kline, Redman, and Butler 2001). This takes hours instead of days, and the PCR primers are labeled with different colored dyes, removing the need for probing to discover the fragments. Moreover, a mix of PCR primers can be added to simultaneously amplify stretches; for example, THO1, TPOX, AMEL, and CSF1PO STRs can all be amplified using the AmpFISTR Green 1 kit from Applied Biosystems. The green fragments created can be subjected to a very rapid type of gel electrophoresis using a thin capillary to separate by size, and then detected using a laser tuned to the green color of the dye used for the primers. Of course, controls must be run to determine the sizes of the fragments, and these are usually just a mixture of DNA samples of known size that can be mixed in with the fragments. This labeled mixture of DNA fragments are labeled with another color-indicating dye, in this case an orange color, but for ease of reading I have placed them on the same readout as the green peaks instead of in a separate window.

Part II—The Report
Students next read Part II of the case and answer clicker question 1 in this section to assess their understanding of the process of gel electrophoresis.

Part III—More Analysis
I then ask students to read Part III and answer clicker question 1 in that section. Almost every student group routinely gets this question correct but they are still unsure during questioning what the different peaks represent. So, I then lecture briefly on the presence and location of useful short tandem repeats of DNA in the chromosomes of humans and how those STRs can each be amplified using kits to generate different-sized PCR products that can be separated by gel electrophoresis (what they are seeing in the graphic from Part III). I ask students to consider clicker question 2. About a quarter of the groups routinely answer this question incorrectly. I will ask one of the groups that got it correct to explain to the class the logic of this probability and then assess students' comprehension by asking clicker question 3.

An answer key that provides answers to the questions posed in this case study is available on the website of the National Center for Case Study Teaching in Science—see *www.sciencecases.org/druid_dracula/druid_dracula_notes.asp* (Brickman 2006).

Case Wrap-up
I wrap up the case with a description of what really happened. During the arrest of Matthew Hardman, a knife was found in his coat pocket, but there was no visible blood on it. DNA testing of the damaged knife handle, however, revealed two sources of DNA, one matching Hardman and a partial profile matching the victim. In the meantime, further forensics work on the partial profile from the windowsill improved the discrimination to 1 in 5 million and finally to 1 in 73 million. The picture was complete when police searched Hardman's home and found magazines as well as evidence the computer had been used to access internet sites featuring vampires and how to become one. Matthew Hardman was found guilty of the murder of Mabel Leyshon at Mold Crown Court on August 2, 2002, and sentenced to life imprisonment.

REFERENCES

Brenner, C. H. n.d. Cellmark diagnostics allele frequencies for U.S. populations. *http://dna-view.com/cellmark.htm.*

Brickman, P. 2006. The case of the druid Dracula. State University of New York at Buffalo National Center for Case Study Teaching in Science website. *www.sciencecases.org/druid_dracula/druid_dracula_notes.asp*

Dolan DNA Learning Center, Biology Animation Library. Cold Spring Harbor Laboratory: Polymerase chain reaction animation *www.dnalc.org/ddnalc/resources/pcr.html* and gel electrophoresis animation *www.dnalc.org/ddnalc/resources/electrophoresis.html.*

Forensic Science Service Case Files: Mabel Leyshon—The Hunt for a Vampire—n.d. *www.forensic.gov.uk/forensic_t/inside/news/list_casefiles.php?case=13.*

Kline, M. C., J. W. Redman, and J.M. Butler. 2001. Training on STR typing using commercial kits and ABI 310/3100. National Institute of Standards and Technology website. *www.cstl.nist.gov/div831/strbase/training.htm*

Krogh, D. 2005. DNA structure and replication. In *A guide to the natural world.* 3rd ed. Englewood Cliffs, NJ: Prentice Hall.

Online Mendelian Inheritance in Man (OMIM). Johns Hopkins University, Baltimore, MD. MIM Number: 300391: 6/13/2003. *www3.ncbi.nlm.nih.gov/omim*

NOTE

The diagrams in the case are the same that would be generated by using ABI PRISM 310 Genetic Analyzer after using the AmpFlSTR Green multiplex PCR kit from Applied Biosystems.

Section XII

Individual Case Study Methods

Many case studies can be assigned just as easily to individuals as to groups. But some strategies just seem cut out for an individual assignment even if you are dealing with an entire class. This section deals with one such approach: the use of dialogues, where I assigned students the task of writing a dialogue between two intelligent people on a controversial topic. Writing a good dialogue requires that the author have a firm grasp of the facts and simultaneously understand several sides of a sensitive issue—a good way to stimulate critical thinking.

In this section I have included a couple of examples. The first one on cloning has explicit rules on how the student is to approach the topic. Even though the student paper example was written in 1999, not much has changed. The political debate continues today across the world.

Chapter 36 is a student paper on the topic of the Endangered Species Act, noteworthy as it has more than two characters; it is drawn from the archives of the National Center for Case Study Teaching in Science. Such dialogue papers can be read out loud by students as they role-play their part. The paper is also interesting in that the author started out with one opinion and at the end of the paper switched her views. Since the material was written several years ago, a number of issues raised in the paper have been resolved; the Atlantic salmon in eight Maine rivers were declared "endangered" on November 13, 2000. And on December 20, 2005, NOAA's National Marine Fisheries Service announced that the final recovery plan for endangered Atlantic salmon in Gulf of Maine rivers had been published.

Dialogues as Case Studies— A Discussion on Human Cloning

Creating Drama and Controversy in the Science Classroom

By Clyde Freeman Herreid

Dialogues, used in ancient times for philosophic discourse and later as educational devices, are gradually coming into use as an accepted teaching strategy. Dialogues have inherent dramatic power that appeals to students. Using the dialogue method, the dialogue writer and reader can explore different sides of an issue, such as human cloning, the example provided in this chapter.

Plato conversing with a student. At Plato's initiative, dialogues became an inspired form of philosophic discourse, intended to challenge and instruct.

I n reviewing the potential for using case studies in the teaching of science, I have highlighted several different teaching methods (Herreid 1994; 1998). In addition to the classical discussion mode used in business schools, I listed lectures, debates, public hearings, trials, problem-based learning, research teams, and team learning. All have considerable strengths when used appropriately.

Another method of case instruction belongs on this list, not only for its inherent merits, but because it has been used by instructors for thousands of years. This is the dialogue.

Dialogues are recorded conversations between two or more people. As a literary device, they are ancient; we can trace their roots to Sicilian dramas of everyday life written in the early fifth century B.C. by Sophron of Syracuse. In Plato's hands in 400 B.C., they became an inspired form of philosophic discourse, meant to challenge and instruct. It is within the Platonic dialogues that we are introduced to Socrates and his insistent probing of the thought processes of colleagues and slaves, and we see the origin of Socratic questioning, a technique long cherished by law school instructors.

The use of dialogues as educational devices has been sporadic. The dialogues of astronomer Galileo, philosopher Berkeley, Saint Augustine, and Confucius are among the most famous. Dialogues have even found their way into American educational history (Burnham 1987), having been used in the early 1800s to teach children science. In contrast to the use of catechisms whose primary purpose was to impart factual knowledge, "the dialogue format tended to inculcate appreciation as well as learning" (Burnham 1987).

Children's books on science typically would have a young person with whom the reader could identify conversing with an older and wiser individual who would reveal the intricacies of a plant or an animal amid cries of wonderment and awe. It was hoped that the reader was also suitably enthralled. A dialogue in an 1833 children's magazine winds up with its child character saying, "We are greatly obliged to you brother John, for giving us such pleasing information; Botany is a beautiful amusement and not such a dry study as I thought it was: I do not wonder you are so fond of it" (Burnham 1987).

A number of educators have evaluated the use of dialogue in teaching. Some have focused on it as a method of interrogation of students, i.e., the Socratic discussion with students (Shor and Freire 1987; Smith 1987; Julian 1995). Others have considered theoretical concerns (Robinson 1995) or its power to develop critical-thinking skills (Gussman and Hesford 1992; Robertson and Rane-Szostak 1996). Its use as a method for student exposition of ideas has been explored (see exceptions, Davis 1981; Lampert 1985; Smith 1987), but the method deserves much wider recognition.

Dialogues, like plays, press conferences, and debates, have inherent dramatic power that appeals to students. Virtually any topic can be framed as a dialogue—a teacher explaining photosynthesis to a student, a child asking a parent where babies come from, Pinocchio conversing with Jiminy Cricket about leading a moral life. Furthermore, the dialogue method seems especially suited for handling controversy. The method allows both the dialogue writer and reader to explore different sides of the issue such as the case of human cloning, the example used in this article.

Students may act as either writers or readers of dialogues with benefit. Here are four techniques for their use:

- *Controversial topic:* Assign students the task of writing a dialogue on a controversial topic. I give one on human cloning. The assignment rules are explicit, and I give one example of a student paper that grapples with the topic. Writing a good dialogue requires that the author have a firm grasp of the facts and simultaneously understand several sides of a sensitive issue—not a bad approach to stimulating critical thinking.

- *Unfinished dialogue:* If the instructor wishes to exercise more control over the topic, she can set the scene and establish the characters of the dialogue. She can even write some of the first exchanges between the protagonists and then ask the students to finish the dialogue.

- *Incomplete dialogue:* The instructor can write a complete dialogue (or use one of her student's), and then eliminate key responses by one or another characters in the "play." The students' assignment would be to write out reasonable responses for the missing parts. This approach could easily be used during an examination, with the instructor providing the incomplete dialogue as a test question.

- *Dialogues used as traditional cases:* Written dialogues are traditionally used to educate the reader rather than the author. That has been their role throughout history, and they can effectively serve as the basis of a classical case discussion. The characters can mouth many misconceptions as well as "truths" that can be explored in the classroom.

Thus, dialogues that are flawed might in fact be better than the more perfect examples. To illustrate the several uses of dialogue, I include a dialogue assignment that I gave to a recent general biology class. Then I include an example of a freshman's paper. The latter can be used by science teachers as a traditional discussion case for classroom use. It can obviously be used to produce an incomplete dialogue by eliminating certain speeches.

References

Burnham, J. C. 1987. *How superstition won and science lost.* New Brunswick, NJ: Rutgers University Press.

Davis, R. 1981. A plea for the use of student dialogues. *Improving College and University Teaching* 29: 155–159.

Gussman, D., and W. Hesford. 1992. A dialogical approach to teaching introductory women's studies. *Feminist Teacher* 6: 32–39.

Herreid, C. F. 1994. Case studies in science: A novel method of science education. *Journal of College Science Teaching* 23(4): 221–229.

Herreid, C. F. 1998. Sorting potatoes for Miss Bonner. *Journal of College Science Teaching* 27(4): 236–239.

Julian, G. M. 1995. Socratic dialogue—how many? *Physics Teacher* 33: 338–339.

Lampert, K. W. 1985. Using dialogues to teach argumentation. *Exercise Exchange* 30: 6–10.

Robertson, J. F., and D. Rane-Szostak. 1996. Using dialogues to develop critical thinking skills: A practical approach. *Journal of Adolescent and Adult Literacy* 39: 552–556.

Robinson, V. M. J. 1995. Dialogue needs a point and purpose. *Educational Theory* 45: 235–249.

Shor, I., and P. Freire. 1987. What is the "Dialogical Method" of teaching? *Journal of Education* 169: 11–31.

Smith, H. W. 1987. Comparative evaluation of three teaching methods of quantitative techniques: Traditional lecture, Socratic dialogue, and PSI format. *Journal of Experimental Education* 55: 149–154.

Student Assignment: Writing a Dialogue Paper on Human Cloning

Human cloning has been in the news, cartoons, and jokes since the announcement that Scottish scientists produced the cloned sheep, Dolly. This development promises major benefits to society if we are to believe some enthusiasts. But it also threatens major problems according to critics, some of whom are sure this is another step toward moral decadence. The issues are serious, the problems real.

You can earn up to 25 points extra credit if you write a paper about the controversy. The paper is to be written in a particularly novel way. No credit will be given if you do not follow this format:

- The paper must be at least five typewritten, double-spaced pages long. It is not limited to this length.
- The paper must be a dialogue between two people on opposite sides of the question. It should be written in the form of a script or play as shown below:

Sam: Hey, Shirley, the cloning issue has certainly been cropping up in the news a lot. It really drives me crazy to think that scientists have all of this power to control our reproduction. This conflicts with my religious views.

In fact, the Pope just came out with a strong statement about it.

Shirley: I don't understand the problem. What's the big deal? Clones aren't anything different than identical twins, are they?

- There should be at least 20 exchanges between people. That is, as shown in the example above, Sam should speak at least 20 times and Shirley should speak at least 20 times.
- The exchanges must be serious, substantive, and courteous comments made between two intelligent people grappling with an important issue. They should not be "Sam, you're a jerk!" "Oh, yeah?"
- It is not necessary to confine your dialogue to two people, more characters may be involved.
- A short introductory paragraph to the paper should be written indicating where the dialogue is occurring and what the circumstances surrounding the discussion are, i.e., set the scene.
- Write a final paragraph to the paper giving your personal opinion and reasons behind it.
- The paper will be graded primarily on the basis of the number of issues explored and the depth of the coverage. It pays to have your characters speak at longer length than the example between Sam and Shirley.
- A list of references must be written at the bottom of the paper. Each must be complete, with author, date, title of article, journal title, volume number and pages or book title, publisher, and city.

STUDENT PAPER ON CLONING
by Kabir Tambar, SUNY at Buffalo

This dialogue is between two students at the University at Buffalo. Steve is a little uncomfort-

able about cloning, while Sally presents many valid arguments in favor of it. Steve presents many moral questions that Sally answers.

Steve: Hi, Sally. Are you aware that the Scottish embryologist, Ian Wilmut, cloned a sheep from adult cells and now there are many moral, economic, and political questions that must be answered?

Sally: Interestingly enough, I was just reading about this topic in a magazine. I was amazed at the simplicity of the cloning process used by Dr. Wilmut and his colleagues. The process of cloning a sheep begins by taking the cells from the udder of an adult sheep and placing them in a culture with few nutrients. The purpose of this is to starve the cells so that they stop dividing, which switches off the active genes. While they starve these cells, they take an unfertilized egg from a different ewe and remove the nucleus from this unfertilized egg. Then they place the unfertilized egg cell next to one of the original starved cells.

Steve: How do the two cells come together? Does it happen spontaneously?

Sally: No, it does not happen spontaneously. An electric pulse fuses the two cells together. A second electric pulse makes the cell divide. After six days Dr. Wilmut placed this embryo into a different ewe, and after a normal gestation period, the new baby sheep named Dolly was born. She was named after Dolly Parton.

Steve: But cloning is not new. In 1952, researchers in Pennsylvania cloned a live frog. What makes Dr. Wilmut's achievement so special?

Sally: Yes, it is true that a frog was cloned in 1952, but those scientists used an embryonic cell. Dr. Wilmut used an adult cell.

Steve: What is the difference between using an embryonic cell and an adult cell?

Sally: Embryonic cells are "undifferentiated." Undifferentiated cells have not gone through changes that make some cells into skin cells or muscle cells or brain cells, for example. Undifferentiated cells can become any cell in the body because it can activate any gene on any chromosome, but as cells develop the DNA of certain cells fold in particular ways making large portions of the DNA inaccessible. This makes sure that the wrong genes do not get turned on at the wrong time or in the wrong place. This whole process of DNA folding makes adult cells much more difficult to work with.

Steve: If working with embryonic cells is easier, then why use adult cells? Why not make cloning simpler rather than more complex?

Sally: Well, when scientists use an embryonic cell, they cannot be sure how the new clone will turn out. The embryonic cell can develop in different ways, but when using adult cells, the scientists know that the clone will look exactly like the original.

Steve: That is fascinating. In essence, this cloning procedure makes a carbon copy of the original. That sounds scary. When this technology advances towards humans, could some evil, devious mind bring back to life people like Hitler or Stalin?

Sally: Certainly scientists would be able to create a clone that looked like Hitler or Stalin, and the clone would have the same genes, but what you are suggesting sounds like genetic determinism. Genetic determinism is the belief that genes determine everything in a person, and that the environment plays no role in how someone acts. Most scientists think that this belief is false. Identical twins are the same genetically, but they are different psychologically and morally. If we cloned Einstein or Newton or any other great scientist, the clones would not necessarily turn into scientific geniuses because the environment that they are raised in makes a difference, but they would look like the original. A cloned Einstein could pick up a guitar at an early age and become a rock star rather than a mathematician, even though he looked exactly like Einstein.

Steve: Well, I heard that Dr. Wilmut is trying to avoid human cloning.

Sally: That is true. Dr. Wilmut said that although human cloning is theoretically possible, he does not see any good reason why humans should be cloned. He hopes that his new technique will not extend to humans. He sees no ethical reason for it.

Steve: What about religious leaders? I heard that the Pope wants human cloning banned.

Sally: Yes, the Pope called for a ban on human cloning as well. He believes that the creation of life outside of marriage is against God's plan. The Church is against in vitro fertilization even though it is legal in America. In fact, when scientists developed in vitro fertilization, many people spoke out against it, but gradually tension surrounding that topic subsided. Perhaps human cloning will be the same.

Steve: I doubt that, but still it is good to hear the Pope speaking out against human cloning. The clones would be made by humans, and, therefore, they would not have souls. Bringing a creature without a soul into the world is wrong.

Sally: How do you know they do not have souls? They would be normal human beings. If a normal human being has a soul, then the clone would have one as well. I would hope that the Church would accept clones rather than turning its back to them. Isolating the clones from the rest of society would be a travesty.

Steve: How are political leaders responding to the prospect of human cloning?

Sally: Britain has banned human cloning and placed many restrictions on embryological research. Here in America, President Clinton ordered the Bioethics Advisory Committee to investigate human cloning and give him a report in about a month. However, President Clinton has already declared that no federal money will be placed into human embryo research, and two bills are before Congress that will attempt to ban human cloning.

Steve: It is good that all these political and religious leaders are standing up against human cloning. I think that cloning could interfere with evolution. Making people genetically the same decreases the amount of variability, and

I learned in my evolutionary biology class that variability is one of the major causes for evolution. Cloning would decrease this variability, and without evolution, humans will not progress. Other animals that do evolve will take control of the planet.

Sally: It is true that genetic diversity is important for evolution to take place, but cloning will probably not be so widespread to make a difference. Beyond that, evolution takes millions of years. It is not as if human cloning will result in the destruction of the human race in 10 years.

Steve: Well, I still feel uncomfortable about human cloning. What about the clone's feelings? Would the clone feel comfortable knowing his origins? Would he be the object of mockery at school?

Sally: Clones would receive rights just like a normal human being, and you must remember that they are human. They are not aliens. His schoolmates would not be able to tell that he is a clone.

Steve: Beyond this, what about the sibling whose traits are copied? Throughout my life, people have told me that everyone is unique, but this child would lose this uniqueness. He would suddenly have a twin, born years after he was born.

Sally: The sibling whose traits have been copied might feel depressed about losing his uniqueness, but twins are born and they can handle this genetic sharing. The parents would probably discuss the procedure with their child before making such a big decision.

Steve: That's interesting, but we are talking about the consequences of cloning. Why would someone want to clone?

Sally: There are many positive applications for cloning. Human cloning could be used for organ donations. If a child needed a new liver, for example, scientists could clone the child and transplant the new liver.

Steve: You keep telling me that clones are human beings just like you and me, and if this is the case, then transplanting organs from a human clone to his counterpart is evil. According to you, a clone is a human being. You cannot raise a human clone, and then at a mature age, remove his liver. If you had twins, would you take out one child's heart to save the other? Who would give the clone a new heart? It would be different if scientists could clone the heart or any other organ, but raising a child just to eventually kill it is morally wrong.

Sally: Well, there are other applications for it. Cloning could also help scientists understand mysteries of science, such as heart or brain cells that do not regenerate after they die. This could help stroke patients or heart attack patients who are crippled by this phenomenon. Scientists could also look into cancer cells that go back into embryonic stages of development and reproduce uncontrollably. Strokes, heart attacks, and cancer are major causes of suffering for many people.

Steve: This is true, but there are more bad applications for cloning. What if a rich businessman wanted to clone himself to carry on his name after he died? This is a misuse of science. It should be banned in America as it is in England.

Sally: You do not understand, Steve. Cloning is so simple that if it is banned in America as it is banned in England, some wealthy company will emerge in a country where it is not banned. Human cloning is inevitable. Banning it in some countries will only add to the fears of those who believe that an army of malevolent clones can emerge if cloning is used for evil. Beyond this, it will probably be too difficult to ban cloning in America. If the government gives no monetary support to human cloning, it will probably go on in the private sector.

Steve: What if some kind of *Island of Dr. Moreau* appears where a rich man owns an island and develops clones that get out of control? The private sector should be feared.

Sally: I think that the pros outweigh the cons. You must remember that *The Island of Dr. Moreau* is just fiction. What are the chances that some crazy-minded maniac who happens to be extremely wealthy would buy an island and create a massive army of clones who he has trained from birth to kill? And supposing this did occur, what are the chances that America or any other international superpower would not find out about this scheme and end it?

Steve: Well, maybe that is far-fetched. What about animal cloning? Why does Wilmut favor animal cloning but not human cloning?

Sally: Cloning animals could help alleviate world hunger. Scientists could clone animals in enormous numbers to feed developing nations.

Steve: Helping alleviate world hunger is good, but what if a leather producer used cloning to help his business? As an animal rights activist, I would not want to see that. Again, cloning can be used for evil.

Sally: Yes, but it could also help farmers. If the farmer found a particularly good cow, for instance, this cow could be cloned and the productivity of his livestock would be enhanced. This helps everyone. The farmer makes more money and the quality and the quantity of the food increases.

Steve: What if someone cloned elephants only to remove their tusks so that the ivory could be sold? This is a greedy misuse of science.

Sally: If a private citizen has enough money to clone elephants, he probably would not need to sell elephant tusks to make a living. The pros outweigh the cons. Another good application for cloning is to protect endangered species by cloning any species that risks extinction. In this way, cloning is adding diversity rather than taking it away. I have to go to class now. Bye.

▶   ▶   ▶

My personal opinion is that cloning animals to prevent world hunger or enhance cattle productivity is good, but human cloning is bad. There do not seem to be many ethical reasons to support the cloning of a human. It is a fascinating idea, but the consequences must be evaluated before this technology proceeds further. Ian Malcolm, chaos theoretician in Michael Crichton's book *Jurassic Park,* said in reference to dinosaur cloning, "They were so busy seeing if they could do it, that they didn't stop to think if they should do it."

If scientists propose ethical reasons to proceed with human cloning, they must also think of the clones. The clones would be human beings, and they should have the same rights as any other normal human. They should not be used in any experiments that normal humans would not be subject to.

Life is precious and should not be taken lightly. Human cloning should be restricted and not allowed to run out of control.

References

Krauthammer, C. 1997. A special report on cloning. *Time* 10 (March): 29–30.

Nash, J. M. 1997 The Age of Cloning. *Time* 10 (March): 25–29

Wachbroit, R. 1997. Human cloning isn't as scary as it sounds. *Washington Post* (March 2): 10.

Student Paper on the Atlantic Salmon Controversy

By Helena Bokobza

J oe and Anju, two teaching assistants, sit quietly in the biology laboratory, preparing for the arrival of their students. It is the day that they are to dissect fish, and the students had to do some reading ahead of time. This Tuesday afternoon would be just like any other, except for the fact that Joe initiates an interesting conversation. "Anju," he says, "did you read about that Atlantic salmon controversy? Some of the students are sure to have picked up on that. It's all over the press."

Anju: Yes, I did. Is it true that the ESA won't be used to protect the Maine salmon since they couldn't pass the DPS test and become an ESU?

(A student enters, confused by the conversation)

Student 1: What is the problem with the salmon? Where did the alphabet come from—ESA, DPS, ESU?

Joe: The ESA is the Endangered Species Act. It was originally passed in the early 1970s, but it has been amended several times.

Student 1: How does it work?

Anju: Well, first a species has to be listed as either endangered or threatened. An endangered species is one in danger of extinction, while a threatened species is one likely to become endangered. Once a species is formally listed, it is protected by Section 9 of the ESA, which prohibits the "taking" (killing, hunting, harassing) of any members of the species. To help the population recover, Section 4 makes certain that there is enough critical habitat for the species to expand and recover. Section 10 requires people who want to do anything that would get in the way of an endangered species or its habitat to acquire an "incidental take permit."

Student 1: But weren't you guys talking about salmon? What does the ESA have to do with them?

(Another student enters and begins to listen)

Joe: Quite a lot actually. Usually the ESA issues broadly to protect a whole species—you've probably heard about the resounding success of the bald eagle, which has expanded from a mere 500 pairs to a much more respectable 4,000. In 1978, though, an amendment was passed allowing the ESA to apply to certain individual populations.

Student 2: How do they decide which populations? It's not like some are "better" than others.

Anju: They go by "evolutionary significance."

Student 2: Isn't that kind of subjective?

Anju: It is. That's why they've formalized the Distinct Population Segment (DPS). It has to be reproductively isolated from other populations, and it must be evolutionarily important to the past and future of the species: an ESU, or Evolutionary Significant Unit.

Student 1: But, I repeat, what does all this have to do with Atlantic salmon?

(More students enter)

Joe: Several river populations of Atlantic salmon in Maine are in questionable status—are they really a distinct population? How different are they from their Canadian salmon?

Student 3: They're totally different! I just read on the Anadromous and Marine Fish Home Page that these salmon are reproductively isolated from the Canadian ones. Most of the differences are subtle and hard to analyze because of a lack of specimens, but it is clear that the Maine salmon are distinct and require special protection.

Student 2: That's not what I read in *Science* magazine. An article said that Canadian and Maine salmon are not reproductively isolated and that they share many of the same alleles. According to this, the Maine salmon are clearly not distinct and don't deserve special protection.

Anju: Those are both good sources, and obviously, this is a complex issue. You have to ask yourself whether genetics should be the sole factor in making these decisions, or whether the cultural worth of a species should be considered.

Student 1: How bad is the salmon situation anyway?

Joe: It's not looking good. In 1995, only 120 salmon returned to the Maine rivers to spawn. And last year, just 250 commercial fishermen somehow killed over 30,000 salmon!

Student 3: Commercial fishing, is that the root of the problem?

Joe: Partially, but there's a lot to it. Offshore netting is a huge threat, and the salmon's main food source, small fish-like capelin, are in decline.

Anju: Don't forget about those hydropower dams. They lower the water level, reducing the flow, which can limit the amount of oxygen available to the salmon, increase the water temperature, or stop migration all together. Dams have fish ladders, ascending pools that are supposed to help the salmon swim over the dams, but many fish have a hard time locating them, and often don't want to ascend.

Joe: Industrial endeavors have also hurt salmon terribly. Toxic chemicals affect the gills of the salmon and often kill its food. Radioactive waste is an obvious threat. Acid rain, an indirect result of the burning of fossil fuels, decreases the pH of a river. If the pH goes below 4.5, the salmon eggs will die. Forestry has an affect on the salmon too—forest management can result in decreased shade and increased water temperature. Even blueberry cultivation affects the salmon due to the pesticides required.

Student 1: Isn't anyone doing anything to stop all this?

Anju: Actually, people are working really hard. They're limiting the number of fishing licenses issued, constructing fish channels to help salmon cross dams by swimming a series of steps, and adding limestone filters to reduce the amount of acid in rivers. Still, the problem won't go away, and these salmon need to be classified as an ESU to receive special considerations under the ESA.

Late coming Student: So, the ESA just applies to salmon?

Joe: No way! The ESA has all kinds of aspects and implications, and is extremely controversial. For example, some people are saying that the ESA saves plants and animals at the expense of humans. In the Pacific Northwest in the early 1990s, the "owls versus jobs" controversy reigned. People believed that using the ESA to protect the Northern Spotted Owl reduced the allowable timber and hurt the industry, affecting local jobs, and possibly costing the federal government twenty million dollars in timber sales. Anju, the truth is though that twenty million is a huge exaggeration, and the major cause of the loss of local jobs was automation, not the owl.

Student 2: I heard that driving through mud puddles is illegal because it harms the habitat of the endangered fairy shrimp.

Joe: What? You must know that's too strange to be true. Do you want to hear something about the ESA that's also strange, but may really be true? Some people claim that the ESA is actually causing landowners to destroy habitats of endangered species! Many landowners have been practicing "shoot, shovel, and shut up"—a practice in which they destroy habitat rather than discover an endangered species and become subject to the ESA's zoning laws. This is destroying individual organisms as well as habitat.

Anju: I read about a good example of this phenomenon. A timber owner in North Carolina was liquidating timber stands left and right, simply to prevent them from housing the red-cocaded woodpecker. Apparently, he already owned 1,000 acres of forest where the woodpecker already lived, and since he couldn't harvest timber from those acres he was losing millions.

Student 2: That's a really good argument against, or at least for, reform of the ESA. I have another one actually. If the whole point of the ESA is to maintain genetic diversity, we have to consider that wiping out one species does little to hurt overall diversity. More importantly, today's technology has begun to develop genetic material from scratch. This makes the fear of losing the cure for cancer by destroying one plant species really archaic.

Student 3: That's not true! There are maybe 30 million species on Earth. Only a little over a million have been named, and far fewer have been examined for medical potential. Only 2% of the 250,000 plant species we know of have been tested. We need the ESA

to maintain biodiversity for medical reasons, if nothing else. Think of the new drugs that have been found in plants. Taxol, the drug used for cancer therapy, was discovered in the bark of the Pacific yew tree. Just before Taxol's life-saving properties were discovered, the Pacific yew was burnt as "slash" during logging operations. Maybe you've heard of cyclosporin, a drug used in organ transplants; that comes from a Norwegian fungus. And what about morphine, found only in the opium poppy? Chemists can't make it in the lab. We need the ESA to protect these organisms and their habitats, perhaps for the sake of our own lives.

Student 4: That's a really good argument. Who knows what we could find in the jungles or on coral reefs. What are we doing to protect them?

Anju: A program called the Habitat Conservation Plan (HCP) has been developed. Any developer who wants to begin a project that would destroy some habitat belonging to an endangered species must get a permit from the ESA. In exchange for the permit the developer agrees to abide by an HCP, which details ways to minimize harm to the species in question. These ways could involve relocation of organisms, the setting up of nature preserves, and so on.

Student 1: This all sounds expensive. How much does it cost?

Joe: The budget proposal for all Fish and Wildlife Service's endangered species programs in 1996 was $57 million. This may seem like a lot, but consider the fact that in 1994, $1.3 billion was spent on movie theater popcorn!

Student 2: Aren't we all avoiding the real issue here though? Bottom line, is the ESA working?

Anju: While some people try to play down its success, the ESA has achieved many goals. In a mere 20+ years, eight species have been delisted completely, and 41% of the total number of species in question are stable or improving. The mere fact that 99% of these endangered species still exist is testimony to the success of the ESA.

Joe: Oh, look at the time! Time to get started on the lab!

PERSONAL OPINION

When I first began this assignment, I felt that I had already made up my mind. I have never been able to muster up the environmental fervor of my peers and I felt certain that this project could not change that. However, I am wholeheartedly surprised by my findings. Every argument raised by those against the ESA was obliterated by its supporters. It is difficult to argue with the facts. In particular, I found one article, "Wild Medicine," regarding the medicinal potential of species, to be extremely persuasive reading. I now wholeheartedly support the ESA and applaud what it accomplishes on such a meager budget and in the face of such powerful opposition.

FURTHER READING

Bean, M. J. 1994. Naysayers downplay Species Act. *Insight on the News* 10 (22): 20–23.

Byrnes, P., and T. H. Watkins. 1995. Wild Medicine. *Wilderness* 59(210): 28–34.

Kocik, J., and R. Brown. 2001. Atlantic salmon. NOAA's National Marine Fisheries Service. Available online at *www.nefsc.noaa.gov/sos/spsyn/af/salmon*.

Lipske, M. 1998. Giving rare creatures a fighting chance. *National Wildlfe* 32(2): 14–24.

Malakoff, D. 1998. Atlantic salmon spawn fight over species protection. *Science* 279: 800.

Michaels, P. 1993. Environmental rules should be based on science. *Insight on the News* 9 (15): 21–22.

Nelson, R. H. 1995. Shoot, shovel, and shut up. *Forbes* 156 (13): 82–83.

Sampson, N. 1994. It's time to reform ESA. *American Forests* 100 (5): 6–8.

Stern, E. 1996. Endangered species list: Extinct? *Mother Earth News* 15: 12–14.

Taylor, B. 1998. Saving the wild salmon: Immediate action or extinction. *ASF Communications* (March). Available online at *www.asf.ca/Communications/March98/editMr11.html*.

Watkins, T. H. 1996. What's wrong with the Endangered Species Act? Not much—and here's why. *Audubon* 98 (Jan/Feb): 36–42.

Section XIII

Hybrid Case Methods

Faculty are ingenious. Their case studies don't always fit into neat categories. Here are a collection of cases that are a mixture of methods. I have noted below what their hybrid approaches entail.

HYBRID CASE METHODS

- Chapter 37: Alien Evolution—A Futuristic Case Study: The Return of the Cambrian Explosion [Problem-Based Learning With Debate]

- Chapter 38: What to Do About Mother: Investigating Fetal Tissue Research and the Effects of Parkinson's Disease [Discussion With Group Role Playing]

- Chapter 39: The Galapagos: A Natural Laboratory for the Study of Evolution [Problem-Based Learning, Role-Playing, and the Jigsaw Method, where groups of experts are assembled on a topic, then rearranged with different experts in new groups]

- Chapter 40: Structured Controversy: A Case Study Strategy [Debate and Whole Class Discussion]

- Chapter 41: A Word to the Wise? Advising Freshmen [Small Group Analysis, Class Discussion, and Individual Work]

Alien Evolution— A Futuristic Case Study

The Return of the Cambrian Explosion

By Shoshana Tobias and Clyde Freeman Herreid

J ay looked at the seas and land that peeked out from beneath the clouds of P-L5. He was anxious to get home to Earth, but he couldn't help but wonder at this beautiful and mysterious planet.

"P-L5," as it was termed, had been home to a small colony of humans and a thriving tourist industry for over a century when the inhabitants fled to neighboring systems almost 100 years ago. Now Jay and his colleagues would be deciding whether or not to start a new colony on P-L5. They didn't have long to decide either—with all the chaos and overpopulation on Earth, no projects were getting much funding these days.

Luckily, K&P Securities had offered to sponsor the side trip and a crew had been thrown together. The captain gave them a tantalizing description of the planet they would be investigating:

"Many of you have heard of P-L5. Some of you may even have had family that once lived there. Let it stand as a reminder in your future travels never to underestimate and ignore the environment around you. The earliest record of this planet dates from the year 2400 when the Fifth Quadrant was discovered. The description is of a simple beautiful planet ideal for human habitation—moderate oxygen levels around 5%, clear blue seas, and land for building. The only native life was a harmless collection of chemoautotrophs, photoautotrophs, and passive filter feeders. With a few environmental adjustments, the planet was settled in 2460 and became a mecca for tourists and for industry, at one time supporting a water distillation plant, farms, factories, schools, libraries, and research facilities.

"Then," the captain continued, "for reasons still unclear, things began to change. The inhabitants fled to new planets, leaving their towns and belongings behind. These ghost towns now stand very much as they were left 100 years ago when people still lived there. This is a two-day stopover. Enjoy the beach, look around, but be careful—we still don't know exactly what happened down there. I will expect a full report in three days detailing environmental and biological conditions on the ground as well as a decision on re-colonization."

As soon as they landed, Jay burst out of the shuttle ready to start exploring. The first thing that hit him was the fresh air. Oxygen. The early colonists had prepared the planet by pumping oxygen into its atmosphere to raise the O_2 concentration to Earth's level—standard procedure back then. He walked toward the cluster of hulking buildings. The iron railings had begun to show signs of rust. He swung open the unlocked doors and stepped into the municipal building. He hoped he would find a clue to this mystery among the scattered government documents.

He picked up a binder marked "water supply." Early water tests showed high oxygen content, moderate calcium carbonate levels, and low sulfur, nitrogen, and phosphates. Cyanobacteria were also present. Interesting. A memo dated 2480 complained of flat soft-bodied organisms, some up to one-meter long, getting jammed in the deep-sea intake pipes.

Flipping through the entries, he came across later complaints: One memo about 50 years later noted tourist complaints about water taste and cloudiness, which the plant manager blamed on phosphate, sulfur, calcium carbonate, and nitrogen runoff from "those damn farms" and years of deep-sea dumping by one of the offshore factories. Later reports recorded an increase in harder bodied organisms being caught in the sea intakes. He pocketed several of the sketches.

It was starting to get dark, so Jay decided to take a quick walk to the shore before boarding the shuttle for the night. Walking through the empty streets, he wondered what had happened. Obviously the environmental change had been rapid, and he had a hunch the alien organisms had probably changed quickly as well. Rapid evolution was not unknown. He remembered once having to move camp ev-

ery night to avoid a riverbed that changed course by morning, or his aunt's flowerbeds on Pentarch that came up in different shapes and colors every year. It would not surprise him if the change here had been fast—probably catching the colonists unprepared.

His boots crunched along the shore as he scanned the beach. A thin film of dirt covered the old water intakes in the distance, and the murky water hid its secrets from view. He noticed what appeared to be deep burrows, several inches long, as the waves receded. He took out the sketches. The planet's jelly-like, flat-bodied early life could not have made these; they lacked the firmness, strength, and three-dimensional body shape to tunnel. Whatever was living in these burrows was closer to the strange hard-bodied creatures that came later.

He bent down to examine the tide pools that foamed around his feet. Maybe the waves had washed something ashore. He scooped up a tiny shelled creature no bigger than his thumb—it looked as if it had been bitten in half, and so did many of the larger life forms he found along the beach. So much for the harmless autotrophs; predation had obviously begun. Drawing a quick sketch of what he had found he ran back to the shuttle determined to fit together the pieces to this planetary puzzle.

"Hey, Jay," one of his friends called out. "Since when did you start taking evolutionary biology? Nice sketches, but the trilobite looks a little funny."

"You know what these things are?" Jay asked in surprise.

"Sure, look up Earth's Late Pre-Cambrian, a.k.a. Vendian or Ediacaran period, and the Cambrian period (543 to 510 million years ago) that came after it. You can use my computer."

"You know, I think I will."

HERE'S THE SITUATION
You have two days before you and your colleagues must decide the fate of this planet and

the hundreds of people who are waiting to re-colonize it. Before you come to any conclusions, however, you need to find out exactly what happened on this planet, why it happened, and what the future possibilities are. Start with sources on Earth's Late Pre-Cambrian, a.k.a. "Vendian" or "Ediacaran" period, and the Cambrian period (543 to 510 million years ago). By the time you return to class to solve this case, you will need to know:

1. What was the Late Pre-Cambrian environment like on Earth?
2. What were the Ediacaran organisms like and how were they adapted to their environment?
3. How is Earth's Pre-Cambrian similar to P-L5's initial environment and organisms?
4. What was the "Cambrian Explosion"?
5. How did the environment and organisms change and adapt during the "Cambrian Explosion"?
6. What causes lead into the "Cambrian Explosion"?
7. Could any of those Earth conditions have been mimicked on P-L5? How?
8. Assuming that this alien planet was going through an "Alien Cambrian Explosion" that mimicked Earth, what do you think will happen next?

ALIEN EVOLUTION: PART II

Jay could hardly wait for dinner to end. His mind was racing with a hundred theories and ideas. It had taken the colonists less then 100 years to dramatically change the planet. Could the colonists' planetary "adjustments" have adjusted more than they intended? How had it affected the native creatures? Could the murky water be hiding new animals? Predators perhaps? And why had the people fled? Once at the computer console, Jay logged into his old biology book. What he found shocked him:

The Ediacaran Period (also referred to as the Vendian or Late Pre-Cambrian) occurred from approximately 700 million years ago until 543 million years ago Earth time. The period was noted for its simple soft-bodied Ediacaran fauna, mainly autotrophic, chemo- and photoautotrophs, symbionts, as well as filter feeders and passive nutrient absorbers, all inhabiting the deep oceans (see "Burgess Shale"). Oxygen levels were low (approx. 5%) at this time, although Cyanobacteria (blue green bacteria) were slowly raising the O_2 concentration.

Great environmental and biological changes began that would have far-reaching impact. Massive glaciers dumped tons of sediment rich in nitrogen, sulfides, calcium carbonate, and phosphates into the seas, encouraging new life forms that grazed on the bacteria-covered nutrients, and providing the calcium carbonate and phosphates that would later be used to make shells. The rise in oceanic and atmospheric O_2 concentration reached toxic levels for some life forms while allowing others to raise their metabolic rates and thrive (see "Oxygen Revolution").

The appearance of early predators toward the end of the Pre-Cambrian signaled the shift in feeding styles from autotrophs to heterotrophs, which is associated with the predator versus prey "evolutionary arms race." This intensified struggle to survive encouraged faster mobility (possible because of O_2 metabolism), shells and claws (i.e., increased mineral content of sea), and the development of sophisticated nervous systems (nerve nets to ganglia and eventually brains). Together these environmental and biological factors led to the "Cambrian Explosion," a period of fantastic evolutionary change and diversity lasting over several million years and beginning approximately 543 million years ago. In that short period, all but one of the major phylum and body patterns evolved.—Online text: *Evolutionary Biology: Earth and Beyond*, 2660.

Now he was getting somewhere. Jay took the creased sketch paper from his pocket and compared the strange drawings to the textbook illustrations. Sure enough, the paper almost exactly matched the ancient fossil illustrations from the screen. Jay looked at the simple drawings in awe. How, he wondered, could creatures from the Earth's distant past have surfaced on an alien planet millions of years in the future? Although the planet had originally seemed to fit Pre-Cambrian Earth's calm description, there had been no major glacial events, no undersea volcanoes, nor millenniums of oxygen-building bacteria. Could the colonists have inadvertently tipped a planet on the edge of an "Alien Cambrian Explosion"?

Jay was beginning to feel uneasy. Let's assume, he thought, that the early colonists found conditions here similar to Earth's Pre-Cambrian, and that this simple planet was indeed changing as Earth had. Let's also say that the colonists speeded up the process exponentially by dumping in oxygen and sediments. Then the environment and organisms may have been able to evolve at an incredible speed—"break-neck evolution" was a recognized phenomenon on some alien planets. If the path of evolution on P-L5 had followed that on Earth, seas would have turned murky with sediment and "Ediacaran fauna" would have given way to a host of shelled, swimming, and burrowing creatures clogging the water pipes. Predators like Earth's three-foot-long *Anomalocaris* would have scared tourists and residents alike.

Perhaps a frightened populace decided to get out before it was too late, before the new creatures emerged from the sea to take their first steps on land as Earth's creatures had later done. Tomorrow he and his colleagues would have to make a decision that would affect hundreds of people and an entire planet. Should they re-colonize P-L5 or leave it for good?

What he needed was information—enough to convince an entire team of scientists, investors, judges, and colonists of just what they were getting into.

Discussion Questions

How were the Ediacaran organisms adapted for their environment?

- What major changes were occurring in the environment around the time of the "Cambrian Explosion"?
- Which of these changes were affected by the organisms themselves; which were purely geological trends?
- On P-L5, humans changed the environment in ways that reproduced the forces on early Earth. Do you really think that Earth-like animals would have evolved again? Why or why not?
- Assuming that this planet was undergoing an "Alien Explosion" similar to the "Cambrian Explosion" on Earth, what would you expect to evolve next?
- Is the planet safe for colonization? Why or why not?

Tomorrow you will be expected to present a full report on the environmental and biological conditions on P-L5 as well as a decision on re-colonization. Each member of your group will represent one interest in this decision such as scientist, colonist, investor, etc., and will have to support your group's decision before a preliminary court. Be prepared to justify your decision with theories on evolution as well as actual examples from Earth. In addition to other materials, you will need to know:

- What were the initial conditions on P-L5?
- How were those conditions similar to "Vendian" Earth? How were they different?
- How did the colonists change P-L5? Why did they change it and what effects did those changes have on the planet and native organisms?
- What led to Earth's "Cambrian Explosion"?
- Could the "Alien Explosion" on P-L5 be slowed or controlled? Could the planet be made safe for re-colonization?

Thank you and good luck! Thousands of people are awaiting this mission's final decision.

Your participant role assignments (Detailed information on each follows):

- High court judges
- Biologist for re-colonization
- Biologist against re-colonization
- Chemist for re-colonization
- Chemist against re-colonization
- Geologist for re-colonization
- Geologist against re-colonization
- Civilian for re-colonization
- Civilian against re-colonization
- Investor for re-colonization
- Investor against re-colonization
- Intern for re-colonization
- Intern against re-colonization

Teaching Notes

This case was written for freshman biology and introductory geology courses. It has been taught in both of these settings with excellent results. Detailed teaching notes are available at SUNY at Buffalo's National Center for Case Study Teaching in Science at *http://ublib.buffalo.edu/libraries/projects/cases/case.html*.

The case is designed to be taught using Problem-Based Learning or another cooperative strategy where teams of five to six students work together throughout the term. Students should have some background in evolution and perhaps ecology by the time this case is used. It is introduced in one class period when students discuss the case in their teams and search out answers to the questions.

During the next class, teammates compare notes and clarify the issues. They are then given the second part of the case and the instructor informs everyone that a debate over the colonization question will be held in a following class period. There will be a "For Re-Colonization Team" versus an "Against Re-Colonization Team." Within each of these teams there will be a particular role for each student. The students choose one of the roles listed at the end of Part II of the case. There are detailed instructions for each student role at our website giving background information as well as references.

When the great debate occurs, a panel of High Court Judges (with their specific roles described—see our website for details) listen to the various individual experts present their side of the argument within a three- to five-minute time limit. The judges have an opportunity to ask questions of all participants before they finally render a judgment whether or not to re-colonize. In addition, it has been our practice to ask for an individual vote of all students and to require written follow-up reports. Students have unanimously enjoyed this case.

Participant Roles for Alien Evolution

Below are instructions for students who will be role-playing during the Alien Evolution debate. The number of players and their roles can be easily modified depending upon the circumstances. Each student receives a sheet of instructions for individual roles. At the end of each sheet there is a set of references such as that shown at the bottom of the judges' page. They have been eliminated here to save space.

High Court Judges—Official Memorandum

To: Esteemed Judges of the Starfleet High Tribunal on Re-Colonization
From: Supreme Court Justice Smith
Re: Re-Colonization of P-L5

I understand that you are going to be reviewing a re-colonization case for a planet in the Fifth Quadrant, P-L5. I would remind you that this is the first such "re-colonization" attempt in 30 years, and your decision carries great importance. I would also warn you that special interests are attempting to influence the case on both sides. It is your duty as judges to investigate the evolutionary matter thoroughly so as to be sure of the evidence and arguments presented in court. I would urge you to familiarize yourself with the various facts and theories of evolution and question both sides of the presenters freely. I have placed a large group of specialists on hand to advise you in your decision. Feel free to call on them to explain a fact or point out a discrepancy in the lower court's argument. I will be watching this case carefully. Good luck!

W. B. Smith,
Supreme Court Justice
Leads and Sources

Magazines and Articles

Bottjer, D. 2005. The early evolution of animals. *Scientific American* (August): 42–47.

Bromham, L. 2003. What can DNA tell us about the Cambrian explosion? *Integrative Comparative Biology* 43: 148–156.

Erwin, D. 1999. The origin of body plans. *American Zoologist* 39: 617–629.

Falkowski, P., M. Katz, A. Milligan, K. Fennel, B. Cramer, M. Aubry, R. Berner, M. Novacek, and W. Zapol. 2005. The rise of oxygen over the past 205 million years and the evolution of large placental mammals. *Science* 309: 2202–2204.

Gee, H. 1995. The molecular explosion. *Nature* 373: 558.

Gould, S. J. 1998. On embryos and ancestors. *Natural History* (July/August): 20.

Gould, S. J. 1994. The evolution of life on the Earth. *Scientific American* (October): 85.

Hurtgen, M. 2003. Ancient oceans and oxygen. *Nature* 423: 592–593.

Kerr, R. 2002. A trigger for the Cambrian explosion? *Science* 298: 1547

Knoll, A. 1996. Breathing room for early animals. *Nature* 382: 111.

Levington, J. 1992. The big bang of animal evolution. *Scientific American* 18–26.

Morris, S. C., and S. J. Gould. 1998. Showdown on the burgess shale. *Natural History* 107 (10): 48–55.

Nash, J. M. 1995. When life exploded. *Time* (December 4).

Oliwenstein, L. 1996. Life's grand explosions. *Discover* 17: 42–43.

Internet Sites

The Divisions of Precambrian Time

www.ucmp.berkeley.edu/precambrian/precambrian.html

Life of the Vendian

www.ucmp.berkeley.edu/vendian/vendianlife.html

Learning about the Vendian Animals

www.ucmp.berkeley.edu/vendian/critters.html

Cambrian Explosion: As of August, 2006, there were 440,000 sites catalogued on Google for the Cambrian explosion. Here are two:

www.carleton.ca/Museum/camex/1ahome.html
www.ucmp.berkeley.edu/cambrian/camb.html

Books

Gould, S. J. 1989 *It's a wonderful life: The burgess shale and the nature of history.* New York: Norton.

Knoll, A. 2003. *Life on a young planet: The first three billion years of evolution on Earth.* Princeton: Princeton University Press.

McMenamin, M., and D. McMenamin. 1990. *The emergence of animals: The Cambrian breakthrough.* New York: Columbia University Press.

Morris, S. C. 1998. *The crucible of creation: The burgess shale and the rise of animals.* Oxford: Oxford University Press.

Schopf, J. W. 1999. *Cradle of life: The discovery of Earth's earliest years.* Princeton: Princeton University Press.

▶   ▶   ▶

Biologist for Re-Colonization

Like the other crewmembers, you explored P-L5 carefully before coming to your decision. This planet was ideal for colonization. The expensive O_2 priming, landscaping, and infrastructure were done a hundred years ago. Looking at the place even now, people could move right in tomorrow! As for the "critter problem," a couple of primitive snails and crabs don't trouble you. If your calculations are correct, it would take hundreds and hundreds of years before these "sea slugs" ever made it to land even with an accelerated evolutionary rate. Imagine the research possibilities. A glimpse into Earth's primitive past. The science facility is already fully equipped and capable of supporting a research team—led by you, of course. Maybe it would be a good thing if colonists weren't brought in just yet; it would give you time to study the planet and do some groundbreaking studies. The best plan would probably be to support re-colonization and apply for a grant to study the planet. If you handle this right, you might just get the break of the century.

▶   ▶   ▶

Biologist Against Re-Colonization
To: Alex Kelly, Biologist
From: Scientists Against Space (SAS)
Re: P-L5

We are at a profound crossroads in our history as a species. With the current push to move populations off Earth and into surrounding planets, our galaxy has been contaminated as never before. Settlements are not only a risk to any colonists, but to the planets and ecosystems we invade. P-L5 is a prime example of this crisis. Against the advice of we scientists, the planet was "adjusted," polluted, and colonized. Oxygen levels were rapidly increased. The very chemical concentrations of its once beautiful seas were changed and foreign organisms were introduced. Is it any wonder that the seas turned murky and the native species frightening? We have already started this once harmless planet down an uncertain path, with new species and phyla that might one day threaten us. To re-colonize this planet would only put hundreds of people in danger and destroy what is left of this fragile ecosystem. As fellow scientists we urge you to convince the judges to ban re-colonization of P-L5.

Thank You!

Kim Menicken, Columbia PhD, Extraterrestrial Biology

Jim McCay, Boston U. PhD, Biotics

Nada Rachim, SUNY Buffalo. PhD, Astro Paleontology

Sam Goldwin, Harvard PhD., Marine Biology

J.K Nafemaya, NYU PhD, Chemical Philosophy

Jim McCay, Boston U. PhD, Biotics

Lu Wang, Lunar South PhD, Physics

Shifra Kayle, Oxford PhD, Dynamics

P.M Cay, U. Mass PhD, Geobiology

▶   ▶   ▶

Chemist for Re-Colonization
Why does everybody always seem to forget the chemistry of evolution? The fears of the timid are misplaced. We can control the process! Left alone, it takes eons for major evolutionary changes to occur. Shells and skeletons require complex processes to turn calcium carbonate from the sea into shells on the backs of animals. The "Oxygen Revolution" didn't happen overnight. Yes, it changed life on Earth, allowing higher metabolism (Krebs Cycle) and displacing anaerobic life forms but it created open niches. Nitrogen and phosphate also contribute to evolution because they allow animals to diversify and grow. DNA changes can't be ignored either, nor can the switch to heterotrophic feeding that allowed animals to grow in volume instead of spreading out for yet more surface area. And we haven't even begun to talk about the way the organisms themselves affect their chemical environment and how that environment then affects the organisms. All of these things can be monitored and regulated. P-L5 is like a test tube: Control the reactants in the environments and you control the organisms that are produced. To convince the judges to re-colonize you will have to explain the chemical theories of evolution and the "Cambrian Explosion" and how you would limit them. Good luck!

▶   ▶   ▶

Chemist Against Re-Colonization
Why does everybody always seem to forget about the chemistry of evolution? Shells and skeletons require complex processes to turn

calcium carbonate from the sea into shells on the backs of animals. The "Oxygen Revolution" changed life on Earth, allowing higher metabolism (Krebs Cycle) and wiping out life forms. Nitrogen and phosphate also contribute to evolution because they allow animals to diversify and grow. Can we control these planetary cycles? We didn't do well on our own plane. Why think we can do it on P-L5? DNA changes can't be ignored either. And we haven't even begun to talk about the way the organisms themselves affect their chemical environment and how that environment then affects the organisms. Evolution is very much like a series of reinforcing cycles that once begun are too complicated and powerful to stop. Besides, trying to chemically regulate this planet would be like trying to put out a fire with lighter fluid—who knows what effects it would have on the ecosystem here? Instead of harmless trilobites we might end up with all kinds of mutant life forms completely alien to our understanding and far beyond our control. It was a mistake to "adjust" this planet once for humans and doing it a second time would only create more problems. P-L5 is better left alone! We should have done so in the first place.

Geologist for Re-colonization

First of all, this notion that P-L5 is going to go down the same evolutionary path as Earth's is absurd. Back in the 20th century Steven Jay Gould made the point emphatically when he said that even on Earth the evolutionary process would never be repeated the same way. If we played the tape over again it would be different. And P-L5 is quite different than Earth. Speaking as a geologist, the right conditions just aren't here. There are no undersea volcanoes or plate tectonics, no glacier activity or limestone deposits on the sea floor. Even if a few organisms have indeed adapted to the new "Earth-like" con-

ditions, it is statistically impossible that those creatures should simply repeat step-by-step the same changes and shifts that took place millions of years ago on Earth. This is politics pure and simple. Whatever is going on, somebody has an interest in keeping P-L5 uninhabited. It is up to you to convince the judges that a rapid explosive evolution where tens of millions of years are collapsed into a few decades is ridiculous.

Geologist Against Re-Colonization

When the voyage to evaluate P-L5 had been announced, you hadn't been able to resist signing on. It had been a long-running family joke that Great-Grandpa Jim had depopulated an entire planet in his younger days by hanging a fish outside the mayor's bedroom window. By the time Grandpa Jim was born, P-L5 was already a dying planet. Years of murky water, "critter sightings," and poor advertising decisions had turned the once booming tourist center into one big vacancy. Townsfolk had been leaving for years for brighter, busier planets, selling their businesses and homes to a financing company. When Great-Grandpa hung one up of those big funny-looking fish that used to wash up on shore, the townspeople decided they had had it.

This planet didn't sound too dangerous in Grandpa's stories, but to you as a geologist it is quite unlike Earth: no undersea volcanoes or plate tectonics, a weak magnetic field, no glacier activity or limestone deposits on the sea floor. Something is obviously going on here and the seawater is turning brown with polluting chemicals. Not only that, but this planet is definitely "hot" and the radioactivity might be speeding up evolution. Geological forces similar to Earth's might be awakening, and who knows what is crawling around down there? The sooner everybody leaves the better.

Civilian for Re-Colonization

When you agreed to be an impartial civilian participant on this voyage, you were just hoping to escape Earth for a little while and P-L5 was a way out. But once you saw this beautiful planet, you couldn't help but get involved. P-L5 was everything you had always dreamed of as a kid in the closed-in metropolises of Earth. Compared to Earth this place was the Garden of Eden. Fresh air, open space, plenty of land. Houses! Real houses, like in your Grandma's old photos—no dirty tenements and 70-story complexes. Some of the other crewmembers worried about "alien monsters" and things, but all it turned out to be was a couple of sea predators and simple trilobites. What were they compared to the viruses, animals, and gangs that ravaged Earth? You have only a few days to learn enough about evolutionary biology to convince a panel of judges that P-L5 should be colonized.

Civilian Against Re-Colonization

Yes, before you signed on to this trip you had heard all the praises of this strange planet, but there still seemed to be a tiny little detail everyone was glossing over—it takes a heck of a lot more than a little trilobite to send thousands of people packing. Walking through the ghostly city by the shore you came upon government files left unlocked, empty homes, and vacant businesses. These people had left homes, factories, and businesses behind, and despite all their reassurances, the investigative team still doesn't know exactly what had made those early colonists leave. You have only a short time to figure out what happened on this planet and convince the re-colonization committee that P-L5 is better left alone.

Investor for Re-Colonization

To: Investor J. C. Hartley
From: K&P Securities Inc.
Re: Investments

I don't think I need to remind you of the importance of this decision. P-L5 once brought two trillion dollars a year into our company finances and we cannot afford to miss this opportunity. Resettlement must begin at once! The initial investment needed to rebuild this colony is incidental when compared to the trillions of dollars it would take to locate, study, and prepare a new planet. The entire infrastructure, buildings, roads, and landscaping are intact. As for the "Alien Problem," we humans have been dealing with far more complex and dangerous life forms for millenniums on Earth—why should we jump at the sight of a few trilobites? So the people can't go to the beach—we'll build a "Cambrian Park" that will knock their socks off! And if the things evolve again, well, we'll just put in a couple of strategic fences. I have compiled a short list of resources you might find useful. I don't care what you argue so long as you convince those judges to re-colonize.

Finally, let me warn you that the judges are likely to take the easy way out and do nothing. They will want to study the problem further. The scientists will be overjoyed with this. This approach would spell disaster for us.

You must therefore make the strongest possible case for re-colonization. This should include that (1) there are no serious dangers—no one can know the future anywhere in the galaxy. This is no different. There is no known danger. Period! If we had shied away from the unknown, we would never have left Earth centuries ago. (2) There are known mineral deposits on P-L5 that would bolster the economic wealth of the Earth. (3) Earth itself has enormous population pressures, global warming, pollution problems, and an entire city of people that has already signed up to immigrate to P-L5. The problems would be alleviated immediately, if we could seriously establish a sustainable colony on P-L5. Moreover, P-L5 could serve as an easy way station to the Andromeda galaxy. (4) Most important, K&P Securities will only offer to help in the financing of this re-colonization for the next six months. After that, we will shift our interests elsewhere and will openly campaign against any judges that have thwarted the development of Earth's economy and the alleviation of her citizens' serious problems.

I'll be waiting,
J.D. Kaper, CEO K&P Securities

Investor Against Re-Colonization
To: Investor K.K.K Xiu
From: L&R Financing
Re: P-L5

I don't need to remind you how seriously the judges' decision tomorrow will affect our future—and yours. L&R Financing financed the original P-L5 colonization in cooperation with our former partners, K&P Securities Inc. However, since the abandonment of the colony almost 100 years ago, we have maintained a discreet and highly lucrative Californium mine on the far side of south island. Should re-colonization begin, we would not only have to abandon and cover up our operations, but face possible environmental charges in the future. The press would savage us if they knew we've been leaking radioactive waste into P-L5's seas for over a hundred years.

But, if re-colonization is denied, everyone goes home and we can maintain our operations. Your job is to convince the judges to veto re-colonization. I have spoken to several specialists in evolution issues and they all agree you can make a good case. You can in good conscience argue that the planet is unsafe and dangerous due to both (1) the chemicals in the ecosystem and (2) the uncertainty of the organisms and their rapid evolution. (Incidentally, if *Anomalocaris* were to wash up on shore that would definitely have an impact on the decision.) Evolution here is too far advanced to be controlled. According to Gould, chance plays such an important role in evolution that using Earth as a "future forecast" is foolish. Gould was certainly right. If we played the evolutionary tape over again, the results might be disastrous. I don't really care what you argue

as long as you win this case. P-L5 must not be colonized! I've had my secretary type up a list of resources that might help you tomorrow. Remember, we're counting on you.

One final thought. It seems likely that the judges will have difficulty balancing the pros and cons of this argument. So, they will probably want to take the easy way out and declare that we must delay and study the question further. If they do that, though not an optimum solution, it will be a victory for us. Studies by committees have a way of dragging on forever. The longer we can delay this decision the better. Trillions of dollars hang in the balance.

Larry Czetsky III
Managing Director, L&R Financing

Intern for Re-Colonization
Well, this was turning out to be one boring summer job. When you signed on as an undergraduate intern with the team of resident Starfleet Scientists, you figured fame would soon follow. What followed were endless hours of thankless lab work, coffee serving, and errands. If you are ever going to emerge from your team's shadow, now is the time; but reading up on some widely known scientific theory on the Vendian, Ediacaran, and Cambrian is not going to get you far. What you need is to come up with some ideas on evolution that will convince people why Starfleet should re-colonize P-L5. A quick glance at *Nature* and *Scientific American* reassures you that there are plenty of interesting theories to choose from. Of course, it is unlikely that you will stumble across any new ideas. Still it is worth thinking about. Can you think of a new approach?

The worst problem is that one of the biologists you are working for does not want colonization, under any circumstances, although he pretends otherwise. He says P-L5 is safe, and he believes it. But, he just wants to have this planet for his own private research project. In fact, he seems to be willing to fudge results in order to make this happen. You wonder if you should tell someone about this—perhaps the investors who are footing the bill for this so-called exploratory trip. Then again, perhaps you should keep quiet about this until the Judicial Council's hearing, and then, spring this information. Otherwise, the information might never become public

▶   ▶   ▶

Intern Against Re-Colonization

Well, this was turning out to be one boring summer job. When you signed on as an undergraduate intern with the team of resident Starfleet Scientists, you figured fame would soon follow. What followed were endless hours of thankless lab work, coffee serving, and errands. If you are ever going to emerge from your team's shadow, now is the time; but reading up on some widely known scientific theory on the Vendian, Ediacaran, and Cambrian is not going to get you far. What you need is to come up with some ideas on evolution that will convince people why Starfleet should not re-colonize P-L5. A quick glance at *Nature* and *Scientific American* reassures you that there are plenty of interesting theories to choose from. Of course, it is unlikely that you will stumble across any new ideas, but it is worth trying. Is there a new approach?

What has you troubled most of all is that a chemist that you are working for is willing to suppress the results of the water pollution data. Dangerous chemicals are clearly coming from a plant on the other side of the planet. On the one hand, this is a good reason to abandon the colonization process, but this is not a fair and ethical approach to the problem. If the data were released, there is no reason why the pollution problem couldn't be overcome. You are sorely tempted to go public with this information. Your career would be in jeopardy but clearly the data should be known to the judges. This would definitely encourage the pro-re-colonization side. If you revealed this to your team, they would probably encourage you to keep quiet. Maybe you should surprise everyone at the Judicial Council's hearing with this revelation; otherwise, the information might be suppressed.

What to Do About Mother

Investigating Fetal Tissue Research and the Effects of Parkinson's Disease

By Ann Fourtner, Charles Fourtner, and Clyde Freeman Herreid

Gretchen was 62 years old when she first noticed the weakness in her right hand. She was enjoying a winter sunset from her terrace overlooking Teague Bay on the island of St. Croix.

Her neighbors had joined her, bringing snacks on a fine Wedgwood plate. As the appetizers were passed, she dropped the plate, spreading fragments and food on the tile floor. She felt terribly embarrassed. Her friends chalked it up to fatigue and stress as Gretchen's husband had recently died after a five-year battle with bone cancer.

Gretchen was vigorous, independent, and refined. She walked two to three miles each day and was an avid golfer. She was adjusting to her husband's absence and didn't depend on her three adult sons for support or advice. However, after she returned to Boston for the summer months she noticed a tremor in her right hand. She was soon diagnosed with early stage Parkinson's disease.

Gretchen was frightened. Her brother-in-law had died of pneumonia brought on by the effects of Parkinson's. At the end stage of his Parkinson's, he had developed contractures on his right side. His right arm would push his hand into his throat, causing him to have trouble breathing. He received physical therapy to help prevent these episodes, but the breathing became more difficult and he was not able to successfully fight off pneumonia.

Gretchen consulted several physicians and then her sons. Her oldest son, Duffy, a financial planner with Anderson Associates, advised his mother to sell the villa in St. Croix as well as the town house in Boston, and purchase an apartment in a long-term-care senior citizen complex. Her youngest son, Geoff, an insurance salesman with Lincoln Life, was in denial. He did not want anything to change. He insisted that the diagnosis was wrong—that she was fine and simply suffered from a nervous tremor due to her age.

Her middle son, Frank, a computer analyst with Computer Associates, was always curious and inquisitive. Once his mother was diagnosed, he searched the medical school library at the University of Massachusetts (via the internet) beginning with the *Merck Manual of Diagnosis and Therapy*. After becoming familiar with the language and the physiological effects of the disease, Frank was able to seek out and understand some of the latest results in ongoing research.

He then used the *Directory of Medical Specialists* to find a doctor that he felt was "on the cutting edge" of diagnosis and therapy. Frank encouraged Gretchen to use the internet for information and support.

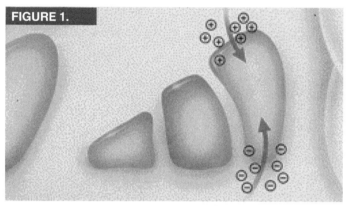

FIGURE 1.

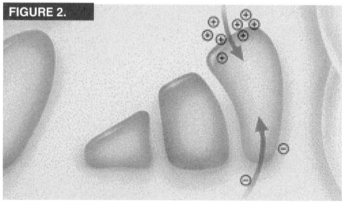

FIGURE 2.

In the normal brain (Figure 1), dopamine (-), the primary chemical that transmits messages about movement, is in balance with acetylcholine (+), another important chemical transmitter influencing movement. In patients with Parkinson's disease (Figure 2), deteriorating nerve cells result in a loss of dopamine and an imbalance of the chemical transmitters (dopamine [-] and acetylcholine [+]) affecting movement.

THE SCIENCE

Parkinson's disease is a common and severe neurodegenerative disorder brought on by a progressive loss of dopamine neurons in the nigro-striatal system of the brain. Symptoms vary in each patient and may include akinesia (inability to move), tremors, weakness, poor balance, loss of dexterity, reduced sense of smell, depression, swallowing and speech problems, and double vision.

Current treatment, which is based on drugs increasing dopamine in the affected areas, is effective in the early stages of the disease. After four to 10 years, the capacity to produce the desired result is reduced due to severe side effects caused by the drug treatment. Consequently, after 10 years of drug treatment, the majority of Parkinson's patients are not able to maintain any sort of quality of life and eventually die of complications. This factor has led to a search for alternative treatments that can halt the disease's progression and/or restore function.

A logical approach in the search for an alternative treatment was to see if the deficient cells of the brain could be replaced. The transplantation of nerve tissue had been first tested in humans in 1905 (Shirres).

By the mid-1980s, techniques for transplanting brain tissue from fetuses had been worked out in rodents and in primates. Human clinical trials were initiated in Europe, Central and North America, and China. By the end of 1990, over 100 Parkinson's patients had received grafts of fetal dopaminergic neurons. By 1994, studies had shown that "patients experienced prominent clinical benefits beginning 6–12 weeks after the transplant procedure with continued improvement over the three-year observation period" (Lindvall).

The technique of transplanting nerve tissue is still in an exploratory phase. Researchers have learned that several factors influence the likelihood of success: donor age, method of tissue storage, type of graft, site of implantation, use of immunosuppression, source of tissue, and patient selection. Other treatment programs are in the wings.

Currently, the Food and Drug Administration is considering the "Activa system," where doctors drill through the skull and implant an electrode into the thalamus, the message relay center in the brain. A wire is run just under the scalp down to the collarbone, where a pacemaker-sized "pulse generator" is implanted. It sends electrical waves to the brain that blocks tremors by emitting constant, small electrical shocks. Activa is already sold in Europe, with over 2,000 patients wearing implants since 1995.

Another procedure being refined for Parkinson's patients is called postero-ventral pallidotomy (PVP), where a small metal probe is inserted into the skull, deep into the globus pallidus of the brain, to surgically deaden a few of the cells in the critically overstimulated pathways.

ETHICAL QUESTIONS

Tissue transplants in humans raise ethical questions. Should women who abort to end unwanted pregnancies be allowed to donate the fetus for use in medical research or for therapy?

Many researchers have insisted that the abortion and subsequent transplant use must remain clearly separated in all respects, that the decision to terminate a pregnancy must not be influenced by the possible use of the fetal tissue. Thus, neither the fetal age nor the subsequent use of the fetus should ever be a factor in the procedure of abortion. Consent is always required and whenever possible before the abortion. (NECTAR guidelines, see *www.bm.lu.se/~nectar/eth.1.html.*)

Other knotty problems include: Should fees be paid for procurement, transportation, or storage? (Most guidelines established have forbidden profit or remuneration.) Should a fetus be kept alive for future use as tissue transplant? (Guidelines unanimously prohibit this; however, tissue can be stored in a "hibernation" medium.)

Is it possible that the need for fetal transplant tissue may lead to planned pregnancies and abortions to produce fetal tissue? (Two possible scenarios may lead to such a decision. One possibility may arise if fetal tissue transplant proves to be a successful therapy for diseases. Another may occur if the demand becomes greater than the supply available from abortion clinics.)

Advocates for fetal tissue transplant research are driven by their search for ways to alleviate the pain and suffering of the disease victims and the possibilities of relief for future generations. Opponents of fetal tissue research are motivated by their concern over the exploitation of women and pressure for increased numbers of abortions. They are troubled by the prospects of doctors benefiting financially for their surgical service in abortion and the fact that the opponents see the fetus as a living human being who is being sacrificed for another person's welfare.

DIRECTIONS FOR THE CASE

In a class period we will have an extensive discussion of Parkinson's disease and the case of Gretchen and her three sons. Each team of students in the class will be asked to consider the problem from the viewpoint of one of the sons. Their profiles are below. Your team will be assigned one of these roles to research and discuss. Please, be prepared to "solve" the family dilemma.

PROFILES

Duffy has accepted his mother's fate and is concerned that she be made as comfortable as possible by caregivers who can see to her physical needs. He has little respect for the medical community, believing that their primary concern is treatment of the disease, prolongation of life at all costs, and financial gain. Duffy has read extensively on the utility of group homes and is searching for one such home dedicated to individuals suffering from

Parkinson's. Useful websites include: *www.apdaparkinson.com* and *www.parkinsons.org*.

Frank has thoroughly investigated the medical and scientific nature of the disease and is convinced that a cure for Parkinson's is "just around the corner." He is convinced that the new procedures using fetal tissue transplants and the newer ideas of cell farming, in which specific lines of cells are grown in large numbers, will give Gretchen the needed neurons to cure the disease or at least alleviate most of her symptoms. Useful web sites include: *http://neuro-chief-e.mgh.harvard.edu/parkinsonsweb/Main/PDmain.html* and *http://www.mssm.edu/neurology/research.html*.

Geoff and his wife Marcia are extremely religious and, although not confirmed Christian Scientists, believe that good living and the grace of God will see a person through most of life's misfortunes. They know that Gretchen is aging and that children must care for their parents. Geoff does not understand the abandonment of parents proposed by Duffy. Furthermore he doesn't accept scientific explanations of disease and treatment that so fascinate Frank. Useful web sites include: *http://neuro-chief-e.mgh.harvard.edu/parkinsonsweb/Main/Surgery/surgical.html and http://apdaparkinson.com*.

REFERENCES

Backlund, E. O. et al. 1985. Transplantation of adrenal medullary tissue to striatum in parkinsonism. First clinical trials. *Journal of Neurosurgery* 62(2): 169-73.

Bjorklund, A. et al. 1983. In tracerebral grafting of neuronal cell suspensions. Introduction and general methods of preparation. *Acta Physiologica Scandinavica*. Supplementum 522:1–7.

Freeman, T. B., and J. H. Kordower. 1991. *Intracerebral transplantation in movement disorders,* eds. O. Lindvall et al., pp. 163–184. New York: Elsevier.

Lafferty, K. Statement to Fetal Tissue Transplantation Research Panel, National Institutes of Health, September 15, 1988.

Lindvall, O. et al. 1994. Evidence for long-term survival and function of dopaminergic grafts in progressive Parkinson's disease. *Annals of Neurology* 35(2): 172–180.

Shirres, D. A. 1905. Regeneration of axons of the spinal neurons in man. *Montreal Medical Journal* 34: 239–49.

Stein, D. G., and S. Brailowsky. 1997. *Brain repair*. New York: Oxford University Press.

TEACHING NOTES

Introduction

This is a real case dealing with one of the medical problems besetting the aging population—what to do when family members are no longer able to care for themselves? It deals with a cutting-edge research problem (the use of fetal tissue transplants) and the attendant social issues of abortion. A more detailed version of the case and teaching notes may be found at *http://ublib.buffalo.edu/libraries/projects/cases/case.html*.

We have taught this case in two different courses, both for nonscience majors. In both situations, the students convened in small cooperative-learning teams where group work figured in the grading. In spite of the obvious sophistication of the material, it was within reach of the average student with a little background in neural function.

Objectives

The case was designed to achieve the following objectives:

- Teach the fundamental principles of neurophysiology and neuropharmacology.
- Teach specific information about brain injury and brain repair mechanisms.
- Consider the physical and psychological effects of a degenerative disease (Parkinson's) on a patient and family.
- Consider cutting-edge research for the possible "cure" of the disorder.
- Explore the ethical questions surrounding the use of fetal tissue in research.
- Consider the sociological implications of an aging population.

Key Issues

This case study has two major scientific concerns: the use of fetal tissue for research or clinical application and the etiology of Parkinson's disease. For this case students must investigate the established guidelines for the use and sources of fetal tissue and compare the treatments that are currently available.

Students can also evaluate the evidence supporting the use of fetal tissue for research in a number of different applications and the evidence regarding the technology itself. They can compare fetal tissue sources to other sources such as cell tissue banks (tissue cultured cells).

There is also a social concern that we ask the students to address—the effect of the disease on the "healthy" family members. Since Parkinson's is a long-term disease in which the ill individual will progressively become weaker and less able to care for herself, the family typically becomes the caretaker. We ask the students to consider the family interactions in handling the medical treatment, long-term physical care, and the financial problems as the disease progresses.

Another social ramification is the source of fetal tissue. This issue begs the question of the legality of abortion and the use of abortive tissue. For example, should the tissue of "spontaneous abortions" and/or "therapeutic abortions" be made available for research and clinical treatments?

TEACHING THE CASE

Before the Case

Just prior to teaching this case, we assigned our small class of students readings in a textbook, *Brain Repair* by R. Stein, S. Brailowsky, and B. Will (NY: Oxford Univ. Press, 1997). The chapters of importance deal with "Regeneration, Repair, and Reorganization" (Chap. 5), "Brain Transplants as Therapy for Brain Injuries?" (Chap. 8), and "The Pharmacology of Brain Injury Repair" (Chap. 9).

In the class period before the case was run, three teams of students were assigned three questions to discuss: (1) What is the probability of successful treatment of Parkinson's disease using fetal tissue? (2) What is the likelihood that fetal tissue will be permitted for research in the United States? (3) Is it a better approach to rely solely on drug therapy for the disease, including drug treatment of psychosis and mental depression that can accompany the disorder?

These questions occupied the teams for 10 minutes, then two people from each group (the scribe and presenter) went to the blackboard to write a summary. At this point, the instructor ran a general discussion of the questions while the students were still at the board. This experience highlighted many of the essential talking points that would emerge in the case.

The students received the case about 20 minutes before the end of class. The groups received instructions about the roles they would play in the case when the class next met.

Each group had to adopt the role of one of the three brothers. A brief personality profile and a couple of references were supplied to each group. They were told that they must approach the case in the persona of the brother they were assigned. They had a brief conversation at the end of class to get a start on their strategy. We advised them to try and get together outside of class as well.

The Day of the Case

At the beginning of the case we gave the students 25 minutes to refine their group positions by talking among themselves. After 15 minutes of this activity we quietly asked one student from each group to withdraw and meet with us privately. This three-person team was then told that they had to play a new role—the part of "Mom." They were told to quietly discuss among themselves how they would feel about their disease, the coming crisis, and the impending decision.

This lasted 10 minutes; then the whole class was brought to order.

The instructor asked a representative from each brother's group to go to the board and write a summary of their group's decision of "What to do about Mom." The instructor ran a discussion emphasizing and clarifying the brothers' positions. The groups were then asked to reconvene and reconsider the problem in light of the other brothers' views. This lasted about 10 minutes.

At this juncture, the instructor asked representatives from each group to explain their position, starting with Geoff, followed by the views of the other brothers. The entire class was allowed to participate at this point while the instructor wrote down the salient points, and a vigorous debate ensued.

At a suitable point, when compromise seemed unlikely, the instructor sprang his surprise. "I have a fourth group here. Here's Mom!" He turned to the three students who considered this problem from Mom's perspective and asked their views. This phase of the discussion lasted perhaps 10 minutes.

The strong statements of the brothers presented earlier suddenly softened. No one wanted to argue with Mom! The financial arguments of Duffy became less relevant. Frank's treatment suggestions became more conservative. The offer of Geoff to care for Mom in his home tended to swing the decision his way.

We finished up the case by asking the students to imagine a point seven years in the future when Mom is largely without motor control and has extreme trouble breathing (the instructor can role-play this). We then asked, "Did you do the right thing?"

Another way to reach closure is to take a straw poll of the class asking them to vote on which option they would choose. A follow-up essay can be assigned where the students must choose an option and defend it.

The Galapagos

A Natural Laboratory for the Study of Evolution

By Nancy A. Schiller and Clyde F. Herreid

Using problem-based learning and role-playing, students analyze the geological origins of the Galapagos Islands, their colonization, species formation, and threats to their biodiversity in this story of a student caught between local fishermen and government officials fighting for control of the islands' natural resources.

PART I: IN THE BEGINNING

Kate stood on the edge of the *caldera* and peered down into the shadows. She could barely make out the movement a thousand feet below. But there, she was sure, was the tortoise she had named Alfredo, slowly making his way among the lava rocks toward the water pool.

Kate marveled at the volcanoes around her. Before she had started this journey, she had read about the Galapagos and their volcanic origins. But she hadn't expected to be so emotionally moved by the islands themselves, by their stark scenery.

A young graduate student, she was about to embark upon a four-year study of the biology of the longest living animals. Alfredo had been around long before Darwin had arrived in the islands—and here he was still, ambling among the lava.

The origins of the Galapagos were similar to the origins of the Hawaiian Islands, but the Galapagos clearly were younger, more stark and barren. Kate had read that the Galapagos were a chain of islands, some of which no longer broke the surface of the water. How were these islands formed, she wondered. Was it from a hot spot at the bottom of the ocean bubbling up magma at periodic intervals? Somewhere in the sea nearby in the Galapagos Rift there were hydrothermal vents belching sulfurous gases. Some biologists believed these vents were the sites of the origin of life.

Made up of 13 large islands and dozens of smaller ones, the Galapagos straddle the equator in the eastern Pacific Ocean, some 600 miles off the coast of mainland Ecuador. Large, jagged outcroppings of lava alternate with small sandy beaches. Isolated patches of mangroves along the shore give way to cactus in the arid lowlands of the islands, then lush cloud forests in the moist upper regions, and finally tree ferns and scrubby grasses in the otherwise barren uplands.

But it was the astonishing array of animals that took Kate's breath away. Like every other visitor to the islands, she was struck by the strangeness and tameness of the fauna. Scores of sea lions lazily sunned themselves on the beaches. Masked boobies courted practically under foot. Among the rocks at the water's edge lived the black iguana, the only marine lizard in the world. In the surrounding seas were stingrays, white-tipped sharks, sea turtles, and the Galapagos penguin. Dozens of endemic species were found here and nowhere else on Earth.

And here she was, standing where Charles Darwin had stood 150 years before. Darwin's theories had depended heavily on his insights into the origins of the life forms on the Galapagos. He had questioned where these animals had come from. How could the flora and the fauna of islands so near one another be so different and yet strangely so similar? Each island seemed to have its own variety of tortoise, its own type of marine iguana, even its own form of prickly-pear cactus.

The finches were particularly interesting. These relatively nondescript birds had beaks with amazing adaptations to eat different types of food. Although most of them were seed-eaters, Darwin had discovered that one of the finches had specialized by using small sharp sticks to probe the recesses of cactus plants for grubs. A woodpecker finch he called it. How could these animals and plants be due to simple creation? Wasn't it more reasonable to think that mainland species had arrived on the islands eons ago and became specialized for different environmental conditions on the different islands?

Kate knew the answers now to Darwin's questions, and yet the islands didn't seem old enough to account for the spectacular diversity she saw all around her. She knew that the Grants, the husband and wife team from Princeton University, were working on a nearby island to resolve the question of the speed of evolution. She had heard at the Charles Darwin Research Station that they had been impressed with the rapid changes that seemed to be brought about by the El Niño climate shifts in the last couple of decades. She resolved to look into this more closely. But right now she had to get back to the station—gray storm clouds were closing in fast.

QUESTIONS

1. How did the Galapagos Islands come into existence? Were plate tectonics involved?
2. How old are the Galapagos Islands?
3. What kinds of animals and plants are endemic to the islands?
4. How do species become endemic?
5. Where did the original colonists come from and how did they get to the Galapagos?
6. What kind of special adaptations do the animals and plants have? How do adaptations evolve?
7. How did these islands figure into Darwin's ideas on evolution?

PART II: DARWIN'S FINCHES

"So, Kate, what do you think of the islands?" asked Miguel.

"I think they're fantastic. The Spanish were right to call them 'The Encantadas'." Kate had just entered the library of the Charles Darwin Research Station to find its director sitting at a table.

"Yes, 'The Enchanted Isles' does seem to suit them. The volcanoes have always seemed bewitched to me. Sit down and tell me how your plans are shaping up." Miguel gestured toward a chair across from him.

"Well, I was on Albemarle two days ago, and I think I could get my research done up there. The chance to study character displacement on the five volcanoes is really exciting. Imagine, five different species of tortoises on the same island. A lot of the tortoises seem to have already been marked by previous researchers, and you seem to have a good handle on some of the history already."

"Yes. In addition, we have some good DNA data on the tortoises here, especially those in our breeding pens. You've seen them, I'm sure."

"Yes, I have. I think it's a terrific breakthrough that at last you can identify which islands some of these animals came from. In fact, it should be possible to identify the parents if enough data were collected. But who's doing this work? Is it done here at the station?"

"No. We send tissue samples out to labs in the United States for DNA fingerprinting. We don't have the facilities here to do Southern Blot procedures or PCR. But tell me, are you committed to working on the tortoises? There are a lot of easier things to study here. The iguanas and the birds are more accessible."

"I've thought about that, especially since the Grants have been so successful working on the finches. How's their work coming?" Kate leaned forward eagerly.

Miguel removed his glasses, tilted his chair back, and began: "I'm sure you know that Peter and Rosemary started trapping and banding all of the finches on Daphne Major over 20 years ago. Sometimes they had only 200 birds on the island; sometimes there were over 2,000. And they could recognize them all! The Grants have been able to watch evolution happen, something that Darwin could only imagine."

"He thought evolution was too slow to see," Kate said. "In fact, Creationists have argued that neither evolution nor Divine Creation could be tested. The Grants' work certainly puts a lie to that."

"Yup. Darwin certainly underestimated the speed of evolution. These islands appeared less than five million years ago, and life is evolving here as fast and furiously as the volcanoes because life forms are trapped on separate islands. The top of each volcano is a prison for most of the creatures."

"There never was a bridge to the mainland, was there?"

"No. Anything that has arrived here had to cross at least 600 miles of water from South America. That's how the first finches arrived here, presumably blown off the mainland during a storm."

"So, in the space of a few million years all of the different species had to have adapted to the different conditions on the different islands."

"That's true, but realize the differences are not all due to adaptations and natural selection. I figure a lot of it has to do with genetic drift."

"Of course. But whatever was going on, no one figured it would be as fast as the Grants have discovered. I think one of the neatest techniques that the Grants brought to their study was a way of measuring how the seeds of the different plant species vary in hardness."

"I agree with you, Kate. Peter and an engineer at McGill University designed a nutcracker, a sort of pliers with a scale attached. They found small soft seeds of Portulaca needed only a force of 0.35 newtons to be cracked. Any of the finch species could do that. But the big hard seeds of *Cordia lutea* needed 14 newtons force and only a few large finches

can muster that much force. Once they knew how to measure hardness, the Grant team could check the abundance of the seeds and see exactly what the birds selected and ate."

"But that varied with the season, didn't it?"

"Exactly. In the wet season, when small seeds were abundant, the average seed hardness was 0.5, but in the dry season it jumped to over 6 newtons. Lots of finches couldn't eat many of those seeds. If it hadn't been for the fact that the six species began to switch to other foods, severe starvation would have occurred. A great example of resource partitioning—one of your pet subjects, Kate.

"In fact, Rosemary Grant found that switching even occurred among individuals of a single species. In times of plenty, all cactus finches eat the same seeds, but when these seeds are scarce, things change. Those with long beaks open the fruits and probe the cactus flowers, while those with larger, deeper beaks crack the big tough cactus seeds, and those with still deeper beaks strip the bark from the trees to get grubs."

"Everything gets worse when a severe drought happens, doesn't it? Natural selection really gets intense."

"Absolutely. It virtually wipes out the birds with the smaller beaks. The great drought of 1977 taught the Grants that. The population plunged to 200 birds. Before the drought, the average beak size of the *fortis* species was 10.68 mm long and 9.42 mm deep. After the drought, it was 11.07 mm long and 9.96 mm deep. Variations too small to see with the naked eye made the difference between life and death. It altered the sex ratio, too, since males have larger, stronger beaks. After the drought, there were seven times more males than females! In the years following the drought the competition between males for mates was fierce. Amazingly, the females started choosing the males with the largest beaks for breeding. The smaller-beaked males didn't have a chance to mate at all."

Kate nodded. "That's a perfect example of sexual selection in action. Both natural selection and sexual selection were working in the same direction: producing birds with large beaks. But were these genetic differences or were they due to the food supply? I mean, wouldn't you expect the well-fed birds to have larger bills, and then they would be the ones to breed and successfully raise young?"

"Of course. One of their graduate students wanted to test that, but it didn't work out, so they have had to resort to indirect evidence to demonstrate that the changes were genetic.

"But let me tell you about the big El Niño events of 1983," Miguel continued. "A huge amount of rain fell that year, a once-in-a-century event! The island went from a desert to a jungle in a few weeks. Food was everywhere. The birds started breeding like crazy and there were suddenly 2,000 finches on Daphne Major. When normal, dry conditions returned; there wasn't enough food to go around. The birds had overshot the carrying capacity of the island.

"But here's the interesting part: Now birds with smaller beaks were favored. Big males and big females started dying because of insufficient food. That's because there were a lot more small seeds than large ones lying around. The floods of El Niño had washed many of the large seed-producing cactus trees away. Even though the big birds could eat small seeds, they were at a disadvantage because of their size. They had to eat more to survive."

"A lot of hybridization started occurring after El Niño, didn't it?" Kate said.

"Yes, to everyone's surprise. Hybrids were rare during the lean years. The reproductive barriers kept the species distinct. The isolating mechanisms were primarily differences in song and beak size. But once the conditions dramatically improved, diversity was favored. A lot of finches began to breed with individuals of different species. They didn't seem to care as much what kind of song or beak their mate had. Some people even speculated that the mutation rate actually increased when environmental conditions shifted dramatically.

"Take a look at the finches outside the window," Miguel added. "Here at the Research Station it's hard to separate the different species because of the hybrids. They sort of fuse together here, where conditions are always good because people feed them. Kate, if you really want a great thesis problem, you couldn't do much better than studying finch hybridization around the village.

"I'm sure that humans are having a terrific impact on both speciation and extinction."

Questions

1. What is DNA fingerprinting and how is it done?
2. What is the difference between natural selection and evolution?
3. What is genetic drift and how could it be involved in evolution?
4. What is resource partitioning and character displacement?
5. What is sexual selection?
6. What are reproductive isolating mechanisms and how do they evolve?
7. Must populations of finches be separated in order to evolve into different species?

Part III: The Tortoise and the Sea Cucumber

Kate was tired. The last few nights she had stayed on late at the station, typing up her field notes. Her research on the breeding practices of tortoises in the wild was going well. She had been observing them for a four-month period, primarily in the Alcedo Volcano area on the island of Isabela, home to about 4,500 tortoises. But she was worried that mounting tensions between local fishermen and the Ecuadorian government might disrupt her work. The year before, in response to a decision by the president of Ecuador to cut short the sea cucumber season, armed fishermen had stormed the research station and taken several scientists hostage.

Kate's biggest concern at the moment, however, were the goats on Isabela. With human settlement of the islands had come new kinds of animals—cats, rats, dogs, donkeys, pigs, and goats. The number of goats on Isabela had increased from less than a dozen in 1982 to over 100,000. They were literally eating the tortoises out of house and home, foraging on the shrubs and bushes on the mountain's slopes, competing with the tortoises for food, causing widespread erosion of tortoise habitat.

Besides the damage done by goats, wild dogs and pigs dug up the tortoises' nests and ate their eggs in addition to preying upon their hatchlings. On Pinzon Island, another introduced species, the black rat (*Rattus rattus*), had killed every tortoise that had hatched on the island in the last 100 years.

The Galapagos had been named in 1535 by a Spanish navigator for the then-prevalent giant tortoises. When Darwin visited in 1835, he had reported tortoises on all of the islands. Since then their populations had dwindled at an alarming rate, and several subspecies had become extinct. Lately Kate had begun to feel almost a personal responsibility to save the endangered animals. She considered the plight of Lonesome George, perhaps the most famous resident at the Charles Darwin Research Station, so named because he was the last surviving member of his subspecies, *G. e. abingdoni*. One of the major initiatives of the research station was its captive breeding and rearing program, which was already racking up successes.

The tortoises of the island of Espanola (*G. e. hoodensis*) had been teetering on the verge of extinction. When captive breeding began for this subspecies, only two males and twelve females remained. Later, a third male was returned to the islands by the San Diego Zoo. Since then well over 300 young tortoises had been bred and repatriated, and some of these were now breeding back on the island. Kate was proud that her fieldwork was part of this effort.

Kate switched off her computer. She decided she would stop by her friend Stephen's house on her way home. Stephen had been a full-time rancher, part-time naturalist in New Zealand before visiting the Galapagos some 15 years before. Enchanted by the place, he had simply stayed on, becoming one of the first government-licensed tour guides.

Much of the islands had been designated a wildlife sanctuary in 1934 by the government of Ecuador. Uninhabited areas were declared a national park in 1959. In 1986, the Galapagos Marine Resources Reserve was created, administered by the Ecuadorian government with the help of the research station. The reserve made up about 97% of the islands' land and 50,000 square kilometers of the surrounding seas. Tourism throughout the islands was strictly controlled. Tourists weren't allowed to wander around. Instead, they had to be accompanied by a licensed tour guide when visiting wildlife sites, and they had to stay on assigned paths. Many islands were off-limits entirely.

As she walked to Stephen's house, Kate thought it ironic that one of the few places on Earth where aboriginal man never existed, one of the least-visited corners of the Earth for much of modern history, should be practically overrun now by human beings. Last year, over 50,000 tourists had visited the islands. Although conservationists were concerned about the impact of tourism on the islands, most scientists agreed that 15 years of tourism hadn't done one-tenth the damage of the recent fishing boom and the mass immigration from the mainland that came in its wake.

Although certain fisheries were long es-tablished in the Galapagos and sanctioned by the government, the sea cucumber fishery had become a sort of "gold rush" phenomenon. Fishermen from the mainland had descended on the islands to harvest them illegally from the protected waters. Considered a delicacy in Asian cuisine, they were also in demand throughout the Orient for their purported aphrodisiac properties. Kate thought them one of the most unattractive animals she'd ever encountered. Ranging in length from two inches to five feet, they had soft bodies and a leathery, somewhat slimy skin. Some species were warty.

The role they played in ocean ecology wasn't fully understood. Marine biologists likened them to earthworms. They spent most of their time on the sea floor, where they sucked up mud and sand, from which they extracted nutrients. Kate had overheard one of the researchers at the station saying that sea cucumbers often made up 90% of the animal biomass in marine systems. Many scientists feared that a rapid decline in their numbers might have serious consequences for the survival of other species in the food chain.

Harvesting of the Isostichopus fuscus sea cucumber had begun in the waters surrounding the Galapagos in 1988 but had been banned by the government in 1992, although illegal fishing continued. The Ecuadorian government simply didn't have the resources to effectively patrol miles of open ocean. In response to increasing pressure from local fishermen, the government lifted the ban and granted a three-month season for harvesting sea cucumbers, beginning in mid-October of 1994. The total take wasn't supposed to exceed 550,000 sea cucumbers, but in the first two months alone an estimated seven million were harvested.

The government stepped in and shut down the fishing season a month early, touching off a series of violent protests that had culminated in several fishermen, wielding axes and machetes, taking hostages at the research station. Government troops had been called out, and the hostages—including Lonesome George—were freed without further violence. In the weeks that followed, the Ecuadorian government placed a moratorium on the sea cucumber fishery until scientists could determine an annual catch that wouldn't wipe out the species. The government asked ORSTOM, the French overseas research agency, and the Darwin Foundation to study the problem.

When Kate got to Stephen's house she found him all worked up over the media's coverage of the crisis. He was upset because the news stories seemed to imply that all of the inhabitants of the islands were anticonservationists.

"Tourism brings in over $50 million a year in revenue," he said. "Fishing isn't a major economic factor in the lives of most people who live here. Believe me, people here are not fools. They're only too aware that they must conserve the islands if they are to protect their livelihoods. These people—the fishermen and the politicians who support them and their violent tactics—don't represent the majority. They certainly don't represent me!

"The problems that beset these islands are not simple—they're very complex. We've been left to deal with the aftermath of an uncontrolled mass migration. We've gone from a population of 5,000 in the early '80s to over 15,000. This population explosion is putting enormous pressure on the islands—on other aspects of our economy, for one thing, like our traditional fisheries, which could be at risk next. And now that this ban has put our newest immigrants out of work, we've got rampant unemployment, and hard on its heels, an increase in crime.

"I'm sympathetic to the plight of these people," Stephen continued. "I know the poverty they're fleeing from on the mainland is terrible. But I'm not sympathetic to their "get-rich-quick" mentality or their strong-arm tactics. The people from the mainland haven't grown up with an appreciation of the uniqueness of the reserve or the goals of the research station, or an understanding of the tradition of sustained subsistence fishing on the islands. They're just not as sensitive to the extraordinary biodiversity and the natural resources of these islands.

"The Galapagos economy, like that of the rest of Ecuador, is based on its natural resources. Victory for the conservationists is not a defeat for Ecuadorians. What many claim is a war against our own people is simply a refusal to defend the Galapaguenos' right to destroy their own future."

Kate sighed. She agreed with Stephen but couldn't help thinking of her neighbor Emilia, who had been so kind to her. Emilia's husband Adolfo was the head of the fishermen's cooperative on Isabela. According to Adolfo, the sea and its bounty were "the only way out" for the local people. Adolfo had cornered Kate a week ago, almost shouting at her as he waved his arms and argued his point: "The conservationists have to take into account that if they don't allow the development of any other industry, there is no way for us to survive. How are we going to feed our kids? We need to live!"

As Kate got ready to leave, Stephen asked her if she had heard that the Darwin Foundation had finally issued its report: "It recommends restoring traditional fisheries in the Galapagos and helping poor fishermen return to mainland Ecuador. They intend to make the moratorium on the sea cucumber fishery a permanent thing. That could mean more trouble. Be careful, Kate."

That night Kate slept uneasily. Early the next morning she was wakened by the sound of someone banging on her door. It was Emilia, carrying her youngest daughter in her arms. Emilia looked frightened. Kate had to ask her twice to repeat herself. When she finally understood what Emilia was trying to tell her, she was horrified. Apparently Congressman Eduardo Veliz and the fishermen he represented had taken over the islands' fisheries and the research facilities. And now they were threatening to set fires, take tourists hostage, and kill rare animals (tortoises, Kate figured) unless the government complied with their demands to reopen the sea cucumber fishery and give local inhabitants of the islands more control over the national park.

Questions

1. Should Kate have chosen to work on a different species than the tortoises that are being threatened? Her thesis work might be destroyed by the politics of the islands.
2. Should Kate get involved in the politics of saving the islands, the way Dian Fossey did in trying to save the mountain gorilla?
3. Should fishing, tourism, or inhabitants be allowed in the islands?
4. How should the Ecuadorian government deal with the conflicts over the islands?
5. Extinction is a natural phenomenon. Why should we worry about whether a few species on some remote islands in the Pacific survive or not?

Instructions to Students

During the discussion period, each team of students will assume the role of a particular interest group vying for a piece of the action in the Galapagos: fishermen, storeowners, tourists, scientists, Sierra Club members, and politicians in Ecuador. When you receive your roles, you should research the case from your particular perspective and talk over your position within your group, developing a position paper.

When we are ready for a general discussion, members of each interest group will be split up to meet with people from other interest groups, i.e., the instructor will form new consensus-seeking groups, each of which will have one member from each of the interest groups present. So, a consensus group will have a fisherman, a storeowner, a tourist, scientist, Sierra Club representative, and politician. The politician's job is to run a discussion to see if their group can come to some consensus on how to resolve the crisis and to write a position paper laying out their group's plan.

TEACHING NOTES

This case was designed to be taught in an introductory biology courses where the focus is on evolution. It involves one of the most famous events in the history of biology: the discovery of the Galapagos Islands as a natural laboratory to study evolution.

Beginning with Darwin's landing in 1835 and his subsequent realization of their importance in illuminating how species were formed, up to the present-day studies by researchers such as Peter and Rosemary Grant and their work on the Galapagos finches, these islands have proved invaluable to science. They are not only sites of spectacular biodiversity and havens for hundreds of endemic species, but today they are also the focus of a dramatic confrontation between various interest groups vying for political and economic control of the islands and their natural resources.

In the Galapagos we have a microcosm of conflict that is being repeated all over the globe. Scientists and conservationists wish to keep the islands pristine and pure, while economic interests wish to exploit their special nature for personal and political gain.

Objectives

- The overall objective is to learn about the process of evolution and the ongoing threats to biodiversity on the planet; specific objectives are:

- To examine the geology and the formation of volcanic islands and how they are colonized.
- To consider the process of species formation on islands and island biogeography.
- To consider how competition leads to character displacement and resource partitioning.
- To compare the effects of natural selection and sexual selection with genetic drift as driving forces in evolution.

- To learn how DNA technology is used to develop a species phylogeny and individual genealogies.
- To grapple with questions of extinction and our obligation to preserve biodiversity.

MAJOR ISSUES

This case is divided into three parts. Each focuses on a different major issue.

Part I: Formation and Colonization of the Islands

The current Galapagos Islands are no more than five million years old. They are the tops of volcanoes that project up from the ocean floor and break the water's surface at varying heights. Recently it has been discovered that there were earlier volcanoes (perhaps 20 million years old), but that these have long since eroded away and are now rubble heaps on the ocean floor. The marine iguanas and some of the other Galapagos species probably got their start on these earlier, now vanished islands.

The volcanic islands of the Galapagos are like the islands of the Hawaiian archipelago. They were formed as the tectonic plates moved over hot spots that drilled holes in the plates moving above them, bubbling hot magma up through the crust at periodic intervals. The oldest submerged islands in the Galapagos are on one end of the chain and the youngest (about one million years old) are on the other.

Darwin believed birds that were blown off course during storms colonized the islands, finding sanctuary on the islands' deserted shores. These immigrants would have specialized into distinct endemic species during their "splendid isolation" from their mainland counterparts. Today there are more than 50 breeding species of birds on the islands, half of which are endemic.

Many of the plants undoubtedly reached the Galapagos by drifting there as part of large mats of vegetation washed away from the mainland. Darwin observed such rafts of vegetation being swept out to sea from the jungle rivers. These vegetative rafts carried small land animal immigrants as well as plants. Darwin argued that other plants were carried as seeds to the islands on the feet and feathers and in the digestive tracts of birds flying from the mainland. Today, there are more than 700 different species of plants on the Galapagos; about 200 of these are endemic.

Part II: Species Formation in Evolution

The work of Peter and Rosemary Grant serves as a major springboard for discussion in this part of the case. The book, *The Beak of the Finch* (Jonathan Weiner 1994), is a marvelous summary of their work. Below are brief remarks that relate to the study questions.

Evolution can be due to natural selection, sexual selection, or genetic drift working on the variations within a population. All probably played a role in the biological evolution on the Galapagos. Darwin thought of natural selection as environmental effects on the organisms bringing about differences in the types of individuals that lived or died. The struggle for existence was due to the struggle with the physical elements—rain, sleet, snow—and the struggle between organisms—parasites, competitors, and predators. The survivors were the ones who could pass on their traits to the next generation.

Darwin claimed that changes could also be brought about by sexual selection. Sexual selection is of two types: (1) combat between males for the right to breed with the female (the larger and smarter ones usually prevail), and (2) female choice (females choose the "most attractive" male for their mates). Sexual selection clearly can affect the genetic constitution of the next generation.

Genetic drift is a random process that can produce evolution even without selection. The effects are most pronounced in populations under 500 individuals—clearly the situation on the Galapagos.

For example, if a pregnant bird with a small beak were blown from one island to a deserted island, the resulting population on that island would have small beaks. This chance event is called the "founder effect." Or, if by luck, a storm killed a disproportionate number of birds with large beaks, this would have a profound influence on the number of large beak genes in the population.

Intense competition between finches appears to make them more distinct through time; i.e., two closely related species will tend to specialize on different foods and become more distinct. This topic of character displacement and the partitioning of resources were raised by David Lack when he studied the Galapagos' finches. He noticed on those islands with only one species of finch that the birds tended to have a broader range in beak size than when this species lived on another island with a similar species. Thus, the species became more distinct when in competition.

The Grants observed that things changed when there was an abundance of food. Species started to interbreed, suggesting that there are few genetic differences among the finch species. Indeed, hybridization threatened to cause complete fusion of the birds into what is known as a "hybrid swarm." The normal reproductive isolating mechanisms (song and beak size) were no longer as important in mate selection. The females became more liberal in their choice of mates in times of plenty, leading to more hybrids.

The question of whether populations of finches must be physically separated in order to evolve into different species is unresolved. Classically, most species formation is believed to be allopatric, i.e., populations first become geographically isolated from one another, for example, by being separated on different islands. In time, differences appear in these populations due to selection or genetic drift. If these differences are great enough, even if the populations are rejoined, they will no longer interbreed. Reproductive barriers will have developed. This is the type of species formation that was believed to produce differences among finch species.

The other main type of species formation, sympatric speciation, or ecological speciation, requires that populations of finches would specialize for different lifestyles while remaining in the same habitat. In view of the Grants' observations of hybridization, this method of speciation appears unlikely in the case of "Darwin's finches."

Part III: The Crisis

This part of the case focuses on personal and societal concerns having to do with questions revolving around biodiversity. Students

explore the logic and concerns of different interest groups on the islands. Fishermen on the islands want to be able to harvest sea cucumbers without restrictions for economic gain and the survival of their families. Scientists want the islands to be left in a pristine condition so that they may continue to study the natural environment. Marine biologists have found that the surrounding waters are a treasure trove of novel species and, as a result, scientists and conservationists have become increasingly concerned about the activities of fishermen and their potentially negative impact to the ecosystem.

Tourists flock to the islands in increasing numbers each year. As a result, there is more and more disturbance to the animals and to habitat. Tour boat operators, tour agencies, and storeowners all have a stake in maintaining the tourist industry.

Politicians in Ecuador paid little attention to the Galapagos Islands until they became a tourist attraction. The government of Ecuador established the islands as a national park in 1959, ruling many of the islands off limits to tourism. On those islands where tours are allowed, tourists must stay on specified dirt trails. The government licenses the park rangers who conduct these tours.

Since most of the tourists arrive by plane and then transfer to a tour ship with a park ranger on board, there is reasonably tight control over the traffic on shore. Only a couple of islands were colonized prior to the government's restrictive policies. With tourism rising, there has been pressure on the government to loosen up the regulations on development and immigration to the islands. With the sea cucumber crisis, politicians have been under the gun to solve the Galapagos' problem.

CLASSROOM MANAGEMENT

This case was designed to be taught using the Problem-Based learning method in a class of about 25 students working in small permanent groups of four or five students. We have used it late in the semester after students have some knowledge of the principles of evolution.

The case is best taught over four days, in class periods of 70 minutes. Each day the students cover one of the three major sections of the case. On day one, the groups receive Part I of the case along with the study questions. They have about 30 minutes to read the case and identify the learning issues (i.e., decide what definitions and concepts to look up) and divide up the workload among their teammates for research in the library or on the internet.

On day two, the members of each group share information with their teammates. The instructor can then lead a general discussion of the major issues with the entire class. Alternatively, the instructor may ask the students to write up and hand in a summary of their answers. When this activity is over, Part II of the case is handed out. Again, the students' job is to identify the learning issues and divvy up the research.

On day three, students share their research results within their groups, and again the instructor has the option to have them hand in a written summary of their answers or hold a general discussion. Following this, the students are given Part III of the case to analyze for learning issues. In this part of the case, they are to look at the problems that beset the Galapagos from the viewpoint of a particular interest group. The instructor assigns each group a particular role. One group will represent the sea cucumber fishermen. Other groups will be tourists, storeowners, scientists at the Darwin Research Station, Sierra Club members, and Ecuadorian politicians from the mainland.

Each group must try to identify the central concerns of their interest group and do a literature search on the topic for the next class. During the next class, the individual groups will be split up to form negotiating teams; each person will go to a different team to represent the interest of their home group. This is the well-known jigsaw technique of cooperative learning.

On day four, the home group members spend 30 minutes sharing their information and writing down a list of their "demands," which they will present to the representatives of the other groups when they meet to negotiate a settlement over the future of the Galapagos. After these points have been decided, the negotiating teams are arranged.

A politician, who chairs the group, leads each negotiating team. His job is to negotiate a settlement that is acceptable to all interest groups. The other members of the negotiating team will be a fisherman, tourist representative, storeowner, and conservationist. In the remaining time of the class, about 40 minutes, these individuals must strike some bargains and reach an agreement. The politicians must write up a summary report giving the particulars of their settlement. In our case, we graded this report and gave each member of the negotiating team the same grade.

And what about Kate? She can be ignored and left wandering the volcanoes in the Galapagos. Or the instructor may wish to round out the case with a brief discussion of Kate's options, finally asking the students to write a short paper on the subject.

Photo Identification

The following are the names of the species pictured in this chapter. The images are identified in the sequence in which they appeared. All species named here are native to the Galapagos Islands.

1. Masked Boobies
2. San Cristobal
3. Sea Lion
4. Marine Iguana
5. Galapagos Penguin
6. Pink Flamingos
7. Pelicans

Structured Controversy

A Case Study Strategy: DNA Fingerprinting in the Courts

By Clyde Freeman Herreid

Science has always been filled with controversy, whether the issue is the Big Bang hypothesis versus the steady state universe, the cold fusion debate, or the wave versus particle theories of the nature of light. It is the nature of the business to question, debate, and argue. Science is not special in that regard. Human society as a whole is besieged by debate and probably always has been. It is personified by Adam and Eve arguing with the serpent. It is Galileo Galilei at the Inquisition. It is Bob Dole versus Bill Clinton.

Formal debate technique is part of a lawyer's arsenal. The seeds of the adversarial approach to problems are sewn in law school classrooms, nurtured in moot courtrooms, and reach full bloom in the criminal and civil courthouses of America. Whatever else it does, the adversarial system hones the wits of the participants and brings the issues of any problem into sharp focus. However, it leaves little room for compromise. Indeed, it seems the debaters are often more interested in winning the argument than seeking justice or truth. Furthermore, much of life is not a zero-sum game where there is a winner and a loser. Many would argue that cooperation and negotiation towards a compromise is a better model for life. In fact, many of the great debates in science ended with a compromise solution, which brings us to the technique at hand.

Structured controversy is a teaching technique that uses the strengths of conventional debate and ends with two sides seeking ways to resolve the conflict through compromise. Its virtues in the classroom have been championed

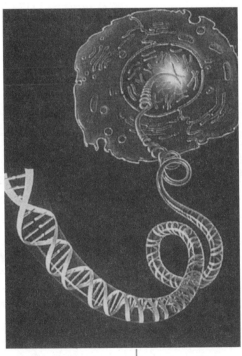

The now familiar image of the double helix.

and summarized by Johnson and Johnson (1989) and Johnson, Johnson, and Holubec (1992). Compared to most other methods of instruction, structured controversy results in greater student mastery and retention of the material and a greater ability to generalize the principles learned (Johnson and Johnson 1988).

There are at least four major critical thinking skills required by the controversy structure (Johnson and Johnson 1989, 1992):

- Students must collect data and analyze the research in order to present evidence supporting a position.
- Students must evaluate and criticize the opposing position using rules of logic and evidence. At the same time, they must repel the attack of their opponents and shift and refine their own positions.
- Students must see the issue from both perspectives.
- Finally, students must synthesize and integrate the best evidence from both sides and reach a compromise consistent with both positions.

Two Versions of Structured Controversy

Johnson, Johnson, and Holubee (1992) summarize the major steps used in structured controversy in the classroom.

- *First*, a controversial topic is proposed by the instructor (e.g., nuclear power plants should form the basis of our nation's energy policy; logging operations should cease in our national forest and parks).
- *Second*, students are coupled in pairs to research literature and prepare arguments for either the pro or con side of the issue.
- *Third*, opposing teams meet and give their "best case" arguments to one another, courteously debating the issue.
- *Fourth*, the opposing teams reverse their

roles presenting the opposite view as convincingly as possible.

- *Fifth*, the opposing teams abandon their advocacy roles and write a compromise report.
- *Sixth*, all individuals in the class take a written test based on the material and receive bonus points if all members of their compromise team score over a set criterion.
- *Seventh*, the teams give a 10-minute oral report on their compromise to the class with all team members participating.

Johnson and Johnson's structured controversy method is a powerful technique that can be applied to case study teaching. It clearly achieves the learning goals I summarized earlier.

Nevertheless, the technique requires a large investment of classroom time; six class periods are recommended. Barbara Watters of the State University of New York at Oswego (Watters 1994; 1996) has recently developed an alternative approach that meets many of the above goals, yet it can be accomplished in one or two classroom periods. It requires a minimum of 75 minutes to complete.

Watters's model works this way:

- *First*, a controversial topic is assigned.
- *Second*, each student works alone, searching the literature and writing two position papers, one for the pro and another for the con side of the controversy.
- *Third*, during class, small groups of students are formed. Half of the groups role-play the pro side and half role-play the con side. Each group chooses its three best arguments.
- *Fourth*, the instructor then calls on a pro side group to present its top argument, identifying its assertion and evidence to support it. Con-group members are asked to comment on the pro argument. Rebuttal is permitted. Then, a con group presents its best argument.

Pro commentary follows with debate. This process is repeated with pro and con teams alternating their arguments.

- *Fifth,* the instructor asks the groups to abandon their advocacy roles and to try to come up with a compromise statement that might be found reasonably acceptable by the opposing groups. These solutions are listed on the board, with commentary by each group.
- *Sixth,* the instructor or a student closes with a summary analysis.

The structured controversy method is excellent for dealing with cases that are highly charged and should be added to the list of techniques for teaching case studies (Herreid 1994). It forces all parties to analyze the best evidence on both sides of the question and then to search actively for a compromise solution. The method is best understood by showing an example of a recent case using DNA fingerprinting, which received notoriety in the O. J. Simpson murder trial.

When using this technique, the instructor must be sure to give clear instructions in order to get good written and oral responses. Students must understand how to write individual position papers on the pro and con sides of arguments and the proper rules of debate conduct.

To start the students out with the right strategy, I give them handouts on the *Elements of Argumentation*, which is drawn from Govier (1992), Hinderer (1992), and Zeidler, Lederman, and Taylor (1992). Then, I assign a topic with instructions on how to proceed. I also include an abbreviated example of a student paper on a different topic.

An example of a student assignment on the use of DNA fingerprinting in forensic medicine begins on page 288. See also the follow-up teaching notes, starting on page 292.

REFERENCES

Govier, T. 1992. *A practical study of argument.* 3rd ed. Belmont, CA: Wadsworth Publishing Co.

Herreid, C. F. 1994. Case studies in science–A novel method of science education. *Journal of College Science Teaching* 23 (4): 221–229.

Hinderer, D. E. 1992. *Building arguments.* Belmont, CA: Wadsworth Publishing Co.

Johnson, D. W., and R. T. Johnson. 1988. Critical thinking through controversy. *Educational Leadership* (May): 58–64.

Johnson D. W., and R. T. Johnson. 1989. *Cooperation and competition: Theory and research.* Edina, MN: Interaction Book Co.

Johnson, D. W., and R. T. Johnson. 1992. *Creative controversy: Intellectual challenge in the classroom.* Edina, MN: Interaction Book Co.

Johnson, D. W., R. T. Johnson, and E. J. Holubec. 1992. *Advanced cooperative learning* (Revised). Edina, MN: Interaction Book Co.

Watters, B. L. 1994. Teaching peace through structured controversy: Applications of debating theory to college-level psychology courses. Paper presented at What Works: Building Effective Collaborative Learning Experiences. State College, PA.

Watters, B. L. 1996. Teaching peace through structured controversy. *Journal on Excellence in College Teaching* 7 (1): 107–125.

Zeidler, D. I., N. G. Lederman, and S. C. Taylor. 1992. Fallacies and student discourse: Conceptualizing the role of critical thinking in science education. *Science Education* 76: 437–450.

STRUCTURED CONTROVERSY STUDENT ASSIGNMENT

AN EXAMPLE OF THE USE OF DNA FINGERPRINTING IN FORENSIC MEDICINE

Write an analysis paper of the arguments surrounding the use of DNA evidence in courts of law. In order that you gain an understanding of both sides of the issue, and acquire experience in identifying assertions and evidence, please structure the paper in the following manner.

TITLE: e.g., DNA Evidence Should Be Used in Forensic Medicine

AUTHOR: Your name

INTRODUCTION: Several sentences briefly introducing the controversy.

PRO-SIDE OF THE ARGUMENT: Here you should lay out four of the major assertions and evidence that would be used in arguing in favor of the proposition stated in the title.

A note on assertions: Those that are short are often more easily defended than longer, more complex assertions. Good assertions are falsifiable in principle; that is, they can be tested and we will know if they are wrong.

A note on evidence: Be sure that the evidence that you use speaks directly to the assertion you make and meets the conditions of a good argument. The evidence must be adequate, relevant, and succinct. Finally, when you refer to data in the literature, proper citations should be appended to the paper.

CON-SIDE OF THE ARGUMENT: Here, you should write four major assertions and offer supporting evidence against the proposition in the title, using references where appropriate.

POSSIBLE COMPROMISES: Here, try to find any compromise statements or positions that both sides of the argument might agree to include.

PERSONAL OPINION: Write your personal views on the proposition.

REFERENCES CITED: Write out complete references to papers that you have cited.

A short version of a student paper follows.

DNA EVIDENCE SHOULD BE USED IN FORENSIC MEDICINE

INTRODUCTION: Technology concerning DNA fingerprinting has been developed for use in forensics. However, some believe this technology is unreliable and may in fact cause a false positive reaction, thus causing the imprisonment of an innocent person. The admission of DNA evidence into court has been extremely controversial, as was seen in the O. J. Simpson case.

PRO: Yes, DNA fingerprinting should be used in forensic medicine.

ASSERTION 1: DNA-based identification is more reliable than other forms of identification, such as blood groups and enzymes.

EVIDENCE 1: "If enough tissue or semen is available, forensics laboratories can perform tests to determine the blood or tissue type. However, such tests have limitations... there are many people in the population with the same blood type or tissue type...this approach can only exclude a suspect...DNA testing, on the other hand, can theoretically identify the guilty individual with certainty because the DNA base sequence of every individual is unique" (Campbell, Mitchell, and Reece 1994).

"DNA-based identification has been so widely embraced by the judicial system because... a suspect can for all practical purposes be positively identified" (McElfresh, Vining-Forde, and Balazs 1993).

"Another problem with traditional forensic methods is that, during the weeks or months [of the investigation], evidence may have to wait before being examined by a forensic scientist and proteins can become degraded or denatured so their antigenic properties are lost. For examination in forensic samples, DNA is more suitable than protein because DNA remains intact in the environments where such evidence generally is found. Indeed, small fragments of human DNA have been isolated and cloned from the tissue of a 2,400-year-old Egyptian mummy. Although the length of these DNA fragments was too small for RFLP analysis, this work does illustrate the impressive stability of the DNA molecule" (Moody 1989).

ASSERTION 2: Statistical analysis has shown that it is almost impossible for two people to share the same DNA unless they are identical twins.

EVIDENCE 2: No two people have the same DNA (nucleotide sequence) unless they have an identical twin (Campbell, Mitchell, and Reece 1994). Even family members do not carry an identical genetic make-up. They share some of the markers, but there are genetic differences that are specific to each person (McElfresh, Vining-Forde, and Balazs 1993). The main purpose of DNA-based identity is to take evidence and compare the similarities or differences to that of the suspect.

DNA tests are so variable that "an almost infinite number of genotypes across several loci can be identified" (McElfresh, Vining-Forde, and Balazs 1993).

Inheritance of DNA patterns is independent among loci, thus the probability of each is multiplied to find the total probability. "It is not unusual for a four-locus DNA pattern to have individual loci with average probabilities of 1 in 100 and therefore a combined probability of 0.1 in 100 million" (McElfresh, Vining-Forde, and Balazs 1993).

ASSERTION 3: DNA fingerprinting is generally accepted by the scientific community.

EVIDENCE 3: "In most states, scientific evidence is admissible only when it has 'gained general acceptance' in the scientific community" (Witkin 1994). "Forensic DNA testing has been adopted not only throughout the United States, but in Canada, Europe, and elsewhere. Similarly, paternity testing, which uses identical methodology, has been accepted for years" (Devlin, Nail, and Roeder 1993). DNA fingerprinting has met the requirements of scientific evidence allowable in court.

DNA fingerprinting, as the process is called, is a complex, high-tech forensic test that can link a suspect to the commission of a crime—or establish his innocence. "While still controversial, use of the test is gaining acceptance in American courtrooms" (Cray 1994).

▶   ▶   ▶

CON: No, DNA fingerprinting should not be used in forensic medicine.

ASSERTION 1: There are inherent errors in the techniques used to determine a DNA fingerprint.

EVIDENCE 1: Possible sources of error include band shift, DNA degradation, partial restriction digesting, and inconsistencies in the electrophoretic gel. "Forensic samples are different in origin, storage, and collection from the standards. Such differences between the samples may be reflected in mobility differences between the DNA bands. It is just as probable that band shift could move away from a match as into one, and there is no way to predict which will happen" (McElfresh, Vining-Forde, and Balazs 1993).

In the RFLP method, restriction enzymes break the DNA strands at specific sites, resulting in variable fragment lengths between individuals. However, "heat, humidity, bacterial contamination, and UV light damage DNA by causing random breakage of the helix" (McElfresh, Vining-Forde, and Balazs 1993). This will result in random fragment lengths that may cause errors in the DNA fingerprint produced. Slight inconsistencies in the electrophoretic gel can skew the positions of the DNA fragments. "Occasionally, restriction bands do not separate completely, or they end up at slightly different positions in different gels" (Campbell, Mitchell, and Reece 1994).

In addition to the inherent errors in the techniques, there is always the possibility of human error. "The largest source of error lies in poor laboratory practices" (Roberts 1992). "The lab error is the most likely place to get a false incrimination of an innocent person or a guilty person going free" (Nowak 1994).

ASSERTION 2: A lack of consensus is often evident when interpreting DNA typing results.

EVIDENCE 2: Each forensic lab has defined its own "match criteria." LIFECODES Corp. of Stanford, Connecticut has established that two bands would be declared a match if they fall within 2.8% of each other in size. This is based on their calculated standard deviation, which derives from empirical data. The FBI has determined that, based on their empirical data, matching bands exist if two bands are within 2.5% of each other in size (McElfresh, Vining-Forde, and Balazs 1993).

Lack of defined protocol or criteria leads to a lack of consensus in interpretation. In a 1989 court case, a LIFECODES Corp. forensic sci-entist calculated the odds of a random match between the evidence and the suspect to be one in a million. Other forensic scientists who examined the same data calculated the odds to be 1 in 24 (Neufield and Colman 1990). "Most scientists with training in molecular biology and population genetics would accept DNA typing as probative, but most also view it with some caution since it involves the confluence of many theories and techniques" (Ayala and Black 1993).

ASSERTION 3: DNA evidence is at best circumstantial.

EVIDENCE 3: All DNA evidence admitted to court consists of a "visual/measured interpretation of the pattern of DNA bands on the autoradiography and if the patterns have been declared to be the same, a mathematical declaration of the probability of finding that DNA pattern in a given population" (McElfresh, Vining-Forde, and Balazs 1993). These probability estimates are a function of the number of VNTR loci examined but "the variation in the frequencies ranges from 1 in 400,000 to 1 in 4,000,000" (McElfresh, Vining-Forde, and Balazs 1993).

It is interesting to note that, while these probability estimates for a perfect match may be compelling, up to 400,000 people can expect to pass within 10 blocks of a rape incident in New York City's Central Park on a typical business day, and 4,000,000 people within three miles of the crime. Viewed in this light, when the suspect falls within the "high probability" range of being the perpetrator, it becomes problematic to correlate "high probability" with "highly likely" without taking into account such things as population density within the area of the crime scene.

Circumstantial evidence "consists in reasoning from facts which are known or proved to establish such as are conjectured to exist" (Garner 1990). Now, it is a relatively simple matter for scientists to establish the "fact" that the probability of a given suspect committing a crime is 1 in 1,000 or 1 in 2,000,000, but given this fact, it is still necessary for a jury to infer, given other evidence, that this probability is compelling enough to establish guilt. By definition, then, since estimates of genotype probabilities are, as yet, never equal to one, the legal community must (through conjecture) establish guilt or innocence via other evidence. DNA evidence is thus circumstantial at best.

POSSIBLE COMPROMISE: Statistical analysis shows that the probability of a false positive match varies from 1 in 400,000 to 1 in 4,000,000 people. Although at first this number seems sufficient enough to convict the suspect, when considering that 4,000,000 people can be found within a small geographical region in densely populated areas, this ratio becomes unconvincing. Therefore, DNA evidence can never prove with certainty the guilt of a suspect.

In light of this, DNA evidence should be used only to corroborate other evidence to implicate a suspect or, conversely, to exonerate that person. Further, regulations should be passed and enforced establishing universal techniques and standards in processing DNA. This would include private and FBI labs.

PERSONAL OPINION: We believe that DNA fingerprinting is a very useful tool in the field of criminal justice. It has been shown to be very powerful and exact in determining the identification and guilt or innocence of a suspect. Like any method, however, DNA fingerprinting is subject to error, and these possible fallacies must be regulated and insured against to warrant the validity of DNA testing.

We feel that research should be conducted to define the frequency of a particular DNA fingerprint occurring in the population in order to reach consensus in the scientific community, that DNA tests should be standardized to avoid the scrutiny that follows due to variations in methods and results, and DNA labs should be regulated, either by the federal government or some other body, to insure the exactness and validity of results.

REFERENCES

Ayala, F., and J. B. Black. 1993. Science and the courts. *American Scientist* (May/June): 233.

Campbell, N. A., L. G. Mitchell, and J. B. Reece. 1994. *Biology: Concepts and corrections*. Redwood City, CA: Benjamin/Cummings.

Cray, D. 1994. Order in the lab. *Time* (8 August): 46–47.

Devlin, B., R. Nail, and K. Roeder. 1993. Statistical evaluation of DNA fingerprinting: A critique of the NRC's report. *Science* (5 February): 748–749.

Garner, B. A., ed. 1990. *Black's law dictionary*. 6th ed. New York: Macmillan.

McElfresh, K. C., D. Vining-Forde, and I. Balazs. 1993. DNA-based identity testing in forensic science. *Bioscience* (March): 149–157.

Moody, M. D. 1989. DNA analysis in forensic science. *Bioscience* (January): 31–35.

Neufield, P. J., and N. Colman. 1990. When science takes the witness stand. *Scientific American* (May): 47–48.

Nowak, R. 1994. Forensic DNA goes to court with O. J. *Science* (2 September): 1352–1354.

Roberts, L. 1992. DNA fingerprinting: Academy reports. *Science* (17 April): 300–301.

Witkin, G. 1994. Science takes the stand. *U.S. News and World Report* (11 July): 29–31.

TEACHING NOTES

Is This Really a Case?

I have called this a case study method and in spite of the facts, the approach does not appear to tell a story. Yet, because the assignment is in the context of the O. J. Simpson civil trial, there is an underlying story line. Nothing more is needed for the student. In the student paper and in the classroom debate that follows, the trial pervades.

In addition, I set up a story context in two other ways. First, I gave the students handouts or literary references to the O. J. Simpson trial where expert witnesses debate the problems of DNA fingerprinting. Students are told they must include additional references if they are to receive an A. Second, I do a "lab exercise" marketed by Ward's Scientific which is a "DNA Whodunit Kit" designed for 30 students. It consists of a hypothetical murder mystery involving the "blood" from a victim, a murderer, and five suspects. Students, using popbeads, first build DNA models that vary among the suspects. Then they proceed to go through simulated steps of the DNA fingerprinting process with "restriction enzymes," "electrophoresis," and "radioactive probes," finally identifying the murder. College students in my Evolutionary Biology course found this exercise exciting and it can be done in any classroom in a period of 75 minutes. Together with the structured controversy assignment, there is no doubt as to the story line.

Blocks of Analysis

In a traditional case study where the instructors include an extensive description of a particular murder or dilemma, traditional blocks of analysis would be found here. But this is not about the O. J. Simpson trial or any other trial. The student has been asked to write a series of assertions and evidence statements using the literature, some of which the instructor may not have seen. Consequently, there is the possibility of more surprises with the structured controversy approach than with most other case study teaching methods. Yet, there are still clear blocks of analysis that we can predict given that the case is to be used in a science class.

DNA Structure

This case, especially if the instructor uses the "Whodunit Kit," provides clear opportunities to get the DNA structure indelibly printed in the mind of the student. This will not likely come up directly in the debate unless the instructor asks the students to clarify or amplify some points of evidence. But if the instructor spends too much time asking questions on this or any other point, the spontaneity and drama of the debate itself is easily lost and the instructor reverts to the role of Socratic discussion leader.

DNA Fingerprinting

There exist excellent drawings, descriptions, and models of the various steps of the DNA fingerprinting process. If these are made available to students in the handouts, there should be little difficulty understanding the process. Questions about the method, however, frequently appear in the debate, as do questions about the use of Polymerase Chain Reaction (PCR) in amplifying nucleotide chains and the use of electrophoresis and probes.

Genetics

The structural discussion of DNA is a natural platform to discuss variability in the genome and the uniqueness of the individual. Topics of mutation, junk DNA, and hypervariability lurk not far behind, along with the use of DNA fingerprinting to detect genetic disorders and gene replacement.

Ethical Considerations of Genetic Engineering

Screening methods for genetic disease and the potential for gene therapy naturally evolve into questions of "What do we do with this information?" Are abortions an option if we detect an abnormality? Do we inform patients? Employers? Insurance agents? Will we permit parents to manipulate their child's genetic makeup at will? These questions, although off the mainline of DNA fingerprinting, are close at hand and it will take an alert instructor to avoid some of these issues if they are not on the agenda for discussion.

The Uses of DNA Fingerprinting

By now the public knows that murder, rape, and paternity cases can be solved with a small amount of DNA. Less well known is the role of DNA in detecting evolutionary relationships, determining family connections in animals, and identifying animal carcasses in cases of poaching of endangered species. These topics are interesting sidelights to the case.

A part of these discussions will focus on the issue of misidentification, which is an especially grievous error in criminal cases. Lab procedures, security measures, and cross-checking between labs are all discussion points, as are questions about how the age and condition of a sample can affect analysis, how band shifting might occur on electrophoresis gels, and how clearly DNA fragment lengths can be identified ("the bin size problem").

Probability Theory

Much of the discussion involving DNA fingerprinting centers on the probability of making a correct match of suspect to crime. This issue is touched upon in the accompanying student paper. An extensive analysis of the probability of finding matches in certain ethnic groups is central to the discussion. It will be important for the instructor to ask how we can decrease the chances of making such an error. Part of the answer should be to increase the number of identifying probes. Certain to be part of the discussion will be how one calculates the probability of a match and the use of the "product rule." The conflict involving the use or nonuse of the "ceiling principle"

advocated by the National Research Council is appropriate here.

In a normal discussion case found in law or business schools, these blocks of analysis would be managed in controlled ways by the instructor. Considerably less control exists with structured controversy cases.

Running the Class

One of the greatest strengths of structured controversy is that the students come to class highly prepared. They have studied the literature and written papers on both sides of the argument and therefore know the issues.

At the beginning of class, after brief introductory remarks by the instructor, teams of four or five students should be rapidly assembled. (In classes where cooperative or collab-

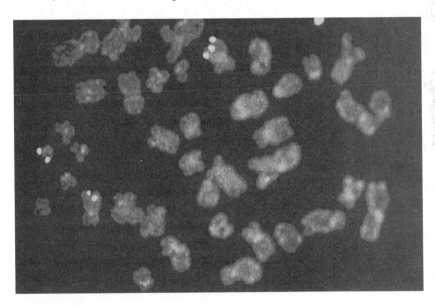

orative learning is routine, groups probably already exist.) After this, the instructor splits the class in half, perhaps by drawing an imaginary line down the center of the room. Teams to the left of the line are assigned the pro-side of the argument and teams to the right are assigned the con-side. The instructor tells each side's teams to decide upon three of their best arguments (assertions and evidence). This takes about 20 minutes.

Video photography of assembled karotypes.

The instructor working at the chalkboard or overhead projector asks one of the teams from the pro-side to mention its first assertion and evidence. The instructor writes this down rapidly in an abbreviated form then asks for comments from the con-side of the room. There will usually be several groups volunteering to criticize the pro argument. Normally, they will challenge the quality or quantity of evidence or present counterevidence.

Sometimes there will be challenges to the chain of reasoning used or fallacies of logic exposed. It is remarkable how vigorously students will argue and role-play a particular position, which may be contrary to their personal views. Instructors can either stand back and let the debate rage or intervene periodically. I recommend intervention.

Students have a hard time concentrating on one particular assertion and its evidence. They often want to bring up other arguments and broaden the debate. If this tendency is not stopped, the debate will spin out of control and little will be accomplished. So, the first job of the instructor is to keep the discussion focused on the assertion and evidence on the board. The second job is to see that the advocacy role is not taken so seriously that students begin to act like Perry Mason, delivering impassioned speeches to the jury. The instructor must stop them from using *ad hominem* attacks and jibes. The third job is to look for opportunities to help develop particular points about key issues. This should be done by asking appropriate questions rather than stopping the discussion and delivering a mini-lecture.

After the pro-side has given one of their arguments, members of the con-side are asked to discuss one of theirs. Again, the instructor writes the assertion and evidence on the board. Then he asks for commentary from the pro-side and friendly debate should follow. This process is repeated one or two more times, alternating between the sides. This phase of the class should be finished 20 minutes before the class ends.

The instructor then asks the teams to leave aside their advocacy roles. The students are instructed to come up with at least one suggestion for a compromise between the two sides. After a five-minute discussion, the instructor should list these on the board either with or without soliciting comment by other teams. If commentary is accepted, be prepared for periodic outbreaks of debate to erupt again. This may not be productive, especially if you are under a time constraint and are trying to close the discussion.

If time permits, the instructor could try a more interesting and fruitful way of compromising. The instructor could tell each team to send half of its members to the opposite side of the room, thus ending up with new teams composed of half-pro and half-con members. These new teams look for at least one compromise position on which they might agree. After a few minutes of discussion the instructor asks for the teams to report on their successes. This serves as a nice finale to the discussion.

A Word to the Wise?

Advising Freshmen

By Jessica Dudek, Nigel Marriner, and Clyde Freeman Herreid

Freshmen frequently struggle with major decisions both in and out of school. Even if they attend required advisement sessions, they do not always have a clear idea which questions to ask and which information to share with the adviser. And this is true even for many science students who have career goals and a clearly delineated set of requirements. (Keep in mind that more than 50% of the engineering majors change fields and that most premedical wannabes alter their plans after the first couple of years.) Often, unasked questions have profound effects on students' curriculum choices and can affect their success in school. Large numbers of students make poor choices and have unfortunate experiences as a result.

To focus attention on some of the important choices that freshmen must make, we designed a case study to sharpen freshmen honors students' understanding of the advisement process. We have run this exercise in six honors sections involving 500 students just before their mandatory advisement sessions. It has been beneficial for them, and this case can be used in general science courses early in the semester as an icebreaker, especially in situations where case studies will be used. Students are interested in other students' problems, particularly when they have a personal stake involved.

CLASSROOM MANAGEMENT

At the beginning of class, we hand out Figure 1 to teams of five students each. The simple instructions given at the beginning direct students to list three main questions that each of the four students (Eric, Carl, Helen, and Sabrina) should ask their advisors. We also suggest they jot down any suggestions they think the advisor might have as answers. About seven minutes is adequate for this step.

Because students work in teams of five, we assign each group two profiles to consider—either Eric and Helen or Carl and Sabrina. They could evaluate all four profiles, but two per group works well given the time constraints. We tell each group to compile a list of the top concerns for their assigned students, which takes about five minutes.

Next, we have the various teams report their findings. As they do, we list the findings on the blackboard under the names of the four students (Figure 2). We first list the problems Eric faces and then move on to the concerns of the others. As we do so, we comment on the questions as they emerge. This takes about 20 minutes.

FIGURE 1.

Advising case study profiles.

Here are the profiles of four freshmen. They report many of the typical concerns of any first-year student. Some will be familiar to you. These students are about to visit their advisers to ask about their careers and course work plans. Some are eager about the visit, and some couldn't care less. As you read these profiles, please list the central issues that each student should bring to the adviser's attention. Write down at least three questions that each student should ask. What advice might you expect the advisers to offer? Are there any important generalizations that you can see among these four students?

ERIC. With no idea what he wants to major in, Eric is sick of people asking him. He is interested in a lot of different subjects and sees no problem in exploring his options for a while. He understands his general education requirements and already has some of them fulfilled through advanced placement credit he received in high school. He figures he can take a nice mix of general education credits and exploratory courses for the first three or four semesters and then decide on a major. There are a few interdisciplinary majors that he would like to pursue, but it doesn't look like this school offers them. He already talked with an adviser over the summer when they registered him for his fall courses. Because nothing has changed since then, he doesn't see the need to rehash it all again. Plus, things are going great. He gets along with his roommate, likes all of his classes and professors, and has an on-campus job working 20 to 25 hours per week.

CARL. Carl doesn't want to close any doors. He has always loved English but feels that business management will give him some tangible "hands-on" skills that he could use once he graduates. He would prefer not have to choose one or the other. He really wants to see if it is possible to do both. He feels like he is wasting his time taking general education requirements. He sees them as a big pain and doesn't like the feeling that he is taking courses he doesn't want or need. He is very happy that he doesn't have to take a foreign language (because he is in business management), but he still thinks that there is a lot of other "junk" that he has to take. To rectify this, he has decided that he isn't going to take any general education courses. He is just going to take his English and business management courses; those are the courses he is "really here for" anyway. He is going to sign himself up for a bunch of upper-level English courses and try to weasel his way into a finance course that he thinks looks interesting. Besides, one of Carl's brother's friends graduated from the same school and told Carl that honors students who are double majors can petition to get out of some of their general education requirements. Carl has decided that he will just nod his head and be complacent in his academic advisement meeting, but after it's over will do his own thing anyway.

HELEN. Because she has wanted to be a physician since she was five years old, Helen decided to major in biology. Other students and her parents told her it was the best major for getting into medical school and preparing for the MCATs. She and her parents know all about the early assurance program with the university's medical school, and Helen plans to have half her pre-med requirements completed by the end of the sophomore year so that she is on target for acceptance. She intends to spend all of her free time this semester studying so she can have the highest grade point average possible for her early assurance application. Because she feels she knows all about med school and what she needs to do to get there, she is not convinced that she will get much out of her advisement session. However, Helen has been under a lot of stress lately for some reason. She has gotten into a few arguments with her parents already on how preparations for med school are going. Between commuting and studying, she has had a hard time meeting other pre-med students. In the back of her mind she wonders if this doctor thing is really going to make her happy and what she would do if she didn't go to medical school.

SABRINA. As a chemical engineering student, Sabrina thinks that maybe this whole advisement thing is a bit of a joke. Her classes will be so regimented that there isn't much need for any kind of discussion. Classes like Chemistry 101 are followed by Chemistry 102, which is followed by Chemistry 201, and so on. She's in the honors program; how stupid do they think she is? Rather than going to this wasteful advisement session she could use that time to deal with a couple of other issues in her life. She was disappointed that her physics class was not more challenging. She would like to take something more demanding, but there don't seem to be any other options. The second issue in her life is her roommate, who is starting to get on her nerves. She doesn't hate her roommate, but she needs to initiate a serious discussion about their living arrangements. She has talked to the Resident Assistant who lives on her floor, but would like to get some other input before sticking her neck out on this! If only there was somebody she could talk to….

Finally, we ask all of the students to write their own profile, preferably in the third person. We also ask them to list the questions that they should ask their advisers when they meet with them. This takes about seven to ten minutes. We collect these profiles for our advisers to have when they meet with their students. These serve as an excellent starting point for a serious advisement session.

If this exercise were to be done in a science classroom, the profiles of Eric, Carl, Helen, and Sabrina could be suitably altered to bring out other important points that the instructor wished to emphasize. He or she could collect the student profiles, read them, and make general comments in the following class or in one-on-one meetings. Alternatively, the students could simply keep them for their own use and reflection. Other possibilities include using them for role-playing exercises.

WHERE DOES THIS GO?

In our advisement sessions, students are often reluctant to bring up sensitive or nonacademic issues and questions that they write in their own profile. Once the adviser initiates a discussion of that particular topic, however, it often becomes apparent that it is, in fact, an important issue for the student.

In a few cases, our honors students were advised before we had read their profile. After the advisement sessions, the advisor read the profiles and noted that frequently the student did not voice some of those important issues in the advisement meeting. Such instances pointed to the value of the advising case study and individual profiles. This exercise allows students to see how sample advisement sessions work, to think about their own advisement appointment in advance, and to articulate their questions and concerns in a nonjudgmental environment.

FIGURE 2.

Major issues faced by the students.

ERIC. Eric's overriding issues are his lack of focus on a particular field or major, his uncertainty about what majors are available, and his skepticism regarding the advisement process. We emphasize the value of an advisement session for Eric. An advisor can go over Eric's major options and tell him about majors he hadn't thought of or known about. His adviser can also review his general education requirements and explain exactly which ones are fulfilled by particular advanced placement courses. Finally, instructors may want to call attention to Eric's work hours and suggest that he cut back his hours during midterms and finals.

CARL. The main issues for Carl are his pursuit of a double major, his disregard for his general education requirements, and his reliance on friends for academic advice. We use Carl's case to explain to students the differences between a double degree and a double major and how to fit two majors into a four-year span. We point out that students should not get advisement from fellow students, and we explain the proper procedure for petitioning. Instructors may also want to discuss the benefits of general education courses and the wisdom of taking upper-level courses as freshmen.

HELEN. Many of our students are pre-med, and Helen's case highlights important issues for these freshmen. In class we explain that biology is not the only acceptable pre-med major, and we outline the pre-med requirements. We also use Helen's case to emphasize other key factors in medical school admissions, including volunteering and extracurricular activities. We talk about our school's pre-professional health adviser and the pre-health listserv, which provide essential information to pre-med students. Finally, we underscore the value of an academic backup plan for pre-med students in the event that they do not or cannot attend medical school. Instructors may also want to focus on Helen's struggles as a commuter and her disagreements with her parents.

SABRINA. The majority of our students begin as engineering majors, much like Sabrina. Because they don't have much choice in their course selection, they question the value of an advisement session. In class we explain that, although the engineering curriculum is regimented now, students will have more choices in their upper-level electives. We also emphasize the many clubs, internships, co-ops, study abroad, and research opportunities available in the School of Engineering. Sabrina's case also allows us to point out the existence of special honors sections of physics, chemistry, and calculus. Additionally, instructors may want to use Sabrina's case to discuss how students may resolve roommate issues and with whom to talk if they are encountering difficulties in the residence halls.

Section XIV

The Directed Case Method

The Directed Case Method is a mixture of an individual assignment and a structured whole class discussion led by the teacher. It has particular appeal to teachers of anatomy and physiology courses and other classes where there is a strong emphasis on content. This method delivers the goods. These are cases where questions are asked at the end of short scenarios. These questions have real answers, important facts, and principles that the instructor wants the students to learn. Another of its appeals to teachers coming from the lecture method is that there is a lot of good old lecturing involved.

The Directed Case Method

Teaching Concept and Process in a Content-Rich Course

By William H. Cliff and Leslie Nesbitt Curtin

Many instructors think that by incorporating case study analysis into the science classroom they will sacrifice course content. The directed case method, however, is a proven strategy for deepening and solidifying understanding of facts and concepts when used as a teaching adjunct within a content-rich course.

Researchers and educators universally acknowledge that modern science education should foster higher-order thinking among students. They also widely recognize that the process of higher-order thinking is enhanced by active-learning strategies.

Teachers of content-rich courses, however, often resist incorporating active-learning methodologies into their classrooms because of the perceived risk to the substantive content of the course. To achieve a satisfactory reconciliation, instructors need an active-learning strategy that deepens and reinforces knowledge of the subject matter as it promotes the process of higher-order thinking.

The directed case study is one such strategy: a case method designed primarily to enhance the student's understanding of the essential concepts of a course and secondarily to encourage critical thinking.

The method is remarkably simple. The instructor creates short, dramatic case scenarios and splices them into each major unit of a traditional lecture course. Each case is accompanied by a set of pertinent, didactic questions that can be answered from the textbook or lecture. Both the case scenario and the case questions are shaped by a set of learning objectives that encourage the student to consider the facts, figures, and principles underlying the subject.

"Welcome to the House, Bro" (see p. 305), an example of a directed case, is drawn from a course we teach in human anatomy and physiology. It illustrates the pedagogic goals, structure, and value of the directed case method.

The scenario is an amalgam of a real circumstance pieced together from a series of short newspaper articles and clinical descriptions found in medical reference texts. It is not important whether the scenario describes an actual, fictitious, or composite event. What is crucial is that the scenario presents students with a salient problem or issue that requires them to apply their knowledge of a particular subject to its resolution while deepening their understanding of the underlying facts and concepts.

QUESTIONS

1. Based upon the signs and symptoms of your patient and the events that led to his illness, what is the pathological condition that is associated with his urinary system? Outline the steps that led to the development of this condition.

2. How does the patient's creatinine clearance compare to the glomerular filtration rate (GFR) of a normal adult? What does this indicate about your patient's renal function?

3. One of the primary forces determining GFR has been altered in such a way as to cause the measured changes in creatinine clearance. Identify which force it is and explain how its alteration has led to the observed change in GFR.

4. List each of your patient's pathological signs and symptoms. List the normal functions of the kidney. Correlate the two lists. Be sure that you can describe how alterations in renal function resulted in the signs and symptoms you listed.

5. An abnormal level of which plasma constituent could account for the abnormalities in cardiac function? How is this abnormal level related to a change in kidney function that you identified in question 4?

6. Changes in three aspects of body fluid homeostasis (plasma volume, glomerular filtration, interstitial volume) account for the development of peripheral edema. Trace out the sequence of events that properly describe the cause-and-effect relationship among them.

7. What type of acid-base disturbance does your patient have? Briefly explain your reasoning. From your patient's condition, what does the nature of the acid-base disturbance tell you about its origin?

8. What approximate pCO_2 would you expect for your patient? Explain how you obtained this value.

9. What acid-base compensatory mechanism (renal or respiratory) accounts for the patient's pCO_2? Explain briefly.

TEACHING NOTES

Underlying this scenario are three separate but interrelated topics in a human anatomy and physiology course: urinary function, fluid and electrolyte balance, and acid-base balance. The scenario outlines the problem of acute renal failure caused by nephritis and describes the consequences of this condition on normal physiology.

Students must draw together their knowledge of the normal physiology of the kidney, fluid and electrolyte homeostasis, and acid-base balance in order to comprehend the significance of the clinical signs and symptoms that accompany the disease. In the process, the students' understanding of these topics grows.

Students bring essential facts and important concepts to bear on the problem by following a series of questions that the instructor carefully constructs in accordance with predetermined learning objectives. In this way, the instructor is able to direct the course of student learning. However, the process of question construction is constantly evolving: The questions are written and honed as the objectives are modified and sharpened, resulting in the most effective match between the case questions and learning objectives.

By a judicious combination of learning objectives and relevant questions, the instructor has the ability to determine the scope of the case. Case questions constructed around a restricted set of learning objectives provide the student with a detailed, focused examination of a topic or subject area. Alternately, case questions with far-reaching objectives force the student to survey a much broader area of study and integrate his or her knowledge of one topic with understanding of others.

OBJECTIVES

- To define glomerular filtration and its relation to urine production.
- To name the transcapillary forces that determine glomerular filtration.
- To explain how changes in these forces influence glomerular filtration.
- To describe the normal functions of the kidney, including how they correlate with aspects of normal homeostasis of fluid, electrolytes, and acids.
- To determine how potassium balance is maintained.
- To identify the relation between kidney function and normal extracellular fluid volumes.
- To name the properties of the various acid-base disturbances.
- To recognize the role of the kidney and the respiratory system in maintaining normal body fluid pH.

DISCUSSION

To successfully analyze the case, students will benefit from a textbook (such as Martini's *Fundamentals of Anatomy and Physiology* 1998) that provides detailed and specific connections between disease states (such as acute renal failure) and the normal functions of the organs/organ systems afflicted (e.g., the kidney/urinary system).

Answer to Question 1: To identify acute renal failure as the correct pathological condition, students need to associate the poisoning with information that indicates that exposure of the kidney to toxic substances from the blood can lead to a sudden reduction in urine output (oliguria). By outlining these steps, students learn an important concept of body fluid homeostasis, i.e., that once toxic substances enter into the body fluids, they inevitably are handled by the kidney as the body attempts to get rid of unwanted substances. By correctly identifying acute renal failure as the ultimate cause for the patient's condition, students recognize that all the other pathological signs and symptoms are manifestations of the underlying renal dysfunction.

Answers to Questions 2 and 3: These two questions direct students to use their knowledge of glomerular filtration and the transcapillary hydrostatic and osmotic forces to comprehend the problem of renal failure. As a result, they examine how the major forces acting across the capillary wall of the renal corpuscle produce net filtration. The students receive blood and urine measurements of a clinically relevant marker of glomerular filtration, i.e., creatinine and the urine flow rate. Using information about creatinine clearance found in the textbook, the students make a quantitative estimate of the glomerular filtration rate (GFR) of the patient.

When students compare their calculations with the rate of normal filtration from the textbook, they detect the drop in GFR that accompanies renal failure. Furthermore, by correlating the calculated reduction in GFR with the observed reduction in urinary output, they see a practical and important illustration of the fact that glomerular filtration is the first essential step in the process of urine production. After making this calculation and considering its significance, students identify the transcapillary forces responsible for net filtration and determine the change responsible for the drop in GFR.

The students must now combine their understanding of how transcapillary forces normally interact to cause filtration with the pathological changes that occur in the kidney during the nephritis. In so doing, the students achieve a more realistic understanding of how these forces interact and affect GFR than if they had simply memorized the definitions.

Answer to Question 4: This question highlights the consequences of renal failure on other aspects of regulatory physiology. By associating the diverse pathological symptoms with one or more aspects of normal kidney function, the students realize the importance of the kidney in regulating fluid, electrolyte, and acid-base homeostasis.

Answer to Question 5: By identifying potassium as the answer, students show that they have reviewed the textbook descriptions of the different electrolyte imbalances and have correctly associated the abnormalities in the ECG with hyperkalemia (elevated levels of potassium). This association enables students to appreciate that actions of the kidney in electrolyte balance have consequences for the normal function of other body organs such as the heart.

Answer to Question 6: After identifying the sequence whereby a drop in GFR leads to an increase in plasma volume and therefore an increase in peripheral edema, the students see the role of the kidney in the regulation of body fluid volumes and the interrelation between a change in the volume of one extracellular fluid compartment (plasma) and the volume of another (interstitial).

Answer to Question 7: Students deduce the type of acid-base disturbance by comparing the observed pH and bicarbonate levels in the plasma with normal values and correlating these changes with descriptions of the various acid-base disturbances provided in the textbook. Identifying metabolic acidosis as the disturbance, students recognize the normal function of the kidney in ridding the body of the fixed acids generated by metabolism.

Answer to Question 8: Referring to a nomogram in the textbook that correlates carbon dioxide with bicarbonate and pH of the blood, students can determine the correct plasma pCO_2. In this exercise, students gain experience interpreting a graph and examining the relationships among the three important components of the bicarbonate buffer system.

Answer to Question 9: In correctly recognizing that the pCO_2 is below normal from question 8, students are poised to understand that respiratory compensation (via hyperventilation) is the appropriate response to acute renal failure. Students can confirm this conclusion by observing that the patient's breathing rate is markedly elevated.

Some of the questions listed above focus on content, which calls for students to turn to their store of facts and concepts to solve the problem. Others stress higher-order thinking skills and process, which require students to apply newly acquired knowledge to address novel situations or arrive at new understandings based on a synthesis of already-familiar concepts. Using a mix of different styles of questions, the instructor establishes a balance of fact recall, conceptual understanding, and synthetic thought and application that is best suited for the student learning desired.

CLASSROOM MANAGEMENT

Students receive a case study at the beginning of the one- or two-week lecture series on each new course topic (i.e., major organ system). In a typical two-semester sequence, the students work through a series of five to eight cases each semester. Students complete the case analysis outside of class, either independently or in groups, using information available from lecture, textbook, and supplemental materials, and submit their answers prior to an in-class review of the case.

The in-class review is an important aspect of the directed case method. During the review, which encompasses a complete class period, each case question is examined by having students explain their answers to the class. Within this framework, the instructor initiates a class discussion about each answer, during which time the instructor is free to make additional comments about the case, and the students can raise specific concerns about the subject material. This format al-

WELCOME TO THE HOUSE, BRO

A Case Study in Body Fluid Homeostasis

In a notorious hazing incident in 1994, male pledges to a fraternity at Cortland State College had their backs coated with a paint mixture that included gasoline and other toxic substances. Traces of these substances were absorbed into their bodies and, as a result, several students required hospitalization. Suppose you were a resident internist at a hospital in Syracuse, NY, treating one of the new fraternity brothers. In the three days since the incident, his blood pressure has risen from 120/80 to 140/100. He has developed enlarged neck veins and peripheral edema. You note the sudden onset of oliguria during the first day after the incident. The patient becomes increasingly disoriented and restless and says he feels a progressive weakness in his muscles. His ECG shows occasional arrhythmias. You notice that his resting breathing rate is markedly elevated. Blood and urine tests reveal the following values (urine output equals 15 ml/hr):

Substance	Plasma or Serum Value	Urine Value
Creatinine	60 mg/l	1500 mg/l
pH	7.2	5.0
Na	130 mEq/l	
K	8 mEq/l	
HCO_3	8 mEq/l	

lows students to clarify misunderstandings, review related facts, and reinforce and re-emphasize subject material. Frequently, the comment or question of one student leads other students to offer their thoughts and questions, promoting increased student participation and interaction.

Instructors of content-rich courses might be reluctant to devote class time for case review that would otherwise be used to present new material. In this circumstance, we suggest adopting a case that addresses the same topic that the instructor would have covered during lecture. In so doing, the instructor is assured that students are learning the material as they analyze the case.

When used in this fashion, the directed case study promotes student learning beyond the level of fact recall or concept recognition. The problem solving associated with this approach lets students practice critical analysis—the very process of higher-order thinking. Nevertheless, the principal goal and one of the fundamental benefits of this method are to encourage the student to deepen and reinforce the understanding of the course content that he or she is already expected to learn.

REFERENCES

Cliff, W. H., and A. W. Wright. 1996. Directed case study method for teaching human anatomy and physiology. *American Journal of Physiology* 270 (*Adv. Physiol. Edu.*15): S19–S28.

Martini, F. H. 1998. *Fundamentals of anatomy and physiology.* 4th ed. Englewood, NJ: Prentice Hall.

Little Mito

The Story of the Origins of a Cell

By Stephanie Vail and Clyde Freeman Herreid

In this directed case study on the structure of the cell and functions of the major organelles, students examine one of the most important events of evolution: the origin of the eukaryotic cell. Students research the two major hypotheses involved and examine the relative merits of each.

Little Mito grew up in a one-room house in the Eukaryote family. His neighborhood consisted of one-room houses just like his, and everyone got along really well. He grew up with his sister, Chlora, his older brother, Flag, and his cousins, ER and Nuc. Each of them had their own chores, and the housework was done quickly and efficiently.

Chlora was in charge of gathering energy and converting it to carbon compounds and oxygen. She did this by soaking up the rays all day, making carbohydrates in a process called photosynthesis. It doesn't sound like a tough job, but everyone knew she was the breadwinner in the family—as long as the sun was shining. If not, then it was up to little Mito to do the job. He took his responsibilities seriously. He took the carbon compounds that his sister had made and broke them down to get energy to run the household.

He needed to breathe in oxygen to do the job. He felt like he was a little furnace, burning up the fuel and letting the energy out. Folks called what he did "cell respiration," and it made him feel proud to know he was doing his bit to contribute to the family's welfare.

Flag was the "mover and shaker" in the household. His job was to help the family move whenever they felt the need to see the countryside. He accomplished this by poking his tail out of the house and doing his undulating dance without a care for what the neighbors thought!

ER and Nuc had their own duties. ER was in charge of distribution and storage. He maintained the household supplies, seemed obsessed with moving things about in the house, and always remembered Chlora, Flag, and Mito's lunch money. Nuc was the head honcho of the Eukaryote family, and his responsibilities involved the organization of the family documents and information and leadership. He told everyone what to do and when to do it, even when they didn't want to. He was particularly busy on those occasions when they needed to build a new addition to the house for their expanding family. But that's another story.

The family was happy and set in its ways for many years until one day Mito heard a rumor about his past. A friend on the playground mentioned something about his great-great-grandfather being in the Prokaryote family. Mito wasn't sure what this meant, but he knew it might be important, so he went to the library to do some research. He never knew that genealogy could be so fascinating. But what he found out was shocking and it troubled him greatly.

Apparently, Mito had a questionable past. He almost felt illegitimate! There was a big argument among academicians. There were two completely different ideas about his family's origins: One was something called endosymbiosis and the other was called autogeny. Autogeny was a familiar concept to him, being as that was what he was taught his whole life. This was the legend that all of his relatives, Nuc, ER, Chlora, and Flag, had come from a prokaryotic cell ancestor who got too big for his britches and decided to infold his plasma membrane. This happened over thousands of generations. Slowly, but surely, he folded his surface and produced a whole bunch of membranes inside the cell. Some of these pinched off and made all of the family. As they floated around in the cytoplasm, they started to specialize with certain tasks and household jobs.

This sounded reasonable to Mito; he was just a kid after all. He knew that Nuc had a swell double membrane folded around him like a comfy blanket. Chlora and he also had double membranes, but their insides were just chock-full of them too and these let them make energy for the house. And there was ER and a bunch of other relatives, like the Golgi cousins and brothers Ves and Lys. All of them were just membranes, membranes, and more membranes. Then there was Flag. No one really knew where he came in—they just didn't talk about it. You know, a family secret.

But here was this other weird idea, endosymbiosis, which must have been what his friend was talking about. The book he found stated:

Eukaryotes arose principally through a series of events wherein certain prokaryotic cells were engulfed by other larger phagocytic prokaryotes, those whose membranes evolved the ability to take in food through phagocytosis. Perhaps because digestive machinery was not yet particularly efficient, or the prey had developed defenses against the predator's enzymes, some of the ingested organisms survived and continued living within the predator.

This was absolutely mind-blowing! It contradicted everything that he had been taught in school about his origins. Mito thought: In the beginning, my great grandfather Mito wasn't part of a family; he did EVERYTHING ALL ALONE. And Grandpa was once an aerobic bacterium and not a Mito at all. Then one day he got eaten by a bacterial predator and, according to this book, he was too strong for them. But he found it was pretty cool living inside the predator. That's my Grandpa! Always looking for a good deal. As long as he did his share for the predator and kept producing extra energy, he was living in the lap of luxury. He didn't think of himself as a parasite or anything, it was more like a buddy system. I'll wash your back and you wash mine—that sort of thing. In the book they called it a mutualistic relationship.

But that wasn't the end of it! The book said the predator host did it again and maybe even again. That's how his sister got here too. She had been a blue-green alga who was gobbled up. Awesome! His brother, Flag, the book said, maybe came from spirochetes that started living all over the host's body. The scientists weren't real sure about that one though. Mito had always thought that Flag was a little strange. He was pleased to read that the book thought so, too. All the books agreed that Nuc and ER came about through traditional membrane infolding. If his cousins Golgi and the twins, Ves and Lys, found this out, he would never hear the end of it. Good grief, he thought, I'm living with a bunch of strangers. We aren't related at all!

Mito was shocked and disturbed, but most of all he was curious. What did this mean, and where did he really come from? Which theory was correct?

QUESTIONS

(1) What are Nuc, Flag, ER, Mito, Chlora, Golgi, Ves, and Lys short for? What does each of these organelles do in a cell?

(2) What is the autogenic hypothesis of the origin of the eukaryotic cell?

(3) What is the evidence that supports the autogenic hypothesis?

(4) What is the endosymbiotic hypothesis?

(5) What is the evidence for the endosymbiotic hypothesis?

(6) What are the comparative strengths and weaknesses of the two hypotheses?

TEACHING NOTES

This is an example of a directed case, that is, one where correct answers are to be given to the questions. It is suited to an introductory biology class and could be readily used in a high school setting. The case deals with the structure of the cell and several major organelles, but its primary thrust is to examine one of the most important historical events of evolution: the origin of the eukaryotic cell. Two major hypotheses are involved—the autogenic versus the endosymbiotic versions.

Objectives

- To learn the major functions of some of the cell organelles.
- To learn the relative merits of the two major hypotheses of the origin of the eukaryotic cell and to understand the evidence supporting each.

Classroom Management

This case is straightforward, as is usual with directed cases. It is distributed with a series of questions that need to be answered by the students with the aid of the textbook, the internet, and journals. Students are expected to hand in their answers to the instructor. The instructor then runs a review of the questions in class, asking students for their answers. If they cannot adequately answer the questions, they receive a low grade on their response, regardless of what they put down on their paper, which, of course, they could have copied from anywhere.

Clearly, there are more creative ways to use this information, such as having students role-play the various organelles with them arguing who is the most important organelle to the survival of the cell. Alternatively, on the question of evolution, a debate could be arranged between two sides arguing the "parentage" issue; whose "children" are the chloroplasts and the mitochondria? Or this case could easily be used as an exam question.

DISCUSSION

Answer to Question 1: There is no mystery here that can't be cleared up by referring to any biology text. Nuc stands for nucleus and is a membrane-bound organelle that houses the chromosomes in the eukaryotic cell. It is filled with a watery fluid called nucleoplasm plus other assorted structures including the chromosomes, ribosomes, and nucleolus. The function that students will undoubtedly choose to mention will be the chromosomal DNA's function "to regulate the cell by directing protein synthesis," or words to that effect.

Flag stands for flagellum, the whip-like organelle that extends from some cells, though not normally from body cells in a multicellular eukaryotic organism. In the latter we frequently find cilia present in cells lining tubular organs such as the respiratory system and in the oviduct. The basic 9 + 2 microtubular structure is present in both cilia and flagella of eukaryotes. It is absent in prokaryotic flagella; they lack the microtubular structure, have a protein core, and are a fraction of the size of the flagella found in eukaryotes. The function of either flagella or cilia in single-celled organisms is to propel the organism through their environment just as a sperm cell is driven along by its flagellar tail. When ciliated cells line a body cavity, they move the body fluids past the cells, often moving particulate matter as well. So in the human reproductive tract, cilia line the female oviduct and help move the eggs to the uterus.

ER stands for endoplasmic reticulum and is the tortuous membranous network found throughout the cytoplasm of eukaryotic cells. The membranes are basically a plumbing system throughout the cell—channels through which synthesized molecules pass from place to place. The rough ER consists of membranes with attached ribosomes that synthesize proteins and then pass into the pipeline. Smooth ER lacks the ribosomes and is the site of synthesis of nonprotein materials.

Golgi stands for the Golgi Apparatus or Golgi Body. This is a flattened series of membrane sacs connected to the ER. There may be hundreds of these in cells of endocrine or exocrine organs that are specialized to produce secretions. The membranes at one end of the stack receive substances produced by the ER. At the other end of the stack the Golgi selects and packages them into small bubbles surrounded by a membrane—vesicles (Ves). These then migrate up to the plasma membrane where they merge and are released to the outside world. Vesicles are also formed that stay inside the cell such as those harboring digestive enzymes—these are known as lysosomes (Lys).

Chlora stands for chloroplast, the organelle responsible for photosynthesis in eukaryotes. The photosynthetic pigments are positioned along stacks of membranes, thylakoid discs, where light energy is trapped and converted into chemical energy, ATP, and carbohydrate products such as starch. Photosynthesis in bacteria that lack chloroplasts occurs throughout the membranes within the cell.

Answer to Question 2: Also known as the membrane-infolding hypothesis, it states that one line of prokaryotic cells evolved into eukaryotic cells by the infolding of its plasma membranes. The argument runs that there are selective advantages to being large (e.g., you are harder to eat and a tougher competitor), so some prokaryotes evolved large bodies. But if you are going to get large, you need a larger surface area for gas, waste, and nutrient exchange. This necessitates an infolding of the cell surface to communicate with the interior. So the endoplasmic reticulum is merely an extension of the cell surface and is connected to the nuclear membrane as well, communicating with the nucleoplasm. The other organelles that make up the novel features of the eukaryotic cell are membranous structures; they could have been extensions of the cell membranes that have pinched off from the ER. This then explains the nuclear membrane, mitochondria, chloroplasts, ER, Golgi Body, vesicles, lysosomes, and vacuoles—all membranous structures. Even the cilia/flagella could have been extensions of the cell membrane into which microtubules have grown.

Answer to Question 3: There is little direct evidence that supports the autogenic hypothesis except that the above structures are membranous. Also, some electron micrographs suggest that the endoplasmic reticulum does indeed connect with the plasma membrane and the nuclear membrane and provides an extensive surface area for exchange. Furthermore, the hypothesis seems reasonable and there is no competing hypothesis for the origin of the nuclear membrane, ER, Golgi, vesicles, lysosomes, and vacuoles. The latter regularly are seen to pinch off from the ER. As to the origin of the mitochondria, chloroplasts, and maybe flagella, there are better ideas.

Answer to Question 4: The endosymbiotic hypothesis states that eukaryotic cells have evolved from several prokaryotic cells coming together in a mutualistic relationship. A large host prokaryotic cell might have originally taken in other bacteria as food, but instead of being digested, the bacteria stayed on as symbionts. Thus, an aerobic bacterium was consumed and became the mitochondrion. A blue-green bacterium was consumed and became a chloroplast. Spirochete bacteria came to live on the host's surface and became cilia/flagella.

Interestingly, evidence now exists that the chloroplasts of some organisms were not obtained directly by a host cell engulfing cyanobacteria (primary endosymbiosis), but rather the chloroplasts are eukaryotic algae (with their cyanobacteria) that were consumed by a host (secondary endosymbiosis).

Answer to Question 5: The evidence that mitochondria and chloroplasts were once bacteria in the distant past is incredibly strong, and most biologists accept this view.

Similarities between chloroplasts, mitochondria, and bacteria include:

- All are similar in size, 5–10 micrometers.
- Mitochondria and chloroplasts are the only organelles (beside the nucleus) that have their own DNA. They and bacteria all have genomes that are small and are arranged as one double circular strand of DNA that lacks proteins. This is quite unlike eukaryotic nuclear DNA, which is arranged in multiple linear chromosomes of DNA and proteins.
- Mitochondria and chloroplasts have double external membranes as if they were engulfed in a food vacuole; that is, the plasma membrane of a predator folded inward around a soon-to-be-mitochondrion or chloroplast, resulting in two membranes around the structure.
- All have small ribosomes, in contrast to the larger ones found in the cytoplasm of eukaryotes. Thus, chloroplasts and mitochondria can manufacture proteins on their own, as do bacteria. Also, hybrid ribosomes (i.e., pieces of bacte-

rial and chloroplast ribosomal subunits mixed together) work just fine!

- Protein synthesis in all three is inhibited by the chemical chlorem-phenicol. This chemical doesn't stop protein synthesis in the eukaryotic ribosomes in the cytoplasm. The reverse is true for cyclohexamide, which stops eukaryotic synthesis but not prokaryotic synthesis.
- All have electron transport proteins on their inner membranes.
- All reproduce by binary fission. The mitochondria and chloroplasts look like bacterial cells when they divide, and they do so independently of when the host cell divides.

Many other examples of intracellular symbiosis are known where bacteria live inside other cells. Kwang Jeon of the University of Tennessee made a wonderful set of observations demonstrating the way that this type of symbiosis could develop. He had been working with amoebae for years when he received a new batch in his lab and placed them near other bowls with amoebae from other parts of the world. Soon his many amoebae began to die in one bowl after the other. Not all of the individuals perished, however. Some only got sick, growing and dividing slowly. Jeon looked at the dead amoebae under a microscope and noticed they were infected by thousands of rod-shaped bacteria, which the new bacteria had brought with them. Over five years Jeon kept the colonies going, and the descendents of the infected colonies progressively improved and soon were back to growing at the normal rate. But they still had their bacteria.

Jeon went further. He got some uninfected amoebae from friends who had samples of his original colonies. He was able to remove the nuclei from infected and uninfected amoebae using a tiny hooked glass needle and he switched them. The infected amoebae with new nuclei survived just fine. But the "clean" amoebae with nuclei from infected amoebae died in a few days. The nuclei were unable to survive in a "clean" cell. They seemed to need their bacterial infection.

Jeon tested this notion by injecting a few bacteria into the cytoplasm of the doomed amoebae just before they would have perished, and they rapidly recovered. Also, Jeon was able to show that the amoebae now depended on their bacteria. He put the antibiotic penicillin into the water. Penicillin will normally kill bacteria but not amoebae. But in this case where the amoebae and bacteria had been living together for many generations, penicillin first killed the bacteria and then the amoebae died. As Margulis and Sagan put it in their book *Microcosmos* (p.123 where they described Jeon's work), "Dangerous pathogens can become required organelles in less than a decade—very suddenly...." (1997).

The evidence that spirochetes gave rise to cilia/flagella is weak and most biologists are not convinced by the meager data. The argument suggesting spirochetes gave rise to cilia/flagella includes the following remarkable symbiosis: There is a protozoan that appears to be covered with cilia. Upon closer inspection this *Mixotricha paradoxa,* which lives in the digestive tracts of termites and digests the wood the termites eat, has dozens of spirochetes attached all over the body, and they beat together in synchronous waves giving the impression of cilia. Also, there is recent evidence that DNA has been found associated with the base of the flagella/cilia. (See Margulis and Sagan 1997, p. 278.)

Answer to Question 6: Neither hypothesis offers a good explanation of chromosome evolution nor a really convincing explanation of where cilia/flagella come from. The endosymbiotic hypothesis only deals with mitochondria, chloroplast, and cilia/flagella evolution. It says nothing about the other organelles such as Golgi, ER, vacuoles, vesicles, lysosomes, and the nuclear membrane. The autogenic hypothesis is far inferior to the endosymbiotic hypothesis in dealing with the evolution of mitochondria and chloroplasts, but it seems to be a reasonable explanation of the other membranous structures in the eukaryotic cell. Perhaps the most reasonable approach today is to combine the two hypotheses.

Finally, there are some recent new ideas about the origin of the eukaryotic cell. Some of these are nicely summarized by Jeremy Mohn at *www.geocities.com/jjmohn/endosymbiosis.htm.*

REFERENCES

de Duve, C. 1996. The birth of complex cells. *Scientific American* (April): 50–57.

Margulis, L. 1981. *Symbiosis in cell evolution*. San Francisco: Freeman and Co.

Margulis, L., and D. Sagan. 1997. *Microcosmos*. Berkeley: University of California Press.

Martin, W., and M. Muller. 1998. The hydrogen hypothesis for the first eukaryote. *Nature* 392: 37–41.

Palmer, J. 2000. A single birth of all plastids? *Nature* 405: 32–33.

Ridley, M. 2000. The search for luca. *Natural History* (November): 82–85.

Sagan, D., and L. Margulis. 1987. Bacterial bedfellows. *Natural History* (March): 26–33.

The Death of Baby Pierre

A Genetic Mystery

By Clyde Freeman Herreid

On March 7, 1964, the baby known as Pierre was born in a remote part of Quebec Province in Canada. He appeared to be a healthy six-pound, twelve-ounce child, except he did not eat well. Over the weeks after his birth, he became progressively more lethargic, vomiting periodically. Most peculiarly, his urine smelled of rotten cabbage, and soon the smell permeated his clothes and body. By the time he was admitted to the hospital on September 14, his muscles were weak and his ribs were showing. Baby Pierre had only gained half a pound in the six months since his birth. The doctors kept him alive by feeding him through a tube threaded through his nose and into his stomach. He gained weight and strength for a while, and then suddenly took a turn for the worse. On November 30, baby Pierre vomited blood and died.

It soon became increasingly apparent that other babies in the Chicoutimi area of Quebec Province had similar symptoms, and people recalled similar deaths in this remote area 120 miles north of Quebec City. Some families lost several children to Pierre's disease. In those families stricken, it soon became clear that the parents were normal, but about one quarter of their children were afflicted. Boys and girls were equally afflicted. Specialists soon concluded that all of the facts indicated that this was a genetic disorder.

1. If a genetic disorder was the cause, which answer is most likely correct?

   (A) A pollutant is causing mutations.
   (B) Multiple alleles are involved.
   (C) The disease is caused by a dominant allele.
   (D) Baby Pierre's parents are homozygous for a recessive allele causing the disease.
   (E) The disease is due to an autosomal recessive.

Explain the reason for your choice.

(To be answered after question 1 is handed in)

Baby Pierre and the other stricken children were victims of hereditary tyrosinemia. This is caused by an autosomal recessive disease. The children lacked the normal gene that produces a liver enzyme that breaks down the amino acid tyrosine. Without the enzyme, tyrosine builds up in the liver and kidneys leading to the cabbage-like smell of the urine. Lethal side effects follow. (A liver transplant is the only long-term treatment of the disease as of 1997.)

Both parents avoid this fate because, although they carry one copy of the defective gene, they carry a normal gene that produces more than enough enzyme for normal liver function. The parents are unwitting carriers of the disease. In genetic terminology they are heterozygotes, while Baby Pierre was a homozygous recessive.

Below is a pedigree of three generations of Canadians.

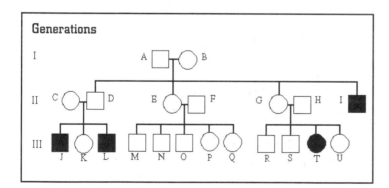

2. Using the symbols of "a" for recessive and "A" for dominant normal allele, write the genotype for the following individuals:

A _____   I _____

D _____   K _____

E _____   R _____

3. Is the above pedigree consistent with a sex-linked trait?

4. What is the likelihood that female K will have a normal child if she marries a normal person who is a carrier for tyrosinemia?

5. What is the likelihood of female K having a normal child if she marries her cousin M?

6. Hereditary tyrosinemia is usually quite rare, affecting only 1 in 100,000 newborns. The situation in the French Canadians in Chicoutimi, Quebec, is dramatically different: 1 birth in 685 can be expected to produce a child with the disorder. From the answers below, what is the most likely reason for the large number of tyrosinemia cases in Chicoutimi? Explain the reason for your answer.

(A) A high mutation rate.

(B) A selective advantage for tyrosinemia in this part of Quebec.

(C) Founder effect.

(D) Nutritional patterns in the people; large quantities of tyrosine in the diet.

(E) Pleiotropy, where the allele for tyrosinemia has beneficial effects as well as harmful effects.

Reason for your choice:

7. The Hardy-Weinberg equation allows us to make some calculations about the local population.

(A) What is the frequency of "aa" individuals?

(B) What is the frequency of the "a" allele in the gene pool?

(C) What is the frequency of the "A" allele in the gene pool?

(D) What is the frequency of heterozygous individuals?

(E) Assuming random breeding, what are the chances that two carriers will marry?

TEACHING NOTES

Introduction

Case studies used in business schools are typically dilemma or decision cases where a business manager is faced with a problem that must be solved. The students' job is to analyze the problem and come up with possible options and solutions to the problem. *There is no one answer to the problem* in good cases. The discussion is necessarily open-ended.

Case studies used in teaching medicine also are generally dilemma cases where a physician must diagnose an illness and prescribe a treatment. But unlike the business case, *there usually is a right single answer*. So the case analysis is focused upon discovering the nature of that problem. The discussion is necessarily closed-ended.

In designing cases for science courses, both closed- and open-ended cases may be desirable. If it is facts and principles that you are after as an instructor, then closed-ended cases may be preferable. One of the most useful of these is the directed case study. Here a story is written and given to the students along with a number of questions about the case. The questions are structured to elicit answers which expose general principles. William

Cliff and Ann Wright have written about their use of this method in the teaching of human anatomy and physiology (*Advances in Physiology Education* 15(1): 519–528, 1996).

"The Death of Baby Pierre" is a directed case study intended for a general biology course. The case is based on an article by Jared Diamond entitled "Founding Fathers and Mothers" in *Natural History* magazine, June 1988 (pp. 10, 12–15).

Objective

To develop or test skills in analyzing pedigrees and genetic problems

Classroom Management

Classroom management is simple in this case, as with all directed cases. The material is handed out to the students at the beginning of a lecture section on genetics. Over the next several days as lectures are given, the students ferret out the answers and hand them in sometime later. At that time, a discussion is held where the teacher runs over the questions and answers and picks up on any interesting or difficult topics.

As the case is structured, the fact that question #1 needs to be answered first before the remaining questions are given to the students makes this case a little awkward to handle. The problem can be solved by merely eliminating the question and giving the whole case to the students at once.

I have used the case as part of an exam for a course in general biology. The case can be easily modified and presented in the middle of a class where personal response systems, "clickers," are used (see chapter 33 for more on clicker cases).

Answers to Questions

1. If a genetic disorder were the cause, which answer is most likely correct?
   (A) A pollutant is causing mutations.
   (B) Multiple alleles are involved.
   (C) The disease is caused by a dominant allele.
   (D) Baby Pierre's parents are homozygous for a recessive allele causing the disease.
   (E) The disease is due to an autosomal recessive.

Explain the reason for your choice.

There is no reason to suspect that answer (A) is correct from the data given. Pollutants are highly unlikely in remote Quebec and they are not likely to cause specific mutations.

The fact that 25% of the children are afflicted when the parents aren't suggests a simple 2-allele system involving a defective recessive allele, so answer (B) isn't likely.

Answer (C) can't be correct because if a dominant allele causes the disease, the parents would also show it.

Answer (D) can't be correct because the parents cannot be homozygous for the disease causing recessive; if they were, they too would have the disease.

Answer (E) is the correct choice. The disease clearly is recessive and since females and males were equally afflicted, it is autosomal and not a sex-linked trait.

2. Using the symbols of "a" for recessive allele and "A" for the dominant normal allele, write the genotype for the following individuals.

A   *Aa*
D   *Aa*
E   *AA (or Aa since F probably Aa)*
I   *aa*
K   *Aa (67% chance of this normal genotype) vs. AA (33% chance)*
R   *Aa (67% chance) vs. AA (33% chance)*

3. Is the above pedigree consistent with a sex-linked trait?

No, since males and females are equally affected in this case. In the typical sex-linked pattern such as color blindness or muscular dystrophy, males are normally the only sex afflicted. These traits are carried on the X chromosome. Since males have only one X chromosome, if the trait is present, they will surely show it. Females, on the other hand, will usually not display the trait even if they are carriers. They have two X chromosomes and the normal X will compensate for the "defective" X. If the trait shows up in a female (a very rare occurrence), both X chromosomes will have the trait.

4. What is the likelihood that female K will have a normal child if she marries a normal person who is a carrier for tyrosinemia?

If K is AA, then all children will be normal (50% will be AA and 50% will be Aa). If K is Aa, then Aa x Aa gives a probability of 3 normal children per 1 diseased child or 75% normal.

5. What is the likelihood of female K having a normal child if she marries her cousin M?

Cousin M could be either AA or Aa just like K could be AA or Aa.
With combinations:

AA × AA} all normal children will result
AA × Aa} all normal children will result
Aa × AA} all normal children will result
Aa × Aa} 75% normal

6. From the answers below, what is the most likely reason for the large number of tyrosinemia cases in Chicoutimi? Explain the reason for your answer.
   (A) A high mutation rate.
   (B) A selective advantage for tyrosinemia in this part of Quebec.
   (C) Founder effect.
   (D) Nutritional patterns in the people; large quantities of tyrosine in the diet.
   (E) Pleiotropy where the allele for tyrosinemia has beneficial effects as well as harmful effects.

Reason for your choice:
   There is no reason to expect a high mutation rate (answer A) or selective advantage (answer B) for tyrosinemia in Quebec. Since it is a genetic disease, answer D is unlikely. Answer E is conceivable but why should it show up only in Chicoutimi? (C) is the most likely answer since it is reasonable to predict Chicoutimi is a small community. (In fact, the Canadian geneticist Dr. Claude Leberge found the Chicoutimi region was settled by a few dozen families who migrated north from Quebec's Charlevoix County. Most people living there are descendants of the original settlers. The tyrosinemia victims can be traced back to one couple, Louis and Marie Gagne, who emigrated from France. It seems likely that either Louis or Marie had the gene for tyrosinemia and passed it to some of their nine children, and innumerable grandchildren, at least two of whom moved to Charlevoix. Their progeny later moved to Chicoutimi. The significant inbreeding produced a high proportion of people who carried the tyrosinemia gene. This is a classic example of the founder effect.)

7. The Hardy-Weinberg equation allows us to make some calculations about the local population.
   (A) What is the frequency of "aa" individuals?
      Given 1/685 children have the disease and are aa, this means $q^2 = .00146$

   (B) What is the frequency of the "a" allele in the gene pool?
      $q = .0382$

   (C) What is the frequency of the "A" allele in the gene pool?
      Since $p + q = 1$ and $q = .0382$, then $1 - .0382 = p = 0.9618$

   (D) What is the frequency of heterozygous individuals?
      $2pq = .073$, or 1 person in 14 are Aa individuals.
      The frequency of aa (homozygous recessive) $q^2 = .00146$
      The frequency of AA (homozygous dominants) $p^2 = 0.925$

   (E) Assuming random breeding, what are the chances that two carriers will marry?
      $.073 \times .073 = .0053$, or 1 marriage in 190 will involve two carriers

The Case of the Dividing Cell

Mitosis and Meiosis in the Cellular Court

By Clyde Freeman Herreid

The Honorable Judge Cellular is presiding over the case of the State v. Egg Cell Number 6624223. As the prosecuting attorney calls each witness to the stand and the courtroom drama unfolds, students learn about the stages of mitosis and meiosis and their particular characteristics, and how cell division in prokaryotes differs from that in eukaryotes.

PART I

The first day of testimony: Mitosis exposed.

"Hear ye. Hear ye. The Honorable Judge Cellular now presiding. All rise."

The judge in his black robes came silently into the courtroom amid the usual bustle that attended one of the special sessions. He slid into his high-backed chair, glanced at the papers on the bench before him, and gazed at the defendant over his spectacles. Then, after giving the same attention to the prosecution, he looked over the jury. If he could have pursed his lips, he would have done so, for he wondered greatly at this particular jury that was filled with prokaryotic cells.

Prokaryotic cells? It hardly seemed fitting that they would be sitting in judgment of a eukaryotic matter. Hardly fitting at all. Oh, well, both the prosecution and the defense seemed to want it that way. So be it. He knew that the attorneys wanted to be impartial, but this was unseemly. Prokaryotes, what did they know about eukaryotes? Harrumph.

The judge adjusted his plasma membrane over his shoulders and began speaking with a voice that seemed to resonate from the bowels of his endoplasmic reticulum. "Ahem, let us see now. This is the case of the State v. Egg Cell Number 6624223. This presents an unusual situation involving an alleged capital offense. The defendant is charged with being an undesirable mutant in the body politic. The penalty is death. This is the most serious of matters, and it requires undivided attention. So let us begin, but let us begin with the presumption of innocence. Please councilors, let us have the opening statements. But, please keep your comments brief and to the point. The prosecution first, arguing the position for the State. I believe it is Councilor Liv, is it not?"

"Yes, thank you, Your Honor. Members of the jury, I come to you today as a member of our cellular community. I come from a long line of cells that stretches back to a time when the world was once filled with only prokaryotic cells like yourselves. For over a billion years you ruled the world. We eukaryotic cells are but recent upstarts. For the most part we live in colonies making up the bodies of animals, plants, and fungi.

"I, in fact, am a liver cell, one of several trillion cells living in a human I'll call Martha. It is essential that we all live in harmony with one purpose in life—that is, survival. If Martha doesn't survive, we all die—I, and the rest of the liver cells, the kidney cells, the muscle cells, the nerves, and all of the others that make up this grand human being.

"Yet, this is not all. Our individual survival is only part of the story. We would not be here except for the fact that we all are descendents of untold numbers of other organisms, many of them complex colonies of cells, for the last 700 million years. And we have relied on sex. Yes, I know that concept is one you asexual cells hardly understand. But as you have certainly read, in humans like Martha, the ovary cells produce some unusual cells called eggs. And in Martha's husband there are some cells called sperm. If these two cells get together, they produce a fertilized egg that may grow up to be another colony of cells we call a baby.

"Now, the point of all of this is that to produce a perfect baby, the sperm and the egg must be perfect. This brings me to the central issue of this crime. The defendant on the stand today is one of Martha's cells. We all love Martha—some of us have lived with her for years—but as we will show, she has been alive for 43 years and this has led to trouble. Many of her eggs are flawed. And this is exactly the case with our defendant, Egg Cell Number 6624223. SHE IS NOT PERFECT.

"It is our contention that she should be destroyed by apoptosis. She is not just con-taminated by a simple point mutation. She is disfigured by having an extra chromosome 21. This invariably leads to Down syndrome. She should be destroyed so that a pure lineage can go on. We believe that you will see the wisdom of this solution by the end of the trial and trust in your good judgment."

"Thank you, Councilor Liv. Now, Councilor Oocyte, would you give your opening remarks?"

"Thank you, Your Honor. Cells of the jury, you have heard the remarks of my colleague. Her argument that my client is flawed is based on unsound logic. We will stipulate that my client is unusual, but that does not mean she is flawed or damaged. In every part of Martha's body there are unusual cells. Some cells in the lining of her digestive tract are triploid or have even higher numbers of polyploidy. Her liver cells, and perhaps Councilor Liv herself, are filled with unusual numbers of chromosomes. Some have three, four, five, six, seven, or more sets of chromosomes. Councilor Liv here appears to be in the pink of health! What's there to be troubled about? These cells are all living healthy lives and contributing to Martha's welfare.

"There is hardly a reason to get upset with my client who has a single extra chromosome 21. And, as is well known, even if a Down syndrome baby is the result, that child can live a happy, wholesome life. We will clearly demonstrate to the jury that death is hardly a reasonable remedy, and that, in fact, there is no crime that has been committed at all."

"Thank you, Councilor. Now Councilor Liv, call your first witness."

THE FIRST STATE WITNESS

Mr. Nuclear Membrane explains the secrets of mitosis.

"Your Honor, I call Mr. Nuclear Membrane of the Epidermis to the stand."

"Bailiff, administer the oath."

"Do you swear to tell the truth, the whole truth, and nothing but the truth so help you DNA?"

"I do."

"I am calling Mr. Nuclear Membrane here as an expert witness on the process of cell division."

"I object Your Honor. Mr. Nuclear Membrane cannot serve in this capacity, as he is simply an expert in the topic of cell division that occurs in skin cells. This is hardly the same as that which occurs in the sex cells. And that is the subject of the case. Although cell division in the skin cells is just like cell division almost everywhere else in the body, cell division is entirely different in the ovaries and the testes where the sex cells are manufactured. The skin cells divide by mitosis. The sperm and eggs are produced by meiosis—an altogether different process."

"Councilor Oocyte objects. Councilor Liv, what do you say?"

"I am not calling Mr. Nuclear Membrane as an expert in meiosis but as one on mitosis. I wish to lay the groundwork for making the distinction between the two."

"Then I withdraw my objection, Judge, and will so stipulate that the gentleman is an expert in mitosis and nothing else. Go ahead, this should be interesting."

"Now, Mr. Membrane, please describe the events of simple cell division that occurs in the skin. I believe you have some diagrams to show the jury that will help."

"Yes, Councilor Liv, I do. First, I want to stress that the normal skin cell divides repeatedly in its life. Skin cells are always being wiped away when Martha's hands rub against anything. We do indeed have a busy time keeping up with the wear and tear of everyday living.

"When Martha's cells get ready to divide, the genetic information has to be copied. If you're going to make another cell just like yourself, you've got to make sure that the next generation knows what to do; you've got to send the right information. So the cell has to make a copy of the instructions in the DNA—you know, the genetic material.

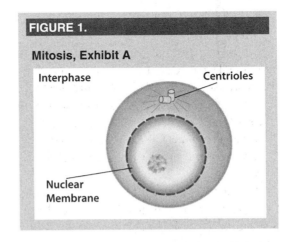

FIGURE 1.

Mitosis, Exhibit A

Interphase · Centrioles · Nuclear Membrane

"So here's the deal. The scientists who study this stage in our life call it 'Interphase,' and that's what's shown in Exhibit A (Figure 1). This is the time when we're really livin' it up, growing like crazy, making proteins like there's no tomorrow, and making little organelles. But then things change in a big way. The cell has gotten too big, you might say. It's got to divide. And that's when the DNA makes a copy of itself.

"Now take a look at the diagrams that show the next steps. All of 'em have special names. They are early and late Prophase, Metaphase, Anaphase, and my favorite, Telophase."

"Please, tell us the overall gist of what is happening."

"Well, it's no mystery. Look here at Exhibit B (Figure 2). The DNA that has made an extra copy of itself gets all wrapped up into wads you call chromosomes. But each chromosome has two parts, you know, the original part and the copy. They're called chromatids—the parts, that is. The two parts of each chromosome are linked together at a point in their middles."

"So, what happens next?"

"Well, in Exhibit C (Figure 3) you see the chromosomes lining up in the center of the cell, and then in Exhibit D (Figure 4) the pairs of chromatids split apart and go off to opposite sides of the cell. They're pulled there by fibers. All of the chromosomes are doing the same

FIGURE 2.

Mitosis, Exhibit B

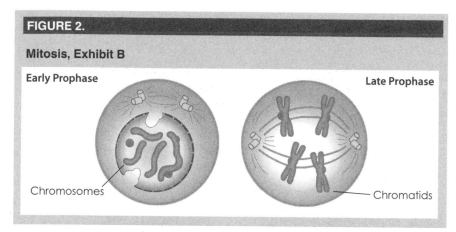

Early Prophase

Late Prophase

Chromosomes

Chromatids

FIGURE 3.

Mitosis, Exhibit C

Metaphase

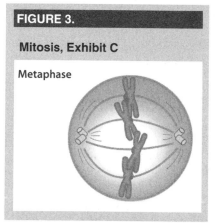

FIGURE 4.

Mitosis, Exhibit D

Anaphase

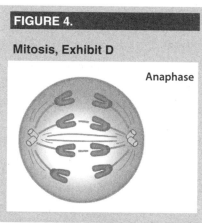

FIGURE 5.

Mitosis, Exhibit E

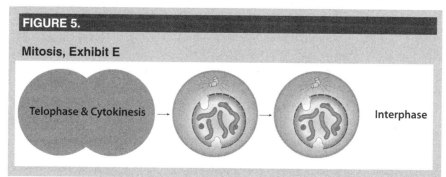

Telophase & Cytokinesis

Interphase

"Objection. That's hearsay, Your Honor."

"Objection sustained."

"Let's try this again, Mr. Membrane. What have you seen yourself?"

"The chromatids are separated and dragged to the opposite sides of the cell, and that's when I reappear—see, that's me, right here in Exhibit E (Figure 5, lower left)—in two places, actually. I make a nuclear membrane that surrounds the chromosomes on both sides of the cell. You know, that's my job, to surround the DNA for the two new cells. I'm making two nuclei for the next generation of cells."

"Let me be sure I have this right. The chromosome material—the DNA—makes a copy of itself, then bundles itself up so it can move to the center of the cell more easily. The two copies of the DNA are wound into separate bundles called chromatids that are bound together. They line up in the center of the cell and then become separated by some fibers that seem to pull them apart. So one set of chromatids (I presume you call them chromosomes at this point) goes to one side of the cell and the other set goes to the other side of the cell."

thing, all at once. Half of their chromatids go to one side and half go to the other. That way, each side of the cell gets a complete set."

"Just a moment, Mr. Membrane, where did these fibers come from? It looks like they come from the centrioles."

"That's right, but I'm not quite sure as I've never been around to see that. I've been told that..."

"That's right. You see, when the cell starts to divide, that is, when the cytoplasm in the center of the cell begins to pinch off the two parts, both sides get a complete set of chromosomes. In humans, there are 46 chromosomes. So every time a skin cell makes a copy of itself, both cells get a complete set of 46 chromosomes. Then each cell reverts to Interphase. It's wonderful, don't you think?"

"Yes, I do. Thank you for your testimony. Now, Councilor Oocyte, the witness is yours for cross examination."

CROSS EXAMINATION

"Thank you, Judge. Now just to be sure I have this right, Mr. Nuclear Membrane, do I understand that you disappear during this process and reappear at the end?"

"That's right, Councilor Oocyte. I have to sort of break apart in the early Prophase so that the chromosomes can move to the center of the cell. They couldn't do this if I were in the way, could they?"

"No, I don't suppose they could, Mr. Nuclear Membrane. Then the next time you see anything is when you reassemble around the two new sets of chromosomes on opposite sides of the cell. That's the reason Telophase is your favorite time, isn't it? So everything else you have told us about in between these two times is mere scuttlebutt, isn't it?"

"I would hardly call it that. It is well known that..."

"Let's move on to another question, shall we? Tell me, when the DNA makes a copy of itself, is the copy always perfect?"

"Well, you know, most of the time. It has to be. Otherwise, the cell might be sick, become cancerous or something."

"But that isn't what always happens, is it?'

"Ah… no. I guess not."

"Isn't it true that many cells have so-called 'imperfect copies' of DNA during mitosis and things aren't disastrous? In fact things are often pretty good, aren't they? Sometimes these somatic mutations turn out well. I'm thinking of cases where a hair cell on the head of a person like Martha mutates and the person has a nice stripe of white running through their hair. That's pretty striking, isn't it? You wouldn't say that is bad would you? Or abnormal? Or a reason to destroy Martha or her mutant cell? No? I thought not, it depends upon the situation, doesn't it?"

"Yes, I guess so."

"No further questions, Your Honor."

"You may step down, Mr. Nuclear Membrane. And I believe we have had enough testimony for today. We will resume tomorrow at the same time. Court is in recess."

QUESTIONS FOR STUDENTS

After reading the court proceedings, students answer the following questions:

- What are the major events that occur during each of the stages (Interphase, Prophase, Metaphase, Anaphase, Telophase, and Cytokinesis) in the life cycle of a cell such as a skin cell? Assume you are a court reporter who has to explain these stages to your readers with as little jargon as possible.

- How does cell division differ in prokaryotes and eukaryotes? Clearly, these differences may be difficult for the prokaryotes in the jury to follow unless you show the similarities and differences.

PART II

Court Is Back in Session

MEIOSIS EXPOSED

The jury filed back into the courtroom, hardly visible to the spectators seated on the benches. Their tiny prokaryotic bodies seemed to bounce along to some inner music. There had been three days of testimony and the jury had become comfortable with the routine. Once seated, they started whispering among themselves and court reporters could catch snatches of their conversations:

"God, I feel so small. I know what you mean. What do you think about that mitochondrion that testified? He looked sort of cool. Look at all of that stuff in their bodies. I mean really … to see all of those membranes inside. I mean, it grosses me out. I really shouldn't be prejudiced, after all they have invited us here, but it really is a bit too much. Shh, here comes the judge."

"Hear ye. Hear ye. . ." With preliminaries over, Judge Cellular peered over his glasses and stated, "I do hope we can move this trial along more rapidly, councilors. We really don't have to burden the jury with hearing from every organelle in the eukaryotic galaxy; surely the testimony is quite adequate to show how mitosis works. And, no, we don't have to hear from the plant cell witnesses. I'm sure we all understand it sufficiently well. Now, Councilor Liv, at our last session we left off with the witness for the prosecution having been sworn in. Was it Mr. Spermatocyte?"

"Yes, Your Honor. He is a primary spermatocyte and the defense has already stipulated that they will accept him as an expert witness for the process of meiosis. You will recall that he comes from Martha's husband Sam and his testes. He has been involved with the meiosis process ever since Sam's puberty."

"Very well. Mr. Spermatocyte, please come back to the stand. Come on sir, don't hang back. No need to swear you in again. Let's get on with it, Councilor Liv."

STATE WITNESS MR. SPERMATOCYTE EXPLAINS HOW SPERM ARE FORMED

"Now, sir, I believe you were explaining the cell division process that occurs in the testes. It is different than in the skin and other parts of the body. Right?"

"That is quite correct, Councilor. The cell division in the sex glands doesn't lead to two identical cells like we typically find in mitosis. No, indeed—it leads to four sperm cells, each absolutely unique. Quite special. Quite."

"How so, Mr. Spermatocyte?"

"Let me remind you that all cells in the human body start out with 46 chromosomes, but actually these are not really 46 completely different chromosomes. They are two sets of 23 chromosomes; one set has come from Sam's mother and the other set from his father. Put them together and you have Sam's 46 chromosomes all jumbled up in the nucleus running the business of his cells."

"But if it's the case that all cells in Sam's body have the same set of chromosomes, why do the cells act differently? Why do skin cells act like skin and nerve cells act like nerves and not vice versa. I should think that…"

"I object to this line of questioning, Your Honor. This is immaterial and irrelevant to the case."

"Overruled, Councilor Oocyte. It is necessary for the prokaryotic jury to understand how the cells in the colony differ from one another even though they have the same set of instructions. You may answer the question, Mr. Spermatocyte."

"Gladly. You see, even if all cells have the same chromosomes and the same genes, not all of the same genes are turned on! A muscle cell has only the muscle genes working, while the skin has only skin genes working. That's all there is to it."

"That's fine, Mr. Spermatocyte. Now continue with what happens when the sperm cells are formed."

"Certainly. Now, you will remember when Mr. Nuclear Membrane testified, he said that

FIGURE 1.

Meiosis, Exhibit A

Prophase I

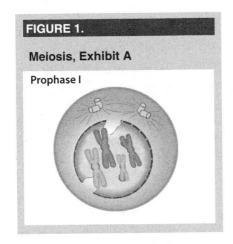

FIGURE 2.

Meiosis, Exhibit B

Metaphase I

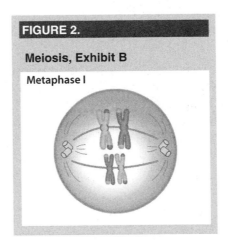

FIGURE 3.

Meiosis, Exhibit C

Anaphase I

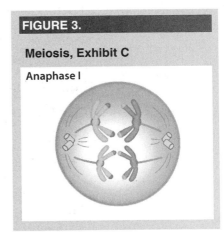

during mitosis all of the chromosomes moved to the center of the cell in a line. Well, the chromosomes also line up during meiosis, *but they line up in a different way!* In fact, everything is different when we sex cells do it! We are the only ones in the body that go through meiosis. We have a special job to do. We have to make sperm and eggs. We are certainly not your run-of-the-mill sort of cells. All the other cells go through mitosis; they are simply making clones of themselves. We, however, are out to make something unique! It is rather clear, isn't it, how special we are? Let me illustrate what happens when the sperm are formed. Naturally, I have brought my own set of diagrams along. They show what happens in my human, Sam."

"I might've known."

"I'll have none of that nonsense in my courtroom, Councilor Oocyte. The bailiff will set the diagrams up on the easel for you, Mr. Spermatocyte."

"Very well. I'll continue. Now you really have to notice this. Take a look at how the chromosomes line up during meiosis. Just look at that, won't you! See, it isn't random at all. There aren't 46 chromosomes in a row. No sir, there are 23 pairs of chromosomes in a row, although I can only show two pairs in Exhibit A (Figure 1). But look how Sam's chromosomes from his momma have paired up with his dad's set; the number 1s are together, and 2s, and 3s, and so on. And if you look closely you can see that each chromosome is composed of two chromatids, just exactly like we saw for the skin cell demonstration."

"I need a little clarification here for my poor judge's brain. Are you saying that when sperm are going to be made, the cell starts off in pretty much the same way as when a skin cell or a muscle cell is going to be made? That is, each chromosome's DNA first makes a copy of itself and the nuclear membrane disappears during Interphase?"

"That's absolutely correct, Your Honor."

"And what you're telling me I see in Exhibit B (Figure 2) is that the chromosomes move to the center of the cell, but this time they're lining up with the mother's and the father's side by side. That is, I could look inside and see the two number 2 chromosomes next to each other and a little further along I could see the two number 16s and so on down the line? Why, if I looked close enough, I would see the chromatids. In fact, they would look like teams of four chromatids."

"That's it, Your Honor! You have it precisely!"

"And, so? Please explain the relevance of that arrangement to me and the jury. I can see them puzzling along with me."

"Yes, indeed. But I must digress a moment. I need to..."

FIGURE 4.

Meiosis, Exhibit D

Telophase II

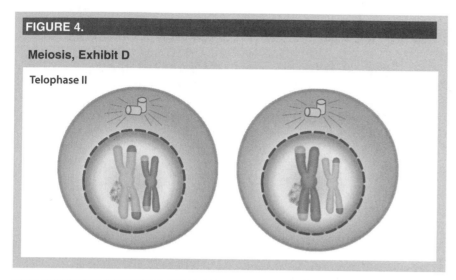

FIGURE 5.

Meiosis, Exhibit E

Prophase II

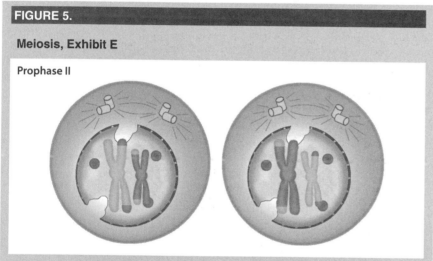

FIGURE 6.

Meiosis, Exhibit F

Metaphase II

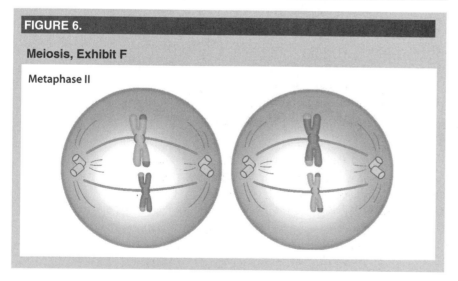

COUNCILOR OOCYTE OBJECTS: WHAT DOES THIS HAVE TO DO WITH EGGS?

"I do object, object, object! What is this, a biology lesson? Surely, we have listened patiently about all of this coming and going long enough. We all get it. Mitosis is different than meiosis. Isn't that sufficient? Let's move the trial along. My client is different than other little gametes. We have granted that. She is on trial for her life! Why are we listening to this lecture about sperm? My client is an egg cell, for God's sake!"

"Sit down, Councilor Oocyte. I will have no further outbursts in my courtroom or I will cite you for contempt. Do you understand?"

"Yes, Your Honor. But this is extremely frustrating, and I am sure that the jury is as disturbed as I. Just look at them. My objection still stands. What is your ruling, if you please?"

"Councilor Oocyte, your point is well made. Councilor Liv, are you going to connect this up in some way? Why are we talking about sperm instead of eggs?"

"The formation of sperm and eggs are essentially the same, Your Honor. But it is easier to explain if we first look at the simpler sperm formation. We will make the connection in a moment."

"Very well, then. Continue with your testimony, Mr. Spermatocyte. I will withhold my ruling for the present."

"Thank you. The point I was making is that when these pairs of chromosomes lie side by side they touch at many points. That's when they sometimes swap parts, and you can see that represented too in Exhibit B (Figure 2). Pieces of Sam's mother's chromosome number 7 can exchange pieces with Sam's father's number 7. It's quite like a mix and match affair. You see it gives variability to the chromosomes. This is called 'crossover' by the geneticists."

"Does it occur often?"

"Oh, absolutely! In fact, in humans at every meiotic tetrad (that's what the four chromatids are called) there are about 10 crossovers. So by the time that crossover is finished, the individual chromatids can hardly be thought of as mother's or father's any more. They are a hybrid of the two."

"Let us now return to the main point, Mr. Spermatocyte. What is the result of this peculiar arrangement of the chromosomes?"

"Well, just like in mitosis, there are some threads that are formed in the cell that attach to the chromosomes. These are the spindle fibers. They act to pull the sets of chromosomes apart—look at Exhibit C (Figure 3). This time though the chromatids of the chromosomes won't be separated. Only the pairs of mother and father chromosomes are separated."

"Do you mean that all of the mother's chromosomes go one way and the father's go another and end up in different cells?"

"Oh, dear me, no. Did I say that? No, no…. Oh, I see where the trouble is! I didn't make a crucial point, and the diagram might be slightly misleading. When the father and mother's chromosome pairs lie together that doesn't mean that they line up so that all of the mother's are on one side and the father's are on the other. Nothing could be further from the truth. No, they can be on either side. It is just chance that the mother's number 10 is on the right side of the cell and the father's is on the left. It could have just as easily been the opposite. So the end result is that it is simply a mixture. The only thing that counts is that each side gets a complete set of chromosomes."

"That's this variability point again. It sounds like each cell is going to be a unique collection of genes. What happens next? Complete sets of

---

FIGURE 7.

Meiosis, Exhibit G

Anaphase II

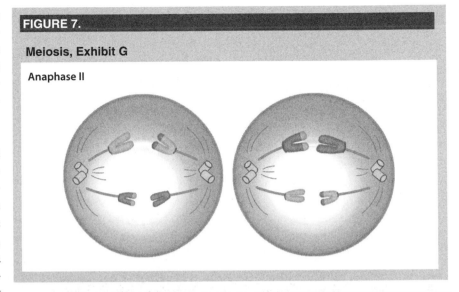

FIGURE 8.

Meiosis, Exhibit H

Telophase and Cytokinesis Complete

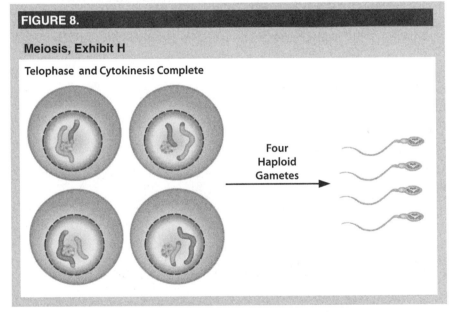

Four Haploid Gametes

chromosomes are on each side of the cell; does that mean that the cell is going to divide?"

"You are quite correct, Councilor Liv. Two cells are formed each with its own collection of 23 chromosomes, as represented in Exhibit D (Figure 4). But wait, things are not over. The chromosomes still have their chromatids. Remember them? Now the cells go to work to pull these apart."

"An excellent explanation, Mr. Spermatocyte. I surmise that you are about to tell me that they now go through the same steps as mitosis—that the chromosomes line up in the center of the cell and then the spindle fibers pull the chromatids apart so that...."

"Hold it, hold it, I object. Your Honor, I've been patient long enough. Who is the witness here and who is the attorney? It's a cute routine that they're putting on, but come on now, this is clearly leading the witness."

"I agree, Councilor Oocyte. Objection sustained. Councilor Liv, please do not lead the witness. Rephrase your statements."

"All right. Mr. Spermatocyte, please tell us what happens next."

"Well, you definitely are correct. In Exhibit E (Figure 5) you see the nuclear membranes again dissolving, and in Exhibit F (Figure 6) the chromosomes are lining up in the middle of the cell, just like in mitosis and it doesn't matter how they get into a line as long as they do it. Then the spindle fibers attach to their chromatids and Exhibit G (Figure 7) shows the fibers pulling them apart. This way each side of the cell gets a complete set of instructions. Then, the cell divides. That's it. Meiosis is finished. If everything is perfect, each cell at the end has one complete set of instructions. Each sperm has 23 chromosomes. And, of course, there are four of them produced. In the first stage of meiosis we produced two cells, and then in the second stage each of these divided again and produced two. That makes four, doesn't it?

"After all, that really is the basic idea of meiosis, isn't it? To have a normal cell with

46 chromosomes go through duplication and then instead of dividing only once, it divides twice. This makes four cells, each with a set of chromosomes instead of dividing only once and having a cell with two sets of chromosomes, and that's what you see in Exhibit H (Figure 8)."

"Yes, indeed."

"Your witness, Councilor Oocyte."

COUNCILOR OOCYTE CROSS EXAMINES: WHAT ABOUT MUTATIONS?

"I hardly know where to begin. This explanation is so confusing that I don't wonder that the jury is baffled about what is going on here. You are telling us that meiosis leads to four cells, not two like we saw previously in mitosis. Right? And you seem to be suggesting that, with all of this crossover and mixing of chromosomes, each sperm cell is unique. If that is so, am I correct in saying that one variation is just as normal as the next?"

"Well, I'm not sure I would say that. I guess I would say that some cells are more normal than others. If there is a mutation, I would say that cell is, uh, suspect."

"Why is that?"

"Because most mutations decrease the chances that a sperm will survive. Most mutations are bad."

"But not all. Right?"

"Right."

"Fine, now let's get the picture of what happens in the egg. In the formation of sperm, meiosis leads to four cells, each with a set of chromosomes. I take it that these four cells are really called sperm when the process is finished. Sperm, is that right?"

"Absolutely. They are sperm with great wonderful tails and great potential, I must say. In fact, I've got some more fascinating diagrams."

"No! I mean, no, that's quite all right. I think we've seen quite enough of those. Please continue."

"Oh. Okay, well, in the formation of the egg, exactly the same process happens. The primary oocyte will eventually form an egg. You will go through the two steps of chromosome shuffling and at the end four cells will be formed. The only real difference is that three of the cells will be tiny and one will be huge. The tiny ones are called polar bodies and they just disintegrate. The huge one is the egg and it has all of the nutrients and cytoplasm saved for itself. See for yourself how loaded the defendant is with nu-...."

"Please, Mr. Spermatocyte, confine your remarks to the general situation and refrain from making personal asides. Now, one more question, sir. Is it true that many egg cells that develop in an older woman like Martha don't go through exactly the same steps? That lots of times there are differences?"

"You are definitely correct. Older men and women seem to have more mutations and...."

"That will do for the moment, Mr. Spermatocyte. Now, tell me what were the events that have lead to the special chromosome pattern that we see in the defendant, Egg Cell Number 6624223?"

"As I understand it, she has an extra chromosome 21. This can happen in a woman's egg as it is developing, especially an older woman. It is a simple mistake."

"Please, don't refer to it that way as there are thousands of women who produce these eggs each year."

"I object to Councilor Oocyte leading the witness. If the witness says it is a mistake, then that is what he means. He has been certified as an expert witness, Your Honor."

"Objection sustained."

"Please, tell us then how this situation occurs to millions of women each year."

"It is simple, really. Everything is fine through the first stage of meiosis. The chromosomes make copies. They line up in the center and the pairs of chromosomes separate. We now have two cells with 23 chromosomes with chroma-tids. Then the trouble starts. When the chromosomes line up again in the center, this time for the chromatids to separate, all goes well except that chromosome 21 doesn't always separate completely. If this happens to the egg, then it will end up with an extra copy of 21."

"It sounds like if this egg is fertilized by a normal sperm cell with its 23 chromosomes, then the baby that results will have an extra chromosome 21."

"Yes. The condition is called trisomy and leads to a baby that has Down syndrome. About one baby in 600 has three copies of 21, but in women over the age of 45, one baby out of 50 will have Down syndrome."

"This sounds pretty common to me. It's hard to imagine that one would want to...."

▶   ▶   ▶

The transcript of the trial stops here. Missing is the testimony of the remaining witnesses for the prosecution and the all-important defense witnesses. Newspaper accounts of the proceedings indicate that there continued to be fireworks between the two attorneys. Most importantly, there was a surprise character witness for the defense, a population geneticist who was a prokaryote. Here was a bacterial cell speaking about the value of mutations in the course of evolution. Councilor Liv tried to discredit him, but only succeeded in alienating the jury. The final decision of the jury is not recorded as the courthouse files of the proceedings have been destroyed in a mysterious fire. So we are left with mere speculation as to the verdict in this trial.

Recorded by Researcher E. coli number 53623.

QUESTIONS

After students read the trial proceedings, they should answer the following questions:

- Record the stages of meiosis in eukaryotic cells, keeping in mind that there are two cell divisions involved, each having its particular terms and characteristics.
- List the key differences between mitosis and meiosis.

- Do prokaryotes have mitosis or meiosis?
- Crossover occurs between homologous pairs of chromosomes, but can it occur between two different chromosomes, say between number 1 and number 17?
- Was it an evolutionary necessity for meiosis to evolve at the same time as sexual reproduction?

The teaching notes for the Mitosis half of the case and Meiosis half of the case are posted on the website of the National Center for Case Study Teaching in Science at *http://ublib.buffalo.edu/libraries/projects/cases/case.html.*

Section XV

How Not to Teach With Case Studies

It is easy for things to go wrong in the classroom—especially if a teacher is trying out something new. In this section we'll look at some of the problems that case teaching can pose. Most of the problems occur because of the lack of experience—of both instructors and students.

In general, the more one teaches with cases, the better one becomes. This goes for students too. While it is reasonable to think an instructor should start out case teaching slowly, this has a downside: If a teacher only runs one case in an otherwise lecture-based course, the students won't know what to make of it. Most likely they will think of it as a lark, nothing to be taken seriously. Neither the professor nor the students will be very good without more practice. Accordingly, it is probably better to try out several case studies even in the first semester an instructor is exploring the case method.

In this section, three chapters parade a host of mistakes before the reader. These are only a few of the pitfalls that await the unseasoned novice. Fortunately, they can all be avoided with some planning.

Return to Mars

How Not to Teach a Case Study

By Clyde Freeman Herreid

When the Trojans let a Greek wooden horse through their city gates, that was a mistake.

When the Chicago Tribune said Thomas Dewey was elected President of the United States in 1948, that was a mistake.

When General Custer attacked Chief Crazy Horse, that was a mistake.

Mistakes, as we all know, are an integral part of our lives. They vary from the trivial spilt milk to the devastating Challenger explosion caused by a defective O ring, to the momentous events that unfolded as Columbus headed west for the East Indies.

Mistakes appear in every chapter of human endeavor, from computers (The "Y2K" problem), to cars (Edsel), to politics (Bay of Pigs), to business (dropping "classic" Coca Cola). Whole professions such as law, plastic surgery, or insurance are devoted to correcting or mitigating the effects of mistakes. Other professions capitalize upon mistakes in interpretation or perception as magicians and con men know.

Science is not free from mistakes. Some are happy ones as with Flemming's accidental discovery of penicillin or tragic as with thalidomide. Some are debacles as with Pons and Fleishman's claim of cold fusion.

In education, we have had our share of mistakes as critics of the New Math and the teaching of reading without phonics will attest. Teachers of case studies are not free from mistakes either. I don't think Salvador Dali's advice is quite on the mark when he says, "Mistakes are almost always of a sacred nature. Never try to correct them. On the contrary: rationalize them, understand them thoroughly. After that, it will be possible for you to sublimate them." Indeed? I prefer journalist Walter Lippman's admonition: "The study of error is not only in the highest degree prophetic, but it serves as a stimulating introduction to the study of truth." Or, Nikki Giovani when she says, "Mistakes are a fact of life. It is the response to error that counts."

In this chapter, I consider some of the common mistakes case study instructors make. I can think of no better way, though a humbling experience, than to offer a recent example of my errors in trying out the "Life on Mars?" case we published in the March/April 1998 issue of *JCST* (pp. 307–310). To recap the case, Bruce Allen, a geology student, and I wrote about the recent brouhaha over the NASA report that there were purported fossil bacteria in a Martian meteorite. The case involved a fictional young NASA scientist, Michael King, who had serious doubts about the evidence and was pondering whether to participate in a sudden press conference. After teaching the case three times in different courses, we reported in the *JCST* article how a successful case might work. We didn't report the mistakes we made on our first attempt. Now we come clean.

The "discovery of life on Mars" event was so dramatic and relevant to several courses that we hurriedly wrote the case and wanted to try it out at the first available opportunity. We foisted ourselves on a colleague teaching a planetary geology course that was in full swing. He was more than willing for us to try the case out on his general education class. The case material was clearly appropriate as there was plenty of prior discussion of the solar system and meteorites. Also there was a scheduled class period in the syllabus on the topic of NASA's *Viking Lander* project. Perfect, we thought.

There was a downside to the arrangement, however. The course was taught by the lecture method. What we were proposing to do was go in as strangers and run a discussion-based case study, something that those students had probably never seen before. In addition, the instructor was not willing to have this experience count for any credit. We could not, for example, require that a short paper be written by the students. Although this might seem a recipe for disaster, we thought we had a good chance at accomplishing this task, but it would take careful planning, courage, and dumb luck.

Here is how we attacked the problem: In the class period prior to our case study, Bruce Allen, who was going to run the case, visited the class for the last 10 minutes to hand out the two-page case and to explain what we were planning. Since only about half of the students were present (a common situation in most lecture-based general education courses), we knew that preparation would be an issue. We asked them to seriously read the case and consider the questions where we asked how scientists knew that the "rock" was a meteorite from Mars, how they knew its age, and how they knew that it contained fossils.

On the day of the class we decided to take half of the 90 minutes class time to show a video of the NASA press conference announcing there was evidence of past life on Mars. We believed this would set the stage for the discussion even if people had not read the case. Also, since students frequently come in late to lecture classes, showing the video would allow the latecomers to become involved. Beforehand, we gave preliminary instructions about the plan for the day—to analyze the evidence mentioned by NASA scientists and to report on the dilemma faced by the hero of the case study.

After the video, we asked the students, about 35 out of a 70-person class, to gather together in groups of four or five. This required some shifting of seats because students were spread all over the 150-person auditorium. As with other teaching amphitheaters of today's modern university, the fixed seats made it awkward but not impossible to group together for conversation.

When the grouping was accomplished, we asked the teams to spend about 20 minutes reviewing the evidence surrounding the press conference and addressing the questions at the end of the case. The purpose of this session was to get people engaged in the problem in a small group setting before facing a full class discussion. Most groups complied, although there were obvious strains and embarrassed silences. Some groups, consisting of students who knew one another, drifted off task. But for the most part, things went well.

At the end of this small group session, Bruce Allen led an open class discussion. He posed questions about the NASA scientists' evidence on the questions surrounding the meteorite's origin, age, and composition and worked on the blackboard to summarize the students' thoughts. This period lasted perhaps 20 minutes and was simply a hurried listing of the lines of evidence.

This left us with a handful of minutes to deal with the personal dilemma faced by Michael King, the hero of the case. We asked for brief comments on what his concerns would be and his possible course of action. We finished by asking for a show of hands by the students as they voted their preferences. Class dismissed. This was hardly an ideal way to run a class. We made five classic mistakes and numerous faux pas in handling the case.

- *Lack of clear goals.* If you don't know where you are headed, how do you know when you have arrived? Like many case instructors, we were initially captured by the excitement and potential of an event that we knew in our hearts would capture the students' attention. After all, the world was captivated by the Mars press conference. There would be many opportunities to discuss issues in astronomy, geology, biology, ethics, and career discussions in science. The case would work for various courses, although the issues would have different emphases.

When it came time to teach the case we decided to hit all issues to see what worked. It was a little like eating Louisiana gumbo hoping to pull out a tasty morsel without knowing what lay in its gooey depths. Of course, in all first attempts at a case we should expect uncertainty, but our goals for the students were too diffuse. Part of this may be excused because of our eagerness to seize the moment. Part of it may be excused because we did not have control of the course and course content. Yet all cannot be excused. On our third try in another general education course called Scientific Inquiry, we got our act together and focused only on two questions: Why the NASA team believed there were fossils and why scientists shouldn't hold press conferences before publication.

Moral: Be sure you know what you want to accomplish in the case, what facts, principles, view-

points the students should cover. Without clear, prioritized goals we consumed a thin broth rather than rich gumbo (to keep the soup metaphor alive.)

- *Lack of time.* Some cases are so rich and complex that one cannot deal with the issues in the available time. That was our problem in Planetary Geology. Sometimes the lack of time can be solved neatly by editing or focusing the case, but that isn't always possible. As a colleague of mine is fond of saying, "You can't shorten a nine month pregnancy by putting nine women on the job."

There is another approach to the time issue. We could have chosen the strategy of some case instructors who simply do not take the issue of coverage so seriously. They let the class discussion follow its own course and stop whenever time runs out. Then it is on to another case. This *laissez-faire* approach will not appeal to most instructors.

The Mars case is best handled by devoting more than one class period to its analysis and having time for students to do outside reading and work. The Problem-Based Learning strategy is particularly effective; students use parts of three class periods to discuss the case, and between classes they do literature searches and interesting assignments. For example, in our latest teaching of the case, we had the students show the case to a scientist and then interview the scientist about the ethical and career questions facing the hero. This greatly enhanced student discussion, for young students have seldom considered such issues.

Moral: Some cases are snacks, others are banquets. Be sure you give each the proper attention.

- *Lack of preparation.* The Boy Scouts' motto, "Be Prepared," is an ideal aspiration not only for America's youth but for us veterans of academia. Truth to tell, exquisite preparation for a class is not always possible. In spite of the advertisement by Orson Wells saying he will drink no wine before its time, sometimes we must sip the drink that is served or not drink at all. In our case, as instructors, we felt we wanted to capture a "breaking" news story and did not have time to choose the ideal conditions for the case.

Then there were students. Students do not always prepare adequately for class. Surprised? While it is hardly noticed in a lecture class, a lack of preparation is debilitating in discussion-based courses. The students rapidly learn this. If discussions are held regularly, any delinquency will be detected. There are consequences for laziness, especially if peer evaluation is used.

In our Planetary Geology experience we had to live with the results of no preparation. We tried to make the best of a bad situation by showing the NASA press conference video. This helped a great deal but used so much time that minutes were in short supply. Small group discussion also helped because information could be shared among teammates. But permanent groups are even more powerful. There the group pressure to prepare and participate is enormous.

Moral: Even the best-laid plans may go astray, but no preparation at all is a recipe for disaster for students and faculty.

- *Lack of experience with the case method— it takes time to get good at anything.* Learning how to analyze a case study and to participate in discussions is no exception. When I have used only one case study in a semester, students are often uncertain how to prepare and how to interact in class. The more cases, the better they get. So we should not be surprised that we encountered trouble in our first trip to Mars.

The geology students did not have a clear understanding of what this break in the routine was all about. A case study? What is that? They did not know what to do, or what their role

should be. Placing students into small groups for a preliminary discussion and giving them explicit instructions about which questions they were to address definitely helped. Awkward though it first seemed, in this setting students had a chance to try out a few preliminary ideas to see how they would fly. Yet, as was evident in the general discussion, their analysis was superficial. For example, when asked to tell why scientists believed that the meteorite spent 16 million years in space or 13,000 years on Earth before its discovery in the Antarctic, they felt they were finished when they answered, "by radioactive dating." It takes significant experience for students to recognize what is an adequate answer.

This only comes from frequent interaction with an instructor pushing and probing for a greater depth of analysis. How long does it take? Unfortunately, it requires at least a third to half a semester for noticeable improvement, but there will be exhilarating moments along the way.

Moral: Give more than one case study and be incredibly explicit about what you wish them to do. Do not simply say, "OK, discuss this among yourselves," and expect miracles. Those are the province of gospel tents and prayer meetings, not classrooms.

- *Lack of commitment or involvement in the case—unless the students have a stake in the outcome of the case, the results will be mediocre.* One way to fail is to write a case that is without relevance to their interests. We think we bypassed this error because the NASA press conference received such attention in the press and we had students who had voluntarily chosen the course, Planetary Geology. Yet, because the case was given by strangers with no leverage in the course and no way to influence their grades, we had to rely solely upon the basic curiosity of students and their tendency to generally go along with authority figures. Not surprisingly, many students had attitudes of "Who cares? It doesn't count anyway," or, "Entertain me."

There was not the kind of intensity and interest in understanding that the case study approach demands and normally gets. Indeed, case study classes, especially those involving small group work, have almost 100%. So as Gypsy Rose Lee, famous for her chutzpah as well as her physical endowments in burlesque, was fond of saying, "You've gotta have a gimmick." Without it the patrons won't show. Nor will the students. Without an interest-grabbing case or a reason for the students to care, case study teaching is no more likely to result in learning than will poor lecturing.

Moral: Without a carrot or a stick, neither mules nor students are inclined to move. Give them a reason to get the train moving and they can pull heavy loads.

There you have the five classic errors and some solutions. In spite of our errors, there was some good news: From the students' viewpoint, we had reason to believe that some received an insight into the questions of the "Life on Mars" debate. One student rushed up afterward and effused that she loved the case and said it was the best class she had attended. That's not bad. From our viewpoint, we clearly accomplished one of our private goals: to try out the case and see how to modify it for future classes.

And modify it we did, with decided improvement. Still, case studies are always elusive and each time they are taught there are surprises. The potential for mistakes is always present. Nonetheless, let us hope that Danish poet and scientist Piet Hein is correct when he says,

"The road to wisdom?—Well, it's plain and simple to express:
Err
and err
and err again
but less
and less
and less."

So a return to Mars should be even smoother next time.

Why a "Case-Based" Course Failed

An Analysis of an Ill-Fated Experiment

By Clyde Freeman Herreid

F ailure is a part of life, but when it affects hundreds of students in an elite private institution, there is no satisfaction in that platitude. It is especially painful when that failure becomes public knowledge—as it did when Duke University attempted to use the "case study method" in its introductory chemistry class (Introductory Chem. 21).

A report in the August 26, 2002, *Chemical & Engineering News* lays out the story (Zurer 2002). I was drawn to this account because case study instruction was tainted by misadventure; this is an important cautionary tale for all of us involved in innovative teaching.

Let me summarize the article. In the fall of 2001, Duke's well-intended chemistry department chairman John Simon initiated an innovative, team-taught course using what he called "case studies." Previously, James Bonk, a respected veteran of the classroom, had lectured to the Introductory Chem. 21 course three times a week for 43 years. The clarity of his lectures was legendary and, to be fair, he was a hard act to follow.

Simon's plan was to immerse first-year students in a course that was exciting and relevant. In a true experimental mode, the students were split into two class sections. One section, with 300 students, was taught in the traditional way by one instructor. The other, with 270 students, was taught with a "case-based" approach that Simon believed was common in law school. (Never mind that such mega-courses are not the norm in law school, nor is the lecture method used.)

The case course was taught by a series of faculty members who "talk[ed] about issues of current importance and themes from the chemical research, relating them to underlying basic principles"(Zurer 2002, 32). They spent two weeks on combustion, a few lectures on the greenhouse effect, a few more on the Antarctic and gas laws, and so on. It did not appear to have been a cohesive approach. And so it seemed to students. By midsemester, the fat was in the fire, and there was a whiff of triglycerides in the air.

Soon, students were complaining to anyone in earshot, including the president of the university, about their confusion and frustration. They complained that they were guinea pigs without any say in the experiment. They complained about multiple teachers who had different teaching and exam styles.

Simon was said to have been unsympathetic. "They were only concerned about grades.... Many of these kids have never gotten anything less than an A. They have never been challenged. They come to Duke expecting us to smooth the road for them between high school and medical school. They need to learn how to learn in all different environments. Instead, they are really angry that we have made them work" (Zurer 2002).

The TAs were critical too. They reported that lectures, labs, and recitations were fragmented and that they were not informed about the cases being presented in lecture. They felt helpless to assist students.

At the end of the semester, students were supposed to take an assessment test to determine the approach's effectiveness. This proved to be futile because the test was not counted as part of their grade. Not surprisingly, the students vented their frustrations by writing expletives on their papers and filling in random answers. The assessment was worthless.

The second semester was calmer—faculty reverted to the lecture style or tried hybrid approaches. These efforts were unknown to the course organizers, which emphasizes the lack of coordination and cooperation present and is the reason why no serious analysis can be made of the data because of the hodgepodge of methods tried; no assessment was even attempted.

Last year, the lecture method returned to Duke and all became quiet. The chair of the chemistry department vows to revisit the issue after thoughtful contemplation. "We are going for a year of stability.... We'll still bring applications and research into the freshman course in some way, but I want a year to think about what happened and to find out what other people around the nation are doing" (Zurer 2002, p. 32). Amen.

SURVEYING THE DAMAGE

What went wrong? What didn't go wrong? It's hard to know where to begin, but let's start with what wasn't necessarily wrong—the faculty's apparent lack of training in the use of case studies. They did not seem to be using the standard case method approach at all, but rather to simply be restructuring their lectures using contemporary problems as a hook into the basic principles.

There is nothing wrong with that approach if the topics are coordinated. After all, the great James Conant, premiere chemist and president of Harvard, initiated this sort of lecture-based case method in the 1940s. Although rarely used afterward, it is a captivating technique, but it must be done well, especially if the students are young and inexperienced and have different expectations. And especially if they are premeds who have a great stake in the outcome. After all, they should do well. They are part of the elite class that has been selected for their intellectual qualities—qualities that have gained for them entrance into Duke. They are champions at receiving wisdom from the traditional teaching method—the lecture.

One aspect of this approach that clearly was a problem, however, was having multiple instructors. Whenever this is tried, it appears to be a recipe for disaster for the very reasons the students named—different styles, different expectations, and different tests, all on top of a brand new teaching method. Even in medical school where this *ad seriatim* faculty parade is the method *du jour*, students often complain bitterly.

No wonder the freshmen did the same. The problems can be especially grievous if the faculty members involved do not attend each other's presentations or hold frequent meetings to share what is happening. This apparently didn't happen—otherwise it is hard to explain how the faculty started bastardizing the approach without anyone noticing.

Even with careful attention, innovation is hard to introduce. There are usually two major barriers to its success:

- *The faculty*. They have to be convinced and prepared to do the necessary work, and they must believe in the approach. They must show no fear or hesitancy in introducing the method and should not in any way suggest that this is an experiment. The students will sense any uncertainty and be immediately on the defensive. And the faculty must be prepared and structured. Perhaps one might muddle through a lecture that he or she has given a hundred times without more than a moment's preparation, sweeping up old yellowed notes from the filing cabinet before heading for class. This won't do for anything new. Serious preparation must be done or the mental cracks will show through.

- *The students*. Students at Duke probably had never heard of the case method and, like all students, would have been highly skeptical of anything that smacked of innovation. You can't blame them. They had been highly successful in their old ways, and new ones were deeply threatening. To offset this skepticism, the professors should have spent significant time at the course outset explaining exactly what was planned and giving students time to discuss their concerns and ask questions.

But this is not enough. Periodically, it is essential to revisit the topic using classroom assessment techniques such as those that have been collected by T. Angelo and P. Cross in their book, *Classroom Assessment Techniques* (1993). It is essential that students know you are listening to them and responding to their concerns. But even with a serious effort in this direction, innovators almost always have to swim upstream, especially when they are following a headline performer.

Duke's chemistry department had a major problem on its hands when it switched professors. Never mind that they switched teaching methods too. They had a legendary professor, James Bonk, drop out of the lists. Probably, anyone who followed would have suffered by comparison. That will always happen.

So please note, the easiest time to be innovative is when you are starting a brand new course. Then there can be no comparisons. Naturally, if there were a previous course that was pitifully taught, then an innovative replacement would be a godsend. Also, if the course is a nonmajors' course, the faculty will have less a stake in the outcome, so innovation may be ignored, at least by the faculty.

But woe to you if the course is a requirement for the premeds and their ilk—then, well then—you can expect a steady drumbeat of complaints. Especially when the complainers can talk to all of their friends, fraternity and sorority brethren, and perhaps their fathers and mothers who took the course before and loved it. Then you will have the problem seen at Duke.

So, is there a moral to the story? Perhaps there are several. Pick and choose your favorite. One thing I am sure of is this: The devil is in the details. The Duke Blue Devil mascot was not designed to poke his pitchfork at his own campus, but surely, as the Introductory Chem. 21 course unfolded, it often felt like that to the faculty involved.

I hope they simply didn't blame the students for the turmoil. I am forever paraphrasing the Swiss developmental psychologist, Jean Piaget, on this point. He said something along the lines of, *every teacher should be an animal trainer at sometime in his life, because when the animal doesn't do the trick, you don't blame the animal*.

Finally, to all of us dedicated case study teachers, I believe one moral is clear: It is plain that the case study method should hardly be blamed for this misadventure. Let us hope that better days lie ahead for both the Blue Devil students and the faculty.

REFERENCES

Angelo, T., and P. Cross. 1993. *Classroom assessment techniques*. San Francisco: Jossey-Bass.

Zurer, P.S. 2002. An educational experience. *Chemical & Engineering News* 80 (34): 31–32.

DON'T!

What Not to Do When Teaching Case Studies

By Clyde Freeman Herreid

"**D**on't" was one of the first words we ever learned at (or over) our mother's knee. It stands right up there next to "No" as our first brush with negative advice in the parental lexicon. Close behind are admonishments of "can't," "shouldn't," and "never do that again."

With this historical baggage, I am a bit hesitant to write a column entitled "Don't," knowing that its use, like an odor in a Proust novel, may trigger memories of youthful indiscretions. Furthermore, I am reminded that saying "don't" had little effect on my own children.

Yet, some of us never tire of giving advice. Ann Landers, Dr. Ruth, and I are forever urging our readers to eat your spinach, clean up your room, and don't let the dog lick your face.

So be warned, I am about to unleash a baker's dozen of "don'ts" for aspiring case teachers willing to try running a classroom discussion armed with only a couple of pages of a story and a lot of chutzpah. I am fortified with the knowledge that by saying "don't" to you, I will be not only joining your saintly mother but a long line of "don't-sayers." Here are a few famous "don'ts" from the pages of history.

- "Don't fire until you see the whites of their eyes." William Prescott at Bunker Hill, 1775. (Perhaps good advice for teachers as well as soldiers.)
- "Don't give up the ship." James Lawrence on board the U.S. Frigate Chesapeake, 1813. (Another chary quote relevant to teaching.)
- "Don't look back. Something may be gaining on you." Satchel Paige, in his autobiography. (Baseball and teaching have a lot in common.)

Having prepared you with these historical anecdotes, I hope you will be considerate of my attempts at sharing some cautionary thoughts. So, to set the scene, picture yourself teaching tomorrow's class completely by discussion. What should and shouldn't you do, assuming, of course, you are ready for a great teaching adventure.

DON'T FAIL TO PREPARE.

Some teachers never adequately prepare. This is a recipe for disaster in all teaching. Unfortunately, the problem for new case teachers is often that they don't know what kind of preparation to do. They don't have a clear understanding of their objectives for using the case. They don't know how to ask the right questions. They don't come into the classroom with a planned board outline or a way to connect the major issues together. And they won't have prepared the students or themselves for this major break from the traditional lecture format. They are under the illusion that a good discussion will just happen. (Boy, are they in for a surprise.)

DON'T START A DISCUSSION WITH A CLOSE-ENDED QUESTION.

The first question that the teacher asks is crucial. The primary criterion is to get students to talk, preferably thoughtfully. If you start with a question that is too obtuse, too formidable, or looks like a trick question, no one will answer. But there is another way to start off on the wrong foot. It is by asking a question that has a definite answer, such as, "What is the chemical formula of glucose?" Most students will be afraid of answering this even if they think they know it. They don't want to risk failure, so they busily put their heads down, avoid eye contact, and write furiously in their notebooks. Moreover, when some brave soul does venture an answer, where does this put you in a discussion?

The best opening questions are open-ended, where there are multiple reasonable answers, or where the question is neutral and simple to answer. Let's say that the case is about the genetic engineering of crops and the scene is at a dinner table where a family argument is in full swing (see "Torn at the Genes" at *http://ublib.buffalo.edu/libraries/projects/cases/ubcase.htm*). Now, a nonthreatening beginning might be to ask the students to identify the family members and indicate what their positions on the topic seem to be. Another, riskier but sexier beginning would be to ask, "Should Marsha eat the tomato?"

A poor question might be, "How do scientists transfer genes from one organism to another?" I would hate to answer a question like that at eight o'clock in the morning and so would the students.

DON'T DEAL WITH CONTROVERSIAL EMOTIONAL MATERIAL UNTIL YOU HAVE ANALYZED THE FACTS.

The safest way to discuss a case is to be sure that everyone has a clear understanding of the facts. If students are confused on these, it will be rough sledding ahead. It is best to get all the facts straight at the outset. For instance, in the transgenic crop story, by getting the names of all of the participants and their positions established, the teacher can then turn to the question of, "What is the evidence the protagonists have for their beliefs?" Here's where you'll get the facts out.

This eventually will lead to a discussion of, "Is genetic engineering in the best interests of the people in the world?" If you start off with a question like this, however, there is a good chance that the facts will get lost in the barrage of attacks and counterattacks that ensue. Even the provocative question, "Should Marsha eat the tomato?" is perilous, and you have to have great skill as a discussion leader to uncover the facts underpinning the case before Marsha languishes in a hail of invective.

If I haven't convinced you yet, consider this problem: Suppose you are discussing the Tuskegee syphilis study on black patients in Alabama who were not informed that treatment was available. Suppose, further, that you have a racially mixed class. Now what would your first question be? (To find out what I would suggest, see *http://ublib.buffalo.edu/libraries/projects/cases/blood_notes.html*)

DON'T FORGET TO USE THE BLACKBOARD IN AN ORGANIZED WAY.

Students always want to know, "What is going to be on the test?" This is especially thorny in a discussion course. One solution to the problem is not to give tests, but to grade solely on the quality of their discussion. (Oh boy, let's save this one 'til another day.)

If you do give tests, your use of the blackboard will help save the day. Before you go into class, develop a blackboard plan. Decide how to organize the case. One common strategy is to write the facts of the case on the left side of the board as they emerge in the discussion. In the center of the board you might group the major issues of the case as they are analyzed. Finally, if you are dealing with a dilemma case where the protagonists have to make a decision, their possible choices and consequences could be enumerated on the right side of the board.

What you and your students get out of this exercise is that there is a sense of order to the case—and you have visible evidence that you have accomplished something. Additionally, it gives the inveterate note-takers in the class something to take home and study for the exam.

DON'T EXPECT TO HAVE A GREAT DISCUSSION UNTIL THE STUDENTS KNOW ONE ANOTHER.

It isn't tough to get adults to speak, especially faculty who make it their business; students are another matter. Getting them to engage on scientific questions isn't a cakewalk. Part of the problem is that they know you are evaluating them. So are their peers. No one wants to look stupid. You have to make the classroom safe for their conversations. This doesn't happen right away. People have to get to know each other and develop a certain level of trust.

One essential aid is to find out their names and use them! On the first day of class I have students wear nametags, or I have them prepare small signs that they prop up in front of them if they are at a table. Faculty in business or law school where there may be 70 students frequently use a seating chart.

It is not enough to have their names; you must use them on every possible occasion. It won't be long before everyone in the room knows everyone else's name and this will greatly facilitate discussion. Still, it often takes one-third of a semester before things really get good.

DON'T FORGET TO CALL ON DIFFERENT PEOPLE.

How easy it is to call on the eager student who is always waving his hand, especially if he usually has good things to say. "Take not the easy path," says Yoda, our *Star Wars* guru.

I think it is essential to try to get everyone into the act, to get diversity into the discussion. One way is to simply keep your eyes open and watch student body language: Are they leaning forward, nodding their heads, frowning, opening their mouths as if beginning to speak? We all have these so-called intention movements when we have something to say. Watch for these clues and call on these people.

Another way is to encourage students to look at the problem from another perspective, using questions such as, "Jessica, what do you think of this proposal? What might someone say who opposed this plan?" I try to steer clear of calling on the same person repeatedly, especially one who wants to dominate the discussion. In fact, I may have to say something to him outside of class if it is a serious problem.

DON'T FORGET TO LISTEN TO THE STUDENTS AND RESPOND TO THEM.

Speaking and listening are social arts—they go together. Philosopher Mortimer Adler makes the analogy that, "The catcher behind the plate is just as active a baseball player as the pitcher on the mound." Good discussion requires that the participants play both positions well. They should do more than simply wait their turn to speak; they need to connect their ideas with the ones that have gone before.

For the teacher, it means that he should periodically try to paraphrase students' points saying, "John, do I understand correctly…." The teacher should not make the discussion a glorified quiz show where he or she runs through a series of questions, saying "right" or "wrong." Nor is this discussion a lecture in disguise. The moderator must connect one student's ideas with another. He or she should ask John how his ideas square with Claudia's earlier point. To do this he must listen.

The instructor should operate at several levels during the discussion. At the first level he or she must be aware of the case material and how to get the content out. At the second level he or she must be aware of the process; thinking about whom to call on next to spread the discussion about; how to resolve the conflict that has just exploded; how to stop the private conversation in the corner; how to move to engage the bored student sitting on the right; when to shift tempo.

And on the third level he or she is thinking of the bigger picture, how these people are doing in the course and how this case fits into the overall curriculum. He or she will be thinking how asking a particular question might affect a particular student; how to be encouraging to Jennifer and yet skeptical of Philip; and how this will impact on their personal development. To be successful at all of these levels requires careful listening both inside and outside of class.

DON'T LEAVE THE SEATS IN A ROW.

Today's classrooms are seldom arranged for good case teaching. They are designed for the lecture method, often in fixed-seat amphitheaters. Business and law schools still run cases in such settings but these would challenge Socrates himself.

Ideally, a U- or horseshoe-shaped seating arrangement works best. The open part of the U should face the blackboard. This permits the professor to walk into the U with the blackboard at his back and the students at his front and sides. This arrangement permits all of the students to see one another. This array must be modified, however, if the number of students is much more than 20. A solution is to have a second and third row of students behind the first.

DON'T STAND IN ONE PLACE IN THE CLASSROOM; MOVE ABOUT.

It is almost unnecessary to make this point to a case teacher. It is hard to stand still. You have to write on the board. You have to move forward to listen seriously to a speaker or move to the side to let students engage one another. There should be no lectern to hide behind. You gotta move.

Also, consider this: You don't always have to be in the center of the horseshoe. You can move out of the U altogether and go behind the students so that you are looking over the backs of students on one side and into the faces of those on the other side. This technique works well when the students are talking to each other and you simply want to get out of the way.

DON'T FRET IF THE DISCUSSION ISN'T ENTHRALLING.

It takes time to get good at anything. This goes for case teaching. The students need practice and so do you. Trust me, you'll get better.

Here is an important point: Instructors often believe that the easiest way to break into case teaching is to try one each semester. This appears to be a sensible approach and the students will undoubtedly enjoy it. Nonetheless, they probably will not consider the case anything more than a diversion if it is used this way—certainly not something that they should remember for the exam. No, the only way that you will have cases taken seriously and to get that enthralling discussion is to run several cases during the semester; then everyone will be comfortable with the method.

DON'T EXPECT TO HAVE A GREAT DISCUSSION IN A 50-MINUTE PERIOD.

It takes time for students to settle down and focus. It takes time for announcements and assignments. By the time that these things have been attended to there simply isn't enough time left out of a 50-minute class to get into a subject deeply. Everyone, and especially you the instructor, will feel frustrated. To do it right requires at least 90 minutes. Two hours is better.

DON'T JUST HAVE STUDENTS DISCUSS THINGS, HAVE THEM PRODUCE A PRODUCT.

Discussions can often leave students and instructors with an unsatisfied feeling. Both may wonder what they really did accomplish. Board work isn't always enough. Giving the students a follow-up assignment usually does the trick. Have them write up a summary of the case, write a letter to their congressperson, or develop a strategic plan. These are all good homework exercises. You don't have to have each student hand in a paper for each case. They might write up something for, say, half or a third of the cases. This approach makes the workload more manageable for everyone.

There you have a dozen "don'ts" for your consideration. They aren't all there is to the case method, of course. There are a bunch of "do's" as well. But the "don'ts" are enough for the moment. This brings you to the point where you should be ready to take the plunge into case teaching. Caution is needed, yes, but only so much can be done ahead of time. It is necessary to get some field experience as this anonymous rhyme highlights:

> Mother may I go out to swim?
> Yes, my darling daughter.
> Hang your clothes on a hickory limb
> And don't go near the water.

Enough caution. Aspiring swimmers and case teachers have to dive in sometime. Make it soon, but just remember a final "don't":

Don't blame me if everything isn't perfect and you don't get promoted. Life isn't always fair.

Section XVI

How to Write Case Studies

The best cases are the ones that a teacher makes up for her or his own class. This should come as no surprise. Each course is different and each teacher is unique; hence, it is always best to customize a case for a particular class. Nonetheless, many teachers don't have time to write a beautifully crafted case. Fortunately, there are several alternatives to this:

1. As I mentioned in chapter 14 in the essay on Michael Crichton's book *State of Fear*, novels and books in general are great case material—no writing on the teacher's part is necessary.

2. In that same chapter I pointed out that scientific journal articles can be used too. It is easy to copy graphs and tables from an article, give them to students, and ask them to tell you what the graphs and tables suggest, how the data could have been collected, and to even write an abstract for a paper.

3. As Frank Dinan reports in chapter 49, the media are a ready source of cases. It is easy to rip out an article from the local newspaper, walk into class, and have a great discussion.

4. Videos and movies work well as case material, and so can reports from television news programs. Material for case studies is everywhere.

But having said that, there are a host of other questions to consider, especially if we are writing our own cases. Just how does someone go about writing a case? How much information should be included? Should the case be real or fictional? What are the virtues of having questions in the case that have real answers versus a case with multiple options? Should we deal with controversial subjects in our cases and if so, how should they be handled? And so on. Many of these questions are addressed in the chapters that follow.

Case Studies and the Media

By Frank J. Dinan

In the fall of 1975, I went to the Shorham Hotel in Washington, DC, to see the political comedian Mark Russell. His routine focused on the Watergate scandal, the comic/tragic drama that was unfolding at that time. It was an uproariously funny evening and I recall Russell saying, "I don't have to write any of this stuff, I just cut it out of the newspaper and read it to you." Of course, this was an overstatement. It was Russell's eye for humor that allowed him to see it where his audience saw the tragedy of those turbulent times.

I believe that, like Russell, we can also use the media as a great source of material. But what we, as case study teachers, should be looking for in the media are "hooks," events that will grab our students' interest and allow us to develop a case that will relate to our discipline.

Unlike Mark Russell, many of us, when we are trying to come up with good ideas for a case study, are inclined to go to material directly related to our discipline as a source of ideas. Of course, what we are really trying to do is to find an interesting and discipline-appropriate story to use as a lure to interest our students in some aspect of our discipline that we wish to teach using a case study. A sometimes overlooked, rich source of case study ideas resides in the wealth of media messages that bombard us every day. To take advantage of this source of inspirational material, we need to develop what I refer to as a "case study mindset," an ability to see potentially interesting case study outlines in the everyday reading and viewing that we do as part of our daily lives. Not only the technical journals that we read within our disciplines, but also our newspapers and magazines, the television programs and the movies that we see, even song lyrics can act as the "hook" that leads us to a case study premise.

NEWSPAPERS AS A SOURCE

Let me tell you about one of the most ingenious uses of the media in the construction of a case study that I am aware of. Michael J. Hudecki, a professor at the State University of New York at Buffalo, was teaching an Honors course in which his students' participation was not as good as he had hoped for—not an unusual problem for many of us. While reading the *New York Times*, Mike came across the following short article:

Memory Loss in Mice

A biochemist, Eugene Roberts, and researchers at the City of Hope Medical Center [in Duarte, California] discovered that injecting fragments of a brain protein called beta-amyloid into the brains of mice caused the mammals to forget chores they had just been taught [Flood, J. F., *et al.* 1991. Amnestic effects in mice of four synthetic peptides homologous to amyloid B protein from patients with Alzheimer disease. *Proc. Nat. Acad. Sci.* 88 (8): 3363–3366, Apr 91]. "This is really the first correlation between the presence of [beta-amyloid] in the brain and the loss of memory," said Rachael Neve, a molecular biologist at University of California at Irvine.

Mike, to his everlasting credit, saw the potential for a case study on the scientific method in this article. With considerable trepidation he made copies of the article, distributed them to his students, and asked a few simple questions. The problem that he faced with his class immediately changed from trying to get student participation to trying to get a word of his own into the whirlwind of student ideas and interpretations that filled the entire class. I have seen Mike teach this case and it is impressive, to say the least. I have even tried it myself, and found that it works well even in my considerably less gifted hands. Mike surely proved that smaller can be better when it comes to cases.

Mike's experience makes it clear that great newspapers may also be great case sources, but let's also look at the other end of the spectrum. A colleague of mine, Joe Bieron, brought my attention to an article in the *Fort Erie (Ontario) Times*, a newspaper that he read while vacationing in Canada. Now there is nothing wrong with the *Fort Erie Times*, but it just isn't the *New York Times*. The article that Joe showed me claimed that gasoline in Canada was cheaper than gasoline in the United States. This was not consistent with

Joe's experience and a few "back of the envelope" calculations proved that he was right. We used the *Fort Erie Times* article in our introductory chemistry course for a case study that centered on the inter-conversion of units of measurement to teach factor analysis. The case, "Gas Pains," asked our students to determine whether the newspaper article was correct and what the real cost difference was between a U.S. gallon of gas in American dollars and the same volume of gasoline listed in liters-per-Canadian dollar. This required our students to use the factor labeling method to make a number of measurement and currency valuation inter-conversions before they could arrive at their conclusion. Working in small teams, they had to submit a brief but detailed report that supported their conclusion.

Yet another major newspaper, the *Wall Street Journal*, provided an article that led Joe Bieron and me to formulate a case that focused on a professor who had "challenged" his students to calculate the cost of *a single aluminum atom* in a roll of aluminum foil. The professor's students were puzzled about how to do the calculation, but he consistently told them that they had all of the information they needed to do it and refused to discuss the problem further. Two of his students objected and took their objections to the administration, where they were also told that they should be able to do the calculation without the professor's help. Given our litigious society, their next stop, of course, was a lawyer's office. The case went to court, and amazingly, at least to me, the judge hearing the case ruled in the students' favor and awarded them restitution of their tuition costs and compensatory damages. This struck us as the ultimate hook—students suing their instructor over an assignment and *winning*. What could be better?

We wrote a case study titled "Avogadro Goes to Court" (Amadeo Avogadro is the name of the Italian scientist who determined the key concept needed to do the calculation that is central to this case) that challenged our students to do the very same thing the ill-fated professor had asked his students to do. We have used the case many times, and our students never fail to rise to the challenge. Also, at least so far, we have managed to stay out of court!

SCIENTIFIC JOURNALS AS A SOURCE

The periodical *Science News* is a magnificent, highly versatile source of ideas for case studies, one that I rate highly. It appears weekly and provides first-rate summaries of important happenings in science, engineering, and mathematics. Its articles are clearly written and intended for the nonexpert. They range from short summaries of important recent happenings to longer (generally three page or less) features dealing with major issues and controversies in these fields. *Science News* articles always include leading references that allow an interested reader to purse a topic back to its original literature sources.

One *Science News* feature that was written when the United Nations was considering a proposal for a worldwide ban on the manufacture of the insecticide DDT formed the basis for a case study titled "To Spray or Not to Spray" that Joe Bieron and I wrote. The hook for this case was the fact that nothing currently is as effective for mosquito control as DDT, yet it is not being used while millions die each year from malaria infections. The case asks its student audience to choose between the *potential* for future environmental damage posed by the use of DDT in a limited way to control malaria to the *certainty* that malaria will cause millions of deaths each year if DDT is not used to control mosquito populations in subtropical regions of the world. It points out the irony that whereas environmentally oriented organizations generally oppose DDT's use, the United Nations' own World Health Organization favors the use of DDT under controlled circumstances to prevent this massive loss of life.

We have used "To Spray or Not to Spray" in both honors and nonscience majors courses to contrast two very different methods for making technological decisions: Risk Benefit Analysis and the Precautionary Principle. The case requires a high level of critical thinking. It invariably generates an intense debate that highlights not only important value issues, but also demonstrates the starkly different conclusions to which these two decision making techniques lead.

DON'T FORGET TELEVISION

As it reports current events of all sorts, television news is, of course, also a rich source of potential cases. A classic case study, one that I have long admired and have often used in my nonscience majors course, "The Benign Hamburger" was inspired by media reports on the death of at least one person and the hospitalization of many others as a result of *E.coli* food poisoning at a California-based restaurant chain. This case introduces the concept of nuclear radiation and considers the risks and benefits involved when this energy source is used for food purification. It also looks critically at the ways in which single-issue pressure groups exploit the (often unfounded) concerns of the public to influence policy decisions in their favor. The case forces analytical consideration of the potential risks and benefits that a business or a government agency faces when deciding whether or not to use a technology that is technically safe, but is one which the public does not understand.

We could cite countless other media inspired cases. In fact, such cases may be the most prevalent of all of the cases found on the National Center for Case Study Teaching in the Sciences website. I hope though that by describing these relatively few media-inspired cases, I have illustrated their abundance and ready availability. They are out there waiting for you to find them and to use them. Happy hunting.

Cooking With Betty Crocker

A Recipe for Case Study Writing

By Clyde Freeman Herreid

Measure into mixing bowl ½ cup of warm water, 2 pkg. dry yeast. Add 1¾ cups lukewarm scalded milk. Stir in 7 cups sifted flour, 3 tbsp. sugar, 1 tbsp. salt, 2 tbsp. shortening. Beat with a spoon, cover, knead, let rise. Shape into loaves. Bake at 425°.

—Betty Crocker recipe for white bread, two loaves

There are more books published on the subject of cooking than on any other topic. Wander into any bookstore and you will witness the culinary literature yourself. Face to face you will meet Betty Crocker, Fannie Farmer, Julia Child, James Beard, and their culinary buddies waiting to charm you into gastronomic imaginings and entreating you to plunk down $29.95 for their newest literary repast.

Not too far away, on nearby shelves, you will find books on how to garden, how to play the guitar, how to meditate with the latest guru, how to repair your Honda, and how to get right with God. There are instruction manuals for everything from becoming a magician to becoming, well, yourself.

There are even books on how to become a great teacher. Yet at Barnes & Noble or Borders you are unlikely to find them. In spite of the growing numbers of books on this topic, they are poor sales prospects for the bookseller. These books will hardly ever be touched by the average college teacher who probably doesn't even know of their existence, much less have one on his or her cluttered bookshelf.

Bearing in mind this neglected niche of publishing, and the flood of articles on education written each year that will never be seen by the practitioners in most classrooms, I am still ready to add another few thousand words, this time on the topic of how to write case studies.

I do believe that somewhere, somehow, an occasional person will actually read them and just possibly find something of use. It is akin to the wish that a person standing on a pier might have as he scribes a note and pops it into a bottle, caps it, and hurls it into the sea, wondering if anyone will ever find it.

In keeping with the cooking theme and addressing our concerns to case study teaching, let us pose the following question. Is there any recipe for creating a case? Is there something as dependable as a white bread approach to cases? Straightforward. Nothing fancy. Fortunately, the answer is yes. But before we start cooking, let's lay down a few principles.

Normally when teachers gets inspired to write a case, they have a course in mind. They know the students taking the course, their numbers, and background. They know the guests that are coming to dinner, but they haven't decided on the meal. What they don't know is how this case that they hope to concoct is going to fit in. (After all, it isn't written yet.) Nor do they know what it will teach exactly or what it will replace on the syllabus. Take a tip—don't worry about this yet. It's too soon to know.

Now that the general background is known, it is useful to point out that there are two general approaches. One method is to start out listing general principles that you wish to teach, then start looking for a good story that might teach them. The other approach is to spot a good story that seems an appropriate fit for your course, then ask yourself what principles you can illustrate with the case.

Whichever avenue you choose, you must choose reasonably soon what type of case-teaching method you will use. Will it be Problem-Based Learning (PBL) with small groups, or discussion based, or a debate, or any other number of strategies? This decision can be put off for a time while you do some research on the topic, but it can't be delayed too long because your writing will be largely driven by the case method of choice.

There is one other set of principles to review before beginning. They are ones that I listed in a previous column, "What Makes a Good Case?" (chapter 7). A good case tells a story, is set in the past five years, creates empathy with the central characters, includes quotations, is relevant to the reader, serves a pedagogical function, requires that dilemmas be solved, has generality, and is short. These rules are not sacrosanct but they work most of the time. So let's suppose you decide to write a case study. What steps can you take to get the job done?

- First, you have to *decide on a topic*. If you already have a story line that intrigues you, this isn't a problem, but let's suppose that that isn't the situation. The next best option is to think of one or more topics that are important to your course. Is there any conflict, controversy, news item, or personal experience that is associated with the topic? If so, all the better. Ask yourself: Can the topic be linked to any contemporary problem such as global warming, environmental disaster, social issues? This is the hook (interest-provoking item) into the case.
- *Review and research the topic* and the hook into the material so that you can see further connections and possibilities.
- *Rapidly write down all the possible principles that you might teach using this topic* in your class. Don't evaluate these ideas at this time; you are brainstorming. But remember that when you start writing you are going to try and slip as many of these delicacies into your dish as possible.
- *Make a list of all the possible characters* (fictional or real) who could be possibly affected by this topic or incident. Do any of these people have problems to be solved?
- *Write a draft of a case from the viewpoint of a person caught in the thick of the case problem.* If there is a crisis looming, great. The case can be written in a straightforward narrative, although techniques used by short story writers (e.g., flashback and dialogue) are welcome.

If you are writing for PBL courses, then the story line must be broken into two or three parts. In PBL, the students receive a page or two of the opening, then they need to do research before receiving subsequent pages.

- As you write these sections *look for opportunities to introduce terms or concepts that are important to your course.* Not all of these must have been covered previously. You want the students to research these items as part of their preparation for the class.

- After you have a draft, *go through the case again and list the major and minor topics that are likely to come up in a discussion of the case.* Hopefully, you will be surprised at the number of topics that you have slipped in, some that you originally had not planned.

- After you have a reasonable version of the case, *write a series of discussion questions* to include at the end of each section. These study questions will assist your students to recognize the important issues embedded in the case.

With some revision here and there, your case is finished. There is still the issue of how to manage the case in the classroom. That will take careful planning. It may be straightforward, or it may be elaborate with role-playing and student research. We'll leave that for another day. Here I would like to illustrate how we developed a recent case using the above steps. You will notice right away that the steps didn't come in the order that I mentioned above, yet the steps are all there.

Let me set the scene. A librarian (we'll call her Nancy) wanted to try writing a case study for my freshman Evolutionary Biology class. She had been interested in the Galapagos Islands for some time and was aware that they had played a significant role in Darwin's ideas on evolution. She thought that the topic ought to be a natural for a case. She knew little more at this point.

I thought the Galapagos theme was intriguing and encouraged her to do some reading.

I didn't have a clue what might come of it. Over the course of many weeks, when Nancy could squeeze in the time, she began to unearth some basic facts about the islands: the unusual nature of the organisms, their docility, the dramatic increase in tourism, the havoc caused by introduced goats, cats, and rats on the native organisms, and the presence of a scientific research station.

And she found an unexpected crisis. Ecuadorian sea cucumber fishermen had been ordered to stop encroaching on the protected waters. They responded by taking over the Research Station and holding scientists hostage for several days, along with "Lonesome George," the only surviving member of a species of the giant tortoises! Now, here was a real hook.

I asked Nancy to try and start writing up her thoughts about the Galapagos. Could she think of a central character? Certainly there were many possibilities: a fisherman, a tourist, a tour boat captain, a park ranger/guide, a scientist, and so forth. She settled on a young scientist, Kate, who was there as a visiting research scientist studying the Galapagos tortoise, thrown into the turmoil of the political crisis. I suggested that we make Kate a young graduate student in search of a thesis project, to make the case more relevant to the students. So Kate was demoted.

In Nancy's first draft, she was able to slide in information about the history of the island, the tourists, the animals, the scientists and fishermen, and the conflicts. It read well, but where was the science? This is always a central problem with any case having an ethical, social, or political hook. The author will ultimately be faced with how to get the science up front. The other "stuff" is so enticing to talk about that all too often the science gets left out. The same thing can happen in the classroom. The teacher must be sure that the science gets discussed first, before the students get enthralled with the politics and ethics. If you don't do the science first, it is likely to be lost altogether.

It was now up to me. Nancy had gone as far as she could. After all it was my course. But what, if anything, could I do with this writing? I sat down and brainstormed all of the topics that I could think of that might come from the Galapagos studies. The list was impressive, including the geology of the volcanic islands and their remarkable formation, plate tectonics, the Galapagos rift and the formation of life in hydrothermal vents. There were obvious connections to history via Darwin, questions about where the organisms came from, and their adaptations. And there were a host of questions about species formation and extinction.

As I developed the list, I recalled the wonderful book called the *Beak of the Finch,* by Jonathan Weiner. It discussed the remarkable studies on the Galapagos finches led by the husband and wife team, Peter and Rosemary Grant. Working for over 20 years on a couple of uninhabited islands, they had watched the ebb and flow of evolution in the birds through drought and El Niño deluge. They had collected striking data. Surely that would be part of the story.

Here is where I had to finally come to terms with the case structure. I now knew that I could blend in a number of major course topics with the case. I also knew that I could use this in my summer school class of 25 students where I employ cooperative learning with permanent small teams. It was a natural step to say that I would set up the case in three stages using PBL strategies. I felt the case was too rich and complex to try in a single discussion or even two class periods.

It was easy to decide how to partition the case. First, I would deal with the geological origin of the islands, their description, and Darwin's visit and musings on the colonization of the islands. I decided to do this having Kate standing on the edge of a volcano and thinking back over their history, telling only parts of their past and alluding to others. The study questions sharpened the focus on these items.

The second part of the case, given to the students on their next day in class after sharing information with each other, dealt with the rate of evolution and selective pressures. Here I drew heavily upon *Beak of the Finch,* raising questions and problems that faced the Grant research group. I decided to write this in dialogue form between Kate and the director of the Darwin Research Station. He was trying to talk Kate into focusing her research on the birds or iguanas rather than the tortoise, thus giving students the opportunity to discuss the Grants' work. Again, a series of study questions focused attention on problems of speciation.

The final section was Nancy's piece. Here we find Kate fully committed to her tortoise project and weeks into research. Suddenly, the sea cucumber crisis erupts into an open debate in Ecuador and is described for the first time in the case. The student groups are asked to take the view of one interest group (e.g., scientists, fishermen, tourists, conservationists) and examine its position, concerns, strengths, and weaknesses. Then after 20 minutes, the groups are shuffled (jigsaw) so that there is a mixture of people from different interest groups placed together. With a "politician" running each group discussion, these people must try to reach an acceptable compromise. After suitable time, a whole class discussion led by the instructor winds up the case and students turn in follow-up papers.

So how did Kate get into this mess of being drawn into the politics of Ecuador and watching her research career possibly go down the drain? We did it to her in a series of well-measured steps. First, we chose a general story topic that appealed to us. The Galapagos had possibilities. Second, after some research we listed a bunch of course principles and terms that could be linked to the theme. Third, we created a character whom we dropped into the middle of the mess, wondering about the ways of the world. Kate was born. Fourth, now that we had a personality, we gave her a voice to tell the story from her viewpoint. That story was divided into several chapters, like a Saturday movie serial or the *Star Wars* movie, with the audience knowing there were more adventures in store. Finally, we wrote a series of study questions for each episode to focus attention on the science of the case. (You can see the final version of this case at *http://ublib.buffalo.edu/libraries/projects/cases/galapagos1.html*.)

There you have it—a white bread approach to writing cases. It is direct and familiar. Nothing fancy. It gets the job done. You can throw in a few raisins or some cinnamon to perk it up (like the role-playing exercise at the end), but it is still white bread. Dependable.

There are other ways to plan the meal. There are recipes galore to dream about for case writing and cooking. Just the other day I was thinking of this Texas barbecue approach.

Take 3 lbs. of spare ribs. Mix 2 tbsp. brown sugar, 1 tbsp. paprika, ¼ tsp. chili powder, 2 tbsp. Worcestershire sauce ....

Too Much, Too Little, or Just Right?

How Much Information Should We Put Into a Case Study?

By Clyde Freeman Herreid

"Say when." That expression, usually reserved as an inquiry by a solicitous dispenser of party libations, is apt for the serious case writer. In both cases it is meant to find out how much is enough. How much liquid or information should we dole out to our vessels? Can we find a Goldilocks solution to the problem, when everything is "Just right?"

Starting me on this quest was a recent e-mail from Dakin Burdick at Purdue. Writing to the POD network, the professional organization of faculty development specialists, he wrote, "I'm working with a team here to create some case studies, and I'm wondering if there is research on the amount of extraneous, complicating, or contradictory data that can be introduced into a case without negatively affecting student learning. I'm imagining that there is some sort of tipping point at which students get so lost in the extra data that they actually make the wrong decisions more often than they make the right ones. Now, I know they can learn from those mistakes, but if the work is intended to build upon each, one experiential learning module on top of another, those wrong turns will significantly slow down students' overall progress. In addition, I can imagine that students might lose confidence if they get lost too often. Anyone done any research on this one? If not, does anyone have a ballpark figure for me? Right now I'm guessing at about three times as much useful information as useless/complicating/confusing data."

WHAT A GREAT QUESTION

I responded, "In general, it makes a difference what grade level students are in. Freshman, who are often functioning at the lowest levels of the Perry Model (dualist thinkers), cannot take much contradictory or extraneous information. They need straightforward problems to analyze. As students mature, they can progressively handle more ambiguity and longer cases. I know of no research on this question.

"My approach to the problem is that you must clearly know what the goals of your case are before you start to write it. In many (most) instances, the straightforward approach without contradictions poses enough challenge without confusing asides and red herrings. Also, it depends on how much experience students have with cases. Are they seeing cases for the first time? If so, they have to first learn how to prepare for them and how to deal with the teaching method in class. Further, it makes a difference whether the teaching is done in a general discussion or small groups and if questions are posed at the end of the case or not. Questions and helpful teammates can lead students through the case in a structured fashion even if the information in the case is ambiguous."

In short, it depends on how much structure is present either in the case or in the method of teaching and the degree of experience of both the teacher and students. And of course, it depends on how many class periods are going to be allotted to the case and how long those class periods are. And how much preparation time is available before the case is to be used in the classroom.

Burdick then added another dimension to the question, writing, "Thanks for the reply! Another answer that came in (via the POD network) mentioned that one should give students too little data, so that they have to extrapolate and become creative. It was an unusual idea for me, since as a modern historian we always are wading through far too much data. But my medievalist colleagues have a similar approach to the use of evidence."

I have thought this before—yes, the too-little-data approach is also a common technique. In the method called Problem-Based Learning (PBL), especially used in medical schools, the case is given in stages. In the first step, a patient comes in with a problem; some symptoms are given, and students work in groups to decide what they know and what they don't know but need to find out. They go to the library and the internet and look up certain information and come back and share it with their group members. Then they are given more data and again analyze what they know and what they need to find out. Back to the library—the third time they meet they make their diagnosis and report their conclusions. Then they are given another case and repeat. This minimalist approach can also be done in a single class, feeding students bits of information in stages using the interrupted case method. Both of these techniques use what is known as progressive disclosure.

Both PBL and the interrupted case method mimic the way scientists (indeed all scholars) go about their day-to-day work. They confront a problem, form questions, and look for data to answer the questions. They are constantly working with insufficient information and, like the historian, are bombarded with mounds of extraneous data. But they press on gathering more information and refining their views. So when this approach is used in the classroom, it tends to increase the skills of the students to identify problems; PBL encourages students to learn how to find out the answers to problems—to become independent learners.

Back to the question again. Some years ago, James A. Erskine and Michiel R. Leenders of the University of Western Ontario devised what they called a Case Difficulty Cube (Figure 1). It has three dimensions—analytical, conceptual, and presentational. Cases can be simple or complex along each dimension.

Along the analytical scale, the simplest case would be one in which you give students both a problem and solution and then ask them if the solution fits the problem or if there are alternatives. (Say, a dog is suspected of having rabies and the owner decides to shoot the animal. Is this the appropriate response?) The second degree of difficulty is to give a problem (rabid dog?) and ask students for a reasonable solution. The third degree of difficulty is to present a situation and ask students to identify the problems and solution.

The conceptual dimension refers to the difficulty level that your case is trying to present. The simplest level would be a case that has a single straightforward concept (a dog is foaming at the mouth and acting strangely). The more concepts you introduce, the greater the difficulty. (Maybe the dog has bitten a child. Or, at a higher level, the dog has bitten a child and the child loves the animal and the animal is a dog show champion. Still higher, a wolf has bitten your dog and several days later your dog has bitten your child. Neither wolf nor dog is showing symptoms. You are a microbiologist, backpacking out in the wilderness without contact with the outside world and requiring several days to travel back to civilization. You have waited years to make this trip with your son, who seems okay and didn't bleed much.) So the third level of difficulty requires significant explanation, clarification, and repetition for most students.

The presentational dimension deals with the question with which I started this essay—how much information should the case contain and how clearly should it be presented? The simplest level will have only the data that is needed and will be clearly presented in text, table, or graph and the case will be short. The second level is longer and has some irrelevant data. The third level is still longer and may have considerable extraneous information, require significant data sifting, and perhaps have missing pieces.

So, using the Case Difficulty Cube model, the most difficult case will be at 3, 3, 3—hard, hard, and hard along all dimensions. Conversely, the simplest would be at the 1, 1, 1 level.

FIGURE 1.

Case difficulty cube.
From J. A. Erskine, M. R. Leenders, and L. A. Mauffette-Leenders. *Teaching with cases.* 3rd.ed. London, Ontario: Ivey Publishing, University of Western Ontario. Reprinted with permission.

AXIS	DIMENSION	RANGE
X	ANALYTICAL	1-3
Y	CONCEPTUAL	1-3
Z	PRESENTATION	1-3

This case you might give to a beginning student who has never seen case studies and is in the early part of an introductory course. As the student matures and the curriculum advances, so would the cases shift in complexity.

I personally like to design cases that do two things—support and challenge students. Cases support students when they fit in their comfort zone. Cases that challenge them would force them to stretch a bit along the cube's scales. So, if students are *dualists*, as in the Perry Model, meaning they think all questions must have a right or wrong answer, I would give them a case that has such elements but add a piece that is more open ended—which has several reasonable alternatives. For instance, in a case that I have co-authored called "Life on Mars. A dilemma case study in planetary geology," we investigate the claims of a team of NASA scientists who found a meteorite with evidence that suggests there was life on Mars. Students have no problem evaluating the claims and evidence. But the case also deals with whether the hero should attend a press conference with his teammates and leader who are about to state that the data strongly support that life existed on Mars. What should our hero do if he is skeptical of their conclusions and given the fact that there are far-ranging consequences for his future? There are multiple approaches to the dilemma. This is challenging for students.

So to return to the question: How much is enough? There is no simple dualist answer to the question. It depends on the situation, of course. I leave it in your hands, but remember this—support and challenge. If cases are too complex, there is nothing but frustration for everyone; but if they are too simple, they are boring as the devil. Look for the Goldilocks solution.

The Way of Flesch

The Art of Writing Readable Cases

By Clyde Freeman Herreid

I was browsing in the Santa Fe Public Library not long ago. I walked into the little nook where they house books donated to the library for resale. There, for a piddling amount of money, were a few gems: yet another unauthorized biography of Barbra Streisand; a copy of an old John Updike novel that mined the middle-aged psyche of Bech; Carl Sagan's last book of essays finished shortly before his death and appropriately called *Billions and Billions,* something he claims he never said in his TV series *Cosmos;* and a little sleeper of a paperback on writing. The title intrigued me: *The Art of Readable Writing.* Linguist Rudolf Flesch wrote it. He had been consultant to the Associated Press, where he cajoled the news staff to throw off the straitjacket formula of writing their stories with the traditional "Who-What-Where-When-Why-and-How" approach. He asked, "How can readers absorb the main facts of the news" if this tired approach "is subordinated to the human interest treatment?"

We can ask the same question about case studies that so often are overburdened with the formal writing style we learned in graduate school—that scientific and dreadful boring way of writing in the passive and third-person voice.

This 50-year-old book is chock-full of great advice about writing. I'd like to share some of its wisdom because it is useful for any kind of writing, including case studies. Central to Flesch's theme is the axiom "Write as you speak." Be straightforward in your sentences. Unfortunately, some academics speak just as poorly as they write, so this advice won't always work. But the idea, "write as you speak," is sound advice for case writing. Before diving into Flesch's recipe for success, let me hasten to say that many fine cases have been written using a formal style. But I am convinced that many more fine cases will be written by following Flesch's advice than will be written by ignoring it. So consider this chapter a book report with my kibitzing thrown in.

KNOW YOUR AUDIENCE

Writing for elementary school children isn't the same as writing for insurance agents. The problems are different. So are the language and the traditions. Here's Flesch's version of Aristotle pointing out the difference between young and old:

Young men have strong desires...
they are fond of victory, for youth likes
to be superior... they are sanguine...
they live their lives in anticipation...
they have high aspirations... they are
prone to pity... fond of laughter...

Elderly men... are cynical...
suspicious... they aspire to nothing great
or exalted, but crave the mere necessities
and comforts of existence... they live
in memory rather than anticipation...
they are mastered by love of gain...

Or, as Flesch puts it,

Young people like romance, adventure,
and daydreams, and old people like
practical, down-to-earth, bread-and-but-
ter stuff.... So, when you want to convey
information to the young, take a hint:
make it a story—with a happy ending.

NOT JUST THE FACTS

You may recall the old television show *Dragnet*
where Detective Joe Friday cuts off any asides
that a witness tries to make with his favorite line,
"The facts, ma'am, just the facts." Flesch argues
that if you don't use examples, dashes of color,
"and a good assortment of useless information,"
the reader won't remember the facts.

POINT OF VIEW

For your writing to be readable, you must
have a point of view. You must have a hero
who undergoes trials and tribulations. You
can write cases with a stooge asking questions of a hero, a Dr. Watson playing up to
Sherlock Holmes. You can write the case
from the vantage point of a typical member
of a group faced with a problem—the generic victim. But the hero must have a name.
And I argue that in cases, especially cases
with a serious theme, the names should not
be cute. Don't call the physician treating a
case of lung cancer, Dr. Cough, or a forensic

pathologist, Bill Crimeboy. This trivializes
the case and reduces it to little more than
a joke, something that teachers should try
hard to avoid. Even with fictionalized cases,
make them as real as possible.

The best heroes are ones that you can
identify with. But they don't have to be
people. They could be animals. I have had
veterinarians write excellent cases from the
viewpoint of a dog with a heart problem or
a horse with a broken leg. I haven't yet seen
a case written from the viewpoint of a para-
mecium or a liverwort, but there isn't any
reason why they can't be written. Flesch re-
minds us that the U.S. Army fought malaria
in World War II with a booklet about Ann
the Anopheles Mosquito, and the state of Alabama produced a pamphlet about Hubert
Hookworm.

Personalization can be extended to parts of
the body. Years ago *Reader's Digest* published
a series of articles with titles like "I am Joe's
Heart" and "I am Joe's Pancreas" written in
the first person. It is even possible to person-
alize inanimate objects. Kipling wrote poems
from the viewpoint of machines and ships.
And let's not forget that there is a rich history
of storytelling from unusual viewpoints—remember Aesop? Any children's book, such
as *The Little Engine That Could,* or Saturday
morning cartoon tells a story. Why not try it
in case writing?

HUMAN INTEREST

Flesch has a yardstick for measuring the human interest in your writing. Count up all the
personal names in a piece you have written.
Then count the personal pronouns, skipping
any *it* or *they* that refers to things not people.
Count all of the nouns like *aunt*, *widower*, or
guy where the gender is clear. Skip words like
students or *teacher* where the gender isn't obvious. Then count the number of times you
used the words *people* or *folks*. The total of
these words calculated, as a percentage of
the total number of words in your text, will

FIGURE 1.

Reading Ease Formula.

Reading ease is calculated by combining the length of words and the length of sentences:

Average length of sentences multiplied by 1.015	_____
Number of syllables in 100 words multiplied by 0.846	_____
Sum	_____
Subtract from 206.835	_____
Reading ease score	_____

---

give you a good measure of how strong the human interest element is. In a dull scientific piece, the percentage will be zero. In a fast-paced novel where characters' names abound, it will be around 20. In readable nonfiction magazines, such as *Time* or *Newsweek,* it ranges between six and eight.

USE DIALOGUE

Virtually any writing can be turned into dialogue. People will choose to read dialogue over almost any other writing style. Flesch argues that "a seasoned popular nonfiction writer knows that to interest his readers he must not only turn most of his material into narrative, but he must go one step further and turn a large part of that narrative into dialogue." The percentage of dialogue varies enormously in different kinds of writing. In technical papers the percentage will be zero while in popular magazine articles it will be between 12% and 15% and can reach 50%. Which would you rather read?

USE CONVERSATIONAL WRITING

If you were to write the way you speak, you would use a lot of contractions. You'd write *you'd, can't, shouldn't, I've, we'll, don't, didn't,* and *let's* instead of their more formal counterparts. You would write *who* instead of *whom.* You would write, "Can I go?" instead of "May I go?" You would use *like* whenever you'd like. You wouldn't give a fig if you split an infini-

tive or dangled a participle. And you'd say, "It's me!" when it is you.

If you were writing real dialogue, you wouldn't worry if you used the same word twice in a sentence and repeated yourself, because that's the way real people speak. Here are Hillary Clinton's comments at a press conference disclaiming any involvement in her husband's presidential pardons. "You know, it came as a complete surprise to me.... You know, I did not have any involvement, you know, and I'm just very disappointed.... Oh, you know, as I have said in the past, there were many, many people who spoke to me or, you know, asked me to pass on information...." But use some sense here. If we really put in all of the "duhs" and "ahhs" and gibberish that we mouth, it wouldn't be readable.

SENTENCE LENGTH

Professor L. A. Sherman from the University of Nebraska discovered back in 1893 that there has been a striking decrease in the length of sentences over time. In Elizabethan times written sentences averaged about 45 words. They may have been elegant, but surely, no one ever spoke that way—certainly Shakespeare didn't. Victorian sentences were down to 29 words, and in the 1890s, they were 20. Today, popular writing averages 17 or 18 words per sentence.

Short sentences are easy to read and easy to comprehend. However, too many of them in a

---

FIGURE 2.

Human Interest Formula.

Human interest is calculated by taking the sum of the following factors:

Multiply the number of "personal words" per 100 words by 3.635   _____

Multiply the number of "personal sentences" per 100 sentences by 0.314   _____

The sum is the human interest score   _____

---

row gives a jerky staccato flavor, which is fine if you wish to give your writing a breathless quality, but it can get irritating if it goes on too long. Use complex sentences now and again, but punctuate them well to avoid finding yourself in a James Joycean syntactic sinkhole.

GREAT BEGINNINGS AND STRONG ENDINGS

"Call me Ishmael" is the famous opening line of *Moby Dick*. It is memorable and personable. It immediately captures your interest. You wonder who this guy with the exotic name is. Another brilliant opening is Tolstoy's beginning for *Anna Karenina*: "Happy families are all alike; every unhappy family is unhappy in its own way." They are grabbers. You want to read more. So you do. The author has your attention.

Mystery writer Edward D. Hoch says that the ideal opening will do three things: grab the reader, introduce a character, and establish a setting. Here is Graham Greene doing all three in his first sentence of *Brighton Rock*: "Hale knew, before he had been in Brighton three hours, that they meant to kill him."

You don't even have to wait until the first sentence. Capture the readers with a catchy title or a quotation right off the bat even before they get to the opening words. No matter how you do it, you have to get their attention right away. That's where the hook should be.

So you have a great beginning, now what? The answer: just carry on. It's best to continue the story in chronological order. Soon you will be in the middle; that's where the meat of the case is, and I'll leave that to you.

But I do have something to say about the ending. Cases may not really have a distinct ending where everything is wrapped up with the hero and heroine walking happily into the sunset. This is especially true of dilemma or decision cases where you are asking the students to create the end of the drama. However, you shouldn't just let the story peter out. Bring the problem to a head. Try to make the end of the case interesting and worth thinking about, if not dramatic. Otherwise, who cares?

AVOID HEAVY SOUNDING WORDS

There are simple ways of saying things and there are convoluted ways. Choose simple. Flesch gives a list of some of his favorite "too heavy" prepositions and conjunctions along with their simple alternatives. Here are a few:

- Along the lines of = like
- For the purposes of = for
- For the reason that = since, because
- From the point of view that = for
- Inasmuch as = for, because
- In case of = if
- In the neighborhood of = about
- With the result that = so that

Here are a few "too heavy connectives" that we ought to avoid: *accordingly, consequently, hence,* and *thus.* All of these can be replaced by the tiny word *so.* Instead of *in addition,* use *also.* Don't write *moreover* or *nevertheless,* write *now* and *but*. These changes will lighten up your writing and make it more enjoyable. Remember, "write like you speak." Don't be ponderous.

Flesch winds up by showing how a piece of writing can be evaluated by two scores, a "reading ease score" and a "human interest score." The reading ease score will fall between 0 and 100 with 0 meaning "practically unreadable" and 100 meaning "easy for any literate person" (see Figure 1). It shouldn't surprise you to learn that Flesch found that comics rank 92, *Reader's Digest* 65, *Newsweek* 50, *New York Times* 39, and a standard auto insurance policy 10.

The human interest score is calculated using the number of "personal words" (which I mentioned earlier) and the number of "personal sentences" (see Figure 2). Such sentences include dialogue; questions, commands, requests directly addressed to the reader (like "This is a point you must remember."); exclamations (such as "That's ridiculous!"); and incomplete sentences whose meaning has to be inferred from the context (such as "an absolute genius," or "Well, certainly he would.").

The human interest scale ranges between 0 (no human interest) and 100 (full of human interest). Scientific journals score numbers suggesting that they are downright "dull." There's no surprise here, is there? The *Reader's Digest* ranks about 40 or "interesting," the *New Yorker,* at 60, is "very interesting," and novels can approach 100 and be "dramatic."

Back to case studies. Don't we want case studies to be both readable and have human interest? Sure we do! The case studies that the students like best are those that rank high on both scales. Of course, there are other factors involved in making great cases: the content we want to cover; the type of subject we have chosen (sex and scandal work here just like in the rest of the world); and the quality of the basic story. We can take any case, topic, or story and write it—readable or unreadable—interesting or uninteresting. Which would you choose?

If you want to have some fun, try calculating the readability and human interest scores for chapters in this book or for some of your own writings. It's scary, I know. It might interest you to know that this case chapter that you are reading now ranks high on both scales. I don't want to tell you how high, but thank goodness! Otherwise, I'd have to go back and do some quick rewriting!

Twixt Fact and Fiction

A Case Writer's Dilemma

By Clyde Freeman Herreid

What shall it be, a real case connected to the real world with blood, sweat, and tears or a fantasy, a twice-told tale by a spinner of yarns around a campfire on a summer night? When a teacher sits down to write a case, he is lured by the former and charmed by the latter. What to do: Write a case about actual events or fabricate a story to fit the occasion? This is a perennial question that many nascent case writers ask as they face the intimidating task of planning their first case.

For starters, think about this: What do we remember longer, the tale of Snow White or a news story about a child who has run away? *Star Wars* or the actual moon landing? Which character do we remember best: Sherlock Holmes or J. Edgar Hoover? There clearly is a place in our hearts for Dorothy of the *Wizard of Oz*, Harry Potter, Ali Baba, and Babar. But let's not get carried away by the fictional heroes and villains, the supermen and Draculas, before we hear from the side of the argument peopled by Mozart, Marie Curie, and Abraham Lincoln.

Let's hear it for reality! Students *do* like real cases, especially if they involve celebrities. Cases that have a connection to their world and its events are grabbers. But it is not enough for a case to be about actual events. Some things are simply more fascinating than others, even in research. "All things being equal," study whales before you study sunfish; study gorillas before you study shore crabs. Whales are simply more "sexy" than sunfish, and gorillas have it all over shore crabs. If you had a choice, which seminar would you go to: "The evolution of whales" or "The evolution of sunfish?" Or how about "Gorillas in the Mist" versus "Shore Crabs in the Mist?" No contest here. Whales and gorillas win hands down. The same is true about dinosaurs, pandas, elephants, and Madonna. Sand flies in Uganda can't compete. So if you have a choice, choose Madonna over sand flies.

But wait: There are some problems with real cases. One is the problem of liability. If you use a person's real story, you may have real legal problems—or moral ones. There probably won't be any difficulty if you use a true story of a public figure whose story has been splashed across the newspapers of the world and on CNN. You are especially safe if you paraphrase quotations taken from the press as part of your story line. But even here you must be careful; the print media may have copyright issues at stake.

Students like cases based on the stories of real people, such as Mozart, Abraham Lincoln, and Marie Curie.

Most cases that are used in business schools are based on fact. Harvard and Western Ontario University have thousands of such *real* cases. How do they get away with it? How can they use cases that involve real people, real companies with real documents? Answer: very carefully. They do innumerable interviews and review countless documents to get the story right. But—here is the important part—they first get permission to do all of these things; then they get everyone to sign off on the accuracy of their case. It's not just the accuracy that is involved; the case must be written in such a way that the folks in the case are not going to look like they are nincompoops. If I were a CEO, I certainly wouldn't approve of a

case about my company that makes anyone look bad, no matter how truthful it was.

All of this takes time—lots of it, months or years. This means money—lots of it. No wonder that these cases cost money to use. Those of us in the science case writing business are not usually faced with such choices. Most science teachers don't know what cases are, much less how to use them in their classes, and they are a far cry from writing one themselves.

Back to the reality issue. There *are* real stories to be told that seem perfect for a case study: Chernobyl, Three Mile Island, the Valdez oil spill, global warming, cold fusion, and ozone depletion. What about these? These are part of the public record. Why not use them? The answer is, of course you should.

FICTIONALIZING A TRUE STORY

Most faculty know some good stories about science. Some involve famous individuals, perhaps the race between Watson and Crick and Linus Pauling to decipher the structure of DNA; tennis pro Arthur Ashe contracting AIDS through a blood transfusion; Janet Reno and Michael J. Fox and Parkinson's disease; cyclist Lance Armstrong and testicular cancer. All are perfect stories. There should be no problem in using them. The details of their tales are well known and in the public record. As long as you don't infringe on someone's copyrighted story or commit libel, you are on safe ground.

But what about that heart-rending true story you know of child abuse, or one about degenerative spinal disease, or of a folic acid deficiency during pregnancy that happened to a friend down the street. Then what? You can try to get permission to tell their tale. But this may be at best awkward. There is another option: fictionalize the story. Change the names, the setting, and the genders. Such changes aren't always reasonable, of course. If it is a tale about the Eiffel Tower it has to be Paris, not San Francisco. If it is about pregnancy, a gender change won't work.

Let's assume you are going to change things. How much change is enough to avoid libel or embarrassing your loved ones? This is the same problem that faces any writer of fiction. Authors don't always make the right choices and do get caught. The best dictum is change as much as possible: Give your characters cigars to chew upon, chiffon dresses, and Southern accents. Yet remember the other side of the equation. How much can you change your characters before the story line itself becomes less engaging or less powerful? A case about an unwed mother considering abortion is hardly the same if we make her unemployed with three children by different men versus making her a 40-year-old woman who is a CEO of a Fortune 500 company.

GENERIC CASES

The more we change the protagonists, the more we slide along the slope of making it a generic case. Yes, we have avoided the libel questions, but we are now in danger of making our case so bland and uninteresting that the readers become alert to the fact that this just isn't real. It is a classroom exercise. It is just another puzzle that the instructor has posed.

This is the problem with most medical cases. They start out in the most awful way I can imagine: "A twenty-year-old female presented the following symptoms...." When I see this kind of opening, I think: "Who in the world cares?" Even if it is based on a real case, there is no personality here. What is her name? Does she have a dog, a husband, and a child? What kind of a person is she? What will happen to those around her if she dies of this dreaded disease? I know that the formal language and the gutting of the particulars from the case allow the physician to concentrate on the physical aliments, which are, after all, his or her prime concern. But frankly, that is one of the troubles that I see in the whole medical profession itself. They are often focused on the "plumbing problems" and not the person.

NAMING NAMES

Using names in cases is important. We need them if we are going to care about the people. Their absence in medical cases weakens the emotional power of the story enormously. So, be sure that your characters have names. Real ones. Do not be cute with the names of your characters, especially if the subject matter is serious. Do not name a pilot Bill Flyboy or a woman with breast cancer Mary Hurtchest. This kind of "creativity" doesn't belong in cases if you want people to believe in the characters. More importantly, it undermines the seriousness of the issues you are discussing. It trivializes important issues. Don't do it.

Jean-Jacques Rousseau

PURE FANTASY

I believe there is a place for fantasy in case writing. I have used it myself. I recently wrote a genetics case using the story of Peter Rabbit and his siblings, Flopsy, Mopsy, and Cottontail. I know of a veterinarian who wrote a cardiovascular case from the viewpoint of a pet beagle. I can remember *Reader's Digest* articles written from the viewpoint of Joe's heart, and I have coauthored a case that was written from the viewpoint of a human fetus. There is nothing wrong with this. Here we aren't trying to palm off an ersatz case on the reader. It is out in the open. We are telling an engaging tale in its own right. Whether it is the *Wizard of Oz* or *Harry Potter*, no one is fooled. Still there are lessons to be learned in any parable. We are Aesop on a mission, giving lessons of loyalty, persistence, pluck, friendship, and maybe even some science.

With cases of pure fantasy, no one will ever ask you the dreaded questions: "Is this a real story?" and "What happened to the boy who was dying?" You will not have to guiltily answer, "Sorry, this isn't a real case." The students will not have to leave disillusioned once more that the educational process isn't about the real world, just another classroom exercise, with no need to invest any emotion here. Let's not do this to students once again. If it is fantasy, make it clean and obvious. They will enjoy it and remember it.

So, what is the bottom line on real versus fictional cases? Both will work. But I argue: Students prefer the extremes, either real stories or complete fantasy. These are easiest to digest. The generic ones in the middle are less satisfying and "less filling." Unless such cases are written with skill, the students sense the deception. They care less. They work less. And, I believe, they learn less.

As Jean-Jacques Rousseau said:
The world of reality has its limits; the world of imagination is boundless. Not being able to enlarge the one, let us contract the other; for it is from their difference alone that all the evils arise which render us really unhappy.

An Open or Shut Case?

Contrasting Approaches to Case Study Design

By William H. Cliff and Leslie M. Nesbitt

The hallmark of an open-ended case study is the possibility of multiple outcomes to the problem at hand. This adds to its realism, provokes higher-order thought, and attracts many instructors to case analysis. Yet, there are circumstances in which a closed-ended approach, having a single correct answer, may be preferred. Here, we weigh the advantages and disadvantages of both approaches. Read on!

Looking at Case Studies

In a 1998 issue of the *Journal of College Science Teaching*, Clyde Herreid outlined a scheme for classifying case study methodologies. His taxonomy rested on the teaching method that the teacher might use for a case and the relative contribution of the student and the instructor to the work of analysis. In this column, we view case studies from another angle—one that draws attention to the elements of case study design.

Following Herreid's suggestion (1997), we propose that case designs can be sorted by the degree to which they are "closed" or "open." Is there a single correct answer to the questions that the teacher poses? We also focus on the case study learning objectives—the educational goals that cases serve.

For the sake of simplicity, we'll begin by imposing a dichotomy on our viewpoint. Case designs will be seen as either fully open or fully closed. In many respects, this simplification is analogous to the distinction between the design of ill-structured and well-structured problems—another pedagogical domain that is rich in instructional possibilities (Jonassen 1997).

Comparing Approaches

The open-ended case design begins with the recognition that, in many situations, people don't know or cannot get all of the necessary or relevant information to solve a problem. Knowledge is in flux, or certainty cannot be obtained (Table 1). Open-ended cases are messy and have a real-world feel about them. They evoke multiple lines of i nquiry and have many possible solutions.

TABLE 1.

Features of closed- and open-ended case designs.

Closed	Open
Knowledge defined	Knowledge in flux
Content-driven	Context-driven
Single acceptable outcome	Multiple acceptable outcomes (situational)

As an example, a case study might force students to make a decision about expanding the electrical power generation capabilities in a local region. Should the new plant be nuclear, fossil fuel, solar, or wind-driven? Or should the plan involve some combination of the four? Surely, to fully answer such a question students must address ecology, technology, ethics, politics, religion, and culture. They must weigh reasonable alternatives to arrive at a satisfactory outcome. Successful resolution of open cases depends on the context in which they are situated, described, or analyzed. And reasonable people might differ.

Because the instructor does not foreordain a single outcome, open-ended cases are student-directed. Arrival at any one of the many legitimate outcomes is satisfactory. Success depends crucially on the student's analytical abilities. The student must demonstrate that he or she can build the "best case" argument for why his or her answer or solution is preferred. In short, *process* is the focus.

Conversely, a closed-ended case design is focused on *content*. It begins with the premise that all the knowledge that the student might need to solve a particular aspect of the case is accessible (Table 1). The questions, issues, or concerns raised in the case typically converge toward definite correct answers. For instance, we wrote a case about a 1994 hazing incident in which a college student had his back coated with gasoline and other toxic substances (Cliff and Nesbitt 2000). We included data collected at the hospital to which the young man was admitted and asked students in our anatomy and physiology class to answer a series of questions about expected changes in kidney function and fluid and electrolyte balance. There were single, correct answers to these questions. We wanted the students to reinforce their understanding of key concepts underlying the case. The design is essentially instructor-directed. We (as instructors) set the content outline to be mastered, and we decided what the criteria would be for success.

EDUCATIONAL OBJECTIVES

Given these differences, how should an instructor determine whether to select an open-ended or a close-ended approach to case design? This question calls for us to consider the educational objectives that can guide case analysis (Bloom 1956). Open-ended cases are context-specific. Learning outcomes center on the critical-thinking abilities that students gain or improve during analysis (Table 2). Learning facts and definitions are not as important as enhancing the thinking skills used to gain them. If an instructor wishes to emphasize higher-order process skills such as evaluation and synthesis, then an open-ended design is preferable.

Alternately, content drives the closed-ended design. The teacher wants the student to solidify his or her knowledge and comprehension of the underlying science (Table 2). In a perfect world, a student strives to integrate the underlying facts and concepts into a coherent portrait of the situation or problem presented by the case study. The instructor is concerned that the student successfully accomplishes this task—that he or she constructs a satisfactory mental model of the subject domain underlying the case (Michael and Modell 2003). This construction is evident when the student can marshal the appropriate facts and concepts and produce astute explanations of the case's scientific foundations. If this is the goal, then the instructor should choose a closed-ended approach.

CLOSED-ENDEDNESS

Given the realism and intellectual richness of an open-ended design, why would an instructor ever consider using a closed-end one? First, some designs are inherently closed. Some stories do have a single answer—the actual murderer is identified at the end of a crime mystery, for instance. For a case that involves a patient suffering from insulin-dependent diabetes, we want our students to arrive at a correct diagnosis of the disease and to be able to correctly distinguish it from other metabolic disorders that may have similar features but different origins. This is particularly important if we wish them to focus on the underlying physiology of the pancreas or the liver, rather than on the subtle nuances of clinical diagnosis.

Second, the instructor may want to retain greater control of the classroom discussion than is often afforded in an open-ended design. This too depends on the instructor's educational objectives for using case analyses. If content is at stake and the instructor wants the case analysis to promote definitive understanding, then it is essential that he or she ask specific questions, so that students solidify these relevant features and correct flawed aspects of their mental models. (Remember, there can be correct answers.)

Also, a closed-ended design can encourage students to advance to the application and analysis stage; they must use their knowledge to make sense of the novel scenario offered by the study. When this occurs, students achieve meaningful learning, because correct application and analysis provides evidence of such understanding (Michael and Modell 2003).

In addition, the instructor may want to guide the trajectory of student learning to a

TABLE 2.		
Pedagogical properties of closed- and open-ended case designs.		
Closed		**Open**
	Educational objectives	
Product oriented		Process oriented
Knowledge		Synthesis
Comprehension		Evaluation
	Student capabilities	
Intellectually formative		Intellectually mature

greater degree than is usually offered by an open-ended design. Rather than leaving the student to work through the case on his or her own, the instructor provides guideposts that students can follow as they make their way toward a satisfying resolution. In effect, the instructor suggests, "Follow me as I lead you through a successful way of thinking through this problem. You may find this approach to problem solving to be useful when you face similar problems in the future." This may be particularly helpful for students who are intellectually formative. They are ill-prepared to tackle challenging problems within some subjects. By careful design of the sequence of questions in a closed-ended case, the instructor provides an intellectual template or a "way of knowing" that students can adopt to improve their ability to reason through more difficult problems and challenges.

Last, it may be worthwhile to use a closed-ended design for the sake of efficient learning. Time constraints may preclude students from having the fullest opportunity to find what they need to know to solve an open-ended case. Primary reliance on student-directed pathways of learning can be prohibitively time consuming. A closed-ended case design limits the possibilities and constrains the avenues. This may be particularly important in a course where a certain amount of content coverage is essential.

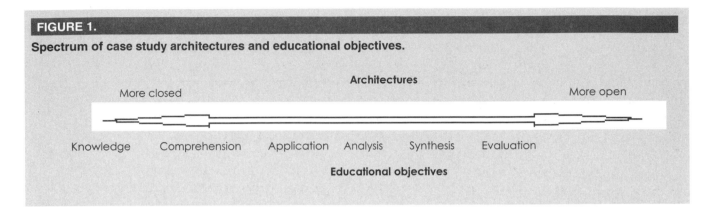

FIGURE 1.

Spectrum of case study architectures and educational objectives.

Architectures

More closed   More open

Knowledge   Comprehension   Application Analysis   Synthesis   Evaluation

Educational objectives

PEDAGOGICALLY RICH CASES

Stepping out of our simplifying dichotomy, many case studies are neither completely open-ended nor fully closed. The degree of openness springs from the decisions that the case designer makes as the case study is fashioned—by the emphases, thought-provoking queries, prompts, and probes crafted into it. Pedagogically rich cases often take both approaches.

For example, the case study about local power expansion may have open-ended features because its analysis might require students to weigh a number of sociopolitical, ethical, and environmental concerns. Nevertheless, when aspects of the engineering science of power generation are examined, most of these issues are closed-ended. Alternately, a case study on the biology of limb development may contain closed-ended elements that help students understand the relations between a well-established series of developmental events. Yet, it may also have open-ended aspects that invite students to address ill-defined questions about the control of these events at the cutting edge of developmental biology.

This being so, how do we decide which closed and open-ended features to build into a case? For starters, we must consider our educational objectives. Let's consider our objectives when plotted along a spectrum of closed-ended to open-ended designs (Figure 1). Do aspects of the analysis make it important for students to concentrate on forming, reinforcing, or deepening factual knowledge and on comprehending underlying concepts? If so, we will pursue a more closed-ended approach to help solidify the correct mental models. Do other aspects make it important for students to develop the skills of synthesis or evaluation? If so, then we will create more open-ended features that promote critical thinking.

Another consideration is "the problem of sequence" (Wiggins and McTighe 1998). How should we match the order of the tasks performed during case analysis with the most effective progression of student learning? How can we maximize the likelihood that students will accomplish as many of our learning objectives as possible? This question of sequencing confronts us whether we are planning student analysis of a single case or the analysis of a series of cases over the span of an entire course.

Let us consider the sequencing of the case involving electrical power expansion. The instructor could start off by asking questions designed to help students master the key features of the engineering science. This approach might require students to determine the thermodynamic efficiencies and specific energetic costs of nuclear energy, fossil fuel, and wind-driven power generation. Having arrived at a single, correct outcome for these closed-ended parameters, students would then be prepared to evaluate more open-ended aspects related to public policy. This might entail an analysis of the tradeoffs between the environmental and economic aspects of power generation and the politics involved.

If we used this approach, students would first solidify what they knew about the underlying science and technology of the case to use this information to address ill-defined aspects of the implementation of policy decisions. This would help them scale a hierarchy of educational objectives over the span of a single case analysis. Alternatively, the instructor may start the case with an open-ended question, say about public policy. This approach obliges students to obtain the required closed-ended competency to resolve the more provocative, open-ended dilemmas.

We can apply the same sequencing tactics to a series of case studies over the course of a semester. Initially, we might assign case studies dominated by closed-ended architectures. Throughout the semester students would progressively analyze more integrative cases characterized by increasingly open-ended challenges. In doing so, our students would move from formative to more mature capabilities.

As case study practitioners, we have compelling reasons to incorporate both closed- and open-ended approaches into our designs. It is our responsibility to capitalize on the strengths of these two approaches in creating the most effective case studies. This effort to become better case study designers finds its parallel in the quest to become better storytellers. And good storytellers know that, even if they begin at the same starting point, they discover that a variety of worthwhile tales can develop as different plot lines converge or diverge over the course of the story. Anything is possible when you start with "Once upon a time…."

In storytelling, it's up to the raconteur, guided by his or her muse, to bring each tale to a fitting ending—a denouement best suited to its intended effect on the listener. In case study design, it's up to us, guided by carefully considered learning objectives, to craft the open-ended and closed-ended facets of our case studies so that they end up offering the greatest pedagogical benefit to our students.

References

Bloom, B., ed. 1956. *Taxonomy of educational objectives: The classification of educational goals: Handbook 1: The cognitive domain.* New York: David McKay.

Cliff, W. H., and L. Nesbitt Curtin. 2000. The directed case: Teaching concept and process in a content-rich course. *Journal of College Science Teaching* 30 (1): 64–66.

Herreid, C. F. 1998. Sorting potatoes for Miss Bonner: Bringing order to case-study methodology through a classification scheme. *Journal of College Science Teaching* 25 (5): 236–239.

Herreid, C. F. 1997. What is a case? *Journal of College Science Teaching* 25 (3): 92–94.

Jonassen, D. H. 1997. Instructional design models of well-structured and ill-structured problem-solving learning outcomes. *Educational Technology Research and Development* 45 (1): 65–94.

Michael, J. A., and H. I. Modell. 2003. *Active learning in the secondary and college science classrooms.* Mahwah, NJ: Lawrence Erlbaum.

Wiggins, G., and J. McTighe. 1998. *Understanding by design.* Alexandria, VA: Association for Supervision and Curriculum Development.

Racism and All Sorts of Politically Correct *Isms* in Case Studies

What Are We to Do?

By Clyde Freeman Herreid

Not too long ago I received an unsettling letter from a consultant for a teaching and learning center. The writer claimed that a case study that I had written was racist. Now to be truthful, this irritated me. To be accused of racism, even inadvertent racism, is troubling, to say the least.

What was this all about? The letter writer suggested that I rewrite a case to remove, in her mind, a clear bias against Asians. The case in question was one I had written about alleged cheating in a classroom in which both of the suspects were Asian.

As described in the case, one student was apparently signaling his friend the "correct" answers during a quiz. Another student reported their "presumed" intransigencies to the professor. This posed a difficult dilemma for the instructor, as you can imagine: What to do given the evidence and the fact that the semester was virtually over? For interested readers, the case is available online at *http://ublib.buffalo.edu/libraries/projects/cases/cheating.html* and in chapter 7 of this book.

The letter writer had a suggestion—why not change the ethnic background of the suspects in the case to something less *ethnic*? Make them anything except Asian, because making them Asian was, according to the letter writer, stigmatizing of the worst type.

I don't know what the letter writer had in mind. What I do know is what my colleagues and I have gleaned from years of experience—Asian students often work cooperatively. Throughout their education, they are encouraged to work together on projects—indeed, this is the norm in Asian societies. Now, here we have an apparent cheating case in an American classroom; could this mean that even though the teacher told the students that they were supposed to work alone on tests that the Asian students couldn't understand the directions? Surely, if the instructor took this attitude, wouldn't she be stereotyping? Aren't these legitimate problems to be discussed in the case? In no time I was flummoxed about the whole affair.

So, I had the letter. What to do? Well, I made a mistake. I threw it on a pile of difficult-to-impossible-problems-to-be-dealt-with-later in the corner of my desk, and it sat there for the longest time. I was reminded of the pile moldering in the dark recesses of my writing table months later when an e-mail came from out of the blue. It reported the most improbable thing—the letter writer was arguing at her school that they should not advertise our upcoming case study workshop at a nearby campus because they could not support our racist policies. Egad! What had I wrought?

Well, to cut to the chase, I wrote back these words:

"Thank you for your concern regarding the issue of racism in the case called 'A Case of Cheating?' My apologies for taking so long to respond to your letter. This case is based on an actual incident and was written for a series of brown bag lunches [for faculty]. As you know, cases are designed or chosen to promote the analysis of serious often-controversial issues. Indeed, [at the National Center for Case Study Teaching in Science] we have cases dealing with cloning, stem cell research, abortion, global warming, the Tuskegee syphilis project, and a host of other sensitive issues. Discussion of race and culture is an important part of the cheating case, since understanding the cultural expectations and background of students lead to improved teaching. This case also presents opportunities for faculty to discuss how to deal with problems among students in small group settings. Given your concern however about misunderstanding regarding the use of this case, I will create a teaching note to accompany this case.

So, let me emphasize a couple of points, starting with a question: First, does it matter that this is a true incident? I think it does. This cheating scenario is exactly the type of a problem that can crop up in any classroom. This case is not a figment of a case writer's imagination. It is real. Given that, there follows a fundamental question that has to be addressed by the teacher: Is her solution going to be colored by ethnic considerations and all of the terribly thorny issues that lie in wait for the unwary tourist? Or not? In fact, that is a fundamental question that must be considered in this case.

Other questions are also important. The behavior of the teacher and the teaching method she employs are prime targets for discussion. Then there is the matter of establishing adequate grounds for determining if cheating has occurred, and so forth.

But there is the larger issue, which is the reason that I bring it to the attention of the readers of this journal. The letter writer seems to have missed the reason that case studies are written at all.

Case studies typically do not promulgate a particular viewpoint about a subject. They may, however, take a particular stance on an issue—one the author does not necessarily personally support or believe in—to challenge students to examine a difficult subject from all vantage points.

As I mentioned in my response to the letter writer, cases exist on all sorts of subjects—the more controversial the better, if we believe the students who sit through them. Abortion, cloning, AIDS, biological warfare, euthanasia, global warming, genetic engineering—bring 'em on! In fact, if the case doesn't have the societal issues embedded within it, the student interest drops greatly. Our job, it seems to me, is not to shy away from such subjects where science intersects with societal problems but to engage students with real-life situations. Surely, we are clever enough as teachers to teach science in context, aren't we? Tell me I am not wrong. If we are to believe the surveys, students frequently leave the sciences exactly for this reason—because we eschew such real-life topics. Thankfully, the National Academy of Sciences in its plea for "Standards" recognizes such folly and argues strongly for integration of science with other disciplines. Would that it were so.

So, back to the letter writer: Who cannot sympathize with her plea for the abolishment of racial stereotyping? But the best way to attack the problem is to examine specific cases in which the issue may arise and deal with it—fairly and honestly—and recognize that in many decisions that race is *not* involved at all.

Ignoring controversial topics and striking a politically correct pose in our thinking does *not* solve the problem. Where is the learning in that?

Section XVII

How to Write Case Study Teaching Notes

Cases aren't much good without teaching notes. I recall a case study by Michael Hudecki (*Journal of College Science Teaching* 31: 57–60, 2001) that was nothing more than a single paragraph taken from the *New York Times* reporting on research involving a study of memory loss in mice. The study had implications for patients suffering from Alzheimer's disease. Looking at the newspaper paragraph did not help me in the least to figure how Mike used this in the classroom. It was only his detailed case study notes (basically, a lesson plan) that allowed me to understand how he handled the case and for me to see how I might do it too. In the chapter in this section I suggest that we can use the business school model for writing teaching notes. Indeed, at this point in the book, the reader who has read some of the cases that I include throughout should well be acquainted with the tactic.

And All That Jazz

An Essay Extolling the Virtues of Writing Case Teaching Notes

By Clyde Freeman Herreid

There was something in Bobby that wanted to do it all. He wanted to play the part, dance the part, conduct the orchestra, produce the play. It was a kind of an obsession with him.

—Robert Whitehead

Bob Fosse died on the streets of Washington, D.C., on September 23, 1987, in the arms of his dancer wife, Gwen Verdon. He was within sight of the National Theater where his dancers were dressing for a revival of his show *Sweet Charity.*

Fosse was a Broadway legend, starting his career as a teenage hoofer in Chicago. As fine a dancer as he was, it was as a choreographer that he made his mark with shows like *Cabaret, Pajama Game, Damn Yankees, Chicago, Pippin,* and, of course, *All that Jazz.*

Choreographers are the case teachers of the dance world. The modern greats like Martha Graham, George Balanchine, Jerome Robbins, and Agnes de Mille take a musical score, a line of a poem, or an image and create a terpsichorean masterpiece that can inspire, provoke, titillate, irritate, or enrapture audiences. Unlike past masters, today's choreographers leave notes and videos to help others see their vision.

There is something ironic, though, about giving explicit instructions on how to play or dance to jazz. My father, a vaudevillian and jazz pianist who banged about the country with dance bands in the 1930s, put it to me this way: Jazz is for the moment. It should never be written down or recorded. It is a once-in-a-lifetime thing. It's never the same the next time

Broadway legend Bob Fosse rehearsing with dancers. Choreographers, like Fosse, are the case teachers of the dance world.

you play it. It is for the musicians who play it and the listeners who are there at the moment. It is for the now. The moment that you regiment it, it's no longer jazz.

And yet, we do record it and regiment it, at least to varying degrees. Even jazz musicians need a melody line to guide them through their riffs. So it is with case teachers. That's what case teaching notes are—a melody line to show the way. They can be used as gospel, as a big band leader might insist, or ignored entirely.

Most of us seek a little guidance, especially newcomers, folks who like the style but cannot spend years in a Chicago bar or a New Orleans brothel to capture the rhythm and tone of a Jelly Roll Morton. Perhaps we are not destined to be a Dizzy Gillespe, but we still can learn how to play a reasonable jazz number or run a case. We don't have to accept Louie Armstrong's dreaded pronouncement in reply to the question, What is jazz?—"Man, if you gotta ask, you'll never know."

Ignoring Satchmo's admonition, or at least not generalizing it to include case study teaching, I have in several columns attempted to answer the question, What is a case? Here, I commit the further effrontery of suggesting how one can help others teach cases by writing good teaching notes. After all, as teachers, explaining is our business. So let's have at it. Here is how you can create teaching notes so that people can run a case, even if they can't be the Bob Fosses of the classroom.

How to Write Teaching Notes

The tradition of including teaching notes along with cases is long standing. They were included practically from the beginning for one key reason: New case teachers wanted them! The naive reader wished to know what the author had intended, not that he expected to follow the author's intentions slavishly, but at least he didn't want to miss some key point.

Moreover, the novice needed all the help she could get. She welcomed the views and experience of the seasoned veteran who knew the strengths and weaknesses of the case. She wished to know the traps and pitfalls to avoid, places where students were apt to travel, the quagmires that were ahead. She needed notes, not just as a security blanket, but needed them to survive.

Teaching notes are not only for the tyro; veterans find them helpful too. Seasoned practitioners use them to explore possible angles they might have missed. They can examine any new case much more rapidly, especially unfamiliar material, if they have the author's roadmap in hand.

To see what teaching notes are all about, one can do no better than to turn to the business-school approach. Cases have been used there since the early days of the century. So the headings below are derived from that venue.

Outline for Writing Case Teaching Notes

I. Introduction/Background

All teachers are helped by knowing how the author has put a case to use in the past, in which course they have tried it, where in the semester it has been used, and what type of background the students will have when they encounter the case. This information belongs in this section. It doesn't mean that the case is limited to the author's experiences, but it gives the reader a chance to understand why some topics and readings are included and why others are not. Thus, the instructor interested in using the case can adjust his or she style, reading list, or comments appropriately.

II. Objectives of the Case

This section is important. Seldom do instructors in traditional courses take the time to think about what they are really trying to do in the lecture classroom—except to give students the facts, the principles of the field. Most lectures (at least in science classes) are at the lowest level of Bloom's Taxonomy of Knowledge. Instructors often think they have done their job when the students can regurgitate the details of the lecture on a multiple-choice test. The true responsibility is not so easily discharged or evaded by case study teachers. No, they must deal directly with the meaning of the information in the context of real-life situations. Ideally, teachers should be able to list exactly what the students should know and be able to do after they have finished the case that they didn't know and couldn't do before they went through the case. This is the purpose of this section of the teaching notes: to force the instructor to be explicit about his or her goals and objectives.

This isn't the place for platitudes, such as, "the students will learn how to think critically" (don't we wish?). This is the place for specific statements, such as these examples: Students finishing the case will be able to (1) take the data in table 3 and graph it appropriately, (2) write a critical essay about the pros and cons of genetic engineering in crops, (3) write a persuasive letter to their congressional representative about the benefits of cloning, (4) solve the equation $p2 + 2pq + q2 = 1$ given the following information . . . , (5) design an experiment that will test the following proposition . . . , and so on.

III. Major Issues

In business-case literature this section is referred to as blocks of analysis or issues for discussion. Under this heading the case author should identify the major issues in the case that the students should analyze. The case author should clearly indicate which issues he thinks will (should) come up and what information he expects to help extract from the students. There may be explicit questions that must be addressed. If so, then the author should give a synopsis of a reasonable answer. This part of the teaching notes is apt to be the most extensively developed.

IV. Classroom Management

This section is a must, for it tells the reader just how you used the case in a classroom situation. The explanation must be presented in detail. What did you do first, second, and last? How long did certain activities take, for example, 15 minutes for a group activity followed by a 5-minute summary of each group's findings. Put it all down; what appears second nature to you will be inscrutable to others.

All cases can be run with different strategies. The traditional discussion method employed by law and business schools is only one approach. Using small groups, such as in Problem-Based Learning or other cooperative-learning methods, is another favorite approach. Whatever method you use, spell it out.

There may be limitations as to the length of the case and notes. For instance, the *Journal of College Science Teaching* has limits for articles in the range of 2,500 words. Many cases and notes clearly exceed this. A solution is to publish the case and a truncated version of the notes and have a more detailed description of the latter on a website such as the National Science Foundation-supported site at the State University of New York at Buffalo: *http:ublib. buffalo.edu/libraries/projects/cases/case.html*.

Under the heading "Classroom Management," the author must indicate what pre-class assignments he or she may have given before the students see the case. If the instructor is using the discussion method, it is extremely helpful to have a list of questions that may be used for study and during class. Also, this is the place to put any follow-up assignments that you might suggest be used after a discussion of the case is finished. Assignments may include:

- *Study Questions.* These are questions that are listed at the end of various sections of the case to help students focus on particular critical issues. There should not be so many as to overwhelm the student. These questions may or may not be directly addressed in the general discussion of the case. Nonetheless, they are there to serve as signposts of important topics. The teaching notes should at least briefly state reasonable answers to these queries.

- *Questions in the Classroom.* Teaching notes frequently provide a list of questions that can be asked in any discussion of the case. Naturally, these are chosen to get at certain prime issues in provocative ways and are designed to facilitate discussion. Sometimes they are categorized as Introductory Questions, Challenge Questions, Decision Forcing Questions, and Summary Questions.

Generally, case practitioners in science classes find that it is best to first ask questions that get at the facts of the case. So, if we are dealing with a case on global warming, early in the discussion an instructor would surely ask: What is global warming? What is the evidence that it is occurring? What is the counter evidence? Only after such factual questions are addressed is it safe to turn to social issues.

To illustrate the dangers of starting with the more social or personal issues, let's take a case that two colleagues and I wrote called Bad Blood, which we published in *JCST* in 1994. This deals with the Tuskegee Syphilis Project, where African Americans in Alabama were denied treatment for the disease. Consider what might happen to the discussion if we started with an opening question such as, "Do you believe that there was racial prejudice involved in the Tuskegee study?" Chances are you might never get to the science at all! My rule of thumb is: When dealing with controversial social issues, cover the science first. This sets the tone for a reasonable discussion and guarantees that you will cover the facts as well as the emotional issues.

- *Board work.* Students new to case study work often wonder what they have learned from a given case. They are apt to think that it is merely hot air they are hearing from their compatriots. There is one good way to overcome this attitude. Write important concepts on the board or overhead projector as they

emerge from the discussion. The very act of writing key points says that the instructor values a student's contribution, especially if the name or initials of the contributor are jotted down next to the idea. Board work gives structure to the discussion, demonstrating it is not aimless rambling in which we are engaged. Students who are passionate about notes will cherish you.

If, as I am arguing, blackboard work is essential to the success of a case and forms a pivotal part of determining how a student sees its worth, then it follows that an instructor had better give serious thought to how she is going to lay things out ahead of time. He or she might decide that factual points should be written on the left side of the board, perhaps developing a concept map as points are brought up. Later in the discussion, when the conversation turns to the possible decisions that the protagonists in the case might make, the teacher might plan to list these on the right side of the board under headings such as Short-Term Solutions and Long-Term Solutions. The pros and cons of these topics can be interspersed along the way. In short, if board work is important to your case (and I am arguing it should be, especially if you are using the discussion method), then give the case reader a hint or two how you do it here in the Case Notes.

- *Closure.* Most students want closure on a case. They want someone to pull together the fragments and tidbits of the discussion and ignore any silliness that happened during the hour. They don't want a canned speech so much as a true summary of what went on. This can be done by the professor or a student.

Teaching notes are often enhanced by a short summary statement about the case, including how the case impinges on other topics in the course or on problems in society. Thus, after a case on global warming, a summarizer might note how the ambiguities in the case fit the general pattern of environmental problems in that we frequently do not have enough information and still must make decisions with imperfect data.

Not all case writers are keen on closure. Some prefer that cases be left hanging, like an unresolved C 7th chord. They like leaving the students with the nagging problem, believing that the students will continue to ponder the question further. (Hope springs eternal.)

V. References

Everyone appreciates a list of references to follow up particular lines of thought, especially if they are annotated. Today, it is especially valuable to include internet addresses as well. Don't leave these out of your lovingly developed teaching notes.

AND ALL THAT JAZZ

So I return to the bistros and dance halls and theater lights. Case writers are indeed much like choreographers as they lay their plans. Both recognize that no performance is like any other: the audience matters—a great deal; some days are good; some days are bad. But when things are going well, there is a synergy that can occur that transforms any work when a performer is ignited by the excitement provided by the audience.

Like jazz, cases are never played the same way in any two settings. That is what makes them unique. They are for the now—for the moment. Sometimes they are unforgettable.

Section XVIII

How to Grade Students Using Case-Based Teaching

Grading students is an onerous task. It seems particularly irksome for beginning case study teachers. They are especially bothered by the prospect of grading participation in class discussions. Coupled with this, they are not sure what kinds of tests they ought to be giving to their students. The students in turn are perplexed by what should they be getting out of the case study experience and what to study for exams.

In this section I deal with the issues of peer evaluation and grading participation. But I do have biases on the other issues too. I argue that *if you teach with cases you should test with cases*; nothing, it seems to me, is more unreasonable than to train students with one method in the classroom and then turn around and evaluate their performance with another method. I have seen many examples of this duplicitous process in my career. I cannot for the life of me understand why faculty would do this. I think it must be due to carelessness rather than meanness.

On the issue of what students should study: Obviously, with enough experience they will probably figure it out. And so will you. But by that time, the semester might be over. To help bridge the difficulty, many teachers choose to briefly summarize their cases to emphasize essential points. Further, they tell them straight out at the beginning of the semester what to expect—perhaps giving them examples of questions or even showing them past tests. It will be harder for you to do this if this is your first time doing case studies because it is quite possible that you will not know what to do yourself. But try to think ahead and help them all the way along. Have pity.

When Justice Peeks

Evaluating Students in Case Study Teaching

By Clyde Freeman Herreid

n mid-December 2004, in the wake of the great "hanging chad" debate when the fate of the U.S. presidency had not yet been decided, politicians and demonstrators were in the streets and in front of the camera calling for "justice!" The courtroom had replaced the ballot box in deciding who would win and who would lose. While the patient public waited for judicial wisdom and a sensible conclusion, we all hoped for a nonpartisan ruling—the sort of judgment one would expect from an impartial judiciary. This is the ideal, isn't it?

Somewhere around every courthouse in America, I suppose you can find the symbol of that legal ideal: a statue of a robed woman holding the scales of justice in one hand and a sword in the other to smite the transgressors of the law. The lady of justice comes to us moderns from the pre-Hellenic pantheon. She is Themis, adviser to Zeus, who became an oracle at Delphi and was known as a goddess of divine justice. There are other pretenders to the scales and the sword, including the Egyptian goddess Maat and the Roman goddess Justitia, but I stand with the Greeks on this one. Themis it is, and she is without corruption, avarice, prejudice, or favor. She is blindfolded. This is to ensure that she is impartial and fair. But can she be fair without peeking?

GRADES AND EVALUATION

The thing I most dislike about teaching is assigning grades. In one breath I know what I mean when I do it—John gets an A and Sarah a C. In the next breath I think it ridiculous, for I do not know what John and

Sarah know or what they grasped. Moreover, both John and Sarah may actually think I know what I am doing, yet hate me for it. And maybe I deserve it—sometimes.

Evaluation is an odious affair. I can even remember a time when faculty refused to do it wholesale. During the Vietnam War when pubescent youths were conscripted into the armed forces if they didn't maintain their grades, there were faculty who abandoned grading altogether, giving all-comers As so they would not have "blood on their hands." They couldn't abide sending young men into battle because of their academic misdeeds. Instead, other men died in their place. We are still laboring with the grade inflation that resulted.

I recall the arguments of those turbulent days. We teachers should forsake evaluation altogether. Our job should be solely to teach. We argued with a certainty that only young faculty can muster. Our role was to act as a library—a source for people to gain wisdom and to leave enriched. Let others judge the result of our educational endeavors. No more this Janus face looking back and front, welcoming our students yet looking away from them when they need our support. The dual role of faculty as instructor and evaluator is odious indeed.

The voices of those days are gone, and we have not shed the onerous duty of evaluation. Given our unhappy lot, what are we to do with this unenviable task, especially when we are thrown into the unfamiliar and discomforting role of evaluating students in a case study class? If we think there is uncertainty in the normal classroom, what an imbroglio lies in wait for us in the case study classroom.

EVALUATION IN THE CASE STUDY CLASSROOM

How do you grade students in classes with case teaching? There are a host of possibilities. I'm only going to deal with a couple. Let's start with the toughest.

- *Evaluating class discussion*. Business school case teachers do it all the time. It's not uncommon for them to base the final course grade on 50% class participation. And this with 50–70 students in a class! This sends shudders up the spines of most science teachers. Yet, what's so tough about the concept? We are constantly making judgments about the verbal statements of our colleagues, politicians, and even administrators. Why can't we do it for classroom contributions?

Most of our discomfort comes from the subjective nature of the act, something that we scientists work hard to avoid in our work-a-day world. It may be that we are even predisposed to become scientists because we are looking for a structured and quantifiable world. Flowing from this subjective quandary is the fact that we feel we must be able to justify our grades to the students. We are decidedly uncomfortable if we can't show them the numbers. This is one of the reasons that multiple-choice questions have such appeal for some faculty.

But let's take a look at how the business school people evaluate case discussion. Some of them try to do it in the classroom, making written notes even as the discussion unfolds, using a seating chart, and calling on perhaps 25 students in a period. As you might expect, this usually interferes with running an effective discussion. Other instructors tape-record the discussion and listen to it later in thoughtful contemplation. Most folks, however, sit down shortly after their classes with seating chart in hand and reflect on the discussion. They rank student contributions into categories of excellent, good, or bad, or they may use numbers to evaluate the students from 1 to 4, with 4 being excellent. They may give negative evaluations to people who weren't prepared or were absent. These numbers are tallied up at the end of the semester to calculate the grade. And that's as quantified as it gets.

I especially like mathematician/philosopher Blaise Pascal's view of evaluation: "We first distinguish grapes from among fruits, then muscat grapes, then those from Condrieu, then from Desargues, then the particular graft. Is that all? Has a vine ever produced two bunches alike, and has any bunch produced two grapes alike?

"I have never judged anything in exactly the same way, " Pascal continues. "I cannot judge a work while doing it. I must do as painters do and stand back, but not too far. How far then? Guess . . . ."

- **Ask for a product.** The simplest solution to casework evaluation is to forget classroom participation and grade everything on the basis of familiar criteria, such as exams and papers. This puts professors back in customary territory without the sweat of novelty. Even business and law school professors use this strategy as part of their grades. I'm all for this. In fact, I always ask for some written analysis in the form of journals, papers, and reports. Along with an exam, these are my sole bases for grades. I don't lose sleep over evaluating class participation.

A word about exams: You can give any sort of exam in a case-based course, including multiple choice, but doesn't it make sense to have at least part of the exam a case? If you have used cases all semester and trained students in case analysis, surely you should consider a case-based test. Too often we test on different things than we have taught.

- **Peer evaluation.** Some of the best case studies involve small group work and group projects. In fact, I strongly believe teaching cases this way is the most user-friendly for science faculty and the most rewarding for the students. Nonetheless, even some aficionados of group work don't like group projects. They say, how do you know who's doing the work? Even if they ask for a group project, they argue against grading it. They

---

TABLE 1.

Peer Evaluation Form

Name _____   Group # _____

This is an opportunity to evaluate the contributions of your teammates to group projects during the semester. Please write the names of your teammates in the spaces below and give them the scores that you believe they earned. If you are in a group of five people, you each will have 40 points to distribute. You don't give yourself points. (If you are in a group of four, you'll have 30 to give away. In a group of six you'll have 50 points, etc.) If you believe that everyone contributed equally to the group work, then you should give everyone 10 points. If everyone in the group feels the same way, you all will receive an average of 10 points. Be fair in your assessments, but if someone in your group didn't contribute adequately, give him or her fewer points. If someone worked harder than the rest, give him or her more than 10 points.

There are some rules that you must observe in assigning points:
- You cannot give anyone in your group more than 15 points.
- You do not have to assign all of your points.
- Anyone receiving an average of less than seven points will fail the course.
- Don't give students a grade that he or she doesn't deserve.

	Group members	Score
1.	_____	_____
2.	_____	_____
3.	_____	_____
4.	_____	_____
5.	_____	_____
6.	_____	_____

Please indicate why you gave someone less than 10 points.

Please indicate why you gave someone more than 10 points.

If you were to assign points to yourself, what do you feel you deserve? Why?

---

rely strictly on individual marks for a final grade determination. I'm on the other side of the fence. I believe that great projects can come from teams, and if you don't grade the work, what is the incentive for participating? Moreover, employers report that most people are fired because they can't get along with other people. Not all of us are naturally team players. Practice helps. So, I'm all for group work including teamwork during quizzes where groups almost invariably perform better than the best individuals. But we have to build in safeguards like peer evaluation.

"Social loafers" and "compulsive workhorses" exist in every class. When you form groups such as those in Problem-Based Learning (PBL) and Team Learning (the best ways to teach cases, in my judgment), you must set up a system to monitor the situation. In PBL it is common to have tutors who can make evaluations. Still, I believe it is essential to use peer evaluations. I use a method that I picked up from Larry Michaelsen in the School of Management at the University of Oklahoma.

At the beginning of every course I explain the use of these anonymous peer evaluations. I show students the form that they will fill out at the end of the semester (see Table 1). Then they will be asked to name their teammates and give each one the number of points that reflects their contributions to group projects throughout the course. Say the group has five team members—then each person would have 40 points to give to the other four members of his or her team. If a student feels that everyone has contributed equally to the group projects, then he or she should give each teammate 10 points. Obviously, if everyone in the team feels the same way about everyone else, they all will get an average score of 10 points. Persons with an average of 10 points will receive 100 percent of the group score for any group project.

But, suppose that things aren't going well. Maybe John has not pulled his weight in the group projects and ends up with an average score of 8, and Sarah has done more than her share and receives a 12. What then? Well, John gets only 80% of any group grade and Sarah receives 120%.

There are some additional rules that I use. One is that a student cannot give anyone more than 15 points. This is to stop a student from saving his friend John by giving him 40 points. Another is that any student receiving an average of seven or less will fail my course. This is designed to stop a student from doing nothing in the group because he is simply trying to slip by with a barely passing grade and is willing to undermine the group effort.

Here are some observations after many years of using peer evaluations:

Most students are reasonable. Although they are inclined to be generous, most give scores between 8 and 12.

Occasionally, I receive a set of scores where one isn't consistent with the others. For example, a student may get a 10, 10, 11, and a 5. Obviously, something is amiss here. When this happens, I set the odd number aside and use the other scores for the average.

About one group in five initially will have problems because one or two people are not participating adequately or are habitually late or absent. These problems can be corrected.

It is essential that you give a practice peer evaluation about one-third or one-half of the way through the semester. The students fill these out and you tally them and give the students their average scores. You must carefully remind everyone what these numbers mean, and if they don't like the results, they must do something to improve their scores. I tell them that it is no use blaming their group members for their perceptions. They must fix things, perhaps by talking to the group and asking how to compensate for their previous weakness. Also, I will always speak privately to any student who is in danger. These practice evaluations almost always significantly improve the group performance. Tardiness virtually stops and attendance is at least 95%.

When I look back at the essential methods of case evaluation, I am struck by the fact that they are a mixture of objective and subjective elements. Some things are readily quantifiable and others are a struggle. Just as in courts of law where there are conflicting personalities, evidence, and judgment calls, teachers carry their own prejudices and experiences into the classroom. The image of a blindfolded justice rendering verdicts in an unbiased, impartial way has always struck me as unrealistic and, in fact, impossible. Justice, to be perfectly honest, must peek now and then and see who the participants are and what their histories are before making a judgment. So should teachers.

Section XIX

Assessment and Evaluation of the Case Study Process

Case-based teaching has been around for about a century. Its virtues are widely lauded throughout the fields of law, business, and public policy, where literally thousands of cases have been published. Nonetheless, in these fields assessment studies are few in number or nonexistent. For that matter, the formal assessment of the lecture method has been poorly studied too. We know that swarms of students do poorly, without a clear set of reasons why. Our educational system is a Darwinian process and we teachers are the survivors. Not all are so lucky.

Here is where we are on the assessment question: Some data are available for the case study approach in science, especially for Problem-Based Learning. And the news is good as seen from a few personal highlights and numerous literature citations.

- I compared 20 years of data in my general biology lecture course with those from a team learning/case study–based course that I taught on the same subject. Attendance in the lecture course varied from 67–85% throughout the semester while the team-learning/case course was 95–100%. The average grade was a C for the lecture course and B+ for the team-learning/case course.

- I asked the Survey Research Laboratory at SUNY/University at Buffalo and an independent research firm, Ciurczak & Co., to survey the success of the case method in faculty trained at workshops of the National Center for Case Study Teaching in Science. In May 2002, they reported data from 152 faculty across the United States, testing the use of case studies in their classes:
  - 97% reported students learned new ways to think about an issue due to the use of case studies.
  - 96% reported students receive additional educational benefits from the use of case studies.
  - 95% reported students take a more active part in the learning process when they use case studies.
  - 92% reported students are more engaged in classes compared to when no case studies are used in that class.
  - 84% reported students in classes using case studies are glad case studies are being used.

This work has been repeated by Aman Yadav and colleagues at Michigan State University with similar findings and is mentioned in chapters 59 and 60 by Mary Lundeberg and Aman Yadav.

- Dinan and Frydrychowski (1995) reported that using Team Learning (one method of case study teaching) in an organic chemistry class at Canisius College in Buffalo, New York, actually covered more material and their students received higher grades in a national exam than when they used the lecture method.

- At the University of Pennsylvania, Diamond and Kozak (1994) used team learning with case studies in chemical engineering for non-science undergraduates. Students taking exams in groups performed 15% higher then when tested as individuals. Pre- and posttests using a Scientific Process Survey indicated strong statistically significant differences in student knowledge in experimental design, statistics, and scientific process by the end of the course.

- Cliff and Wright (1996), at Niagara University and Canisius College, respectively, used the Directed Case method in an undergraduate course and reported the students said the use of cases made it easier to learn the subject (74%), and deepened their understanding (70%). Statistical differences were measured showing improvement in student test scores when cases were used.

- At State University of New York (SUNY), Scannapieco and Herreid (1994) used case studies with team learning in a dental class. They found similar learning on standardized tests with the case versus lecture approach but a remarkable difference in attendance (100% versus 50%) and a much better performance in clinical activities with the case approach.

- Walters (1999) used cases in an endocrinology class at Tulane University School of Medicine and reported enthusiastic feedback. Student ratings improved when cases were integrated into the standard lecture course.

And of course we have the overwhelming evidence of the superiority of active learning strategies over the lecture method seen in the papers below.

- A meta-analysis of over 1,200 studies in which researchers compared the performance of students educated using cooperative learning strategies (including case studies) versus those taught by the lecture method shows: In verbal, mathematical, and physical skills, cooperative learning promoted greater learning and greater retention. Students enjoyed the experience more, had a better attitude toward the subject, developed better social skills, became more articulate, and became more tolerant of differing viewpoints than with the lecture style (Johnson and Johnson 1989; 1993).

- A multiyear study involving several faculty and hundreds of students was published by Udovic and colleagues (2002). Lecture teaching was compared to active learning methods showing dramatic improvements in conceptual understanding of the material with the latter.

- Hake (1998) compared data from 6,000 students in introductory physics classes and reported students enrolled in lecture-intensive courses perform poorly on a variety of measures as compared to students in interactive-engagement courses.

In this section we tackle the question of assessment again, for we simply do not have enough information. There are so many different types of case study methods with different strengths and weaknesses. And there are so many ways to go wrong when one is trying to run studies on people.

REFERENCES

Cliff, W. H., and A. W. Wright. 1996. Directed case study method for teaching human anatomy and physiology. *Advances in Physiology Education*15: S19–S28

Diamond, S. L., and A. I. Kozak. 1994. A course on biotechnology and society. *Chemical Engineering Education*. 28 (Spring): 140–144.

Dinan, F. J., and V. A. Frydrychowski. 1995. A team learning method for organic chemistry. *Journal of Chemical Education* 72(5): 429–431.

Hake, R. R. 1998. Interactive-engagement vs. traditional methods: A six-thousand-student survey of mechanics test data for introductory physics courses. *American Journal of Physics* 66: 64–74.

Johnson, D. W., and R. T. Johnson. 1989. *Cooperation and competition: Theory and research*. Edina, MN: Interaction Book Co.

Johnson, D. W., and R. T. Johnson. 1993. Cooperative learning: Where we have been, where we are going. *Cooperative Learning and College Teaching Newsletter* 3(2): 6–9.

Scannapieco, F. A., and C. F. Herreid. 1994. An application of team learning in dental education. *Journal of Dental Education* 58: 843–848.

Udovic, D., D. Morris, A. Dickman, J. Postlewait, and P. Wetherwax. 2002. Workshop biology: Demonstrating the effectiveness of active learning in an introductory biology course. *Bioscience* 52: 272–281.

Walters, M. R. 1999. Case-stimulated learning within endocrine physiology lectures: An approach applicable to other disciplines. *Advances in Physiology Education* 276: S74–S78.

Coplas de Ciego

By Clyde Freeman Herreid

I just received an e-mail message from Angel M. Pastor in the Departamento de Fisiologia y Zoologia Facultad de Biologia in Seville, Spain. He wrote to me about the medieval Spanish custom in which blind storytellers went from town to town telling stories (sung as mantras) of murder, impassioned love, and pestilence to the villagers as a means of sustaining themselves. The stories were called coplas de ciego, or blind tales.

The performances could be elaborate, sometimes involving musical instruments, sometimes accompanied

by *lazarillos* (guiding children) who would dance and collect coins, and sometimes incorporating a cartooned story. For the presentation, the storyteller would synchronize his monotonic story by precisely pointing with a walking stick. At this point in his description of the coplas de ciego, Professor Pastor rhetorically asked me how they could point precisely? Maybe they were not that blind, he said. And he suggested that maybe they were like us professors who vaguely point in the direction of slides as we try to convey explanations drawn from our yellowish brains.

Let me carry the metaphor further. So often in classes we tell our own coplas de ciego. As teachers, we weave our own tales about the rules and facts of science. We go blithely on our way, blind to the audience, gesturing with our walking sticks (LED pointers) at our PowerPoint cartoons.

Unlike the Spanish storytellers, who got feedback from their audience in the form of coins, we teachers seldom construct a way of determining how we are doing. We are oblivious to the pleadings of people like Patricia Cross and Tom Angelo, gurus of classroom assessment, who argue that we must gauge our teaching effectiveness by monitoring what is going on in the classroom—not just with tests, but with all sorts of classroom research techniques. As Homer Simpson, would say, "D'oh!"

Which brings me to two points: Once again, Nancy Schiller and I, directors of the National Center for Case Study Teaching in Science, are privileged to edit and publish in *JCST* some wonderful stories in the form of case studies—perhaps not about impassioned love, murder, and pestilence, but exciting ones just the same. We hope you can use them in your classrooms.

But, we have a special plea to make; we have a crying need to assess the effectiveness of using case study teaching. Despite the fact that case study teaching has been used for more than a hundred years in law, business, and other disciplines, there have been few attempts to evaluate the method's effectiveness in science teaching. This needs to be corrected—for our own good. We need data and evidence to show our colleagues and granting agencies the virtues of case study teaching.

If we are going to argue that the storytelling approach has value—not that it is just value-added, but is a better way to teach—we must collect data on its effect on student learning and attitudes toward science. We must collect the coins after the tale is told. We need to know how many there are. None? Or dozens? Only then will we know if we are telling blind tales or tales with a vision.

Assessment of Case Study Teaching

Where Do We Go From Here?
Part I

By Mary A. Lundeberg and Aman Yadav

WHY DO ASSESSMENT?

In recent years, a number of National Science Foundation and National Research Council reports have advocated the need to improve undergraduate science instruction and enhance science literacy for all students (NRC 1996; 2002). Many undergraduates, especially women and traditionally underrepresented groups, avoid higher-level science and mathematics. Several students who switch from science and mathematics majors in college report "poor teaching by faculty" as a significant reason for switching (Seymour and Hewitt 1997, p. 32). Examples of poor teaching in the science fields at the undergraduate level include an emphasis on memorizing facts, lack of application of concepts, dullness, and failure to encourage connections among concepts (Kardash and Wallace 2001).

One effort to improve the learning of science is through case study teaching. Teachers use realistic or true narratives to provide opportunities for students to integrate multiple sources of information in an authentic context, and may engage students with ethical and societal problems related to their discipline (Lundeberg, Levin, and Harrington 1999; Herreid 1994). Although such methods are being used in some university-level courses in the fields of science, mathematics, business, and education, relatively little empirical research has examined whether and how these case-based teaching approaches have the desired effects of promoting deep understanding, enabling transfer of ideas to new contexts, and making learning more motivating or valuable for certain student populations, especially traditionally underrepresented groups (Lundeberg, Levin, and Harrington 1999; Lundeberg et al. 2002). What happens in classes that use case study teaching? Do students learn more in case-based science courses? Are they able to make more connections among concepts? Can they apply these concepts to real-life situations? How might case study teaching in science promote scientific literacy in students?

We propose that empirical research, particularly well-designed classroom experiments, has the potential to lead to a strong line of research regarding case-based teaching in science. In this chapter, we illustrate how such experiments might be

	Unit A: Infectious Disease	Unit B: Genetics
	TABLE 1. **Research design involving two instructors and two classes.**	
Class 1	Use of case-based instruction	Use of traditional lecture method or other control
Class 2	Use of traditional lecture method or other control	Use of case-based instruction

done, describing what needs to be measured and how this approach is superior to much of the current research on case study teaching. We urge faculty to think systematically about principles of scientific inquiry in education (Shavelson, Towne, and the Committee on Scientific Principles for Education Research 2002), to use a research design that will provide valid and reliable evidence for claims they want to make and/or processes they want to better understand, to carefully consider measurement issues, and to avoid common problems in evaluation.

Why Do Investigations in Classrooms?

Shavelson, Towne, and the Committee on Scientific Principles for Education Research (2002, p.2) propose that the basic core of scientific inquiry is the same in all fields, including education, and that the scientific enterprise is guided by the following set of norms, or principles, that shape inquiry:

- Pose significant questions that can be investigated empirically.
- Link research to relevant theory.
- Use methods that permit direct investigation of the question.
- Provide a coherent and explicit chain of reasoning.
- Replicate and generalize across studies.
- Disclose research to encourage professional scrutiny and critique.

Linking classroom investigations of case study teaching to prior research and relevant theories is essential for posing significant questions that lead to quality research. Research questions fall into three categories:

1. Description—What is happening?
2. Cause—Is there a systematic effect?
3. Process or mechanism—Why or how is it happening? (Shavelson, Towne, and the Committee on Scientific Principles for Education Research 2002, p. 99)

Ideally, research questions drive the research design, and methods for investigation are chosen to answer the questions and eliminate alternative explanations. However, one crucial difference in educational research is the importance of context in inquiry. Although scientific research in the lab generally follows a particular paradigm and is carefully controlled to advance or dispute a specific theory, classroom research presents complexity that is not readily illuminated by a single theory nor measured by a single method. "Most educational interventions can probably be captured better with diverse theorizing and multiple methods…. Educational intervention research should be diversely theoretical because single theories never fully capture complex phenomena" (Pressley, Graham, and Harris, Forthcoming).

Berliner (2002, p. 18) called education research the "hardest science of all." He pointed out that educational researchers face particular problems that are context sensitive, which limit generalizations and theory building. Any teaching situation has many variables that influence the interactions among and between the teachers and students. Such variables include students' motivation to learn, their socioeconomic status, whether they have been given choices among cases, and their academic major. Indeed, research in education needs to "account for influential contextual factors within the process of inquiry and in understanding the extent to which findings can be generalized" (Shavelson, Towne, and the Committee on Scientific Principles for Education Research 2002, p.80).

Establishing strong research depends on selecting insightful questions that fill a gap in the knowledge base, by referring to prior research, relevant theory, and classroom practice (Shavelson, Towne, and the Committee on Scientific Principles for Education Research 2002). Researchers studying case-based science teaching might ask multiple questions in conducting rigorous evaluation research. For example, in seeking to understand whether case-based teaching had an effect—caused improvements in the outcome of interest, such as motivation or student understanding—a classroom experiment that minimizes unconfounded comparisons would add to the knowledge base. However, to capture the context of how cases were used in the classrooms under investigation, detailed descriptions ("What is happening?") and investigations into how case-based teaching influenced outcomes ("How is it happening?") are necessary (Shavelson, Towne, and the Committee on Scientific Principles for Education Research 2002).

Classroom-based experiments generally have more external validity than randomized experiments in education; university settings rarely permit random assignment to courses, and research conducted within course settings may have very different results than educational research conducted within a laboratory setting (Lundeberg and Fox 1991). However, for researchers interested in designing classroom experiments, we caution them to pay attention to internal validity. Internal validity refers to how con-

fidently we can conclude that the change in the dependent variable was as a result of the treatment (independent variable) and not some extraneous variable (see Campbell and Stanley 1966 for explanations of the eight extraneous variables that can impact a study's internal validity—history, maturation, testing, instrumentation, statistical regression, selection, experimental mortality, and selection interactions). Pressley and Allington (1999, p. 4) also raised valid questions that might help researchers assess whether internal validity criteria have been met:

- Did the control group receive an intervention?
- Were the control participants exposed to the same material as the intervention participants?
- Was there counterbalancing of instructors and experimental condition?
- Were the treatment conditions explicitly described so that replicability studies could be carried out?
- Was there equivalent instructional time in the intervention and control treatments?
- Was there an evaluation of whether the intervention and control treatments were delivered as intended?
- Was the sample size sufficiently large to detect meaningful effects?
- Was the false-positive error rate controlled appropriately and were the analyses appropriate?
- Were the effect sizes reported?

RULES OF THUMB FOR DESIGNING A GOOD STUDY

To investigate the potential of emerging case-based approaches, it is important to develop theoretical understandings of case-based teaching in science, including theories of learning and problem solving in classroom settings. Researchers are advised to design a classroom experiment using counterbalancing to avoid confounding comparisons. A powerful classroom experiment also requires a careful consideration of measurement issues.

ONE EXAMPLE OF A GOOD STUDY DESIGN

A research design for a study involving two instructors teaching the same course to two different classes might look something like Table 1.

In this design, the two science classes are counterbalanced for the use of case-based instruction to teach units A and B. Thus, an instructor teaching Class 1 will teach Unit A (Infectious Disease) using the case-based method, while the instructor teaching Class 2 will be using a traditional lecture-based method (or another control such as a lab) to teach Unit A. When the two instructors teach Unit B (Genetics), the two instructors will switch the teaching method, with the students in Class 2 experiencing the case-based teaching and Class 1 being taught with a traditional method. Ideally, this would be replicated one more time during the semester with units C and D to add additional data. Thus, the units are balanced for the method of teaching (case-based versus lecture-based) to minimize potential instructor bias, balanced over two or more units to control for subject effects, and balanced over two courses containing different students to control for student effects. Such a research design isolates the impact of case-based instruction on students' conceptual understanding and may help avoid any instructor bias that might have been present had there been only one instructor.

HOW AND WHAT SHOULD WE MEASURE?

Research with case-based instruction goes beyond the research design. We need to consider how to assess the impact of case-based instruction on student understanding and be confident that our measures assess what it is that we want to assess. The development and use of methodologically sophisticated, qualitative methods—interviews, journal entries, observations and case studies of particular students—should be considered as alternatives to performance data, such as standardized objective tests or constructed case analysis tests. Such methods would allow us to access students' cognition and understanding of science concepts, and to understand more about how and why cases affect student understanding in science.

To assess the impact of case-based instruction, familiarize yourself with educational theories of student learning, and think carefully about what you want to know about how cases are potentially affecting students. Do you want to assess instructional outcomes such as student performance, and/or other outcomes such as motivation, persistence, and attendance? Do you wish to measure students' conceptual understanding and their ability to transfer their understanding to new contexts, rather than their ability to remember facts and figures? These kinds of assessment tools may not be readily available and are unlikely to be typical course exams provided by textbook companies. If you are going to develop open-ended assessments then you must use a reliable, valid rubric, give pre- and postassessments blind to the time of testing, and collect data demonstrating the reliability of the rating system. You should use multiple measures to provide more insightful kinds of evidence illuminating what (and how) cases may be affecting student performance. Be sure the measures can be replicated and have an absence of ceiling and floor effects.

We support the advice provided by Pressley, Graham, and Harris, (Forthcoming):

"As a general rule of thumb, the more implementation and process data collected, the better the chance of explaining why interventions work relative to comparison conditions, when they do, and, why they fail, when they do not. Without such data, the researcher can only conjecture about why the intervention produces the effects it produces...."

We think that the most informative educational intervention research programs of the future are going to use multiple research approaches, with analyses complementing one another to provide information about various aspects and impacts of the intervention.

Let's consider the previous example of assessing the impact of case study teaching in science on students' understanding of Infectious Disease (Unit A) and Genetics (Unit B). Measures of student understanding in this study might include pre- and posttests of conceptual understanding (e.g., typical problems) and use of two more cases to measure transfer of knowledge to new situations not discussed in class, one for each of the two units. Thus, the students from Class 1 and 2 would be given a case on infectious disease and genetics (different from the one Class 1 discussed in the class), and this case would serve as a transfer case. The students would then be asked to solve the problem posed in the transfer case. Because only Class 1 uses case-based instruction for infectious disease principles, such a measure would assess student understanding of infectious disease concepts and the impact of case-based instruction on students' conceptual understanding, as compared to the control group of students. Similar procedures would be used to assess whether students acquired conceptual understanding of the genetics concepts and the impact of case-based instruction.

Ideally, the conceptual tests as well as the transfer tests should be scored by both instructors who would be blind to whether the tests were pretests or posttests. Moreover, the instructors would code inter-rater reliability to ensure that their scoring was consistent. The instructors might videotape the case discussions, and conduct focus-group interviews with the students to add additional insight into how and what students were learning from the case situations. They might trade classes to conduct the focus-group interviews, since students might be more honest with a person other than their course instructor. An additional point of data might be to give students their own pre- and posttests to compare and ask them to analyze and reflect on changes in their performance.

We encourage science professors to collaborate with education professors and/or educational psychologists to investigate the use of case study teaching in science. Such collaborations lead to stronger designs and the accumulation of research that will strengthen the field. Finally, we encourage professors to collaborate across sections of courses and across institutions to investigate the efficacy of case study teaching in science.

This is Part I of a two-part series dealing with the assessment of case study teaching. Part II will look at the problems with previous studies and what we know in spite of the difficulties.

REFERENCES

Berliner, D. C. 2002. Educational research: The hardest science of all. *Educational Researcher* 31 (2): 18–20.

Campbell, D. T., and J. C. Stanley. 1966. *Experimental and quasi-experimental designs for research.* Chicago: Rand McNally.

Herreid, C. F. 1994. Case studies in science—A novel method in science education. *Journal of College Science Teaching* 23 (4): 221–29.

Kardash, C. M., and M. L. Wallace. 2001. The perceptions of science classes survey: What undergraduate science reform efforts really need to address. *Journal of Educational Psychology* 93 (1): 199–210.

Lundeberg, M. A., and P. W. Fox. 1991. Do laboratory findings on text expectancy generalize to classroom outcomes? *Review of Educational Research* 61 (1): 94–106.

Lundeberg, M. A., B. B. Levin, and H. L. Harrington. 1999. Reflections on methodologies and future directions. In *Who learns what from cases and how: The research base for teaching and learning with cases,* eds. M. A. Lundeberg, B. B. Levin, and H. L. Harrington, 231–240. Mahwah, NJ: Lawrence Erlbaum Associates.

Lundeberg, M. A., K. Mogen, M. Bergland, K. Klyczek, D. Johnson, and E. MacDonald. 2002. Fostering ethical awareness about human genetics through multimedia-based cases. *Journal of College Science Teaching* 32 (1): 64–69.

National Research Council (NRC). 1996. *National science education standards*. Washington, DC: National Academy Press.

National Research Council (NRC). 2002. *Investigating the influence of standards*. Washington, DC: National Academy Press.

Pressley, M., and R. Allington 1999. What should reading instructional research be research of? *Issues in Education,* 5 (1): 1–35.

Pressley, M., S. Graham, and K. Harris. Forthcoming. The state of educational intervention research as viewed through the lens of literacy intervention. *British Journal of Educational Psychology.*

Seymour, E., and N. M. Hewitt. 1997. *Talking about leaving: Why undergraduates leave science*. Boulder, CO: Westview Press.

Shavelson, R. J., L. Towne, and the Committee on Scientific Principles for Education Research, eds. 2002. *Scientific research in education*. Washington, DC: National Academy Press.

Assessment of Case Study Teaching

Where Do We Go From Here?
Part II

By Mary A. Lundeberg and Aman Yadav

Most of the research on case-based science teaching at the university level involves comparative studies, which contrast student perceptions of case-based science teaching with more traditional teaching. Sometimes this type of research is being done to convince colleagues that case-based science teaching is equally effective if not better than traditional teaching. Such research has also been "reactive," where proponents of case-based instruction gather evidence to support their position and counter criticism from opponents (Williams 1992), rather than attempting to understand the dynamics and processes of case-based teaching. And, of course, all instructors who are trying innovative teaching methods are interested themselves in knowing if the time and energy they are investing in the new method is worth the effort.

But whatever the motivation for the research, there are many ways to go wrong. For example, sometimes instructors teaching only one class will conduct a pretest and a posttest without collecting any process data. In this situation we cannot tell without additional qualitative data on processes whether the gain is due to the case, practice with the test, or other uncontrolled factors (Campbell and Stanley 1966; Pressley, Graham, and Harris, Forthcoming).

It is natural for faculty to select paradigms with which they have familiarity, and in the sciences, measurement is a careful, precise aspect of the research method. In science we have had a bias toward counting, as expressed in this quote from Sir William Thompson, Lord Kelvin (1824–1907):

When you can measure what you are speaking about, and express it in numbers, you know something about it; but when you cannot measure it, when you cannot express it in numbers, your knowledge of it is of a meager and unsatisfactory kind; it may be the beginning of knowledge, but you have scarcely, in your thoughts, advanced it to the stage of science.

However, measurement is not as precise in educational research as in the sciences, and a strict focus on quantitative measurement may limit methodology as well as research questions.

In the social sciences and education, such quantitative measures are sometimes difficult to generate; in any case, a statement about the nature and estimated magnitude of error must be made in order to signal the level of certainty with which conclusions have been drawn. Perhaps most importantly, the reasoning about evidence should identify, consider, and incorporate, when appropriate, the alternative, competing explanations or rival "answers" to the research question. (Shavelson and Towne 2002, p. 68).

Williams (1992) highlighted problems teachers face in assessing student learning when using case-based and problem-based approaches. First, even though the students are learning via the case-based method, they are often being assessed using standardized objective tests, predominately multiple-choice assessments. Second, classes with a large number of students make it difficult to use written tests of performance skills throughout the semester. However, because it is important to investigate whether students are able to abstract the general principles from the study of cases so that they are able to apply those principles and transfer them to other situations, we need to develop better and more efficient methods for assessment.

A factor that influences the design of classroom research is a bias toward comparison conditions, or what some researchers refer to as "horse race" studies—that is, research examining which approach "wins" in terms of student perceptions or achievement. The "winner" in these studies varies, depending on the kind of knowledge measured. For example, comparing two classes of students, one that experienced case-based teaching and one that experienced traditional lectures, might show no differences on a standardized test of critical thinking or the standard multiple-choice exam. How are we to interpret this? Without pretest information, it is impossible to judge gains between the two groups. Moreover, if the assessment task is not aligned with the goals of case study teaching, the results will not be valid.

In the following three examples, we illustrate some problems with comparative studies that are not well controlled for instructor bias, not well planned to measure particular outcomes (comparing apples to oranges), and have such weak interventions they yield data impossible to interpret.

Examples of How Not to Do a Study

Scenario I

One kind of problematic study involves instructor bias that influences students' responses to survey items, leading to self-report bias. A typical example would be an instructor who uses case-based instruction for the first time and is very enthusiastic and decides to survey students to see if their perceptions of the value of case-based teaching match his own. The instructor quickly constructs a brief questionnaire, often with leading questions and/or questions that call for judgments based on experiences students may not have gained. After the class is concluded, this instructor might ask students whether the discussions he led in case-study teaching required them to think critically. If he was explicit about this being one of his course goals, and had developed good rapport with the class, students may agree with this perception, just because they want to tell him what they know he wants to hear, regardless of their awareness of any growth in critical thinking on their part. This can be problematic, especially if students have "operationalized" critical thinking totally differently than the instructor.

Another difficulty with surveys is given in the next example in which the instructor might ask students whether they liked his case-based instruction more than they would have liked traditional lecture. This is an impossible question for students to answer accurately, since they have not experienced a traditional lecture with that particular class. A variation on this same theme is asking students to compare a previous biology course to this one; this kind of leading question is not likely to provide meaningful information, due to the inherent time bias and memory problems associated with prior schooling. Moreover, students generally respond positively to this kind of question because they do not really know how they might have liked traditional lecture in a particular class and may want to please the instructor, given the instructor's obvious bias toward cases.

Scenario II

In this second example, the instructor compares grades from the case study section that she taught with grades from all sections of introductory biology. She hopes to show that the case study section had fewer Ds, Fs, and withdrawal grades than the sections taught with more traditional lectures, and to argue that the case study section provided evidence that students who do not traditionally do well in introductory science courses learned more with case study teaching. Now, suppose the case study section does meet her expectations. Let's presume that the instructor did not use tests; rather, her students completed open-ended assignments she scored with rubrics. Clearly there are several problems here: Different kinds of tests (open-ended essays or projects or papers) may produce different grades than multiple-choice tests. Furthermore, different instructors have different levels of enthusiasm, knowledge and clarity, as well as different levels of skill in facilitating student ideas. Given these kinds of extraneous variables, it is difficult to know precisely what grade comparisons among sections of a particular course really mean if that is the only kind of data collected.

Scenario III

This type of problematic study uses an intervention that is both too weak and too brief to make a difference. For example, an instructor who is new to the case method decides to try one case discussion in one section of a course and to use a lab that he has used for years in another section of the same course. To see whether cases improve students' critical thinking, he administers the multiple-choice exam he has always used that primarily tests for factual scientific knowledge of terms at the end of the unit.

This design is troublesome for four reasons: First, a brief exposure to a case is unlikely to have a strong effect on student thinking or knowledge. Second, the instructor is comparing a pedagogical method in which he is inexperienced (cases) with a method (labs) he is very experienced in using, so his skill may be a confounding factor. Third, the instructor is using the same assessment without considering whether that test measures the kind of critical thinking or conceptual understanding he assumes cases are developing. Finally, if the instructor had consulted the literature, he would have found a meta-analysis showing that the type of exam given to students generally determines gain-score effects in their critical thinking (Dochy, Segers, Van den Bossche, and Gijbels 2003).

Comparative studies of whether case treatment is better than control treatment (typically large lecture) may not add to the knowledge base on case study teaching unless we also examine in what contexts, with what populations, and under what conditions these interactive methods affect learning and/or motivation. Furthermore, to demonstrate whether significant differences are practical, meaningful differences, researchers also need to supply effect size information to augment statistical tests. Effect sizes provide a perspective on the importance of a treatment effect, independent of sample size.

WHAT DO WE KNOW IN SPITE OF THE PROBLEMS?

Because they have been easy to count, we have considerable information about faculty and student perceptions of the value of case-based teaching, student attendance in class, and perceptions of changes in student learning and motivation. In a recent national survey we found faculty believed that students' critical thinking increased and their understanding deepened when learning via case-based instruction (Yadav et al. 2006). Faculty reported students in the classes using case studies demonstrated stronger critical-thinking skills (89.1%), were able to make connections across multiple content areas (82.6%), and developed a deeper understanding of concepts (90.1%). Most of the faculty perceived when they used case-based teaching that students were better able to view an issue from multiple perspectives (91.3%), and were more engaged in the class when using cases (93.8%).

Research by Hoag and colleagues (2005) has shown that students tend to attend class more on days when cases, rather than lectures, are used. However, on days in which students discussed cases, Hoag gave points for turning in responses to the cases, so this extraneous variable (points) is a confounding factor in interpreting these results. Furthermore, students believe that content is easier to remember and apply and they enjoy it more when using case studies (Hoag, Lillie, and Hoppe 1999). While perceptual outcomes based on self-report data have been relatively easy to measure, a greater challenge has been to study what students actually learn using the case study teaching approach (Lundeberg 1999).

Performance in learning (other than overall grades) is not often assessed in case-based teaching because it requires careful construc-

tion of appropriate measurement tasks to assess student understanding and academic performance. Do students learn more from a case study approach to teaching science as compared to a more traditional approach using primarily lectures? The answer depends on how one measures learning. According to a recent meta-analysis examining 43 research studies on Problem-Based Learning (PBL) (one variation of case-based teaching used primarily in medical schools), there are significant differences on skills gained (that is, clinical application of knowledge and higher-order thinking). All of the skill differences favored Problem-Based Learning. However, there were no significant differences in knowledge on standardized measures of accumulated knowledge gained in medical school (Dochy, Segers, Van den Bossche, and Gijbels 2003). Given that the case study approach focuses on depth of understanding rather than breadth, this result is not surprising. When the assessment task was open-ended (e.g., recall, short answer, simulation, oral, essay) and/or when the assessment task measured critical thinking rather than basic knowledge, students in the PBL group showed higher gains in performance as compared to the traditional group. Essentially, the higher the level of knowledge and thinking required on the assessment task, the more likely that case-based teaching will produce greater gains in student understanding.

To measure critical thinking requires careful formulation of questions, and to construct such questions may require preliminary research. For example, a group of physicians and faculty teaching physiology (Michael et al. 2002) collected open-ended written explanations from students to discern reasons for some prevalent misconceptions in physiology. From this qualitative research, they constructed a two-tier test that assessed both misconceptions as well as reasons for these misconceptions. In physics, Mazur (1998) advocated assessing students' understanding of basic physics concepts using what he called *paired problem* testing. In the paired problem testing, students are assessed using a traditional problem and a qualitative conceptual problem. Mazur found that students would solve the traditional problems easily by plugging the numbers into right equation. However, they did not fare well when solving the conceptual problems, indicating that students had little understanding of what the equations used to solve traditional problems really meant. We have also found in our research on teaching with multimedia cases in biology that the kind of assessment task matters greatly. Tests that require students to engage in higher-order thinking, such as interpreting data from simulations and cases, generally produce higher performance among students than do traditional multiple-choice course exams (Bergland et al. Forthcoming).

Creating assessments such as the ones described above provides a way to assess whether students form conceptual understanding of important, complex principles. Einstein reminded us, "Not all that counts can be counted; not all that is counted, counts." Rather than relying on tests that can be easily scored, or simply calculating differences in grades among sections, researchers may need to begin with more open-ended assessments to understand students' reasoning and their application of knowledge.

FUTURE QUESTIONS WORTH INVESTIGATING USING CLASSROOM RESEARCH

With cases being used more and more for science instruction, it is important to address what kind of research questions we might ask and what gaps in the literature need to be filled. There has been very little empirical research investigating *how* students learn from case-based teaching. How do students represent knowledge in a particular discipline? Previous research has indicated that problem solvers represent problems by category and these categories in turn have an influence on problem solving. Ex-

perts and novices differ in their categorization of problems, the process of inquiry, and problem-solving techniques (Chi, Feltovich, and Glaser 1981). Researchers studying case-based instruction might explore the influences of group tasks, social processes, and the social influence on group effectiveness when using cases. If we want to understand case-based instruction, we need to know more about who learns what from cases and why. Examples of fruitful questions to pursue include the following:

- What misconceptions do students bring to instruction, and how are they affected by different case-based approaches designed to dispel them?
- When in the instructional process are case-based approaches most promising?
- More specifically, how much background knowledge is necessary for case-based learning to be effective?
- Are some case-based approaches particularly appropriate for online or computer-based settings versus discussions led by the instructor?
- Are these approaches more appropriate in some disciplines and contexts than in others?
- Under what conditions do video, computer simulations, and other emerging representational tools enhance or interfere with the case-based learning experience?

Future research in case-based instruction might also promote a deeper understanding of case-teaching approaches that make science accessible to all students, promote the learning of disciplinary concepts and habits of mind, and portray science in relevant, interdisciplinary contexts (Lundeberg and Moch 1995; NRC 1996; Handelsman et al. 2004). In all such studies, important questions concern how case-based methods facilitate understanding and engagement for different student populations (Lesh and Lovitts 2000).

Faculty members use cases in a variety of ways, so it is important to understand the kind of cases used, how a case is presented, and how student learning is assessed. For example, we are investigating how learning might be affected by the use of video cases about HIV/AIDS compared to text-based cases (Dirkin et al. 2005). We, the authors, argue that it is important for researchers to describe the context of case study teaching, including the kind of cases used, in order to understand the issues and processes surrounding the use of case-based instruction.

REFERENCES

Bergland, M., M. A. Lundeberg, K. Klyczek, D. Hoffman, J. Emmons, C. Martin, K. Marsh, J. Sweet, J. Werner, and M. Jarvis-Uetz. Forthcoming. Exploring biotechnology using case-based multimedia. *American Biology Teacher.*

Campbell, D. T., and J. C. Stanley. 1966. *Experimental and quasi-experimental designs for research.* Chicago: Rand McNally.

Chi, M., P. Feltovich, and R. Glaser. 1981. Categorization and representation of physics problems by experts and novices. *Cognitive Science* 5 (2): 121–152.

Dirkin, K., A. Yadav, M. Phillips, M. Koehler, K. Hilden, and M. Lundeberg. 2005. Is the movie better than the book? Differences in engagement and delayed recall of video and text cases in science. In *Proceedings of world conference on educational multimedia, hypermedia and telecommunications 2005,* 4196–201. Norfolk, VA: AACE.

Dochy, F., M. Segers, P. Van den Bossche, and D. Gijbels. 2003. Effects of problem-based learning: A meta-analysis. *Learning and Instruction* 13 (5): 533–568.

Handelsman, J., D. Ebert-May, R. Beichner, P. Bruns, A. Chang, R. DeHaan, J. Gentile, S. Lauffer, J. Stewart, S. M. Tilghman, and W. B. Wood. 2004. Scientific teaching. *Science* 304 (5670): 521–522.

Hoag, K. A., J. K. Lillie, and R. Hoppe. 2005. Piloting case-based instruction in a didactic clinical immunology course. *Clinical Laboratory Science* 18 (4): 213–220.

Lesh, R., and B. Lovitts. 2000. Research agendas: Identifying priority problems and developing useful theoretical perspectives. In *Handbook of research design in mathematics and science education,* eds. A. Kelly and R. Lesh, 45–71. Mahwah, NJ: Lawrence Erlbaum Associates, Inc.

Lundeberg, M. A. 1999. Discovering teaching and learning through cases. In *Who learns what from cases and how: The research base for teaching and learning with cases,* eds. M. A. Lundeberg, B. B. Levin, and H. Harrington, 3–24. Mahwah, NJ: Lawrence Erlbaum Associates, Inc.

Lundeberg, M. A., B. B. Levin, and H. L. Harrington. 1999. Where do we go from here? Reflections on methodologies and future directions. In *Who learns what from cases and how: The research base for teaching and learning with cases,* eds. M. A. Lundeberg, B. B. Levin, and H. Harrington, 231–240. Mahwah, NJ: Lawrence Erlbaum Associates, Inc.

Lundeberg, M. A., and S. Moch. 1995. The influence of social interaction on cognition: Connected learning in science. *Journal of Higher Education* 66 (3): 310–335.

Mazur, E. 1998. Moving the mountain: Impediments to change. In *Proceedings of the third annual NISE forum,* ed. S. B. Millar, 91–93. Washington, DC: NISE.

Michael, J. A., M. P. Wenderoth, H. I. Modell, W. Cliff, B. Horwitz, P. McHale, D. Richardson, D. Silverthorn, S. Williams, and S. Whitescarver. 2002. Undergraduates' understanding of cardiovascular phenomena. *Advances in Physiological Education* 26: 72–84.

National Research Council (NRC). 1996. *National science education standards.* Washington, DC: National Academy Press.

Pressley, M., S. Graham, and K. Harris. Forthcoming. The state of educational intervention research as viewed through the lens of literacy intervention. *British Journal of Educational Psychology.*

Shavelson, R. J., L. Towne, and the Committee on Scientific Principles for Education Research, eds. 2002. *Scientific research in education.* Washington, DC: National Academy Press.

Shulman, L. S. 1992. Towards a pedagogy of cases. In *Case methods in teacher education,* ed. J. H. Shulman, 1–33. New York: Teachers College Press.

Williams, S. M. 1992. Putting case-based instruction into context: Examples from legal and medical education. *The Journal of Learning Sciences* 2 (4): 367–427.

Yadav, A., M. A. Lundeberg, K. Dirkin, N. Schiller, and C. F. Herreid. 2006. National survey of faculty perceptions of case-based instruction in science. Paper presented at the annual meeting of American Educational Research Association, San Francisco, CA.

Section XX

The Future of Case Teaching

Finally, I wish to deal with the future of case teaching. Where are we headed and what does it mean to the individual teacher?

There is a revolution in teaching going on. Quietly and relentlessly, large numbers of instructors are eagerly seeking something better in the world of instruction. Echoing the words of actress Shirley MacLaine as she and her comrades belted out their laments in the 1969 movie musical *Sweet Charity*, "There's Gotta Be Something Better Than This," teachers (the ones who are paying attention) have recognized that the lecture method simply doesn't get the job done for most students.

> *"There's gotta be something better than this,*
> *There's gotta be something better to do.*
> *And when I find me something better to do,*
> *I'm gonna get up, I'm gonna get out*
> *I'm gonna get up, get out and do it!"*

That's why "active learning," in all of its various guises, is so passionately embraced by many of the nation's innovative teachers. They believe that students learn best when they are actively doing something in the classroom besides listening. Case-based learning is a model that resonates with their vision. But it is only one method of instruction. One size does not fit all. Or fit every situation. The method(s) is only one arrow to have in our teaching quiver—an arrow to be drawn when the situation seems right.

So let's look to the future. Here I deal with a couple of issues: (1) the future of case-based teaching in the life of a professor—how she or he copes with a new method in her or his own career and (2) how the future of cases—and teaching in general—will unfold in the years ahead. There is a lot of crystal gazing here but if, as the last chapter suggests, Socrates is keeping an eye on us, our future promises to be exhilarating!

Paul Seymour, Assistant Professor

A Dilemma Case in Teaching

By Clyde Freeman Herreid

The numbers were staring him in the face. Paul Seymour looked at them again, irritated and troubled. A third of the semester was over in his Molecular Evolution course, and he had just taken his first survey of the students' reaction. Now the results were in. There was no avoiding it. The students weren't happy. They didn't like the new teaching methods he had introduced. The students weren't used to working in collaborative groups. They didn't want discussion. They didn't like group papers or group tests, or case studies. They simply wanted the facts. As one intense young man had told him:

"You're getting paid to teach us, and all you do is stand around. We do all the work. How can I fill out an evaluation for you? You aren't doing anything."

Paul Seymour had finished his PhD three years before at Duke University with the world-renowned Torkel Gustafeson, arguably the generation's best physiological ecologist. From there he traveled to Johns Hopkins for a postdoc with Mary Craxton, whose DNA fingerprinting work on coral reefs had garnered both excellent reviews and scholarly recognition. Paul's research credentials were impeccable. In his short career he was fortunate enough to have published ten papers, two of which had appeared in *Nature* and one in *Science*. He was on his way. In fact, he had thought more than once of a fellow postdoc's comment. Fred Smothers, a graduate of Cornell University, used to say, "If you haven't made it by the time you have been out 10 years, you aren't going to make it." By that criterion, Paul had made it. Here he was recently hired in Chicago, his research career was beckoning, and yet....

Paul had discovered the joys of teaching. His undergraduate days had been spent at Colorado College, where excellent teaching was the norm. The reason he had gone to graduate school was because a young assistant professor had taken enough personal interest in him.

At Duke, Paul had been a teaching assistant and found that he loved to explain things. His research seminars were always enjoyable to prepare and give. He received well deserved compliments on his clever presentations. Perhaps his colleagues were right. He was a born teacher.

At Johns Hopkins the die was cast. Dr. Mary Craxton, his postdoc mentor, had been recently experimenting with a new teaching method she had seen. She called it collaborative learning. Students worked in teams on projects and received group grades. Not a lot of lecturing occurred in Mary's classes, but discussion was intense. Paul started attending Mary's classes when his research permitted. He soon found himself a regular participant. The discussion method of teaching Advanced Molecular Biology seemed intriguing. He was determined to try it when he got his own classes.

The State University at Chicago was perhaps not the ideal place to try collaborative learning, but Paul thought he could manage it if he prepared ahead. After having his first semester off to set up his lab, Paul thought he was ready to teach Molecular Evolution. His class consisted of 40 juniors, most of them premed students who had survived organic chemistry last year and were looking ahead to the agonizing MCATs.

Paul could still remember that first day when he explained the course rules: 50% of the course would be individual work and 50% group scores, with peer evaluation being part of the grade. He was met with skepticism and even downright hostility. Today, five weeks later, he was having second thoughts. The students weren't happy. And it was clear they had been talking to other faculty: some of his new colleagues in the Department of Integrative Biology had made passing comments to him. The chairman, Distinguished Professor David Montague, seemed to have heard things as well, for he was more than casually interested in the fact that Paul didn't seem to be getting much grant writing done. Paul was feeling pretty depressed.

CASE TEACHING NOTES

Introduction/Background

This is a realistic case that poses two important issues that confront many faculty when they first begin to use case study teaching—or

for that matter any novel teaching method—early in their career. The first issue is how to introduce a new method into the classroom successfully where both the instructor and the students are novices. The second issue concerns the possible consequences of focusing heavily on teaching in an environment where teaching is not the primary criterion for promotion and tenure.

The case was written as an exercise for faculty attending case study workshops as a way for them to evaluate some of the major problems facing young faculty when they try out new teaching methods. The case works well in any faculty meeting, such as a luncheon seminar focused on the problems of teaching.

Objectives

- To examine some pitfalls in teaching case studies, especially where students are accustomed to the lecture method.
- To examine the main forces that impinge on young faculty who are strongly interested in teaching and pursuing a research agenda.

Seminar Management

The case is short and can be read in a few minutes. In a workshop situation I ask the faculty to work in groups of four to five people. I ask them to read over the case and then in groups to look at the situation from different vantage points. I typically ask one group to look at the problem from Paul's viewpoint and another group to analyze the case from the vantage point of the chair of Paul's department. A final group I assign to look at the situation from the perspective of Paul's dean. Other possible groups can be established: Paul's colleagues, the students' parents, the granting agency, etc. If there are many participants in the workshop, I will have several groups playing each role.

When the workshop participants are finished reading the case, I ask each group to consult with their teammates to see if they can reach a consensus as to how they might react in their roles as Paul, the chair, or dean. Then I as a facilitator run a general discussion.

First, I ask the group that is role-playing as Paul to give us their thoughts. They usually talks about Paul's concerns about teaching and defend why he is teaching in this new way, making the point that he is adapting as he goes and that things will get better in the future with a few adjustments.

Then I say to the chair group, "Suppose that you have a student that comes to you and complains about the teaching of Dr. Seymour, what would you say to the student?" The "chair" typically replies that "s/he" will look into it. I then ask the chair what else s/he might you do? The group usually says that they would talk to Paul to indicate their concerns. This usually spills over into a conversation about Paul's tenure and promotion issues and brings up the fact that his dedication to teaching might jeopardize his career. I often ask someone in the chair group to have a conversation with a person from Paul's group. This is a role-playing experience that is played out between two individuals in a realistic fashion.

Following this exchange, I turn to the dean's group and ask: "Suppose that you had a contingent of students come directly to you and complain that this new professor, Paul Seymour, is not teaching them anything. He is expecting them to do all of the work. Moreover, he is jeopardizing their acceptance into medical school by inflicting this unorthodox teaching method upon them. Given this, what would you do?" Typically they respond with appropriate dean-like statements such as "I'll look into it." And when they follow up with a phone call to the chair, the chair responds by saying s/he has already talked to Paul, etc.

By working back and forth between groups, I as a facilitator can expose the key problems that Paul and the administrators face. Ultimately, Paul must come to grips with his dilemma. He has some choices to make: modify or radically change his behavior or face the consequences. What are the issues and what will (should) he do?

Major Issues/Blocks Of Analysis

There are two key issues in the case: Paul's difficulty with the new teaching methodology and the fact that his research program seems to be in jeopardy.

TEACHING ISSUES

As far as the teaching issue goes, Paul is experiencing many of the same problems that all instructors face when introducing new methods, in this case Team Learning and case studies (Herreid 2002). There is always student resistance. For students, the novelty factor often makes them worry that their previous methods of studying might not work. This is a serious threat to students who have been successful with traditional methods. So Paul needs to spend significant time at the start of the semester explaining his reasons for the new methodology. And this must be done more than once. He needs to mention that cooperative learning strategies lead to better grades, not poorer grades. He needs to make that point by saying that over 1,200 studies have been done showing that groups outperform individuals, that students using cooperative methods retain the information longer, are more articulate and more tolerant of diverse views than students in lecture classes (Herreid 1998), and that learning to work together in teams is essential for success (surveys of CEOs indicate that 90% of the people who are fired from their jobs lack people skills), etc. Also, I find it useful to stress that many medical schools are now teaching using cooperative learning methods such as Problem-Based Learning and that most physicians work in group settings so that going through a team-based class will give them an advantage in the health professions.

Paul, as a new teacher, has another thing working against him. He does not have a long history of teaching experience to fall back on. Young teachers encounter a host of common student problems and excuses. The instructor will eventually figure out how to solve and answer these. But in the beginning, s/he can be at a loss. What should the instructor do when a student is tardy or hands in a paper late or claims he can't take an exam because of a death in the family or has to appear in court or...or...or? Eventually s/he will have answers, but in the beginning, coming on top of trying out a new approach to teaching, any vacillation on the part of a new instructor makes her/him appear weak and incompetent—easy prey for a suspicious and argumentative student looking for a scapegoat for an inadequate grade or unusual assignment.

Key trouble spots for students are the group activities and especially the peer evaluation. Many good students have been stuck in poor groups where they have felt abused and have ended up having to do all of the work. They hate this. Moreover, they hate to depend on other people and their different time schedules. Students find it very difficult to meet to do group work outside of class, especially given their work and family schedules. There are ways to avoid or reduce the difficulties. One of these is simple: Don't assign outside group work.

Second, always create group assignments that are either too large or too complex for a single student to accomplish in the time allotted. Students get rightfully annoyed if they see that they could accomplish the task faster and more efficiently working alone.

Third, be sure that students understand the role that peer evaluation plays in their grade. They need to see its value; it gives them an opportunity to be sure that everyone is doing their bit in group projects. Peer evaluation must be described on the first day of class and the forms used for it shown. The students must have a chance to do a practice peer evaluation part way through the semester. This practice evaluation allows students to see

that any individual who is not pulling her/his weight in the group projects will be punished by her or his teammates. This gives the social loafers a "reality check" and provides them an opportunity to rectify their behavior (for details on how to conduct peer evaluations, see Herreid 2001, 2002).

So what are Paul's options? These should be explored and evaluated in the seminar or workshop setting. There are short-term solutions and long term. He can give up the new teaching style altogether or he can try to make adjustments on the fly. If he is going to make adjustments, he should consider involving the students. One solution is to suspend normal class activities one day and have the students working in their groups: (1) list the positive things that have come out of this new approach and then (2) list concerns they have about what is happening in class. If these group papers are handed in, Paul will have a chance to evaluate the points. It is usually not wise to open up the class for discussion at this point. Tempers need to cool. In the following class, Paul should address the key issues, clarifying problem areas, discussing how he will or will not modify his procedures, and explaining the reasons for his decisions. This direct approach will almost invariably reduce the tension. Even though not everyone will be happy, the problems are no longer smoldering in the background undermining the class. Paul has shown his concern and taken the students seriously and should be able to survive the semester. In the long run, if Paul is going to experiment, he will need to correct his approach the next time around, that's for sure.

RESEARCH ISSUES

As far as the research issue is concerned, Paul is in serious trouble. He apparently is in a Research I University. He was probably hired largely on the basis of his research potential and he is beginning to slip. His tenure and promotion seem to be dependent on grants, publications, presentations at national meetings, and giving research seminars. Teaching typically is given short shrift in this setting. Indeed, in some university environments, receiving a teaching award may be the kiss of death. Paul has been captured by the allure of teaching and has found that it takes a major commitment to be good, especially if he is going to move away from traditional lecturing. He simply must face facts. The talks with the chair, colleagues, and perhaps the dean will help him get a grip on reality. But make no mistake, this is a crisis. If he doesn't make major adjustments in the way he spends his time, he will be looking for another job soon.

Among his choices: He can give up the new methods altogether or more likely he will try to modify his teaching somewhat, hoping he can still be successful in his teaching and continue his research. He wants to do it all. But there is another alternative, of course; he can always choose to go elsewhere, to a teaching institution and chuck the research career—but as young assistant professor and productive researcher he is unlikely to come to that conclusion at this point in his career.

If you were Paul Seymour, what would you do?

References

Herreid, C. F. 1998. Why isn't cooperative learning used to teach science? *Bioscience* 48: 553–559.

Herreid, C. F. 2001. When justice peeks: Evaluating students in case study teaching. *Journal of College Science Teaching* 30: 430–433.

Herreid, C. F. 2002. Using case studies in science—and still covering content. In *Team based learning: A transformative use of small groups*, eds. L. Michaelson, A. Knight, and L. Fink, 109–118. Westport, CT: Stylus Pub.

Teaching in the Year 2061

By Clyde Freeman Herreid

"My interest is in the future because I am going to spend the rest of my life there."

—Charles Kettering

I am going to talk about the future. I do this for two reasons. First, like Charles Kettering and everybody else, I'm going to spend the rest of my life there; and second, because I believe that we're passing through a revolution so profound that it rivals that of the discovery of fire or writing or the printing press. It is the technological revolution led by the transformation of our world by computers. Music, art, entertainment, medicine, and science are being changed before our very eyes by technological Merlins waving silicon wands. And so is teaching.

Why do I choose to focus on the world of 2061? The answer: This is when Haley's Comet returns to Earth. About 10 years ago, the American Association for the Advancement of Science decided to launch an educational initiative to produce a scientifically literate America by the time Haley's Comet returned to Earth. (Hope springs eternal!) They knew this would be a tough job, because only 5% of today's population is judged scientifically literate. I think that they put this far enough into the future not only so that there would be enough time to reach their objective, but also because they thought none of us would be around to check up on them. So, taking a page from their book, I, too, want to talk about 2061. But to get there, we have to travel through the intervening years.

Before donning our seven-league boots, let's recognize that trying to predict the future is fraught with pitfalls. For every H. G. Wells and Leonardo da Vinci who correctly predicted the invention of the atomic bomb and the submarine, there are countless Jean Dixons and astrologers who have trouble even predicting tomorrow. Isaac Asimov, the biochemist polymath who became perhaps the world's greatest science fiction writer, told a marvelous cautionary tale about the vicissitudes of prognostication. He pointed out that at the time of the moon landing, no one was particularly surprised at the event. After all, people had been writing about it for generations. Even the Buck Rogers cartoons of the 1930s had shown space travelers wearing space suits very similar to those worn by our astronauts. Yet, with all of our foresight, no one anticipated the most amazing thing of all about the moon landing: When it occurred, the whole world would be watching—on television!

TODAY'S CLASSROOMS

Claude Bernard, our society's patron saint of experimental science, would recognize today's classrooms. They haven't changed much over the centuries. Students sit dutifully, taking down the words of the master as he lectures to them from yellowed notes. In fact, Plato and Socrates would be fairly comfortable too. They wouldn't have much trouble seeing that that drawing on a blackboard or on an overhead projector isn't much different from drawing in the sand. But a PowerPoint presentation might give them pause and the internet—By Apollo! This would be a world apart. Imagine being able to tap into the world's knowledge and read your very own *Republic* electronically.

I think that e-mail might give them trepidation, especially if they taught 500 students in an amphitheater like I do. Of course, they would be initially enamored with the possibility of being in touch with their students 24 hours of the day, but they would soon become jaundiced having to spend as much as 20% of their time answering messages like some of my colleagues. When would there be time to think great thoughts?

I don't think that electronic bulletin boards or distribution lists would be too novel, but listservs and chat rooms would certainly stagger them. Just think, they could run their symposia not with just a handful of colleagues reclining on cushions and imbibing on *vino ordinaire*, but they could commune with a cacophony of buddies and strangers. In fact, the Plato of today would have written his dialogues in an electronic chat room with a cyber Timaeus, Crito, and Phaedo. Surely, they would soon discover, like many professors of today, surviving listservs and chat rooms with freewheeling students is challenging to the hardiest educators. It is better to set up scheduled office hours on chat rooms to limit the dialogue.

Then there are webpages. What might our classic personages say about these? Gadzooks! At least a third of my university's courses now have webpages, and most students have the computers to access them. In my evolutionary biology class, students not only can log in and see class notices, policies, and the course syllabus, but can hear lectures they have missed, view the slides and overhead displays, take practice quizzes, see video demonstrations, and take practical exams on virtual anatomical dissections (however, I must note, with apologies to Bill Gates, that despite all this electronic jazz, I have not found a trace of improved learning).

And what of computers in the classroom? Here, a latter-day Claude Bernard, instead of taking hours to set up a dog to run an experiment only to have time to get one run through, can run dozens of simulations and collect data to analyze. Genetics students can play Mendel and run simulated crosses of pea plants without digging a weed or planting a seed. Ecologists and meteorologists can run computer models of the different scenarios of global warming without the glaciers melting or sea levels rising. But as amazing as all of this would be to our visiting scholars from the past, I think they would be most astounded with the potential of distance learning.

FROM CORRESPONDENCE COURSES TO VIRTUAL CLASSROOMS

Remember the days when you could take a correspondence course on practically any subject, everything from becoming a pianist to becoming a brain surgeon? Correspondence courses are still doing well, thank you very much, but in a new form known as distance learning. It was a small step for schools like Pennsylvania State University to go from running television courses for 2,500 students in 1960 to setting up TV classrooms around the state. From the school's television studio, the grand professor could pontificate and his message would speed across the airways to remote sites where students and their facilitators would discuss the wisdom of the latest missive.

Now that computers are here, it is another small step to have the students tune in electronically. Classmates can be anywhere. The teaching can be "synchronous," where teacher and students are online at the same time, or "asynchronous," where the professor's lessons are prerecorded and may be accessed at any time, day or night, a great boon to the working student. In the last few years, there has been an enormous jump in the development of these "virtual classrooms."

Here is just a sampling of the many institutions now engaged in distance learning. The State University of New York has 40 of its campuses linked together using virtual learning. The Virtual College of Texas has 70,000 community college students using virtual learning. Sixteen southern states with their 260 campuses are joined together into something called the Electronic Campus of the Southern Regional Education Board; they offer 3,000 courses in distance learning. Then there is the Open University operating out of the United Kingdom with 160,000 students in 40 different countries; 35% of their distance learning courses are computer-based. And this is only the beginning of a worldwide trend,

the switch to computer education. How far this trend will take us away from our traditional ways can only be appreciated by looking at the future of computers.

THE FUTURE OF COMPUTERS

Gordon Moore, the inventor of the transistor and later the chairman of Intel, noted that the number of components that could be placed on a computer chip was doubling every two years. This increase has occurred because of improvements in optical lithography used to position the transistors on silicon chips on an ever-smaller scale. The resulting exponential rise in the number of calculations per second that can be achieved by our computers has become known as Moore's Law of Integrated Circuits (Figure 1). Consequently, computers today are 100 million times more powerful per unit cost than they were 50 years ago. Says MIT's Ray Kurtzweil: "If the automobile industry had made as much progress in the past 50 years, a car today would cost one hundredth of a cent and go faster than the speed of light."

The end is not in sight. Computer experts argue that the ever-tighter packing of transistors onto silicon wafers will continue to follow

FIGURE 1.

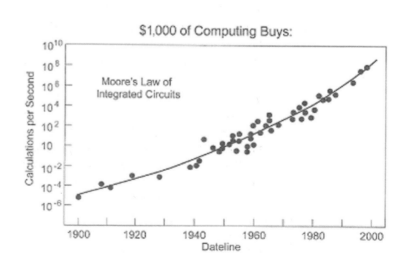

Moore's Law for the next 15–20 years. Well before their limit is reached, other innovations will be in place to keep the exponential rise going. Here are a few of the promising innovations waiting in the wings:

- Three-dimensional chips. Traditional chips are flat. Some venture-backed companies are now beginning to pack circuitry into layers to produce cubes.
- Optical computing. Recently, people have been working with streams of photons rather than electrons to produce faster computers.
- Molecular computing. DNA computers promise to be more flexible than electronic or optical computers where massive numbers of solutions must be evaluated and assembled.
- Computers as crystals. Data can be stored as holograms where as many as a trillion bits of information can be stored in each cubic centimeter.
- Nanotubes. Recently discovered elongated carbon molecules, called nanotubes, can perform all the electronic functions of silicon units used in our current computers. Because of their small size (50,000 laid side by side would equal a human hair), nanotubes promise to lead to a revolution in miniaturization.
- Quantum computing. Considered to be the Holy Grail of the computing industry, quantum computing is not a digital system like those just mentioned. Bits of information are not encoded as either off or on but may be simultaneously both zero and one at the same time and potentially much more powerful. It has been said that quantum computing is to digital computing as the hydrogen bomb is to a firecracker.

A Look Into The Future

"If we were to go back in time 100 years and ask a farmer what he'd like if he had anything, he probably would tell us he wanted a horse that was twice as strong and ate half as many oats. He would not tell us he wanted a tractor."

—Philip J. Quigley

"When inventing movable type. Gutenberg wasn't thinking of the revolution that would follow it. He certainly didn't anticipate Adam Smith's Wealth of Nations, *Charles Darwin's* Origin of Species, *or Adolf Hitler's* Mein Kampf. *Nonetheless, his device changed everything, and it changed everything forever."*

—Gregory J. E. Rawlins

Prognostication is not for the timid, and Ray Kurtzweil of MIT is anything but timid. His 1999 book, *The Age of Spiritual Machines: When Computers Exceed Human Intelligence,* is filled with exactly the kind of predictions one needs if we are to envision how rapidly the world will change in the next decades. Among Kurtzweil's accomplishments is the development of voice-recognition computer systems. Recipient of nine honorary degrees and the 1999 National Medal of Technology from President Clinton, Kurtzweil has identified some notable benchmarks ahead that I have modified slightly.

Dateline 2010

- A $1,000 PC (1999 dollars) will perform a trillion calculations per second.
- PCs will range in size from those small enough to be inserted in watches up to the size of thin books.
- PCs will be increasingly wireless, and vocal interaction between computers and people will be common.
- Most routine business transactions (reservations, purchases) will occur between a human and a virtual personality, such as an animated human face.
- Traditional classrooms still exist, but intelligent interactive software is now a common method of learning.

DATELINE 2020

- A $1,000 PC has the computational ability of a human brain.
- Miniaturized computers are embedded everywhere: in furniture, appliances, walls, jewelry, and our bodies.
- Three-dimensional virtual reality displays embedded in eyeglasses are common.
- High-resolution virtual reality with visual, auditory, and tactile sensations enable people to do practically anything with anybody anywhere.
- Communication with computers is largely by voice or gesture.
- Papers and traditional books are rarely used and traditional libraries are anachronisms.
- Most learning occurs via intelligent simulated software-based teachers.
- People are beginning to develop personal relationships with computers as friends, teachers, and lovers.

DATELINE 2030

- A $1,000 PC has the computing capacity of 1,000 human brains.
- Neural implants are beginning to be used to enhance visual, auditory, and tactile perception, interpretation, memory, and reasoning. These are merely extensions of the cochlear and retinal implants used in the year 2000.
- All literature, music, and art will be scanned into the computer network.
- All knowledge will be theoretically available to anyone's PC.
- There will be no jobs for receptionists, bookkeepers, general physicians, family lawyers, or schoolteachers as their skills can be easily automated.
- Automated agents are now learning on their own, and knowledge is being created by machines with little human intervention.
- Computers will routinely pass the Turing Test, whereby people cannot tell if they are talking to a machine or a human.
- Machines will claim to be conscious and people will begin to believe them. (A page out of Isaac Asimov's robot stories will have come true.)

DATELINE 2061

- $1,000 PC has the computing power of all human brains.

VIRTUAL REALITY

The word *virtual* is becoming cant for anything that is simulated. *Virtual reality* means more than that. It refers to a simulated environment in which everything seems real. It started with the military and its interest in training pilots. The Link Trainer was originally designed to simulate the cockpit of a fighter plane so that aviators could gain the necessary fight experience without the expense or danger involved in flying a real plane. As airplanes became increasingly complicated, so did the flight simulators, with their computer-generated scenery and combat missions. Simulators are now used to train ship and submarine crews, tank and artillery operators, and missile battery teams. Their cousins are found in arcades and home computer games.

Today, virtual reality is being used in research labs around the world. There are single-wall systems that appear as large cinema screens with three-dimensional images dancing out at the viewer as seen through goggles. Chemists are able to manipulate giant molecules floating in space with the wiggle of a wand and can walk into their innards like a human enzyme. Architects and civil engineers are able to stroll through their buildings and cross their bridges before they are built. Of course, this is already possible with some computers and software systems, but the ultimate goal is not to sit in front of a computer screen, but to move freely about in a virtual world. "Caves" are the closest answer to this total immersion. These are rooms built with computer screens on all four walls, floor, and ceiling. There are fewer than a hundred worldwide in operation at the moment, but don't be surprised to find them in the living rooms of the next generation.

The new technology can only get better. By linking a robot's senses with our own, we will be able to project our *telepresence* into distant worlds. Surgeons will operate on patients in other countries or cruise through the circulatory system. Miners will dig ore under oceans, and astronauts will explore alien planets without ever leaving home. The better the simulation of sight, sound, touch, and smell, the more we will begin to believe we are actually in the other world.

More than that, we will be able to create worlds that do not exist at all. Think how far we have come in the last couple of decades. Consider motion pictures. Recall the computer animations that we have witnessed in *Jurassic Park, Star Wars, Terminator 2,* and *The Matrix.* Or consider the animated humanoids in the arcades and home computer games like Sony's PlayStation 2. Certainly, we can still tell the difference between the real people and the simulated. But, these distinctions won't last long. Right now, real people from past movies are being plugged into new scenes; we have commercials with Humphrey Bogart in scenes he never played and Fred Astaire in dances he never danced. We have a fictional celluloid Forrest Gump meeting real American presidents from the past. Special effects experts warn us that movie moguls are well on their way to devising a virtual movie actor will be indistinguishable from a real person. They warm to the prospect of paying virtual salaries instead of the real ones they do now.

WHAT WILL THIS MEAN TO TEACHING? EVERYTHING

We will be able to train students in "real-world" problems because we will be able to simulate the real situation. Novice surgeons will practice on virtual patients without killing or maiming a real one. Students will dissect virtual animals without being harassed by animal-rights activists. Fledgling scientists will mix chemicals, manipulate genes, and alter ecosystems. Those of us who think that case studies are the way to teach will be able to immerse the students directly into the virtual situation and have them *become* the person who must solve the problem or suffer the consequences. The sights will be there. The sounds will be there, the touch and the smell, giving new meaning to the phrase "experience is the best teacher."

Virtual reality will not be confined to "caves" or special rooms in the future. Originally virtual reality required the use of special helmets, then goggles. Right now there are PCs that have been reduced to the size of eyeglasses. By 2020, three-dimensional display systems will be provided by contact-lens systems and implanted retinal-imaging devices. Later in the century, these systems will be connected directly to the brain by neural implants.

So if we can create simulated movie actors, why not simulated teachers who will act as customized guides to knowledge?

But who needs teachers if all knowledge has been scanned into the computer network and we have miniature PCs embedded in our bodies? All knowledge is essentially within our grasp. We will have become cyborgs—a synergy of human and machine—part of a cyberhive of beings.

We can say that it will never happen. We don't like the vision. Things will never move this fast.

Never say never. As Gregory Rawlins in his book *Moths to the Flame* points out, recall that only 35 years separate our discovery of DNA from the first patented artificial animal. Only two generations separate the Wright brothers' *Kitty Hawk* from rockets to the moon or water wheels from nuclear power plants or fireworks from hydrogen bombs.

"Given the present stupendous rate of technological change, it is almost useless to extrapolate twenty years into the future, far less fifty. Provided that we don't destroy ourselves first, the world of fifty years from now may be as different from today's as our era is from the Stone Age. The world of a hundred years from now may as well be from another planet. And the human race may still call itself human, but it may as well be a new species."

We may lament that change is coming; but come it will. The world of 2061 and its computer technology will cause the demise of our universities and libraries as we know them, just as surely as the printing press displaced hundreds of scribes in the 1500s. As the scribes before them, faculty and librarians will wail and gnash their teeth and argue that it can't come to pass. But as Gregory Rawlins has put it, commenting on a similar historical moment:

"They were kings of the hill. They dominated every ecosystem. But for them, as for all life, there is only one rule: adapt or die. As they roamed the veldt and the marshes and the seas, living life as they had for millions of years, an asteroid was entering the atmosphere. Things were about to change greatly. And the dinosaurs had no idea."

Then again, we may choose to take one day at a time. Perhaps Albert Einstein had the right attitude about this prediction business all along when he commented, "I never think of the future. It comes soon enough."

From Advances in Physiology Education 24: 1–7 (2000). Used with permission.

E-Mail From Socrates

By Clyde Freeman Herreid

Subject: Case Studies
Date: 3/15/06
From: Socrates@ElysianFields.com
To: herreid@buffalo.edu

My Dear Professor Herreid:

I hope that you do not mind my contacting you by e-mail. I am apprised that cyber communication is the modern way of conversation on Earth. We have been doing something like it here for quite some time. Naturally, we do not use the keyboard as you do. We simply meditate on what we wish to say and the missive is sent. That has been sufficient for the two millennia that I have been here. I suppose that it will not be long before you too will graduate to wireless systems and eventually have neural implants in your brain. Then all of this typing will not be necessary, but let us leave that to the future.

I contact you because I have been hearing about these case studies you have been lauding. Am I to understand that one of their strengths is that you believe students learn better if information is put into the form of stories? Do I perceive your meaning correctly?

Sincerely, Socrates

Subject: Re: Case Studies
Date: 3/16/06
From: herreid@buffalo.edu
To: Socrates@ElysianFields.com

Dear Philosopher:
This is a surprise! I have had the pleasure of reading the many dialogues that your student, Plato, has written where you are featured, but I hardly expected that one day I would hear from you.

About cases, yes, you are correct. I believe that humans are storytelling animals and that we learn best when things are put into an experience or a story. Teachers seem to think they can just lecture about the principles that they believe govern the world and the students will remember them. This is in spite of much evidence to the contrary. They ignore the fact that large numbers of their students fail or barely pass their courses using the techniques of lecturing. I argue that students learn best on a need-to-know basis—when they are presented with a story that engages them.

I would be delighted to learn your thoughts on the subject. Perhaps it would be best if we continue this conversation in a chat room. May I suggest we adjourn to one known as The Academy?

My regards, C.F.H.

Later, online at The Academy:

SOKRATZ: IMHO, this, indeed, is a much better venue for our deliberations, Professor. I am indebted for your wisdom.

On the question of case studies: As you may have observed, I have been the protagonist in some stories myself. Plato's dialogues were essentially stories in a conversational format meant to stimulate the consideration of serious philosophical subjects. Yet, I am perplexed that you really have not deigned to credit him in the manner he deserves. Surely there is a priority involved. Is there not some obligation to mention the ancients who used stories to make a point? Was not Aesop a parablist? And should you not consider Homer's epics as illustrating great truths? These are not merely stories for children; they are not just told for entertainment but for the eternal wisdom embedded within them.

CFH: Certainly, you are right. I am sorry you feel that I have slighted your compatriots. Yet as you realize, even they are not the first to use stories to teach. All societies, even those without a written record, have a long tradition of storytelling with moral lessons. Stories are ways of passing on knowledge from one generation to the next.

SOKRATZ: So then, you appear to agree that there are questions of priority to which one needs to pay homage. That speaks well for you. But on another point: Do you deem that some stories are better than others?

CFH: Absolutely. Ones with danger, fear, murder, and mayhem are those that we remember best. Homer's epics fit the bill well. They touch the fundamentals of emotion. We had better remember stories like his if we are to survive.

SOKRATZ: Perhaps that is the reason that your television programs that depict violence and sex are the most watched shows. Is there not an irony here? If the Professor agrees that strong emotion is the essence of a good story, why is it that so many cases lack these passions? The writing seems dry and relatively uninteresting. Even case writers in medicine who would seem to have ideal material for such cases seldom place any emotion into their stories. To my untutored vision they appear to have removed the very parts of the story that would inspire interest on the part of the reader. Physicians instead write, "A 33-year-old male was admitted into the emergency room, presented a low blood pressure, and complained of prolonged dizziness...." Why do they write "presented"? Why do they not use names for the patients? There is no personality to their patients. Indeed, where are the blood and guts, the very thing you say makes for a good story?

CFH: What you say is true, Socrates. Medical case writers have sucked all the drama from their cases. I imagine they do this in order to give the illusion they are objective "scientists" in search of the truth. I think this comes from their long tradition of presenting case histories to hospital staff after the death of one of their patients. They don't want emotion to cloud their judgment.

SOKRATZ: But is this not antithetical to what they say on other occasions? Have not physicians argued that medicine is an art more than a science? That was the sentiment held by Hippocrates.

CFH: I accept your logic. Physicians pay homage to their past, but today I think they want us to believe that science is at the forefront of their profession. The clinical language helps support that view. But you are right; it dehumanizes the cases. Also, I think that most physicians and scientists in general are not trained in this style of writing. We learned to write in the passive voice, saying things like "The experiments were run" rather than "I ran the experiments." Using the personal pronoun *I* was frowned upon by journals. Even if you were a single author of a paper, you would be encouraged to use the term *We*.

SOKRATZ: Does this not smack of the royal *We*, the imperial decision? "I am the philosopher-king. Do not question me."

CFH: It is interesting that you would say this since you have argued that a democracy is not to be trusted, that power is better appropriated by those born to rule. Science is the antithesis of this. Our discoveries are truly democratic. It matters not who proposes an idea; it must survive the challenges of all comers before it is seen as "truth." And this idea may be overthrown again if a better one comes along. Truth is not the province of a single person but the product of thousands of scientists. I am sure you know the famous statement of Sir Isaac Newton: "If I have been able to see so far it is because I have stood on the shoulders of giants." Science is truly democracy in action. No, the use of the pronoun *we* does not stem from an imperial posture, rather it is an attempt to emphasize the objective nature of science. That is, an event is independent of the observer; it would appear the same to all people regardless of who they are or where they might be. Unfortunately, I believe this notion is carried too far, especially in case studies where we wish to engage students. In fact, the lecture method simply reinforces the wrong view of science—that there is no discussion allowed. This method is what drives many students away from science. It is flat out boring and misrepresents the way that science is done.

SOKRATZ: You sound very much like Plato's young student, Aristotle. He was not so empirical when he was young. Are you suggesting that we ignore the Social Contructivists who argue that science is a cultural phenomenon and its observations are colored and perhaps determined by the observer and the time period in which he or she lives?

CFH: Isn't this carrying us away from your original inquiry into cases?

SOKRATZ: I am not so sure. Reality does seem to have a subjective quality about it, does it not? In the *Republic* Plato has written that human beings cannot perceive reality directly. It is as if we live in an underground cave with its mouth opened toward the light. We have been there since childhood and have our legs and necks chained with our backs to the outside world. We cannot move and can only see shadows of images thrown on the walls by the firelight behind us. What we see is like a screen that marionette-players have in front of them as they show shadows of puppets to the audience. The world that we inhabit is indeed a mere shadow of the ideal world, which we can never see.

CFH: The image that Plato presented in the *Republic* has held powerful sway over ages of scholars and students, I grant you. Yet I don't believe the metaphor is apt. Most scientists that I know believe that the world is something real and that we are progressively getting closer to understanding it. We are not doomed to be forever sitting with our backs to reality seeing mere shadowy reflections on the wall.

SOKRATZ: You do me an injustice here. I too believe that there is a real world, an ideal world. Nonetheless, I am not persuaded that humans can throw off their chains and turn around to see the real world. We are too dependent upon our particular sense organs. Our eyes can only see certain degrees of light; the bee does not see the same colors of the flower as do my friends Crito and Protagoras. Our ears can only hear certain sounds; I do not hear the squeal of the mouse yet my dog hears the rodent quite clearly. Our brains can only interpret the world in limited ways. Tell me, then, how we can really appreciate what it means to be a bat that uses only the sounds of the night to find its way through the darkness? Or, to be a sponge without eyes? Each of us senses the same world, but is it not true that our interpretations differ?

And what of the future? You say that scientists are moving ever closer to discovering the true nature of the universe. Yet, do you not think that the use of virtual reality in the computer world will remove reality even further? Electronic shadows of shadows of shadows.

CFH: Virtual reality will definitely change the world of teaching with case studies. Today, we write case studies with story lines to engage students. The best cases are ones that students know are true rather than made up. Totally fabricated story lines simply aren't as compelling. If you are writing a case about a fictional person, the students won't care much about the outcome of the case. Real cases, real people, real events are best.

SOKRATZ: Apparent reality. You will appreciate my skepticism here. Not in the sense of a Sophist but merely because I still await your instruction as to how it is that people can ever hope to see the real world.

CFH: Whether or not we can see the "real world," as you call it, the students believe the cases *are* relevant to their world. I don't think we should be too surprised that they are interested in stories about AIDS and drugs and rock stars. They will be more likely to study science if there is some rhyme or reason for remembering the facts and principles that we insist on drilling into their heads. Information is more likely recalled if there is a context. Students often complain that the lack of such a framework pushes them out of science.

SOKRATZ: I see you do not wish to refute me on the reality of the world. So let us turn to the students. I understand their lack of enthusiasm for science. Plato shared my antipathy. Nonetheless, his student Aristotle was a convert, as you undoubtedly know. But I would like to return to the future of case studies. I gather that you believe that computers will improve the cases. You have complained about the lack of verisimilitude in many of the cases. The writing, I gather, leaves something to be desired. How do you think that computers will change things?

CFH: Interactive cases are the wave of the future. Imagine this case: An unconscious patient is brought in by helicopter from a mountain climbing expedition. Now, suppose that the instructor asks a physiology class to evaluate the patient after receiving only a limited amount of information that might be available to an emergency medical physician. They can order any number of tests that cost varying amounts of money. They can interview the companions on the expedition. They can obtain the medical records of the patient, and so on. Suppose all of this information is available on the computer along with physiology papers on various aspects of cardiovascular, pulmonary, and kidney function that might be related to this patient's problems. Now we can turn students loose to research every lead they can think of to save the patient. There will be videotapes available of the mountain climbers describing the climb. There will be the clinical results of relevant and irrelevant tests. The students will be graded on their diagnostic success not only by seeing if they get the correct diagnosis but also on their ability to choose the cheapest way to accomplish the task. So, the interactive phase of the case becomes critical.

SOKRATZ: I surmise that you will plead that with the coming of virtual reality the student will eventually be immersed in the case. He will actually believe that he is the doctor, or the patient, or one of the friends.

CFH: Yes. That is what I see ahead. It will be an immense breakthrough for realism in case studies. I even envision a time when it will be possible to develop an Electronic Virtual Socrates with whom a student can converse.

SOKRATZ: And do you further surmise that the miniaturization of computers and their eventual implantation into the human brain will allow the simulation of practically every human sensation and emotion? And this will be realism?

CFH: That is a reasonable assumption.

SOKRATZ: That should make it difficult if not impossible to distinguish the real from the electronic, will it not?

CFH: You have a point.

SOKRATZ: So, then do I have it correctly: The cave analogy may be apt in such a setting, with human beings sitting in a cybercave with their backs to the real world watching electronic shadows dance on the walls that they believe to be real?

CFH: Philosopher, I sense we have come full circle, an appropriate tribute to the Ptolemaic views you hold.

SOKRATZ: I see you avoid the question, Professor. Remember, the unexamined life is not worth living.

Now, forgive me, I really must depart. I hear the music of the spheres calling. I will be watching your case study work with interest.

And I will be in touch—virtually, of course.

Appendix I
About the Authors

At the time of writing, **Bruce C. Allen** was a graduate student at the University at Buffalo, State University of New York.

At the time of writing, **Helena Bokobza** was an undergraduate student at the University at Buffalo, State University of New York.

Peggy Brickman is an assistant professor in the Department of Plant Biology, Division of Biological Sciences at the University of Georgia in Athens, Georgia.

William H. Cliff is an associate professor, Department of Biology, at Niagara University.

Leslie Curtin is an adjunct professor, Department of Biology, at Niagara University.

Frank J. Dinan is a professor in the Department of Chemistry and Biochemistry at Canisius College in Buffalo, New York.

Jessica Dudek is assistant administrative director of the University Honors Program at the University at Buffalo, State University of New York.

At the time of writing, **Kristie DuRei** was an undergraduate at the University at Buffalo, State University of New York.

Ann Fourtner is a science writer living in Getzville, New York.

Charles Fourtner is professor of biological sciences, University at Buffalo, State University of New York.

Clyde Freeman Herreid is a Distinguished Teaching Professor in the Department of Biological Sciences and director of the National Center for Case Study Teaching in Science at University at Buffalo, State University of New York.

At the time of this writing, **Arnold I. Kozak** was a graduate student at the University at Buffalo, State University of New York.

Mary A. Lundeberg is a professor and chair of the Department of Teacher Education at Michigan State University in East Lansing, Michigan.

Nigel Marriner is assistant administrative director of the University Honors Program at University at Buffalo, State University of New York.

Frank A. Scannapieco is professor and chair, Department of Oral Biology, School of Dental Medicine, at the University at Buffalo, State University of New York.

Nancy A. Schiller is co-director of the National Center for Case Study Teaching in Science and associate librarian, Science and Engineering Library, University at Buffalo, State University of New York.

At the time of writing, **Shoshana Tobias** was an undergraduate student at the University at Buffalo, State University of New York.

At the time of writing, **Stephanie Vail** was an undergraduate student at the University at Buffalo, State University of New York.

At the time of writing **Aman Yadav** was a doctoral candidate in the Learning, Technology, and Culture Program in the Department of Teacher Education at Michigan State University in East Lansing, Michigan. He is now an assistant professor in the Department of Educational Studies, Purdue University, West Lafayette, Indiana.

Appendix II
Original Chapter References

The references below are to the publications in which these articles originally appeared. The numbers correspond to the chapter numbers in this book.

1. Herreid, C. F. 1995. Chicken Little, Paul Revere, and Winston Churchill look at science literacy. *Perspectives* 25: 17–32.

2. Herreid, C. F. 2001. The maiden and the witch: The crippling undergraduate experience. *JCST* 31 (2): 87–88.

3. Herreid, C. F. 1999. Saint Anthony and the chicken poop: An essay on the power of storytelling in the teaching of science. *JCST* 29 (1): 13–16.

4. Herreid, C. F. 2001. Storyteller's box. *JCST* 31 (1): 6.

5. Herreid, C. F. 1994. Case studies in science: A novel method of science teaching. *JCST* 23 (4): 229–239.

6. Herreid, C. F. 1997. What is a case? *JCST* 27 (2): 92–94.

7. Herreid, C. F. 1997. What makes a good case? *JCST* 27 (3): 163–165.

8. Herreid, C. F. 2005. The business end of cases. *JCST* 35 (1): 12–14.

9. Herreid, C. F. 1998. Sorting potatoes for Miss Bonner: Bringing order to case study methodology through a classification system. *JCST* 27 (4): 236–239.

10. Herreid, C. F. 2004. Can case studies be used to teach critical thinking? *JCST* 33 (6): 12–14.

11. Herreid, C. F. 2002. Naming names. *JCST* 32 (3): 162–163.

12. Dinan, F. J. 2006. Opening day: Getting started in a cooperative classroom. *JCST* 35 (4): 12–14.

13. Herreid, C. F., and A. I. Kozak. 1995. Using students as critics in faculty development. *Journal on Excellence in College Teaching* 6 (1): 17–29.

14. Herreid, C. F. 2005. Using novels as bases for case studies: Michael Crichton's *State of Fear* and global warming. *JCST* 34 (7): 10–11.

15. Herreid, C. F. 1994. Journal articles as case studies: The *New England Journal of Medicine* on breast cancer. *JCST* 23 (6): 349–355.

16. Fourtner, A.W., C. R. Fourtner, and C. F. Herreid. 1994. Bad blood: A case study of the Tuskegee syphilis project. *JCST* 23 (5): 277–285.

17. Herreid, C. F. Case study teaching in science: A dilemma case on "animal rights." *JCST* 25 (6): 413–418.

18. Herreid, C. F. 1998. Is there life on Mars? *JCST* 27 (5): 307–310.

19. Herreid, C. F. 1998. Why isn't cooperative learning used to teach science? *Bioscience* 48: 553–559.

20. Herreid, C. F. 1999. The bee and the groundhog. *JCST* 28 (4): 226–228.

21. Herreid, C. F. 2000. I never knew Joe Paterno: An essay on teamwork and love. *JCST* 30 (3): 158–161.

22. Herreid, C. F. 2005. The pima experience: Three easy pieces. *JCST* 34 (6): 8–13.

23. Herreid, C. F. 2003. The death of problem-based learning? *JCST* 32 (6): 364–366.

24. Herreid, C. F. 1998. The petition: A global warming case study. *JCST* 28 (2): 82–86.

25. Herreid, C. F. 1996. AIDS and the Duesberg phenomenon. From the archives of the National Center for Case Study Teaching in Science. Available online at: *http://ublib. buffalo.edu/libraries/projects/cases/aids.htm.*

26. Herreid, C. F. 2005. The interrupted case method. *JCST* 35 (2): 4–5.

27. Herreid, C. F. 2005. Mom always liked you best. *JCST* 35 (2): 10–14.

28. Herreid, C. F., and K. DuRei. 2006. The intimate debate method: "Let's make marijuana legal!" New to this book.

29. Herreid, C. F. 2003. Larry finally wrote his book. *JCST* 33 (1): 8–9.

30. Herreid, C. F. 2002. Using case studies in science—And still covering the content. In *Team-based learning: A transformative use of small groups in college teaching*, eds. L. Michaelsen, A. Knight, and L. Fink, 109–118. Wesport, CT: Praeger.

31. Scannapieco, F. A., and C. F. Herreid. 1994. An application of team learning in dental education. *Journal of Dental Education* 58: 843–848.

32. Schiller, N. A., and C. F. Herreid. 2001. Of mammoths and men: A case study in extinction. *JCST* 31 (1): 52–56.

33. Herreid, C. F. 2006. "Clicker" cases: Introducing case study teaching into large classrooms. *JCST* 36 (2): 43–47.

34. Brickman, P. 2006. The case of the druid Dracula: A directed "clicker" case study on DNA fingerprinting. *JCST* 36 (2): 48–53.

35. Herreid, C. F. 1999. Dialogues as case studies: A discussion on human cloning. *JCST* 28 (4): 245–249.

36. Bokobza, H. 1998. Student paper on the Atlantic salmon controversy. From the archives of the National Center for Case Study Teaching in Science. Available online at: *http://ublib.buffalo.edu/libraries/projects/cases/Bokobza.html*.

37. Tobias, S., and C. F. Herreid. 1999. Alien evolution—A futuristic case study: The return of the Cambrian explosion. From the archives of the National Center for Case Study Teaching in Science. Available online at: *http://ublib.buffalo.edu/libraries/projects/cases/alien/alien_evolution.html*.

38. Fourtner, A.W., C. R. Fourtner, and C. F. Herreid. What to do about mother: Investigating fetal tissue research and the effects of Parkinson's disease. From the archives of the National Center for Case Study Teaching in Science. Available online at: *http://ublib.buffalo.edu/libraries/projects/cases/fetal_tissue.html*.

39. Schiller, N. A., and C. F. Herreid. The Galapagos: A natural laboratory for the study of evolution. *JCST* 30 (1): 56–63.

40. Herreid, C. F. 1996. Structured controversy: A case study strategy. *JCST* 26 (2): 95–101.

41. Dudek, J., N. Marriner, and C. F. Herreid. A word to the wise? Advising freshmen. *JCST* 34 (5): 10–12.

42. Cliff, W. H., and L. Curtin. 1991. The directed case method. *JCST* 20 (2): 64–67.

43. Vail, S., and C. F. Herreid. 2002. Little mito: The story of the origins of the cell. *JCST* 32 (1): 60–63.

44. Herreid, C. F. The death of baby Pierre: A genetic mystery. From the archives of the National Center for Case Study Teaching in Science. Available online at: *http://ublib.buffalo.edu/libraries/projects/cases/pierre.htm*.

45. Herreid, C. F. 2004. The case of the dividing cell: Mitosis and meiosis in the cellular court. *JCST* 33 (4): 10–13; 33 (5): 12–18.

46.   Herreid, C. F. 1998. Return to Mars: How not to teach a case study. *JCST* 27 (6): 379–382.

47.   Herreid, C. F. 2003. Why a case-based course failed: An analysis of an ill-fated experiment. *JCST* 33 (3): 8–11.

48.   Herreid, C. F. 2001. Don't! What not to do when teaching case studies. *JCST* 30 (5): 292–294.

49.   Dinan, F. J. 2006. Case studies and the media. *JCST* 36 (3): 18–19.

50.   Herreid, C. F. 1999. Cooking with Betty Crocker: A recipe for case study writing. *JCST* 29 (3): 156–158.

51.   Herreid, C. F. 2005. Too much, too little, or just right? How much information should we put into a case study? *JCST* 35 (1): 12–14.

52.   Herreid, C. F. 2002. The way of Flesch: The art of writing readable cases. *JCST* 31 (5): 288–291.

53.   Herreid, C. F. 2002. Twixt fact and fiction: A case writer's dilemma. *JCST* 31 (7): 428–430.

54.   Cliff, W. H., and L. M. Nesbitt. 2005. An open or shut case? Contrasting approaches to case study design. *JCST* 34 (4): 14–17.

55.   Herreid, C. F. 2004. Racism and all sorts of politically correct *isms* in case studies. What are we to do? *JCST* 34 (3): 10–11.

56.   Herreid, C. F. 2000. And all that jazz: An essay extolling the virtues of writing case teaching notes. *JCST* 29 (4): 225–228.

57.   Herreid, C. F. 2001. When justice peeks: Evaluating students in case study teaching. *JCST* 30 (7): 430-433.

58.   Herreid, C. F. 2004. Coplas de Ciego. *JCST* 33 (4): 6.

59.   Lundeberg, M. A., and A. Yadav 2006. Assessment of case study teaching: Where do we go from here? Part I. *JCST* 35 (5): 10–13.

60.   Lundeberg, M. A., and A. Yadav 2006. Assessment of case study teaching: Where do we go from here? Part II. *JCST* 35 (6): 8–13.

61.   Herreid, C. F. 2006. Paul Seymour, assistant professor: A dilemma case in teaching. From the archives of the National Center for Case Study Teaching in Science. Available online at: *http://www.sciencecases.org/seymour/seymour.asp*.

62.   Herreid, C. F. 2000. Teaching in the year 2061. *Advances in Physiology Education* 24: 1–7.

63.   Herreid, C. F. 2006. E-mail from Socrates. *JCST* 35 (7): 12–15.

Index

Page numbers in **boldface** type refer to tables and figures.

using too weak or too brief interventions in, 415–416

what is known from, 416–417

Astaire, F., 434

Astin, A. A., 8

Atlantic salmon controversy, student paper on, 237, 247–250

Avogadro, A., 352

B

Bacon, F., 85

Bad Blood: The Tuskegee Syphilis Experiment, 104

Baker, J. N., 101

Balanchine, G., 387

Barrows, H. S., 36

Beak of the Finch, The, 280, 358

Beecher, L., 181

Bell Curve, The, 10

Bennett, J., 46

Benveniste, J., 32

Berliner, D. C., 408

Bernard, C., 430

Bible stories, 1, 55, 68

Bieron, J., 352, 353

Billions and Billions, 365

Blackboard work for cases, 344–345, 390

Blattner, W., 158

Blocks of analysis for cases, 389

Bloom, B. S., 31, 91, 224

Bogart, H., 434

Bonk, J., 339, 341

Boyle, R., 181

Brailowsky, S., 269

Brain Repair, 269

Breast cancer and insurance coverage case study, 90–98, **95–97**

Brickman, P., 225

Brighton Rock, 368

Bringing Problem-Based Learning to Higher Education: Theory and Practice, 151

Burdick, D., 361, 362

Bush, G. H. W., 8

Business cases, 42–43, 49–52, 57, 83

definition of, 50

requirements for, 50–51

selling of, 50, 51

structure of, 51, **51**

teaching of, 50–51

Buxtin, P., 103

C

Cambrian Explosion, 255–256

Cannabinoids. *See* Marijuana

Capuana, J., 67

Carbon dioxide emissions, 162, **162,** 164–166

Careers in science, 5

Carillo, C., 19–21

Carnegie, D., 68

Carroll, L., 156

Case(s)

based on journal articles, 89–98, 349, 353

based on newspaper articles, 351–353

based on novels, 85–87, 349

based on television news programs, 353

blackboard work for, 344–345, 390

characteristics of a good case, 45–48, 356

clicker, 224–225, 227–234

closed- and open-ended, 43, 375–379, **376–378**

closure of, 390–391

conflict provoked by, 46

contemporary, 46, 83

coplas de ciego, 405–406

decision forced by, 46

definitions of, 27, 41, 43, 50

educational objectives of, 376–377, 388–389

empathy created by, 46

factual vs. fictional, 371–374

first-person oral narratives, 148

futuristic, 253–263

general applicability of, 46–47

generic, 373

goals of, 84

historical, 83

how much information to include in, 361–364

interactive, 441

interest of, 46

length of, 47, 389

pedagogic utility of, 46

Science, 5, 151, 157, 158, 248

Science and Engineering Indicators survey, 7

Science and Social Issues, 33

Science education

   areas of concern in, 3–7

   deficiencies in, 1, 29

Science for All Americans, 29

Science literacy, 1, 407

   of American adults, 3, 6–7, 128

   dimensions of, 9

   reasons for low rates of, 3–7

   standards of, 8–9

   teaching to increase rate of, 7–10

Science News, 353

Scientific American, 22, 158

Scientific information explosion, 10–11

Scientific process, 9, 36–37

Scientific research team format, 36–37

Scientist, The, 157

Seating arrangement in classroom, 346

Sensenbremmer, J., 166

Sequencing tactics for cases, 378–379

Sexual selection, 274, 280

Seymour, E., 5

Shakespeare, W., 22

Shavelson, R. J., 408

Sherman, L. A., 367

Simon, J., 339–340

Simpson, O. J., 12, 287, 292

Simulation-based training, 433

Skeptical Inquirer, xv

Skepticism, 64–65, 199

Small group methods. *See* Cooperative
      learning

Smith, A., 22

Smith, K., 129, 142

Social skills, in cooperative learning groups,
      128–129, 133, 143–144

Societal issues in case studies, 382

Societal relevance of science, 9–10, 31

Socrates, 421, 437–441, **438**

Socratic questioning, 33, 41, 43, 240

Spence, L., 190

Spermatogenesis, 324–328

Stabler, R., 56

Standardized science test scores, 1, 4, 127

Standards of science literacy, 8–9

State of Fear, 85–87, 349

Stein, R., 269

Stewart, B., 5

Stories, 19–21, 45. *See also* Case(s); Case study
      teaching technique

Storyteller's box, **25,** 25–26

Structured controversy, 285–294

   case study of DNA fingerprinting in
         forensic medicine, 287–294

   critical thinking skills required for, 286

   Johnson and Johnson's model of, 286

   Watters' model of, 286–287

Student response systems. *See* Clickers in the
      classroom

Students

   barriers to cooperative learning, 132–133

   calling on, 345–346

   dislike of science, 221

   dropping out of science studies, 1, 4–5, 128

   freshman advising case study, 295–298

   learning names of, 67–69, 345

   listening and responding to, 346

   preparation for college science courses,
         1, 4

   product creation by, 347, 397

   research projects for, 36–37

   standardized science test scores of, 1, 4,
         127

   support network for, 5

   using as critics in faculty development,
         75–82

Study questions for cases, 389–390

Survivor, 142

Syphilis, 33, 99–110. *See also* Tuskegee Study
      of Untreated Syphilis in the Negro
      Male

T

Tarnvik, A., 69

Taylor, S. C., 287

Teachers

   barriers to implementation of cooperative
         learning strategies, 130–132

   importance of learning students' names,
         67–69, 345